# LITHUANIA

## SALLY CHAMBERS
### WITH LINAS ŽABALIŪNAS

www.bradtguides.com

Bradt Guides Ltd, UK
The Globe Pequot Press Inc, USA

**Bradt** GUIDES
TRAVEL TAKEN SERIOUSLY

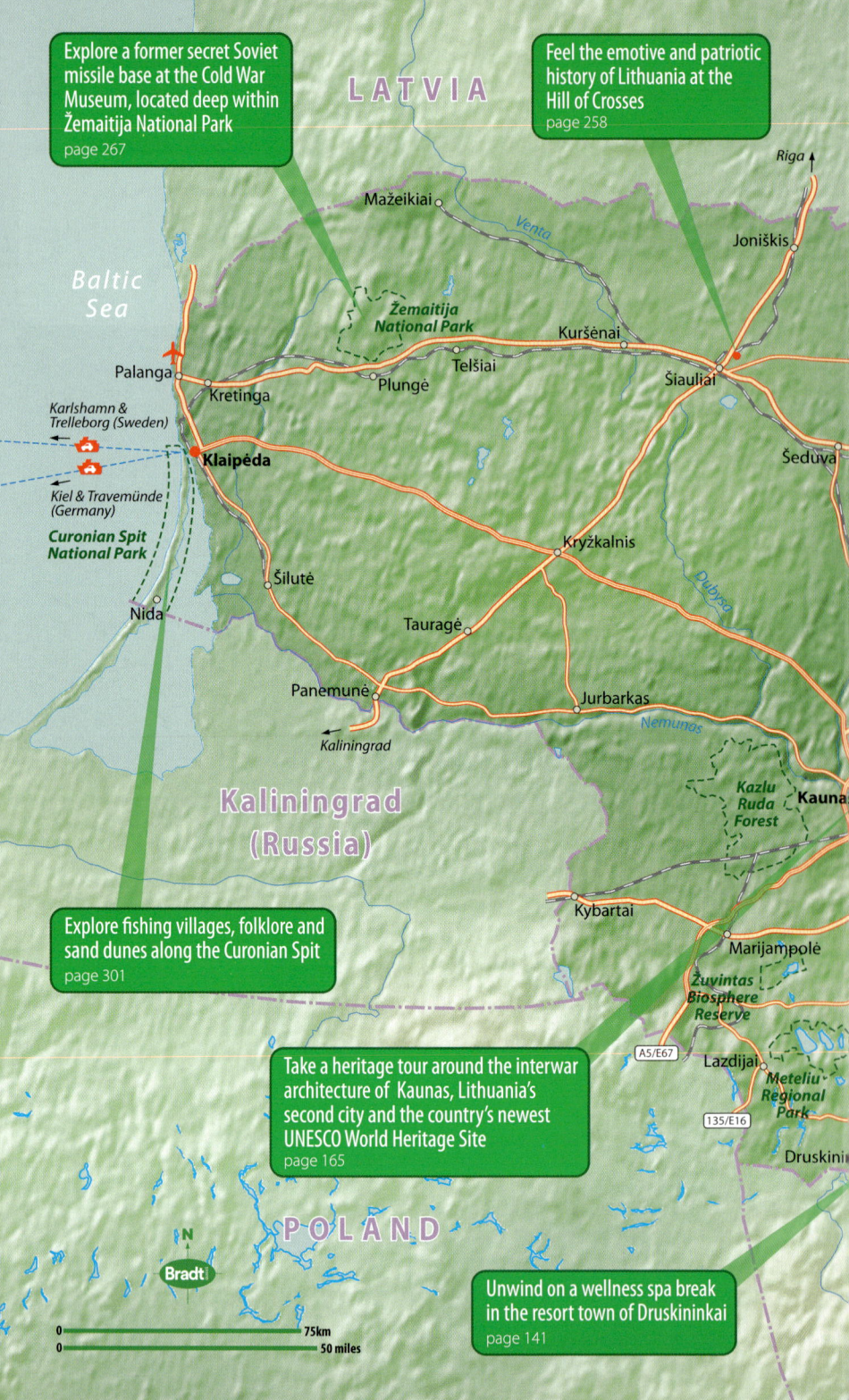

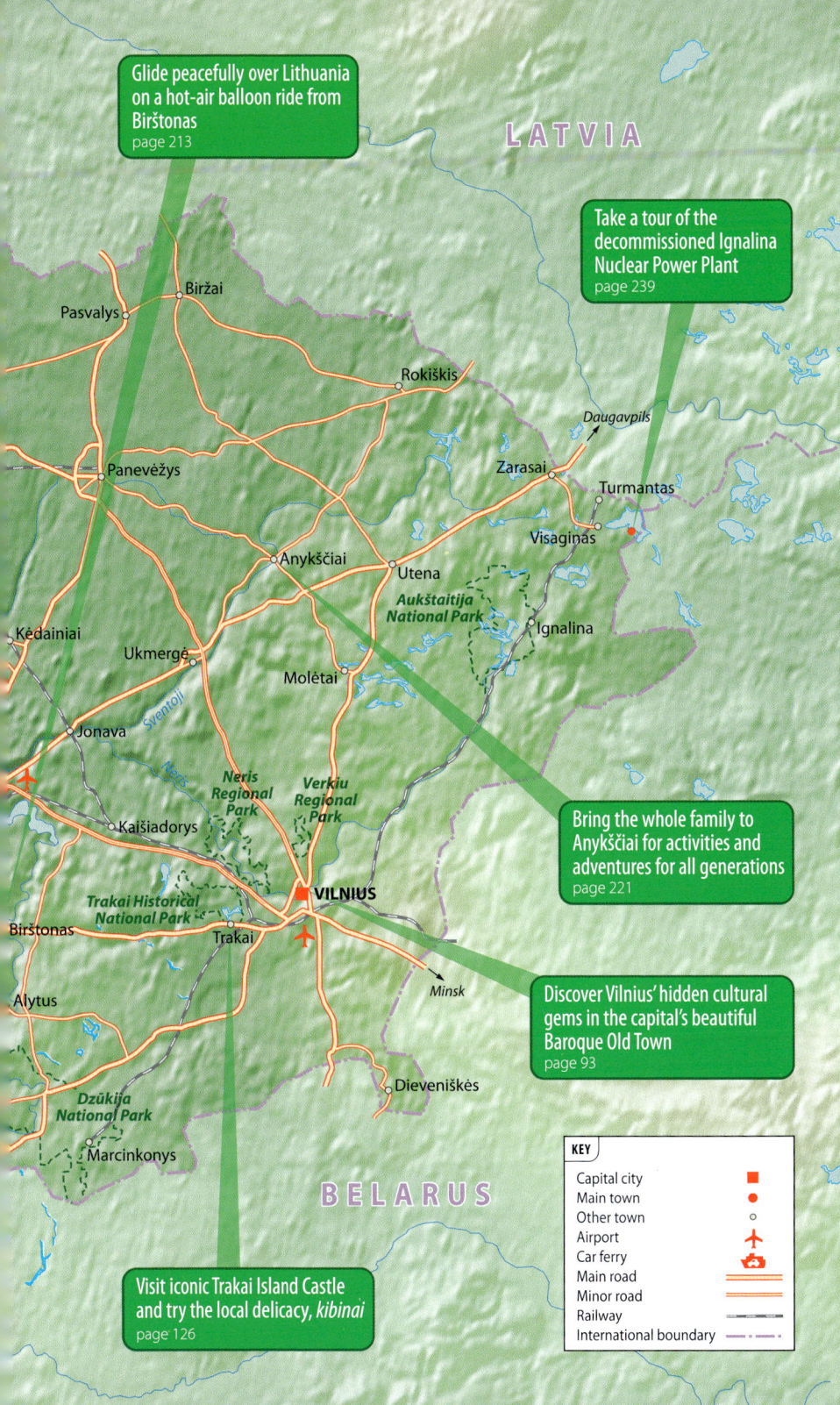

# LITHUANIA
## DON'T MISS...

### FORESTS
Lithuania's extensive forests are revered for their cultural, economic and ecological roles; visit Dzūkija National Park to breathe pure forest air, go hiking, forage for mushrooms and spot birds and other wildlife PAGE 147
(LZ)

### BEACHES
White sandy beaches stretch the length of the Baltic Sea coastline, including the UNESCO-listed Curonian Spit PAGE 301
(Z/S)

### LAKES
Lithuania is dotted with thousands of lakes, for swimming, sailing or fishing, but by far the most-visited surround the historic and iconic Trakai Island Castle PAGE 126
(PVW/S)

### FESTIVALS
The Lithuanian Song and Dance Festival is the nation's most spectacular cultural celebration, held every four years PAGE 67
(AV/S)

### LEGACY OF SOVIET OCCUPATION
The Cold War Museum, a former Soviet missile base in Žemaitija, is one of many legacies that now serve to educate about the period of Soviet occupation PAGE 267
(SC)

# LITHUANIA
## IN COLOUR

above right (SF/S) — Mindaugas was the first Grand Duke of Lithuania and only crowned King of Lithuania; his statue stands in Vilnius nearby to the reconstructed Palace of the Grand Dukes PAGE 94

above left (GA/LT) — The TV Tower in Vilnius is both an icon of resistance and home to the daredevil Edge Walk PAGE 117

below left (LC/LT) — The Gates of Dawn in the capital's Old Town is a popular pilgrimage site PAGE 106

below right (SC) — Browse the vast array of stalls in Halės turgus market hall in Vilnius PAGE 90

above (P/S)

Vilnius is one of few capital cities over which you can fly in a hot-air balloon PAGES 92 & 213

below (SC)

The impressive skyline of Vilnius' new business district on the north bank of the Neris River PAGE 113

# BALTIC
## HOLIDAYS

*Sally and Linas are the author & researcher of this book!*

## Tailored Travel Experiences

The Baltic states, Scandinavia & Eastern Europe

- Lithuania travel specialists since 1999
- Exceptional guides & drivers
- Discover Lithuania with local experts

"Just back from a great holiday in Lithuania organised by Baltic Holidays. From the moment we arrived, everything ran like clockwork. Excellent guiding, comfortable hotels and a good balance between organised outings and self-guided exploring. Lithuania is a fantastic destination!"

Tripadvisor Travellers' Choice Awards 2025

www.balticholidays.com ▪ info@balticholidays.com
📞 UK 0161 818 7140 ▪ 📞 USA (315) 636 5329
👥 @balticholidays

## AUTHOR

**Sally Chambers** is an expert in travel to Lithuania and co-owner of specialist tour operator Baltic Holidays (w balticholidays.com). For over 25 years, she has been promoting Lithuania as a travel destination and encouraging visitors to explore beyond the main sights on tailor-made tours. Having moved to Lithuania in 1999, she lived in Vilnius and worked for a local travel guide publishers, and volunteered for a British charity engaged in environmental projects in the northern town of Žagarė. When not in Lithuania, she lives with her family in her native Cumbria, UK.

## CONTRIBUTOR

Born and raised in Kaunas, **Linas Žabaliūnas** grew up during the Soviet occupation of Lithuania. His first taste of tourism was immediately after Lithuanian independence in 1991, when his family opened their own hospitality business, inspired by an English B&B during a trip to Devon. An expert in personalised off-the-beaten-track experiences full of local Lithuanian traditions, culture and history, Linas has been guiding visitors to Lithuania since 1999. He is a very well-respected personality in Lithuanian tourism and a former president of various Lithuanian tourism associations. He and his wife, Jurga, are co-owners of Baltic Holidays, along with Sally, and they run the Natur Camp campsite in Birštonas.

### FEEDBACK REQUEST

At Bradt Guides we're aware that guidebooks start to go out of date on the day they're published – and that you, our readers, are out there in the field doing research of your own. You'll find out before us when a fine new family-run hotel opens or a favourite restaurant changes hands and goes downhill. So why not tell us about your experiences? Contact us on 01753 893444 or e info@bradtguides.com. We will forward emails to the author who may post updates on the Bradt website at w bradtguides.com/updates. Alternatively, you can add a review of the book to Amazon, or share your adventures with us on social:

BradtGuides & balticholidays
BradtGuides
BradtGuides & vilniusally

First published November 2025
Bradt Travel Guides Ltd
31a High Street, Chesham, Buckinghamshire, HP5 1BW, England
www.bradtguides.com
Print edition published in the USA by The Globe Pequot Press Inc,
PO Box 480, Guilford, Connecticut 06437-0480

Text copyright © Bradt Travel Guides Ltd, 2025
Maps copyright © Bradt Travel Guides Ltd, 2025; includes map data © MapTiler
© OpenStreetMap contributors
Photographs copyright © Individual photographers, 2025 (see below)
Project Manager: Susannah Lord
Cover research: Pepi Bluck, Perfect Picture

Thank you for buying an authorised edition of this book published by Bradt Travel Guides. For over 50 years, Bradt Travel Guides has encouraged adventurous, immersive and responsible travel, and this is only possible because of the support of our readers. By purchasing our books, you are enabling us to continue to commission expert authors who genuinely know and love the places they write about, and who write their books after thorough, on-the-ground research.

The author(s) and publisher have made every effort to ensure the accuracy of the information in this book at the time of going to press. However, they cannot accept any responsibility for loss, injury or inconvenience resulting from the use of information contained in this guide. All rights reserved. No part of this book may be reproduced, scanned or distributed by any means without the written permission of Bradt Travel Guides, nor used or reproduced in any way to train artificial intelligence technologies/models. Bradt Travel Guides and the author(s) unequivocally reserve this work from the text and data mining exception, as per Article 4(3) of the Digital Single Market Directive 2019/790.

ISBN: 9781804692417

**British Library Cataloguing in Publication Data**
A catalogue record for this book is available from the British Library

**Photographs** Alamy Stock Photo: Jurgita Vaicikeviciene (JV/A); Linas Žabaliūnas (LZ); Lithuania Travel: Andrius Aleksandravičius (AA/LT), Giedrius Akelis (GA/LT), Laimonas Ciūnys (LC/LT), Simas Bernotas (SB/LT); Sally Chambers (SC); Shutterstock.com: Arnoldas Vitkus (AV/S), Birute Vijeikiene (BV/S), Lukas Jonaitis (LJ/S), Michele Ursi (MU/S), MNStudio (MNS/S), photovideoworld (PVW/S), proslgn (P/S), Renata Apanaviciene (RA/S), Rokas Tenys (RT/S), Sokolov Alexey (SA/S), Stockcrafterpro (SCP/S), Stoniko (S/S), Svet foto (SF/S), trabantos (T/S), Vaidotas Grybauskas (VG/S), Yevgen Belich (YB/S), zayatsphoto (Z/S).
*Front cover* View of Gedimino Avenue in Vilnius, with Vilnius Cathedral and its bell tower (JV/A)
*Back cover, clockwise from top* Landscape of Kernavė State Cultural Reserve (LC/LT); handwoven traditional Lithuanian cloth (BV/S); 'Edge Walk' participants at Vilnius' TV Tower, and the view below (SB/LT)
*Title page, clockwise from top right* Painted weathervanes, Nida (T/S); Kulionys lake (AA/LT); traditional Lithuanian wooden carving (SC)

**Maps** David McCutcheon FBCart.S. FRGS, assisted by Simonetta Giori

**Typeset by** Ian Spick, Bradt Guides; and Geethik Technologies, India
**Printed in india by:** Imprint Press
**Digital conversion by** www.dataworks.co.in

## AUTHOR'S STORY

When I moved to Lithuania in late 1999, I had the second edition Bradt guide to Lithuania tucked in my bag. I still have it – full of notes, ticket stubs and memories. Little did I know the impact Lithuania would have on my life; without any family connection or Lithuanian love interest, it was purely the people and place that won me over. Living in Vilnius for two years and exploring the region extensively was a privilege and the basis to becoming an accidental expert in Lithuania travel. The fickle finger of fate was often at work those days and upon my return to the UK, I was asked to man the fort at a friend-of-a-friend's start-up travel company specialising in Lithuania. Over 20 years later, we're still devoted to promoting Lithuania, albeit without a fax machine, and we no longer share one computer in a spare bedroom.

Over the years I have spoken with hundreds of people at travel shows to promote Lithuania, arranged research trips for journalists from around the world, shared Lithuania on social media, and still yearned to do more to raise Lithuania's profile. It was an honour to be commissioned to write a new Bradt guide to Lithuania, made even better by involving my colleague and good friend Linas, and specialist contributors who have all been part of my Lithuania journey. Bradt guides encourage you to delve deeper into a destination, to explore beyond the obvious, and learn about the country and its people. This is my goal when designing a tour at Baltic Holidays, hoping that people will take the risk and visit a lesser-known place because unexpected experiences often become a memorable highlight.

Friends and family know this book to be my love letter to Lithuania, tempered only to allow the reader freedom to navigate their own journey through this feisty little nation. I would be delighted if this new Bradt guide becomes a souvenir of your own travels in Lithuania.

## HOW TO USE THIS GUIDE

**AUTHOR'S FAVOURITES** Finding genuinely characterful accommodation or that unmissable off-the-beaten-track café can be difficult, so the author has chosen a few of her favourite places throughout the country to point you in the right direction. These 'author's favourites' are marked with a ✳.

**PRICE CODES** Throughout this guide we have used price codes to indicate the cost of those places to stay and eat listed in the guide, as follows:

**Accommodation price codes**  Average price of a double room in high season:

| | |
|---|---|
| €€€€€ | Over €200 |
| €€€€ | €120–200 |
| €€€ | €80–120 |
| €€ | €40–80 |
| € | Less than €40 |

**Restaurant price codes**  Average price of a main course, including side dishes:

| | |
|---|---|
| €€€€€ | Over €25 |
| €€€€ | €15–25 |
| €€€ | €10–15 |
| €€ | €6–10 |
| € | Less than €6 |

**ADMISSION FEES** Where admission fees are shown in this guide in the format eg: €15/10, the first price refers to the adult rate and the second to the concessionary rate.

**MAPS**

**Keys and symbols** Maps include alphabetical keys covering the locations of those places to stay, eat or drink that are featured in the book. Note that regional maps may not show all hotels and restaurants in the area: other establishments may be located in towns shown on the map.

**Grids and grid references** Several maps use gridlines to allow easy location of sites. Map grid references are listed in square brackets after the name of the place or site of interest in the text, with page number followed by grid number, eg: [85 C3].

# Acknowledgements

Thank you to Andy, Jack and Ben for patiently supporting me and offering to go away on adventurous holidays to give me time to write – I am not missing another family holiday! A big thank you to my parents, Anne and Ian, who waved me off to Lithuania in 1999 calmy hiding any concerns and trusting me to make the most of the experience. Thank you to my friends for moral support and to my colleagues at Baltic Holidays who saw considerably less of me during the writing process. Special thanks to my colleague Linas who has been integral to the research, facts and content checks for this guide – now we have a lasting legacy of our dedication to Lithuania tourism! We both thank Jurga, Ema and Kamilė for their behind-the-scenes help. I am grateful to fellow Bradt author and Baltic specialist Neil Taylor for recommending me to write this guide; and to the Bradt team for guiding me as a complete novice – thank you Claire Strange and Susannah Lord.

Our sincere thanks for their support go to Lithuania Travel and the regional tourism information centres in Vilnius (Justina and Lina), Kaunas (Raimonda and Ernesta), Palanga (Rasa and Aušra), Klaipėda (Romena and Mindaugas), Nida (Angelina), Molėtai (Daiva), Šakiai (Birutė), Šiauliai (Rūta), Telšiai (Egidijus), Plungė (Sandra), Druskininkai (Rimantas), Visaginas (Anastasia), Birštonas (Rūta) and Riešė (Aida).

In addition, for their contributions to the book, I thank Alex Gibb, Matt Kovalick, Sarah Mitrikė, Vika Ross, Emmett Russell, Richard Schofield, Ruta Sepetys, Rachel Suddart, Renata Sutovaitė, Neil Taylor and Phil Teubler.

# Contents

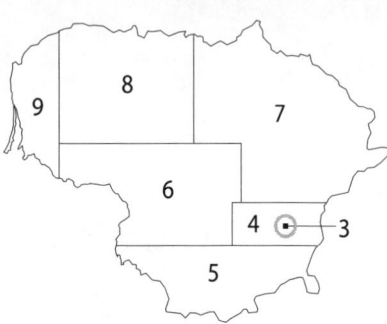

|  | Introduction | viii |
|---|---|---|
| **PART ONE** | **GENERAL INFORMATION** | **1** |
| Chapter 1 | **Background Information**<br>Geography 3, Climate 4, Natural history and conservation 4, History 9, Government and politics 23, Economy 23, People 25, Language 26, Religion and beliefs 27, Education 32, Culture 32 | 3 |
| Chapter 2 | **Practical Information**<br>When to visit 43, Highlights 44, Suggested itineraries 44, Tourist information and tour operators 46, Red tape 47, Getting there and away 47, Health 51, Safety 52, Travelling with a disability 53, LGBTQIA+ travellers 54, Travelling with kids 54, What to take 55, Money and budgeting 55, Getting around 56, Accommodation 58, Eating and drinking 60, Public holidays and festivals 62, Shopping 65, Arts and entertainment 66, Opening times 68, Media and communications 68, Cultural etiquette 69, Travelling positively 70 | 43 |
| **PART TWO** | **THE GUIDE** | **71** |
| Chapter 3 | **Vilnius**<br>History 73, Getting there and away 76, Getting around 77, Tourist information 78, Where to stay 79, Where to eat and drink 84, Entertainment and nightlife 87, Shopping 90, Sports and activities 91, Other practicalities 93, What to see and do 93 | 73 |
| Chapter 4 | **Around Vilnius**<br>Trakai Historical National Park 120, Trakų Vokė 128, Paneriai 128, Kernavė 129, North of Vilnius 132, Medininkai 134 | 120 |
| Chapter 5 | **Dzūkija**<br>Druskininkai 137, Dzūkija National Park 147, Northeast Dzūkija 155, Western Dzūkija 157 | 136 |

| Chapter 6 | **Kaunas and around**<br>Kaunas 163, Kėdainiai 197, Nemunas River Valley 200,<br>South of the Nemunas River 203, Birštonas 210 | **163** |
|---|---|---|
| Chapter 7 | **Aukštaitija**<br>Anykščiai 217, Utena 224, Molėtai 226, Around<br>Molėtai 228, Aukštaitija National Park 231,<br>Visaginas 236, Zarasai 240, Around Zarasai 242,<br>Rokiškis 243, Biržai 245, Panevėžys 247,<br>Ukmergė 249 | **217** |
| Chapter 8 | **Žemaitija**<br>Šiauliai 251, Joniškis 260, Žagarė 261, Northern<br>Žemaitija 264, Žemaitija National Park 265,<br>Plungė 269, Telšiai 272 | **251** |
| Chapter 9 | **The Coast**<br>Palanga 279, Around Palanga 288, Klaipėda 290,<br>Around Klaipėda 300, The Curonian Spit 301,<br>South of Klaipėda 314 | **277** |
| Appendix 1 | **Language** | **321** |
| Appendix 2 | **Further Information** | **329** |
| **Index** | | **333** |
| **Index of Advertisers** | | **341** |

## LIST OF MAPS

| | | | |
|---|---|---|---|
| Anykščiai | 220 | Klaipėda: Old Town | 295 |
| Aukštaitija | 218 | Lithuania | 1st colour section |
| Birštonas | 210 | Nida | 310 |
| The Coast: Palanga, Klaipėda | | Palanga | 280 |
| and the Curonian Spit | 278 | Šiauliai | 254 |
| The Curonian Spit | 302 | Trakai | 122 |
| Druskininkai | 138 | Vilnius: city centre | 82 |
| Dzūkija | 136 | Vilnius: Old Town | 85 |
| Kaunas: city | 170 | Vilnius: overview | 72 |
| Kaunas and around | 162 | Vilnius, Around | 120 |
| Klaipėda: city | 291 | Žemaitija | 252 |

# Introduction

A new Bradt guide for Lithuania is here! Since the last edition in 2008, Lithuania has continued to flourish as a creative, innovative and spirited country on both the European and global stage. How things have changed for visitors: while once they showed text-heavy displays, museums now showcase exhibits using captivating interactive technology; quirky new attractions have captured international attention as film locations, such as Ignalina Nuclear Power Plant in Aukštaitija region, or Lukiškės Prison in Vilnius; and the inclusion of 34 Lithuanian restaurants in the Michelin guide in 2024 bestowed much-deserved recognition on the country's outstanding gastronomic scene. Creativity thrives, with traditional and contemporary fairs and festivals the backbone of the cultural calendar, interspersed with music concerts, art installations, impromptu performances and celebrations popping up regularly. Transport links continue to improve Lithuania's connection to the wider world, with Kaunas airport a busy low-cost airline hub and Vilnius airport recently opening a new departures terminal. Train connections between Vilnius and Warsaw, and Vilnius and Riga have increased in regularity, a small step towards the eagerly awaited Rail Baltica line scheduled to open in 2030. On a local scale, access to nature has never been better, with new educational trails leading visitors further into the Lithuanian wilderness than they would have dared ten or 20 years ago.

Few know that Lithuania was once the largest country in Europe. Stretching from the Baltic to the Black Sea, the Grand Duchy of Lithuania incorporated lands of Lithuania, Poland, Belarus and Ukraine under a multi-cultural society at its peak during the 15th century. Having later been occupied by the Russian Empire, Nazi Germany and the Soviet Union, it was feisty Lithuania that was the first of the Soviet republics to declare independence from the Soviet Union in 1990. Today, evidence of Soviet occupation educates new generations of Lithuanians and visitors; the Museum of Occupation and Freedom Fights in Vilnius and the Ninth Fort in Kaunas both serve to inform the world about the realities of Russian occupation while respecting the victims. It is easy to understand why Lithuanian support for Ukraine is steadfast. Currently, Lithuania's borders with Belarus and the Russian exclave of Kaliningrad attract media attention; but the borders have never been more closely guarded and patrolled, being also the external borders of the EU and NATO. This has caused some people to have a wobble about visiting, but those undeterred are not disappointed – it is a fabulous time to explore Lithuania.

Lithuania's birth certificate exists in the form of a script written by St Brunon in 1009, describing a frosty reception when pagan Lithuanians threw rocks at him. We can attest that hospitality has improved considerably. Not only are the main cities of Vilnius, Kaunas and Klaipėda bustling centres with boutique hotels and fine dining, but exceptional smaller destinations are emerging too. The spa resorts of Birštonas and Druskininkai offer more than just rest and relaxation, with fun activities and access to nature particularly popular with families. The national parks of Aukštaitija, Dzūkija and Žemaitija are idyllic locations for forest walks, lake swimming, water sports, foraging and rural culture. On the coast, the Curonian Spit National Park is a haven of sandy dunes, pine forests and colourful fishing villages. Lithuania is perfect for a 'coolcation' beach holiday.

At the heart of the country is a rich heritage of traditions, culture and national identity that has survived and now thrives. Many small regional museums present their once-suppressed local heritage proudly, the open-air Museum of Lithuanian Ethnography (Rumšiškės) is a charming reminder of bygone days, and every four years the Lithuanian Song and Dance Festival represents the pinnacle of ethnographic traditions and national pride, when thousands of participants perform in spectacular vibrant events. Rather than taking a short, snappy city break to Vilnius or a whistlestop visit on a Baltic tour, trust Lithuania for a full holiday – this guide encourages you to stay longer and discover more.

Small countries must shout loud to attract attention and visitors. Decades ago, I was gifted a T-shirt emblazoned with the words 'Lithuania. Mmm…but where is it?' This theme was followed up by GoVilnius with their headline-making campaign 'Vilnius. The G-spot of Europe. Nobody knows where it is but when you find it - it's amazing'. If you feel the fun from these campaigns, you will love the artistic soul of Lithuania.

## KEY TO SYMBOLS

|  |  |  |  |
|---|---|---|---|
| —·— | International boundary | ♀ | Bar |
| ⊒☐⊨ | Railway, station | ☆ | Nightclub/casino |
| 🚗🚢 | Vehicle/passenger ferry | ♗ | Pub |
| 🚤 | Boat tours/small ferry | ✝ | Church/cathedral/monastery |
| ✈ | Airport | ☐ | Cemetery |
| P | Parking | 🗼 | Lighthouse |
| 🚌 | Bus station | ▸ | Golf course |
| 🚲 | Bike hire | 🎢 | Theme park |
| ℹ | Tourist information | ⚲ | Beach |
| 🏺 | Museum/art gallery | ➤ | Birdwatching |
| 🎭 | Theatre/cinema | ❀ | Gardens |
| ♪ | Music venue | 🏃 | Sporting facility |
| 🏰 | Castle/fortress | ▲ | Summit (height in metres) |
| 🏛 | Historic building | ● | Other place of interest |
| 🏛 | Ancient city gate | ～ | Dunes |
| 👤 | Statue/monument | | Pedestrian area |
| $ | Bank | | Marsh/wetlands |
| ✉ | Post office | | Urban park |
| ✚ | Pharmacy | | National park/protected area |

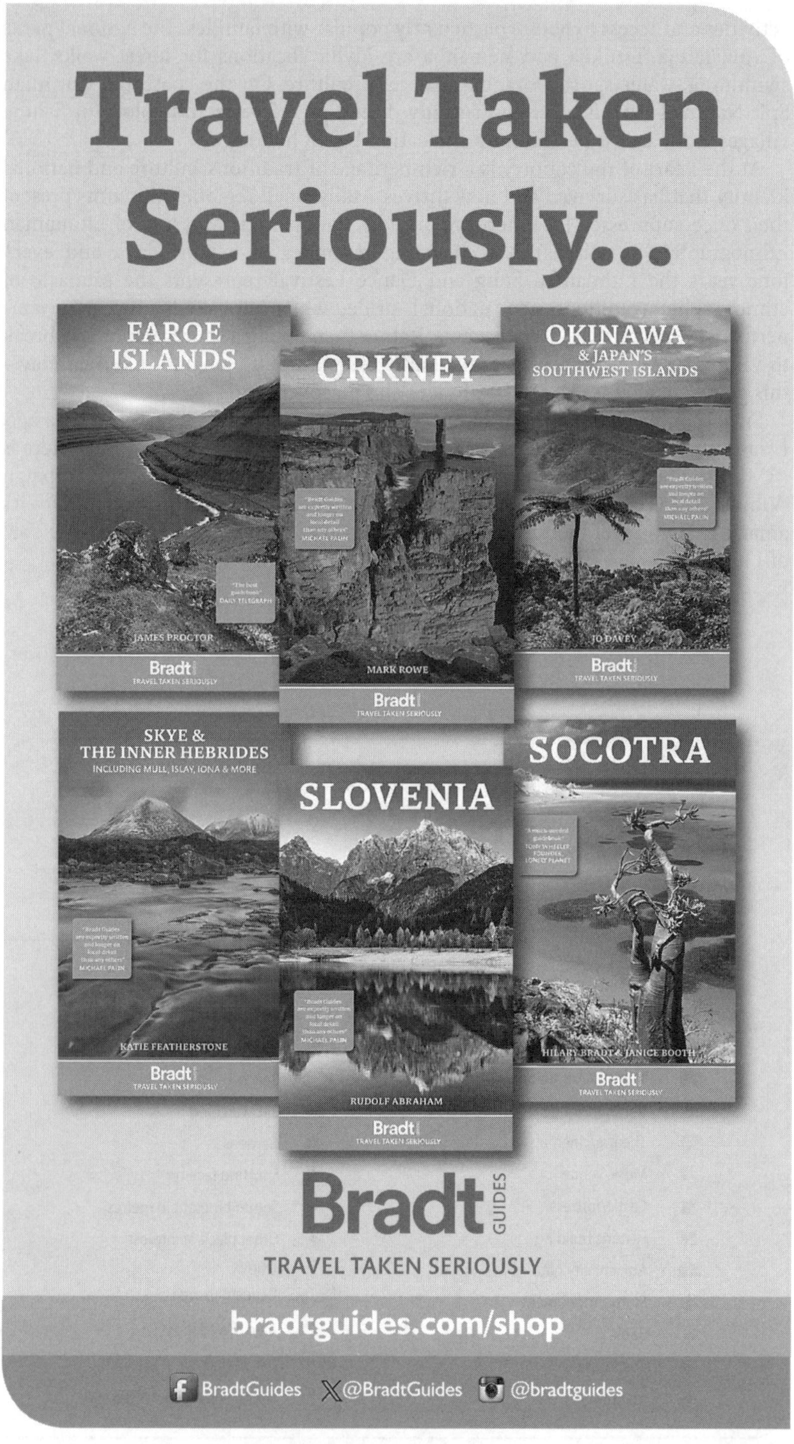

# Part One

## GENERAL INFORMATION

## LITHUANIA AT A GLANCE

**Location** Northern Europe, borders with Latvia, Belarus, Poland and Russia (Kaliningrad). Vilnius, the capital, is 262km from Riga, 394km from Warsaw and 1,723km from London.
**Size/area** 65,300km$^2$ – similar size to the Republic of Ireland
**Climate** Marine/continental temperate
**Status** Republic of Lithuania, parliamentary democracy
**Population** 2.8 million
**Life expectancy** Men 71.5 years, women 81 years
**Capital** Vilnius (population 569,700)
**Other main towns** Kaunas (population 375,000), Klaipėda (193,000), Šiauliai (131,000), Panevėžys (117,000)
**Language** Lithuanian, belonging to the Baltic branch of the Indo-European language family
**Religion** Predominantly Roman Catholic
**Currency** Euro
**Exchange rate** £1 = €1.15, US$1 = €0.85 (August 2025)
**International telephone code** +370
**Time** GMT and BST +2hrs
**Electrical voltage** 220 volts/50Hz AC; European two-pin plug
**Weights and measures** Metric
**Flag** Three horizontal stripes of yellow, green and red
**National anthem** 'Tautiška giesmė' (The National Hymn) written in 1898 by Vincas Kudirka
**Coat of arms** Vytis the white knight on horseback with his sword aloft and the double cross of Grand Duke Jogaila on his shield
**National flower** Common rue (*Ruta graveolens*; *ruta* in Lithuanian)
**National bird** White stork (*Ciconia ciconia*; *gandras* in Lithuanian)
**National sport** Basketball
**International memberships** European Union, NATO, Schengen Area
**Native name** Lietuva
**Public holidays** 1 January, 16 February, 11 March, 1 May, 24 June, 6 July, 15 August, 1–2 November, 24–26 December

# 1

# Background Information

## GEOGRAPHY

Lithuania is a northern European country with an area of 65,300km$^2$, making it similar in size to the Republic of Ireland. International borders with Latvia to the north and Poland to the south are internal European Union and Schengen Area borders, open to cross freely by all forms of transport; while to the southwest lies Kaliningrad (Russia) and to the east Belarus, both of which have secure international borders. Prior to the Russian invasion of Ukraine, it was possible to visit Kaliningrad and Belarus on tourist visas, and there was much bilateral activity for trade and personal visits. At the time of writing the borders are closed, strictly monitored and being reinforced in some regions.

The Lithuanian landscape is one of predominantly fertile glacial plains formed by the last ice age, and never exceeding 300m in altitude. The highest point is Aukštojas Hill (293.84m) near Medininkai (page 134) in the east of the country close to the Belarus border. The eastern border region is an area of highlands, along with the Žemaitija uplands in northwest Lithuania, all formed by glacial deposits creating morainic hills. Geological legacies of the glacial period can be found across Lithuania in the form of erratics – huge, isolated boulders that were carried by the ice and deposited when it thawed. Barstyčiai stone (*Barstyčių akmuo*), also known as Puokė stone (*Puokės akmuo*), is the largest glacial erratic boulder in Lithuania and, along with many others claiming a ranking, is a major draw for visitors in search of a selfie. The geological composition of Lithuania is rich in minerals. Mineral spring water is considered very important to national health – Druskininkai and Birštonas are the main health resorts centred around their mineral spring sources and attract those in need of rest and recuperation. In the Biržai region of northern Lithuania there are an estimated 9,000 sinkholes, caused by a natural system of underground water eroding layers of gypsum. The most famous and largest sinkhole, Karvės Ola (or Cow Cave), which lies only 3km west of Biržai city (page 247), appeared around 200 years ago.

Approximately 60% of Lithuania's land is used for agricultural purposes, a medley of large-scale commercial farm businesses and small subsistence farms (of the country's 200,000 farms, 40% cover an area of less than 5ha). Over 30% of Lithuania is forested predominantly with pine, spruce and birch species. This is a fraction of the established forests that existed prior to the mass deforestation in the 18th century. The largest forest is Dainava Forest, approximately 1,290km$^2$ of primeval woodland in the Dzūkija region, preserved because the land is too sandy for agricultural use.

Lithuania is a land of lakes, with more than 3,000 of them dotting the landscape. Often interspersed with extensive marshes and ancient peat bogs, these areas provide vital habitats for wildlife. Under the authorities of the Soviet Union and their push for industrialisation, wetlands were drained and peat extracted on an unsustainable scale. Today these habitats are being sensitively restored by local and EU initiatives and a balance reached between wildlife conservation and human recreation. The largest lake is Lake Drūkšiai in the northeast, a factor that influenced the building of Ignalina Nuclear Power Plant on its shore (page 239). 'Kaunas Sea' is Lithuania's largest artificial lake created in 1959 by damming the Nemunas River to create the Kaunas Hydroelectric Power Plant.

The Nemunas is the longest river in Lithuania. Its source is in central Belarus, and its total length is 937km, 359km of which are in Lithuania. The widest point is 500m and the greatest depth is 5m. The Nemunas River basin drains more than 20,000 smaller rivers and covers 72% of Lithuania's territory. The Nemunas has always been a natural border – whether between ancient tribes, Prussia and the Russian Empire, Nazi Germany and Soviet Russia – and today a stretch of 116km forms the border between Lithuania and the Russian exclave of Kaliningrad. The Neris River flows through Vilnius, also originating in Belarus, and converges with the Nemunas River at Kaunas, from where it continues west as the Nemunas and discharges into the Curonian Lagoon. The vast Nemunas River Delta and Curonian Lagoon form an important habitat for migrating birds. The constantly shifting sands of the Curonian Spit and shallow fresh water of the Curonian Lagoon are unique; here, humans and nature have shaped the natural and cultural landscapes (page 301).

Lithuania is home to three triangulation points of the Struve Geodetic Arc, an almost 3,000km arc that stretches from northern Norway to the Black Sea mapping the Earth's meridian arc and calculating our planet's shape and size. Another point of interest, and often a source of debate, is that Lithuania is officially the Geographical Centre of Europe (page 132).

## CLIMATE

Lithuania's climate is a combination from west to east of maritime and continental conditions. Lithuania in Lithuanian is 'Lietuva', which translates as 'land of rain', but this is a misnomer. Precipitation is neither perpetual nor persistent and more likely to be in the form of short bursts of heavy downpours in the warm summer months (July and August are the wettest months). In winter, heavy snowfall comes and goes but rarely lasts more than a couple of days before melting. The warmest month of the year is July, with an average temperature 18.3°C; the coldest is January when average temperatures are around -2.9°C. Extreme temperatures do occur for short spells, reaching daytime peaks of 35°C in summer and -25°C in winter. In June, daylight lasts over 17 hours, whereas in December daylight lasts just over 7 hours. The west of Lithuania gets slightly more hours of sunshine per annum – for example, the Curonian Spit might receive approximately 1,900 hours of sunshine per year compared with 1,700 in Vilnius.

## NATURAL HISTORY AND CONSERVATION

Soviet occupation (page 12) left deep scars on the Lithuanian landscape as a lack of sentiment allowed centralised plans for collective farming and large-scale industry to be pushed through, with little concern for the environment or those dependent on it. When independence was restored in 1991, a surge of national pride, identity and freedom saw the establishment of five national parks across Lithuania. An additional 30 regional parks have been established since 1992,

## ETHNOGRAPHIC REGIONS

Lithuania is divided into five official ethnographic regions, delineated on grounds of cultural traditions, lifestyle, dialect, folk songs and dances. For the purpose of this guide, we have divided the book into navigable regional chapters suited to most visitors exploring the country. While several chapters are named after ethnographic regions, they are not true to the official designated ethnographic areas. For example, Aukštaitija ethnographic region covers a larger area of Lithuania than the chapter of that name.

**AUKŠTAITIJA** Covering the northeast, Aukštaitija is the largest ethnographic region. From Švenčionys it tracks the Belarus border and the Latvia border all the way round to west of Žagarė, then extends south to the Nemunas River, encompassing most of Kaunas as it cuts eastward, then northeast up to Švenčionys.

**DZŪKIJA** Dzūkija covers the southeast of Lithuania and is contained by the Poland and Belarus borders as far as Švenčionys, then extends west slightly north of Vilnius, Elektrėnai, Birštonas and Lazdijai.

**SUVALKIJA** Suvalkija is defined by the Nemunas River to the north and east until south of Birštonas, where the boundary tracks southwest to approximately the midway point of the Poland–Lithuania border. To the south and west, the region runs along the Poland and Kaliningrad borders. Suvalkija is sometimes referred to as Sūduva after the ancient Baltic tribe of Sudovians, but this is rather ambiguous as their territory extended further south than the present ethnographic region of Suvalkija.

**LITHUANIA MINOR** Lithuania Minor (Mažoji Lietuva) is the smallest ethnographic region and encompasses the former Prussian lands, including the Curonian Spit, the city of Klaipėda, the Nemunas Delta and the sliver of land adjacent to the Nemunas River and Kaliningrad border until just west of Jurbarkas.

**ŽEMAITIJA** Also known as Samogitia, Žemaitija in the northwest of Lithuania covers the coastal area from Palanga up to the Latvian border, along the border until just after Naujoji Akmenė, running south to Šiauliai, east of Raseiniai and down to the Nemunas River, where it borders the river until west of Jurbarkas and curves up to Palanga, including Tauragė and Kretinga regions.

and numerous reserves have been established to protect natural and cultural heritage, and fragile biospheres. Over 12% of Lithuanian territory is a protected environment. The management of national species is overseen by the Ministry of the Environment, which publishes the Red Data Book of Lithuania listing the rare and threatened species of animals, plants and fungi in Lithuania.

The designation of national and regional parks was the beginning of a long journey to address environmental damage, to establish a legal framework for conservation and protection, and to raise ecological and environmental awareness. Membership of the EU in 2004 brought positive change in the form of financial incentives, support for environmental improvements, and laws to enforce environmental protection. The restoration of property rights also created many new private landowners, who took pride in their property and also took advantage of subsidies designed to encourage an environmentally friendly approach. Ongoing challenges include water pollution from fertiliser use and inadequate waste-water treatment, dependence on landfill and a move towards a circular economy, and reduction of greenhouse gases.

The close connection between Lithuanians and the natural environment stems from their pagan heritage, the still-prevalent subsistence farming of older generations, an appreciation of local, seasonal food and drink, and strong cultural traditions using nature's resources. The younger generations had not veered away from these traditions before they appeared in contemporary society as fashionable, with farmers' markets popping up alongside vintage clothing shops and a wave of young professionals regenerating rural village properties as they look for work–life balance and healthy lifestyles for their families. This individual respect for the environment will no doubt help the country develop a healthy national approach.

Access to nature has significantly improved in recent years. From a legal standpoint, the forests have always been open to all unless clearly stated that there is a danger due to forestry operations, military training zones, or border territory.

### NATIONAL PARKS

If you plan to visit one of Lithuania's national parks, contact the relevant national park administration office for advice about accommodation, activities and events. Services and facilities are often run by small local providers, and the information centres can help you connect with some special local experiences. Visitors are encouraged to purchase a State Park Visitor Ticket (w saugoma.lt/en/state-park-visitor-ticket; €1), a voluntary donation that goes towards the upkeep of the national parks.

**AUKŠTAITIJA NATIONAL PARK** Located in Lithuania's northeastern region, Aukštaitija National Park is dominated by lakes and historic villages. It is the oldest national park, having been established in 1974 under the Lithuanian SSR authorities (page 231).

**CURONIAN SPIT NATIONAL PARK** Curonian Spit National Park covers the Lithuanian side of the Curonian Spit, a long stretch of sand dunes, forests and fishing villages between the Baltic Sea and the Curonian Lagoon (page 305).

**DZŪKIJA NATIONAL PARK** Characterised by quaint historic wooden villages and deep forests perfect for mushrooming and berry-picking (page 147), Dzūkija National Park is in the south of the country.

**TRAKAI HISTORICAL NATIONAL PARK** Trakai Historical National Park is by far the most visited by international visitors owing to its close proximity to Vilnius (page 120). It is also the only national park awarded for its historical importance due to the Trakai Castle complex and town.

**ŽEMAITIJA NATIONAL PARK** The most ethnographic of the national parks, Žemaitija is alive with ancient traditions, wooden churches and road shrines, while also being home to the largest lake in Lithuania (page 265).

Marked trails, purpose-built paths and boardwalks have improved access for people of differing ability, with road signs and car parking also much improved. The introduction of **cognitive trails** offering a clearly marked hike with information boards and art along the way has been very successful. The construction of 35 **observation towers** across the country, each one artistically unique and offering sweeping panoramic views to those fit enough to climb the stairs, was an ingenious way to reconnect people to activities in nature and offer locals a new angle from which to appreciate their relatively flat homeland.

**FLORA** Forests (*miškės*) are spiritual places of huge cultural significance and importance. Since ancient times they have provided Lithuanians with sources of food, places of sanctuary and essential materials. Several months of the Lithuanian calendar are named after trees; the month of June is *birželio* (birch) and July is *liepos* (linden).

**Oak** (*ąžuolas*) is the national tree, and you will find it represented in all forms of art and folklore. The oak was a sacred tree in pagan times, the hardest and strongest of all trees, never to be damaged and to be worshipped with respect. Oak trees were planted on farmsteads as an offering to the gods and for luck – when travelling through the countryside, you will often see a lone oak in an expanse of fields, marking the spot where a farmstead once stood. When the surrounding land was nationalised for collective farming, the farmstead would be destroyed, but locals could not bring themselves to cut down a sacred oak tree. The oldest tree in Lithuania, at approximately 1,500 years old, is the Stelmužė oak in Aukštaitija region.

**Foraging** is a national pastime in Lithuania, and from September onwards if you hear rustling in the forest, it is more likely to be someone scouring the ground for mushrooms (*grybai*) than an encounter with wildlife. The forest floor provides the perfect conditions for lichens, mushrooms and fungi to flourish – this includes both poisonous and non-poisonous varieties, so be sure to embark on mushrooming with an expert in tow. The most common species of edible mushrooms found are the boletus (*baravykai*) and chantarelle. You get special points if you find a 'witches' cauldron' (*Sarcosama globasum*), but they are very rare and should not be picked. Wild berries also grow in abundance, including wild strawberries, cranberries, blueberries and cloudberries. If you prefer to leave the foraging to the locals, you can always buy a tub of mushrooms or berries from one of the ubiquitous roadside sellers. In springtime, birch trees are tapped for their sap (*beržo sula*), a sweet elixir rich in antioxidants, which is also sold by the roadside, or available in supermarkets if you are in the city and want to sample it.

Another joy of the Lithuanian landscape through the warmer months of June to August are **wildflower meadows**, particularly in the Nemunas River delta region. Across the whole country you will see plentiful crop fields edged with vibrant poppies, daisies, lupins and cornflowers. Less conspicuous are Lithuania's threatened flora, including several species of aquatic and semi-aquatic plants, and three species of rare orchid found in the Katra River valley in Dzūkija region.

## FAUNA
**Birds** The Katra River valley is a biodiversity hotspot providing habitat for rare birds, including spotted crakes (*Porzana porzana*), water rails (*Rallus aquaticus*) and black grouse (*Lyrurus tetrix*). Two very rare European birds breed in Lithuania, the aquatic warbler (*Acrocephalus paludicola*) and the great snipe (*Gallinago media*) – there are approx 200–300 pairs of each. Osprey (*Pandion haliaetus*) can be spotted fishing in the many lakes (30–40 pairs currently in Lithuania), and the white-tailed

eagle (*Haliaeetus albicilla*) is making a healthy comeback with 40–50 breeding pairs. The forests are home to numerous bird species, including rare species of woodpecker: three-toed (*Picoides tridactylus)*, white-backed (*Dendrocopos leucotos*), middle spotted (*Leiopicus medius*) and grey-headed (*Picus canus*), among others.

The most iconic of Lithuania's birds is not the rarest, however, but one that reliably returns every year and deserves its accolade as the country's national bird – the **white stork** (*Ciconia ciconia*), or *gandras* in Lithuanian. Stork-spotting becomes an addictive sport for visitors in summer; the birds tend to like nesting on top of electricity poles, chimneys and roofs, so many farmsteads and villages have installed purpose-built platforms to encourage the storks to nest safely and more conveniently. It is believed that white storks mate with the same partner for life and return to the same nesting site each year. The male returns first and about a week later the female joins him, resulting in Lithuania having the highest density of nesting white storks in the world. Their migratory routes have changed in recent years; an increasingly milder climate means winter migration to Africa is unnecessary and Portugal is warm enough for them to overwinter. Every year Gandrinės, or Stork Day, is celebrated on 25 March to welcome the birds, and on 24 August they are bid farewell on Gandrų išskridimo diena, or Stork Leaving Day, which occurs around St Bartholomew Day 'Šv. Baltramiejaus diena'. Lithuania is also home to the more elusive black stork (*Ciconia nigra*); these birds are shy and nest in the forests away from humans.

**Mammals** The largest mammal resident in Lithuania is the **moose** (*Alces alces*) with a population of around 7,000 – though it is rather a shy creature and you should count yourself lucky if you see one. The most prolific mammal is the **roe deer** (*Capreolus capreolus*) whose population has exploded in recent years and countrywide management of the species' population of over 120,000 is planned. **Wild boar** (*Sus scrofa*) are widespread in Lithuania with a population in the region of 20,000, although sightings are rare. They are found in areas of fertile soil, predominantly the central northern and southwestern parts of the country. The **wolf** (*Canis lupus*) population in Lithuania has been steadily increasing, from an estimated 200 wolves in 2013 to more than 700 in 2023. They reside mainly in the northern and western regions in thick forest and are currently Lithuania's largest predator. **Brown bears** (*Ursus arctos arctos*) are currently not permanent residents in Lithuania, though the odd one sometimes wanders in from Belarus or Latvia. It is expected that Lithuania will see brown bear populations re-established in the future as the burgeoning populations in neighbouring countries are forced to relocate further afield. A thriving population of over 50,000 **beavers** (*Castor fiber*) are managed through hunting licenses in order to balance their positive creation of habitats for biodiversity and their incidental damage to agricultural land.

Having become extinct in the 19th century and been reintroduced in the late 20th century, Lithuania now has several viable herds of **European bison** (*Bison bonasus*) which are bred in captivity with the intention of slowly releasing them into the wild. Visit the Stėgalis Bison Reserve (page 154) in Dzūkija National Park to see these magnificent beasts up close.

**Wildlife management** Wildlife management in Lithuania usually involves close collaboration with the country's official hunting clubs, which have an obligation to control their local wildlife populations and are responsible for cleaning up roadkill. Hunting in Lithuania is allowed only as part of an official hunting club and only in winter, outside of the breeding season. Gun ownership is carefully

> **BEEKEEPING**
>
> There is a beautiful word in Lithuanian, *bičiulis*, which translates as 'bee friend' and is also the name given to a beekeeper. In ancient Lithuania, bees were considered sacred, revered for their production of honey and beeswax, which had medicinal properties and brought the only sweetness to a tough life and plain diet. It was a lucrative economic activity, generating income for the beekeepers and benefitting the local church through taxes. The goddess of bees, Austeja, was worshipped and associated with family and fertility. Ancient beekeeping involved hives in hollowed-out pine tree trunks and a dangerous ascent by the beekeeper to scoop the raw honey out by hand. A visit to one of the ancient beekeeping museums is recommended if you find yourself nearby Musteika in Dzūkija National Park (page 154) or Stripeikiai in Aukštaitija National Park (page 234).
>
> Today the word *bičiulis* also means a close friend.

managed with training in gun handling, psychological tests and secure storage, and only guns for self-defence and sport are allowed to be kept at home. While the plentiful deer population are in the spotlight for culling, wild boar numbers are significantly down since a plague outbreak depleted the population; meanwhile wolves that were reintroduced and protected are now able to be hunted under license in certain areas.

## HISTORY   Neil Taylor

Lithuania has been an independent country with its current borders only since 1990. From 1918 until 1939, it was also independent but with a much smaller area, excluding Vilnius and a large area of the northeast, so the Polish border extended to Latvia. Prior to the mid-13th century, there was never a predominant power, unlike in many other parts of Europe. Tribes moved back and forth across what is now Poland, Lithuania, Belarus and Latvia, but left few permanent settlements. These were in any case largely constructed from wood, given the easy availability of this material in the area, although there was sufficient metal for weapons and tools.

**1253–1918** In a formal sense, the state of Lithuania dates from 6 July 1253, when Grand Duke Mindaugas was crowned its king. Mindaugas was born in 1219 and spent most of his adult life ruthlessly fighting not only neighbouring tribes but also internal rivals. He was happy to convert to Catholicism to win sufficient support for his kingdom and then to maintain it. Catholicism would continue to be the national religion, which, eight centuries later, it still is. Mindaugas and two of his sons were killed in 1263, but his third son was able to reclaim the throne briefly in 1265 until his death in 1267. The concept of an independent Lithuania was born, although achieving this would not prove easy. It reached its greatest extent under Grand Duke Vytautas in the early part of the 15th century, when the Grand Duchy of Lithuania stretched from the Baltic coast to the Black Sea. In 1569 the Grand Duchy of Lithuania was united with the Kingdom of Poland, creating the Polish–Lithuanian Commonwealth until 1795, when the whole territory saw the third partition of Poland-Lithuania by its three surrounding empires, Austria, Prussia and Russia, and, therefore, the collapse of the Polish–Lithuanian Commonwealth. Lithuania became part of the Russian Empire.

The 19th century was not a good time for Lithuania: uprisings in 1830 and 1861 were ruthlessly supressed, with Vilnius University being closed in 1832 by Tsar Nicholas I, and in 1864 it became illegal to use the Roman alphabet for writing Lithuanian. Only the Cyrillic alphabet could be used, a policy which was abandoned in 1904. (This press ban resulted in considerable book smuggling from East Prussia, where printers were more than happy to take on this extra business; page 38). Serfdom was abolished in 1861, but this did not lead to much change in the countryside. In the towns, there was not the development of a new middle class, as there was in Latvia. Tsarist Russia would attempt to impose Orthodoxy and Soviet Russia attempted to impose atheism, both with little success, despite the ruthless methods employed. Just one border would remain constant from 1422 until 1923, that between the Prussian Memelland, the area along the coast around what is now Klaipėda, and the hinterland controlled then by a mixed Lithuanian and Polish aristocracy.

The potential of Lithuania as a nation had very little resonance abroad before its official existence after World War I. Apart from the occasional folklorist and linguist, only one Western scholar, the Dane Meyer Benedictsen (1866–1927) took an interest in the country overall, following his first visit in 1893. His book *Lithuania, The Awakening of a Nation,* which first appeared in Danish in 1895, was then regularly updated and published in most European languages. It remains the classic on that theme, and his description of the Russians has a very modern ring to it: 'All the Russians have done and will do in the future is to impede the national development of the people, confuse their ideas and make them unhappy.' Because most knowledge of the area came from Russian or German writers, who were happy to propagate an image of Lithuanians as illiterate alcoholic peasants, which some of course were, they ignored the gradual increase in an urban educated Lithuanian middle class. We are fortunate that Benedictsen took a different approach, best summed up on the inscription on his tombstone: 'The interpreter of oppressed nations'.

**1918–44** In the West, because an armistice was signed on this date, 11 November 1918 is usually accepted as representing the end of World War I, with the Versailles Treaty formalising the new borders the following year. Earlier than that, on 16 February 1918, independence had actually been declared in Vilnius with the signing of the Act of Independence of Lithuania, and this day is still a national holiday as a result. However, fighting continued on the Eastern front and was particularly acute in all three Baltic countries. It was difficult to predict what the result for Lithuania would be: a union with Poland, a union with a future Soviet Union, incorporation into a new Germany, or independence. Only the last was what the Lithuanians wanted. To the north, Latvia and Estonia had equally to fight the Germans, the White Russians and the Bolsheviks, but frontiers agreed by 1920 would last through the first independence period, the Soviet era and then with minor adjustments into the current period of re-independence.

With the signing on 12 July 1920 of a treaty with Soviet Russia, independence was assured but on very different boundaries to those expected by those who had fought so courageously for it. The main dispute was with Poland, over the area around Vilnius and north to the Latvian border, which the Poles seized in October 1920 and kept until 1939. A state of war, in a formal sense, existed between Lithuania and Poland until 1938, so the border between the two countries was firmly closed. Travel from one to the other had to be through Latvia or East Prussia. Fortunately, there was no fighting between the two countries, but had relations between them been better, they, together with the other two Baltic countries, might well have been able to form an effective alliance free from either German or Soviet influence.

A border dispute with Latvia was resolved by James Young Simpson (1873–1934) who originally made his name through zoological research in Siberia but then joined the Foreign Office, where his work involved frequent visits to Russia, before and during World War I. He was part of the delegation to Versailles after the war, taking a particular interest in the Baltics and Finland. Not having any ethnic links with the area, he was seen as an ideal arbitrator. As the son of a gynaecologist, he said he saw the need to alleviate 'the birth pains of the two young countries'. The dispute centred on the port of Palanga, which, as part of the historical region of Courland, was seen naturally to belong to Latvia. However, with it being at the time the only possible outlet to the sea for Lithuania, and the large port of Liepāja being 75km to the north, Simpson granted it to Lithuania, with Latvia being compensated by other territory inland. A treaty was signed on 30 March 1921, and there have been no further disputes since.

**Memel becomes Klaipėda** The situation around the former Prussian/German port of Memel (now Klaipėda) would remain difficult throughout the duration of prewar Lithuania. Although it was on the edge of the German Empire, by the end of the 19th century it had become an important port and business centre. From 1867, Memel could be sure of a high profile in the Reichstag, being represented by Field Marshall von Moltke until his death in 1891. (Von Moltke was responsible for the Prussian defeat of France in 1870). While all senior government posts, and those in the business community too, were taken by Germans, Lithuanians were increasingly involved at middle-management level and were able to set up their own businesses.

During the negotiations at Versailles, there was agreement that Memel and the surrounding province should be taken from Germany but no decision was taken as to its future. The new country of Poland was eager to take over a fully functioning port, as was the equally new country of Lithuania, since neither had one in their likely future boundaries. Pending a solution, the League of Nations sent a French military contingent to run it. Realising that this contingent had little interest in their work, the Lithuanians invaded and seized the territory in January 1923. If other countries were interested in the issue at all, they took the view that Lithuania was now satisfactorily compensated for the loss of Vilnius. With the benefit of hindsight, it is clear why the integration would not work effectively. Memel was rich, urban and protestant. The rest of the country was rural, poor and Catholic. Racism came to the fore in many descriptions from that time. Some writers talked about travelling from Memel into the Lithuanian countryside as being akin to returning from the 20th to the 19th century; others compared the difference to travelling from Europe to Asia. In the 1930s, the Nazis would soon realise the potential this situation offered them. The German community never accepted the Lithuanian name of Klaipėda, continuing to use Memel.

**Kaunas: temporary capital** In 1920, following the seizure of Vilnius by Poland, the Lithuanian government was forced to move to Kaunas, which would be designated as the 'temporary' capital, in the hope that it would soon return to Vilnius. However, a cursory glance around the town centre shows an array of buildings of a size indicating that, at least from the late 1920s onwards, there was an unofficial acceptance of Kaunas being more permanent. Perhaps a parallel can be drawn with a similar development in Bonn from the late 1950s, when a reunited

Germany with Berlin as its capital seemed equally improbable. The square outside the modest presidential palace has statues of the three interwar presidents, of whom Antanas Smetona was the most important. He seized power in 1926, which he kept until the Soviet invasion in June 1940. Similar coups would take place throughout eastern Europe over the next few years, largely as a reaction to the weak coalition governments that preceded them. Like his opposite numbers in Latvia and Estonia, Smetona can perhaps best be described as a benevolent dictator who did not attempt to interfere with education, the arts or religion. The hagiographical way in which he was described by exile authors during the Soviet occupation, and then to a lesser extent in Lithuania itself after re-independence, reflects this as does the complete contrast to the one-year Soviet regime that ruled from June 1940 to June 1941, the Nazi regime that followed until 1944 and then the restored Soviet regime which would rule from then until 1990.

**World War II** While Lithuania made repeated concessions to the German community in Klaipėda, it became clear during 1938 that the local community would largely welcome a 'Heim ins Reich', a return to German sovereignty, which seemingly had taken place so smoothly in Austria and Czechoslovakia. Presented with an ultimatum on 20 March 1939, the Lithuanians delayed agreeing to it for two days while they sounded out the British and French governments; but once it was clear that no support from them would be forthcoming, surrender was the only option. The German army followed, with Hitler sailing in on 23 March to proclaim to an ecstatic local population that Memel had now returned to the Reich. Jews and most Lithuanians had to flee at once. At the time, Lithuania seemed to be a safe haven for Jews, and was fully open to them, while other European countries were doing their best to prevent further Jewish immigration, despite the desperate situation they were facing in Germany.

On 1 September 1939, Germany attacked Poland, which started World War II. A week earlier, Germany and the Soviet Union had signed the Molotov–Ribbentrop Non-Aggression Pact, named after their two foreign ministers. This pact divided eastern Europe into two areas of influence with the aim of ensuring peace between both powers. The Soviet Union attacked eastern Poland on 17 September and by 6 October, the country had ceased to exist, by then being divided between the two occupying powers. This was relevant to Lithuania as the Red Army seized Vilnius and a large surrounding area, which since 1920 had been part of Poland, but which they then returned to Lithuania. This was formalised in a misnamed Mutual Assistance Treaty signed on 10 October, which allowed the Soviet Union to station 20,000 troops in Lithuania, a number roughly equivalent to the entire Lithuanian army. These troops stayed largely in their barracks, and there were few incidents between them and the local population. In fact, there was some initial gratitude to the Soviet forces for ending the Polish occupation. However, the Red Army, as would become their custom later in the war throughout eastern Europe, stole many works of art and stripped factories of their machinery as they left Vilnius. Behind the scenes in Moscow, plans were being laid for a full-scale occupation of the three Baltic countries. Despite rumours of this reaching Lithuania, the government started to move back from Kaunas to Vilnius. Through the winter of 1939–40, Soviet forces were fighting the Finns; they lost 150,000 troops during that war, which probably gave the Baltics a few extra months of freedom.

**The first Soviet occupation** The fall of Paris to Germany in June 1940, combined with the successful invasions a month earlier of Denmark and Norway, encouraged the Soviets to implement the full occupation of the Baltic countries. Knowing that Britain would now be fighting the Germans alone, and that the US government had no wish to join them, the Soviets could be sure that there would be minimal resistance to their plans. The German promises given in the Molotov–Ribbentrop Pact gave them further assurance. The German government, through the Lithuanian Embassy in Berlin, made it clear that they would not offer help to any resistance the Lithuanians might hope to organise. Having initially thought that opposition to the Soviets might be possible, and given the strength of the Soviet army – 240,000 troops, 1,500 tanks and 1,100 aircraft allocated just to the invasion of Lithuania, not to the Baltics overall – President Smetona soon accepted the inevitable. He fled to Germany, before settling in the USA. Most of his cabinet members, together with many others active in what the Soviets would call 'bourgeois Lithuania' would be arrested; some would be executed immediately whereas others would be sentenced to long periods of imprisonment in gulags, where many would of course die. The meaningless charge under which they were arrested was committing 'counter-revolutionary crimes'.

Juozas Urbšys, foreign minister in 1940, was relatively fortunate in that he was allowed to return to Lithuania in 1956 and lived until April 1991, translating 20th-century French fiction into Lithuanian. In the last few years of his life, he could take advantage of the *perestroika* era in the Soviet Union to publish his memoirs and to give interviews to foreign journalists. His views on possible resistance in 1940 had not changed: had it been attempted, the subsequent occupation would have been even worse.

The three Baltic countries were occupied in a similarly brutal way, with bogus elections calling for incorporation into the Soviet Union, which was of course 'accepted' by Moscow. By the middle of August 1940, they were all Soviet republics. Russian officials took all the major decisions in ministries and in factories; in libraries, they purged any books – and there were many – that were regarded as anti-Soviet, and they imposed a very specific syllabus for school history lessons. Some farmers were initially pleased to see the arrest of their landlords, which they assumed would give them their own land, but they soon learned the reality of Soviet agriculture as collective farms began to be forced on them.

The Soviets were keen to eliminate any symbols of the former government, being completely oblivious to the hostility this would arouse. Displaying the Lithuanian flag was forbidden, trade agreements with companies abroad had to be authorised in Moscow, and on 25 November 1940 the rouble started to replace the litas as the National Bank of Lithuania no longer had a role. An artificially low exchange rate was fixed to impoverish anyone who had not already spent their litas. On 25 March 1941 the rouble became the sole legal tender. Few can have predicted that three months later, the German invasion would remove the rouble from circulation, to be replaced by the Reichsmark. During the year which this first Soviet occupation lasted, the immediate aim was to introduce a uniformity which had since 1918 been imposed on all the Soviet republics established then. No consideration was given to the fact that Lithuania, and its two Baltic neighbours, had run successful nations based on private enterprise and international contacts.

To reinforce Lithuania's new status as a Soviet province, all foreign embassies and consulates were told to close and so to withdraw their staff. A Dutch honorary consul, Jan Zwartendijk, and a Japanese diplomat, Chiune Sugihara, resisted this policy for a crucial ten days at the end of July 1940, which enabled them to issue visas to several thousand Jews who had escaped from Germany and from what had been Poland (page 191). Soviet attempts to close all Lithuanian embassies failed. Some of the countries where they were situated, such as the UK and the USA, would never recognise the occupation, so staff could remain en poste to liaise with the ethnic communities who would arrive after the war and to ensure that their cause was not forgotten by their hosts. Their presence at diplomatic functions would cause constant embarrassment to Soviet officials, who tried to avoid any contact with them. If Soviets did not attend an event, others would ascribe their absence to 'Baltic flu'. Some of these staff were still alive and working at the time of re-independence in 1990, so could immediately resume normal diplomatic activity.

Haphazard arrests of so-called enemies of the people or counter-revolutionaries, followed often by executions or long terms of imprisonment, were a characteristic of Soviet life from the foundation of the Soviet Union in 1924. By the end of July 1940, there had been 500 such arrests in Lithuania, but by early June 1941, this number had increased to 11,000. Around 70% of those arrested were ethnic Lithuanians, around 20% were Poles and around 10% were Jews. Much worse was to come, however, when at 03.00 on 14 June 1941, with no warning, the Soviet authorities revived the Tsarist tradition of deportations to Siberia from each of the three Baltic republics – but on a massive scale. Over the following four days, 17,000 people were rounded up across the country and sent to Siberia. Some 21,000 people had been listed for this fate, but 4,000 were spared by the intervention of the German invasion.

**Nazi occupation** The Soviet Union should have been ready for Operation Barbarossa, the German invasion that took place on 22 June 1941. They received warnings from around the world, even from their major spy in Japan, Richard Sorge, and the German build-up close to the border was obvious for all to see, but Stalin refused to believe these warnings until the day before the attack was launched. The deportations on 14 June had been meticulously planned and were ruthlessly efficient. What followed a week later, from the Soviet point of view, was complete chaos, with Lithuania and much of Latvia occupied within a week.

For many non-Jews, the German invasion was treated almost as a liberation, as there were no positive memories of the Soviet year of occupation. There were hopes that a Lithuanian government could be re-established, but the Germans soon made it clear that Lithuanians were second-class citizens who would have minor roles under their occupation, and as the situation worsened from the German point of view, Lithuanians would be conscripted into the army or for work in German factories. To stress their racial policies, many public buildings had a sign at the entrance: *'Hier spricht man nur deutsch'* (Only German spoken here). With ever-increasing demands from the Germans for agricultural produce and for the output from factories, the standard of living fell both in the towns and in the countryside, and there was an increasing fear that, when Soviet forces returned, as clearly they would do, all the horrors of their previous occupation in 1940–41 would return with them.

The start of the Holocaust is normally associated with a conference held in Wannsee, just outside Berlin, in January 1942. It codified the measures needed for a 'final solution to the Jewish problem'. In fact what happened in Lithuania during the first week of the German occupation in June 1941, and then continued until their defeat in 1945, equalled in horror the mass murder of Jews throughout eastern Europe. The Nazi propaganda about Judeo-Bolshevik conspiracies clearly found resonance among elements of the Lithuanian population in the aftermath of the Soviet occupation, so there is no doubt that there was support and involvement from them for this 'Final Solution', as there was in most other countries which the

## SOVIET DEPORTATIONS  *Ruta Sepetys*

In 1939, the Soviet Union established four military bases in Lithuania. By 1940, the country was fully occupied. Shortly thereafter, the Kremlin drafted lists of people considered anti-Soviet who would be executed, sent to prisons or deported to forced labour camps in Siberia. Innocent Lithuanian citizens – teachers, librarians, doctors, academics, lawyers, military servicemen, writers, business owners, artists, musicians and more – were all branded anti-Soviet and added to the growing list for banishment. The first deportations took place on 14 June 1941.

Meanwhile, back at home, cultural landmarks and churches were destroyed – an attempt to erase memory as well as identity. In 1945, at the post-war conferences of Yalta and Potsdam, the Baltic states were left within Stalin's purview, and the country of Lithuania disappeared from maps.

Many who were exiled spent up to 15 years in Siberia. When they returned in the mid 1950s, many found their homes, belongings and, in some cases, even their names were being used by the Soviets. Everything was lost. The returning deportees were treated as criminals, forced to live in restricted areas and often under surveillance by the KGB, formerly the NKVD. Speaking about their experience could result in imprisonment or deportation back to Siberia. As a result, the horrors they endured remained a painful secret for nearly half a century. Some brave souls, who feared the truth might be lost forever, buried journals and drawings on Lithuanian soil; they risked severe consequences if their testaments were discovered by the KGB. Many Lithuanians channelled emotion and fear into art, music, poetry and dance – a way they could express themselves and keep their nation alive in their hearts.

Nearly every Lithuanian family was touched by the deportations; not only Lithuania but also the Baltic states of Latvia and Estonia all lost a sizable part of their population during the Soviet period. The forced population transfers also impacted Poland, Romania, Finland and other countries.

Some wars are fought with bombs, but the people of Lithuania armed themselves with belief. In 1991, after 50 years of forced Soviet occupation, Lithuania regained its independence, peacefully and with dignity. Through 'The Baltic Way', they chose hope over hate and displayed to the world that even through the darkest night, there is light – and that sometimes – love is the most powerful army. Lithuania's older generation, who lived through the Soviet period, hold a living archive of survival and resilience. They are history's true witnesses. Visitors who have the honour of meeting them will leave both inspired and forever changed.

*Ruta Sepetys (w rutasepetys.com) is an internationally acclaimed and number one* New York Times *bestselling author of historical fiction.*

---

Nazis occupied. The extent of this collaboration is still a matter of dispute among both Lithuanian and foreign historians, but it must not obscure the number of courageous non-Jews willing to risk their lives by opposing this policy. The Yad Vashem Memorial (w yadvashem.org) lists 918 Lithuanians. Many senior members of the Church and the former prime minister Kazys Grinius made public pleas for the slaughter to stop, all to no avail.

## 1944–90

**The second Soviet occupation** From the summer of 1944, with the Allies having established a bridgehead in Normandy following the D-Day landings, western European countries could look forward to the defeat of Nazi Germany and the return of their independence. Sadly for the Baltic countries, the prospect was simply a renewal of the horrors of the 1940–41 Soviet occupation. There were hopes that the Western powers would 'encourage' the Soviets to leave, but these soon turned out to be misplaced. For six months, from the summer of 1944, Lithuania was a bitter battleground between Soviet and German forces, as the former slowly fought their way from Vilnius to the coast. Lithuanians had been conscripted by both sides, and others hid and resisted from the forests, taking advantage of the fact that only they had detailed knowledge of the landscape. Those who had the opportunity to retreat with the German forces often did so, hoping that their exile would be temporary. After several years in displaced persons camps in Germany, they would scatter across the world, in particular to the UK, the USA, Canada and Australia. Most would never see Lithuania again, although younger ones could and did return eagerly after re-independence in 1990 (including Valdas Adamkus, later elected President).

Given that 118,000 is the figure usually quoted for the number of deportees taken from Lithuania to Siberia between 1948 and 1953, it is clear that no attempt was made by the Soviet authorities to win the hearts and minds of the local population. Brute force and terror were the only languages they knew, and this was most evident in the countryside where several years were needed to impose collective farms. The last week in March 1949 was the most terrifying for Lithuania when about 30,000 people were deported, such was the opposition to collective farms. Factories were re-established more easily, assuming that the skilled staff had not fled the country or been murdered. Soviet propaganda alleged that poor farmers were being oppressed by their landowners, which might have been believed thousands of miles away beyond the Urals, but not by anyone actually living in Lithuania.

**Freedom fighting** Anti-Soviet partisan activity began as soon as Soviet forces started to reconquer Lithuania during the summer of 1944. Armed resistance groups called 'Forest Brothers' (page 205) were established throughout Lithuanian territory, hiding out in bunkers in remote forests. By 1953, Soviet control of day-to-day life was so intense, with ration cards, job allocations, censored post and tapped telephone lines, it was impossible to remain hidden in the forest with necessary supplies of arms and food. As this control increased during the nine years from 1944, different tactics had to be used. About 30,000 is the figure usually quoted for the number of partisans active in 1944–45, but this does not include many others who used their jobs as a cover to deliver information and supplies. When they disbanded, about 250 were left. Clearly, given the secrecy needed, records could not be kept, and regular liaison around the country was impossible. Early on, small, pitched battles were possible at a time when hardware had been abandoned by the fleeing Germans and the Soviets had not yet established guarded and properly supplied bases. Later, haphazard attacks on individual soldiers, transport installations and telephone wires would prove more effective. Regular references in the Soviet press to 'bandits' showed the extent to which they were disturbing the occupiers and so could not be ignored. It was of course rare in the Soviet press to mention such failings.

The death of Stalin in March 1953 provided an easier atmosphere throughout the Soviet Union; it would be far too early to talk of a thaw, but most of those still alive in Siberia were able to return home. Culturally, Lithuania's most famous composer and painter, M K Čiurlionis (1875–1911; page 188) was no longer a 'non-person', so the gallery in Kaunas dedicated to him before World War I was reopened. Historical themes and nature returned to poetry and prose, and stained glass reappeared, no longer having the stigma of it being exclusively linked to the Church. Yet Nikita Khrushchev, the Soviet leader in 1961, stopped the renovation of Trakai Castle, presumably because it brought attention to the empire that Lithuania once was.

The Soviets could probably claim correctly that they had dealt with the 'bandits' by the mid-1950s and that the 1949 deportations had removed most farmers unwilling to accept collectivisation. However, they were never able to supress the Catholic Church or incorporate it into a communist regime in a manner similar to the successful coercion imposed in Russia on the Orthodox community. In the Soviet Union, other denominations as well were forced to 'repent' but Catholics in Lithuania largely avoided this, despite constant harassment, which took such forms as police taking photographs of congregation members and the names of children attending catechism classes. The Soviets did manage to arrest some priests not willing to 'repent', who then suffered sentences appropriate for violent crimes, but certainly not for engaging in normal religious activity which elsewhere would be taking place openly every Sunday. One of the most famous dissident priests was Juozas Zdebskis (1929–86) who showed his defiance with his final statement at one of his many bogus trials: 'We must obey God rather than men' (Acts 5:29). Some priests were sent to so-called psychiatric hospitals, where the 'treatment' would be even more brutal than that in prisons, as attempts would be made to 'cure' priests of their beliefs. Their consolation would be that the persecution of any priest or teacher would have the opposite effect to what the authorities had intended. Their congregations would immediately increase.

There is detailed knowledge of the activities of the church in Lithuania thanks to the 81 issues of *The Chronicle of the Catholic Church in Lithuania* produced secretly between 1972 and 1989. Very fortunately, the Keston Institute in Britain (w keston.org.uk) had been established three years earlier, in 1969, for the study of religion behind the Iron Curtain. A highly efficient smuggling service ensured that every single issue of *The Chronicle* quickly reached Britain from where it could be broadcast back to Lithuania both in Lithuanian and in Russian, so ensuring a circulation far higher than was possible through the 600 issues or so printed surreptitiously in Lithuania itself. The year 1972 also saw the circulation of what became known as *The Memorandum*, a document addressed to the Kremlin with a very simple message, namely that the many religious leaders currently in prison should be released and that, as granted in the Soviet Constitution, freedom of conscience should be openly respected. Some 17,000 people signed the document, and a copy of the original reached Britain so its contents could be repeatedly broadcast back to the Soviet Union – and eventually returned to Lithuania. The 1960s and 1970s saw very slow developments towards renewed contact with the outside world. A few members of the émigré community were allowed to visit, but only to Vilnius and usually as part of an Intourist group package visiting several other towns as well. (Kaunas would have been of greater interest, as Vilnius had a very small Lithuanian population between the wars when it was under Polish occupation.) Some Lithuanians in the cultural field could join delegations abroad or even the Soviet diplomatic corps. This was of course during what is often called the stagnation era in the Soviet Union, when three party first secretaries in succession died in office, having done little or nothing in the last years of their lives. In the communist world, this could be contrasted to what Deng Xiaoping initiated in China at the same time.

Pope John Paul II, elected in 1978, is often credited with bringing down communism, perhaps not on his own, but his public profile in Poland combined with the influence of the Solidarity movement were major factors in Poland showing how new forms of protest could unsettle governments previously sure that violence would always be sufficient. Lithuanians inevitably became aware of this activity just beyond their border and would use churches as bases for dissent. Traditional forms of dissent, such as public marches by students, remained ineffective as they could so easily be halted by Soviet troops who were always available in large numbers. In Kaunas in 1972, 19-year-old student Romas Kalanta burned himself to death in public, and was followed by one or two others; but it has to be doubted whether these isolated incidents had any long-term effect. More famous academics who did not hide their anti-communist views were usually exiled abroad, and many would go to the USA.

Antanas Sniečkus (1903–74) was the Communist Party secretary from 1936 until his death. Before 1940, he had had to act clandestinely as the Party was banned under the Smetona regime. He retreated with the Soviet forces in 1941 but then returned in 1944 as the Soviet takeover of his country unfurled. He undoubtedly schemed better for his country than did his opposite numbers in Latvia and Estonia. He prevented an influx of ethnic Russians and also turned down a Moscow request that his province, as it now was, should unite with Kaliningrad, which would have ensured that Lithuanian culture might well have been obliterated. Petras Griškevičius (1924–87), his successor, was a complete non-entity, a Brezhnevite to the end, who was fortunate to die when he did. He would not have been able to relate to either of the emerging Lithuanian or Russian governments.

**Towards independence** Ronald Reagan was first elected to the office of US President in 1980 and was happy to lend his name to ceremonies linked to Baltic Freedom Day (14 June – chosen because it was the date of the first large-scale Soviet deportations in 1941). The first of these ceremonies took place in 1981; for the second one in 1982, Reagan invited 200 representatives from the three Baltic communities to the White House and made sure this was well publicised. However, towards the end of his presidency, he was faced with the dilemma of wanting to encourage Soviet liberalisation while satisfying the ever-stronger Baltic lobby in the United States. The problem would in the end be solved in Lithuania, not in Washington, with the population moving ever faster towards independence.

Mikhail Gorbachev became the Soviet leader in March 1985, and the two words associated with his policies, *glasnost* and *perestroika*, quickly went around the world and gave him instant fame. It took around two to three years for groups to form in the Baltic republics to calculate how *perestroika* could be used. 'Restructuring' need not have involved a direct threat to the Communist Party, but from 1988 groups active in many different fields made sure that it was. While there was rarely any formal cooperation with similar groups in Estonia and in Lativa, people eager for change often discussed plans with their opposite numbers there. Lithuanians had the advantage that they could more easily become aware of developments in Poland, where change began in the early 1970s; on television they could not avoid seeing film of a Polish pope or of striking workers in the Gdansk docks. From then on, event after event (all peaceful except for one) brought independence closer.

In 1984, Vytautas Landsbergis was elected Chair of the Musicologists Section of the Society of Composers, hardly it would seem an appropriate stepping-stone to leadership of his country six years later. However, it was a good testing ground for battles with authorities which would in due course lead to independence. An old guard will always oppose innovation, in music as much as in literature, so it has to be disguised; in this case church music was described as 'medieval' so could be included in a concert programme. In June 1988 the first opposition party, Sajūdis, was formed with the aim of 'promoting *perestroika*' so as to be acceptable to Moscow. The founding committee of 35 people was a subtle cross-section of Lithuanian intellectuals who had all, like Landsbergis, become famous in their respective fields. Some were Party members, so had clout, some were young so had initiative, and some were artists or writers so could effectively network and publicise. Landsbergis was not a Party member, but in the summer, he would be elected as Chair of Sajūdis because he had these three qualities in abundance. On 23 August 1987, an attempt to hold a commemoration for the signing on this date in 1939 of the Molotov–Ribbentrop Pact was banned because it was classed as being 'anti-Soviet'. On this date in 1988, nearly 150,000 people attended a rally in Vilnius organised by Sajūdis, where Lithuanian flags were flown in abundance and the national anthem was sung. Landsbergis gave a speech revealing the true contents of the pact, which had been a totally taboo subject. There could now be no turning back to the Soviet era, but exactly what would replace it and how, was still in doubt. No guidance would come from Moscow, only occasional threats.

On 23 August 1989, the 50th anniversary of the Molotov–Ribbentrop Pact, approximately 2 million people created a Baltic chain, a continuous line from central Tallinn to Cathedral Square in Vilnius. If anyone was not aware of the link with 23 August 1939, and perhaps could not recognise the three national flags, they would be after this demonstration, organised of course before mobile phones and when very few private cars were available. This was the only occasion towards the end of the Soviet era when the three Baltic republics worked closely together despite the effectiveness of cooperation within the three countries and abroad.

In January 1990, Mikhail Gorbachev came to Vilnius and had the courage to walk among local people, which he must later have regretted. His security team could not prevent one member of the crowd reaching him and telling him that Russia had exploited Lithuania for the previous 50 years. Gorbachev quickly retreated to his limousine without providing an answer. The following day he addressed what he assumed would be a carefully selected audience of 1,000 Party members. He naively asked, 'Do you really want independence?' The unanimous roar back made the answer clear. He immediately cut short his visit and flew back to Moscow. Gorbachev lived on until 2022, never comprehending why the regime he led was so detested throughout the Baltics. He was similarly inept wherever else the issue arose in the Soviet Union, whether in say Kazakhstan, Georgia or Nagorno-Karabakh. On 11 March 1990, Lithuania signed the Act of the Re-establishment of the State of Lithuania. It was the first of the Soviet republics to declare independence from the Soviet Union between 1990 and 1991, resulting in the eventual dissolution of the Soviet Union on 26 December 1991.

**1990 TO THE PRESENT** In any discussion of recent Lithuanian history, the name 'Loreta' is of equal significance to that of any politician. Loreta Asanavičiūtė (1967–91) was one of 13 protestors killed on 13 January 1991 as they tried to prevent Soviet forces from taking over the Vilnius TV Tower. She was run over by a tank and detailed filming was taken, ensuring that no Soviet lies would gain currency in Lithuania or abroad. Had the First Gulf War not been taking place at the same time, much wider international coverage would have been guaranteed. Sadly, the Soviet army was similarly active in Riga a week later, but Boris Yeltsin was able to prevent a third such attack taking place in Tallinn. Landsbergis can personally claim much of the credit for the television coverage that did take place in central Vilnius and at the TV Tower, which ensured at the time and subsequently that no excuses put out by Moscow would hold water.

International recognition and consolidation of independence soon followed. On 11 February 1991 the Icelandic parliament was the first to recognise Lithuania officially as an independent nation. No-one was expecting the failed coup attempt that took place in Moscow on 20–21 August that year. We are often reminded of the pictures of Boris Yeltsin standing on a tank beside the Moscow White House. Less well-known is what he said: 'Remember the people of Vilnius. They showed us the way.' The emerging Russian government had already recognised the Lithuanian government on 27 July, the USA recognised Lithuanian independence on 2 September, and the declining Soviet one would do so on 6 September, after most European countries had done so during the previous two weeks.

Over the next few years, Lithuania had to be transformed from a country rigidly controlled from Moscow to one where businesses had much more freedom than would be the case in the West, a period referred to as the 'wild west' of the 1990s. Those in 'non-jobs' were quickly made redundant and many tempted by business

## LITHUANIA HISTORY TIMELINE    *Neil Taylor*

|  |  |
|---|---|
| **1009** | Lithuania's first mention in written sources; the *Annals of Quedlinburg* covers St Brunon's mission to Lithuania (Litua). |
| **1236** | The pagan Samogitians defeat the Livonian Brothers of the Sword at the Battle of Saulė (the Sun) near Šiauliai. |
| **1253** | 6 July: Founding of the Kingdom of Lithuania by King Mindaugas. 6 July is a public holiday in Lithuania. |
| **1569** | Union of Lublin Treaty founds the Polish–Lithuanian Commonwealth. |
| **1579** | Founding of Vilnius University. |
| **1795** | Following the partition by Austria, Prussia and Russia, Lithuania and Poland cease to exist as independent countries. Lithuania is absorbed into the Russian Empire. |
| **1832** | Closure of Vilnius University by Tsar Nicholas I, following uprisings throughout the country. |
| **1861** | Abolition of serfdom. |
| **1862** | Completion of a rail link to St Petersburg with Warsaw and Vilnius. |
| **1864** | Use of the Cyrillic alphabet becomes compulsory in all publications printed in Lithuania. |
| **1904** | The Roman alphabet is again allowed for publications in the Lithuanian language. |
| **1918** | 16 February: Declaration of Lithuanian Independence. |
| **1920** | 12 July: In the Treaty of Moscow Soviet Russia recognises Vilnius as part of Lithuania. |
| **1920** | October: Poland invades Lithuania, annexing Vilnius and a swathe of eastern Lithuania. The two countries remain in a state of frozen conflict until 1939. Kaunas becomes Lithuania's temporary capital. |
| **1922** | 21 August: Adoption of Constitution. |
| **1923** | 9 January: Memel/Klaipėda is occupied by Lithuania. French troops are withdrawn. |
| **1926** | 17 December: Antanas Smetona seizes power in a coup. |
| **1939** | 22 March: Klaipėda/Memel is seized by Nazi forces and reincorporated into the German Reich. |

after watching Western soap operas could easily fail. Others took advantage of the chance to work abroad and the birthrate dropped as women had greater freedom to put a career before starting a family. As a result, the population in 1991 of 3,700,000 had dropped to 2,800,000 by 2020, at which level it has stabilised. Many who worked abroad have been happy to return to better salaries and an environment ever closer to that of western Europe or the United States. Given the universal use of English in any internationally orientated business, foreigners have become increasingly willing to settle in Lithuania. At the time of writing in early 2025, it is of course impossible to predict the futures of refugees from Belarus and Ukraine now living in Lithuania; in due course, they may wish to move further west or to return home.

Various milestones from 1990 onwards should be noted. Clearly the Russian rouble had to be withdrawn, as did the Soviet troops based in Lithuania. By the end of 1993, the troops had gone and the litas had been introduced as the new currency, with a fixed exchange rate to the US dollar (from 2002 it would be tied to the euro, which would in turn replace the litas in 2015). Pope John Paul visited in 1993, to be followed by President George W Bush in 2002 and Queen Elizabeth II in 2006.

| | |
|---|---|
| **1939** | 10 October: Following the occupation of Poland by Nazi and Soviet forces, Vilnius is restored to Lithuania. A so-called Treaty of Mutual Assistance is signed with the USSR which allows for 20,000 Soviet troops to be stationed in the country. |
| **1940** | 15 June: Total occupation by Soviet forces. |
| **1940** | 3 August: Lithuania becomes a Soviet province. |
| **1941** | 14 June: The first deportation trains depart, forcefully taking the families of Lithuanian officers, doctors, priests, landowners, intellectuals and anyone opposing Soviet occupation to Siberia. Around 18,000 Lithuanians are deported over the course of several days. |
| **1941** | 22 June: Operation Barbarossa, the German attack on the Soviet Union, is unleashed. The whole of Lithuania is conquered within a week. |
| **1945** | 28 January: The fall of Memel/Klaipėda replaces a German occupation of Lithuania with a Soviet one. |
| **1949** | 24 March: A second wave of Soviet mass deportation sees some 30,000 Lithuanians deported to Siberia. |
| **1988** | 8 June: The steering group Sąjūdis is formed. |
| **1989** | 23 August: A Baltic chain of over a million people lines the road from Vilnius to Tallinn, commemorating the 1939 signing of the Molotov–Ribbentrop Pact. |
| **1990** | 11 March: Lithuania declares independence. |
| **1991** | 20–22 August: A failed anti-Gorbachev coup in Moscow enables all Baltic countries to achieve independence. |
| **1991** | 17 September: Lithuania joins the United Nations. |
| **1993** | 25 June: The litas is re-introduced as Lithuania's national currency. |
| **1993** | 31 August: Final withdrawal of Russian troops. |
| **2004** | 29 March: Lithuania joins NATO. |
| | 1 May: Lithuania joins the EU. |
| **2015** | 1 January: Lithuania joins the euro. |
| **2025** | 7–8 February: Lithuania leaves Brell, the Russian-controlled electricity network, to join the European one. |

In 2004 Lithuania became a member of both NATO and the EU. There had been a referendum in 2003 on joining the EU, with 91% of voters in favour of joining, on a 63% turnout. After centuries of occupation, Lithuanians could finally make up their own minds on whom they wanted to work with. Joining the euro took longer than planned, being introduced in 2015. The final break with Russia occurred on 9 February 2025 when Lithuania left BRELL, the Moscow-controlled electricity network, and joined the continental European electricity distribution system.

A new relationship with the Russian exclave of Kaliningrad became necessary, now that a journey from there to Russia necessitated travelling through Lithuania and Belarus. In the 1990s, residents of Kaliningrad could travel freely to Lithuania and Poland, and travel in reverse was equally possible. But this was no longer allowed after Poland and Lithuania joined the EU in 2004, and visas were introduced in both directions. The outbreak of the Ukrainian War in 2022 curtailed travel even further, and Kaliningrad returned to its Soviet isolation. Having borders with Belarus and Kaliningrad is of course concerning, although Lithuania's third border, with Latvia, is comforting given that both countries are loyal EU and NATO members. Lithuania is a small but feisty country that demonstrated its bravery and integrity when clearly stating its position against Russia's invasion of Ukraine. Along with Latvia and Estonia, Lithuania was catapulted on to the global stage as being vulnerable, responding with remarkable determination and leadership, and earning a new following of people determined to support these plucky nations by visiting and learning more. Only those over 50 years old will remember what Lithuania used to be like when life was a mix of fear, boredom and a struggle for basics. If a chapter like this is allowed a prediction, it can be that Lithuania will now stay pleasantly normal, fully protected by, and enjoying its close relationship with mainstream Europe.

## FREEDOM AND DEMOCRACY — Emmett Russell

During the six years I was involved in school exchanges with students from the United States and Lithuania, a significant truth emerged from the historical tours, the interviews with locals and the relationships formed across distance and time: freedom isn't free and the right to self-determination depends on democracy. From the freedom fighters of World War II resisting Soviet occupation out of bunkers hidden in the forests, to unarmed citizens confronting Soviet tanks at the Vilnius TV Tower in 1991, reminders of the historic and more recent fights for freedom are strewn throughout Lithuania's history and landscape. At the Hill of Crosses near Šiauliai, our students placed their personal crosses alongside hundreds of thousands of others, defiant symbols of one's right to religious, as well as political, freedoms. In the shadows of a mud yurt and a cattle car used to transport Lithuanians to Siberia during the 1940s, students interviewed survivors of Soviet deportations in the Museum of Lithuanian Ethnography before discovering a secret nuclear bunker and an underground printing press still in operation as late as 1992 in the city of Kaunas. These relics of past political tyranny stimulated the imagination and hearts of students to think about current threats to democracy and to appreciate the courage of ordinary men and women who valued their freedom more than their lives. From within a nuclear missile silo at the Cold War Museum and a former KGB prison, now the Museum of Occupations and Freedom Fights in Vilnius, students saw the remnants of terror from unlawful interrogation, torture and execution, not to mention the threat

## GOVERNMENT AND POLITICS

Since the restoration of independence in 1990, Lithuania is an independent democratic parliamentary republic. The head of state is the president, who resides in Vilnius at the President's Palace (page 110). It is an elected role, voted for by all citizens of Lithuania aged over 18 years. The term of office is five years, and the president can be elected for no more than two consecutive terms. Parliamentary elections occur every four years. The prime minister and 14 members of cabinet who form the government are selected from elected MPs by the ruling parliamentary party, or coalition if there is no majority. Parliament then votes to ratify the selection, and the prime minister and government form the country's executive body. Lithuania's foreign policy is carried out by the president and the government. Incidentally, Lithuania was one of the first countries in the world to grant women the right to vote in elections: it was included in the 1918 constitution and enacted in 1919.

## ECONOMY

Throughout the tumultuous ancient and medieval periods, Lithuania was steadfastly an agrarian economy based on hunting, farming, forestry and fishing. Whether peasant or nobility, fortune and survival were dependent upon the land regardless of what invading power was threatening the region. During the period of occupation by the Russian Empire (1795–1918), industrialisation was slow, held back by serfdom (abolished in 1861) and lack of land reform. The interwar years were seen as stagnant but resilient led by national optimism, a mood that was quashed by the brutal post-war incorporation of Lithuania into the Soviet Union.

of nuclear war from missiles aimed at Europe in the 1960s and 70s. Then, sitting in the Seimas, Lithuania's Parliament, American students joined Lithuanians and celebrated a memorial to freedom fighters who lost their lives resisting Nazi and Soviet forces. Now, one need only peer over the barbed wire and chain-link fence into the Russian exclave of Kaliningrad from the safety and beauty of Nida on the Lithuanian coast to realise the fragility of freedom and the importance of taking up Liberty's torch from the hands of the deportees, from the Forest Fighters, and from democratic friends far and wide to fight for and to preserve our treasured freedoms. On 23 November 2002, George W Bush said, 'You (the Lithuanian people) have known cruel oppression and withstood it. You were held captive by an empire and you outlived it. And because you have paid its cost you know the value of human freedom. Lithuania today is true to its best traditions of democracy and tolerance and religious liberty, and you have earned the respect of my nation and all nations.'

Travelling across Lithuania, our students did indeed learn to respect not only each other but also the lessons of the past and to embrace their responsibility for the future.

*Emmett Russell is an MA graduate in Literature. He has taught at Montgomery Bell Academy in Nashville, Tennessee, in the US since 1996 and began leading trips with teachers and students to Lithuania in 2014.*

A centrally planned economy orchestrated from Moscow implemented the Soviet masterplan for collectivisation and mass industrialisation. Lithuania produced unfinished parts and components that were fed into wider USSR markets, keeping them reliant and dependent on the central economy of Moscow.

When the USSR collapsed in 1990, the ensuing unleashed chaos and the following decade of turmoil is often referred to as the 'wild west'. The remnants of a centrally planned economy had to adjust and transition to a market economy against a backdrop of political and social upheaval. During this decade decisions were unauthorised, developments proceeded with disregard of any rules, money was power, and the black market thrived. As domestic politics struggled to find control and stability, external influences provided the necessary support. In June 1995, Lithuania signed a pre-accession agreement with the EU. This came into force in 1998 and was a strategic programme under which the EU provided Lithuania with the expertise and financial support to meet the standards and adopt the rules necessary to become a member of the union. The early 2000s saw rapid investment and growth driven by anticipated EU membership and membership of the World Trade Organization in 2001. On 1 May 2004 Lithuania became a full member of the European Union alongside fellow Baltic neighbours Latvia and Estonia, giving access to one of the world's largest markets and improving their appeal to global investors. The economic boom of the 2000s across the three Baltic nations became known as the Baltic Tiger.

Today, Lithuania is the largest economy of the three Baltic states. The main industries include the longstanding traditional sectors of petroleum refining, food processing (with emphasis on the frozen fish market), fertiliser production and animal feed. Several industries have transitioned to added-value products; for example, the timber industry has developed from raw timber exports to processing and manufacturing, including a successful furniture industry. IKEA has several plants in Lithuania, and if you look closely when you're next constructing a Billy bookcase, you may spot the Lithuanian words *kairė* (left) and *dešinė* (right). Recent years have seen impressive growth in technology sectors. Biotech and life sciences are particularly strong, attracting international investment and with ambitious goals to be a world-leading hub. Fintech is powering ahead owing to investor confidence and a very strong start-up sector with regular success stories, including Lithuania's very first unicorn, Vinted, in 2019.

Lithuania's economy showed remarkable resilience during the Covid-19 pandemic (2020–23), leaving it relatively well prepared to face the impact of Russia's full-scale invasion of Ukraine from February 2022. More than willing to cut ties

### TOWN TWINNING WITH LITHUANIA

Town twinning has long been a way to build connections throughout the world and Lithuania has an impressive list of such partnerships including these with the English-speaking world:

Alytus – Rochester, NY, USA
Kaunas – Los Angeles, CA, USA
Klaipėda – Cleveland, OH, USA and North Tyneside, UK
Rokiškis – Sherborne, UK
Šiauliai – Omaha, NE, USA
Vilnius – Chicago, IL, USA and Madison, WI, USA
Ukmergė – Worcester, UK

with Russia, Lithuania promptly sourced new energy partners in Poland and Sweden (finally disconnecting, along with Latvia and Estonia, from Moscow's central energy grid in February 2025) and navigated EU sanctions on Russian interests. Numerous businesses are affected by Russian sanctions, including several large fertiliser plants, while trade with Russia and Belarus has ceased and businesses are establishing new markets with the West and further afield with new global democratic partners.

## PEOPLE

Lithuanians are from the Baltic branch of the Indo-European nations and are often referred to as the 'Italians of the north', in part due to their more outgoing character compared with their northern Baltic neighbours, but also because of their strong Catholic traditions and family-centred lifestyle. Lithuanians are welcoming and friendly, and although committed to their traditional heritage they embrace innovation and are curious and open to connecting globally.

Lithuania has been multi-cultural since medieval times when Grand Duke Gediminas invited traders from all over Europe to come and settle in Vilnius. Recent official statistics (2023) report a demographic breakdown of 83.6% Lithuanian, 6.4% Polish, 5.1% Russian, 1.7% Belarusian, 1.6% Ukrainian and 1% other. Waves of demographic change have left their mark on Lithuania. It is not uncommon for the largest ethnic minority in a country to be from a neighbouring country, but in Lithuania the situation was exacerbated by Poland's occupation of a swathe of southern Lithuania, including Vilnius during the interwar period (1919–39). Most people who identify as Polish are living in Vilnius and to the east of the city, calling their community *tutališkes* which also identifies as the most religious (Catholic) area of Lithuania. Under Russian occupation, strategic immigration of Russian citizens into Lithuania was the norm. For example, when Moscow needed to demolish areas of housing to construct new facilities for hosting the 1980 summer Olympics, Muscovites were rehoused in Lithuania. The promise of a new life in newly built sleeping suburb tower blocks on the edge of the cities lured them. Most of Lithuania's Russian-speaking population live in the northeastern city of Visaginas, a purpose-built city for housing nuclear specialists and engineers who moved to Lithuania explicitly to work at the nearby Ignalina Nuclear Power Plant (page 239).

The largest event to affect Lithuania's demographics was the Holocaust. Before World War II Lithuania was home to approximately 160,000 Jewish people (7% of the total population), and Vilnius was often referred to as 'Jerusalem of the north' on account of its large Jewish community. Those who were fortunate fled Lithuania, but most of Lithuania's Jews were executed or sent to concentration camps. Today, Lithuania has a small active Jewish community with heritage projects underway and a sensitive approach to documentation and commemoration of Jewish history. Find more information about Jewish Lithuania on page 28. Less well known are the 130,000 Lithuanian citizens who were forcibly deported to Siberian gulags under Stalin's reign of terror between 1941 and 1953, as well as the tens of thousands murdered and imprisoned. Lithuania's demographics have all too often been at the mercy of brutal invading powers, including the dramatic exodus of German Lithuanian Lietuvininkai who fled southwest Lithuania as the Red Army approached from Russia in early 1945.

Since joining the EU in 2004, it is estimated that up to 750,000 Lithuanians have emigrated, most of whom are of working age. But recent years have seen the trend reversing with 15,000–20,000 emigrants returning every year, often bringing back

> **FAMOUS CONNECTIONS**
>
> Musician Bob Dylan's maternal grandparents were Jewish Lithuanians from Kaunas; actor Charles Bronson's father was born in Druskininkai; Jason Sudeikis of *Ted Lasso* fame has Lithuanian ancestry via his grandfather, whose parents where from Tauragė and Raseiniai; American actor Sean Penn's grandfather was from Merkinė; and The Killers' lead singer Brandon Flowers' grandmother was Lithuanian. There are more…including Victor David Brenner, who was born as Viktoras Baranauskas in Šiauliai in 1871 but emigrated to the USA in 1890. As a professional engraver, he designed the Lincoln Cent, the longest-running coin design in the USA (you can see his initials VDB on the coin). Lithuanians have certainly made their mark on the world.

wealth, skills and young families all ready to contribute to the Lithuanian economy. There is a sense of renewed appreciation for what Lithuania has to offer, not just family ties but also an increasingly good standard of living, a healthy natural environment, and opportunities. In the 2024 World Happiness Report, Lithuania was ranked the world's happiest country for people under 30 years old. Investment is evident all over the country, including in small, forgotten villages where young professionals are renovating family properties or investing in second homes.

The Lithuanian diaspora is currently estimated at 1.3 million people around the world. The Global Lithuanian programme (❋ GlobaliLietuva), founded in 2012, was established for Lithuanians and those of Lithuanian descent living abroad to build links with the homeland.

## LANGUAGE

Lithuanian is an Indo-European language, retaining archaic features that can be traced back to Sanskrit (the long-extinct language of ancient India), of which Lithuania is very proud. Lithuanian and Latvian are the only two extant Baltic languages and, although they are closely related, they have diverged through time and speakers of one language do not automatically understand the other. Over the centuries, shifting borders and occupying powers restricted the Lithuanian language, but the more it was oppressed, the greater its importance and role became in national identity and pride. During the medieval Grand Duchy years, Old Slavonic and Latin were spoken. Polish was the language of noble society during the Polish–Lithuanian Commonwealth, while Lithuanian was spoken by rural workers and agricultural labourers. Under Prussian rule, German influenced the local dialect of western Lithuania while Russian was imposed on the rest of Lithuania ruled by the Russian Empire, Lithuanian being banned between 1864 and 1904. The interwar period welcomed the revival of native Lithuanian. Following Lithuania's incorporation into the Soviet Union, Lithuanian remained the official state language, but Soviet authorities pushed Russian language dominance under a programme of Russification, predominantly in the areas of official governance, education and news. At home, Lithuanian continued to be the main language.

Today within Lithuania there are two dominant dialects: Aukštaitian (highland Lithuanian) and Žemaitian (lowland Lithuanian). These were considered uneducated and inferior by Soviet authorities, resulting in them almost disappearing, but recent years have seen a revival and introduction of local signage in both Lithuanian and local dialect. There are quite marked differences between Lithuanian and Žemaitian

> ### LITHUANIAN NAMES
>
> Learning Lithuanian is challenging, with its archaic grammar including multiple cases and complex declensions of adjectives, nouns and pronouns. There are some easy patterns to pick up: for example, masculine words always end in -as, -us or -is, while feminine words end in -a, -ą, -e or -ė. This also applies to names, for example the male first name of Simonas, and the female Simona; the male name Giedrius, and the female Giedrė. Many Lithuanian first names originate from the names of ancient gods, goddesses, or significant historical figures. If you have one of these names, it comes with the benefit of a dedicated 'name day' on the same day every year, which is celebrated like a mini-birthday, often with a cake or flowers. It can be fun browsing in a bookshop for the Lithuanian translation of book names including *Harry Poteris*.
>
> Surnames also follow a distinct pattern and traditional format distinguishing gender and also indicating a woman's married status. For example, the wife of a man with the surname Jankauskas would be called Jankauskienė (married to Jankauskas), their daughter would be called Jankauskaitė (daughter of Jankauskas and unmarried) and their son would have the same name as the father, Jankauskas. International marriages are confusing the system as they are not consistent with the Lithuanian format, and discussions are ongoing about tradition versus modern equality with some wanting the marital status of a woman not to be prominent in her surname.

(Samogitian), which can be seen in the following examples: the name Telšiai in Lithuanian and Telšė in Žemaitian/Samogitian; mosquito in Lithuanian is *uodas* and in Žemaitian/Samogitian *kuisis*; duck in Lithuanian is *antis*, but in Žemaitian/Samogitian *pylė*. Aukštaitian is much closer to standard Lithuanian, but still has marked phonetic differences, such as in the question 'What colour is Utena church roof?' In Lithuanian, this is '*Kokios spalvos yra Utenos bažnyčios stogas?*' But in Aukštaitian, it is '*Kokias spalvas Utenas bažnyčias stagas?*' And the answer '*Raudonos spalos*' and '*Raudonas spalvas*' respectively. (The roof is red by the way!)

Since independence, English has quickly usurped Russian as the second language and is spoken widely by younger people particularly in the cities and in tourism services. Older generations still use Russian as their second language, especially in rural areas. You will find a concentration of Russian speakers in the town of Visaginas in northeastern Lithuania because of the immigration of native Russians who were moved here to work at the Ignalina Nuclear Power Plant in the 1980s (page 239). In Lithuania Minor, the coastal and Nemunas Delta regions, you will find a knowledge of German helpful owing to their Prussian past and predominantly German visitors.

## RELIGION AND BELIEFS

Lithuania is overwhelmingly Catholic, with 77% of the population practising Catholicism, according to the 2021 census. All other religions and beliefs present in Lithuania represent 17% of the population and include Orthodox (Russian and Ukrainian), Old Believers, Evangelical Lutherans, Evangelical Reformed, Jews, Muslims, Greek Catholics, Karaites, Jehovah's Witnesses, Pentecostals/Charismatics, Old Baltic faith communities, Baptists, Seventh-day Adventists,

## JEWISH LITHUANIA
*Richard Schofield*

The Lithuanian Jews were a mostly Yiddish-speaking people of predominantly Ashkenazi descent, who just over a century ago numbered almost 250,000 souls, and who less than four decades later were almost entirely annihilated during the Holocaust. Their presence as a recognisably homogeneous group dates back in written sources to the 14th century. In 1388, Vytautas the Great issued the first in a series of privileges to the Jews of Trakai, or Troki as it was known at the time, which would ultimately lead to several hundred years of neurotic and unpredictable legislation marked by everything from pogroms and expulsions to the occasional period of exceptionally favourable treatment. The following information barely lifts the lid on an extraordinarily rich and abundant culture, whose traces continue to be literally seen and figuratively felt in every town, village and city in the country.

**THE SHTETL IN A NUTSHELL** Synonymous with pre-World War II eastern European Jewish life and culture in general, the *shtetl* was the quintessential Jewish market town that existed throughout the region from at least the 13th century until the Holocaust. Each different in its own way, a *shtetl* was – and, in many cases in Lithuania, remains – ultimately recognisable by the various buildings and other locations that community needed according to Jewish law, or Haskalah, most notably a cemetery to bury the dead, a *mikvah* or bathhouse for regular ritual cleansing and at least one (Orthodox) synagogue, or *shul*, where the local rabbi would oversee the community's combined religious and educational needs. Also crucial in every *shtetl* was a place for trade and commerce in the form of the central marketplace, where the local farmers would descend once a week to sell their produce and spend their earnings in the Jewish-owned shops that surrounded it. Numbering more than 400 at their peak, and in some cases almost entirely populated by Jews, almost every town in Lithuania was once such a place. Many remain fairly intact and are fascinating places to explore once the basics of how they were laid out is understood.

**BETWEEN THE WARS** In return for helping negotiate Lithuania's independence at Paris after World War I, the Lithuanian Jews were awarded a wealth of freedoms and concessions they'd never experienced before. After the enlightened Lithuanian Ministry for Jewish Affairs was quietly abolished in 1924, however, the so-called Golden Age for the Lithuanian Jews came to an abrupt end. Gradually forced out of business with the assistance of Antanas Smetona's right-wing authoritarian government, the 1920s and 30s are notable for their high rates of Jewish emigration. Squeezed between the Soviet Union and Nazi Germany, the fledgling Lithuanian nation was soon swallowed up by its powerful neighbours on either side of its borders. On 15 June 1940, a full-scale invasion of Lithuania took place from the east. Shortly after, the Republic of Lithuania became the Lithuanian Soviet Socialist Republic (LSSR).

**THE HOLOCAUST** Nazi Germany invaded the LSSR on 22 June 1941. With the often-enthusiastic cooperation of local collaborators, by the time the last German soldiers left on 28 January 1945, over 90% of the country's 200,000 Jewish men, women and children had been robbed, humiliated, starved, raped, tortured and murdered. Although the country's brutal participation in the Holocaust remains a seemingly irredeemable stain on its reputation, it's important also to remember that many Lithuanians risked everything to save their Jewish friends and neighbours.

**ALL THAT REMAINS** Unable to endure life in a postwar Soviet regime that expressed no desire whatsoever for a Lithuanian Jewish renaissance, the vast majority of the country's 15,000 or so Holocaust survivors took every available opportunity after 1945 to leave the USSR forever, an enterprise that was so successful that today it's almost impossible to find a Jew in Lithuania whose family were living in the country before World War II. Thus today's Lithuanian Jewish landscape is almost exclusively composed of atmospheric and abandoned Jewish cemeteries, repurposed synagogues and an increasingly large number of Jewish-themed tourist 'experiences'. All of the following are highly recommended.

Dating from 1801, the wooden former **Summer Synagogue in Pakruojis** (page 255) is situated in one of the most challenging places to reach in the country, with just three buses a day leaving from Vilnius and no direct public transport from Kaunas. Its extraordinary primitive painted interior, however, makes even walking there more than worth the effort. Run by the local children's library, there's no website to speak of.

Boasting nine surviving former synagogues, including the still-working Ohel Jakov Choral Synagogue at Ožeškienės gatvė 13, **Kaunas** was home to more than 30,000 Jews before World War II. The ensemble of 1920s and 30s architecture in its compact centre was largely built and inhabited by Jews. Several thousand European Jews were transported to their deaths at Kaunas's **Ninth Fort** (page 192), which today features a museum.

The main branch of the **Aušros Museum** in Šiauliai (page 256) is located inside a villa, formerly owned by a Jewish family and includes lots of information about the city's vanished Jewish past. Some of the best-surviving former Jewish marketplaces can be found in **Kėdainiai**, where there is also a combined cultural centre and museum inside the former Great Beit Midrash (1857) at Paeismilgio gatvė 12B (page 199); **Telšiai**, also home to a museum inside the former **Telšiai Yeshiva** (page 274); and **Rokiškis**, where the staff at the local regional museum (page 244) will be more than happy to help you get the most out of a your visit.

**FURTHER INFORMATION**

**Camera Obscura** w cameraobscura. lt. A celebration of pre-war Lithuanian Jewish photography run by a local Brit. Contains a growing collection of more than 600 biographies with links to thousands of historical photographs.

**Jewish Heritage Lithuania** w jewish-heritage-lithuania.org. A good source of information for tourists.

**Lithuanian Jewish Community** w lzb.lt. This website is a good place to learn more about the last relics of Lithuanian Jewish life & culture. Visiting in person visits requires an appointment.

*Richard Schofield is a leading expert on pre-World War II Lithuanian Jewish photography. Find out more about his work at* w *cameraobscura.lt.*

Methodists, The Church of Jesus Christ of Latter-day Saints, and the neo-pagan religion of Romuva. Six per cent of the population have no religious affiliation.

**PAGANISM** In the 1321 Mappa Mundi (world map) of Pietra Vesconte, an inscription reads 'Letvini pagani' – Lithuanian pagans. Proud to be the last pagan country in Europe, Lithuania finally converted to Christianity in 1387. A long time has passed since then, but you can still sense an undercurrent of pagan traditions here.

Lithuanian paganism was a polytheistic belief system that worshipped an array of gods and goddesses, including the supreme god Dievas (god of the sky), Perkūnas (god of thunder), Gabija (goddess of fire) and Saulė (goddess of the sun). Worship would take place at an *alka* (sacred site), often atop a hill or close to groves of ancient oak trees, believed to be the sacred abode of the gods. Open-air ceremonies were led by a *krivis* (priest) who also conducted rituals and sacrifices, and an eternal fire, guarded and kept alight by priestesses called *vaidalutės*, was central. Today, one alka with an eternal flame still exists, nestled on a remote hilltop and overseen by a rota of committed volunteers who have their own personal motivations for guarding the flame.

During occupations by foreign powers, peasant culture was generally accepted as unthreatening. But it was during these periods of oppression that Lithuanians looked to their heritage for identity and spiritual guidance, with a revival of ancient folklore, paganism and mythology hidden within traditions and customs. The founder of the neo-pagan Romuva revival was Vydūnas (1868–1953), who actively promoted the movement in the face of oppression and an all-out ban in 1940 by the Soviets. Members were lost to deportation and execution, but pagan belief was strengthened and traditions well preserved. Even Catholicism was a soft power that allowed people to commune with nature through their daily lives, inadvertently continuing the pagan theme of focussing on the natural world and people's place within it. During the crusades it was common for pagan folklore to be altered in order to promote a new anti-pagan narrative, laying the path for Christianity, but it failed to eradicate important traditions. Many pagan characters have lived on in Lithuanian folklore, myths and legends, passed down through generations and are still central to Lithuanian traditions and customs today.

In 2024, Romuva gained state recognition as a religion. They are focused on a pagan love of nature, having left the other attributes of paganism in the Dark Ages.

**CHRISTIANITY** In 1385, Grand Duke Jogaila of Lithuania married Jadwiga, daughter of Louis I, King of Poland. The marriage created a union between Lithuania and Poland, a show of strength against the Teutonic Order and the first steps towards the creation of the Polish–Lithuanian Commonwealth. One of the marriage terms was for Jogaila to convert to Catholicism, in order to become the King of Poland. In February 1387 he returned to Lithuania and oversaw the strategic conversion of Lithuania to Christianity, to the Catholic Church.

During the Soviet era, when all religion – being against communist ideology – was banned, the Catholic Church was persecuted through the confiscation of property, debasing churches (often turning them into warehouses), banning religious publications, arresting and deporting priests, and stopping religious education in schools. The pilgrimage site of the Hill of Crosses also fell victim to Soviet anti-religion (page 258). After the collapse of the USSR, religion rebounded, and repression turned into free speech and the freedom to practise religion. While Lithuania today is a secular state, neutral in matters pertaining to religion, and its citizens equal and free to practise their religion of choice, it does adhere to the national Christian holidays of Christmas and Easter.

## SCHOOL MEMORIES  *Linas Zabaliunas*

Being born in the late 70s and schooled in the 80s, I was brought up in a generation of change. As a small child, it was difficult to understand the big Communist Party funerals broadcast on state TV channels that brought the country to a complete stop, and visits to the Lenin monument in Vilnius on school trips, but in the years of Soviet occupation in Lithuania these were accepted as normal by a primary school student. Gorbachev's *perestroika* brought new legal private initiatives – to us this meant Donald Duck chewing gum being available to buy from specific market stalls and only on Sundays, and our first pair of jeans bought legally in a shop around 1986, made in Lithuania by Vilkaviškio siuvimo fabrikas, and which lasted forever.

In primary school we had to join the Spaliukai (the Lithuanian name for the Soviet Union's Little Octobrists youth organisation for children in grades 1–4). Members were nicknamed 'the grandchildren of Lenin'. I avoided the Spaliukai summer camps as our family was busy with 'other' things at grandad's place. Going to school in the standard blue boys' uniform made everyone the same across the whole USSR. Our first sense of times changing was when our primary school teacher was allowed to visit relatives in the USA and came back speaking about life on the other side of the Iron Curtain – it seemed unreal. Then came the late eighties with the Sąjūdis freedom movement, the Baltic Way, older boys truanting to avoid registering for military service – especially since the USSR was fighting in Afghanistan and no-one wanted to be conscripted.

On 11 March 1990 Lithuania was restored as an independent state. It was also a year of change for me – finishing primary school and starting the fifth grade, when pupils would graduate from Spaliukai and become Young Pioneers. My year group was the first to refuse to. Between March 1990 and January 1991, there were two parallel worlds: while the new independent state was building its future, the ever-present Soviet Lithuania trundled on. Our refusal to become Young Pioneers was because we were Lithuanian, nothing to do with the USSR anymore; but nobody got rid of the institution in school and our teacher was confused as to why we would not join, telling us we were ruining our future and career, marking our record for life. But nothing changed.

After independence, classes changed dramatically with the introduction and intense teaching of Lithuanian history. Since there were no Lithuanian history books, we used photocopied texts. The introduction of English to the timetable was also new. We would sing along in English to children's songs like 'Skidamarink A Dink A Dink' played on a vinyl record. We had a young music teacher who managed to get a VHS recording of a Billy Idol concert – watching the video during music class was surreal.

There are a lot of memories, a lot of stories to share and they all remind us, especially in the light of current geopolitics, how every small change helped shape our independent nation and erase unwanted Soviet identity. This very important part of our history is being taught in Lithuanian schools today, and the younger generations are encouraged to ask their parents and grandparents for first-hand accounts of how life was in Soviet times. It is important that this history is not forgotten.

# EDUCATION

Full-time education is free of charge and compulsory in Lithuania from 7 to 16 years of age. Between the ages of 7 and 11 years, children attend primary school (*pradinė mokykla*), followed by lower-secondary school (*pagrindinė mokykla* or *gimnazija*) between 11 and 16 years. Higher-secondary school for 16–19-year-olds is often offered at the same school or gymnasium, or at bespoke VET (vocational and educational training) schools. The provision of private schooling and international schools is increasing in response to a demand driven by wealth and aspiration. The school year starts on 1 September, and if that falls on a weekend it is up to individual schools to decide whether to start or wait for Monday. You will see children walking to school on the first day with flowers for their teachers.

Higher education is offered via colleges and universities in the form of Bachelors, Masters and Doctoral degrees. In 2021, 57.5% of young people aged 25–34 years had achieved a higher education qualification, compared with the EU average of 41.2%, although recent figures indicate that fewer people are enrolling in higher education, and vacancies are being filled by international students. Opportunities via international exchanges and the EU Erasmus programme continue to be popular among Lithuanian students, with great emphasis placed on learning foreign languages, experiencing other cultures – and maybe enjoying milder winters.

In response to a declining population predominantly due to emigration, the Lithuanian government introduced generous maternity and paternity rules to incentivise their young, dynamic workforce to also get producing the next generation of Lithuanians. Paid maternity leave lasts for two years (with 60% pay in the first year and 40% pay in the second year) with a third year of unpaid leave also possible, and the recipient's job remaining open for their return over the full three years. Either parent can take this leave. To enable those parents who want to return to work, state and private nursery schools (*darželis*) and pre-schools take children from 0–7 years.

# CULTURE

### PAINTING *Vika Ross*
Landscape, peasant life, folklore, historic battles, pagan symbolism and Christianity are all prominent themes in the Lithuanian art aesthetic. In Soviet times, Lithuanian art took a turn towards rebellion with artists in exile taking creative risks; those artists who remained in Lithuania had to adapt to the strict confines of socialist realism, including the painting of large-scale brutalist murals. Modernist art emerged more prominently from this period. The parallel avant-garde Fluxus art movement was spearheaded by Lithuanian émigré artist Jurgis Mačiūnas, who studied art in the United States and then created the anti-art movement which was intended as a social critique to promote radical freedom of expression and sought to upend the conventions of traditional art. Those wanting to gain more insights into Lithuanian art can get a good overview at the National Gallery of Art (page 115) and other galleries housed under the umbrella of the Lithuanian National Museum of Art (page 114). The Vilnius Art Auction (w menorinka.lt) has an extensive online gallery showcasing a wide variety of Lithuanian art. See also any of the ten galleries affiliated to the Lithuanian Artists' Association (Lietuvos dailininkų sajunga; w ldsajunga.com). For a contemporary view of Lithuanian art and painting, the MO Museum (page 114), also in Vilnius, showcases works from the 1960s to the present.

Notable Lithuanian artists include **Pranciškus Smuglevičius** (1745–1807), whose Neoclassical works focused primarily on religious and historical scenes, featuring themes of Roman antiquity and Italian landscapes. **Antanas Žmuidzinavičius** (1876–1966) was a colourful figure who travelled extensively throughout Europe and had an extended stay in the United States in his younger years. A prolific artist, he was a cultural advocate, patriot, teacher and art collector who donated his Čiurlionis pieces to the M K Čiurlionis Art Museum (page 187). His name is also associated with the Kaunas Devils Museum (page 187; devil folklore abounds in Lithuanian culture): what started as a playful collection of devil figures gifted to the artist has grown into a large-scale display of devil artworks – sculpted and painted – and continues to expand with donations from around the world. **Petras Kalpokas** (1880–1945) was another greatly influential contributor to Lithuania's artistic legacy, both as a prolific artist and a professor of art. Born on a farm in the Biržai district, Kalpokas was a nature lover whose numerous landscape paintings – in predominantly Impressionist and Realist style – reflected his reverence for the natural world. Kalpokas is also known for his self-portraits, portraits of people close to him as well as those of historical figures. He spent extended periods of time in Latvia, Germany, Switzerland and Italy, where his artistic talent was further developed and recognised. **Antanas Gudaitis** (1904–89) was a highly influential Lithuanian Expressionist painter, set designer, art advocate and art professor who was born in Šiauliai and died in Vilnius. Schooled in Kaunas and in Paris, he was inspired by the prominent French painters of his day and known for his use of colourful contrast and broad brushstrokes. **Petronėlė Gerlikienė** (1905–79) was born in Chicago but her family returned to Lithuania when she was a toddler. She spent most of her life in Žemaitija and then joined her artist son in Vilnius in her early 70s when she also began painting and exhibiting her works to quick acclaim. A big name in the style of naïve art, Gerlikienė's striking paintings and tapestries tell the story of small-town life and folk traditions, and also depict moments of human suffering. Her works can be seen at the MO Museum, the Lithuanian Museum of Art and other major galleries throughout the country, along with those of her contemporary, **Monika Bičiūnienė** (1910–2009), another dynamic and exceptionally prolific naïve artist. **Kazys Varnelis** (1917–2010) was a diaspora artist who developed his modern and abstract interpretation of Lithuanian art motifs over decades spent in the United States from 1949 onwards. His pieces are housed at major American art museums, including The Guggenheim Museum in New York and the Art Institute of Chicago. Born in Alsėdžiai, the artist was able to return to Vilnius for his final chapter where his legacy can be discovered at the Kazys Varnelis House Museum (page 114), curated and formerly inhabited by the artist and now affiliated with the National Museum of Lithuania. Varnelis's optical art was part of an exciting exhibition at the Centre Pompidou in Paris which wrapped up in early 2025. Street artist **Vytenis Jakas** (b1980) is known for his cheeky and exuberant style and has become something of a sensation, best-known for the Yard Gallery in Kaunas (page 185). Jakas has turned the popular site into his residence and contemporary art hub.

One of the Lithuanian Art Association's senior members, **Arvydas Každailis** (b1939) is a greatly esteemed artist and champion of art, cultural identity and history in Lithuania. Každailis has lived through Lithuania's tumultuous periods since World War II and has dedicated his life to preserving Lithuania's history through his detailed historical illustrations and other creative endeavours, including the loving restoration of his summer home in the Zarasai region. The long-abandoned homestead had belonged to a famous Lithuanian poet, Faustas

Kirša, who ended up in the US after World War II. Každailis' extraordinarily prolific career has included all manner of graphic art, children's book illustrations, painting using various mediums, etchings, collage, woodcarving, metalwork, heraldry and more. He was also an art teacher for many years at the National M K Čiurlionis School of Art. Much of Každailis' work highlights the battles and struggles that Lithuania has endured both in ancient times and in the 20th century. Každailis is known as the creator of the modern coat of arms of Vilnius and Lithuania, as well as the flag of the President of Lithuania, among others. He has made it his mission to recreate the emblems and coats of arms for numerous towns and cities throughout the country. He has received numerous awards for his artistic contributions to Lithuania, including the Order of the Lithuanian Grand Duke Gediminas in 1999.

## TRADITIONAL ARTS AND CRAFTS  Vika Ross

Lithuania's most renowned painter and composer, Mikalojus Konstantinas Čiurlionis (page 188), once stated that 'folk art is the foundation of a nation's artistic tradition'; and, indeed, one of the defining characteristics of Lithuania's arts and crafts heritage is the organic integration of its folk art. A historically agrarian society, Lithuania continues to produce and value traditional handcrafted everyday items made of natural materials, and with artisan skills passed down through generations. Folk art is alive and well in Lithuania and in its vast post-World War II diaspora, and its techniques protected and encouraged through cultural heritage programmes. Lithuanians are passionate about preserving and reviving age-old traditions and are by nature hands-on, imaginative and amazingly creative. Festivals and fairs usually feature artisans selling their wares. By far the biggest craft fair is the annual Kaziukas Fair in March (page 80). Crafts workshops and small ethnographic museums containing examples of local crafters are ubiquitous across Lithuania, but visitors without Lithuanian language skills will struggle. The Museum of Lithuanian Ethnography (page 196) is an ideal opportunity to visit the workshops of an amber master, a basket weaver and a master of weaving who has inherited the skill from his mother and uses her traditional loom to continue the craft.

**Ceramics and pottery**  Souvenir shops and stalls offer an array of ceramic items, including bell pendants in all shapes and sizes, animal figurines and decorative tableware. Clay whistles in the form of birds are popular and echo the love of music and of the natural world in Lithuanian culture. Earrings and pendants fashioned from clay, candle 'houses', whimsical mythological creatures, Christmas ornaments and angel figures all make lovely gifts. Lithuania is also known for its **black ceramics** – the clay developing its distinctive, lustrous colour through traditional methods of pit-firing using natural materials such as wood and pine needles. Items such as jugs and bowls for daily domestic use were traditionally made using this technique; but archaeologists have discovered that black clay items had religious uses too and containers were used as urns for human remains several thousand years ago. There is a continued interest in preserving this technique in modern-day Lithuania.

**Basketry**  Beautifully handmade using a variety of natural materials, including straw, twigs and thin strips of wood, **baskets** have traditionally been used for mushroom picking, carrying vegetables and other produce to and from markets, and for displaying painted eggs at Easter. Elaborate **straw chandeliers**, or *sodai* (meaning gardens or orchards) were customarily created as wedding decorations and for birthdays, Christmas and other holidays, and this past-time is still very much en vogue. It is believed the chandeliers attract the souls (*sielas*) of deceased family members and so are hung above the family dining table or a baby's cradle to pass on good spirits. Traditional Lithuanian **Christmas ornaments** are made from wheat and rye straw and remain just as popular today. Straw **hats** have been incorporated into daily life in Lithuania for all generations and are also worn as part of national folk costumes, primarily by men.

**Dowry chests** Historically, young Lithuanian women spent years preparing the contents of their dowry chests (*kraičio skrynia*), including a range of items made from linen such as tablecloths, clothes and other practical textiles. These were encased in intricately painted wooden dowry chests with motifs of floral and natural elements and other colourful ornamentation. They would be proudly displayed in the future marital home.

**Metalwork** Dating back to pagan times, metalwork in Lithuania typically features elements of the natural world such as birds and plants and celestial themes such as suns and moons. Sun crosses – an amalgamation of a metal cross with ornate celestial features – represent a fusion of Lithuania's pagan and Christian traditions. With Lithuania's long-standing tradition of cross crafting, some wooden crosses are adorned with metal elements. Metal jewellery has always been popular, with archaeologists unearthing a variety of ancient jewellery items, including some made of silver and bronze – an interesting collection is showcased at the museum of the Kernavė archaeological site (page 129). Many a Lithuanian household has a wrought-iron horseshoe hung over the threshold to bring good fortune and ward-off unwanted or negative events, a custom thought to date from the 15th century. Much to the concern of foreign visitors, the horseshoe is always hung with the open end facing downwards (meaning the horse has walked forwards into the house, so bringing good luck).

**Paper cutting** Dating back to the 16th century, paper-cutting became a popular past-time in the 19th century in Lithuania, mostly for women, and has remained a prominent craft tradition to this day. Although, like many other traditional Lithuanian crafts, it was hindered during Soviet times, paper-cutting has since had a somewhat of a renaissance. Artworks created using scissors or a knife usually depict a rural scene, peasant life or natural objects containing national symbolism.

**Textiles** All manner of textile creations are integral to Lithuania's traditions and crafts. Historically, Lithuanian women would learn to spin and weave from a young age in order to acquire the skills to fill their dowry chests and equip households with items such as bedding, towels and tablecloths. Linen pieces would be embroidered with brightly coloured threads in geometric patterns. Traditional folk costumes are woven in distinctive styles that vary greatly from region to region; woven sashes used as belts for folk dance costumes have also traditionally been created as gifts for special occasions and as decorative items in homes that would be hung on beautiful hand-carved dowels. If you'd like to see a colourful array of folk costume, make sure you go to Lithuania's Song and Dance Festival (page 67).

Lithuanian textile techniques also include crocheting, knitting, wool-making and even beading in the form of regional beaded wrist warmers traditionally worn by all generations both as elaborate accessories for dance costumes and also for warmth. There is also a long-standing tradition of doll-making in Lithuania. Dolls in the various versions of traditional Lithuanian attire are ubiquitous in shops, museums and homes throughout the country.

**Knitting** Lithuanians are passionate knitters, their talents showcased in the complex patterns of the thick woollen socks and mittens for sale on souvenir stalls. Be sure to buy authentic knitwear rather than mass-produced alternatives. Along with most of Lithuania's heritage crafts, knitting stemmed from a practical need and became an integral part of social history representing regional symbolism, family status, love and loss.

**Linen** With its agrarian roots and age-old tradition of flax farming, it's not surprising that Lithuanians have a long-standing tradition of creating beautifully adorned linen tablecloths, napkins and clothing. Lithuania's top designers continue to embrace this material as both functional and fashionable; as such, women, men and children in Lithuania proudly wear a wide range of linen garments.

## AMBER

Baltic amber has been a lucrative commodity since the Neolithic period and was a staple export on the ancient trade routes between the Baltic and Mediterranean seas. It was formed over 45 million years ago during the Eocene epoch, when the surrounding region of Scandinavia was thick coniferous forest before being consumed by the Baltic Sea. The trees exuded resin to heal and protect the bark from insects or disease, running down the trunk in drops and trails. The sticky substance trapped detritus such as soil, seeds and insects (mainly flies and mosquitos but also spiders and ants among others) before hardening and preserving them in an amber grave. These fossilised inclusions are rare and valuable. Most deposits of Baltic amber are found on the Baltic Sea's southern coast, washed from their original location by rivers and tides and having been buried over time in sedimentary deposits before being redeposited by geological activity and washed ashore by wave action.

Traditionally, Baltic amber was collected by hand from the shore or scoured from the seabed with a net on a long pole. Modernisation transformed it into a huge industry with specialist divers and mechanical dredgers increasing both the industrial haul and environmental damage. A walk along the shoreline after a winter storm offers a good chance to hawk some amber in the flotsam. There are more than 250 documented colour varieties of amber, the dominant colours being light yellow to dark brown, but amber can be almost white, green or with a blue tint, transparent or opaque.

Amber jewellery and trinkets are popular souvenirs and if bought from a reputable seller come with a certificate of authenticity. Baltic amber is the only fossil resin to contain succinic acid, which is believed to have therapeutic properties for the wearer. A basic test for genuine Baltic amber is to heat up the amber by rubbing it in the palm of your hand – it should have a delicate fragrance of pine-tree resin.

To this day, amber is the material of choice for traditional Lithuanian jewellery. Next in popularity are amber figurines and even decorative wall art, including intricately assembled nature scenes or a portrait of the Virgin Mary that is a common sight in homes and places of worship around the country. Amber is literally the stuff of legends as told in the tragic love story of Jūratė and Kastytis, which ends with tiny pieces of amber from Jūratė's amber castle washing up to shore after its destruction by the god of Thunder (page 285).

**Woodwork** Woodwork is one of the hallmarks of Lithuanian craft, with numerous everyday items traditionally being made from wood, including spinning wheels, spoons and towel racks, as well as decorative and religious items. Commonly found in Lithuanian households is a *rūpintojėlis* or carved statue of a 'pensive' Christ (the direct translation means 'the one who cares'), considered by some to reflect the many hardships endured by Lithuanians over the centuries. At the other end of the spectrum, popular decorative items, to be hung on the wall or sit on bookcases, include goblins, devils and kitchen witches, along with other mythological creatures. The pagan and mystical elements of Lithuanian folklore have quite literally been carved into the cultural landscape. Wayside shrines can be spotted across the countryside along with chapel posts featuring wooden crosses and depictions of saints and other religious figures, including the pensive Christ. Wooden handicrafts are also incorporated in to folk music and dance traditions from carved wind instruments to wooden shoes which punctuate evocative folk dances. Also quintessentially Lithuanian are spooky-looking Shrovetide carnival masks made for the Užgavėnės festival, as well as ghoulish statues such as the well-known ones found in Juodkrantė's Witches Hill (page 307).

**LITERATURE** *Renata Sutovaitė*
Pagan Lithuania (page 30) did not have its own written word, the nation instead expressing itself through song. During the medieval years, important documents were written in Church Slavonic, Latin or Polish languages, even after the creation of the Grand Duchy of Lithuania during the 13th century. With the arrival of the Reformation in the 16th century, Protestant and Catholic clergymen stopped addressing their congregations in their usual Latin or Polish and began using Lithuanian; religious books and texts in Lithuanian soon followed. Slowly, this created opportunities for non-religious Lithuanian books to be printed; the first, *Catechism* by Martynas Mažvydas, was printed in 1547. Vilnius Jesuits took it a step further. The Renaissance and Baroque movements brought the founding of Vilnius University in 1579 and a profusion of Latin literature was born around Vilnius University and the King's court, giving rise to the region's first famous writer, the Lithuanian Polish *poëta laureatus* of Pope Urban VIII, Maciej Kazimierz Sarbiewski (Motiejus Kazimieras Sarbievijus; 1595–1640).

In the late 18th century, a stunning talent emerged in the form of Kristijonas Donelaitis (1714–80), a village pastor from Stalupėnai (today in the Russian exclave of Kaliningrad). Around 1770, he wrote a 2,997-lined poem titled *Metai* (The Seasons) in Lithuanian hexameter, about rural people and work. *Metai* barely survived the Napoleonic Wars and ended up being published only in 1818, when Romanticism was in full swing around Europe and cultural salons started to care about folk art. Meanwhile, in Vilnius, another literary giant emerged: Adam Mickiewicz (Adomas Mickevičius, 1798–1855). Three nations fought over him for a long time: he was born in the former Grand Duchy of Lithuania in an area now within the borders of modern-day Belarus; he studied in Vilnius and taught in Kaunas, and in his epic poem *Pan Tadeusz* he refers to 'Lithuania, my homeland'; and although he lived in Poland for only seven months, he was the son of a Polish noble and wrote in Polish. Eventually, with tri-partisan agreement he was credited to Poland.

The National Revival movement and the fight for books printed in the Latin alphabet at the end of the 19th century (following the uprising of 1863–64 and ban of the Latin alphabet by Russian tsars) gave rise to Žemaitė (1845–1921), a modest village woman who wrote about the harrowing obedience of women in the patriarchal rural society and rising above it. At a similar time, Lithuania's greatest poet, Maironis (1862–1932), wrote many verses praising Lithuanian nature and encouraging national identity and patriotism (page 181). Both Žemaitė and Maironis were honoured on Lithuanian litas banknotes.

## LANGUAGE BANS AND BOOK SMUGGLING

To restrict the use of a native language is to erode national identity, a linguistic and psychological weapon of choice repeatedly employed by Russian occupiers. In response to the 1863 attempted uprising of Lithuanian nationalists, Imperial Russia banned the Lithuanian language for four decades (1864–1904) to punish, control and strategically smother any rebellion. Russian became the major language and the Cyrillic alphabet replaced Lithuanian Latin characters. It was prohibited to speak Lithuanian in public or to produce any printed materials in Lithuanian. While families continued to speak Lithuanian at home and discreetly teach children their native tongue, an underground movement inevitably developed to supply contraband Lithuanian literature and printed materials. Books and leaflets were secretly printed in East Prussia at printing houses in Koenigsberg (Kaliningrad) and brave individuals called *knygnešiai* – book carriers – hauled books in sacks or covered wagons across the border, usually under the cover of darkness or during winter blizzards to evade the guards. It was an incredibly dangerous role, and the punishment if caught was imprisonment, exile to Siberia, or being shot. If successful, the knygnešiai would leave their haul at a designated place, perhaps in the forest, from where another associate would take the books on to their next place of hiding.

A clandestine network of distributors existed across the country. At first, operations were run predominantly by priests, motivated to obtain religious texts and prayer books for their parishioners and less likely to be suspected and searched. Catholic Bishop Motiejus Valančius (1801–75) was a leading figure who arranged the first large-scale network to smuggle books into Lithuania, posthumously awarded the status of 'greatest Lithuanian personality of the 19th century'. His successor was the peasant Jurgis Bielinis (1846–1918), an advocate for Lithuanian independence and who created the largest book-smuggling operation in Lithuania earning him the title 'King of the Book Carriers'. The brave and important role of the book smugglers is recognised every 16 March (Bielinis' birthday) as Day of the Book Smugglers (Knygnešio diena). Lithuania celebrates Lithuanian Press Restoration, Language and Book Day on 7 May every year to commemorate the lifting of the ban on that day in 1904.

The spirit of resistance printing resurfaced during the period of Soviet occupation. Lithuanian publishing houses were under state control, ensuring Moscow could direct the narrative and push Soviet ideology. Printed publications were an important medium through which the independence movement could reach people and for banned cultural and Christian teachings to be shared, so ingenious and high-risk illegal underground printing houses were constructed. One of the best examples and the only one that evaded Soviet security is the Underground Printing House 'ab' (page 196) in the garden suburbs of Kaunas, where the immensely brave Vytautas Andziulis (1930–2018) and Juozas Bacevičius (1918–95) constructed a covert printing operation in their greenhouse.

Regained independence in 1918 gave Lithuanian writers freedom of expression and access to the larger European literary world. Several writers became diplomats, including French-Polish-Lithuanian Oscar Milosz (1877–1939) – 'I am a Lithuanian poet, writing in French'. Perhaps the best-known female Lithuanian poet, Salomėja Nėris (1904–45) rose to fame but was soon condemned as a traitor to the nation – together with the Lithuanian communists she tagged along to Moscow to bring 'Stalin's sun' to Lithuania and wrote a poem worshipping the dictator. Later she apologised for her mistake but the nation is yet to forgive her.

Imprisoned in the Stutthof Concentration Camp during World War II, Balys Sruoga (1896–1947) miraculously survived and wrote a book filled with brutal truth and dark humour, *Dievų miškas* (Forest of the Gods), about his survival in an inhumane environment. Intellectuals were persecuted by Soviet Russia and many Modernists fled west to New York City. Among them were Antanas Škėma (1910–61), author of *Balta drobulė* (*White Shroud*); Henrikas Radauskas (1910–70), who proclaimed 'I do not believe in the world, but I do believe in fairytales'; poet Jonas Mekas (1922–2019), the 'godfather of American avant garde cinema'; and science-fiction writer Algis Budrys (1931–2008), author of *Rogue Moon*. Eduardas Cinzas (1924–96) settled down and wrote novels in Belgium.

In Soviet-occupied Lithuania, native literature did not stand still. Some skilfully wrote to appease the authorities (Eduardas Mieželaitis; 1919–97); others, like Juozas Baltušis (1909–91), depended not only on their talent but also on their personal background and connections; while others (Marcelijus Martinaitis, Sigitas Geda) did their best to break out of the censorship framework using satire, allegory and mythology. Justinas Marcinkevičius (1930–2011) wrote poetry and dramas that subtly reminded society of national heroes of the past and to fight for freedom. But not everyone managed to remain and navigate these times: poet Tomas Venclova (b1937) and author Saulius Tomas Kondrotas (b1953) emigrated to the United States, and Icchokas Meras (1934–2014), who wrote in Lithuanian, left for Israel.

During the fall of the Soviet Union, censors in 1989 possibly did not entirely understand the brave provocations in the novel *Vilniaus pokeris* (*Vilnius Poker*) by Postmodernist Ričardas Gavelis, while Jurgis Kunčinas, a 'chronicler of Soviet bohemianism and the absurdity of Soviet social life', wrote *Tūla* set largely in Vilnius's Užupis district, and became the greatest Lithuanian writer of the early post-Soviet years.

Modern-day Lithuanian literature contains many excellent historical fiction novels, including Arvydas Šlepikas' novel *Mano vardas Marytė* (*My Name is Marytė*), recalling the ruthless post-World War II years, when thousands of hungry orphans known as *Wolfskinder*, from Prussia (now Kaliningrad), walked into Lithuania asking for bread. Kristina Sabaliauskaitė's *Silva Rerum* explores events relevant to all of eastern and central Europe scarred by destructive wars. Playwrights Marius Ivaškevičius and Sigitas Parulskis' plays fill entire theatres; Renata Šerelytė is famous for her short stories and adventure books for children, while Giedra Radvilavičiūtė was awarded the 2012 EU literature prize for her short stories full of everyday magic. Gabija Grušaitė's *Cold East* appeals to contemporary audiences with themes of identity. *Pietinia Kronikas*, by Rimantas Kmita, about the first, wild, post-Soviet years was written in the highly specific Šiauliai dialect.

On the global stage, Lithuania was made famous in world literature by American Lithuanian Rūta Šepetys's bestseller *Between Shades of Gray* about the devastating exile of Lithuanians to Siberia during the 1940s. And the most notorious 'fictional Lithuanian' of all time – Hannibal Lecter, born, by the will of author Thomas Harris, in a small estate somewhere near Vilnius.

## CINEMA  Matt Kovalick

Since independence, Lithuanian landscapes have served as the backdrop to B-movies and blockbusters proving Lithuania to be an attractive, competitive and talented film location. Trakai Castle and Vilnius University starred in the BBC's *War and Peace* drama while Pažaislis Monastery in Kaunas featured in HBO's *Catherine the Great*. Lukiškės Prison created convincing gulag scenes in Netflix's *Stranger Things*, while the Soviet architecture of Vilnius's Fabijoniškės district provided backdrops for *Young Wallander* and the award-winning *Chernobyl* series, which was also filmed at the decommissioned Ignalina Nuclear Power Plant (page 239). A skilled filmmaking workforce and tax incentives are part of Lithuania's draw, and it also makes for a cheaper and more straightforward alternative to Russia when filming period epics.

Lithuanian documentaries, short films and features are appearing more frequently at international film festivals and returning home with awards and accolades. Laurynas Bareiša, Saulė Bliuvaitė and Alantė Kavaitė exemplify emerging Lithuanian directors who have found success with recent feature-length films and recognition at European and American festivals like Locarno, Cannes, Venice and Sundance. For more information visit the Lithuanian Film Centre (Lietuvos kino centras; w lkc.lt).

In 1925, the film *Naktis Lietuvoje* (Night in Lithuania) by Pranas Valuskis about Lithuanian book smugglers introduced Hollywood to Lithuanian cinema. Creativity was to be stifled for decades during Soviet occupation although film directors, including Gytis Lukšas, Henrikas Šablevičius and Arūnas Žebriūnas, were able to work around censorship and produce valuable films. Notable Lithuanian films include *Vienui vieni* (Utterly Alone; 2004) by Jonas Vaitkusm, based on real-life events in the life of partisan and freedom fighter Juozas Lukša, set in 1950–51, and filmed in black and white. Documentary *The Invisible Front* (2014) by Jonas Ohman and Vincas Sruoginis personalises the Forest Brothers' resistance movement also through the story of Juozas Lukša. Historical drama *Ashes in the Snow* (2018) by Marius Markevičius tells of the forced deportation of Lithuanians to Siberia. Small yet skilful, the Lithuanian filmmaking community interrogates the past with urgency as the generation who lived under occupation ages. New Lithuanian filmmakers turn their lens on society and relationships creating contemporary pieces. Following in the footsteps of Lithuanian-American Jonas Mekas, the godfather of American avant-garde cinema, presentations of Lithuanian and Baltic filmmakers pop up in New York, London and at major cinematic events. The annual Vilnius Short Film festival (Vilniaus trumpųjų filmų festivalis; w filmshorts.lt), which takes place each year in January, and the Vilnius International Film Festival ( w kinopavasaris.lt) in March showcase local and international films at events nationwide.

## MUSIC  Matt Kovalick

Music flows freely through Lithuania and its people. Ask a group of Lithuanians if they sing and they can likely harmonise an impromptu folk song. **Folk music** is an integral part of Lithuania's cultural heritage, with over half a million unique songs officially recorded. These songs are historical records of days gone by – songs about harvest, weaving, war, family life, love and legends, accompanied by traditional instruments such as *kanklės*, a plucked stringed instrument, trapezoid in shape and similar to a zither. Singing is a group activity and still to this day local communities have their own ensembles, styles and accompanying dances. *Sutartinės* is a traditional **polyphonic singing** style that is included in the UNESCO list of Intangible Cultural Heritage of Humanity. It is an archaic form of Lithuanian singing native to the northeastern Aukštaitija region. The songs are performed by small groups of women and follow a simple structure with two to five pitches, creating a powerful sound. Lithuanian diaspora community groups celebrate holidays with songs that nod to a nostalgic, simpler, countryside life back in the homeland. This rich music culture survived and thrived over the last century as a means of expression and identity, allowed in peasant communities even under oppression. Nothing is more patriotic and powerful than the **Lithuanian Song and Dance Festival** (page 67) held every four years. Upwards of 37,000 performers from around the world feature in the multi-day spectacle, all having learned the same songs and dance routines that create a mesmerising scene of swaying singers adorned in national costumes of flowing skirts, linen shirts, and *juostos* (colourful woven belts). Visit the **Kaunas Folk Music Museum** to learn more (page 182).

The godfather of Lithuanian music is **Mikalojus Konstantinas Čiurlionis** (1875–1911), who represented the Lithuanian soul through both his music and art. The Čiurlionis museums in Kaunas (page 187) and Druskininkai (page 142) provide authentic insights into his life and work, guiding you through his unique world from romantic to modern mysticism. As the nation re-emerged in independence, interest and pride in his compositions and accompanying paintings grew. Now, the academy bearing his name produces new generations of talent. If you frequent the classical concert halls of Europe you have probably already heard a touring Lithuanian pianist, violinist or opera singer. Orchestras from both sides of the Atlantic engage conductors like **Mirga Gražinytė-Tyla** and **Modestas Pitrėnas** to lead their symphonies. While, in Vilnius, Kaunas or Klaipėda, enjoying orchestra or opera is easy and not too expensive as halls run full seasons of quality concerts.

Classical crossover talents like accordionist **Martynas Levickis** even sell out arena-size venues, which feature international and Lithuanian pop stars. With rock music banned under the Soviets, 90s rock legend **Andrius Mamontovas** with his band **Foje** burst through first after independence. Along with 2000s groups like Sel, Mango, Biplan and sports arena anthem icon Marijonas Mikutavičius, the spotlight shifted on to a new generation of pop stars. Recent, respectable Eurovision Song Contest entries from **The Roop** and **Monika Riu** caught airplay beyond the borders. Acts well worth a listen online or in person include **Gjan** and **Saulius Prūsaitis** who often tour the country or feature at music festivals like the **Žagarė Cherry Festival** held in July (page 263) or at summer concerts in Palanga.

**SPORT** Matt Kovalick

In Lithuania, **basketball** (krepšinis) transcends sport, often being referred to as the nation's second religion. Basketball has been a source of national pride and a proxy for politics ever since the sport's introduction during the independent interwar years and Lithuania's victory at EuroBasket 1937. The raucous courtside atmosphere of a Žalgiris game at Žalgirio Arena in Kaunas rivals any major sporting event. Today's opponents are teams from the Euroleague or national league, Lietuvos krepšinio lyga (w lkl.lt), but in the Soviet era, battling CSKA Moscow served as a proxy for politics, occupied versus occupier. Few moments shine as bright – or as colourful – in sport and national pride as Lithuania winning the 1992 Barcelona Olympics basketball bronze medal. On the podium, the squad announced to the world that Lithuania was again free and independent while sporting tie-dyed jerseys featuring a dunking skeleton sponsored by the Grateful Dead jam band. The documentary *The Other Dream Team* by Marius Markevičius chronicles this inspirational story through interviews with star players like Arvydas Sabonis and Šarūnas Marčiulionis and portrays their experience pre- and post-independence.

With three Olympic bronzes and three European championship titles, Lithuania continues to produce high-quality talent. The country ranks as having one of the highest number of players per capita in the National Basketball Association (NBA) in the USA.

For a small country, Lithuania produces its fair share of top athletes. For decades they competed under the flag of the Soviet Union, but since the 1992 Olympics have competed as Lithuania. Notable names include swimmer Rūta Meilutytė who won the 100m breaststroke Olympic gold medal in 2012 at the age of 15 and continues to win the 50m event at world-class meets more than a decade later. The current world record holder in discus, Mykolas Alekna broke the Olympic record of his father – two-time gold medallist Virgilijus Alekna – and took home the silver medal at the 2024 Paris Olympics. Also in Paris, newcomer Dominika Banevič 'B-Girl Nicka' secured the first silver medal in women's breakdancing. Sports stars in athletics, shooting, cycling and hockey have also brought home gold and glory.

Beyond the Olympics, Lithuanian strongman Žydrūnas 'Big Z' Savickas has put his country on the map by lifting atlas stones and pulling planes – he has broken world records and won the World's Strongest Man competition four times. And two solo athlete-activists named Aurimas traversed oceans to bring recognition to Lithuania and important causes. In 2023, adventurer Aurimas Valujavičius rowed across the Atlantic from Ayamonte, Spain, to Miami, Florida, in 121 days to commemorate 90 years since the fateful transatlantic flight by Lithuanian pilots Steponas Darius and Stasys Girėnas in 1933 (page 193). He was just days away from completing his 12,000km journey when storm conditions caused by Cyclone Alfred resulted in him needing to be rescued. And in September 2024, under the banner 'Lithuania stands together', Aurimas Mockus set off to row solo across the Pacific from San Diego, California, to Brisbane, Australia, to raise awareness and money for relief efforts in Ukraine.

# 2

# Practical Information

## WHEN TO VISIT

In recent years, Lithuania has confidently become a year-round destination with amenities and entertainment to cater for all seasons. It is a national talent to adapt to the season, be it changing from summer to winter tyres, or from cold soup to hot soup – life carries on regardless of the weather or temperature.

**Spring** has an increasing sense of optimism as the days slowly get longer and brown landscapes garner faint hues of green. March and early April can be a tad drab but festivities like Kaziukas Fair and Easter inject a welcome shot of colour and vigour. It is said that St George's Day (23 April) unlocks nature and one week later Lithuania will be green. Temperatures can be volatile with unseasonably warm days flanked by snow showers. If you visit in spring, always have some change in your pocket for the first time you hear a cuckoo or, according to local custom, the year ahead will be financially tight. Also take sunglasses, woolly gloves and an umbrella.

**Summer** days from late May to early September are long and light with temperatures hovering between 18 and 25°C. Hot spells of 30°C and above are becoming more regular in July and August, often culminating in a thunderstorm at the end of the day. The Curonian Spit lays claim as the sunniest place in Lithuania but a coastal breeze keeps the seaside resorts slightly cooler. Al fresco living is embraced across the country with pop-up terraces and outdoor venues in parks and courtyards. With locals holidaying and international guests visiting, summer is peak season in Lithuania and prices reflect this, but the variety of cultural offerings can be well worth it.

**Autumn** days in a country where ancient woodlands and mixed forests cover a third of the territory is always going to be golden. You don't need to leave the cities to appreciate the season; there are remarkably green spaces with wooded hills, tree-lined avenues and large parks bringing the russet and copper colours into the city. The evenings cut in early, but comfort can be found in cosy bars and restaurants, or you can while away the evening at an opera, ballet or concert performance. Often the weather is mild and settled during the day, with a cold nip in the evening requiring a hat and gloves in addition to your coat.

**Winter** feels long and is all too often wished away, but it too has its moments. November can be grey as the first snow is anticipated, and once it arrives, it leaves just as quickly. Indeed, snowfall in Lithuania comes and goes, with heavy snowfall often followed by a mild period of melting and shovelled piles of snow turn grey with silt and sand. Temperatures average around -5–0°C but can plummet to -25°C for short periods. As always, there is no such thing as bad weather, only unsuitable clothing. Layer up with thermals, a good thick coat and don't forget a good-quality hat, scarf, gloves and socks for the extremities. Waterproof footwear with a good grip is essential. Indoors will be warm and toasty, no matter how cold it is outside

– by the end of your visit you will be an expert at putting on/taking off your winter layers. Christmas Markets and festive street decorations commence at the end of November lifting spirits and attracting seasonal shoppers and sightseers up to the New Year.

For those interested in **birdwatching**, spring and autumn are the optimal times to visit because of Lithuania's location on migratory routes.

## HIGHLIGHTS

A sad but all too commonly heard utterance is 'I've done Lithuania, I went to Vilnius on a city break.' **Vilnius** is indeed brilliantly beautiful, its Old Town a joyous mix of Baroque architecture, creative genius and cultural and culinary highlights; but the capital is also a gateway to the rest of the country with some fascinating cultural gems and plenty to entice nature lovers, outdoor enthusiasts and history buffs alike. Head south from Vilnius to the spa resort of Druskininkai and combine relaxation with hiking through the historic wooden villages of **Dzūkija National Park**, mushrooming, learning about the Soviet occupation at Grūtas Soviet Sculpture Park, or exploring the peripheral towns and villages along the Belarus and Russia borders. Lithuania's second city **Kaunas** was recently granted UNESCO World Heritage status for its unique interwar-period architecture and is surrounded by three major national heritage sites: the Museum of Lithuanian Ethnography (Rumšiškės), Ninth Fort former prison camp and Pažaislis Monastery. Tour along the **Nemunas River valley** for a scenic route through former Prussian lands of Lithuania Minor to the **Lithuanian seaside**, where holidays can be spent on the beach, hiking or cycling, indulging in local specialities and soaking up the regional culture and history. Traverse the north of the country through the ethnographic region of **Žemaitija** with its traditional wooden churches and road shrines and the Cold War Museum missile base, and take the opportunity to relax in nature and sail or scuba dive at **Lake Plateliai**. Northeast of Šiauliai is the awe-inspiring pilgrimage site of the **Hill of Crosses**. Ride the Aukštaitija Narrow Gauge Railway from Anykščiai before venturing into **Aukštaitija National Park** to trek the hiking trails or paddle kayaking routes through interconnecting lakes. Visit the decommissioned **Ignalina Nuclear Power Plant** made famous as a film location for the HBO TV series *Chernobyl*. Head south via the charming towns of Palūšė, Molėtai and Labanoras for a walk in nature, berry picking or to enjoy a local lunch. Last but never least, eat *kibinai* pasties at **Trakai** before crossing the wooden bridges to explore the iconic island castle – or maybe you prefer to soar above the castle on a hot-air balloon experience.

## SUGGESTED ITINERARIES *Phil Teubler*

**A WEEKEND IN VILNIUS** Take a guided walking tour with a local guide who will open your eyes to the city's secrets and stories; or, to cover more distance, take a 2-hour bike tour. Highlights include Gediminas Castle for a panoramic view of the city and the Museum of Occupations and Freedom Fights to understand the Lithuanian experience during Soviet occupation. Stroll the cobbled streets of the Old Town to admire its Baroque façades; visit the independent republic of Užupis, full of artists' studios and sculptures; and make time to enjoy the numerous restaurants, bars and cafés the capital has to offer. Take a trip out of town to Trakai, just 30km away, equally attractive in winter, when you can walk on the frozen lake, and in summer when you can swim or kayak.

**ONE WEEK** After several days exploring Vilnius, travel on to Kaunas on a double-decker express train (50mins; upgrade to first class for just a few extra euros). Spend time admiring the city's UNESCO-listed Modernist architecture, then take half-day trips out of town to the Ninth Fort, Pažaislis Monastery and the Museum of Lithuanian Ethnography (Rumšiškės). Finish off with a cycle ride along the Nemunas River.

**TWO WEEKS** Take a little longer to explore Lithuania's cities, countryside and coast. After four nights discovering Vilnius, travel south via Trakai to Druskininkai. Here, unwind in a spa hotel, visit Grūtas Soviet Sculpture Park, hike, kayak or go mushrooming – and if you're in need of more activity, head to the indoor ski facility and water park open year-round. On the coast, stay in Klaipėda or Palanga for four nights. From whichever town you make your base, you can sightsee, spend time on the beach and take a day trip to the Curonian Spit. Stay in a farmstead in Žemaitija

### BALTIC HIKING TRAILS

Whether you are partial to extreme challenges and physical endurance or are looking to add some pleasant day hikes into your Lithuania itinerary, the **Baltic Trails** are two long-distance routes which traverse Estonia, Latvia and Lithuania as part of longer European trails. The coastal trail is marked with signs of white-blue-white horizontal stripes or blue stickers in urban areas; the forest trail has signs of white-orange-white and orange stickers. Smaller sections of each trail can be done in isolation. For more details, visit the well-organised and clearly presented website: **w** baltictrails.eu.

The **Baltic Coastal Hiking Route** (Jūrų takas) is part of the 10,000km long-distance European Coastal Path (E9) from Cape St Vincent in Portugal to Tallinn in Estonia, which is the longest coastal trail in the world. The Lithuania section starts at Nida on the Curonian Spit and ends at the Lithuania–Latvia border north of Šventoji, including also the Nemunas Delta. Committed hikers will relish the challenge of this 216km trail along the Lithuanian coast. Those looking for a shorter hike can do any number of the individual sections of approximately 20km per day. Each section of the trail offers clear information about amenities along the way and transport options for returning to your starting point.

The **Baltic Forest Hiking Route** (Miško takas) is part of the European Long-Distance Path (E11), which starts in the Netherlands and ends in Tallinn, Estonia. The Lithuania section is 747km long, starting at the Poland–Lithuania border near Lazdijai and passing through the forests and farmland of western Lithuania before entering Latvia north of Skuodas. Highlights include the Dzūkija and Žemaitija national parks. The comprehensive daily itineraries are perfect also for day hikers.

Look out for the sign 'Draugiški žygeiviams' along the trails – this means 'hiker-friendly' and is awarded to establishments offering support services such as drinking water and electric charging points.

The **Camino-Lituano** (**w** caminolituano.com) is another long-distance hiking trail (500km) traversing Lithuania from Žagarė in the north to the Polish border south of Lazdijai. It is part of the Camino de Santiago network of pilgrimage routes that lead to Santiago de Compostela in northwest Spain. Each stage is approximately 25km long and the route is marked with yellow arrows and the scallop shell symbol of St James (Santiago).

National Park or travel back to Kaunas via the Cold War Museum or Nemunas River valley.

**THREE WEEKS** Take all the above and add lesser-known places and some more unusual sights to your itinerary, or slow down by spending more time in nature. Stay a couple of nights on the Curonian Spit in an old fishing village, discover northern Lithuania and local life in Žagarė, take time out in Anykščiai and ride the Aukštaitija Narrow Gauge Railway, overnight in a manor house, or head northeast to visit Ignalina Nuclear Power Plant where the drama series *Chernobyl* was filmed.

## TOURIST INFORMATION AND TOUR OPERATORS

Lithuania's official online tourism portal **Lithuania Travel** (Keliauk Lietuvoje; w lithuania.travel) offers a blog-style overview of the country's main attractions and an online booking tool. For the nitty-gritty details, head to the city and regional tourist office websites listed in the relevant chapters of this guide. Local tourist information centres have benefitted greatly from regional investment and provide up-to-date tourist information and local recommendations; they also have English-speaking staff.

### TOUR OPERATORS
**Lithuania**
**Baltic Bike Travel** w bbtravel.lt. Specialists in cycling holidays around Lithuania.
**Baltic Holidays** w balticholidays.com. Specialists in individual & group tailor-made tours of Lithuania with local drivers & guides. Baltic & Nordic tours also offered. Based in Kaunas, with both Lithuanian & UK teams of experts.
**Jerulita** w jerulita.com. Specialists in Jewish heritage tours of Lithuania.

**Lithuanian Tours** w lithuaniantours.com. Offering an array of countrywide tours & sightseeing day trips.

**UK**
**Naturetrek** w naturetrek.co.uk. Seasonal birdwatching tours of Lithuania.
**Regent Holidays** w regent-holidays.co.uk. Offering group tours, w/end breaks, fly-drives & individual arrangements to Lithuania & the neighbouring Baltic countries.

### FAMILY HERITAGE RESEARCH

If you have Lithuanian ancestry and want to research your roots, these genealogy resources are a good place to start.

**Archeonas** w archeonas.lt. A Lithuanian site, founded by professional historian & genealogist Sigita Gasparavičienė, it is ideal for preparation before a family-research trip to Lithuania, or for follow-up from afar.
**Lithuanian Genealogy** w lithuaniangenealogy.com. A US-based website founded by Angela Sinickas who successfully researched her own Lithuanian family connections & now offers these services to others. The site recommends resources for starting your own online research.
**Lithuanian Society of Genealogy & Heraldry** w genealogija.lt. The website is currently in Lithuanian only, but you are advised to contact them by email & request assistance directly.

**TravelLocal** w travellocal.com. A UK-based website where you can book direct with selected local travel companies, allowing you to communicate with a ground operator without having to go through a 3rd-party travel operator or agent. Your booking with the local company has full financial protection, but note that travel to the destination is not included. Member of ABTA, ASTA.

## USA
**Vytis Tours** w vytistours.com. Individual & group tours to Lithuania & the Baltic countries.

## RED TAPE

**ENTRY REQUIREMENTS** Lithuania is a member of both the European Union and Schengen group of countries, along with its Baltic neighbours Latvia, Estonia and Poland. There are no border controls between these countries and no visas are needed for travellers from other EU and Schengen countries, Australia, Canada, New Zealand, the UK and the USA.

Nationals of non-Schengen countries wishing to travel to Lithuania require a passport that is valid for at least three months after the date of departure from the Schengen area. Passports must have been issued within the last ten years.

Note that, from the last quarter of 2026, citizens of visa-exempt countries, including the UK, USA, Canada and Australia, will be required to pay a fee and obtain an ETIAS travel authorisation (w travel-europe.europa.eu/etias_en) in order to enter Lithuania. A new Entry-Exit System (EES; w travel-europe.europa.eu/ees_en) is also set to be introduced on 12 October, to replace the requirement for stamping passports. This will be rolled out gradually at border crossings over the following six months, with full implementation across the EU by 10 April 2026. Check before you travel.

If you are intending to stay longer than 90 days in Lithuania, you will need to apply for a residence permit via the MIGRIS Electronic migration service( w migracija.lt).

**EMBASSIES** The Ministry of Foreign Affairs maintains a list of Lithuanian embassies around the world at w keliauk.urm.lt/en/embassies, where you can also apply for a Schengen visa if needed. The website also lists foreign embassies and honorary consuls based in Lithuania.

## GETTING THERE AND AWAY

Since the collapse of the national carrier Lithuanian Airlines in 2009, Lithuania is now predominantly served by low-cost airlines for direct flights throughout Europe. Ryanair is often the only choice unless you opt for a more expensive and longer indirect flight with a national carrier. Long-haul flights can arrive to Vilnius or Palanga if flying with Scandinavian Airlines (SAS), allowing for a one-way tour across the country. As flight-free travel becomes more popular in response to the climate crisis, travellers can combine overland travel by bus or train with ferry services operating from Klaipėda port. At the time of writing the borders with Kaliningrad (Russia) and Belarus are closed to tourist traffic.

**BY AIR** Lithuania has three international airports: **Vilnius Airport** (w vilnius-airport.lt; IATA airport code VNO) is located 5km southeast of Vilnius city centre; **Kaunas Airport** (w kaunas-airport.lt; KUN) is situated 14km north of Kaunas; and **Palanga Airport** (w palanga-airport.lt; PLQ) is 6km north of Palanga. All three airports are small and easy to navigate. Kaunas Airport is a low-cost airline hub, with Vilnius predominantly serving the national carriers. Palanga serves both low-cost and national carriers but only a handful of flights per day. At the time of writing, the airlines offering direct routes to Lithuania are as follows.

**airBaltic** w airbaltic.com. The Latvian airline is majority owned by the Latvian government with Riga as its main hub. It operates daily flights from Vilnius to Riga, Tallinn & many other European cities; from Palanga, daily flights to Amsterdam & Riga.
**Finnair** w finnair.com. The Finnish national carrier has 4 or 5 direct flights daily between Vilnius & Helsinki, making it a good option for long-haul connections.
**LOT Polish Airlines** w lot.com. Operates up to 6 daily flights between Vilnius & Warsaw, & is also a popular long-haul option.
**Lufthansa** w lufthansa.com. 2 or 3 flights daily between Vilnius & Frankfurt.
**Norwegian** w norwegian.com. Fly from Vilnius to Oslo & Stockholm 3 times per week. Fly from Palanga to Oslo 5 times per week.
**Ryanair** w ryanair.com. Scheduled flights from Vilnius to London Luton & London Stansted, also Dublin & other European cities. Operates from Kaunas to London Luton, London Stansted, Liverpool, Edinburgh, Bristol & Belfast, also Dublin, Shannon & other European cities. Flies from Palanga to London Stansted & Dublin.
**Scandinavian Airlines (SAS)** w flysas.com. Operates 2 or 3 flights daily from Vilnius to Copenhagen & Stockholm with good long-haul connections. Flights from Palanga to Copenhagen twice daily.
**SWISS** w swiss.com. Flights between Vilnius & Zurich daily.
**Turkish Airlines** w turkishairlines.com. Flies twice daily between Vilnius & Istanbul.
**Wizz Air** w wizzair.com. Flies daily between Vilnius & London Luton, also Kaunas & London Luton. Operates direct flights from Vilnius & Kaunas to several European cities.

**BY TRAIN** Since independence in 1991, rail links to Lithuania have been improving slowly. The EU-funded project Rail Baltica (w railbaltica.org) through which Lithuania and its Baltic state neighbours will be integrated with the European Rail Network is planned to complete in 2030, providing efficient train travel between the three countries and Poland. You must carry your passport or proof of identity with you on all international train journeys.

**From/to Poland** There is a joint Polish Railways PKP Intercity (w intercity.pl) and Lithuanian Railways (page 56) daily train service from Warsaw to Vilnius via Kaunas and vice versa. Although sold as a direct service, you do change trains in Mockava in Lithuania. It is a simple change from one side of an island platform to the other with little or no waiting time, the only inconvenience being the lack of shelter if it is raining. Mockava train station is very basic and in a rural location. If you arrange a pick-up or drop-off there, note that Mockava train station is not in the village of Mockava but further east and close to the village of Zelionka. Bikes can be taken on board the trains, but as space is limited you are advised to make a reservation in advance. There is a 35kg limit on luggage, but extra luggage allowance can be purchased. The Lithuanian train is new with a snack service, while the Polish train is often older livery and you should take your own food and drink just in case. Both trains offer first- and second-class tickets. The journey takes approximately 9 hours and an adult ticket one-way costs €25.

**From/to Latvia** A direct train service operated by Lithuanian Railways runs daily from Vilnius to Riga and back again. The journey takes 4 hours 15 minutes one way and stops at Kaišiadorys, Šiauliai, Joniškis and Jelgava. The trains have seating in first and second class, wheelchair access and bike spaces (€10 per bike, prebooking advised), and snacks and drinks are available to buy. A one-way adult ticket costs from €24 per person in second class (€34 in 1st class).

### LITHUANIA'S RAILWAY LEGACY

Lithuania's internal rail network stems from the mid to late 1800s, when Imperial Russia ruled and constructed the Warsaw–St Petersburg railway which crossed southeastern Lithuania, stopping at Vilnius; a branch line connected Kaunas and Kybartai. After Lithuanian independence in 1918, attempts to continue using the inherited network were marred by poor conditions, with passengers sometimes having to disembark to help collect firewood for the driver. Some modernisation took place with upgraded rolling stock, but one issue persisted – the railway tracks in Lithuania were Russian broad gauge and incompatible with those leading west into Poland. It is said that the Russian gauge was strategically conceived to prevent Western forces from attacking Russia via the rail network. It is also said that it was an error by a Russian spy who measured the German railway tracks incorrectly. When the Soviet Union occupied Lithuania in 1940 the incompatible railway gauges were certainly another form of barrier with the West. After independence from the Soviet Union in 1990, Lithuania constructed a new stretch of European gauge railway from Šeštokai to the Lithuania–Poland border to facilitate a connection with the Polish rail network. For several decades Šeštokai was where passengers changed trains from a Russian gauge train to a European gauge train on the route to Warsaw. In 2001, the three Baltic countries signed an agreement to cooperate on a new pan-Baltic railway. The EU-funded project Rail Baltica (w railbaltica.org) will integrate the Baltic states into the European Rail Network and provide much-needed efficient train travel between Warsaw, Vilnius, Riga, Tallinn and Helsinki (ferry) by 2030, although this date looks likely to be pushed back. Until then, passengers still must change trains when travelling from Poland to Lithuania, but this now occurs at the new station of Mockava. At the time of writing, it is unknown how the new Rail Baltica route will affect the existing stations or railway lines that will not be serviced by the new route. Hopefully they will be kept as local lines.

**Interrail/Eurail** Lithuania is now covered by the Interrail/Eurail scheme (w interrail.eu). You can buy a single country pass for Lithuania for three to eight days' duration (3-day/8-day adult pass €50/113). The pass covers your ticket cost but a seat reservation is compulsory on most routes and will cost an additional €5 per person per journey. Lithuania is also covered on the Interrail Global Pass, which allows travel across 33 European countries, lasting from four days to three months. Compulsory seat reservations also apply.

**BY BUS** International bus services to Lithuania are well developed with several options. A one-way adult ticket from Riga to Vilnius costs from €15 standard class to €30 luxury class. A one-way ticket from Warsaw to Vilnius costs from €19 standard class.

**Ecolines** w ecolines.net. Services from Vilnius & Kaunas to European cities including Warsaw (daily overnight service; 8hrs 45mins), Riga (3 a day; 4hrs) & Tallinn (2 a day; 9hrs 30mins). At the time of writing services to Minsk, Moscow & St Petersburg were still running despite sanctions and tightened security. Services are also running to Ukraine. Buses are equipped with onboard toilet, free Wi-Fi & sometimes a snack service but do not rely on this.

**FlixBus** w global.flixbus.com. A low-cost service with routes from Vilnius & Kaunas to cities throughout Europe & good connections for onward

travel to Klaipėda for the coast. A good option for travel Vilnius to/from Gdansk via Bialystok (13hrs 30mins; adult €25.99 one-way).
**Lux Express** w luxexpress.eu. Regular services from Vilnius to Riga, Tallinn & Warsaw. There's also a direct service from Klaipėda to Riga (3 a day; 4hrs 40mins). Buses have onboard toilet, Wi-Fi, charging points, individual LuxTV screens & snack service. Lux Express Lounge buses offer more luxurious Relax seat upgrades.
**Ollex** w ollex.lt. A local Lithuanian bus company offering regular daily connections from Riga Airport to Lithuanian cities including Klaipėda, Šiauliai, Plungė & Telšiai.

**BY FERRY** Lithuania can be reached by ferry from **Germany** and **Sweden**, with all ferries arriving to the port of Klaipėda in western Lithuania. The ferries are basic commercial ferries used mainly for freight, but they do take private passengers on foot or with their own vehicle. For further details of these sailings, see the **DFDS** (w dfds.com) and **TT-Line** (w ttline.com) websites.

**BY CAR** If driving to Lithuania you will need a full valid driving licence, car insurance certificate valid for driving in Lithuania and the vehicle registration document. Drivers must be over 18. The car must display the national identifier ('UK' for vehicles registered in the UK) either within the car registration number plate or separately as a sticker. You are advised to take headlight converters for driving on the right (for UK vehicles), a warning triangle, fire extinguisher, first-aid kit, reflective jackets for all passengers, a spare bulb and fuse set, and your locking wheel nut.

**From Poland** Driving to Lithuania via Poland is straightforward. This border area is called the Suwałki Gap (page 160), named after the nearby Polish town of Suwałki and Lithuanian ethnographic region Suvalkija. It is unique in having a tri-border point for Lithuania–Poland–Russia (Kaliningrad) at its western end and another for Lithuania–Poland–Belarus at its eastern end. All overland connections from Lithuania, Latvia and Estonia to western Europe pass through this 65km wide 'gap'. Since Russia invaded Ukraine, the Suwałki Gap has made news headlines and has been widely discussed as vulnerable to a Russian and Belarusian strategic attack; this has stirred curiosity in some visitors and there are certainly some interesting sights to see. The A5/E67 is the Via Baltica highway that runs from Warsaw to Tallinn, although the road officially starts in Prague. The highway is a decent dual carriageway and is constantly being maintained and improved; it skirts Kaunas, where you have the option to join the A1 road west to the Lithuanian coast, or east towards Vilnius. The scenic and slightly slower option is via Augustow in Poland's lake district, travelling into Lithuania on road 135/E16, then via Lazdijai and Alytus to Vilnius. When you cross the border from Poland into Lithuania it will be marked by simple country signs as you are already in the Schengen zone of free movement. Think carefully before choosing to cross the border on a minor route as it is likely to be a bone-shaking sandy road, rutted and pot-holed in the middle of the forest with no phone signal.

**From Latvia** The most direct driving route between Latvia and Lithuania is the A10/E67. Just south of Panevėžys it splits into the A2 to Vilnius and A8/E67 to Kaunas. The most popular route for tourists is the A12/E77, via Šiauliai and the Hill of Crosses. Good main roads also connect the countries on the eastern side between Daugavpils and Utena (A6) and on the western coast between Liepāja and Palanga (A13). Even the small roads that cross the Latvia–Lithuania border are of satisfactory quality due to substantial local traffic between the two countries, for example the road crossings between Ezere and Mažeikiai, Augstkalne and Žagarė or Skaistkalne and Biržai.

## HEALTH  with Dr Daniel Campion

**BEFORE YOU TRAVEL** Overall, the standard of health care in Lithuania is good. As an indicator of population health, life expectancy is improving but remains relatively low by EU standards. There are no legally required vaccinations to enter the country, but before travelling you should ensure you are up to date with routine vaccinations including measles, tetanus, diphtheria, influenza and Covid-19. The need for additional vaccinations including hepatitis A, hepatitis B, rabies or tick-borne encephalitis depends upon your lifestyle and planned activities in Lithuania.

Nationals of EU countries plus Iceland, Liechtenstein, Norway or Switzerland should ensure they have a valid European Health Insurance Card (EHIC). UK nationals should have a valid Global Health Insurance Card (GHIC; w nhs.uk). Both cards enable you to receive medical treatment on the same basis as a local resident, but neither should replace adequate travel insurance. They do not cover any other health-related costs that may be incurred, including medical repatriation or private treatments. It is important to take out an appropriate travel insurance policy to cover your needs.

**Travel clinics and health information** A list of current travel clinic websites worldwide is available on w istm.org. For other journey preparation information consult w travelhealthpro.org.uk (UK) or w wwwnc.cdc.gov/travel (USA). All advice found online should be used in conjunction with expert advice received prior to or during travel.

**IN LITHUANIA** Lithuania has several private clinics with English-speaking doctors and a full array of medical services. These include the **Baltic American Clinic** (Nemenčinės plentas 54a; w bak.lt) in Vilnius and **Northway Medical Centres** (w nmc.lt) in Vilnius, Kaunas, Klaipėda and Kretinga.

**Pharmacies** (*vaistinė*) are widespread and are recognised by their green cross or snake and staff symbol. *Eurovaistinė* and *Camelia* are the main countrywide chains. In the cities, it is likely the pharmacist will speak some English.

**Tap water** is safe to drink and you are encouraged to take a refillable water bottle to avoid purchasing single-use plastic bottles of water.

In an **emergency** call ☏112.

**Medical problems** Mosquitoes in Lithuania are not known to carry harmful diseases, but nevertheless they can be a nuisance in the warmer months especially in the forests and countryside. Be sure to take an insect repellent – containing DEET or icaridin – and antihistamine cream or tablets.

**Tick-borne infections** are a greater health concern for visitors to Lithuania. Ticks are found predominantly in rural areas of forests, meadows and long grass but also in city parks, and are most active between early spring and late autumn. It is estimated that 5% of tick bites in Lithuania result in a disease being transmitted to a human when the tick feeds and embeds itself into the skin. When visiting high-risk areas wear long-sleeved tops, long trousers, boots and socks, and a hat. Tight-fitting garments are best and a light colour makes it easier to spot any ticks. Where possible, try to avoid walking through thick undergrowth or brushing against hanging branches. Use insect repellent regularly and inspect yourself and

> **TICK REMOVAL**
>
> Ticks should ideally be removed intact, and as soon as possible, to reduce the chance of infection. You can use special tick tweezers, which can be bought in good travel shops; or failing this, with your fingernails, grasp the tick as close to your body as possible, and pull it away steadily and firmly at right angles to your skin without jerking or twisting. Applying irritants (eg: Olbas oil) or lit cigarettes is to be discouraged as a means of removal since they can cause the ticks to regurgitate and therefore increase the risk of disease. Once the tick is removed, if possible douse the wound with alcohol (any spirit will do), soap and water, or iodine. If you are travelling with small children, remember to check their heads, and particularly behind the ears, for ticks. Spreading redness around the bite and/or fever and/or aching joints after a tick bite imply that you have an infection that requires antibiotic treatment. In this case seek medical advice.

your clothing for ticks after the hike, paying particularly attention to skinfolds and hair. The risk of infection increases the longer a tick is embedded in the skin, so removing it promptly and correctly is very important. A hot shower and use of a washcloth may help remove any unattached ticks.

**Tick-borne encephalitis** is a viral infection spread via the bite of an infected tick and causes inflammation in the brain. The ticks are most active between April and October. Most cases are asymptomatic or mild, although the infection can rarely lead to severe neurological disease or death. If you are planning to spend a lot of time in forests and rural areas in Lithuania, you may want to consider immunisation in addition to bite prevention. In the UK, this is a three-dose vaccine given over 6–12 months. If time is short, two doses 14 days apart can give good short-term protection. Another prevalent tick-borne disease is **Lyme disease**, a bacterial infection for which there is as yet no vaccine. Therefore, it is all the more important to take preventative measures to avoid bites (see page 51 for advice). If you become unwell or develop a rash after a tick bite, seek medical advice. Lyme disease is treatable with antibiotics.

**Rabies** has not been detected in terrestrial wild animals since 2018, and it was last detected in pets in 2013. Bats may still carry rabies-like viruses. Cases in wild animals have decreased significantly due to a national elimination campaign using bait containing oral vaccine. However, the disease exists in neighbouring Belarus and animals don't respect borders: travellers should remain vigilant. As of 2025, the country is still considered to be a rabies risk area by UK public health authorities. If you are bitten, scratched or exposed to the saliva of any mammal, you must clean the wound well, disinfect it and seek medical assessment urgently. If rabies exposure is suspected, you will be prescribed a four-dose rabies vaccination course and may also need treatment with a blood product (rabies immunoglobulin). Antibiotics and a tetanus booster may also be necessary. Those at higher risk of rabies – including adventure travellers and those working with animals – should consider vaccination before travel.

## SAFETY

Overall, Lithuania is a safe country for visitors. By adopting universal safety precautions and common sense, and being aware of some local nuances, visitors should be able to navigate safely and securely.

Lithuania has lower **street crime** rates than many European countries, but it is wise to be vigilant. If possible, lock your passport in the hotel safe and keep a photocopy of your passport separate to the original. Do not leave valuables in the car, or park in dark side streets. Petty crime does occur and you are advised to keep your bag close to you when out and about, especially in bars and restaurants. Using coat hooks and cloakrooms is common in Lithuania (all those big winter coats!), but do not leave anything personal or valuable in the pockets when using these. Be aware that owning any amount of drugs can land you in serious trouble in Lithuania.

**Road traffic** accident statistics are high in Lithuania. If you choose to drive, refer to page 57 for advice. Watch out for e-scooters flying along pavements; and avoid hiring them to get about. We strongly advise against it. Old town cobbled streets have claimed numerous victims, with dental and facial reconstruction surgery being one of the most lucrative businesses as a result in recent years. Never hire a taxi off the street; instead prebook your ride using the Bolt app – as well as getting a better rate anyway, your journey details will be recorded and you can share your journey tracking with a friend.

Generally, in **winter** you must have all senses switched on to the dangers of ice. Wear shoes with a good grip to master the icy ground and, if venturing out of town, consider using shoe spikes. Never walk on a frozen lake unless you are sure it is safe. In towns and cities, look out for incident tape cordoning off sections of pavement – this is probably a warning about icicles overhead that could fall at any time, rather than about broken paving slabs. During periods of thaw, downpipes can channel a lot of water across the pavements, leaving tracks of ice when the temperature drops again.

For **women** travellers, harassment is uncommon but you should always be aware of your surroundings, and take the same precautions as you would in any other European destination. Lithuanian society is steadily becoming more culturally diverse, with more expats living in the country, including those from ethnic minority backgrounds, and tourists visiting from all over the world. But it is still new to some of the older generations of Lithuanians and in rural areas. There may be a bit of curious staring but there are few reports of **racism** and the intolerant minority are not prominent.

In an **emergency** call ☏112.

## TRAVELLING WITH A DISABILITY

There is no denying that Lithuania's old-town cobbled streets and historic sites with limited accessibility will pose a challenge to visitors with mobility issues. In the main cities, however, particularly in newly developed areas, modern shopping malls and on public transport, investment is being channelled into improving accessibility with the installation of lifts or ramps, wider doorways and audio guides or braille information boards usually in Lithuanian and English. While new attractions, or those that have been recently renovated, are more likely to have better access for travellers with disabilities, some sights are still very restricted. Unfortunately, it is also common to see attempts at improved access falling short of required standards.

Most hotels offer rooms with disabled access, but it is worth double checking before you book that all facilities are accessible – the hotel room may be, but there might be steps to the restaurant. As with everything, do not expect smaller towns and rural areas to have made the same progress as in the major cities.

The website **Wheelmap** (**w** wheelmap.org) has an excellent interactive map detailing wheelchair accessible and partially accessible places throughout Lithuania. The UK's **gov.uk** website (**w** gov.uk/government/publications/disabled-travellers/disability-and-travel-abroad) has a downloadable guide giving general advice and practical information for travellers with a disability (and their companions) preparing for overseas travel. The **Society for Accessible Travel and Hospitality** (**w** sath.org) also provides some general information. UK Blue Badge parking permits can be used in some regions of Lithuania, so it is worth taking your documents if you intend to travel by car (for more details, visit **w** disabledmotorists.eu).

## LGBTQIA+ TRAVELLERS

The LGBTQIA+ scene in Lithuania is improving, although it remains a sensitive topic. Lithuania's Pride Festival (**w** gopride.lt) is held annually in June, consisting of a parade and concert, which attracted more than 15,000 participants in 2024. Every three years it is combined with Baltic Pride (**w** balticpride.org), which rotates between the three Baltic countries.

The LGL National LGBT Rights Organisation (**w** lgl.lt) is a non-profit, non-governmental organisation championing inclusivity though education, support and representation for the LGBTQIA+ community. They still have important work to do. Homosexuality was decriminalised in 1993 and, since accession to the EU, equality and non-discrimination laws have been passed, including the equal age of consent being changed to 16 since 2004. However, Lithuania remains one of six countries in the EU without civil unions or equal marriage laws. Attempts have been made to address this, most recently in March 2024, but the Lithuanian parliament removed a draft civil union bill from its agenda due to the likelihood it would not be passed. The case for same-sex marriage or civil partnerships remains tricky, with the Lithuanian Constitution and Civil Code both needing to be changed as they explicitly state that marriage is between 'a man and a woman' and 'with a person of the opposite sex', respectively. Neighbouring Latvia legalised same-sex civil unions in 2024, and trailblazing Estonia has allowed same-sex marriage and civil partnerships since 2013. It is worth noting that Lithuania is the most religious of the three Baltic countries.

While there are some LGBTQIA+ friendly venues in the main cities, small towns and rural areas can be less accepting of LGBTQIA+ travellers. According to a 2020 survey, six in ten LGBTQIA+ people are not open about their identity (EU Agency for Fundamental Rights, Country Data – Lithuania) and sadly online hate crimes and hate speech are often overlooked by the Lithuanian authorities. On a more positive note, Lithuania was represented at Eurovision 2024 by LGBTQIA+ artist Silvester Belt.

## TRAVELLING WITH KIDS

Lithuania is a very child-friendly country. Children are seen as the centre of the family, and you will often see multi-generational families out for lunch or dinner, walking in the park, or attending cultural events. Smoking is heavily restricted in public places, family seating in restaurants includes high-chairs, with children's menus available in most, and there are an increasing number of family-oriented attractions, in addition to the many playpark facilities – though it is fair to say that sometimes health and safety can be a bit lax, so do pay particular attention if you decide to visit a playground. The main cities all have play parks, family-friendly shopping malls, and

> **TRAVELLING WITH YOUR DOG**
>
> If you are planning on taking your beloved pooch to Lithuania, rest assured that you will receive a warm welcome. You will need to plan and book pet-friendly accommodation, which usually involves an additional €10 or so charge per pet, per night. In summer, eating outside in courtyards and terraces with a dog is easy and you can expect a bowl of water to be brought to your table in warm weather. In colder months you will need to do your research and check which establishments welcome dogs. Some dog-friendly venues display a 'Draugiški Gyvūnams' (Pet Friendly) paw sticker on the door. In winter, you also need to consider the very cold temperatures and how long your dog can comfortably be outside and walking on ice or snow. Supermarkets and pet shops sell familiar brands of pet foods, and if a vet is needed it is likely they will speak some English. Dogs travel free of charge on buses but must be on a leash and muzzled; on trains they must be on a leash and you should expect to pay 50% of the adult fare for your dog. Pets entering Lithuania from abroad must be microchipped, vaccinated against rabies and have a current certificate of health from a registered vet.

a host of active leisure opportunities. Hotels often have family rooms or connecting rooms, and cots are usually available on request. It's a good idea to carry a copy of your child's passport or birth certificate to use as proof of age for concession prices at attractions. Car seats are obligatory and determined by height and weight, not age; they should be requested in advance from your rental firm if needed.

## WHAT TO TAKE  Rachel Johnston

A suitably stuffed suitcase will help you enjoy your time in Lithuania. Take enough **prescription medication** to last your whole trip along with a copy of your prescription, or save it to your phone. If you plan to visit countryside or woodland, **insect repellent** is essential as Lithuanian bugs have teeth and like to bite.

Summer temperatures can rocket, so slather on the **sunscreen**; and in winter when the cold sets in, a handy pocket-sized **lip salve** will save you from chapped lips. Whatever the season, **layering** is the key to comfort. Wearing multiple thermal layers (and a big coat) will keep you warm in winter, and allow you to adjust easily to moving indoors, though glasses-wearers will fight the fog (the struggle is real). When temperatures drop, protect your extremities with **hats, gloves and socks**. You can always upgrade to locally sourced versions – hand-knitted mittens and woollen hats make great souvenirs and gifts. In summer, loose cotton layers and a cap or wide-brimmed hat will keep you cool and protect you from summer sun and wind.

Urban or rural, you'll probably cover a lot of miles on foot. Cobbled old-town streets are no friend to the kitten heel – you need **sensible shoes**. If you're visiting at the height of winter, spike overshoes can help you stay upright.

Small denominations of **euros** are handy for tipping. Don't rely on hotels having USB charging points – dig out a **European two-pin plug** adapter for your charger.

## MONEY AND BUDGETING

**MONEY** The currency of Lithuania has been the euro since January 2015, replacing the Lithuanian litas which was the national currency in 1922–39 and 1993–2015.

> **AVERAGE PRICES**
>
> | | |
> |---|---|
> | 1-litre bottle of water | €0.80 (including €0.10 deposit that is redeemed at a 'taromatas' machine found in every supermarket) |
> | loaf of bread | €1.99 |
> | bottle of 50cl beer | €1.45 (including €0.10 deposit) |
> | 1 litre of petrol | €1.43 |
> | McDonald's Big Mac | €4.90 |
> | cappuccino in a café | €3.00 |

The use of **debit and credit cards** has largely replaced cash, with Visa and Mastercard widely accepted. **ATMs** are commonplace in the cities and in most towns, though be mindful that in Lithuania ATMs dispense your cash before returning your card. Next-generation payments by mobile phone apps are now rapidly replacing cards.

It is advisable to always have small denomination cash on you, especially if shopping at the markets and for tipping in restaurants. Most restaurants are unable to add tips to the bill and although some may offer an app for **tipping** via your mobile phone, cash is usually best. Check the menu for whether a service charge is included, if not, and you feel a tip is due the general rule is 10% of the bill.

**BUDGETING** It is no longer valid to describe Lithuania as a low-cost holiday destination, but it does still offer value for money. There is a wide range of accommodation, places to eat and attractions to suit every budget. As a guide, budget travellers staying in a hostel, campsite, cheap hotel or dormitory, should expect to pay €30 per person per night for accommodation, another €20 on food and drink, and €20 on public transport and attractions, making a total of €70 per day which can be easily blown out of the water if tempted by a couple of cocktails for €12 each. On a mid-range budget, expect to spend approximately €145 per day, including €70 for accommodation, €50 for food and drink, and €25 for other costs. A high-end budget could easily breach €120 on hotels, €80 on food and drink, and €50 on entertainment in the main cities, totalling €250 per day. As a rule, the main cities are more expensive not least because they offer temptingly good food, lively bars and entertainment to entice you to spend your euros. For lower prices, look to visit off-peak during the months of November and January to March and stay in resort towns on weekdays.

## GETTING AROUND

**BY TRAIN** Services are run by the state-owned Lithuanian Railways (LTG; Lietuvos geležinkelios; w ltglink.lt), whose website is very clear and user-friendly for schedules and buying tickets online. Tickets can also be bought at station ticket offices or machines, or on the train if the station is closed. New rolling stock on the main routes has made travel by train comfortable and it is still generally cheaper than taking the bus. One drawback for train travel, however, is that stations are often on the edge of town, whereas bus stations are usually more central. The main railway line crosses Lithuania east to west from Vilnius to Klaipėda via Šiauliai (five trains daily; 4hrs 20 mins; adult €35/25 first/second class one way). It is a useful route and particularly busy with beachgoers on Fridays and Sundays during the summer months. Kaunas and Vilnius are connected by a regular **direct service** (hourly, daily; 1hr 15mins; adult €13/10 first/second class one way). Vilnius to

Trakai is the most popular route for tourists visiting Trakai town and castle (page 120). Other routes of interest are: Vilnius to Turmantas, which stops at Visaginas for those wanting to visit the atomic town and Ignalina Nuclear Power Plant (page 239); and Vilnius to Marcinkonys, for a scenic train ride and an opportunity to hike in the forest or visit the ethnographic villages of Dzūkija region – this is fondly referred to as the 'mushroom train' in autumn as it provides easy access for foraging in the forest from the city (page 152). Lithuania once had a dense network of narrow-gauge railways connecting industrial plants and agricultural regions to the main Warsaw–St Petersburg railway. The majority of these were abandoned, falling into disrepair and eventually dismantled. Thankfully, the line between Panevėžys and Anykščiai was saved and the **Aukštaitija Narrow-Gauge Railway** continues to run as a popular tourist attraction to this day (page 222).

**BY BUS** Lithuania has an extensive bus network connecting the main cities and towns to the smaller peripheral villages. For decades, bus travel has been the most popular form of transport; only in recent years with an increase in private car ownership and a steady migration from villages to the cities have services started to be reduced. It is still possible to get to remote places by bus, but you need to embrace a slower pace of travel, plan around local schedules and be sure to check the timings for your return journey to avoid getting stuck. The best website for routes, timetables and tickets is w autobusubilietai.lt. Tickets can also be bought at bus stations and from the driver. On public holidays or festivals, city buses are often free (indicated by '*nemokamai*' on the payment terminals). At the time of writing, a single adult ticket from Vilnius to Druskininkai cost €14, to Kaunas €9, and to Visaginas €20. It is important to note that entering public transport (bus or trolleybus) is strictly via the front door and leaving via the middle or back door.

**BY CAR** Without doubt, if you want to explore beyond the main cities and towns, this is best done by car. Equally, if you are only visiting the cities, a car is best avoided. Instead take a trip out of town on public transport or with a local driver-guide who will navigate the traffic and parking for you. Driving in Lithuania is on the right-hand side of the road, and car headlights are to be switched on all year round. From 1 November to 1 April winter tyres are mandatory on all vehicles. The alcohol limit for driving is 0.4g per litre which you would be wise to translate as zero. Random alcohol testing does occur and fines are considerable. There is zero tolerance for drug-driving. Speed limits are clearly marked and strictly enforced by permanent cameras and mobile police camera checks. Main roads are generally good quality although the more rural you go, the less comfortable the ride becomes driving along bone-shaking gravel roads, and, if following another car, in a dust cloud. Forest roads are often sandy or muddy and riddled with roots and potholes.

Main roads have regular **service stations** with Circle K being the biggest chain. At the time of writing, locals tend to avoid Viada and Baltic Petroleum fuel due to their close connections with Russia and Belarus. Most cars are diesel, with some running on gas (dujos), and electric cars are becoming more popular with charging stations widely available. Always fill up on fuel before venturing into a national park or remote area. It is recommended to carry some small-denomination euros for parking machines, or local parking which could be in someone's garden during an event or festival.

**Car rental** The car-hire scene has changed considerably with the introduction of the **CityBee** (w citybee.lt) app-based car-sharing service. Download the app to your device, register and pass the identity checks, then you are all set up to use the service. CityBee cars are booked online via the app by locating a nearby available vehicle; you then book it, unlock it via the app (the keys will be inside the vehicle) and drop it off at your destination when you are finished. You must leave it parked in an authorised location; these are clearly highlighted on the app map. For example, you can take a CityBee car from Vilnius, drive to Palanga and leave it there. CityBee operates in all three Baltic countries, so for example you can take a CityBee car from Kaunas in Lithuania and leave it in Riga, Latvia or Tallinn, Estonia. You pay for the time you have the car and the kilometres driven. This type of rental is perfect for those with no car and for short A-to-B journeys. **Bolt Drive** (w bolt.eu) is another option for self-drive car sharing along similar lines to CityBee.

For longer periods, a **traditional car hire** company is recommended. Hertz (w hertz.com), Enterprise (w enterprise.com), Europcar (w europcar.com) and Sixt (w sixt.com) all have a presence in Lithuania and have offices at Vilnius, Kaunas and Palanga airports.

For both types of services, you must be over 21 years of age and will need your personal ID and a valid full driving licence.

**BY TAXI AND RIDE-HAILING APPS** Traditional taxi services have been largely replaced by Uber and Bolt drivers, the latter by far the most popular and widely available in Lithuania (it is after all a Baltic success, hailing from Estonia). Before you can request a ride using **Bolt** (w bolt.eu), you are required to download the app to your device, register and connect a card for payment. Ease of communication, payment and the tracking system make Bolt very easy to use and transparent. If you do need to take a **local taxi**, never take a taxi straight off the street as this is an invitation to get ripped off. Licensed taxis are distinguished by a taxi sign on the vehicle roof. It has always been cheaper to call and book a taxi, even if you dial the number on the side of the cab right in front of you. Make sure the meter is switched on before you start your journey, and ensure you have cash to pay the taxi driver.

## ACCOMMODATION

As you might expect, the capital Vilnius has a full array of accommodation options ranging from five-star luxury hotels in characterful Old Town properties, to basic, but well-located, hostels. Chain hotels are mainly in the business district north of the river. Kaunas and Klaipėda have four-star hotels through to hostels. In provincial cities the main overnight option is often the former Intourist hotel, an unmistakable concrete block where foreign tourists had to stay in Soviet times, their comings and goings monitored by a middle-aged woman stationed on every floor noting timings and behaviour. Of course, these hotels have now been renovated and modernised,

### ACCOMMODATION PRICE CODES

Average price of a double room in high season:

| | |
|---|---|
| €€€€€ | Over €200 |
| €€€€ | €120–200 |
| €€€ | €80–120 |
| €€ | €40–80 |
| € | Less than €40 |

> **CITY TAX**
>
> Be prepared to pay a city tax when checking into your accommodation. This is usually €1–2 per person per night. There is no national legislation; rules are made by local municipalities and vary widely. You will be informed about paying city tax and the rate at the time of booking, or when you check-in.

but some still have a whiff of nostalgia about them. Where possible, consider booking a locally owned hotel so your money will support the local economy. New chain hotels have driven prices down and local family-run places find it hard to compete in a harsh business environment. Be aware that cheap self-check-in hotels are basic and rarely have a member of staff available to help should you encounter a problem such as your key card not working or noisy neighbours. Apartment rental, mainly through sites such as Booking.com and Airbnb is well established across the country, but take time to read the reviews especially regarding access and neighbours.

If heading to a **health resort**, factor in the difference between a spa and a sanatorium (*sanatorija*) or clinic (*gydykla*) when choosing your accommodation. New spa hotels focus on wellness and pampering, offering a high standard of accommodation and are popular for weekend breaks. Sanatoriums are clinical rehabilitation centres where people go to recover under doctor's orders (although you can visit, and a medical mud bath treatment is a memorable experience!).

**Rural tourism** is big business in Lithuania with many locals heading to the countryside for weekends, festivals and the holiday season. The range of rural accommodation varies hugely from the most basic homestead (*sodyba*) to luxurious cabins with hot tubs and saunas. Be mindful that cooking facilities will be basic as most locals go to the countryside to grill shashlik outdoors. The water supply to rural properties is often spring water with a high mineral content, making it metallic to smell and taste. You may prefer bottled water for brushing your teeth, drinking and cooking. Properties can be remote, so take everything you might need. Many rural accommodations are venues for weddings, family parties or corporate events especially on weekends and we recommend you check this when booking or you might find yourself awake all night because of the noise, or participating in a strangers' wedding. The Lithuanian Countryside Tourism Association (Lietuvos kaimo turizmo asociacija (Atostogos kaime); w countryside.lt) can help you find a rural place to stay, although they only cover approximately 60% of accommodations.

**Camping** is a relatively new past-time in Lithuania but one that is gaining popularity fast, and the growing number of campsites reflects this. Some are remnants of Soviet pioneer camps and best avoided. Camping is only allowed in designated places especially in nature conservation areas, where a site may consist of just a picnic table and dry toilet in a clearing. The best resources for finding an official campsite in Lithuania are the Lithuanian Campsite Association (w camping.lt) or Baltic Campsites (w campingbaltic.com). Note that the camping season is from Easter to late September with most infrastructure closed outside of this period.

As investment spreads across the country, abandoned **manor houses** (*dvaras*) are being bought up and privately renovated into charming venues and hotels. Some welcome individual guests, but do check who your fellow guests will be – you could be sharing with a rowdy party or you may be the only guest and the kitchen closed with no dinner or breakfast available.

Accommodation **prices** are highest in summer, and during celebrations and festivals in the cities. On a sunny weekend or during school holidays the coastal resorts of Palanga and Nida reach astronomical prices, but in low season during winter you can still find a bargain.

You will need to show your passport or identity document when checking into your accommodation. Please note that a driving license will not be accepted for this purpose.

## EATING AND DRINKING   Alex Gibb

**FOOD AND DRINK** Gone are the days of functional fuel to get you through a day of manual labour with stodgy staples of pork, potatoes and mushrooms. Lithuania now boasts a thriving food scene that celebrates nature's bounty with creativity and pride. Drawing inspiration from the New Nordic movement, Lithuania has rediscovered the art of foraging, fermenting and distilling, creating a distinct culinary identity to whet one's whistle. Inclusion in the Michelin Guide 2024 marked a monumental moment for Lithuania, with 34 establishments earning prestigious accolades and showcasing the emergence of 'New Baltic Cuisine'.

Lithuania's culinary culture is deeply rooted in its natural rhythm, shaped by four distinct seasons. The cold, harsh winters have long necessitated preservation techniques such as pickling, curing and smoking, with smoked meats, dried vegetables, and tart preserves defining winter fare. Spring, on the other hand, bursts forth with optimism, as nettles, sorrel, dandelion, crunchy radishes and fresh cucumbers reawaken the senses. Summer overflows with the sweetness of juicy strawberries, rich ripe tomatoes and the sharp tang of wild garlic; while outdoor

### CLASSIC LITHUANIAN DISHES

A traditional feast often begins with one of the numerous craft beers, from farmhouse ales to dark Baltic porters. For a non-alcoholic option, try **gira** (kvass), a fermented rye bread drink. Pair either with classic beer snacks like **kepta duona** (fried rye bread rubbed with garlic) which awakens the senses and hastens a thirst.

**Herring** (silkė) has long been a staple of Lithuanian cuisine, though climate change poses a growing threat to its availability. It is often prepared as salted, cured or brined offerings. A dollop of sour cream and a few toasted mushrooms can elevate this dish into a spectacular event on its own.

Filling but not as heavy as the next legendary dish, **bulviniai blynai** are shallow-fried potato pancakes traditionally served with the ubiquitous sour cream and bacon bits. Contemporary versions can be found in smaller portions with delicate sauces.

The iconic **cepelinai** (named after its Zeppelin shape) is a gelatinous dumpling, gluey in texture thanks to a combination of raw grated and boiled mashed potato. This dense beast comes filled with mushrooms, curd or mince and dosed with a hearty dollop of sour cream and crispy bacon bits.

**Koldūnai** are dumplings filled with pork, pumpkin, elk, boar or spinach. These little parcels of love will keep you going throughout the year.

**Šaltibarščiai** remains the standout dish of Lithuanian cuisine, even if neighbouring countries claim variations of it. The striking pink colour is as refreshing as its salty, tangy flavour. Made with kefir, beetroot, cucumbers, dill and eggs, this cold summer soup is paired with warm potatoes. A source of national pride, Vilnius hosts an annual Pink Soup Festival (page 81).

> **RESTAURANT PRICE CODES**
>
> Average price of a main course, including side dishes:
>
> | | |
> |---|---|
> | €€€€€ | Over €25 |
> | €€€€ | €15–25 |
> | €€€ | €10–15 |
> | €€ | €6–10 |
> | € | Less than €6 |

grilling becomes a national pastime. Autumn, the season of mushrooms, brings a competitive fervour as Lithuanians flock to their secret foraging grounds. This deeply ingrained connection to the land is both a cultural treasure and a culinary experience to be shared – if you're lucky.

Honey remains a classic that is devoured in tea, slathered on cucumbers and dripped over cheese. Dairy farming has flourished, giving rise to an impressive selection of cheeses, curds and sour milk products that delight both artisanal and commercial palates. Lithuania's beverage culture is rooted in herbal traditions and a close relationship with nature. Herbal teas made from mint, chamomile, linden, berries and forest plants are cherished for both their flavour and medicinal qualities. Sea buckthorn is good as a tea or in a cocktail, birch syrup is a popular seasonal drink, and you may notice notes of caraway, cloves and rye in different drinks.

Back in the day you could spot a Lithuanian on a plane a mile away. They would be carrying an enormous tower of rich eggy pastry. *Šakotis* (tree cake) still prevails at social gatherings and celebrations, often the centrepiece of a special moment. The sight of it being made is a delight, crafted on a lathe in front of an open fire (page 146). *Medaus pyragas* (honey cake) is a layered piece of art with a delicately sweet bent to it; a lovely accompaniment to a strong black coffee. Deep-fried doughnut balls vie with curd treats and various pastry-based nibbles to offer simple, nostalgic pleasures. Apple cheese, a chewy pressed confection, is a surprise for visitors, delivering a sweet (and healthy) hit. Berries and forest fruits remain a popular finale. The various venues along Vilnius's Stiklių gatvė deliver Instagram-worthy creations.

The culinary scene has evolved to embrace modern dietary trends and **special dietary requirements**. Many restaurants cater to gluten-free, lactose-intolerant and vegan diets. Halal restaurants have become more numerous with the arrival of Muslim gig-economy workers from the Caucuses.

Venture out of Vilnius and Kaunas to discover distinct regional specialities. The coastal diet is dominated by fish, eel and herring, both smoked and fresh. Northwestern Lithuania (Žemaitija) is famous for its rustic, hearty cuisine with smoked sausages, stuffed pancakes and sour cream ruling the roost. Aukštaitija in the northeast has more dairy in the diet, coupled with rye breads and curd doughnuts. The southeast region of Dzūkija is forested with sandy soil, perfect for mushrooms, berries and buckwheat dishes. Buckwheat is a gluten-free staple often served at breakfast, lunch or dinner. Suvalkija in the southwest is an up-and-coming gastrotourism destination for heritage farming and food experiences.

Post-independence, farming was a furious race to modernise agriculture, reduce the reliance on subsistence farming and consolidate holdings into larger groups. This widespread adoption of fertilisers increased productivity but was not better in terms of taste and sustainability. Focus is now firmly back on farm-to-table practices, local sourcing, organic farming and a renewed respect for the land and its produce. The anti-fast-food movement is strong; Lithuanians truly value nature and have a deep connection to it, which they attribute to their pagan roots.

**EATING OUT** Dining hours align with continental European norms, with lunch from noon till 14.00 and peak dinner time being 19.00–21.00. Bookings are generally recommended either with the venue directly or using w tablein.lt/en. Waiting staff speak good English and will be happy to chat. **Tipping** is common: leave a few coins as a gesture of thanks or a full 10%, it's up to you.

## PUBLIC HOLIDAYS AND FESTIVALS

When you've been invaded and occupied multiple times over the years, you end up with a lot of public holidays and independence days with good reason to celebrate and commemorate. These public holidays and festivals affect the whole country.

**NEW YEAR'S DAY** (Naujųjų metų diena; 1 Jan; public holiday) The morning after the night before, expect fewer establishments to open and those that do will open up late and operate in slow motion. It is also **Flag Day**, when a new Lithuanian tricolour flag is raised on Gediminas Castle at 14.00 to commemorate the first time it was raised there on 1 January 1919.

**THREE KINGS DAY** (Trys karaliai; 6 Jan) On Lithuania's Twelfth Night, also known as Epiphany, there is a theatrical procession of the Magi in the main cities. In Vilnius this starts from the Gates of Dawn and passes through the Old Town to Cathedral Square. Although a religious holiday, it is a normal working day. On this day it is customary to bless the house by writing 'K+M+B' – representing the Three Kings, Caspar (Kasparas), Melchior (Merkelis) and Balthazar (Baltazaras) – followed by the year in numbers, above the door. You will see this written in chalk above many front doors of houses and apartment buildings.

**DAY OF RESTORATION OF THE STATE OF LITHUANIA** (Lietuvos valstybės atkūrimo diena; 16 Feb; public holiday) This holiday commemorates the signing of the Act of Independence on 16 February 1918 that declared Lithuania's independence from the Russian Empire and established the Republic of Lithuania. The occasion is marked with a ceremony and music concert in the cities. Expect lots of flags and gun salutes (Latvian and Estonian flags are also raised as a show of Baltic solidarity).

**UŽGAVĖNĖS** (7th week before Easter) Užgavėnės is Lithuania's equivalent of Carnival, Mardi Gras or Shrove Tuesday. Although linked by date to the religious calendar and Easter festival, the celebration has archaic roots and is full of ancient symbolism and meaning. Ancient Lithuanian society was agrarian, dependent on the seasons and the fruits of the land, so celebrating the end of winter was an important milestone. The main event is the burning of a giant effigy of winter called Morė, a Baltic pagan deity who symbolises the death of winter and birth of spring, the transition from darkness to light. Festival-goers wear eccentric, somewhat creepy masks and costumes of animals, birds, devils and witches. The largest celebration is held at the open-air museum Rumšiškės (page 196), but smaller events are held all over the country. Wrap up warm, savour pancakes and hot tea, and urge winter to jog on by singing '*Žiema, žiema, bėk iš kiemo!*' (Winter, winter, get out of the yard!).

**DAY OF RESTITUTION OF INDEPENDENCE OF LITHUANIA** (Nepriklausomybės atkūrimo diena; 11 Mar; public holiday) On 11 March 1990, the first freely elected Supreme Council of the Lithuanian Soviet Socialist Republic declared Lithuania independent from the Soviet Union. Moscow authorities attempted to quash the rebellion by sending in Soviet troops amid a bloody crackdown, but as fellow occupied nations followed suit, the USSR collapsed, and the world finally recognised Lithuania as an independent state the following year. Iceland is held in special regard, being the first country to recognise Lithuania's Independence on 11 February 1991. A state ceremony is held and everyone displays their Lithuanian flags (Latvian and Estonian flags are raised too).

**EASTER** (Velykos) As a staunchly Catholic country, Easter is of great significance in Lithuania and observed by many through distinct traditions that draw from the pagan festival of Spring equinox. Celebrating the resurrection of Christ and the reawakening of nature brings out the most passive of believers, making Easter a big event. Holy Week begins on Palm Sunday, a distinctive day when people carry *verbos*, the decorative Lithuanian palm made from twigs of willow, hazel and juniper. In Vilnius region, verbos have become an artform by incorporating dried flowers and herbs of significance, making these highly attractive souvenirs. If you take one home, be sure to follow tradition and playfully pat your housemates with your verbos while chanting 'the palm is beating you, not me!' and then store it safely to protect the home from hardship. Traditionally, the Thursday of Holy Week was a day of cleaning, Good Friday a quiet day of respect, and Easter Saturday a day to prepare Easter eggs. *Margučiai* are traditional painted eggs, laboriously decorated with hot wax patterns and coloured using natural dyes such as tree bark, onion skins, beetroot and flower petals. On Easter Sunday, mass is attended and followed by a lavish meal. You should expect shops, banks, offices and some restaurants and attractions to be closed over Easter.

**LABOUR DAY** (Darbo diena; 1 May; public holiday) For some, this is a legacy of the Soviet Union that should be scrapped. Lithuanians want no reminder of the International Workers' Day pushed during the period of occupation. On the other hand, it is a public holiday at a pleasant time of year, and many are happy to discard the history and enjoy May Day with family and friends.

**MIDSUMMER** (Rasa or Joninės; 24 Jun; public holiday) On the shortest night of the year, 23–24 June, Lithuanians celebrate the summer solstice, successfully combining a Christian festival with pagan traditions. Before conversion to Christianity, midsummer in Lithuania was called Kupolės, named after the herbs gathered that day, or Rasos, meaning Dew Holiday. With the advent of Christianity, the feast was aligned with St John's Day and renamed Joninės, although traditions did not change. Rituals have always been linked to nature, agriculture and prosperity, summoning good luck and love. It is customary to stay up all night, leap over bonfires, sing folk songs and make wreaths to wear from foliage, flowers and herbs. Young couples are encouraged to go into the forest to search for the mythical fern blossom, which only blooms that night and is a symbol of fertility. The cities can feel quiet as locals head out to the country to celebrate and the next day is a public holiday for the country to rest after a national all-nighter. Celebrating midsummer as a visitor can be tricky with venues isolated and transport services limited. The biggest midsummer celebrations are held at Kernavė (page 129) and Verkiai Regional Park (page 133), but you will find small local events too.

**STATEHOOD DAY** (Valstybingumo diena; 6 Jul; public holiday) This day pays tribute to King Mindaugas, the first medieval duke to unify Lithuanian lands and the country's only king to have received a crown from the pope, in 1353. It is also **Lithuanian Unity Day** when all over the world at 21.00 Lithuania time the Lithuanian national anthem is sung. In Vilnius the main event takes place in V Kudirkos Square.

**VIRGIN MARY ASSUMPTION DAY** (Žolinės; 15 Aug; public holiday) Another crossover of the Christian calendar and an ancient pagan festival called Žolinė, this celebration marks the end of the growing season and gives thanks for the harvest. It's also suitably known as Kopūstinė (cabbage day). People are seen carrying bundles of wildflowers or corn to the church.

**ALL SAINTS' AND ALL SOULS' DAYS** (Visų šventųjų diena ir visų sielų diena; 1 & 2 Nov; both public holidays) Lithuania's Day of the Dead festivities span two days and focus on remembering the deceased. Discussions to reduce the holiday to one day are controversial as many people must travel long distances to their relatives' graves and often to several different regions of the country. Be aware that the traffic is heavy on these days, with otherwise occasional drivers venturing out and it is the best time to see vintage Lada and Moskvich cars on the roads. Cemeteries become a hive of activity as people tend graves, lay flowers and light candles. The traditional name for these days is Vėlinės.

If you are in Lithuania for All Saints' or All Souls' Day and time allows, visiting a cemetery, preferably at dusk when it will be lit by the soft glow of candlelight, is highly recommended. If you are in Vilnius on these days, head to one of the city's historic cemeteries (page 111). In Kaunas on 1 November at 17.00 on the main pedestrian street of Laisvės alėja, the public are invited to light a candle in memory of departed loved ones, creating an illuminated 'river of souls'.

**CHRISTMAS** (Kalėdos; 24–26 Dec; public holidays) Christmas Eve (Kūčios; 24 Dec) is the main event for Lithuanians and is another example of the intertwined festivals of the Christian and pagan calendars. The old winter solstice festival centred around a family meal with an extra place set for those in absentia and comprising 12 traditional courses symbolising the months of the year; today these represent the apostles. As this is the end of advent, there is no meat in the meal, anticipation brewing for rich food tomorrow. The table of food is left out until morning so departed souls can take what they need in the night. Legend has it that Christmas Eve is the only time when farm animals can speak in human voices, but you must never eavesdrop or you won't live to see the morning. On the first Christmas Day (Pirma Kalėdų diena; 25 Dec) church is attended in the morning, followed by a social day of festive food and visiting family. On the second Christmas Day (Antroji Kalėdų diena; 26 Dec), time is spent with family or visiting friends. Exchanging Christmas gifts differs between families, but in most cases Father Christmas (Kalėdų Senelis) delivers gifts on the night between 24 and 25 December and gifts are discovered under the Christmas tree on the morning of 25th.

**NEW YEAR'S EVE** (Naujųjų metų išvakarės; 31 Dec) New Year's Eve means party night across the country, with the largest events taking place in the cities. Many venues hold special ticketed functions with food and entertainment provided until the early hours. Restaurants may close earlier than usual to allow their staff to celebrate. It is strongly advised to purchase event tickets or book a restaurant table in advance. In Vilnius, from 22.00, crowds gather in Cathedral Square amid

> ### RAISING THE LITHUANIAN FLAG
>
> Most buildings in Lithuania have a flag stand, usually on the wall on the front of the building. Whether the building is state owned or private, there will be someone responsible for displaying the flag as it is obligatory on some public holidays, state occasions and commemorative days. Banned during the years of occupation, flying the flag is today an important display of national identity, patriotism and independence. Before independence, people would hide their Lithuanian flags in the hope that one day they would be raised again, with some people born during the Soviet era seeing the national flag for the first time only after 1991. Alongside the public holidays listed from page 62, the flag is also raised on the following dates:
>
> | | |
> |---|---|
> | 13 January | Day of the Freedom Fighters; in memory of the 13 January 1991 events |
> | 24 February | Day of Independence of Estonia (Estonian and Latvian flags raised too) |
> | 29 March | NATO Day; honouring Lithuania's accession to NATO in 2003 |
> | 1 May | European Union Day; honouring Lithuania's accession to the EU in 2004 |
> | 9 May | Europe Day; commemorating the end of World War II in 1945 |
> | 15 May | Day of Convening of the Constituent Assembly (first parliament in 1920) |
> | 14 June | Day of Mourning and Hope; remembering the mass deportations to Siberia in 1941 |
> | 15 June | Day of Occupation and Genocide; mourning the beginning of Soviet occupation in 1940 |
> | 15 July | Day of the Battle of Grunwald; commemorating victory over the Teutonic Knights in 1410 |
> | 23 August | Day of the Black Ribbon; mourns the signing of the Molotov–Ribbentrop Pact in 1939 |
> | 31 August | Day of Freedom; marking the final departure of the Red Army from Lithuania in 1993 |
> | 23 September | Day of the Genocide of Lithuanian Jews; marking the destruction of the Vilnius ghetto by the Nazis in 1943 |
> | 25 October | Constitution Day; commemorating the adoption of the national constitution in 1992 |
> | 18 November | Day of Latvian Independence (Latvia and Estonia flags raised too) |
> | 23 November | Day of the Lithuanian Soldier; marking the founding of the Army of Lithuania in 1918 |

a music-and-light-show extravaganza peppered with unofficial fireworks, and masses of jovial people wrapped up in cosy layers welcome in the New Year.

## SHOPPING

The first **supermarkets** in Lithuania opened in 1992. Prior to this everything was bought at the market, local shops and from small kiosks. The first brand was IKI, followed by Maxima who denote their store size by X, XX and XXX with the latter being the biggest. Both brands still dominate the Lithuanian supermarket scene along with newcomers Lidl, Norfa and Rimi. When travelling away from the cities, the local stores of smaller supermarket brand Aibė dominate the towns.

The minimum age to buy alcohol is 20 years old.

**SOUVENIRS** Souvenirs from Lithuania stem from traditional crafts and natural materials, often with a contemporary twist. Souvenir markets are a fun way to browse, though more and more imported tat is appearing on some stalls. During festivals, talented craftspeople descend on Vilnius with unusual and high-quality creations, Kaziukas Fair in March being the leading craft fair (page 80). For high-end crafts look to galleries and boutique shops.

For centuries, **amber** has been a lucrative export for Lithuania and today it is an iconic souvenir. Displays of jewellery and trinkets adorn souvenir shop windows, but for specialist local designers visit the amber galleries. **Linen** or flax textiles now come in contemporary designs and all manner of products are available from bread baskets to bedding. Some specialist shops offer shipping abroad too. **Wooden items** such as hand-carved spoons or chopping boards will remind you of your travels when back at home. An upgrade to local woollen mittens could save your fingertips if you are feeling the cold. **Ceramics** and traditional candle houses are popular but be sure to request extra packaging for the journey home. For more on traditional crafts, see page 34.

For fun and often quirky souvenirs, head to the tourist offices, especially in Vilnius, where you will find bright t-shirts, keyrings, magnets and novelty socks all with iconic symbols and tongue-in-cheek slogans to inspire and provoke a conversation about Lithuania.

If you prefer an edible memento, there is an abundance of Lithuanian **chocolate and sweets**, with Rūta being the main brand and small artisan confectioners becoming widely available too. A unique souvenir to carry home on the plane is the *šakotis* **tree cake**, which will come well packaged and ready to travel. Head to the local market for a real-life shopping experience; though they are becoming more sophisticated and sanitised, they remain fascinating.

## ARTS AND ENTERTAINMENT

The creative arts are held in high esteem in Lithuania, with song and dance playing a central role to national identity and expression. Top-rated performances of ballet, opera and musical concerts can be enjoyed for a fraction of the price compared with other European cities. The arts are well supported and tickets sell out, so it is recommended to buy your ticket in advance from the venue website to ensure a seat. The season for ballet and opera runs from September to June and is based in Vilnius, although Kaunas State Musical Theatre and the newly renovated Klaipėda State Music Theatre host excellent performances. Theatre productions are predominantly in Lithuanian although subtitles are used in some venues (this will be clear on the event website). Lithuania is attracting a growing number of international artists on their European tours, with the main venue being Kaunas' Darius and Girėnas stadium and Vingis Park in Vilnius.

Lithuanians are a creative bunch and alongside their official venues you will find a medley of smaller classical and contemporary concerts being held in galleries, churches and pop-up venues. In summer these move outdoors to

## LITHUANIAN SONG AND DANCE FESTIVAL

In August 1924 the very first song festival (Dainų šventė), called The Song Day, was held in Kaunas. Vilnius at this time was occupied by Poland. Two more song day events followed in 1928 and 1930, but then nothing until 1946 when it was held for the first time in Vilnius, the city having been returned to Lithuania but under the auspices of the new occupying Soviet Socialist Republic of Lithuania. During the Soviet occupation the festival expanded to include both folk song and dance events. The celebrations had to comply with communist ideology but Lithuanian patriotic songs were subtly included and passed off as peasant culture which was deemed harmless by the Soviet authorities. During the 1980s, the independence movement was building, and forbidden patriotic songs were boldly included in the repertoire; the 1985 festival witnessed a record turnout of 38,800 participants. This was the beginning of the **Singing Revolution**, a series of events that led to independence being restored to the three Baltic nations of Lithuania, Latvia and Estonia and the collapse of the Soviet Union (page 18). With independence from the Soviet Union having been declared on 11 March 1990, the song festival held the following July was awash with energy and optimism despite the country being subject to economic blockades and still unrecognised by the international community as an independent nation. The Song Day repertoire of that year featured only music by Lithuanian composers.

In 2003, along with the song festivals of Latvia and Estonia, UNESCO included the Baltic Song and Dance Festivals on their list of Intangible Cultural Heritage of Humanity. They play an important role as both repository and showcase of traditional folk singing and dancing, and expression of cultural identity to be preserved for future generations.

Today, the festival is held every four years and is a week-long festival attracting 150,000 spectators and 37,000 participants. While regional choirs and dance groups from across the country learn the choreography and lyrics, so do those of Lithuanian descent around the world, including the youngest generations of Lithuanian emigres who make the special pilgrimage to participate in the festival in their homeland. The organisation is astounding, resulting in mesmerising patterns created by thousands of swirling dancers and powerful patriotic spine-tingling singing. The main events of the festival are the Ensemble Evening, a combination of singing and dancing held in the evening at Kalnų park in Vilnius; the Dance Day, a visual treat at the football stadium in Vilnius; the joyous procession from Cathedral Square to the festival grounds at Vingis park; and the finale of Song Day, an evening that wraps the week up. For visitors, the song festival is a unique insight into Lithuanian history and patriotism, the regional costumes are stunning, the craft fairs are impressive, and you can certainly feel a part of the celebrations. The centenary celebration was in 2024, but 2028 is expected to be no less impressive.

Find out more at the official website: **w** dainusvente.lt/en.

courtyards and terraces. No matter how much research you do in advance, you are likely to stumble across a spontaneous or unexpected artistic event – that's all part of the magic. To find out what's on, the best website is **w** bilietai.lt.

## OPENING TIMES

**Office hours** in Lithuania are usually 08.00–17.00 Monday to Friday, with banks and other services keeping similar hours. Some bank branches stay open later and on Saturdays. **Shops** tend to open 10.00–20.00 Monday to Saturday, closing later in the big shopping malls. Sunday shop opening hours are shorter, 11.00–18.00. In smaller cities shop opening hours are shorter and likely to be closed on Sundays. Main supermarkets open 07.00–midnight, smaller grocery stores 08.00–22.00. Supermarket chain IKI have introduced autonomous 24/7 shops that are unstaffed and sell basic groceries available any time of day. Note that alcohol can only be bought from shops within certain hours of the day: 10.00–20.00 Mon–Sat and 10.00–15.00 Sun.

**Museums** are generally closed on Mondays, sometimes Tuesdays, but there is no pattern and always an exception to the rule. Winter opening hours are often shorter and outdoor exhibitions or venues usually close during the winter months. Last entry to attractions is usually 1 hour before the closing time. In smaller cities and towns, **tourist information** centres often close for an hour at lunchtime.

**Restaurants** in the main cities typically open from noon until 23.00 or midnight; cafés open earlier and are the best place to find breakfast or brunch. In smaller cities and towns expect restaurants to close earlier. During the winter months and on public holidays restaurant opening hours may be reduced. **Bars** in the main cities stay open until the small hours especially on Friday and Saturday nights.

## MEDIA AND COMMUNICATIONS

**INTERNET** Public internet access is excellent with many places offering free Wi-Fi, and the average download speed is twice that of the global average. The majority of accommodations offer free Wi-Fi for guests, the password shown on your keycard or available from reception.

**NEWS** Following worldwide trends, Lithuania's physical newspaper sales are in decline as people turn to online news portals. The main Lithuanian newspaper, *Lietuvos Rytas* (w lrytas.lt), is no longer printed daily but updated constantly online. Good sources of news in English are *The Baltic Times* (w baltictimes.com), *The Lithuania Tribune* (w lithuaniatribune.com) and the state-owned broadcaster Lithuanian Radio and Television (LRT; w lrt.lt/en).

**POSTAL SERVICES** Lietuvos pastas (w post.lt) is the company responsible for postal services in Lithuania. You will find branches in most cities and towns, though they are becoming fewer. It is becoming commonplace to use parcel delivery lockers located at most supermarkets for sending and receiving parcels.

**TELEPHONE** Lithuania's country code is +370. Most locals use mobile phones over landlines, with the landline telephone network reducing by 300km per year. The last public payphone was taken out of service in 2022.

In 2024, the local **telephone number system** was changed, but this only affects calls made within Lithuania and from a local landline or mobile phone. Every number now starts with the prefix 0. So, for mobile phone numbers that previously started with 6, this is now 06; for landlines, a 0 is added to the start of the existing number. When calling a Lithuanian number from abroad or from a non-Lithuanian mobile within the country the 0 is dropped.

All Lithuanian telephone numbers in this guide include the country code and are in international format ready to dial from a foreign mobile phone whether you are in Lithuania or elsewhere. Remember to activate roaming with your mobile phone provider before travelling to ensure your phone works abroad.

The main local mobile phone operators are Bitė, Tele2 and Telia. You can purchase a local mobile phone SIM card from one of these networks to get a local number and local rates. They are available from supermarkets, petrol stations or Narvesen kiosks. You will need ID to register your details and your handset will need to be unlocked (able to be used on other provider networks).

**TELEVISION AND RADIO** The most popular television channels are the LRT channel TV3 and the commercial LNK. Delfi is the leading cable TV network. In most hotels you will find these accompanied by a selection of German, French and Italian ones with BBC World News the only English-language option. Many young people subscribe to Netflix, and you can swap series recommendations. Popular radio stations are the public-service broadcaster LRT Radijas and commercial stations Radiocentras and M1; all play Lithuanian pop music alongside an eclectic mix of international hits and golden oldies interspersed with news and chat.

## CULTURAL ETIQUETTE

It used to be said that Lithuanians were suspicious of strangers who smiled. Understandable when you have been occupied multiple times and lived alongside collaborators and informers. However, this is not the case anymore, with laughter and smiles regularly on display especially among the younger generations. Lithuanians have been described as the most outgoing of the three Baltic countries, their nickname being the Italians of the north. We couldn't find evidence to support this, but it is worth keeping in mind that Latvians and Estonians are known for being introverts so everything is relative. The World Happiness Report 2024 propelled Lithuania into the limelight for securing top spot as happiest place in the world for under 30-year-olds (ranking 19th for overall happiness).

To keep everyone happy, there are some cultural rules to follow:

- Always buy an odd number of flowers as a gift; even numbers are associated with death and funerals.
- Never shake hands over a threshold and always take your shoes off when entering someone's house.
- Punctuality matters – do not be late, especially in a professional environment.
- Be prepared for Lithuanians' straight talking – this is not intended as rude, purely matter of fact.
- Always say cheers, '*Į sveikatą!*', with eye contact.
- Hang up your coat in a restaurant if hooks are available.
- Never put glass or plastic bottles in the bin; always leave them beside the bin for someone else to easily collect and return them to the deposit scheme.
- If visiting relatives, no matter how distant, be prepared for kisses and hugs.
- And finally, always observe the toilet paper rules of each toilet you visit during your stay – if there is no sign condemning the paper to the bin, flushing is fine.

# TRAVELLING POSITIVELY

It is rightly said that when travelling in nature we should leave nothing but footprints; however, through responsible choices we can also leave an intangible trail of benefits for the local communities, people we meet and environment we have enjoyed. Choose to buy a guidebook by an independent publisher – it will advise and entertain, last longer than your phone battery, and forever be a souvenir of your trip. Book with a local tour operator for authentic recommendations and support. Stay in locally owned hotels to support the local economy. Book guided tours with local experts who will bring your trip to life. Chat with people, listen to their stories, compare views. Stay longer, travel slower, visit beyond the main sights. Support local artisans and artists. Attend local music performances, events and festivals. Take home stories to share and tell the world about Lithuania.

Some visitors like to donate to a local charity; these are our recommendations:

**Gelbekit vaikus** Vokiečių gatvė 8-16, Vilnius; w gelbekitvaikus.lt. The Lithuanian branch of Save the Children provides support across the country to children experiencing challenges.

**Maisto Bankas** Ulonų gatvė 2, Vilnius; w savanoriai.maistobankas.lt. Fundraising, collecting & distributing food aid to those in need. They welcome volunteers to assist with their work.

**Rimanto Kaukėno Paramos Fondas** Dariaus ir Girėno gatvė 21, Vilnius; w kaukenoparama.lt. The Rimantas Kaukėnas Charitable Foundation was set up by Lithuanian basketball star Rimantas Kaukėnas in 2012 to support seriously ill children.

# Part Two

## THE GUIDE

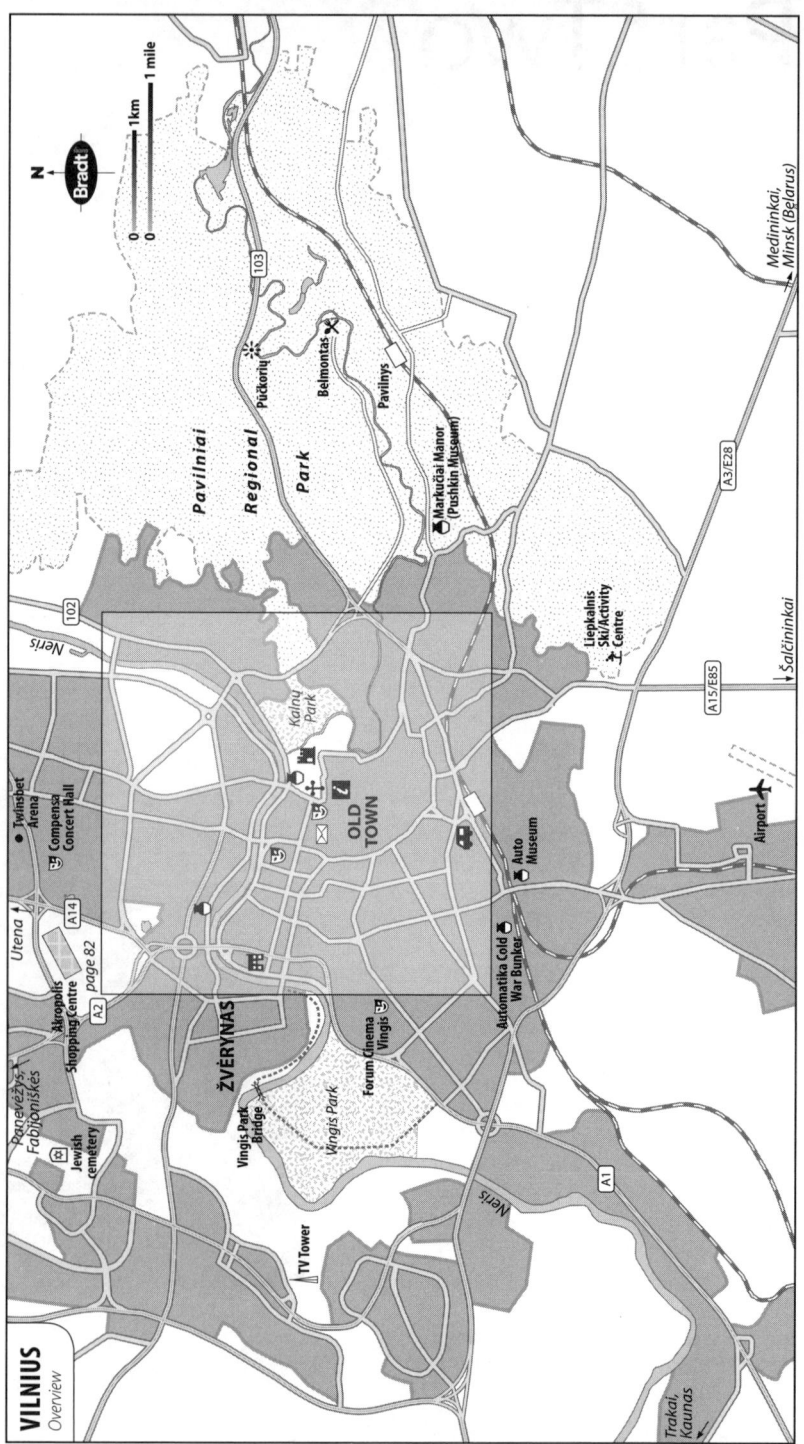

# 3

# Vilnius

Over its 700-hundred-year history, Vilnius has experienced periods both of prosperity and of devastation; it has been a cultural capital and a victim of pan-European conflicts. Vilnius to the Lithuanians, Wilno to the Poles, and Vilna to the Russians and the prominent Jewish community that once lived here, modern-day Vilnius is a city where many cultures have left their mark. In the 30 years since Lithuania regained its independence, creativity, ingenuity and opportunity have flourished, and a youthful spirit leads the way, countering a heavy history with daring, quirky confidence.

Long gone are the days when travellers booked a Vilnius city break with trepidation, their suitcases laden with nylon tights as gifts for tour guides and plugs for hotel sinks. Today, visitors are spoilt for choice with iconic sights, engaging museums, Michelin-starred and -recommended restaurants and artistic events to enjoy. Vilnius' UNESCO-listed Old Town (*senamiestis*) boasts one of the largest assemblages of Baroque buildings outside Rome, alongside masterpieces of Gothic, Renaissance and Neoclassical architecture which line the grand boulevard that is Gediminas Avenue (Gedimino prospektas). While church spires dominate the Old Town skyline, over the Neris River the view is dominated by new glass skyscrapers housing businesses attracted to the city by a young, educated workforce hungry for tech supremacy and start-up success.

Vilnius' rich creative soul is deeply connected to nature – indeed, the city is one of the greenest capitals in Europe. But it is at street level, exploring on foot, that hidden treasures and real local life are revealed. Behind many a restored façade lies a cobbled courtyard, part-suspended in time, home to locals, and where medieval architecture sits side by side with the latest alternative bar. Stroll along centuries-old streets lined with former merchant houses or go hiking in the pagan hills behind Gediminas Castle. Dine on traditional peasant dishes or indulge in a tasting menu accompanied by wine. Sip on a craft beer or glamorous cocktail. Learn about the dark days of occupation from a forward-looking local and enjoy a classical recital or alternative festival. Whatever draws you here, Vilnius is a multi-generational city where everyone can feel at home.

## HISTORY with Benas Petraitis

Archaeological evidence indicates that human settlements have existed at the confluence of the Neris and Vilnia rivers since AD1. Recent excavations on the Kalnų Park hills behind Vilnius Cathedral have unearthed early evidence of pagan communities inhabiting these spiritual mounds and the area lays claim to being the oldest part of the city. According to legend, the area was a sacred forest when Grand Duke Gediminas (1275–1341), ruler of the Grand Duchy of Lithuania, rested here after a day of hunting. He had a vivid dream in which an iron wolf stood atop a hill howling. When he awoke and asked the *krievis* (pagan priest) to translate the dream, the message was clear – he should build a city here, where rulers would reside and represent the Lithuanian lands. Obeying the message from the gods, Gediminas established Vilnius, named it after the Vilnia River and transferred the capital of the Grand Duchy from Trakai to Vilnius.

| | |
|---|---|
| 1323 | The first written reference of Vilnius appears in letters (dated 25 January 1323) from Gediminas to the Hanseatic cities inviting craftsmen, traders, soldiers and monks to come to Vilnius and establish communities and businesses. Those who accept are well received, and a tolerant, multi-cultural society ensues. |
| 1387 | Jogaila, Grand Duke of Lithuania and King of Poland, introduces Christianity to Lithuania and the Diocese of Vilnius is founded. The same year, Jogaila grants Vilnius Magdeburg Rights, allowing its citizens to self-govern, regulate trade and crafts, and guarantee personal and property rights. The 1400s are relatively settled, with action occurring beyond Vilnius as the Grand Duchy defends against western attacks and concentrates on eastward expansion. |
| 1500 | The Gothic masterpiece of St Anne's Church is built. |
| 1522 | The brick defensive wall of Vilnius is completed. Ordered by Grand Duke Alexander, it encircles the densely populated city and protects against impending Tatar attacks. Vilnius flourishes as a centre of merchants and craftsmen. Francis Skoryna, of Prague, establishes the first printing house in Vilnius and publishes the *Little Book of Travels*, the first printed book in the Grand Duchy. |
| 1569 | The Polish-Lithuanian Commonwealth is established via the Union of Lublin; as a result Vilnius loses its role of royal and administrative capital to Warsaw. |
| 1579 | Vilnius University is established. |
| 1604 | The cornerstone of St Casimir Church is laid to mark the patron saint of Lithuania's canonisation. Building is completed in 1618 and marks the beginning of the Baroque era in Vilnius, paving the way for the independent Vilnius Baroque school that emerges throughout the 18th century, led by architect Johann Christoph Glaubitz. |
| 1610 | 30 June–1 July: Vilnius is devastated by one of the biggest fires in its history. |
| 1630–33 | The Great Synagogue is built in Vilnius and becomes the most important spiritual and cultural centre for Lithuanian Jews. During the 17th century Vilnius is home to 40 prominent rabbis and in the 18th century the great sage Gaon Elijah establishes a concentration of Jewish intellectual Talmudists and scholars, resulting in Vilnius being known as 'Jerusalem of the North' (page 25). |
| 1795 | Lithuania is annexed to the Russian Empire and Vilnius loses its capital status. The Lower Castle, part of the Upper Castle and much of the city wall, towers and gates are demolished. |
| 1812 | June: Napoleon marches through Vilnius on his way to Moscow. |
| 1860 | The Warsaw–St Petersburg railway opens and Vilnius train station becomes an important transport hub, leading to industrial, trade and population growth. |
| 1897 | In 1897, more than 40% (some 64,000 people) of the population of Vilnius is Jewish. |

| | |
|---|---|
| **1915** | Vilnius is occupied by the German army until the end of World War I, in 1918. |
| **1918** | 16 February: The Council of Lithuania signs the Act of Independence of Lithuania at the House of Signatories (page 101), proclaiming the establishment of an independent democratic Lithuanian Republic, with Vilnius as its capital, finally ending 123 years of occupation by Tsarist Russia. |
| **1919** | Soviet Russia invades Vilnius on 5 January 1919, proclaiming it the Soviet Socialist Republic of Lithuania. On 19 April, the Polish army led by commander-in-chief Piłsudski drives the Bolsheviks out of Vilnius and captures the city, eventually incorporating it into Poland. |
| **1920–39** | Polish occupation of Vilnius. Lithuania's capital is transferred to Kaunas with most Lithuanians leaving Vilnius. The ethnic make-up of Vilnius becomes predominantly Polish, Jewish and Belarusian, and a state of frozen conflict follows. |
| **1939** | World War II breaks out, and in the September Soviet Russia invades Poland, annexing Vilnius under the Molotov–Ribbentrop pact, signed on 23 August between Germany and the Soviet Union. In October, Vilnius is given back to Lithuania under the Lithuanian–Soviet Treaty of Mutual Assistance, a short-lived false hope of Lithuanian independence. |
| **1940** | June: Lithuania is occupied by and is incorporated into the Soviet Union. |
| **1941** | The first cattle wagons, transporting intellectuals, priests, teachers, doctors and wealthy farmers to Siberia, depart Lithuania on 14 June as Stalin starts his first round of deportations. In Vilnius the first wagons leave from Naujoji Vilnia train station. |
| **1941** | 22 June: Nazi Germany attacks the Soviet Union as part of Operation Barbarossa. Vilnius is occupied by Nazi Germany until July 1944. |
| **1941** | 31 August–2 September: Thousands of Vilnius Jews are murdered in response to the Great Provocation, when two planned gunshots are fired in the Jewish area and it is claimed Jews have killed two Germans. A 'cleansing' of the area begins with the deportation of Jewish citizens to nearby Paneriai for mass execution. A few days later, on 6 September, the remaining Jewish population is forced into two ghettos.  
21 October: Vilnius' Small Ghetto is liquidated; 11,000 Jews are killed. |
| **1943** | 23 September: The Great Ghetto is liquidated; 29,000 Jews are killed. |
| **1944** | July: The Soviet Union 'liberates' Lithuania from Nazi Germany, giving another false hope of independence. |
| **1946** | Soviet deportations resume with the goal of liquidating the bourgeoisie, intellectuals and independence movement. The active Forest Brothers partisan movement and Lithuanian resistance are arrested in large numbers and many are interrogated and executed in the KGB building on Gediminas Avenue (page 111). For decades society is suppressed by fear and the resistance movement is driven underground. |
| **1987** | 23 August: Around 300 people gather at the statue of Adomas Mickevičius in Vilnius to demonstrate against the Soviet occupiers. |
| **1988** | 23 August: A Sąjūdis opposition movement meeting attracts 250,000 people in Vingis Park. |

| | |
|---|---|
| 1989 | 23 August: On the 50th anniversary of the Molotov–Ribbentrop pact, some 2.5 million people form 'The Baltic Way', a 650km-long human chain stretching from Vilnius to Tallinn in Estonia, showing the unity and independent will of the Baltic states. |
| 1990 | 11 March: The Supreme Council of the Lithuanian SSR in Vilnius proclaims Lithuania's independence. Lithuania is back on the political map of Europe after 50 years in the Soviet Union. |
| 1991 | 13 January: Moscow attempts to regain control, sending in Soviet tanks, armoured personnel carriers and armed soldiers to storm Vilnius TV Tower and the Lithuanian Radio and Television building. Fourteen civilians are killed. Huge crowds protect the parliament from Soviet troops, with barricades. The threat is repelled and other occupied states soon follow suit, with the Union of Soviet Socialist Republics (USSR) finally dissolved in December 1991. |
| 1994 | Poland renounces any claim over Vilnius in the Friendship and Cooperation Treaty. |
| 2004 | 1 May: Lithuania joins the European Union. |
| 2009 | Vilnius is European Capital of Culture. |
| 2015 | 1 January: Lithuania joins the euro single currency. |
| 2022 | Vilnius welcomes Ukrainian and Belarusian refugees; national support for Ukraine is unwavering. The street housing the Russian embassy in Vilnius is renamed Ukrainian Heroes Street (Ukrainos Didvyrių gatvė). |
| 2024 | Vilnius continues to build a positive reputation for start-ups and fintech industries, while the nation tops the World Happiness Report (2024–present) for young people under 30. |

## GETTING THERE AND AWAY

**BY AIR** **Vilnius International Airport** (Vilniaus oro uostas; Rodūnios kelias 10A; w vilnius-airport.lt) is located 5km south of the city centre. Take time to admire the ornate details of the historic arrivals hall – yes, sightseeing starts immediately in Vilnius! For information on flights and airlines serving Vilnius airport, see page 47.

### Getting from the airport

**By bus** Exit arrivals and walk along to the bus stops outside the new departure terminal. Bus 88 runs every 20–30 minutes and stops in the city centre before continuing to the business area north of the river. Bus 88N is a night bus running the same route from 22.30 to 05.30 every 30 minutes. Bus 3G runs every 10 minutes via the centre to Fabijoniškės district. Buses 1 and 2 depart every 20–30 minutes to Vilnius bus station. To buy a single ticket (€0.90 for 60mins), use your card or device to pay by contactless at the validation machine in the bus. If a ticket inspection occurs, they will scan your card or device to check you have a valid ticket. Single tickets can also be bought from the driver for €1 (cash only); you must then validate your ticket in one of the machines on the bus. See page 78 for information on multi-use ticket options if you plan to use public transport during your stay.

**By train** The airport station is an easy 350m walk from the arrivals terminal, mainly under a covered, illuminated walkway. A lift or stairs take you down to the track level. Tickets to Vilnius can be purchased at the station ticket machine, on the train or online (w ltglink.lt; €0.80 one way). The journey takes 8 minutes.

The service is most useful if you are travelling to or from elsewhere in Lithuania by train, or if staying close to Vilnius train station.

**By taxi** There is a **taxi** rank immediately outside the arrivals hall supposedly for approved taxi companies only. Only get into a licensed taxi vehicle at the taxi rank or you risk being scammed; have your destination address written down as the driver may not speak English; and expect to pay around €20 to the Old Town – taking a taxi is the most expensive option of getting to the city, and be prepared to pay in cash. Alternatively, using the easy-to-use **Bolt** ride-sharing app will cost around €10 and payment is by card.

**By car** The airport **car rental** centre is in multi-storey parking P4, a short walk straight ahead from the arrivals hall. If picking up a **car share** vehicle from Citybee or Bolt Drive (page 57), you need the outdoor parking area P2. It is a 4km drive to the Old Town and takes between 10–30 minutes depending on the traffic. When exiting the airport complex, turn right onto Dariaus ir Girėno gatvė and follow signs for *centras*.

**BY TRAIN** The **railway station** [83 D8] (Vilniaus geležinkelio stotis; Geležinkelio gatvė; w ltglink.lt) is located on the edge of the Old Town. Trolleybuses 1, 2, 7 and 20 and buses 26, 34 and 53 will take you into the city centre. Use w judu.lt to check the routes, and see page 56 for ticket information. Local taxis are available outside the station, but using the Bolt app is recommended for cheaper rates and easier communication. Station services include luggage storage, a supermarket, a café and charging points.

Waiting for your train need not be boring. **Peronas** (f peronasbaras) is a bar on a defunct platform (*peronas*) below the pedestrian bridge crossing the tracks, serving drinks and snacks under the gaze of a huge statue of Tony Soprano from *The Sopranos* TV series. The Lithuanian Railway Museum (page 118) has an outdoor exhibition visible from the pedestrian bridge. Also of interest is the securely fenced-off international platform through which St Petersburg–Kaliningrad trains pass. A photographic display of the horrors being perpetrated by Russia in Ukraine was constructed along the platform, a vain attempt to reach people through the state-controlled propaganda but the train staff close the curtains.

**BY BUS** The **bus station** [83 D8] (Vilniaus autobusų stotis; Sodų gatvė 22; w autobusustotis.lt) is opposite the train station making this area of the city a busy transport hub on the edge of the Old Town. Both international and domestic services depart from here. Services include the ticket office, luggage store and a waiting area. The Old Town is a short walk away, but if a taxi is required, we strongly recommend using the Bolt app rather than taking a taxi off the street.

## GETTING AROUND

**ON FOOT** Being a small city with places of interest on most streets, walking is the best way to explore Vilnius. Few areas are fully pedestrianised but traffic is restricted on some Old Town streets and others are inaccessible to vehicles. Pedestrians tend to outnumber vehicles in the Old Town and efforts are being made to reduce private vehicle use throughout the city centre. Walking routes prepared by the tourist information centre with different themes, varying distances and covering both the city centre and surrounding countryside are available at w walkablevilnius.com.

**BY BUS AND TROLLEYBUS** Vilnius' public transport system is run on a combination of buses and trolleybuses. Trolleybuses look like buses but are powered by a rod that attaches to the overhead electricity cables and can run only on the cabled routes. The much-loved old trolleybuses have been retired out of service with a fond farewell, some being sold to collectors and private buyers. Their drivers were mainly women who decorated their cab area with curtains and novelties and took no nonsense, often having to get out and hoick the rod back up to the overhead cable when it became detached.

If you plan to take public transport during your stay in Vilnius, download the **Trafi** app (w trafi.com) – this is the main platform for checking routes, schedules, real-time tracking and buying your ticket. A single journey costs €1 every time and lasts for 60 minutes. Or you can buy a one-day (24hr) ticket for €5, or a three-day (72hr) ticket for €8. You must validate your ticket each time you get on a bus or trolleybus using the machine inside. You can also buy tickets at Narvesen kiosks and automatic ticket machines, or from the driver (cash only). Alternatively you can pay by contactless at the machines inside the bus: tap your card or phone when you get on and again when you get off. If there is a ticket inspection, your payment device will be scanned to check you have paid.

Note that buses on public holidays or during festivals are often free – look out for the signs saying '*nemokamas*'. It is worth knowing that G buses are express buses that don't stop at all stops along the route. Note that the website w stops.lt has a very simple public transport trip-planning tool for Vilnius.

**BY TAXI, RIDE-HAILING APPS AND CAR-SHARING SERVICES** Uber is available, but there are fewer drivers than Bolt, making Bolt the better choice here. Download the app, create an account then local travel is a breeze and usually cheaper than a taxi too. See page 58 for advice on taxis.

**Citybee** (w citybee.lt) and **Bolt Drive** (w bolt.eu) are both popular car-sharing services in Vilnius. For visitors they are ideal for a self-drive day trip out of town, a self-catering supermarket shop, or for city sightseeing if mobility is restricted. Register for the app, reserve a car, and pay for the time and kilometres covered during your period of hire (for further details, see page 57). Be sure to leave the car parked in an authorised zone at the end of your hire period.

**BY BICYCLE AND SCOOTER** Exploring Vilnius by bike is a good option, but stick to the cycle paths where possible as other road users are not necessarily accommodating of cyclists. Recommended routes include the Neris River path and visiting the TV Tower. **Velotakas** (page 93) arranges cycle hire and self-guided or guided tours. As fun as electric scooters may seem, they are often incompatible with cobbled streets, potholed roads or broken pavements. Dentistry and facial reconstruction have been big business since the arrival of these pay-as-you-go modes of transport and we urge you to proceed with an abundance of caution.

## TOURIST INFORMATION AND TOUR OPERATORS

The **tourism information centre** [85 C1] (Vilniaus turizmo informacijos centras; Pilies gatvė 7; w govilnius.lt; ⏰ 09.00–18.00 daily) is located on the main pedestrian street of Pilies. They have a VR experience, souvenirs, events listings and a tour booking service, and sell the **Vilnius Pass** which benefits those wanting to visit lots of museums and attractions with free or reduced entry and discounts across the city (24hr pass €37, 48hr pass €47, 72hr pass €56).

## TOUR OPERATORS

**Romantic Vilnius** w romanticvilnius.lt. Offering dreamy tours of Vilnius & also food tours, fully catering for those who believe the way to the heart is via the stomach.

**Valandėlė City Tour** w valandele.lt. Their Vilnius hop-on/hop-off buses include a live guide or audio guide service. Pick up is from Cathedral Sq close to the bell tower. Also arranges private tours by car or walking tours.

**Vilnius City Tour** w vilniuscitytour.com. Operators of a Vilnius hop-on/hop-off sightseeing bus & both group & private day tours to major attractions including Trakai & the Hill of Crosses. Also arranges airport transfers.

**Vilnius Free Walking Tours** w vilniusfreetour.lt. The free tour runs daily at 10.30 & 15.30 from Cathedral Sq, but you must pre-register as the tours only run with min 4 guests.

**Vilnius with Locals** w vilniuswithlocals.com. Free walking tour every day at 11.00 from Vilnius Town Hall. Paid tours include regular themed group tours including Jewish Vilnius, Soviet history & food tasting.

## WHERE TO STAY

Vilnius has an array of accommodation options to suit all budgets, needs and styles. With leisure visitors in mind, we have focused on accommodation close to the Old Town where you will feel immersed in the city with attractions and activities conveniently nearby. More hotel options are available north of the river in the new town, but these are predominantly chain hotels catering to business travellers and lack the unique local flavour and charm you will experience in the Old Town. For those looking for self-catering options, the usual online booking portals are full of rental listings. And if you prefer to combine a stay in the countryside with time in the city, check out the region's resorts (page 127).

### LUXURY

✱ **Hotel Pacai** [85 C3] (104 rooms) Didžioji gatvė 7; w hotelpacai.com. The former 17th-century mansion is now a luxury design hotel popular with visiting heads of state & wealthy Instagrammers. Step back in time as you walk through grand corridors in search of your room. Standard rooms are in the new-build section, & deluxe, superior & suites in the old part characterised by high ceilings, exposed brickwork & frescoes. The restaurant is Michelin-recommended & there is a spa (but no swimming pool). According to legend, Napoleon addressed his troops from the balcony of the Pacai Suite. €€€€€

**Grand Hotel Vilnius** [83 D5] (93 rooms) Universiteto gatvė 14; w hilton.com/en/hotels/vnodeqq-grand-hotel-vilnius. Luxurious lodgings with front-facing rooms offering iconic views of Cathedral Square & Gediminas Castle. Nothing is any trouble for the concierge service, & the spa has one of the largest swimming pools in the Old Town. The Michelin-recommended restaurant, Telegrafas, is named in honour of the building's past life as the main telegraph office. A little-known fact is that beehives on the roof provide fresh honey to the kitchen. €€€€

**Stikliai Hotel** [85 B3] (41 rooms) Gaono gatvė 7; w stikliai.com. What started out as a dream among 3 friends grew from being a café, to a restaurant, to a luxury hotel & a long-time sumptuous favourite of visiting dignitaries. The property has an array of luxurious room categories (but no twin-bed rooms) & 1- & 2-bedroomed apartments, plus a small swimming pool & sauna, fitness room & billiards room. The classic French restaurant Stikliai is Michelin-recommended. €€€€

### FIRST CLASS

**Hotel Neringa** [82 C4] (124 rooms) Gedimino prospektas 23; w neringavilnius.com. This heritage building, noted for its 1917 Modernist architecture & the 1959 murals that adorn the restaurant walls, has been a hotel since 1939. It underwent 3 years of renovation & rebuild, reopening in 2021. The original façade & restaurant were preserved – not many other hotel b/fasts are served in a monument of cultural heritage. To the locals this place is loaded

> ## FESTIVALS
>
> Vilnius is often a-buzz with creative events, from tiny concerts or pop-up exhibitions in a courtyard, to major festivals taking over Cathedral Square. They provide an outlet for the bubbling creative energy that flows through the city and offer the visitor an even greater insight into the city's culture and community.
>
> For details of the Lithunanian Song and Dance Festival, which is held every four years, see page 67.
>
> **VILNIUS FESTIVAL** (Vilniaus festivalis; w vilniusfestivals.lt) A variety of prestigious performing arts festivals are held throughout the year, including jazz, film, theatre, dance and classical music events.
>
> **VILNIUS LIGHT FESTIVAL** (Vilniaus šviesų festivalis; w lightfestival.lt) The Vilnius Light Festival brings colour and energy to the dark days of late January. It celebrates Vilnius' birthday on 25 January – the date in 1325 when Grand Duke Gediminas wrote his letter inviting people to come to Vilnius. Over three days, the capital is filled with creative light installations between the hours of 17.00 and 22.00. They are often in unusual locations, so download the app for the map. The exact dates change but always cover 25 January.
>
> **KAZIUKAS FAIR (ST CASIMIR'S FAIR)** (Kaziuko mugė; w kaziukomuge.lt) On the weekend closest to 4 March (St Casimir's Day), the streets of the Old Town are filled with craftspeople and artisans, local produce and food stalls, entertainment and concerts. This festival has been a winter-warmer harbinger of spring for over 400 years.

with nostalgia & is the place to enjoy authentic chicken Kyiv & herring. €€€€

**Narutis Hotel** [85 C1] (50 rooms) Pilies gatvė 24; w narutis.lt. The oldest hotel in Vilnius is housed in an assemblage of 15th- & 16th-century mansion buildings in an enviable location on the main pedestrian route of Pilies gatvė & opposite St John's Church. Rooms are classic in style with a bit of chintz. The spa in the cellar is free for guests, & the terrace bar is a good spot to watch the world pass by in summer. €€€€

**Shakespeare Hotel** [85 D1] (31 rooms) Bernardinų gatvė 8; w shakespeare.lt. When it first opened in 1999, the Shakespeare Hotel seemed a bit of a branding gamble, but it is still here & as popular as ever. The rooms are named & subtly styled after legendary novelists, playwrights & antagonists including the James Joyce (standard), the Jane Austen (business) and the Shakespeare (superior, of course). €€€€

**Amberton Cathedral Square Hotel** [83 D5] (116 rooms) L Stuokos-Gucevičiaus gatvė 1; w ambertonhotels.com/vilnius. This hotel boasts a prime location – request a room at the front for sweeping views of Cathedral Square. It's popular with groups, so b/fast can be busy. €€€

✵ **Artagonist Art Hotel** [85 C2] (34 rooms) Pilies gatvė 34; w artagonist.lt. A contemporary hotel housed in a 15th-century Old Town building with rooms individually styled by Lithuanian artists, Artagonist is uniquely Vilnius. Note that cheaper rooms have windows that open internally over the reception atrium or are very small. Friendly staff, excellent location. €€€

**Artis Hotel** [85 A1] (118 rooms) Totorių gatvė 23; w artis.centrumhotels.com. Artis's slim, elegant façade is deceptive as the hotel houses not 1 but 2 restaurants & is popular with large groups. In an interesting location next to the Ministry of Defence & opposite the President's Palace. €€€

**OPEN HOUSE VILNIUS** (w openhousevilnius.lt) All sorts of architecturally important closed, official or private buildings are open to visitors for free over this weekend festival of architecture. The date varies every year between late April and early May, so check the website for updates.

**PINK SOUP FEST** (w govilnius.lt/pink-soup-fest) A riot of 'pink' events fill this special day dedicated to the national beetroot-based cold pink soup, *šaltibarščiai*. When šaltibarščiai appears on the menu, you know the longed-for summer has arrived. Visitors can ride the Pink Soup Slide, savour food market delicacies and enjoy the open-air evening concert. The event is held in Kūdros Park at the end of May/beginning of June and, yes, you are encouraged to wear pink!

**CULTURE NIGHT** (Kultūros naktis; w kulturosnaktis.lt) An evening of free arts, dance and music is provided in many different venues across the city in early June.

**VILNIUS CAPITAL DAYS** (Sostinės dienos; w vilnius-events.lt) Centred around Gediminas Avenue, Vilnius Capital Days is usually held over the first weekend of September, around the time of the autumn equinox. Expect artisan and craft stalls, food markets, pop-up entertainment and a main music stage in Cathedral Square.

**CHRISTMAS MARKET** Festive stalls selling artisan wares, culinary gifts including gingerbread and sweets, and warming mugs of hot mulled wine (*karštas vynas*) are set up around the Christmas tree in Cathedral Square from late November to late December – though the Christmas tree stays up until 7 January. Extravagant shop-front decorations adorn the streets of the Old Town.

**Grotthuss Hotel** [85 A5] (37 rooms) Ligoninės gatvė 5; w grotthusshotel.com. This small, classic hotel with a mini-manor-house atmosphere is tucked away on a cobbled side street. Its summer courtyard restaurant is perfect for lazy b/fasts & evening drinks. €€€

✴ **Hotel Vilnia** [83 E5] (79 rooms) Maironio gatvė 1; w hotelvilnia.lt. A classic hotel, Vilnia sits on the boundary between the Old Town with its red roofs & the green space of Bernardine Gardens. The building once housed the Lithuanian Communist Party publishing house, which, until 1985, churned out Soviet newspapers. €€€

**Radisson Astorija Hotel** [85 C4] (119 rooms) Didžioji gatvė 35-2; w radissonhotels.com/en-us/hotels/radisson-collection-vilnius-astorija. Once one of the grandest private houses in Vilnius, the Astorija mixes an air of aristocracy merged with chain hotel vibes. The wellness centre has a pool & sauna. In summer, the rooftop bar offers splendid views & is open to non-residents. €€€

## TOURIST CLASS

**City Gate Hotel** [85 C6] (53 rooms) Bazilijonų gatvė 3; w citygate.lt. Located just outside Vilnius Old Town, across the road from the Gates of Dawn, this is a good economy choice. The courtyard & wooden loggia retain a sense of its former days as a historic inn housing a brewery & stables for passing travellers. Today the offering is a comfy bed & buffet b/fast. €€

✴ **Domus Maria Hotel** [85 C5] (48 rooms) Aušros vartų gatvė 12; w domusmaria.com. This 17th-century former monastery offers monastic simplicity in an unbeatable location in the Old Town. The quad rooms are good for families & groups of friends. €€

**Hotel Apia** [85 B2] (12 rooms) Šv. Ignoto gatvė 12; w apia.lt. A charming family-owned boutique hotel with 12 cosy, individually styled rooms. Note that b/fast is served at the Narutis Hotel, 5mins' walk away. €€

**Radisson Blu Lietuva** [82 C3] (154 rooms) Konstitucijos prospektas 20; w radissonhotels.

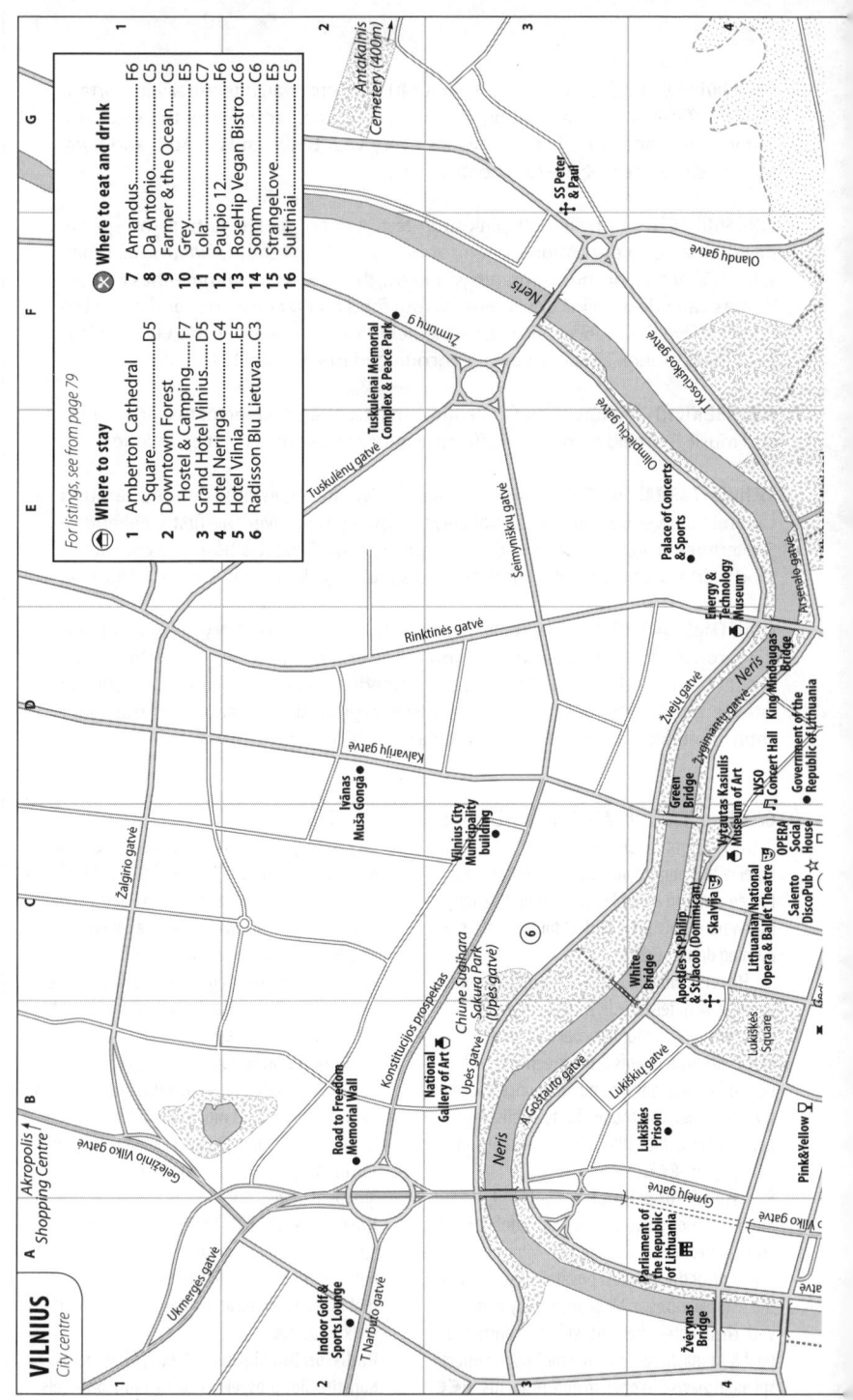

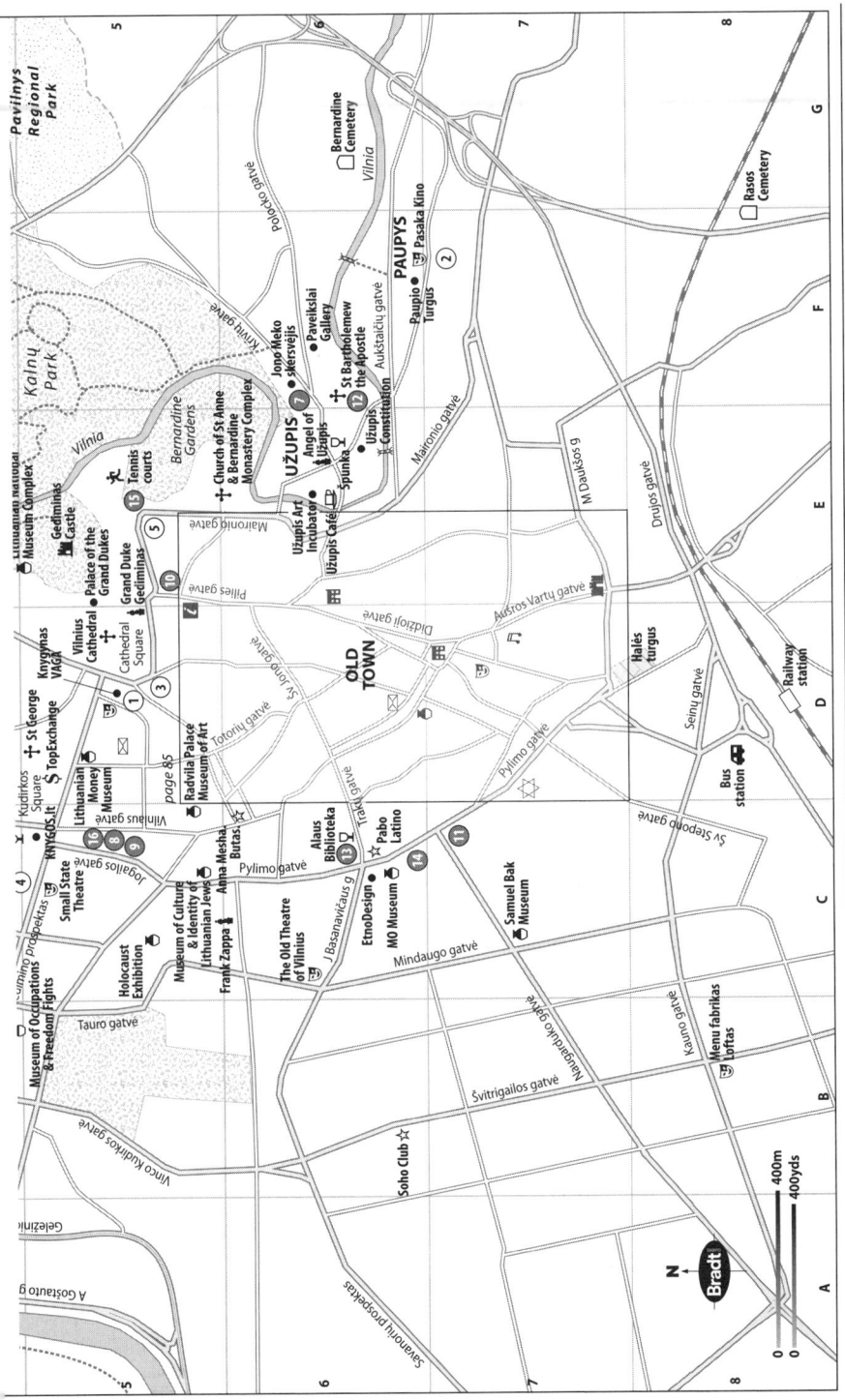

com/en-us/hotels/radisson-blu-vilnius-lietuva. Located across the river from the Old Town, the Lietuva was once the only skyscraper in Vilnius. It took 20 years to build due to poor planning & coordination, finally opening in 1983 & operating under the Moscow-based incoming travel agency Intourist. At that time, all foreigners had to book their travel to the Soviet Union via Intourist, who arranged not only the hotel but all other services too, enabling authorities to keep a quiet eye on guests. Most cities in the Soviet Union had an Intourist hotel, all under heavy KGB surveillance, with dedicated rooms & restaurant tables wiretapped & not-so-inconspicuous women sitting on every landing noting everyone's comings & goings. But there is no evidence of this dark past today. This is a sharp business-class hotel with the popular Skybar on the top floor offering swanky cocktails & sweeping views of the city (non-residents welcome). €€

### BUDGET
**Downtown Forest Hostel & Camping** [83 F7] (28 rooms) Paupio gatvė 31A; w downtownforest. lt. Centrally located in the Užupis area, accommodation options here include private or dormitory rooms & camping pods. It also caters for campers with tents or camper vans. It is a social place with BBQs & events held in the large garden, but quiet time rules 23.00–08.00. €

## WHERE TO EAT AND DRINK

Deciding where to eat or drink in Vilnius gets trickier every year with the burgeoning variety of venues; but, whether you choose street food or a Michelin-starred restaurant, you will be well catered for. There are many more top-notch places than we can list here, including numerous Michelin-recommended restaurants, and hotel restaurants which should not be overlooked. Here are some recommendations.

### LUXURY
**14Horses** [85 B2] Dominikonų gatvė 11; w 14horses.lt; ⏱ 17.00–23.00 Tue–Sat. Awarded a Bib Gourmand by Michelin for their exceptional (organic) farm-to-table dishes, they serve creative, modern cuisine. The style is smart but with a relaxed atmosphere. Choose 2 starters, main & dessert, or 3 starters & main. Wine pairing available. €€€€
**Amandus** [83 F6] Užupio gatvė 32; w amandus. lt; ⏱ 19.00–22.00 Wed–Sat. This Michelin-recommended restaurant in bohemian Užupis combines authentic historical cuisine with youthful creativity in a cosy atmosphere. Your host & chef Deivydas Praspaliauskas has been voted top Lithuanian chef several times. A new tasting menu is introduced each month with dinner reservations starting prompt at 19.00. Amandus Gourmet is their shop next door full of gastronomic goodies to take home. €€€€€
**Džiaugsmas** [85 A1] Vilniaus gatvė 28; w dziaugsmas.com; ⏱ 17.00–23.00 Mon–Sat. Behind the modest façade is an industrial-style interior where the experimental micro-seasonal dishes served add colour & personality. Choose a tasting menu with paired wines or from the à la carte menu. Awarded a Michelin star in 2024. €€€€€

**VILNIUS** Old Town
*For listings, see from page 79*

⊙ **Where to stay**
| | | |
|---|---|---|
| 1 | Artagonist Art | C2 |
| 2 | Artis | A1 |
| 3 | City Gate | C6 |
| 4 | Domus Maria | C5 |
| 5 | Grotthuss | A5 |
| 6 | Hotel Apia | B2 |
| 7 | Hotel Pacai | C3 |
| 8 | Narutis | C1 |
| 9 | Radisson Astorija | C4 |
| 10 | Shakespeare | D1 |
| 11 | Stikliai | B3 |

⊗ **Where to eat and drink**
| | | |
|---|---|---|
| 12 | 14Horses | B2 |
| 13 | Baleboste | B6 |
| 14 | Beigelistai | D2 |
| 15 | Bistro 18 | B2 |
| 16 | Čili Pica | C3 |
| 17 | Cozy | B2 |
| 18 | Džiaugsmas | A1 |
| 19 | Ertlio Namas | C2 |
| 20 | Eskedar | C2 |
| 21 | Etno Dvaras | C1 |
| 22 | Gabi | D1 |
| 23 | Lokys | B3 |
| 24 | Nineteen18 | B2 |
| 25 | Pas Mus | C2 |
| 26 | Pirmas Blynas | D3 |
| 27 | Saint Germain | D2 |
| | Vieta | (see 6) |

* **Ertlio Namas** [85 C2] Šv. Jono gatvė 7; w ertlionamas.lt; ⏲ 17.00–23.00 Mon–Sat. Against the backdrop of a fine historic building & beautifully presented rooms, guests embark on a historical & culinary journey, with each authentic Lithuanian course explained via storytelling. Ertlio Namas was recommended by Michelin in 2024 as being 'for your brain as well as your body'. The 4- or 6-course set menu can be with or without wine pairing. €€€€€

* **Nineteen18** [85 B2] Dominikonų gatvė 11; w nineteen18.lt; ⏲ 18.00–23.00 Wed–Sat. Awarded a Michelin star in 2024 for their creative, detailed dishes inspired by local produce &

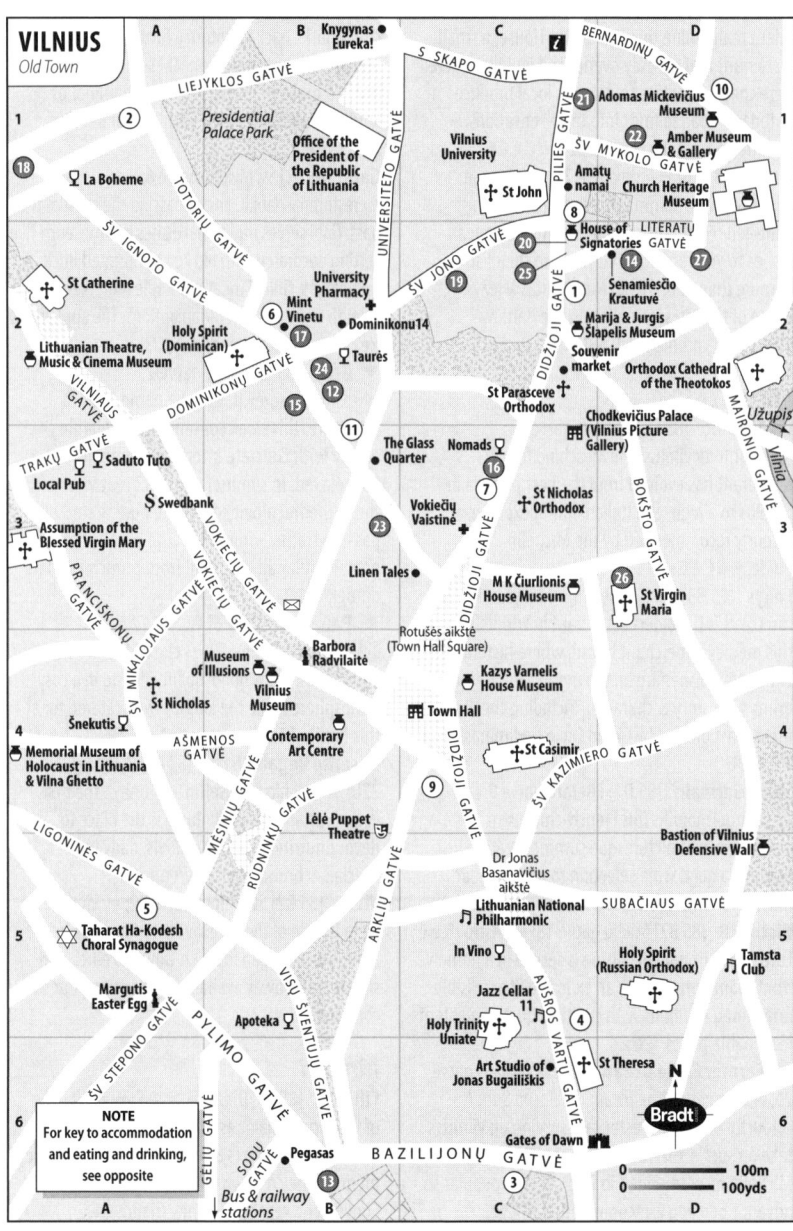

historical Lithuanian cuisine, Nineteen18 is a leader of Vilnius' farm-to-table movement. It is the Vilnius restaurant of the organic Farmer's Circle & Red Brick restaurant near Ukmergė (page 249). Advance booking recommended. €€€€€

**Pas Mus Restoranas** [85 C2] Pilies gatvė 28; w pas-mus-restoranas.tablein.com; ⊕ 18.00–23.00 Wed–Sat. The personal touch & natural talent really shine through at 'Our House', a small restaurant that is easily overlooked on Pilies gatvė. Here chef-owner Vita transforms local produce or today's foraged finds into taste sensations. Awarded a Michelin star in 2024. €€€€€

**Somm** [83 C6] Pylimo gatvė 21; w somm.lt; ⊕ closed Sun. Somm is for 'sommelier' & this wine-led restaurant matches creative European dishes to your preferred wines from their list of more than 500. Owner Narimantas Miežys is one of the top sommeliers in the Baltics. Michelin-recommended. €€€€€

### FIRST CLASS

**Da Antonio** [83 C5] Vilniaus gatvė 23; 📷 daantoniovilnius. The Meschino family restaurant has evolved from the best pizzeria in the 90s to a high-end Italian dining experience recently recommended by the Michelin guide. €€€€€

**Lokys** [85 B3] Stiklių gatvė 8; w lokys.lt. Family-run Lokys is the oldest restaurant in Vilnius. In this medieval merchant house, where historical Lithuanian dishes are on the menu, everything brims with story & character, including the 'Boar meat roast praised by Grand Duke Gediminas'. €€€€€

**Saint Germain** [85 D2] Literatų gatvė 9; w saintgermain.lt. This French-chic bistro restaurant with picturesque summer seating features a good wine selection to partner your mussels or entrecote. €€€€€

**Bistro 18** [85 B2] Stiklių gatvė 18; w bistro18.eu. European/Lithuanian cuisine is served in a homely front room atmosphere; an example of accessible fine dining in Vilnius with creative, quality meals at reasonable prices. €€€€

✳ **Farmer & the Ocean** [83 C5] Vilniaus gatvė 25; 📘 farmerandtheocean; ⊕ closed Sun. A colourful basement restaurant serving up Vilnius's take on surf 'n' turf in a cheery environment. Michelin recommended in 2024, & very popular so advance booking is recommended. €€€€

### MODERATE

✳ **Cozy** [85 B2] Dominikonų gatvė 10; w cozy.lt. Everyone is welcome in this friendly laid-back bar & restaurant, a golden oldie serving consistently good food & drink. €€€

**Etno Dvaras** [85 C1] Pilies gatvė 16; w etnodvaras.lt. The ethnographic rural décor at this branch of the Lithuanian restaurant chain harks back to country farmsteads. Enjoy dishes such as potato pancakes like grandma used to make or national dishes cepelinai or koldūnai, washed down with a local beer or *gira*. €€€

**Gabi** [85 D1] Šv. Mykolo gatvė 6; w restoranasgabi.lt. Encompassing the spirit of the past, Gabi serves traditional dishes in a museum-like setting decorated with old keys, imprinted bricks & saltshakers. Grilled meat is a staple ingredient here, though there are vegetarian options. The apple pie & ice cream is recommended. €€€

✳ **Grey** [83 E5] Pilies gatvė 2; w restoranasgrey.lt. Grey by name but not by nature, this sleek contemporary reliable eatery with concrete interior is sophisticated but relaxed. In summer, enjoy a great view of the cathedral albeit sometime punctuated by passing traffic – from the large outdoor seating area. Popular all day long, from brunch to a late dinner. €€€

✳ **Paupio 12** [83 F6] Paupio 12; 📘 restoranaspaupio12; ⊕ closed Mon. Parents can enjoy good-quality dining in a cosy atmosphere while the kids are well catered for at this family-friendly restaurant. €€€

**RoseHip Vegan Bistro** [83 C6] Pylimo gatvė 22D; w rosehip.lt. RoseHip was one of the first vegan restaurants in Vilnius & is the place to devour nutritious Buddha bowls, daily lunch specials & brunch on the w/end. €€

**Vieta** [85 B2] Šv. Ignoto gatvė 12; w vieta-vieta.lt. One of the oldest vegetarian cafés in Vilnius went vegan in 2022. Down to earth and simple; take-away available if you bring your own containers. €€

### BUDGET

**Čili Pica** [85 C3] Didžioji gatvė 5; w cili.lt. One of the oldest chain restaurants in Lithuania. Think pizzas, burgers & salads on a photographic menu, & they're open until midnight every day. Convenient, reliable & family friendly. €€

**Sultiniai** [83 C5] Jogailos gatvė 8; ⏲ 10.00–18.00 Mon–Fri. For some, this is the place for a nostalgic treat reminiscent of grandma's cooking, for others a quirky throwback to Soviet times. Order off a basic menu at bargain prices through the hatch. €

## CAFÉS

**Eskedar** [85 C2] Pilies gatvė 26; w eskedarcoffee.com; ⏲ 10.00–late daily. Located on the ground floor of the House of Signatories & reminiscent of a time when intellectuals & high society met here to drink coffee & put the world to rights, today the café writes a new chapter for the history books. The owner, Eskedar, arrived in Lithuania as a refugee from Ethiopia & has made a success of her coffee-roasting company & small chain of cafes. €€

✱ **StrangeLove** [83 E5] Barboros Radvilaitės gatvė 6B; w strangelove.lt; ⏲ 08.00–20.00 Mon–Fri, 10.00–20.00 Sat–Sun. When you get a table at this small café you'll feel rather pleased with yourself as it is a popular place. They roast their own coffee to accompany their delicious cakes. There's extra seating upstairs & out the back in summer. €€

✱ **Baleboste** [85 B6] Pylimo gatvė 53; w instagram.com/baleboste.vilnius; ⏲ 10.00–17.00 Tue–Thu, 09.00–21.00 Fri, 08.00–21.00 Sat, 08.00–17.00 Sun. Traditional Lithuanian Jewish Litvak dishes are served at this homely café, where Riva & her team bake the softest bagels – perfect with baba ghanoush. €

**Beigelistai** [85 D2] Literatų gatvė 7; ⓕ Beigelistai; ⏲ 09.00–19.00 daily. Come to Beigelistai for freshly made bagels in a cosy corner of Literatų gatvė surrounded by wall art. The soup & bagel deal is a local favourite. A piano for tinkling the ivories & many books mean you will never be bored. €

**Lola** [83 C7] Naugarduko gatvė 2a; w lolavilnius.lt; ⏲ 08.00–17.00 Mon–Fri, 10.00–17.00 Sat–Sun. A top choice for b/fast & brunch; the shakshuka is highly recommended. €

**Pirmas Blynas** [85 D3] Savičiaus gatvė 15; w pirmasblynas.lt; ⏲ 10.00–19.00 Wed–Mon. Housed on the ground floor of St Virgin Maria's Church (page 104), this is Vilnius' first social restaurant employing people with disabilities. They specialise in delicious pancakes, have outdoor seating in summer & a kids' corner. Affordable & consistently good. €

## ENTERTAINMENT AND NIGHTLIFE

Vilnius' main nightlife area is centred around Vilniaus and Islandijos streets, but there are many fine venues dotted across the city. Live music, theatre, opera and ballet are well supported and performances often sell out. You are advised to buy tickets in advance either from the venue's website or w bilietai.lt.

**BARS** For rooftop bars, see page 88.

### Beer

**Alaus Biblioteka** [83 C6] Trakų gatvė 4; w alausbiblioteka.lt; ⏲ 17.00–midnight Tue–Sun. Indecisive souls may be overwhelmed by the awesome choice of beers here, but knowledgeable staff are on hand to help. The flight samples are recommended.

✱ **Local Pub** [85 A3] Trakų gatvė 13; w localpub.lt; ⏲ 16.00–midnight daily. A simple well-loved bar for craft beers & chat. Beer tasting sessions available.

**Šnekutis** [85 A4] Šv. Mikalojaus gatvė 15; w snekutis.com; ⏲ 11.00–23.00 daily. The story of how Šnekutis brewing legend Valentas, the 'home appliance repair man turned brewer', became an icon of the craft beer scene is a long read on their website. Enjoy it while sipping one of their beers. The bar celebrates that whacky tale via craft beers, hearty Lithuanian food & a visual cacophony of paraphernalia.

✱ **Špunka** [83 E6] Užupio gatvė 9-1; ⓕ saviciaus9spunka; ⏲ 15.00–22.00 daily. This small, bohemian bar in Užupis has an extensive selection of excellent beers & local characters. Seating in the square in summer.

**Cocktails** If cocktails are your thing, be sure to try one with local lore at its heart, such as Krupnikas (honey liqueur), Midus (Lithuanian mead) or Trejos Devynerios 999 (herbal liqueur). Watch out for Žalgiris, which can be mind-numbingly strong. Starka is a vodka matured in oak & pairs beautifully with apple juice, while Žagarės vyšnių likeris (cherry brandy) matches well with tonic, ice & grapefruit juice on a hot day.

✳ **Apoteka** [85 B5] Visų Šventųjų gatvė 5; w apotekabar.lt; ⊕ 18.00–midnight Wed–Thu & Sun, 18.00–02.00 Fri–Sat. A warm & friendly welcome awaits you here, & a creative cocktail menu.

**Nomads** [85 C3] Didžioji gatvė 5 (in the same building as Čili Pica); ⓕ nomadsbar; ⊕ 17.00–02.00 Sun–Thu, 17.00–03.00 Fri–Sat. Small & cosy, serving innovative seasonal cocktails. The bartenders will be happy to chat & help you select a suitable drink.

## Wine

✳ **In Vino** [85 C5] Aušros vartų gatvė 7; w invino.lt; ⊕ 16.00–02.00 Sun–Thu, 16.00–04.00 Fri–Sat. In vino we trust for tapas & wine (& whisky, too). It's a long-standing favourite of locals, with a popular courtyard in summer.

**La Boheme** [85 A1] Šv. Ignoto gatvė 4; w laboheme.lt; ⊕ 17.00–midnight Mon–Thu, 16.00–midnight Fri, 13.00–midnight Sat, 13.00–22.00 Sun. One of the first wine bars in town, located in a grand medieval hall, La Boheme attracts wine enthusiasts, those looking for a romantic dinner & moviegoers before or after their visit to the arthouse cinema above.

**Saduto Tuto** [85 A3] Trakų gatvė 15; w sadutotuto.lt; ⊕ 17.00–23.00 Tue–Thu, 17.00–02.00 Fri–Sat. Intimate bar serving Mediterranean snacks, natural wines & cocktails. Their 'nighttime bites' menu kicks in from 22.00 until closing. Be sure to book a table as it gets busy.

**Taurės** [85 B2] Senatorių pasažas; Dominikonu gatvė 11; w senatoriupasazas.lt; ⊕ 16.00–midnight Wed–Fri, noon–midnight Sat, noon–18.00 Sun. This organic, biodynamic &

## ROOFTOP BARS

Summer decadence in Vilnius is happily paying €12 for a cocktail with a dazzling view. A reservation is recommended at any of these rooftop bars and best done via w tablein.lt or with the venue directly.

**3 Mūzos Rooftop Bar** [83 D5] Gedimino prospektas 4; w 3muzos-rooftop-bar.tablein.com. Enter the National Drama Theatre foyer underneath the Three Muses statue, then take the lift to the 5th floor for one of the best rooftop terrace views of the cathedral & Gediminas Castle.

**Astorija Bar** [85 C4] Didžioji gatvė 35; w astorijabrasserie.lt. Getting a seat on the tiny terrace at the Radisson Astorija Hotel's (page 81) rooftop bar is potluck, but the view, especially at sunset, makes it worth trying.

**Neringa Rooftop Bar** [82 C4] Gedimino prospektas 23; w neringavilnius.com. A classy rooftop terrace on the top floor of Hotel Neringa (page 79).

**OPERA Social House** [82 C4] J Lelevelio gatvė 4; ⓕ OPERAsocialhouse. This is the boho option rooftop terrace, with super views & a youthful hipster vibe. Take the stairs or brave the vintage elevator. There's indoor seating in the old greenhouse.

**Pink&Yellow** [82 B4] Gedimino prospektas 44a; w pinkyellow. lt. Overlooking Lukiškės Square & downtown Vilnius, Pink&Yellow's spacious terrace is the perfect location for quaffing cocktails or dining with a view.

**Skybar** [82 C3] Konstitucijos prospektas 20; ⊕ 18.00–02.00 Fri–Sat, 18.00–midnight Sun–Thu. The top-floor bar of the Radisson Blu Lietuva (page 81), Skybar has the highest views all around. It's all enclosed & open year round.

natural wine bar is perfect for an aperitif before dinner, or a relaxing glass after. If you need immediate sustenance, you can order food from the neighbouring open grill, Muu.

**CINEMA** The out-of-town **Akropolis Shopping Centre** has several big cinema complexes located within it: both **Apollo Cinema** (w apollokinas.lt) & **Multikino** (w multikino.lt) are good for big international movies & are popular with families & teenagers after a day of shopping or on a cold or rainy day.

**Forum Cinema Vingis** [map, page 72] Savanorių prospektas 7; w forumcinemas.lt. Multi-screen cinema complex for the latest blockbusters. Check the website for language & subtitles information.

**Pasaka Kino** [83 F6] Kino Pasaka; Paupio 26; w pasaka.lt. There are 2 Pasaka boutique cinemas in the capital, but this is the best for both English-language screenings & comfort.

**Skalvija** [82 C4] Skalvijos kino centras; A Goštauto gatvė 2; w skalvija.lt. Originally called the Planeta cinema in 1963, Skalvija is the oldest cinema in Vilnius & shows a curated repertoire of foreign-language & arthouse films. Check the website for showings in English or with English subtitles.

### CLUBS
**Anna Mesha. Butas** [83 C6] Vilniaus gatvė 28; annameshabutas; 23.00–05.00 Fri–Sat. A stylish, somewhat elite nightclub where it's worth making a little more effort appearance-wise to get past security.

**Pabo Latino** [83 C6] Trakų gatvė 3; w pabolatino.lt; 21.00–05.00 Fri–Sat. Nightclubs come & go, but this one is a keeper. It attracts a mixed crowd of all ages & nationalities who do their best to dance the night away to Latino tunes.

**Salento DiscoPub** [82 C4] A Vienuolio gatvė 4; SalentoNightClubVilnius; 22.00–06.00 Wed–Thu, 22.00–08.00 Fri–Sat. The party lasts all night long at Salento, with hardcore revellers making their way home as commuters make their way to work. A longstanding venue for a good night of music & dancing.

**Soho** [83 B6] Švitrigailos gatvė 7; sohoclub.lt; 22.00–07.00 Fri–Sat. The longest-running gay club in Vilnius is not only a nightclub but a central hub & safe space for the LGBTQIA+ community.

### CONCERT AND LIVE MUSIC VENUES
**Compensa Concert Hall** [map, page 72] Kernavės gatvė 84; w compensakoncertusale.lt) Venue for visual productions, including ballets, musicals & classical concerts often by touring international performers.

**Jazz Cellar 11** [85 C5] Aušros vartų gatvė 11; w vilniusjazzclub.lt. A live jazz venue where musicians love to perform & jam, conveniently located in the Old Town. Check the website for what's on & to book tickets in advance.

**Lithuanian National Philharmonic** [85 C5] Lietuvos nacionalinė filharmonija; Aušros vartų gatvė 5; w filharmonija.lt. Established in 1940, the Lithuanian National Philharmonic is the oldest state-owned concert venue in the country, committed to promoting Lithuanian musicians, performers & composers while keeping their art accessible to a wide audience. Their diverse repertoire includes classical, contemporary & jazz music. Prices are still very reasonable compared with an equivalent performance in London.

**LVSO Concert Hall** [82 D4] (Formerly the Vilnius Congress Hall) Lietuvos valstybinis simfoninis orkestras; Vilniaus gatvė 6; w lvso.lt. LVSO is the home of the Lithuanian State Symphony Orchestra, who, since their debut in 1989, have come a long way from having no fixed abode for their first 10 years to occupying this newly renovated modern facility. Originally named the Youth Symphony Orchestra they were exactly that, young musicians in a young nation with a spirit of optimism. Their repertoire covers traditional classical & contemporary music, as well as collaborations with **Vilnius City Opera** ( VilniusCityOpera).

**Menu fabrikas Loftas** [83 B8] Švitrigailos gatvė 29; loftasvilnius. 'Art factory Loftas', 15mins' walk from the Old Town, is a former electrical engineering factory, now experiencing its best life as a pop-up arts & entertainment space. The open-air art gallery of murals & street art attracts curious visitors & brings a pop of colour & creativity to this industrial area. Loftas regularly hosts theatre, stand-up comedy, talk shows, live music & DJ nights.

**Tamsta Club** [85 D5] A Strazdelio gatvė 1; w tamstaclub.lt. A venue beloved by music lovers & musicians alike, Tamsta Club attracts both Lithuanian & international acts, especially young, up-&-coming performers. There's live music on Thu–Sat nights with a varied programme of different music styles & genres. Ticketed entry; tables can be reserved only after buying a ticket & are held for free until 19.00 on the day of the performance.

**Twinsbet Arena** [map, page 72] Ozo gatvė 14; w twinsbetarena.lt. Hosts large entertainment & sports events, including basketball games & concerts by international performers.

## THEATRE

**Lėlė Puppet Theatre** [85 B4] Lėlė; Arklių gatvė 5; w teatraslele.lt. The Vilnius Puppet Theatre was founded in 1958 & moved to this 18th-century former palace of the noble Oginski family in 1975. The palace had been adapted for concerts in 1930, & during World War II, when Vilnius was occupied by Nazi Germany, it became the Jewish Ghetto Theatre where imprisoned Jews bravely attempted to retain a sense of community & dignity. Today the puppet theatre stages its own productions & compositions popular with both adults & children.

**Lithuanian National Drama Theatre** [83 D5] Lietuvos nacionalinis dramos teatras; Gedimino prospektas 4; w teatras.lt. Hovering over the entrance of the Lithuanian National Drama Theatre, the gold faces of the *Three Muses* statue by Stanislovas Kuzma represent Drama, Tragedy & Comedy, all of which can be enjoyed here. The repertoire comprises classical, modern & Lithuanian plays mainly in Lithuanian but some performances are subtitled.

**Lithuanian National Opera and Ballet Theatre** [82 C4] Lietuvos nacionalinis operos ir baleto teatras; A Vienuolio gatvė 1; w opera.lt. This mammoth Modernist building is often dismissed as an eyesore, but only by those who do not understand it. You must look closer to appreciate the brave narrative of architect Elena Nijolė Bučiūtė in the 1960s. The welcoming warmth of the glass façade filled with chandeliers & tactile & visual geometric interior design are magnificent examples of Modernist architecture. Seasonal performances of classical & contemporary works are held here. Ticket prices for performances range from €16 to €85. Note that concerts often start at 18.00. Backstage tours can be booked in advance (€14 pp).

**The Old Theatre of Vilnius** [83 C6] Vilniaus senasis teatras; J Basanavičiaus gatvė 13; w vsteatras.lt. In response to geopolitical changes, this theatre, formerly known as the Russian Theatre, is now undergoing a transition to multilingual theatre. Some performances have English subtitles, & these are highlighted on the website.

**Small State Theatre** [83 C5] Vilniaus mažasis teatras; Gedimino prospektas 22; w vmt.lt An intimate theatre with a varied repertoire. Some performances have English subtitles – check this on the website or with the venue directly.

## SHOPPING

The shopping experience in Vilnius ranges from local markets and independent shops, to huge out-of-town shopping centres. Boutique shops can be found in the Old Town and in larger stores on Gedimino prospektas. For more choice, head to a large out-of-town shopping centre. **Akropolis Shopping Centre** (Ozo gatvė 25; w akropolis.lt; ⊕ shops: 10.00–21.00 daily; Maxima supermarket: 08.00–23.00 daily) is Vilnius' mega-mall with shops and services galore, a wide selection of restaurants, indoor ice skating, cinema complexes, soft play and bowling. It's very popular, especially in the colder months when you can be entertained all day in the warmth; it's pet-friendly too.

### MARKETS

**Halės turgus** (Halės Market) [83 D8] Pylimo gatvė 58; w halesturgaviete.lt. People have been bringing their produce and wares to sell at this covered market hall for over a century. It was constructed in 1906 by famous architect & engineer Vaclovas Michnevičius. The food halls have recently been modernised & what was once a very basic market now has an artisan feel, including fish & meat counters, fresh bread, local cheeses & honey. Outside are stalls of fresh fruit & vegetables, flowers, & individual sellers with tubs of foraged berries & mushrooms for sale. Other halls are filled with clothing stalls selling a nostalgic array of polyester pants & cheap trainers, & a selection of other goods including greetings cards, wigs, toys & homewares. If you hunt hard enough, you can still buy a Versace plastic carrier bag like in the early 1990s. In addition to the main market areas, young entrepreneurs have established trendy food outlets selling Uzbek plov, Armenian wine, Middle Eastern sweets & top-quality local produce.

**Souvenir market** [85 C2] Pilies gatvė/Didžioji gatvė; ⏰ daily, during daylight hours. Every day each of the market's fixed booths, decorated with black-&-white photographs of days gone by, open up into souvenir stalls laden with various amber, linen, wooden & woollen wares. Artists display their paintings for sale on wooden stands at the top of the square.

## BOOKSHOPS

**KNYGOS.lt** [83 C5] Vilniaus gatvė 9; w knygos. lt. The physical outlet for an online bookstore, KNYGOS.lt sells a varied section of books including foreign language titles.

**Knygynas Eureka!** [85 B1] Universiteto gatvė 10; w knygynas.biz. This small independent bookshop is run by bibliophiles & has a great selection of English & Lithuanian books. You'll find some nice souvenirs here too.

**Knygynas VAGA** [83 D5] Gedimino prospektas 2; w vaga.lt. Despite the building's nostalgic feel, in essence this is a large commercial bookshop with a wide selection of books, gifts & a café. Also has branches at Gediminas 13 & Pilies gatvė 22.

**Mint Vinetu** [85 B2] Šv. Ignoto gatvė 16; w mintvinetu.com. This small & cosy independent bookshop-café has a calm atmosphere & a small English book selection.

**Pegasas** [85 B6] Pylimo gatvė 53/2; w pegasas. lt. The largest bookshop chain in Lithuania, Pegasus offers a wide choice of titles, including English-language versions.

## HANDICRAFTS AND DESIGN

**Amatų namai** [85 C1] Pilies gatvė 22; w localhouse.lt. 'Local House' is the place to visit for handmade local crafts & souvenirs covering all skills from handmade jewellery to home-produced honey.

**Art Studio of Jonas Bugailiškis** [85 C6] Aušros vartų gatvė 17–10. Enter the 'Melodious World of Wood', which is a charming way to describe this cluttered & eccentric Lithuanian folk artist's workshop & gallery. Come here for authentic wood carvings, metalwork & other obscure items. Opening hours can be erratic.

**Dominikonu14** [85 B2] Dominikonų gatvė 14; w dominikonu14.com. Visit this Baltic design gallery for unique & high-quality art, fashion, jewellery, ceramics & souvenirs.

**EtnoDesign** [83 C6] J Basanavičiaus gatvė 3; w etnodesign.eu. A small company creating charming wooden gifts with stories to tell. Each item, be it a small magnet or larger wall decoration, is fine cut with a laser – the detailed designs feature flowers, birds, the sun & moon, & many other themes, all telling a story from Lithuanian folklore. The story is printed on the packaging & they make excellent gifts or souvenirs.

**Linen Story** [85 C3] Stiklių gatvė 4; w linentales. com. A boutique shop selling high-end linen ware in contemporary designs, including natural, coloured & patterned Lithuanian-made table linen, bedding, clothing & homewares.

**Paveikslai Gallery** [83 F6] Užupio gatvė 19; w paveikslai.lt. Paveikslai sells local artists' work in store & online, as well as offering shipping abroad, so there are no limits to the size of the souvenir wall art you might choose.

**Senamiesčio Krautuvė** [85 D2] Literatų gatvė 5; 📘 SenamiescioKrautuve. A specialist food shop selling foodie souvenirs & gifts, fresh local produce, alongside sweet & savoury treats.

## SPORTS AND ACTIVITIES

In addition to the activities listed below, you can take advantage of the **tennis courts in Bernardine Gardens** [83 E5], excellent tennis facilities in the heart of the Old Town. Book online (w sebarena.lt) or at the courts in person. Equipment is available to hire. For golfing opportunities in Vilnius and nearby, see page 131.

## SAUNA

**Ivãnas Muša Gongã** [82 D2] (Ivan Bangs the Gong) Kalvarijų gatvė 50D; **w** ivanasmusagonga.lt. This chain of modern boutique-style saunas in Vilnius & Trakai offers various sauna experiences in private or group sessions with or without a sauna master overseeing the practicalities. Everything you need is included from towels to sauna hats. The central sauna is handy for Vilnius, but also look out for their pop-up saunas at Lukiškės Prison (page 112) & on the Neris River; they also have a countryside lakeside sauna for up to 10 people in Trakai region. Prices range from €39 pp for a group session to €350 for a private party of up to 6 people. As for the name, legend has it that Ivan was a salt master in Vilnius who would announce a new delivery of salt – a very important commodity at that time – by banging his gong.

## TOURS AND TRIPS

**Pipiro Baidares Canoeing w** pipirobaidares.lt. Kayak & canoe trips around Vilnius, including night-time kayaking on the Neris River with the city illuminated all around. Kayaking on the smaller Vilnia River is also available, but note that this is not for beginners as it is shallow & tricky to navigate, sometimes even too shallow to kayak. They also offer kayak tours to Kaunas & Trakai. Discuss your plans & abilities with them directly.

**Smile Hot Air Ballooning w** hotairballoon.lt. Based in Vilnius & offering flights over Vilnius & Trakai. Vilnius flights are dependent on many factors so keep an open mind about possible cancellation, rescheduling or taking off from

### LITHUANIAN SAUNA

Lithuanians traditionally use steam saunas – hovering around 60°C, these are not too hot, and the air is humid with the steam being produced by pouring water on to hot stones above a wood burner. A whole sauna experience usually lasts 3–4 hours, involving you going in and out of the sauna three or four times. Time spent inside the sauna can include a massage using honey or salt, or being gently beaten with a sauna whisk (a bundle of young tender birch branches called a *vanta*). The use of natural medicinal herbs, plants, honey and even amber is common (there is an amber sauna in Palanga; page 282). Simple sauna hats made of felt can be worn to prevent the head from overheating. It is normal to wear swimwear or a towel in the sauna. Each sauna will have its own dress code rule – in general, you may encounter a participant at a single-sex sauna naked; you are unlikely to encounter someone in the nude at a mixed sauna session unless clearly stated. Saunas are always accompanied by a shower, and rural saunas are often located next to a lake, pond or river, so you can take a dip to cool down in between sessions. There is always a seating area where you enjoy drinks and snacks – after all, this is a relaxing social activity. The best drink to accompany a sauna session is tea made from fresh local mint or thyme, but beer and snacks are also popular.

A true sauna experience is run by a sauna master and can be a real highlight of a visit to Lithuania. When booking, do check the details regarding group size or if it's a private session, naked or not, mixed or single sex, and if English is spoken. Note that hotel saunas are standard saunas with no sauna master or extras unless specifically requested. In rural Lithuania, you will find traditional wood-fired saunas that are extra cosy and almost always next to a source of water for jumping or immersing in. A sauna is sacred time to slow down and switch off. Learn more via the Association of Professional Bathmasters (**w** pirtininkuasociacija.lt) or Lithuanian Steam Bath Fellows (**w** pirtiesbiciuliai.lt).

another location (page 213). You can join a group flight (from €140 pp), or book exclusively for a private group, or a romantic trip for 2 with a glass of sparkling wine to celebrate post-flight (from €699 per group/couple).

**Velotakas Bike Tours** A Stulginskio gatvė 5; w velotakas.lt. Choose from a guided or self-guided city tour or off-road regional park adventure by bike. Bicycle rental including electric or gravel road bikes is provided. Guided group tours cost from €29 pp, & private tours from €35–98 pp depending on group size. Tours start/finish at their office (address above). Prebooking recommended.

**Vilnius Gondola** w gondola.lt. View Vilnius from the Neris River on a small boat cruise, particularly pleasant at sunset. There are daily departures from spring through to autumn from King Mindaugas Bridge (Karaliaus Mindaugo tiltas): at 12.10, then hourly until 20.10. Each tour, with free audio guide, lasts 50–55mins. Tickets are €10 pp; children under 7 years go free. Exclusive private trips are also available for max 12 people (€85 for 1hr, €140 for 2hrs) & must be prebooked. Note that the open-sided gondola operates only in favourable weather conditions.

## OTHER PRACTICALITIES

Bank branches in the city centre have drastically reduced in recent years and you will need to book an appointment for an English-speaking cashier. In the Old Town, try **Swedbank** [85 A3] (Vokiečių gatvė 26) or go over the river to Konstitucijos prospektas for more branches. ATMs are available across town. Banks do not deal in cash, so for currency exchange you will need an exchange office, usually found inside large supermarkets or shopping centres. The most central is **TopExchange** [83 D5] (Gedimino prospektas 9; w topexchange.eu; ⏰ 10.00–20.00 Mon–Sat, 10.00–18.00 Sun).

There are two central **post offices**, one at Totorių gatvė 8 [83 D5] and Vokiečių gatvė 7 [85 B3]. Both are bare bones shops but offer the necessary services though are closed on Saturday afternoons and Sundays.

There are numerous pharmacies across the city but we recommend **University Pharmacy** [85 B2] (Universiteto Vaistinė; Universiteto gatvė 2) and **Vokiečių Vaistinė** [85 C3] (Didžioji gatvė 13). Both are open daily. The larger chains of Eurovaistinė and Gintarė Vaistinė are located on Gedimino prospektas.

## WHAT TO SEE AND DO

**CATHEDRAL SQUARE AND AROUND** Cathedral Square [83 D5] (Katedros aikštė) is the iconic centre of Vilnius, dominated by the cathedral and bell tower, overlooked by Gediminas Castle, softened by neighbouring parkland and encircled with historical facades. It is also the main location for national gatherings and ceremonies, fairs and festivals. Important historical events are subtly acknowledged across the square. Look for **Stebuklas**, the 'miracle' tile embedded in the paving slabs; and once you find it, remember to turn 360° on one heel and make a wish. Once you've completed that task, look for the **Baltic Way Footprint** designed by artist Gitenis Umbrasas and laid in 2013 to commemorate the start point of the Baltic Way (page 76). The tile features the footprints of a participant of the Baltic Way and there is a time capsule for future generations buried beneath it. The same commemorative tiles were gifted to Riga and Tallinn, the cities through which the non-stop chain of people stood, hand in hand, in solidarity in August 1989. Watching over Cathedral Square, sword drawn, is a statue of **Grand Duke Gediminas** (1275–1341) accompanied by his horse; beneath him, carved into the stone, is an iron wolf (Geležinis Vilkas), reminding us of the legend of Vilnius' beginnings (page 73).

**Vilnius Cathedral** [83 D5] (Vilniaus arkikatedra; Katedros aikštė 2; w katedra.lt; ⊕ 07.30–19.00 daily; free) Formerly called the Cathedral-Basilica of St Stanislaus and St Ladislaus, this is the most important Catholic building in Lithuania. Early history suggests the cathedral was built on the site of a pagan temple in 1251 when Grand Duke Mindaugas was embracing his newfound Christianity. Upon his death in 1263, it was returned to the pagans, and only given back to the Catholic church in 1387 when Lithuania converted to Christianity. The current building dates from 1419, but it has been modified over the centuries. The present Neoclassical design is thanks to Lithuania's first architect Laurynas Stuoka-Gucevičius, who also designed the town hall. The cathedral is simple inside, except for the must-see High Baroque Chapel of St Casimir (1458–84). St Casimir was Lithuania's patron saint and the chapel was built in 1636 to house his remains. On the apex of the cathedral roof stand three figures: saints Stanislaus, Helena and Casimir. These are all copies created in 1997. The original 18th-century statues were removed and destroyed in 1950 by the Soviets at the same time the cathedral was confiscated from the Catholic church. For 32 years during Soviet occupation the cathedral was an art gallery, returning to the Catholic church in 1988.

**Crypts** (Katedros požemiai; Katedros aikštė 2; w bpmuziejus.lt/crypts; ⊕ 10.00–17.30 Mon–Sat; €10/6) You must book in advance to visit the cathedral crypts, which are run by the Church Heritage Museum (page 98). A guided tour unveils the secrets of the cathedral history, archaeology and funeral traditions, including the Royal Mausoleum, where rulers are laid to rest. For adrenaline seekers and those of a nimble and non-claustrophobic disposition, there is an extreme adventure tour that involves crawling through formerly closed cavities and squeezing into secret sections with only torchlight to guide you (the narrowest passage is 40cm wide).

**Bell tower** (Katedros varpinė; Katedros aikštė 2; w bpmuziejus.lt/tickets-bell-tower; ⊕ 10.00–19.00 Mon–Sat; €6/4) Originally a tower on the city's 13th-century defensive wall (see the similarities between Gediminas Castle and the lower section of the bell tower), it was extended in the 16th century to become a 57m-tall belfry and remodelled to the current design in the 19th century. The bell tower has become an iconic symbol of Vilnius and is a popular meeting place. For panoramic views you can climb the steep wooden stairs to the viewing platform 45m up. The city's oldest clock keeps the city running on time from the spire of the bell tower, and the six new bells installed in 2002 call people to Mass.

**✳ Palace of the Grand Dukes** [83 E5] (Didžiosios Kunigaikštystės valdovų rūmai; Katedros aikštė 4; w valdovurumai.lt; ⊕ Jun–Aug 10.00–18.00 Tue–Thu, 10.00–20.00 Fri–Sun, Sep–May 10.00–18.00 Tue–Fri, 10.00–20.00 Sat, 10.00–16.00 Sun; €8.50/4.25) It's hard to believe that this palace is a reconstruction, opened on 6 July 2013, the anniversary of the Coronation Day of Lithuanian King Mindaugas. What was a controversial project has been hailed a success. Carefully constructed above the original foundations, this is the result of many years of archaeological research. A fortified wooden settlement existed on the site in the 4th to 8th centuries, developing into a brick-built castle in the 13th and 14th centuries, and transforming into a Renaissance-style palace in the 16th century. Baroque features were added in the 17th century and this period saw the luxurious interiors filled with personal art collections of Lithuanian and Polish rulers. During the mid-1600s during the war with Moscow, the palace was destroyed and eventually torn

### VILNIUS MUSEUMS

Most museums in Vilnius are recently renovated and have been brought into the 21st century with the offer of newfangled interactive exhibitions. Most have permanent exhibitions and temporary or visiting exhibitions throughout the year. Labelling in English alongside Lithuanian, though not guaranteed, is common. Audio guides are often free, either as a physical device available from the ticket office or by scanning QR codes on your phone; and some museums have VR headsets for a truly immersive experience. Free guided tours are often available at fixed times (check on the relevant museum website); almost all museums can provide a private tour in English if arranged in advance, highly recommended if you have a specific interest; and virtual tours are available on some attractions' websites for those who can't visit Vilnius in person.

The Vilnius Pass (page 78) is a great investment if you plan to visit a lot of the city's museums. Combination tickets are offered by some museums, especially those belonging to the National Museum of Lithuania. National museums are free on the last Sunday of the month. Plan around most museums being closed Mondays and/or Tuesdays.

---

down during the 19th century. The idea to rebuild the palace to house the National Art Gallery had been bubbling away throughout the 20th century, and the post-independence years created renewed momentum as the new independent nation lacked the state rooms required to host international forums and state occasions. The museum is an excellent introduction to the Grand Duchy of Lithuania period. The inner courtyard often hosts cultural events – it could be a skating rink in winter or an opera theatre in summer. Tickets are sold for separate routes through the museum: choose from an archaeological exhibition, state rooms or weaponry and an observation tower on the sixth floor.

**Gediminas Castle Tower and Ducal Palace** [83 E5] (Gedimino pilies bokštas; Arsenalo gatvė 5; ⏱ 10.00–20.00 daily; €8/4; officially part of the Lithuanian National Museum Complex, combined entrance tickets are available) The expectation of a good view lures people up to Gediminas Castle, and rightly so. It is free to climb the hill under your own steam between the hours of 07.00 and 23.00. The cobbled path (not suitable for bicycles, wheelchairs or prams) starts from the road alongside the Vilnia River on Trispalvė alėja. Alternatively, you can take the funicular (€2/3 single/return) from the inner courtyard of the Old Arsenal.

The distinctive red-brick structure of Gediminas Castle is a symbol of Vilnius. The only remaining 14th-century tower of the upper castle contains a permanent exhibition focused on the history of Vilnius. The Ducal Palace ruins on the other side of the cobbled summit are closed to the public. In 2017, during maintenance works on the hill slopes, human remains were discovered buried on the hillside, believed to be the bodies of 20 participants of the 1863–64 uprising against the Russian Empire who were publicly executed in Lukiškės Square and secretly disposed of. They were given a state funeral and reburied in Rasos Cemetery in 2019.

**Lithuanian National Museum Complex** [83 E5] (w lnm.lt) A selection of museums are housed in the 16th-century arsenal complex. This was once one of the largest armouries in the region, containing armaments and munitions for the whole of the Lithuanian Grand Duchy strongholds from the Baltic to the Black Sea. Museums are ticketed separately, although some combined ticket options are available; check the website when planning your visit.

**The New Arsenal** (Naujasis arsenalas; Arsenalo gatvė 1; closed at the time of writing for renovation; see the main website for opening & price information) In front of the museum is a **statue of King Mindaugas**. This tribute to the only king of Lithuania, by sculptor Regimantas Midvikis, was unveiled on 6 July 2003 to commemorate the 750th anniversary of his coronation. The New Arsenal is expected to reopen during the lifespan of this guide.

* ***Castellan's House*** (Pilininko namas; Arsenalo gatvė 1; ⊕ 10.00–18.00 Tue–Sun; €6/3) A new exhibition space of the National Museum of Lithuania is housed in one of the best-preserved 16th-century buildings on the complex. The Vilnius

### VILNIUS PARKS

* **BERNARDINE GARDENS** [83 E5] (Bernardinų sodas) Formerly called Sereikiškės Park, Bernardine Gardens is in the heart of Vilnius between Gediminas Castle hill, the Vilnia River and the Bernardine Monastery Complex. It is the oldest park in Vilnius, established in 1469 by Bernardine monks, and the oldest oak tree in Vilnius resides here at a ripe old age of over 400 years. The park has a lot to offer: a quiet area for a picnic, chessboards by the river, children's playground, summer café, tennis courts, a musical fountain, public toilets and a reconstructed monastery garden with edible plants and medicinal herbs.

**KALNŲ PARK** [83 F5] (Kalnų parkas) Encompassing the forested hills that lie behind Gediminas Castle hill, Kalnų Park is a lush natural area of almost 25ha immediately adjacent to the city centre and key to Vilnius' claim to being one of the greenest cities in Europe. From the city centre you can access Kalnų Park from T Kosciuškos gatvė immediately on your right after crossing the Vilnia, or head behind the tennis courts in Bernardine Gardens to cross the bridge and walk with the river to your right until you reach some steps. Kalnų Park is formed of several hills. The most prominent is the Hill of Three Crosses, also known as Crooked Hill (it is believed the Crooked Castle once stood here, destroyed during the power struggle between warring descendants of Grand Duke Gediminas in 1390). The Three Crosses are a memorial to crusader monks who brought Christianity to Lithuania but were killed by pagans. Notice the old concrete remains of the former crosses on your way up – these were blown up by the Soviets in 1950 as they did not want them dominating the city's skyline. The current crosses were erected in 1989. Other cultural objects in the park include the outdoor Mountain Park Stage (Kalnų parko estrada) where events are held including the Lithuanian Song and Dance Festival 'Evening Ensemble', and Grand Duke Gediminas' genealogical family tree sculpture. Information boards explain the history of the hills, including the Hill of Gediminas' Grave, where there is a pagan altar used for gatherings and traditional celebrations. Hiking trails make this a perfect place to stretch your legs, and the viewpoints are particularly popular at sunrise and sunset.

castellan lived here. Appointed by the ruler of the Grand Duchy of Lithuania, he would oversee the construction and maintenance of estate buildings, collect rents and manage disputes between residents. It was an appointment for life. Records exist of 39 known castellans; the last one was killed by soldiers of the Russian Empire. There is an excellent exhibition here explaining Lithuanian history via carefully curated artefacts and interactive displays. The dark room celebrating Lithuanian global connections is a novel exhibit. There are QR codes for audio guides throughout.

**The Old Arsenal** (Senasis arsenalas; Arsenalo gatvė 3; ⊕ 10.00–18.00 Tue–Sun; €5/2.50, free audio guide) Dedicated to the archaeological story of Lithuania, the exposition follows the 12,000-year journey from the melting of the ice fields to the Iron Age when Baltic tribes formed and became the foundation of the Lithuanian state. Highlights of the extensive exhibition of artefacts and archaeological finds include the remains of a pagan priest, who was buried almost 8,000 years ago, and the Stakliškės treasure chest containing a haul of over 3kg of silver. There is a good book and gift shop here, and next door is the **Museum of Applied Arts and Design** (page 114).

**House of Histories** (Istorijų namai; T Kosciuškos gatvė 3; w lnm.lt/en/museums/house-of-histories; ⊕ 10.00–18.00 Tue–Sun; €8/4) The newest branch of the National Museum of Lithuania is gaining an excellent reputation for diverse and high-quality temporary exhibitions. Previous projects have covered conspiracy theories, Kyivan Rus and Lithuanian migration stories. Formerly used as barracks for the Imperial Russian army, the building oozes history and suits its new life as a museum space since 2021.

**Church of St Peter and St Paul** [82 G3] (Šv. apaštalų Petro ir Povilo bažnyčia; Antakalnio gatvė 1; w vilniauspetropovilo.lt; ⊕ 06.00–18.30 daily; free) The church of St Peter and St Paul is the most famous Baroque church in Vilnius and renowned as one of the most beautiful Catholic churches in the world. Considered an architectural masterpiece, the current church was built in 1676 and funded by the wealthy noble Pac family. The interior is a stunning arrangement of more than 2,000 stucco mouldings, frescoes and a Rococo pulpit from the early 19th century. The unknown architect was disappointed with the simple style of local craftsmen, so invited Italian masters Giovanni Pietro Perti and Giovanni Maria Galli to come to Vilnius and create an extraordinary interior. It has survived impeccably well over the years having been carefully renovated numerous times, although the main altar was removed in 1766 and a large painting of *The Parting of SS Peter and Paul* by Pranciškus Smuglevičius hangs in its place. The church is a 15-minute walk along Antakalnio gatvė from the House of Histories.

**AROUND PILIES GATVĖ** Pilies gatvė (Castle Street) is the oldest street in the Old Town of Vilnius and once it was the only cobbled street in the whole city. It was always an important route, whether connecting the castle to the Town Hall square and Gates of Dawn via Didžioji and Aušros vartų streets, or leading south towards neighbouring (ally or enemy) Poland. Kings, queens, dukes and nobility travelled this road to attend to castle business while wealthy merchants and religious orders built residences along the route. The architecture is a mix of Gothic, Renaissance, Baroque and the odd Modernist hiccup along the way. This main thoroughfare is still the focus of church processions, festivals and parades.

**Adomas Mickevičius Museum** [85 D1] (Adomo Mickevičiaus muziejus; Bernardinų gatvė 11; w muziejus.vu.lt) Referred to as both Adomas Mickevičius in Lithuanian and Adam Mickiewicz in Polish, herein lies the first challenge when learning about the poet. Born in Russian-partitioned lands of the former Grand Duchy of Lithuania – which had been part of the Polish-Lithuanian Commonwealth and is now in present day Belarus – Mickevičius (1798–1855) is claimed as a national poet by Lithuania, Poland and Belarus. Practically, he spoke Polish, his father was from Polish nobility, he was an activist for Polish independence and is buried in Krakow, Poland. He considered himself both Polish and Lithuanian and referred to Lithuania as his homeland. You can attempt to untangle his complex life through the paintings, books, photographs and other objects housed in this building where he was a tenant and wrote his poem 'Grażyna' in 1822. At the time of writing, the museum was closed for renovation and is expected to reopen at the end of 2025.

**Church of St Anne and Bernardine Monastery Complex** [83 E6] (Maironio gatvė) Located in the square adjacent to the complex, stands a **monument to Adomas Mickevičius** (Paminklas Adomui Mickevičiui), a 4.5m tall granite statue of the poet, completed in 1984 by sculptor Gediminas Jokūbonis. On 23 August 1987 a crowd of people gathered here silently to condemn the Molotov–Ribbentrop Pact, an important step towards Lithuania's independence movement.

***St Anne's Church*** (Šv. Onos bažnyčia; Maironio gatvė 8; w vilniausonosbaznycia. net; ⊕ 11.00–18.00 Tue–Sun; free) Built between 1495 and 1500 and attributed to the Bohemian architect Benedikt Rejt (1453–1534), St Anne's is a Gothic masterpiece and Vilnius icon. The interior is surprisingly simple compared with the Flamboyant Gothic exterior. Legend states that Napoleon wanted to take the church back to Paris in the palm of his hand, but the sad reality was that his troops caused damage to the interior when using it as a warehouse. The main altar centrepiece is a painting of the patron of the church, Saint Anne, her daughter the Blessed Virgin Mary and the child Jesus. The neighbouring bell tower may look like a natural extension of the church but it was in fact added in 1873.

***Church of St Francis of Assisi and Bernardine Monastery*** (Šv. Pranciškaus Asyžiečio (Bernardinų) parapija; Maironio gatvė 10; w bernardinuparapija.lt; ⊕ 09.00–18.00 Mon, 07.30–18.00 Tue, 07.30–19.00 Wed–Fri, 08.30–18.00 Sat–Sun; free) Bernardine monks arrived in Lithuania during the 15th century and were granted permission to build a wooden church on the current site by Grand Duke Kazimierz. When the original church was destroyed by fire, a much larger brick church was built with imposing Gothic vaulted ceilings, sturdy enough to stand tests of time, fire and war. It was Soviet occupation that caused the worst damage, the church falling into a dilapidated state with restoration still ongoing. Tours in English can be booked via the website for a small donation to the church.

**Church Heritage Museum** [85 D1] (Bažnytinio paveldo muziejus; Šv. Mykolo gatve 9; w bpmuziejus.lt; ⊕ 11.00–18.00 Tue, 11.00–20.00 Wed, 11.00–18.00 Thu–Sat; €8/5) Housed in the Church of Saint Michael the Archangel and former Bernardine convent is the precious treasury of Vilnius Cathedral. It is an opulent collection enriched over the years by generous gifts from royalty, nobility and bishops, but also depleted in size due to theft and confiscation. During the 17th-century war with Moscow, a portion of the treasury was successfully hidden in the cathedral crypts. When war and invasion loomed again in 1939, the treasury was hidden again in the depths of the cathedral – hidden so well that it remained missing until its accidental rediscovery in 1985. The treasure was not reported to the Moscow authorities but kept secret for another five years until after independence. The collection of chasubles, chalices and crowns is impressive, alongside the great monstrance of the Bernardine Church, which was hidden from the Russian army in the convent's garden in 1655. Upstairs on the gallery, a simple-looking set of shallow smooth-glide drawers contain exquisite liturgical vestments that are beautifully preserved. Each drawer deserves a peek inside. A free audio guide is available to accompany you around the museum. Every Saturday at 14.00 there is an open guided tour; you must buy an entry ticket and register for the tour.

**Amber Museum and Gallery** [85 D1] (Gintaro muziejus-galerija; Šv. Mykolo gatvė 8; w ambergallery.lt; ⏱ 10.00–19.00 Wed–Sun; free) Tucked away on the narrow side street of Šv. Mykolo, downstairs is a museum dedicated to the origin, cultural and economic importance and art of Baltic amber. There are some good examples of inclusions – objects preserved in amber, including a mosquito that had fed on blood prior to being consumed by the resin. On the ground floor is the gallery and shop, where you can buy contemporary jewellery and other artefacts that all come with a certificate of authenticity.

**Vilnius University** [85 C1] (Vilniaus Universiteto; Universiteto gatvė 5; w muziejus.vu.lt; ⏱ 09.00–18.00 Mon–Sat; guided tours available) Vilnius university is one of the largest complexes in the Old Town and a major reason why the Old Town retains an authentic atmosphere of a real-life, functional community with historical streets and courtyards untouched by commerce or tourism. Founded in 1579 as a university to advance the existing Jesuit college, it is the oldest university in the Baltic states and existed like an independent city complete with its own law court, brewery, grain mill and book binders. The main teachings were theology and philosophy with staff and students predominantly Jesuits until 1773, when the non-religious Polish-Lithuanian Commonwealth central education authority took over the university. Focus was then steered to science-based learning; medicine, anatomy and veterinary science developed and specialists from across Europe visited to lecture and the teaching staff became more diverse and accomplished.

In response to the attempted uprising in 1832, the Imperial Russian authorities closed the university between 1832 and 1919. University lecturers, students, professors, intellectuals and secret societies were all considered anti-Tsar and needed to be repressed. During this period, the library and observatory remained open, the rest of the university complex being repurposed as a hospital, school and war academy. When it reopened in 1919, Vilnius was occupied by Poland. Most Lithuanian students had fled to Kaunas, so the university was composed predominantly of Polish and Jewish students and staff. Turbulent years followed with the arrival of Soviet Russian troops, the reunification of Vilnius to Lithuania and the arrival of occupying Nazi German troops. Under Nazi German occupation, teaching staff were arrested, deported or killed, and Jewish and ethnic minority students experienced similar fates. There were several acts of bravery within the university. Ona Šimaitė was a librarian who collected books from former students in the Jewish ghetto. She helped deliver food, hid documents for those interred and helped some to escape. Her story is immortalised in the book *Epistolophilia* by Julija Šukys.

It is possible to explore some of the university complex freely without a tour within the given opening hours. The highlights of the university architectural ensemble include the **Great Courtyard** offering a 360° panorama of architectural gems including open arcades and 18th-century frescoes, stunning in the blazing midday sun or illuminated on a dark winter's evening.

The eastern side of the courtyard comprises the façade of **St John's Church** [85 C1] (Šv. Jono bažnyčia; Šv. Jono gatvė 12; w jonai.lt; ⊕ 09.00–19.00 Mon–Sat, 09.00–15.00 Sun). Funded by Grand Duke Jogaila in 1386 as a symbolic statement of Lithuania's acceptance of Christianity, it took 40 years to complete due to its scale and the disruption of war. The main altar is spectacular, a three-dimensional world of ten altars, columns and sculptures that draw you in. In the original designs there were 23 altars! The flair of Baroque was added in the mid 18th century by architect Jan Krzysztof Glaubitz. Soviet occupation was a destructive period for the church with valuables removed, metals repurposed, a vegetable store in the cellars and a ramp built for truck access. After independence, the long process of restoring it began. Access is free but a university guided tour reveals the hidden stories of the church. One of the finest viewpoints over Vilnius is from the adjacent **St John's Bell Tower** (Šv. Jonų bažnyčios varpinė; Šv. Jonų gatvė 12; ⊕ May–Sep 10.00–19.00 daily; €5/3). The original stairs from 1748 are chunky, steep and uneven. There is a lift, but you must climb several steps to reach it and it only goes to the fourth floor, from which there is a view but through wire mesh. To access the top viewing platform there is a rather cumbersome mishmash of wooden stairs with low head height to climb. The view is well worth it, a 360° panorama of red rooftops, forests, iconic landmarks and new developments in the distance.

Guided tours of **Vilnius University Library** (w biblioteka.vu.lt) must be arranged in advance. However, you can visit the library's main attraction, Pranciškus Smuglevičius Hall (⊕ 09.00–17.00 Mon–Thu, 09.00–15.45 Fri), for free and without appointment. The **Astronomical Observatory Courtyard** can be accessed for free without a tour. Its façade inscribed with the university motto, *itur ad astra* (from here we rise to the stars), and peaceful courtyard are its main appeal as the observatory itself no longer functions.

Official **guided tours of the university** last 1½ hours and are available from Monday to Saturday between 10.00 and 17.00 (€8/2). Tours can be booked in advance by emailing e ekskursija@muziejus.vu.lt, or in person at the ticket office (Universiteto gatvė 3). An official tour unlocks the secrets and stories of the university, including the **Nine Muses Hall** by Rimtautas Gibavičius and the *Seasons Fresco* by Petras Repšys depicting Lithuanian mythology.

**Žibintininkas Lamplighter statue** (Šv. Jono gatvė) A mysterious character perched atop a high pedestal; this is Žibintininkas the lamplighter created by sculptor Vytautas Nalivaika. He is raising his lantern to illuminate the night in honour of the lost profession of lamplighters who reliably lit the gas lamps along the streets of the Old Town up until the end of the 19th century.

> **TALKING STATUES**
>
> This project run by MO Museum (page 114) brings more than 20 statues around the city to life. Active statues have a blue sign containing a QR code and web address. Simply scan the code or enter the website into your browser, select your language and you'll receive an incoming call. Answer your phone to hear the statue's story. You'll need Wi-Fi or mobile data for it to work.

**House of Signatories** [85 C2] (Signatarų namai; Pilies gatvė 26; w lnm.lt/en/museums/the-house-of-signatories; ⊕ 10.00–18.00 Tue–Fri, noon–17.00 Sat–Sun; €6/3) On 18 February 1918, in this house 20 members of the Council of Lithuania signed a document declaring Lithuania to be an independent democratic nation. During the years of political upheaval that followed, the original Act of Independence documents were lost and presumed missing. In 2017, a Lithuanian businessman offered a €1 million reward for finding the missing document and donating it to the State of Lithuania before 16 February 2018. In March 2017, Lithuanian historian Liudas Mažylis found one of the missing originals in the German state archives and it returned to the House of Signatories in time for the centenary exhibition. The museum tells the stories and fates of the signatories, several of whom later became president of Lithuania. Those who didn't emigrate became political prisoners and were deported to Siberia; some survived, some didn't. Temporary exhibitions focus on diplomacy, freedom and statehood. The entrance of the museum is via the lift at the rear of the courtyard; take it to floor 2 where the ticket office is located. Free daily tours in English are given at noon every day during summer, meet at the ticket office.

**Literatų Street** [85 D2] (Literatų gatvė) More than 200 works of art by Lithuanian and foreign artists adorn the walls of this picturesque, and photogenic, cobbled street. Each work pays homage to an author or literary masterpiece.

**Marija and Jurgis Šlapelis Museum** [85 C2] (Marijos ir Jurgio Šlapelių namas-muziejus; Pilies gatvė 40; w slapeliumuziejus.lt; ⊕ 11.00–17.00 Wed–Sat, 11.00–16.00 Sun; free) Jurgis Šlapelis (1876–1941) and his wife Marija (1880–1977) resided here and the museum is dedicated to their prominent role in the Lithuanian national revival movement. After the lifting of the Lithuanian language and press ban in 1904, the couple focused on the preservation of the Lithuanian language and opened one of the first Lithuanian-language bookshops in Vilnius in 1906. They founded the first 'lending bookstore', offering more people access to reading materials, and eventually began publishing their own titles. Their work continued throughout the world wars and Polish occupation, until in 1949 the Soviet occupiers evicted them and forced the bookshop to be liquidated. The museum was opened in 1994; exhibits explain the couple's story and their life in Vilnius, alongside the history and challenges posed to the Lithuanian printing press during this time.

**Orthodox Cathedral of the Theotokos** [85 D2] (Dievo Motinos Ėmimo į Dangų katedra; Maironio gatvė 14; ⊕ 07.30–20.00 daily; free) One of the most ancient churches in Vilnius, the Orthodox Cathedral of the Theotokos was built before the Christianisation of Lithuania during the reign of Grand Duke Algirdas for his Orthodox second wife, Uliana of Tver, in 1346. Like most churches in Vilnius its present appearance bears no resemblance to its original form, owing to damage endured over the centuries. The cathedral was transferred to the Russian Orthodox Church in 1865 during the campaign of Russification and remains Orthodox today, attended by ethnic Russian and Belarusian residents of Vilnius.

**AROUND DIDŽIOJI GATVĖ** At the top of Pilies gatvė the road widens into a cobbled square. This is where Didžioji gatvė begins and continues up to the Town Hall. The square is home to the **souvenir market** [85 C2] (page 91). Rather hidden among the stalls on a central island planted with two linden trees is **Ragutis akmuo**, a ceremonial stone with pagan origins containing a perpetual flame in the form of a lit candle.

> ## UŽUPIS AND PAUPYS
>
> Nestled into a bend of the Vilnia River lies the Independent Republic of Užupis, declared by free-spirited Užupis residents on 1 April 1997. If you choose to cross the border into this pseudo-territory, enter via Užupio tiltas from Maironio gatvė to pass the official republic sign. Pop-in the corner shop **Užupio 1 postas - Border Control** (🇫 uzupisbordercontrol) immediately on your right after the bridge for some Užupis souvenirs and a passport stamp (getting your actual passport stamped could result in all sorts of trouble, so best buy a postcard instead for this purpose). Across the road is **Užupio Café** [83 E6] (Užupio kavinė; w uzupiokavine.lt) a regular haunt of artists and creative spirits since 1994 and headquarters of the breakaway republic. Užupis has long been an artistic hub in Vilnius, neglected and run down during the 1990s with a bohemian vibe. Today it is a medley of renovated façades and gentrified luxury properties with real life tucked away in the courtyards and side streets. Underneath the bridge you will see the **Mermaid of Užupis**, the siren who lures you into the republic. Look around and you will spot many more art installations down by the river; this is the **Užupis Art Incubator** [83 E6] area, established in 1996 by a group of artists to create an art community. You can explore the courtyards to discover quirky art installations, sculptures and amusing weird stuff. From the bridge, the main street of Užupio gatvė leads you to a square watched over by the **Angel of Užupis** [83 E6] sculpture by local artist Romas Vilčiauskas. The angel 'hatched' in 2002 from a temporary egg sculpture that distracted from the angel's delayed arrival (the egg is now the **Margutis Easter Egg** sculpture at Pylimo gatvė 43 [85 A5] –

**St Parasceve Orthodox Church** [85 C2] (Šv. kankinės Paraskevės cerkvė; Didžioji gatvė; ⊕ noon–18.00 Mon–Sat, 08.30–18.00 Sun) Set amid the trees behind the souvenir market on Didžioji gatvė, the oldest Eastern Orthodox church in Lithuania catches your eye with its distinctive Neo-Byzantine style. Built in 1345 upon the site of a pagan temple honouring the god Ragutis, the church passed between Orthodox and Eastern Catholic religions and suffered numerous fires over the centuries. In 1705, the Russian tsar Peter the Great prayed here for victory of the Muscovite army during the Great Northern War. Severely damaged during World War II, the Stalinist government opened a Museum of Atheism in the renovated church building and then a museum of Lithuanian folk art. Only in 1990 was it reconsecrated and returned to the Orthodox Church.

**Chodkevičius Palace** [85 C3] (Chodkevičių rūmai; Didžioji gatvė 4) At least eight generations of the influential noble Chodkevičius (Chodkiewicz in Polish) family lived here during the 16th and 17th centuries, until it was sold in 1811. Through the archway of the late-Classicism façade is a large open courtyard, and the surrounding buildings house the Lithuanian National Art Museum administration and the **Vilnius Picture Gallery** (page 115).

**St Nicholas' Orthodox Church** [85 C3] (Šv. Nikolajaus Stebukladario palaikų Pernešimo cerkvė; Didžioji gatvė 12; ⊕ 09.00–17.00 daily) With Neo-Byzantine additions dating from 1865, similar in style to St Parasceve church, and a Catholic tower paired with an Orthodox dome, this is one of the most unusual churches in Vilnius. The original church sited here dates to the 14th century but was constructed of wood and therefore vulnerable to fire (brick churches were whether another angel will hatch one day remains to be seen). Every 1 April, the local Independence Day is celebrated around the angel. The square and streets of Užupis are home to numerous cafés, bars and restaurants, galleries and boutique shops. Continue up Užupio gatvė to visit the quiet contemplative **St Bartholemew the Apostle Church** [83 F6] (Vilniaus Šv. apaštalo Baltramiejaus bažnyčia; Užupio gatvė 17A), check out the latest art installation in the alley at **Jono Meko skersvėjis** [83 F6] (Užupio gatvė 24) and hunt down the *Užupis Cat* sculpture in Užupio skveras.

Every independent republic is governed by rules, and you can read the **Užupis Constitution** [83 E6] (Užupio Respublikos konstitucija) on the wall plaques of Paupio gatvė 3A in more than 40 languages.

From Užupis, continue along Paupio gatvė, crossing the bridge over the Vilnia River and then turn left to discover the newly developed residential area of **Paupys**. Just as the historical façades are easy on the eye, so is this new architectural adventure for Vilnius' new generations. It feels like you've been dropped into architects' plans. For an easy circular walk, follow the foot- and cycle path along the river, and at the pedestrian bridge turn right into Paupys until you get to the main Aukštaitčių gatvė. Turn right and look out for the zig-zag path on the left which leads up to funky food court **Paupio Turgus** [83 F6] (w paupioturgus.lt) for refreshments. This district was a town planner's dream focused on optimising the quality of life for residents. Walk back to the Old Town along Aukštaitčių gatvė and look out on your left for an unexpected gorilla.

forbidden at that time). It was only in 1514 that a brick church was granted under special permissions and until 1865 it was surrounded by other buildings hiding it from view.

**Pacai Palace** [85 C3] (Didžioji gatvė 7) Bought by Mykolas Kazimieras Pacas (1624–82), a military commander of the Grand Duchy of Lithuania, the Pacai Palace became one of the finest residential properties in Vilnius. Famous Italian masters were commissioned to create flamboyant interiors suitable for visiting dignitaries – these included the King of Poland and Grand Duke of Lithuania John Sobieski, tsars of Russia and the French Emperor Napoleon. The last descendant of the Pacas family, Liudvikas Mykolas Pacas inherited the palace in 1797 but his involvement in the 1831 uprising meant he had to flee to France. The palace was nationalised and underwent mundane reconfigurations until 2010, when it was restored and relaunched as the luxury Hotel Pacai (page 79).

**M K Čiurlionis House Museum** [85 C3] (Mikalojaus Konstantino Čiurlionio namai; Savičiaus gatvė 11; w mkcnamai.lt; ⊕ 11.00–17.00 Tue-Fri, 13.00–17.00 Sat; free) Lithuania's national treasure Mikalojus Konstantinas Čiurlionis (1875–1911) lived and worked here between 1907 and 1908. Since 1995 this address has housed a museum and cultural centre dedicated to the composer and painter. For those interested in Čiurlionis and not visiting the main museums in Kaunas or Druskininkai, this will suffice. Seek out the VR experience Angelų takais (Trail of Angels; €20/13), which immerses you into his paintings accompanied by a soundtrack of his compositions. This is a very popular attraction and you are advised to prebook. Look out for their small concert programme too.

**St Virgin Maria's Church** [85 D3] (Švč. Mergelės Marijos Ramintojos bažnyčia; Savičiaus gatvė 15; w ramintoja.lt; ⊕ 18.00–19.00 Mon & Wed, noon–13.00 Sun) This graceful but weathered church was built by Augustine monks in the 17th century, a modest late-Baroque church with the tallest tower in Vilnius. The surrounding monastery buildings now house the European Humanities University. The church symbolises what most churches endured: as occupying powers focused on removing religion and its influence over the population, they desecrated churches by looting treasures and degrading them into warehouses. The restoration process is expensive, time consuming and often controversial; hence, many churches still await their renewal. This church had the usual unwanted visitors: Napoleon stored ammunition here, Imperial Russia stripped the interior to reconfigure it into an Orthodox church, then the Soviets turned it into a warehouse, dividing it up with an irreversible concrete structure. This unique church needs to be innovative. On the ground floor is **Pirmas Blynas** café (page 87), there are community and exhibition spaces, and on the top floor is the simple chapel now within touching distance of the original church ceiling.

**Town Hall Square** [85 C4] (Rotušės aikštė, Didžioji gatvė) Dominated by the columned façade of the **town hall** [85 C4], this area was once the Great Market area and a municipal centre. Today, celebrations and festivals are held in the pedestrianised area, and the summer terraces of surrounding bars and restaurants create a busy vibrant space. Stand in front of the **Vilnius Portal** (recently relocated here from Vilnius railway station), where you can wave in real time at people in Lublin, Dublin and Philadelphia. Notice the plaques on the right side of the town hall façade. One references Vilnius Old Town being inscribed on the UNESCO World Heritage List in 1994, while another quotes G W Bush from his visit to Vilnius on 23 November 2002: 'Anyone who would choose Lithuania as an enemy has also made an enemy of the United States of America.'

**The Glass Quarter** [85 B3] (Stiklo kvartalas) The quaint, narrow Stiklių gatvė leads into this cosy area of winding cobbled streets lined with restaurants and boutique shops. Well known for its colourful art installations and embellished store fronts, it is the home of numerous local design shops and jewellers. The area has always been associated with artisans; in 1495 the Goldsmith's Guild was founded here and in 1547 it was the location of the first glass manufacturer. In the heart of the quarter is the **Stikliai Hotel** (page 79) and **Ponių Laimė** bakery (w poniulaime.eu) the trailblazer of over-the-top creative window (then whole shopfront) dressing. Incorporating surrounding streets including Gaonų and Zydų, the area became the bustling Jewish quarter in 1633, home to Elijah ben Solomon Zalman known as the Vilna Gaon, the Great Synagogue and Matas Strašiūnas Judaistic Library. During World War II, the Jewish quarter was turned into the Little Ghetto in which approximately 11,000 Jews were incarcerated and ultimately murdered (page 28). The Jewish history of the area is acknowledged through street signs in Hebrew and Yiddish, memorial plates and memorial artwork.

**Church of St Casimir** [85 C4] (Šv. Kazimiero bažnyčia; Didžioji gatvė 34) This church is a Baroque beauty, its intricate façade commanding the immediate area and the royal crown atop its central tower dominating the Old Town skyline. Saint Casimir was the son of Lithuanian Grand Duke and King of Poland Casimir. He was born in Krakow in 1458 and lived a life committed to piety and spirituality.

When he died of tuberculosis at the age of 25 in 1484 he was buried in Vilnius Cathedral. He was canonised in 1522, his feast day of 4 March was declared by the pope in 1602 (celebrated at Kaziukas Fair; page 80) and he became patron saint of Lithuania. The cornerstone of the Church of St Casimir was laid in 1604 by Jesuit monks and construction completed in 1618. The St Casimir Chapel in Vilnius Cathedral was completed in 1636 and his remains interred there.

Suffering the same fate as other churches during the Soviet occupation, the interior of St Casimir's was looted and damaged with the altar, paintings, organ and bells all lost as the building was used as a wine warehouse. It was returned to the Church in 1988, since when it has been carefully restored and services have resumed, with Sunday Mass followed by half an hour of religious music and contemplation often featuring famous Lithuanian organists and soloists.

**AROUND AUŠROS VARTŲ GATVĖ** The top of Didžioji gatvė splits at Dr Jonas Basanavičius square into Subačiaus gatvė to the left and Aušros vartų straight ahead. Overlooking the square is the grand façade of the Lithuanian National Philharmonic (page 89). Immediately to your left is Šv. Kazimierio gatvė, a narrow Old Town back street that leads to Bokšto gatvė and the bastion.

### Bastion of Vilnius Defensive Wall
[85 D5] (Vilniaus gynybinės sienos bastėja; Bokšto gatvė 20; w lnm.lt; ⊕ 10.00–18.00 Tue–Sun; €6/3) As Vilnius grew, residents outside the original fortified castle areas were vulnerable and in 1503 Grand Duke Alexander commissioned the building of a stone defensive wall around the new city boundary. The bastion is the wall's only strategic defensive structure, and after suffering extensive damage in 17th-century war it fell into disrepair, even becoming the city rubbish dump. In 1987, after renovation, it was opened as an underground museum telling the story of Lithuania's defence, with displays of weaponry and artillery accompanied with historical legends and facts. There's a great view from the terrace over the Old Town.

### Holy Trinity Uniate Church
[85 C5] (Švč. Trejybės Graikų apeigų katalikų bažnyčia; Aušros vartų gatvė 7B; w uniateheritage.if.vu.lt) Pass through the ornate Basilian Gate, slightly set back and sandwiched between former merchant houses which now house wine bars, cafés and shops. The elaborate gate was built in 1761 and designed by Vilnius' Baroque master Johann Glaubitz. Although its fancy façade is the first thing to notice, you may witness unexpected daily life up there as it is now an apartment. Residents sit out on the balcony and a cat is often spotted precariously pottering about. Continue through the second gate and up the hill into the courtyard. The Holy Trinity Uniate Church, also known as the Ukrainian Church, is central to the yard and surrounded by the Basilian monastery complex. In the 1800s the Basilian monks were expelled and the monastic cells converted into a prison, where those involved in the anti-governmental independence movement, including the romantic poet Adomas Mickevičius (page 98), were incarcerated. While the church suffered badly after being desecrated and used as a vodka warehouse by the Soviets, recent renovations have transformed it and provided a new lease of life and optimism.

### Russian Orthodox Church of the Holy Spirit
[85 D5] (Šv. Dvasios vienuolyno katedra; Aušros vartų gatvė 10) The distinctive, vivid pink gate topped with an Orthodox cross welcomes you into the lush church garden. Note that the Russian Orthodox Cross always has three bars. The long middle bar was where Jesus's hands

were nailed and to the lower bar his feet. The lower bar is always set at an angle, symbolising that there are two ways to go in the afterlife: one end points up to heaven while the other points down to hell. This is the most important Russian Orthodox church in the country as it is home to the Russian Orthodox Diocese of Lithuania. It was rebuilt in 1749 after a fire and the exterior is not typical for an Orthodox church, having been designed by Baroque master Glaubitz. Internally there is a grand Rococo altar serving as a most unusual iconostasis. In front of the altar is a reliquary housing the preserved bodies of saints Anthony, Ivan and Eustachius, their feet visible at the base of their shrouds. They were servants of Grand Duke Algirdas, the last pagan ruler of Lithuania, and were tortured and killed in 1347 for their Christianity.

**Church of St Theresa** [85 C6] (Šv. Teresės bažnyčia; Aušros vartų gatvė 14) Vilnius's most Italianate building was designed by Italian architect Constantino Tencala and built in the Early Baroque style between 1633 and 1652 for the Discalced Carmelite order of the Roman Catholic Church. It is the only church in Lithuania whose weathervane features an angel with a trumpet. The interior is intricate and delicate with soft pink hues, numerous ceiling frescoes and ornate plasterwork highlighted with gold leaf.

**Gates of Dawn** [85 D6] (Aušros vartai; Aušros vartų gatvė 14; w ausrosvartai. lt; ⊕ May–Oct 06.00–19.00 daily, Nov–Apr 07.00–19.00 daily; free) The only remaining gate of the early 16th century defensive city wall. Walk through the gate and look back to see clearly the remnants of the original city wall that skirted the Old Town for 2.5km and had ten gates. In the 17th century, a wooden chapel was constructed by the gate, replaced by a brick chapel after a fire, then in the 19th century reconstructed in the Classic style we see today. The chapel contains a miraculous painting of the Blessed Virgin Mary, Mother of Mercy (the artist is unknown) which attracts Catholic and Orthodox pilgrims from all over the world. The doors of the chapel are regularly opened so she is visible from the street, and it is possible to enter the chapel via the doorway just before the arches on the left. There is a remarkable collection of small silver hearts and other votive offerings inside the chapel.

**AROUND VOKIEČIŲ GATVĖ** Vokiečių gatvė (German Street) is characterised by a wide pedestrian path lined with flower beds, trees, a fountain and parking areas in between the road lanes. This is not primarily the result of urban planning but in response to the bomb damage caused during World War II. The southern side of the street has original architecture and narrow cobbled streets, the northern side consists of modernist Soviet architecture built in the post-war period. This was once a densely populated residential and commercial area like the surviving areas beyond either side; the lost streets are demarcated by different colour paving stones to remember what was once here. Behind the post-war Soviet apartment buildings was Vilnius' main Jewish area and the site of the Great Synagogue (page 28).

**Vilnius Museum** [85 B4] (Vilniaus muziejus; Vokiečių gatvė 6; w vilniausmuziejus. lt; ⊕ 15.00–19.00 Tue–Fri, 11.00–19.00 Sat–Sun; €5/2.50) This recently renovated space welcomes locals and visitors to learn about the capital city. Ever-changing exhibitions cover unusual angles about people and place, not shy of confronting difficult issues faced by the city. The attached **Reading Room and Backstage Café** (⊕ 08.00–20.00 Mon–Fri, 09.00–19.00 Sat–Sun) serves up coffee and snacks while books are available to peruse or purchase.

**Museum of Illusions** [85 B4] (Iliuzijų muziejus; Vokiečių gatvė 8; w vilnil.lt; ⊕ 10.00–19.00 Mon–Fri, 10.00–20.00 Sat, 10.00–18.00 Sun; €13/9) Entertainment with a bit of education thrown in – this museum offers a lot of fun for families with new exhibits added regularly. The optical illusions are full of mystery but a member of staff is on hand to explain the science behind them. Here you will find the only 2D café in town – curious?

**Barbora Radvilaitė statue** [85 B4] (Vokiečių gatvė) Meet Lithuania's lovestory heroine, Barbora Radvilaitė (1522–51) – also known by her Polish name Barbara Radziwiłł – immortalised by sculptor Vladas Vildžiūnas in 1982. Against the will of the Polish royal family, Lithuanian-born and already-widowed Barbora married her true love, Žygimantas Augustas (Sigismund II Augustus), the future successor to the Polish crown. They married in 1547, and in 1550, when Žygimantas Augustas was crowned King of Poland and Grand Duke of Lithuania, Barbora became Queen of Poland and Grand Duchess of Lithuania. There was no happy ending as she died of illness only five months later, but the story lives on – even though it was forbidden to refer to the statue by name under Soviet occupation. This is a talking statue, and you can hear the full story by scanning the QR code (page 100).

**Church of St Nicholas** [85 A4] (Šv. Mikalojaus bažnyčia; Šv. Mikalojaus gatvė 4; w mikalojus.lt) Tucked away down a side street, St Nicholas' is the oldest brick church in Vilnius. It was built for merchants and craftsmen who had relocated to Vilnius from the Hanseatic cities in the 14th century, just before the Christianisation of Lithuania. The brick Gothic exterior is rather modest with its triangular pediment and niches distinct to that period. The interior, too, is without extravagance, the main architectural feature being the star-vaulted ceilings. Mass times are available on the website.

**Church of the Assumption of the Blessed Virgin Mary** [85 A3] (Švč. M Marijos Ėmimo į dangų bažnyčia; Trakų gatvė 9) More commonly known as the Franciscan Church, and surrounded by the Franciscan monastery, the current church building dates from 1764 although it has existed in many different forms since it was first documented in 1387. Bearing the scars of 300 years of misuse, including repurposing as a granary, prison and warehouse, it was only a functioning church during the interwar years 1918–39. After 50 years of being closed, it was finally returned to the Franciscan Church in 1998. The slow and costly process of renovation is now underway, but the church still opens for prayer and public visits with many coming to view (and hear if lucky), the new 'Big Blue' organ.

**AROUND VILNIAUS GATVĖ** An attractive street of historic wealthy mansions connects the Old Town with Gedimino prospektas. The architecture is perhaps best appreciated in winter when the street is quiet and empty. In summer, outdoor seating and terraces for the multitude of bars and restaurants make this a vibrant space to enjoy warm summer evenings.

**Lithuanian Theatre, Music and Cinema Museum** [85 A2] (Lietuvos teatro, muzikos ir kino muziejus; Vilniaus gatvė 41; w ltmkm.lt; ⊕ 10.00–18.00 Tue–Sat, 10.00–16.00 Sun; €5/2) Providing an insight into the cultural world of Lithuania over the years, this is a museum for those who love the performing arts. It is

## JEWISH VILNIUS
*Richard Schofield*

A renowned centre of traditional Talmudic study for several centuries, Vilnius – or Vilna/Vilne in Hebrew/Yiddish – was also home to an immense diversity of secular Jewish life and culture until its population of more than 55,000 Jewish men, women and children were nearly all murdered during the Holocaust. The following provides a mere glimpse of numerous sites in Vilnius that remember the city's Jewish heritage and history.

**HOLOCAUST EXHIBITION** [83 C5] (Holokausto ekspozicija; The Green House, Pamėnkalnio gatvė 12; w jmuseum.lt; ⏲ 10.00–18.00 Tue–Fri, 11.00–18.00 Sat–Sun; €5/2) Originally founded and staffed by a small team of Holocaust survivors who've all since passed away, this wonderfully low-tech museum provides a refreshingly simple overview of the Holocaust as it unfolded throughout Lithuania.

**MEMORIAL MUSEUM OF HOLOCAUST IN LITHUANIA AND VILNA GHETTO** [85 A4] (Žemaitijos gatvė 4; w jmuseum.lt) Located inside the former Vilna Ghetto library and scheduled to replace the Holocaust Exhibition sometime in 2026, this ambitious new museum aims to bring its predecessor up to date while retaining its original spirit.

**MUSEUM OF CULTURE AND IDENTITY OF LITHUANIAN JEWS** [83 C5] (Lietuvos žydų kultūros ir tapatybės muziejus; Pylimo gatvė 4A; w jmuseum.lt; ⏲ 10.00–18.00 Tue–Fri, 11.00–18.00 Sat–Sun; €6/3) Three floors of Lithuanian Jewish history and culture embrace everything from the two major conflicting Judaic faiths that co-existed in Lithuania before 1941 to the unique secular world of Lithuanian Jewish literature, art and music. The top floor is devoted to the life and work of Vilnius-born artist Rafael Chwoles, who was born in the city in 1913 and who passed away in Paris in 2002. Be sure to pick up at least one of the books for sale in the ticket office.

housed in the Small Radvila Palace, which once belonged to the wealthy and influential Radvila family. The building's attractive façade is complemented by an arcade feature overlooking the rear courtyard in which there is a container cinema exposition 'Kino teatras'.

**St Catherine's Church** [85 A2] (Šv. Kotrynos bažnyčia; Vilniaus gatvė 30; f Kotrynosbaznycia) This Baroque beauty built between 1625 and 1743 catches the eye of all who walk past. Heavily damaged during World War II and subjected to the disrespect and pillaging granted a Catholic church during Soviet times, it is now renovated and primarily serves as a cultural venue. If you can experience a music performance here, the backdrop of ornate Rococo sculptures and powerful acoustics are truly memorable. The church is managed by Vilnius Teachers House (w kultura.lt).

**Frank Zappa statue** [83 C6] (K Kalinausko gatvė) Why is there a Frank Zappa statue in Vilnius? Because there could be, once the country was freed from Soviet occupation. The statue is more a symbol of freedom rather than a tribute by die-hard fans to Frank Zappa. It was created by sculptor Konstantinas Bagdonas, formerly known for his Communist Party-approved busts of Lenin, and unveiled in December 1995. A replica was sent to Zappa's hometown of Baltimore, USA,

**SAMUEL BAK MUSEUM** [83 C7] (Samuelio Bako muziejus; Naugarduko gatvė 10; w jmuseum.lt; 10.00–18.00 Tue–Fri, 11.00–18.00 Sat–Sun; €5/2) The apocalypse-themed artist Samuel Bak survived the Vilna Ghetto as a young boy; he now lives in the United States. Several of his original paintings are on permanent display here in Vilnius, inside a former Jewish theatre which also houses several other fascinating and instructive exhibits.

**TAHARAT HA-KODESH CHORAL SYNAGOGUE** [85 A5] (Vilniaus choralinė sinagoga; Pylimo gatvė 39; w jewish-heritage-lithuania.org/synagogue/choral-synagogue-in-vilnius) Built in the so-called Moorish style in 1903 to accommodate the city's Jewish elite, what the interior lacks in architectural magnificence is more than made up for in the stories one imagines it could tell if only it could speak. Do leave a donation if you can. Shabbat services are open to all.

**OTHER SIGHTS, SITES AND RECOMMENDATIONS** Visit Vilnius' historical Jewish quarter and former site of the Vilna Ghetto, starting on Stiklių gatvė and Žydų gatvė, and stretching over to the area around Mėsinių gatvė. See the original Yiddish (and Polish) writing on the fronts of the buildings on Žemaitijos gatvė and above the entrance to the café at Pylimo gatvė 23. Pay your respects to the Vilna Gaon and others at the Jewish cemetery at Sudervės kelias 28 (Vilniaus (Sudervės) žydų senosios kapinės). Created after the Soviet authorities destroyed the city's two original Jewish cemeteries, the new location requires your own set of wheels or a ride from the city centre on bus 43 or 46, getting off at the Buivydiškių stop. Splashing out on a good tour guide to show you around for a few hours is money well spent. David Fishman's 2017 *The Book Smugglers: Partisans, Poets, and the Race to Save Jewish Treasures from the Nazis*, really helps set the scene.

though sadly Zappa never knew anything about his alternative role in Lithuania, having passed away in December 1993.

**AROUND TOTORIŲ GATVĖ** A quieter but no less important route between the Old Town and Gediminas Avenue, passing through the official heartland of the Ministry of Defence and Presidential Palace.

## Dominican Church of the Holy Spirit
[85 B2] (Vilniaus Šventosios Dvasios bažnyčia; Dominikonų gatvė 8) At the top of Totorių gatvė is the calm and undeveloped street of Šv. Ignoto (Saint Ignatius) with its fine stretches of old city wall. On the corner of Šv. Ignoto and Dominikonų gatvė is the Dominican Church. It's easily overlooked on account of its unassuming exterior and being set parallel to the street without a main façade, though the interior is quite remarkable. Filled with playful Rococo statues and ornamentation, Baroque frescoes and 16 altars, this is one of the most lavish churches in Vilnius. After World War II, it was the main church of the city's Polish Community. Behind the church sprawls the former Dominican monastery, which never recovered from Tsarist Russia converting it into a prison during the 19th century. No doubt this sought-after Old Town real estate will one day become luxury apartments with underground parking.

**Office of the President of the Republic of Lithuania** [85 B1] (LR Prezidento kanceliarija; S Daukanto aikštė 3; w pazinkvalstybe.lt) The Presidential Palace has long been a centre of state affairs in Lithuania, regardless of who was in power. In 1795 it became the official residence of the Russian Governor General who ruled Vilna Governorate within Imperial Russia; his famous guests included Tsar Alexander I and Emperor Napoleon Bonaparte. During World War I, the palace was occupied by the German authorities and from 1944 to 1990 it was used by officers of the Soviet army. Since 1997 the palace has been the residence of the President of the Republic of Lithuania. Tours of the Presidential Palace are organised via the Centre for Civil Education (Totorių gatvė 28) and require pre-registration (register at e registracija.vpc@prezidentas.lt); these tours include free hour-long tours in English which run every Sunday between 10.00 and 15.00. The Presidential Palace grounds are regularly opened to the public often hosting seasonal art installations.

**AROUND GEDIMINAS AVENUE** Gediminas Avenue (Gedimino prospektas) stretches over 1.8km from the cathedral to the parliament building. Built during Imperial Russian rule in the early 1800s to house city institutions and wealthy residents, the avenue is formal and grand with architectural anomalies dotted along the way. Its name has changed over time, depending on who was in power: St George Avenue under Russian rule, Mickiewicz Street under Polish rule, and both Stalin Avenue and later Lenin Avenue during Soviet rule. Since 1989, it has been named Gediminas Avenue after the founder of Vilnius.

### THE HOUSE OF BOOKS

A curious church and monastery complex hides away behind Gediminas Avenue, in a sorry state of disrepair. This is St George's [83 D5] (Šv. Jurgio kankinio ir Švč. Mergelės Marijos Snieginės (Pergalingosios) bažnyčia; K Sirvydo gatvė 4), whose current buildings were constructed in 1750 by the noble Radvila (Radziwiłł) family and consecrated in 1765. The church and monastery were closed by the Soviet authorities and transferred to the central state library in 1946 for use as a book archive and repository. It became known as the House of Books.

In 2017 the discovery of a vast Jewish archive hidden in the church made the headlines. Before World War II, Vilnius was home to the Yiddish Scientific Institute (YIVO), and its Strashun Library was one of the most important Jewish libraries in eastern Europe. During the Nazi occupation, a group of Jewish scholars known as 'the paper brigade' were tasked with sorting and protecting these collections. Some manuscripts were sent to safety in Frankfurt, some destroyed and others dangerously smuggled into the Jewish ghetto and hidden. After the war, and the decimation of the local Jewish population, a Lithuanian librarian called Antanas Ulpis hid surviving Jewish documents in the basement of St George's Church. The Jewish archives are now being studied and provide a trove of information and unique insight into the social, cultural, political and economic life of the historic Jewish community. Now cleared of books and boxes, the church interior is hauntingly beautiful as it patiently awaits renovation, though its future is uncertain. The complex is closed to the public and open only on rare occasions.

> **VILNIUS' HISTORIC CEMETERIES**
>
> **ANTAKALNIS CEMETERY** [82 G2] (Antakalnio kapinės; Karių kapų gatvė 11) Once called the Soldier's Cemetery, Antakalnis Cemetery has distinct sections of military graves alongside famous personalities from the arts.
>
> **BERNARDINE CEMETERY** [83 G6] (Bernardinų kapinės; Žvirgždyno gatvė 3, accessed from Polocko gatvė in Užupis) Bernadine is the second-oldest cemetery in Vilnius and one of the most beautiful.
>
> **RASOS CEMETERY** [83 F8] (Senosios Rasų kapinės; Rasų gatvė 32) Rasos is a fascinating and historically rich cemetery with many important literary and cultural figures laid to rest here.

During the evenings and weekends the section between Cathedral Square and V Kudirkos Square is pedestrianised and outdoor seating and people strolling create a relaxed vibe.

## Lithuanian Money Museum of the Bank of Lithuania (Lietuvos banko Pinigų muziejus; Totorių gatvė 2; w pinigumuziejus.lt; ⊕ Jul–Sep 10.00–19.00 Tue–Fri, 11.00–18.00 Sat, Oct–Jun 09.00–18.00 Tue–Fri, 10.00–17.00 Sat; free)

Originally, in 1985, this was the Museum of the History of the State Bank housed in the Lithuanian Republic Office of the USSR State Bank, pushing ideological rhetoric and propaganda, of course. Both bank and museum became defunct with Lithuanian independence, when the national Bank of Lithuania was reestablished. After a long closure, the museum was relaunched in 2010 and improves with every upgrade. Not only is the history of the national bank and money production explained but it is an alternative angle through which to follow the nation's history. Previously the museum has received several awards for being friendly and hospitable. Perhaps try one of their pre-booked guided tours (1hr) – they're free of charge.

Next door is the **Bank of Lithuania**; notice the small bust of Vladas Jurgutis, the first governor of the national bank, the only bust in Lithuania cast from molten 50-cent coins (old litas currency) – over 75,000 of them, to be precise.

## V Kudirkos Square [83 D5] (V Kudirkos aikštė, Gedimino prospektas)

Gediminas Avenue opens into a leafy square at V Kudirkos aikštė, named after Vincas Kudirka (1858–99), the Lithuanian poet and physician, whose statue stands in the centre of the square. Although born in Poland, he moved to work in Lithuania's Suvalkija region and became active in the Lithuanian independence movement, editing clandestine publications and composing 'Tautiška Giesmė', which would become the Lithuanian national anthem. Look around you at the array of architecture on display, trying to ignore the monstrous Novotel building that somehow slipped through planning in the wild, unruly 1990s. At the back of the square, hidden by the trees is the late Modernist building of the **Government of the Republic of Lithuania** (Gedimino prospektas 11; w lrv.lt). V Kudirkos Square is also an important intersection for bus and trolleybus services.

## ✳ Museum of Occupations and Freedom Fights [82 B4] (Okupacijų ir laisvės kovų muziejus; Aukų gatvė 2A; w genocid.lt/muziejus; ⊕ 10.00–18.00 Wed–Sat,

10.00–17.00 Sun; €6/3) Also known as the Museum of Genocide Victims and the KGB Museum, this museum is housed in the former headquarters of the NKVD (later called KGB) Soviet secret police. The first floor has an exhibition about the partisan resistance movement, while the second floor is dedicated to deportations, life in the gulags and KGB activities. Downstairs are the former cells where between 1944 and 1947 prisoners were detained, interrogated, tortured and, in the basement, executed. Fear and terror were used by the Soviet authorities to suppress the local population; you could end up here because of a disgruntled neighbour telling lies, anyone could be an informer and there was no 'innocent until proven guilty'. A guided tour is recommended to truly understand what took place here – book via the website. Note the names and dates inscribed along the façade of the building. These commemorate members of the armed resistance who were murdered here and identified in the mass burial ground at Tuskulėnai Memorial Complex and Peace Park (page 117).

**Lukiškės Square** [82 B4] (Lukiškių aikštė, Gedimino prospektas) Lukiškių aikštė is the largest square in Vilnius and, since being remodelled and landscaped, is a pleasant area surrounded by ministry buildings and shaded by trees in which to enjoy a rest while children run through the water fountains. It was not always so agreeable here. After the January uprising in 1863, this was where insurgents were publicly executed. In 1953 a statue of the former Soviet leader Lenin, the largest in the country, was erected in the square. Soon after independence in 1991, it was removed by crane, and as the statue was dismantled it broke into pieces to the cheers of the watching crowd. However, he has since been reconfigured and now stands in Grūtas Soviet Sculpture Park near Druskininkai (page 145).

**Dominican Church of Apostles St Philip and St Jacob** [82 C4] (Šv. Apaštalų Pilypo ir Jokūbo bažnyčia; Vasario 16-osios gatvė 11; w dominikonai.lt) The church's 17th-century twin towers provide an attractive backdrop to Lukiškės Square and they are a source of aural beauty too. The church contains a 61-bell carillon, the largest in the Baltic states, which rings daily at 13.00 and 19.15. The Vilnius Carillon Festival (w vilniauskarilionas.lt) is held here every summer. During the Soviet occupation, the church was stripped of all its treasures and used to store fruit and vegetables; the neighbouring monastery was transformed into a hospital. It has now been fully restored and retains its main attraction the *Mother of God of Lukiškės*, one of the oldest icons in Lithuania dating from the late 15th century.

✷ **Lukiškės Prison** [82 B4] (Lukiškių kalėjimas; Lukiškių 6; w lukiskiukalejimas.lt; ⊕ noon–midnight; guided scheduled group tours can be booked online up to 2 weeks in advance (max 16 people; 2hrs long; €22 pp) In true Vilnius style, this rough and raw prison complex has been relaunched as an eccentric cultural hub, referred to as Lukiškės Prison 2.0. Built in 1904 under the rule of Russian Tsar Nicholas II, the prison complex housed criminals, political prisoners and exiles over 115 operational years, until its overcrowding and deteriorating conditions became deplorable and the last inmates left in 2019. It was an asset to cruel political regimes who incarcerated social activists, political figures, writers and anyone posing a threat to the occupying power of the time. The building is a cultural heritage monument from the Russian Empire, and now its dark past is open to visitors via official guided tours. This is a world of contrasts. Real stories of prison life, musty cells, uneven floors, dark corners, tales of injustice and dangerous crimes. Over 350 artists' workshops now occupy the former cells, and the courtyard may contain a sauna for hire or an ice-skating rink; event spaces host music concerts, pop-up cinema or artisan markets, and music blasts from the bar as you explore the art installations. Fans of the series *Stranger Things* will be interested to know that part of Season Four was shot here. Night tours are for over 18s only and aim to thrill the visitor with the darkest of tales. Private tours are available on request.

**Parliament of the Republic of Lithuania** [82 A4] (Lietuvos Respublikos Seimas; Gedimino prospektas 53; w lrs.lt) Since its completion in 1980, the Parliament (Seimas) of Lithuania has sat here, albeit sometimes under the auspices of occupying powers and housing a puppet government. But since 1990 it has been the heart of democratic independent Lithuania. Tours can be arranged via the **Parliament Visitor Centre** (Gedimino prospektas 60; ⊕ 08.00–17.00 Mon–Thu, 08.00–15.45 Fri; e visitors@lrs.lt). On the river side of the parliament is a memorial commemorating the tragic events of 13 January 1991, when Russian troops attempted to regain control of Lithuania by force. While the TV Tower was under attack, crowds flocked to protect the parliament. Thousands of people gathered here in Independence Square, hundreds of buses and lorries blocked access, and barricades of concrete, reinforcing steel bars and anti-tank ditches were hurriedly constructed. People came from all over Lithuania to defend their country's freedom, warmed by bonfires and supporters delivering hot food and drink. Meanwhile members of parliament remained inside pushing their plight to the rest of the world and preparing petrol bombs for active defence if needed.

**Žvėrynas district** Continuing over Žvėrynas Bridge (Žvėryno tiltas) at the end of Gediminas Avenue brings you to the district of Žvėrynas. Few visitors venture this far, but if you are interested in exploring suburbia, and in particular wooden architecture, this is the ideal place. More than 108 wooden houses in various states of disrepair and renovation dot this leafy neighbourhood. Other highlights include **Vilnius Kenesa** (Vilniaus karaimų kenesa; Liubarto gatve 6) and **Panama Food Garden** (Vykinto gatvė 17a; f panamafoodgarden) for a lunch stop. If you leave Žvėrynas via the Vingis Park Bridge (Vingio parko tiltas), you can extend your walk into a hike through Vingis Park.

## NORTH BANK OF THE RIVER NERIS
**New town skyline** Between 1983 and 2001, the Lietuva Hotel building was an anomalous and rather pithy excuse for a skyscraper on the north bank of the Neris River. In 2001, the first modern glass skyscraper, nicknamed 'the glass pencil', was opened (though now earmarked for demolition), followed in 2004 by the new Vilnius City Municipality building [82 C3] (famous for being emblazoned with a banner stating 'Putin, the Hague is waiting for you') and Europa Tower, the tallest building in the Baltic states. Contemporary glass structures continue to sprout in response to a prosperous era of fintech, start-ups and banking, leading to Vilnius' north bank resembling a mini-Manhattan skyline (everything is relative).

**White Bridge** [82 C3] (Baltasis tiltas; Upės gatvė & A Goštauto gatvė) In winter, this is a simple pedestrian bridge for crossing the Neris River as quickly as possible, while battling against an icy wind and peering down at eerie ice floes drifting downstream below. In summer, the area becomes a hub of young energy with pop-up cafés and bars, a beach, volleyball, buzzing skatepark

## ART GALLERIES AND MUSEUMS

The **Lithuanian National Museum of Art** (Lietuvos nacionalinis dailės muziejus; w lndm.lt) comprises nine galleries and museums across Vilnius, Klaipėda, Palanga and Juodkrantė, each hosting permanent and temporary exhibitions, often a Lithuanian and international exhibit in tandem. In Vilnius this includes the Museum of Applied Arts and Design, National Gallery of Art, Radvila Palace Museum of Art, Vilnius Picture Gallery and Vytautas Kasiulis Museum Of Art.

**CONTEMPORARY ART CENTRE** [85 B4] (Šiuolaikinio meno centras; Vokiečių gatvė 2; w cac.lt; ⊕ noon–20.00 Tue–Fri, 11.00–19.00 Sat, 11.00–18.00 Sun; €7/4) One of the largest contemporary art venues in the Baltic states, this one is famous for the Baltic Triennial – an ambitious contemporary art event held since 1979 and known for blurring the lines between official and underground art.

**KAZYS VARNELIS HOUSE MUSEUM** [85 C4] (Kazio Varnelio namai-muziejus; Didžioji gatvė 26; w lnm.lt/en/museums/kazys-varnelis-house-museum; ⊕ 10.00–18.00 Wed–Sun, €6/3) Don't be deceived by the small façade. The museum is a labyrinth of 15th-century buildings full of Gothic and Renaissance architectural features and 40 rooms of artwork exhibits. Founded in 1993, the museum houses the collection of Lithuanian artist Kazys Varnelis (1917–2010) who lived in the USA for 50 years before returning to Lithuania post-independence. Varnelis was an abstract painter incorporating optical illusions and geometric patterns, combining elements of Minimalism, Constructivism and Op-Art. He also collected antiques, furniture, maps and art, pieces which now adorn the museum alongside his own works. Other works include etchings by Spanish artist Francisco Goya and a 1631 Radziwiłł map of the Grand Duchy of Lithuania.

**MO MUSEUM** [82 C6] (MO muziejus; Pylimo gatvė 17; w mo.lt; ⊕ 10.00–20.00 daily, closed Tue; €11/6) Created not only to display art but to sweep you up into the world of art, MO Museum aims to prompt conversation and for spaces to feel alive with interaction and the opportunity to linger a while and reflect. The collection of over 6,000 modern and contemporary artworks is housed in a statement building designed by internationally renowned architect Daniel Libeskind, worthy of a recce itself. The museum was a private initiative by Lithuanian philanthropists Danguolė and Viktoras Butkus and opened in 2018.

**MUSEUM OF APPLIED ARTS AND DESIGN** [83 E5] (Taikomosios dailės ir dizaino muziejus; Arsenalo gatvė 3A; w lndm.lt/en/tdm; ⊕ 10.00–18.00 Tue–Wed & Fri–Sat, 10.00–20.00 Thu, 10.00–16.00 Sun; €6/3) The vast halls of this Old Arsenal building have been displaying artworks since 1987, the high ceilings perfect for larger installations. Exhibitions change every three to six months and often feature famous international artists. The museum produces a book about every exhibition to capture it in time; these are available to buy in the museum shop.

and basketball courts. Nearby is where hot-air balloons take off and kayak tours launch. As you walk across the bridge, keep in mind that in September 1999, aerobatic pilot Jurgis Kairys flew his plane under all ten bridges that cross the Neris in Vilnius.

**NATIONAL GALLERY OF ART** [82 B3] (Nacionalinė dailės galerija; Konstitucijos prospektas 22; w ndg.lt; ⊕ 11.00–19.00 Tue–Wed, noon–20.00 Thu, 11.00–19.00 Fri–Sat, 11.00–17.00 Sun; €8/4) The National Gallery of Art houses the national collection of 20th- and 21st-century Lithuanian art, comprising more than 46,000 exhibits including modern and contemporary painting, sculpture, photography, graphic art and film installations, with temporary exhibitions changing regularly. Cultural events, lectures and film screenings are held in the auditorium. The stark modernist exterior of the building does not prepare you for the colour and emotions stirred up by the art inside. A good excuse to cross the Neris River and explore the business district of Vilnius.

**RADVILA PALACE MUSEUM OF ART** [83 C5] (Radvilų rūmų dailės muziejus; Vilniaus gatvė 24; w lndm.lt/en/rrm; ⊕ 11.00–19.00 Tue, Wed, Fri & Sat, noon–20.00 Thu, 11.00–17.00 Sun; €6/3) Built for Jonusas Radvila (1612–55) in the mid 17th century, this was one of the most beautiful residences in Vilnius, the interior adorned with a collection of paintings including western European artworks. The palace was heavily damaged by fire later that century and the valuable art collection stolen. Abandoned in a state of disrepair for many decades, the building was finally renovated in 1967 and began a new era as a gallery in 1990. The palace houses the foreign art section of the National Museum of Art, alongside rotating temporary expositions.

**VILNIUS PICTURE GALLERY** [85 C3] (Vilniaus paveikslų galerija; Didžioji gatvė 4; w lndm.lt/en/vpg; ⊕ 10.00–20.00 Tue, 10.00–18.00 Wed–Sat, 11.00–17.00 Sun; €6/3) Owned by the Lithuanian National Museum of Art since 1994, the picture gallery is housed in an elegant wing of the Chodkevičius Palace, the rest being occupied by administration, archives and art storage. The focus of the picture gallery is the national collection of 16th- to 19th-century fine art. Portraits of noblemen and -women dominate the gallery, but a highlight is the 16th-century wooden sculpture *The Risen Christ*. Once believed to be lost having been smuggled illegally out of the country, it was identified in a Viennese antique shop, and after ten years of diplomacy and law enforcement it was returned to the museum in 2020.

**VYTAUTAS KASIULIS MUSEUM OF ART** [82 C4] (Vytauto Kasiulio dailės muziejus; Goštauto gatvė 1; w lndm.lt/en/vkdm; ⊕ 10.00–18.00 Tue–Wed, 11.00–20.00 Thu, 10.00–18.00 Fri, 10.00–17.00 Sat–Sun; €5/2.50) This museum curates diverse exhibitions of contemporary art on a rotating basis and includes Kasiulis' own works in a permanent exhibition. Kasiulis (1918–95) was one of the most famous Lithuanian artists living in exile in Paris and involved in the School of Paris artist community. Like many other exiled artists, his work was largely unknown in Lithuania until after independence and the museum was opened in 2013. His bright, vivid Impressionist style brought a new dimension to the Lithuanian art scene.

**Chiune Sugihara Sakura Park** [82 B3] (Č Sugiharos sakurų parkas; Upės gatvė next to the National Gallery of Art) In 2001, to mark the 100th anniversary of Japanese diplomat Chiune Sugihara (page 191), Japan gifted Lithuania 200 sakura trees as a symbol of friendly relations. Each spring the Japanese cherry blossoms

> **THE ROAD TO FREEDOM MEMORIAL WALL**
>
> The Road to Freedom Memorial Wall [82 B2] (Laisvės kelias; Konstitucijos prospektas/E272 roundabout, Vilnius) commemorates the peaceful political demonstration of 'The Baltic Way' held on 23 August 1989. Creating a human chain from Vilnius to Tallinn, people of all three Baltic nations stood hand in hand in opposition to the Russian occupiers. The memorial wall is in the colours of the Lithuanian tricolour flag, each brick bearing the name of someone who donated to the project in 2010, and with human shapes cut out of the brickwork symbolising those who participated in the human chain.

burst into flower for about two weeks in late April/early May, attracting people to stroll and pose under the canopy of pink petals.

**Green Bridge** [82 C4] (Žaliasis tiltas; Kalvarijų gatvė) Since the original bridge on this site was built in 1739 and painted green, this river crossing has been known as the 'green bridge'. Over the centuries it was burned down several times and bombed by the Wehrmacht in World War II. The current bridge was constructed in 1952 when Vilnius was under Soviet occupation – it was renamed after a Soviet general and decorated with four cast-iron sculptures depicting Soviet propaganda scenes – student youth, agricultural workers, industry and guard of peace. After Lithuanian independence, its true name was restored and it became a controversial topic whether the sculptures were works of art or Soviet propaganda that should be removed. In July 2015, they were removed temporarily but that extended into a permanent removal. The statues have been in storage ever since, though they have attracted expressions of interest including an offer to purchase them from the Kaliningrad city of Sovetsk, and an offer to display them at Grūtas Soviet Sculpture Park (page 145). Nothing has progressed to date.

**\* Energy and Technology Museum** [82 D4] (Energetikos ir technikos muziejus; Rinktinės gatvė 2; w etm.lt; ⊕ 10.00–18.30 Tue–Sun; €7/3.50) The statue of *Elektra* on the roof summons you to cross the river from the Old Town and visit this impressive hands-on museum housed in the first power plant in Vilnius (in operation from 1903 to 1998). The Energy Exhibition is laid out among the old workings of the steam boilers, turbines, generators and pipework and is full of interactive fun. Downstairs the hi-tech Transformation Hall houses a Faraday cage with two large Tesla coils installed; regular demonstrations are held. The kids' area is excellent and educational, although the big slide is the star attraction. The top-floor roof terrace offers views of the Old Town, a replica of the *Lituanica* airplane (page 193), and in summer the Elektrinė terrace bar is open. There is a museum café, handy should you find yourself staying here longer than expected and in need of refreshments. The museum can also arrange private tours of the Liepkalnis Water Storage Facility, an underground reservoir in use from 1916 to 1987 – and now open for tours while plans are afoot to convert it into an events venue due to its exceptional acoustic qualities and quirkiness. And if you want to know more about *Elektra*, she is part of the MO Museum talking statues project (page 100).

**Palace of Concerts and Sports** [82 E4] (Koncertų ir sporto rūmai; Rinktinės gatvė 1) Guaranteed to raise the question, what is that? Whether viewed from

Gediminas Castle or the riverbank, this Soviet Brutalist legacy attracts attention for its unique shape and dilapidated state. Built in 1971, with a capacity of 4,400 spectators it hosted major basketball games, concerts and shows until closing in 2004 due to safety issues. The future of the site is embroiled in controversy partly because it is a strange architectural monument, but mainly because it was built by the Soviets upon the oldest Jewish burial ground in Vilnius, Piromont Cemetery.

**Tuskulėnai Memorial Complex and Peace Park** [82 F2] (Tuskulėnų rimties parkas; Žirmūnų gatvė 1F; w tuskulenumemorialas.lt) Tuskulėnai Manor was built in 1825 for a noble family in a late classicist style, with the White Manor House and St Theresa Chapel added later. In early 1994, Lithuanian authorities confirmed that prisoners killed in the KGB headquarters on Gediminas Avenue between 1944 and 1947 were buried in the grounds of Tuskulėnai Manor and archaeological investigations began. Between 1994 and 1996, 45 graves were found to contain the remains of 724 people, and in 2004 a memorial chapel-columbarium was built in the park to house their remains. A permanent exhibition in the **White Manor House** (⏲ 10.00–18.00 Wed–Sat, 10.00–17.00 Sun; €4/2) reveals the history and secrets of Tuskulėnai Manor.

## CITY OUTSKIRTS
**Vingis Park** (Vingio parkas; entrances on M K Čiurlionio gatvė & Birutės gatvė, Žvėrynas) *Vingis* means 'bend' or 'curve' in Lithuanian, hence the park is named after the sweeping meander of the Neris River it is nestled in. Within the park once stood the Palace of Zakret, where, during a ball in June 1812, Tsar Alexander I of Russia received news that the French army led by Napoleon had invaded Imperial Russia. Heavily damaged in a fire, the palace was never rebuilt. Today, instead, the park's focal point is the huge stage, where in 1988 the independence movement Sąjūdis held rallies, in 1993 Pope John Paul II celebrated Mass, and every four years the Lithuanian Song and Dance Festival finale is held. Major international stars also perform here from time to time. Vingis Park is popular with locals for walking, cycling and roller-skating on account of its wide asphalt paths, hiking trails and cycle routes. There is also a play area, mini zoo, amusement park and several cafés during summer. Park Run is every Saturday at 09.00, meeting at the M K Čiurlionio gatvė entrance.

**Vilnius TV Tower** (TV bokštas; Sausio 13-osios gatvė 10; w tvbokstas.lt; ⏲ 11.00–21.00 daily; €16/9) This iconic landmark on the Vilnius skyline is the tallest structure in the country at 326.5m high (in terms of TV towers, it ranks 8th in Europe and 26th in the world). It took six years to construct and began operating in December 1980, broadcasting television and radio while also offering the opportunity to dine with a bird's-eye view from the revolving restaurant. On 13 January 1991, while Lithuania was still navigating its declaration of independence from the Soviet Union, Moscow sent in Soviet troops to crack down on the independence momentum. Huge crowds headed to protect the Parliament building and to the TV tower to prevent the Russian troops taking control of the media. Fourteen people were killed at the TV tower that night, crushed by tanks and killed by gun shots. A permanent exhibition on the ground floor of the tower commemorates those who lost their lives fighting for freedom that night. You might notice blue forget-me-not flowers around Lithuania, a symbol of remembrance for these events. A memorial bronze sculpture called *Aukojimas* (Sacrifice) stands outside the tower, a symbol of independence. Nearby is the historic antenna park, including the satellite antenna Nera, gifted to Lithuania by Norway in 1991 and used by Lithuanian leaders to overcome Soviet isolation tactics and secure communication with the world. The TV tower offers stunning views from the bistro, Toliai, on the 67th floor; or visitors can stay overnight in one of the two 'Debesys' (clouds) double-room apartments on the 68th floor (a one-night stay on Friday or Saturday costs €960, or €1,300 on New Year's Eve or Valentine's Day). A popular activity is the **Edge Walk** (adults €39 plus €16 general entry; lasts 45–60min, May–Oct), where you are strapped in securely but are free otherwise to walk around the platform at a height of 170m.

To get to the TV Tower, use the Bolt app (approx €13 from the Old Town) or take trolleybus 16 from the train station to the Televizijos Bokštas stop.

**Automatika Cold War Bunker** (w coldwarbunker.lt) During the Cold War period, more than 300 civil defence shelters were constructed around Vilnius to protect residents from chemical, biological or nuclear attack. The shelters or bunkers were made from reinforced concrete to withstand impact or dangerous contamination and contained necessary survival equipment. Many were destroyed or fell into disrepair, but this is an authentic bunker constructed in 1984, and today it is open to visitors. Opening hours are sporadic and visits must be booked in advance via the website, where you can check dates, times and language of scheduled guided group tours (€13/9). An exclusive self-guided tour takes place in the dark by torchlight while listening to an audio guide. It is quite eerie as you fumble your way around the bunker listening to stories and explanations. At the end of the tour, you meet the guide for any questions (1–2 adults €50, 3–4 adults €60). Private guided tours can also be arranged online; the minimum price is €100. Tours last for 1–1½ hours. Upon booking you will be told where to meet the guide (at a bus stop); do not be late as the tour will not wait and there is no phone signal in the bunker.

\* **Auto Museum** (Auto muziejus; Dariaus ir Girėno gatvė 2; w automuziejus. lt; ⏱ 10.00–19.00 Wed–Mon; €15/5) The Auto Museum is one of Vilnius's newest museums, located on the road to the airport in the former Vilnius taxi park. During Soviet times about 800 city taxis worked from here, a fine retro location for this outstanding private collection of more than 100 exhibits. The sleek multi-storey setting has Bond villain lair vibes and showcases the fine vehicles perfectly. Signs are in English but many exhibits have stories to tell and a guide is recommended. The King of Nepal's car and the brown motorbike 'Kaunas apskritis 97' are just two of many captivating examples.

**Lithuanian Railway Museum** [83 D8] (Lietuvos geležinkelių muziejus; Geležinkelio gatvė 16; w ltgmuziejus.lt; ⏱ 09.00–18.00 Tue–Fri, 10.00–18.00 Sat; €6/3) Located on the second floor of Vilnius Railway Station, the indoor exhibition is a recently renovated hands-on interactive experience, fun for young and old. Experience the challenges of being a train driver via a virtual reality game and learn about the history of train travel in Lithuania from being a province of Imperial Russia to integration with the European railway system. A free audio guide in English is available. To reach the outdoor exhibition, you must cross the train tracks via the bridge. There are 28 rolling-stock exhibits, all from the 20th century and include old locomotives, wagons and a hydraulic water column from 1938.

Railway fans may also enjoy Šiauliai Railway Museum (page 257) and Aukštaitija Narrow Gauge Railway (page 222).

✱ **Markučiai Manor** (Markučių dvaras; Subačiaus gatvė 124; w markuciudvaras. lt; ⊕ 10.00–17.00 Wed–Sun; €3/1.50) Also known as Vilnius's Pushkin Museum, even though Alexander Pushkin the poet never lived here, Markučiai Manor was built by railway engineer Aleksejus Melnikov. The manor was given as a dowry when his eldest daughter, Varvara, married in 1875; but it was her second husband whose legacy lives on here. Grigory Pushkin was the son of the Russian poet Alexander Pushkin and they created a small museum containing his personal belongings brought to Vilnius from the family home in Mikhailovkoye. The manor is one of the best-preserved wooden villas from the 19th century and furnished with authentic interiors. The surrounding park contains a monument to Pushkin, a chapel and family cemetery. If you are lucky enough to attend a recital or music concert in the manor, it is very atmospheric. The museum is a 40-minute walk from the Town Hall or you can take bus 10 from the Užupio bus stop on Maironio gatvė and get off at the final stop.

**Pavilniai Regional Park** Few capital cities have immediate access to expansive natural spaces like Vilnius does. **Pavilniai Regional Park** (w pavilniai-verkiai.lt) can be seen from the heights of Gediminas Castle or St John's bell tower when looking eastwards. It is the extensive area of forest disappearing into the distance – over 2,000ha of accessible nature on the city's doorstep. The park is centred around the Vilnia River valley and within it you will find nature reserves, historical ruins, viewpoints, artworks, hills for sledging and a network of over 21km of hiking trails. One of the most popular routes is the **Pūčkorių Educational Trail** (Pūčkorių pažintinis takas) with options of 2.8km, 3.7km or 5.3km circular trails taking between 1 and 3 hours to walk. Maps for hiking are available from Vilnius Tourism Information Centre (page 78). Look out for the routes that involve taking a train from Vilnius Railway Station to Pavilnys Railway Station and walking back to the city centre. After a pleasant hike, enjoy a leisurely lunch at local restaurant **Belmontas** (Belmonto gatvė 17A; w belmontas.lt; ⊕ noon–23.00 daily; €€€€) in Pavilniai. You can also start the Pūčkorių Educational Trail from here, and car parking is available. What was once a watermill on the Vilnia River is now an entertainment and leisure complex, popular for weddings, parties and conferences. A meal or refreshments can be enjoyed on the summer terrace set next to the river and small waterfalls, or in the historic tavern; both have a menu of traditional Lithuanian fare including grilled dishes in the summer. The next-door **Belmontas Adventure Park** (Belmonto Nuotykių Parkas; Belmonto gatvė 17; w belmontonuotykiuparkas.lt; ⊕ May–Sep) is popular with families and friends tackling the high rope courses (adults €20/2½hrs; students €18/2hrs; children €16/1½hrs) suspended throughout the surrounding forest. To guarantee a place, you should book in advance via the website. At the southern end of Pavilniai Regional Park, the highlight for many is **Liepkalnis** (Minsko plentas 2; w liepkalnis.lt), a mini Alpine-style leisure resort on the edge of Vilnius city centre. It is a popular ski centre in winter featuring ten ski slopes and lifts, ski hire, ski lessons and an apres-ski bar (€27/18 for a 3hr w/end ski pass, €23 full ski-kit hire for 3hrs). In summer it operates adrenaline activities including tubing, summer toboggan, mountain bikes and scooters, trampolines and a café.

# 4

# Around Vilnius

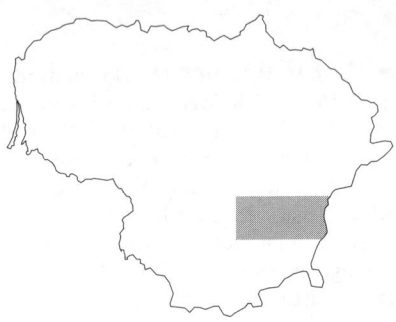

Trakai is by far the most popular day trip from Vilnius, but for those graced with a longer stay in the capital there are numerous other sites worthy of a full-day or half-day trip out of the city. Some of these sites are en route to other destinations and make ideal sightseeing stops.

## TRAKAI HISTORICAL NATIONAL PARK

Trakai Historical National Park is the smallest of Lithuania's national parks with an area of just 8,000ha, yet it is one of the country's biggest attractions. Distinguished from its counterparts by its unique 'historical' title, emphasis is placed on the preservation of the monumental heritage of Trakai alongside the conservation of the local landscape. The region is a melting pot of medieval history, pagan folklore, ethnic influences and natural landscapes – including the park's more than 32 lakes – all of which provide a dramatic backdrop to contemporary activities including hot-air ballooning, rowing regattas, ice-swimming competitions and music festivals.

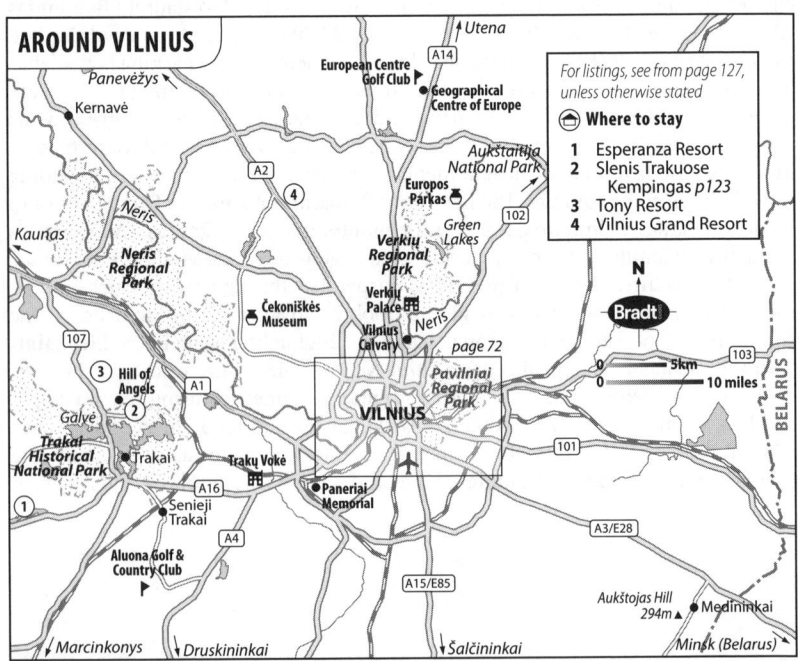

Few international visitors stay longer than a day or explore beyond Trakai town and its island castle, but if time permits you are encouraged to slow down and discover more of the park; perhaps have a sunset barbecue on a lakeshore, take to the water in a kayak or rowing boat, or enjoy a local hike. The park is best explored by car as public transport is limited. If you are dependent on public transport, Trakai will be your main stop.

**TRAKAI** Trakai is a small historical town stretching along a thin peninsula and surrounded by the four interconnecting lakes of Galvė, Skaistis, Luka and Totoriškių. This tiny resort at the heart of Trakai Historical National Park welcomes over a million visitors each year to stroll the streets lined with wooden houses, traverse the bridges to the island castle, browse the souvenir stalls and try the local delicacy, *kibinai*. The island castle, along with the peninsula castle, was once a military stronghold defending the Grand Duchy of Lithuania; now it is a national symbol of independent Lithuania and one of the most visited monuments in the country.

Spending a day in Trakai offers enough time to explore the iconic castle and picturesque town, capture it all on camera and enjoy a local snack. There is much to keep you longer in the national park, including countryside resorts, hiking and outdoor activities, water sports, golf courses and cultural heritage sites. In winter, the crowds are gone and the cold arrives. Snow blankets the castle turrets, the lake freezes and ice-fishing replaces the rowing boats and pedaloes. Cosy cafés remain open alongside the hardiest of souvenir sellers.

### Getting there and around
***By train and bus*** Regular buses and trains run between Vilnius and Trakai every day. Both take about 40 minutes. You can pre-purchase tickets and check schedules for the trains (w bilietas.ltglink.lt/en) and buses (w autobusubilietai.lt/en) via their respective websites. Alternatively, tickets can be bought in person at the Vilnius train and bus station ticket offices, or directly from the bus driver and train conductor. Train is usually the more comfortable way to travel.

Upon arrival in Trakai it is a 30–40-minute walk from the train station (Vilniaus gatvė 5) or 20–30 minutes from the bus station (Vytauto gatvė 90) to the main sights. The walk into Trakai centre can be via the lakeshore (slightly longer) or through the town along Vytauto gatvė. Local taxis (including Bolt) often circle the stations and should cost about €3 to the centre. At weekends and daily during the summer months there is a shuttle bus service from the bus and train stations to Trakai centre. The schedule can be checked at w trakai-visit.lt.

As always, check the return train or bus timetable before getting immersed in sightseeing, or it will be an expensive taxi back to Vilnius centre. Note that Trakai train station is not staffed and tickets can be purchased from the conductor on the train. Amenities at the train station are limited to a vending machine, while the brand-new bus station incorporates shared facilities with a Rimi supermarket.

***By car*** Leave Vilnius city centre on Savanorių prospektas, following signs for the A1 (E85) highway heading west. Take the A4 highway in the direction of Druskininkai, then the A16 (E28) towards Trakai. Driving time is approximately 30–50 minutes depending on traffic.

There are numerous **parking** places around Trakai town in designated car parks and on the street. Parking is priced in zones, the most expensive being closest to the centre at €2.50 per hour. Note that you will need cash for parking machines or be able to pay by mobile phone app. Parking is at a premium during the peak summer months, weekends and festivals, so public transport is recommended at those times. If you do drive, make use of local entrepreneurs waving you into their gardens to park under their apple trees. They will have a P sign at the entrance to the property and will charge a fixed fee for the day. You will need to pay in cash and be sure to ask for a cash receipt as proof of payment.

**By taxi** It is possible to take a taxi or Uber/Bolt from Vilnius for approximately €20–40 one way but beware that you may struggle to get one back to Vilnius.

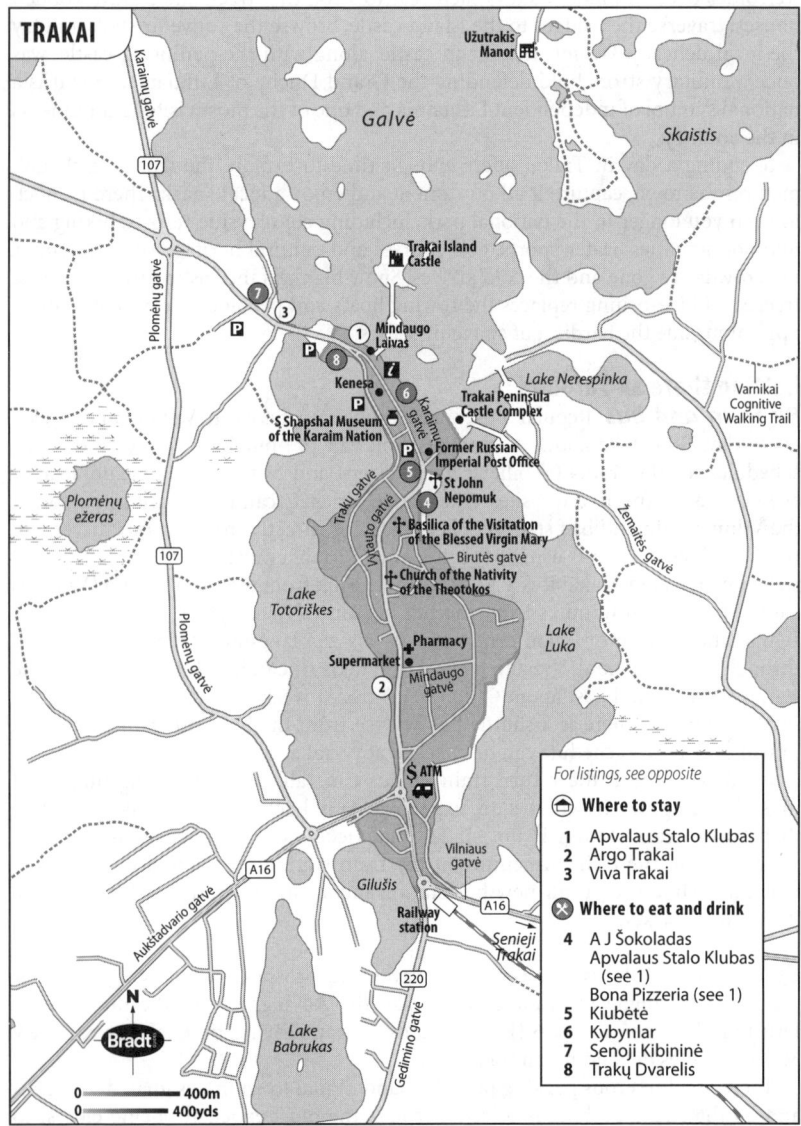

> **FESTIVALS AND FAIRS**
>
> Trakai's festivals include the popular **Trakai Summer Festival** in late May/early June, and also **Žolinės** (Virgin Mary Assumption Day; 15 Aug) when the **Kopūstinė Fair** (Cabbage Fair) takes place on the island of Kopūstinė, which lies in between the two pedestrian bridges across to the castle. In ancient times, the local Karaite population grew cabbages (*kopūstai*) to be harvested and sold at the fair. These days, the Cabbage Fair is a local farmers' and craft market. For further information about Trakai festivals and fairs, visit w trakai-visit.lt.

**Tourist information** The **Trakai Tourism Information Centre** (Karaimų gatvė 41; w trakai-visit.lt; ⏱ May–Sep 09.00–18.00 daily, reduced hours off-season) should be your first stop for local advice, recommendations and tourist literature. Staff can also help with booking local activities and guided tours. Check their website for details of the festivals and regattas held in Trakai throughout the year.

From the information centre, head down to the waterfront, where in the warmer months you will find cafés, souvenir stalls, pedaloes to hire and lots of people promenading along the lakeshore admiring the view across the water to the island castle. Walk beyond the main tourist area for a quieter viewpoint.

## 🏠 Where to stay  *Map, opposite, unless otherwise stated*

In the centre of Trakai and throughout the national park there are numerous self-catering apartments and holiday homes to rent. Standards vary and you should do your research carefully before choosing. See our section on countryside tourism (page 59) for further guidance. There are limited options for camping in Trakai.

**Argo Trakai** (6 rooms) Vytauto gatvė 89; w argo-trakai.lt. Each apartment is individually styled & all have access to the small spa area. The restaurant is well known for its Georgian cuisine. €€€

**Apvalaus Stalo Klubas** (17 rooms) Karaimų gatvė 53A; w asklubas.lt. A French-boutique-style hotel with picture-perfect views of Trakai Castle, a Moroccan spa, terrace restaurant & lakeside location. Choose from economy & standard rooms or luxurious suites. €€€

**Viva Trakai** (4 rooms) Galvės gatvė 1; w vivatrakai.lt. Overlooking Trakai Castle is this small guesthouse, with private sauna available to hire. It's popular for private functions, so you may get caught up in some celebrating, especially if staying over a w/end. €€

**Slenis Trakuose Kempingas** [map, page 120] Slėnio gatvė 1; w slenistrakuose.lt. A lakeside resort located on the northern shore of Lake Galvė directly over the water from Trakai town, this is Trakai's only official campsite. It has space for up to 88 campervans, basic WC/shower facilities, Wi-Fi & a private beach; tent pitches available. 7km from Trakai bus station. Book in advance. €

## 🍴 Where to eat and drink  *Map, opposite*

**Apvalaus Stalo Klubas** See above; ⏱ 15.00–21.00 Wed–Thu, 13.00–21.00 Fri, 13.00–22.00 Sat, 13.00–19.00 Sun, closed Mon–Tue. Housed in the hotel of the same name, their fine dining restaurant serves modern Lithuanian cuisine & was Michelin-recommended in 2024. Note that their tasting menu is not available May–Sep. The location is perfect for dining with a view of the castle & lake, but the exquisitely presented food will be competing for your attention. The terrace is a very popular option in good weather. Advance booking for the restaurant is recommended. €€€€€

✴ **Bona Pizzeria** Part of the Apvalaus Stalo Klubas complex (see above); ⏱ noon–18.00 Tue–Thu, 10.00–21.00 Sat, 10.00–18.00 Sun. This is Apvalaus Stalo Klubas's simple & family-friendly option for a relaxed meal of brunch or gourmet pizzas, overlooking the castle & lake. Take-away kibinai available. €€€

**Kybynlar** Karaimų gatvė 29; w kybynlar.lt; ⏲ 11.00–21.00 Sun–Thu, 11.00–20.00 Fri–Sat. An authentic, traditional Karaite kitchen welcomes you for kibinai & main dishes. Kibinai-making workshops are available for groups if booked in advance. €€€

**A J Šokoladas** Vytauto gatvė 4; w ajsokoladas.lt; ⏲ 10.00–20.00 Mon–Sun. Cakes & chocolates for those with a sweet tooth & a small chocolate sculpture museum for the curious. €€

✳ **Kiubėtė** Trakų gatvė 2D; w kiubete.lt; ⏲ 10.30–22.00 daily. Kiubėtė is ideally located for buying a snack or lunch between the town centre & bus or train station. An alternative to kibinai are their very filling savoury pies. €€

**Senoji Kibininė** Karaimų gatvė 65; w kibinas.lt; ⏲ 10.00–22.00 daily. Enjoy traditional, authentic kibinai & meals in a historic Karaite building, or, if you prefer flat over filled pastry, go for pizza in their new Kibininė Pica next door. They also have a fast-food Kibin Drive on the A1 motorway between Vilnius & Kaunas, should you need another pastry fix on the way home. €€

**Trakų Dvarelis** Karaimų gatvė 54A; w trakudvarelis.lt; ⏲ 11.00–20.00 Sun–Thu, 11.00–22.00 Fri–Sat. Kibinai of course, but they also have a more varied menu, including chicken Kyiv & pancakes at reasonable prices. €€

**Sports and activities** Alongside sightseeing, there is much to keep you entertained in and around Trakai. The nearby **Varnikai Cognitive Walking Trail** (Varnikų pažintinis takas; w trakai-visit.lt/en/varnikai-cognitive-walking-way) is a 5km ecotourism path through ancient woods, meadows and the Ilgelis swamp with rest stops and viewpoints along the way. Bicycle hire is not available locally, but if you bring your bike to Trakai, please note that the **cycling** infrastructure is basic and you should be prepared to cycle on some roads. The 7.5km route round to Užutrakis Manor is popular, returning the same way.

An abundance of **water sports** is available on the surrounding lakes. Local company **Wet Weim** (w wetweim.com) arranges canoeing around Trakai with transfers from Vilnius. **GoSUP** (w gosup.lt) rents paddleboards by the hour at Trakai and offers guided sessions including an atmospheric night tour. An array of whacky vessels can be rented from **Mindaugo Laivai** (w mindaugolaivai.lt), and traditional rowing boats and pedaloes are available to hire along the lakeshore. If you prefer to sit back and relax, **Baltis** (w baltis.lt) offers regular 45-minute cruises around Lake Galvė.

For something special, take a **flight** over Trakai for a birds-eye view of the landscape either by hot-air balloon, helicopter, small plane or glider with a local provider (w trakai-visit.lt/en/flight-over-trakai).

**Other practicalities** You'll find a supermarket, pharmacy and an ATM along Vytauto gatvė, between the train and bus stations and the centre.

**What to see and do** Sightseeing in Trakai starts soon after passing the shops on your walk into town from the train or bus station. Immediately on your right after Maironio gatvė is the Orthodox **Church of the Nativity of the Theotokos** (Švč. Dievo Motinos Gimimo cerkvė), which was funded by Russian Tsarina Maria Aleksandrovna in 1863. Set among the low wooden houses of Birutės gatvė is the **Basilica of the Visitation of the Blessed Virgin Mary** (Švč. Mergelės Marijos Apsilankymo bazilika), a Baroque beacon of worship towering over the surrounding residential area. The Old Town street of Karaimų gatvė begins at the shrine of **St John Nepomuk** (Šv. Jono Nepomuko koplytstulpis), a 14th-century Czech priest who was killed by King Vaclav for not revealing the Queen's confessions. Hands bound, he was thrown from Charles Bridge into the Vltava River in Prague in 1393 and became known as the defender of the confession. He was canonised in 1729. It was the Jesuits who introduced Nepomuk to Trakai in the 18th century and made him the patron saint of the town. Continuing, on your right is the bold blue **Former Russian Imperial Post Office** (Buvęs Rusijos imperijos pašto pastatas), built in 1810 in a traditional wooden style with grand entrance porch columns that imply importance. It is now home to the Trakai Historical National Park administration.

***Trakai Peninsula Castle Complex*** Once part of a mighty defensive system and residence of the Grand Dukes of Lithuania, the Trakai Peninsula Castle Complex

> **THE KARAITES**
>
> The Lithuanian Karaites are an ethnic group of Turkish origin. Their ancestors are believed to be from the oldest Turkish tribes – the Kipchaks – originating from the Byzantine Empire and later the Crimean Peninsula. In the late 14th century, Lithuanian Grand Duke Vytautas returned from a successful military campaign in Crimea accompanied by several hundred Karaite families. Legend has it that he was so impressed with the brave Karaite warriors that he offered them land and a new life in return for their defence of his castle against Crusader attacks. Evidence suggests that there was a special respect between the Grand Duchy and the Karaite people because their community was granted an unusual freedom to practise their own religion and to govern their own affairs. The middle island between the mainland and the castle island is called Karaimka Island, and in 1994 an oak statue of Grand Duke Vytautas was erected there to immortalise his memory.
>
> The community settled in Trakai along the street that is now known as **Karaimų gatvė**. Their **colourful wooden houses** each have three windows overlooking the street, representing 'the worship of God, loyalty to the Grand Duke and that guests are always welcome'.
>
> At Karaimų gatvė 22 is the **S Shapshal Museum of the Karaim Nation** (**w** trakaimuziejus.lt; ⊕ 10.00–18.00 Wed–Sun; €8/4) with displays about the Karaites' history, customs and everyday life.
>
> Unlike the Karaites in Israel, Lithuanian Karaites do not view themselves as Jews, but as an independent religious community. As a result, the Karaites were spared the tragic fate of the Lithuanian Jews in World War II. The Karaim religion (Karaism) is based on the Old Testament and hinges on the ten commandments. Worship is conducted in the local **kenesa** (Karaimų gatvė 30). The original 14th-century kenesa was destroyed and rebuilt several times; the building you see today was constructed in the 19th century. Visitors are not allowed inside.
>
> One of the most enduring legacies of Karaite culture in Trakai is the *kybyn* (plural *kybynlar*) in Karaite, or *kibinas* (plural *kibinai*) in Lithuanian. Kibinai are traditional Karaite pastries filled with juicy mutton and onion, very similar to a British Cornish pasty. They are widely available in Trakai restaurants and these days veggie, vegan or gluten-free options are available. In several of the kibinai restaurants in Trakai you can book a **kibinai workshop** to make (and eat) your own creations. Wash your kibinai down with the traditional Karaim national drink, *krupnik* – guaranteed to warm you up on a cold day and remind you of Christmas (spices and cloves galore).
>
> Although the Lithuanian Karaite community is now greatly reduced in numbers and at risk of disappearing altogether, their culinary heritage is ingrained in Trakai culture.

endured an unsavoury bunch of occupiers over the years – high-profile prisoners and enemies of Lithuania, a police court during the Russian Empire, the German Gestapo during World War II and the KGB in the post-war years. The **Trakai History Museum** (Trakų Istorijos Muziejus; Kęstučio gatvė 4; w trakaimuziejus.lt; ⊕ 10.00–18.00 Wed–Sun; €8/4) is housed in a renovated building of the original castle complex. Few visitors allow enough time to come here on a day trip, naturally gravitating towards Trakai Island Castle first. For those who do, the main attraction is a **Sacral Art Exhibition** of church heritage and ecclesiastical objects in the surviving chapel. In 1779 the Dominicans began to build a church within the castle complex, but a lack of funding resulted in construction stopping at ground-floor level and plans were reworked to build a monastery and chapel instead. The remaining buildings are used by the castle administration or are undergoing renovation. Also within the complex is **Sacrifice Hill**, a 17m-high hill fort and the highest point of the peninsula, offering excellent views. Its name derives from the sacrificial pagan ceremonies that are believed to have taken place here.

*Trakai Island Castle* (Trakų salos pilis; w trakaimuziejus.lt; ⊕ May–Sep 10.00–19.00 daily, Oct–Nov & Mar–Apr 10.00–18.00 Tue–Sun, Dec–Feb 10.00–18.00 Wed–Sun; €12/6) Trakai Island Castle is the jewel in the crown of Trakai Historical National Park. Majestically isolated amid the waters of Lake Galvė, visitors are enticed to cross the wooden bridges and explore. Built in the 14th century by Grand Duke Kestutis and finished by his son and heir Grand Duke Vytautas, Trakai Island Castle was a strategic fortress intended to protect the seat of the Grand Duchy of Lithuania against invaders. It is said that every man coming to Trakai had to bring a stone the size of a sheep's head or larger to contribute to the castle's construction. From the shoreline the castle silhouette is magnificent and would have made any marauder think twice about attacking.

The castle was heavily damaged during the Russian invasion of 1655 and was left to ruin for centuries. Bizarrely, extensive renovation works took place under the auspices of the Soviet authorities between 1951 and 1962 during the occupation. This was a cultural coup for Lithuania, to restore a significant symbol of Lithuanian statehood and national heritage using Soviet money under the guise of it being a 'monument of victory over Nazi Germany'. Comments about the quality of the Soviet-era workmanship do abound. You can clearly distinguish between the renovated brickwork and authentic stonework.

The layout inside the island castle is unusual, with a large open courtyard area within the outer castle walls. Along the western side of the courtyard are former residential quarters now housing eclectic displays of historical artefacts. Exiting the courtyard across a short bridge you enter a detached tall keep that contains the Great Hall, the Treasury and extensive rooms of historical exhibitions connected by narrow passageways and staircases. The Treasury has some fine examples of 'Lithuanian long currency', a stick of silver that was marked and cut into smaller values, the first form of coinage. It is interesting to note the lack of a fireplace in the Great Hall – instead, hot water pipes were laid down to create a (surprising) example of early underfloor heating. The Grand Dukes were ahead of their time.

*Užutrakis Manor* (Užutrakio dvaras; Užtrakio gatvė 17; w uzutrakiodvaras.lt; ⊕ 11.00–19.00 Wed–Sun; €4/2) Known locally as the 'white swan of Lake Galvė', Užutrakis Manor was built by the prominent Tiškevičius family at the beginning of the 20th century. It was a luxurious residence, and Count and Countess Tiškevičius hosted many visiting dignitaries, who always arrived by water. Road access was reserved for agricultural purposes, the route becoming known as 'the potato road' due to the constant deliveries to the large distillery on the manor farm.

It is one of the best-preserved manor houses in Lithuania, which is quite a feat having been nationalised under Soviet occupation and repurposed as a sanatorium, pioneer camp and tourist base. The manor was severely damaged and the surrounding parkland abandoned, but successful restoration continues and visitors can take a guided tour of the interior between May and September, or explore the park estate year-round on foot or by bike. During July and August, evening concerts of classical music are held at Užutrakis Manor (for details, see f Muzikos festivalis „Užutrakio vakarai").

Today, Užutrakis welcomes visitors to arrive by water on organised boat tours of the lake (request stop), or by car via 'the potato road'. Both ways offer stunning views of Trakai Island Castle. Visitors coming by car should stop en route at the **Hill of Angels** (Angelų kalva; free), an open space dotted with finely crafted sculptures of angels and sun-crosses. Established in 2009 to honour Lithuania's 1,000th anniversary, the site has become a spiritual place for many and you are invited to find and embrace the Angel of Kindness.

***Senieji Trakai (Old Trakai)*** According to legend, in the early 14th century, Grand Duke Gediminas was hunting in the area when he happened upon a hill surrounded

## RESORTS AROUND VILNIUS   Map, page 120

Ideal for those who want to stay outside of the city centre, or to extend a city break with some nature or leisure activities, these resorts welcome international guests with good facilities and comfortable standards.

**Vilnius Grand Resort** (240 rooms) Ežeraičių gatvė 2, off the A2 highway 19km north of Vilnius centre; w vilniusgrandresort.com. This luxury resort is very popular for functions, but also for tourists who want a base outside the city centre & a free shuttle bus every 20mins to take them the 19km into town. The complex is vast, with a selection of rooms from standard to presidential suite in both classic & contemporary styles. Guests will not get bored with a choice of restaurants & bars, lounge areas, use of the V Spa & Wellness Centre, & an 18-hole golf course. Ideal for people wanting Vilnius plus spa treatments, a round of golf, or space for the family just 25mins' drive from the capital. €€€€€

**Esperanza Resort** Ungurių gatvė, Paunguriai village; w esperanzaresort.lt. Undergoing reconstruction at the time of writing, but due to open in late spring 2025. A luxury lakeside resort with hotel & cabin accommodation, spa centre & saunas. Popular for weddings, parties & families at w/ends. 15mins' drive from Trakai centre & 50mins from Vilnius. €€€€

**Tony Resort** Anupriškių gatvė, Gratiškės village; w tonyresort.lt. Hidden away in the forest is this small holiday resort featuring accommodation dotted among the pine trees in 2 VIP apartments, 8 family-friendly shingle-clad 2-storey chalets, while 16 standard & 20 economy dbl rooms are available in the main building, along with the restaurant where b/fast is served. The grounds extend to the shore of Lake Gilušis, where amenities include boat rental, volleyball, beach, sauna, tennis, walking trails & bike hire. Winter sports are also available. Day visitors are welcome (€7 per adult). 15mins' drive from & 40mins from Vilnius. €€€

by oak trees. Inspired by the strategic and spiritual location, he instructed a castle to be built and named it Trakai, derived from the word 'trakas' meaning 'a glade in the forest'. The surrounding ditch provided a useful moat and the castle was accessed by drawbridge. For seven years, the castle and surrounding small town of characteristic two-windowed houses were capital of the Grand Duchy of Lithuania. After being usurped by Vilnius after Gedminas's prophetic Iron Wolf dream, Trakai became the capital of the Duchy of Trakai. In 1391 during a battle with the Teutonic Order, the castle was largely destroyed, and never rebuilt. The construction of Naujoji Trakai (New Trakai) on Lake Galvė stole the attention, importance and name from what today is called Senieji Trakai (Old Trakai). The castle-less hilltop is now home to a Neo-Gothic church and monastery rebuilt at the turn of the 19th century. The surrounding monastery buildings are occupied by an order of nuns, but you can visit the church to admire its striking façade and interior sculptures. Externally is a wayside shrine of the Virgin Mary and baby Jesus, the first of nine similar shrines installed along the **Vytautas the Great Road** which extends between Senieji Trakai and Trakai. The dedicated route of shrines was opened in 2000 to commemorate the 570th anniversary of the death of Grand Duke Vytautas, each shrine depicting an important aspect of the Grand Duke's life.

Buses run between Trakai and Senieji Trakai, but bear in mind they run early morning and late afternoon to service people commuting for work. A Bolt ride costing about €4 one way could be more convenient.

## TRAKŲ VOKĖ

In the town of Trakų Vokė, the beautifully restored former palace and landscaped gardens of the noble Tiškevičius family, **Trakų Vokė Manor** (Trakų Vokės dvaro sodyba; Žalioji alėja 2A; ￼ TrakuVokesDvaroSodyba; ⊕ 11.00–19.00 Thu–Fri, 11.00–17.00 Sat, 11.00–15.00 Sun; €5/3), attracts day-trippers, newlyweds on photoshoots and international film crews (it has starred in recent productions of *Catherine the Great*, *Anna Karenina* and *War and Peace*). Built in the late 19th century by Count Jonas Tiškevičius (1831–92), the palace is authentic although damage and theft during wartime left it bare and bereft of the luxurious furnishings and antiques that once filled the rooms. Today the palace hosts exhibitions, concerts and events. The park was designed by landscape architect Eduard André; its layout and many of the deciduous trees that line the park's avenues are original. Picnicking in the grounds is popular and a café is open at weekends. The palace is 15km from Vilnius, parking is close to the eye-catching Red Gate entrance and free of charge.

Take bus 51 from Vilnius to Pagiriai and alight at Eduardo Andrė gatvė in Trakų Vokė. Alternatively, take the Vilnius–Marcinkonys, Vilnius–Trakai or Vilnius–Kaunas train and alight at Vokė station, from where it is a 15-minute walk through the park including crossing a monkey bridge.

## PANERIAI

Between 1941 and 1944, some 50,000–70,000 people were killed at Paneriai. Most of them were Jews from the Vilnius region, but the victims also included Lithuanians, Poles and members of the Roma community – all executed by the Nazis. The forest of Paneriai (also known as Ponar) lies adjacent to the railway line and had recently been developed by the occupying Soviet army for the building of ammunitions warehouses and fuel depots. When the Germans arrived in June 1941, they repurposed the unfinished fuel pits into execution pits for mass murder.

The **Visitors Information Centre of the Paneriai Memorial** (Agrastų gatvė 15, Paneriai; w jmuseum.lt/en/paneriai-memorial; ⊕ Jun–Sep 09.00–17.00 Tue–Thu & Sun, 09.00–16.00 Fri, Oct–May by appointment only; free) was updated in 2018 providing a more informative visit to the site, although the opening hours are rather unreliable. It is managed by the Vilna Gaon State Jewish Museum and the exhibits, which include a sieve used to search for gold in the ashes of victims, heighten an already emotional experience. While the visitor centre has specific opening times, the memorial site is always open. Set within the peaceful forest are several monuments, and the pits where victims were executed and their bodies burned.

Paneriai is 12km south of Vilnius. To visit by car, leave Vilnius via Švitrigailos gatvė, then Dariaus ir Girėno gatvė, turning right at the overhead sign for Eišiškių plentas. Follow Eišiškių plentas until turning right at the brown sign for Panerių memorialas. Turn right at Baltosios Vokės gatvė, then left at Memorialo gatvė (the train tracks are immediately ahead of you). The road ends at the car park. If using public transport, train is the most straightforward option with departures roughly every hour from Vilnius. After alighting at Paneriai, cross the pedestrian bridge, turn right and walk approximately 1km along Memorialo gatvė with the tracks on your right.

## KERNAVĖ

Kernavė is a pleasant small town, dominated by the cultural reserve and museum. As you approach the reserve entrance you pass the imposing red brick **Virgin Mary of the Scapular Church** (Svc. Mergeles Marijos Skaplierines baznycia) built on the site of a 15th-century wooden church between 1910 and 1920 and funded by Lithuanian Americans. There is very little local infrastructure catering to tourists, but if you are looking for a coffee, snack or lunch, try **Kernavės slėnis** (Vilniaus gatvė 14b; f Kernaves.Slenis; ⊕ May–Nov noon–19.30 Sat–Sun; €€).

Bus services to Kernavė are quite limited but with careful planning it is possible. Take the Vilnius–Kernavė or Vilnius–Širvintos (alight at Kernavė) bus, but be aware that buses are more frequent in the first part of the day and late afternoon for commuters; there are only two buses a day at weekends. Ensure you know your return bus time before heading off to explore, or it will be an expensive Bolt ride back to Vilnius.

### WHAT TO SEE AND DO
**Kernavė State Cultural Reserve** (Kernavės valstybinis kultūrinis rezervatas; Kerniaus gatvė; w kernave.lt; ⊕ always open; free) Kernavė is an ancient archaeological site of profound importance to Lithuanian history. The five mounds overlooking the Neris River and picturesque Pajauta Valley were fortified settlements known as hillforts. Named after Duke Kernius, who founded Kernavė as the first capital of the Grand Duchy of Lithuania in c1040, it became a key political and cultural centre, the heart of pagan Lithuania, and remains a symbol of statehood. First mentioned in 1279 in the Livonian Chronicle written by Catholic priest Hermann von Wartberge, Kernavė flourished during the 13th and 14th centuries. But archaeological excavations are testament to human settlements being present here since the Late Paleolithic period (9000BC), the finds of which are on display in the museum. Evidence of sacred sites, rituals, burial grounds and early Baltic civilisation has been profuse and to date only 2% of the area has been excavated.

In 1989 the state cultural reserve was established to exhibit historical and archaeological finds, conduct scientific research and preserve the site. In 2004, Kernavė State Cultural Reserve was declared a UNESCO World Heritage Site, meeting two

> ### KERNAVĖ ARCHAEOLOGICAL DAYS
>
> Kernavė Archaeological Days (w kernave.lt/festival) are held annually in early July. They bring hustle and bustle to the reserve when medieval-style craftspeople, traders, musicians, artists and re-enactment teams set up a traditional camp around the open-air village. Apart from ever-present smart phones, the scene is quite authentic, with professional medieval festivalgoers bringing their wares, crafts and skills to showcase to visitors. They appear truly happy to embrace living in an ancient era. Of course you can buy their goods, and they accept euros rather than gold coins; some will even produce a card payment machine out of their smock. It's a surreal atmosphere to wander among warriors, while kids play barefoot, pots boil on open fires, herbs are crushed, silver hammered, leather stretched, and lutes strummed.

official criteria: 'an exceptional testimony to the evolution of human settlements in the Baltic region over the period of some ten millennia. The property has exceptional evidence of pantheistic and Christian funeral traditions' and 'the settlement patterns and the impressive hillforts represent outstanding examples of the development of such types of structures and the history of their use in the pre-Christian era'.

Footpaths and wooden steps make the steep-sloped mounds accessible for exploring. These natural castle mounds were formed by glaciers and the ideal place to build a fort atop – easy to defend and to keep watch from. Lithuania has approximately 1,000 hillforts and is one of the most hillfort-populated countries in the world! Within the reserve is also the **open-air museum** (⊕ same as archaeological museum; free; see below), a reconstruction of 13th and 14th century huts, streets and yards, similar to those that housed the craftspeople, merchants and warriors whose artefacts have been excavated on site. The tiny wooden **Kernavė chapel** was built in the early 19th century and is a rare example of an octagonal folkloric chapel.

**Kernavė Archaeological Site Museum** (Kernavės archeologinės vietovės muziejus; Kerniaus gatvė 4A; w kernave.lt; ⊕ Apr–Oct 10.00–17.00 Tue, 10.00–18.00 Wed–Sun; €4/2; free on the last Sun of the month) Supporting the Kernavė State Cultural Reserve is this well-presented museum which brings ancient archaeological finds to a 21st-century audience. Here you can see the finds from painstakingly precise excavations, artefacts from the Stone Age to the Middle Ages are innovatively presented and multi-media screens make the history engaging to all ages. A variety of events, performances and festivals are held at Kernavė throughout the year bring the site alive while connecting with its past. Attending traditional celebrations such as Midsummer (Rasos) is special, but logistically you need your own transport so you can decide whether you stay for an hour just to witness, or all night to experience.

## NERIS REGIONAL PARK

The largest regional park that is easily reached from Vilnius, Neris Regional Park encompasses the meandering loops of the Neris River and surrounding mixed woodlands, wetlands and meadows. Numerous marked hiking trails and cognitive walking paths make the area very accessible, with kayaking tours and cycling routes also available. Of note is the 2.3km **Oak Wood of Dūkštas Cognitive Trail** (Dūkštos pažintinis takas), a circular route through one of the largest and oldest oak forests in Lithuania – listen out for the tapping of green woodpeckers and chirping song of European fire-bellied toads, and visit the Airėnai Stone to decode its ancient runes. If you are looking for more active recreation, local activity provider Adventure Academy (Nuotykių akademija; w nuotykiuakademija.lt) arranges seasonal activities including guided hiking, kayaking and husky rides.

### GOLF COURSES IN LITHUANIA

Golf is a relatively new sport for Lithuania and steadily growing in popularity. The landscape lends itself well to rolling fairways interspersed with woodland and water courses. Expect courses to be closed during winter months as play is not allowed after frost or in minus temperatures.

**Aluona Golf & Country Club** Ežeriuko gatvė, Anglininkai village; aluonagolf. A 9-hole golf course, 43km southwest of Vilnius in Trakai region. Par 31 with predominantly open terrain, good for beginners, no luxuries, & open to all via pay-and-play. Book in advance.

**Capitals Golf Club** Sostinių golfo klubas; Vingio gatvė 90, Pipiriškiai village; w capitals.lt. Located 50km from Vilnius, Capitals is named in honour of its location being almost equidistant between the 4 historical capitals of Lithuania – Vilnius, Kaunas, Kernavė & Trakai. Where grand dukes & nobles once hunted for game, now everyone has access to play golf here. The first professional 18-hole course in Lithuania (€65, par 72), it was designed by course architect Peter Chamberlain & features 8 lakes & 67 bunkers. Accommodation (€€€) is available in the clubhouse including 4 dbl rooms & a quad for families.

**European Centre Golf Club** Europos centro golfo klubas; Golfo gatvė 20, Girijos village; w golfclub.lt. An easy drive 28km north of Vilnius & located next to the Geographical Centre of Europe, this 18-hole course (€60, par 71) was designed by a team of Swedish specialists & suits both beginners & professional players. There's also a driving range & clubhouse, & they host tournaments & a summer golf academy for kids.

Indoor golf simulators are available in the centre of Vilnius at their **Indoor Golf & Sports Lounge** [82 A2] (Saltoniškių gatvė 9).

**National Golf Resort** (Golfo klubas 'National'; Tvenkinių gatvė 30, Stančiai village; w nationalgolf.lt) 17km north of Klaipėda, this championship 18-hole course (par 72) opened in 2009. Green fees depend on the season (high season May–Sep €79, low season Oct–Apr €50). There is accommodation €€€ on site for up to 56 guests & additional activities include Padel tennis, footgolf & fishing.

**The V Golf Club** (Vilnius Grand Resort, Ežeraičių gatvė 2, Vilnius; w vilniusgrandresort.com/en/golf. Part of the Vilnius Grand Resort complex (page 127), since 2019 this 18-hole course (€60, par 72) has been a certified CPG Pro-Am & EGA European Team Amateur Men's & Women's Championship course. Facilities include a driving range, putting green, clubhouse, shop & restaurant.

**Wolf Golf Club** (Vilkės golfo klubas; Vilkės gatvė 26, Kamorūnai village; w dzukijosgolfas.lt) An internationally recognised 18-hole Scottish links golf course (€60, par 72) with natural obstacles & sand bunkers, this is the most challenging course in Lithuania, though it welcomes everyone from beginner to professional. 130km from Vilnius; 20km northwest of Druskininkai.

The enthusiastic team at the **Neries Regional Park Visitor Centre** (Neries regioninio parko lankytojų centras; Vilniaus gatvė 3, Dūkštos; w neriesparkas.lt; ⊕ 09.00–18.00 Tue–Fri, 10.00–15.00 Sat) will answer your questions, show you the exhibition, and load you up with all the information you need to explore the hiking trails and tourist routes. Be sure to buy your voluntary state park visitor ticket here for €1; they have locally produced ecological herbal teas, spices, honey, linen and crafts for sale too.

Neris Regional Park is a 30-minute drive from Vilnius, and there is no denying that having a car makes the sights more accessible. It is possible to access the park by train via the Vilnius–Kaunas service, alighting at Lazdėnai station, from here you can cycle or walk along the well-signposted 25km circular **Neris River left bank tourist route**. If you do drive, a quaint stop on the way to or from Vilnius is the **Čekoniškės Museum** (Čekoniškių kaimo verbų ir buities seklyčia; A Mickevičiaus gatvė 179, Čekoniškės village). Don't expect English to be spoken or to spend long, but it is a short-but-sweet insight into rural heritage and always good to support a local museum.

## NORTH OF VILNIUS

**THE GEOGRAPHICAL CENTRE OF EUROPE** (Europos geografinis centras; Golfo gatvė 6, Girijos village; ◧ europos_geografinis_centras; ⊕ always open; free) From Estonia to Ukraine, several places claim to be the geographical centre of Europe, each determined by a different definition of the border of Europe and the accuracy of scientific knowledge and techniques available at the time. Lithuania's geographical centre of Europe was claimed in 1989 when the French National Geographic Institute included the method of gravity centres in their measurements. Their calculations were based on the geometric characteristics of the European continent contours and its ratio to the Earth's gravitation. Gone were the days of finding a midpoint on a map. The importance of this site has grown over the years (literally). In 1992, the surrounding area was designated a reserve, in 1997 a 9-tonne boulder was placed on the exact spot, and in 2004 to mark Lithuania's accession to the European Union a tall white granite pillar topped with a star crown, created by sculptor Gediminas Jokūbonis, was erected. Oak trees line the walk from the car park and European flags line the final stretch to the monument. If the wooden cottage visitor centre is open (⊕ times vary), you may be in luck to buy a certificate proving your visit. The surrounding area is of historic interest and includes several ancient pagan burial sites, although modern life pervades in the form of the neighbouring European Centre Golf Club (page 131).

Located 26km from Vilnius, it is possible to get here by bus from the Pramogų arena bus stop. Take bus 130/132/133/137 going to Paberžė and get off at Radžiuliai bus stop. There are about four buses a day. Travel time is about 30 minutes and tickets can be purchased on the bus from the driver.

**EUROPOS PARKAS** (Europos parko gatvė 302, Skirgiškės village; w europosparkas. org; ⊕ 10.00–sunset daily; €12/11) Also known as the Open-Air Museum of the Centre of Europe, Europos Parkas is an open-air sculpture park featuring works of art by international and Lithuanian artists, including Abakanowicz, Oppenheim, LeWitt and Pepper. Founded in 1991 by Lithuanian sculptor Gintaras Karosas, the park now includes more than 90 works of art by artists from over 27 countries scattered amid the gentle hills, ponds and forest clearings. In 2001, the sculpture 'LNK Infotree' was recognised by Guinness World Records as the largest television sculpture in the world. A labyrinth of vintage TVs symbolises the Soviet propaganda that infiltrated homes during the occupation period. Now weather-worn and lichen-rich, their message is still relevant with today's propaganda being delivered largely via screentime. On site there is a restaurant with outdoor terrace and post office shop for souvenirs and toilet facilities. Parking is an additional €2 per vehicle. Download the app to access the audio guide and hear the stories behind the sculptures. Your ticket will give you discounted access to nearby **Liūbavas Mill and Manor** (Liubavo dvaro malūnas; w liubavas.lt), the highlight of which is the watermill exhibition and a stroll around the small estate. You can take bus 66 from Žalgirio bus stop on Verkių gatvė in Vilnius to Europos Parkas. Buses are regular, running almost every hour.

**VERKIŲ REGIONAL PARK** (Verkių regioninio parkas; Žaliųjų Ežerų gatvė 53, on the entrance road to Verkių Palace; w pavilniai-verkiai.lt; ⏱ 08.00–17.00 Mon–Thu, 08.00–15.45 Fri) Beyond the northern suburbs of Vilnius lies Verkių Regional Park, established in 1992 to protect the sacral significance of the Vilnius Calvary, the cultural complexes of Verkių Palace, and the natural assets of the Green Lakes.

The **Vilnius Calvary** (Vilniaus Kalvarijų Kryžiaus kelias; w vilniauskalvarijos.lt/kryziaus-kelias) is a popular pilgrimage route comprising a 7km Way of the Cross with 35 stations of the cross dotted along the way, including 19 stone chapels, seven wooden gates, one stone gate, a wooden bridge and chapel over the Cedronas River, and the **Church of the Discovery of the Holy Cross** (Šv. Kryžiaus Atradimo bažnyčia; Kalvarijų gatvė 329). The latter is one of Lithuania's most important pilgrimage sites being one of the few churches in Vilnius permitted to stay open during Soviet times. The route also passes the **Church of Trinapolis** (Švč. Trejybės bažnyčia; Verkių gatvė 70), a Trinitarian monastery and church ensemble on the banks of the Neris River. (A shorter route of about 2km is called Mažosios Kalvarijos, or Small Calvary.) As you progress along the route, keep in mind that although established in the 17th century with 22 stations of the cross, by 1962 these had all been destroyed. What you see today is wholly reconstructed and protected as an architectural monument of national significance. To start your own Vilnius 'Way of the Cross' take bus 1G from Vilnius railway station or V Kudirkos aikštė direction 'Santariškės' and alight at Kalavarijos bus stop.

**Verkių Palace** (Verkių rūmai; Žaliųjų ežerų gatvė 49; w verkiai.lt/en; ⏱ 08.00–16.30 Mon–Sat; entry to the palace is only available to prebooked groups & for private events) is one of the most valuable examples of Classicist architecture in Lithuania, and you may hear it referred to as the Versailles of Vilnius – be aware that this is an exaggeration and a half. As charming as Verkių is, it should be judged on its own merits, of which there are many. The restored Wittgenstein interiors can be toured, and cultural events and music performances are often held in the luxurious reception rooms. Wedding receptions are very popular here due to the photogenic backdrop both inside the palace and in the manicured grounds, with celebrations in summer held on the Verkiai restoranas terrace. For individual tourists, a picnic in the park is a popular option, but if you forgot your sandwiches there is a restaurant, Vandens Malūnas (Verkiu Watermill; ⓕ verkiuvandensmalunas; €€€) in the grounds. The historic watermill restaurant serves up traditional dishes of culinary heritage – a cosy pub in the winter and lush terrace in summer. For those in Vilnius over midsummer, celebrations are usually good in the Verkių Palace grounds.

The **Green Lakes** (Žalieji ežerai) are in the north of Verkiu Regional Park, easily accessible from Vilnius city centre by buses 36, 65, 66 and 76 (get off at Verkių Riešė bus stop, then it is a short walk to the lakes). Six lakes are nestled in the forest, all of which are an unusual bright-green colour due to the high mineral concentration of the water. Formed by glaciers carving their way across the landscape, the lakes are up to 40m deep and their sides steep. Lake Balsys is the largest and the best equipped with plenty of facilities for recreation. The well-managed beach is one of the most popular beaches for swimming in Vilnius, which explains the parking carnage that can occur on a hot summer weekend (take the bus). There are barbecue grill places, beach volleyball nets, boat rental, paddleboards, an outdoor café, ice cream for sale, and many kilometres of hiking and biking trails. Nearby to the bus stop on the main road is an Iki supermarket if you need extra provisions.

## MEDININKAI

It takes a more curious visitor to venture east from Vilnius. Most tourists have busy itineraries exploring the main sites around the capital and do not consider taking to the main E28 road, direction Minsk, Belarus. Just 30km drive from Vilnius city centre and 2km before the border with Belarus is the town of Medininkai, located on one of the oldest trade routes in Lithuania and now the eastern frontier of the European Union and NATO. There is a small shop in Medininkai itself and a petrol station close to the Medininkai Memorial, but otherwise no amenities for food and drink, so plan your visit between meals or bring a picnic.

### WHAT TO SEE AND DO
**Medininkai Castle** (Medininkų pilis; Šv. Kazimiero gatvė 2; w trakaimuziejus. lt/en/medininku_pilis; ⊕ 10.00–18.00 Wed–Sun; €8/4) Medininkai Castle was built in the 14th century as a defensive enclosure castle, protecting the important trade route between Vilnius and the eastern regions of the Grand Duchy. You can understand the strategic choice of location when admiring the panoramic view from the tower observation deck, but perhaps we are more sensitive to this today because of its proximity to the Belarus border and current geopolitics. During the 16th century the castle's importance declined, and it was abandoned and left to deteriorate to the point of ruin. Now partially restored, one of the four original towers has been reconstructed and houses displays of weaponry and archaeological finds relating to the medieval Grand Duchy of Lithuania. The huge internal courtyard is enclosed by the 2m-thick, 15m-high defensive wall and often hosts cultural events, including the annual medieval extravaganza Medininkai Castle Games, held on the last weekend of September.

**Medininkai Holy Trinity Catholic Church** (Švč. Trejybės ir Šv. Kazimiero bažnyčia; Šv. Kazimiero gatvė 4) Although the current church was only constructed in 1931, Medininkai was one of the first parishes established in Lithuania during the 14th century. The charming wooden church is serviced by Franciscan monks, the first of whom was Father Kamil Wielemanski in 1961 when returning from Soviet exile. The modest green wooden house next door is the monastery. With a large part of the local population identifying as Polish (notice the street names in Polish and Lithuanian), Mass is held in Polish and is relayed outside by loudspeaker.

**Medininkai Memorial** (Medininkų memorialas; E28 road, just before the Belarus border) You will sense when you are getting close to the border, as a multitude of signs begin to appear alongside lane markings, and perhaps a line of trucks, although the amount of traffic crossing the border has severely reduced since Russia's illegal invasion of Ukraine and sanctions have been imposed on

### A TALE OF TWO HILLS

You would be forgiven for not realising you were in the Medininkai Highlands here – it is a rather subtle elevated area. However, a 5-minute drive (or 35-minute walk) from Medininkai Castle is Juozapinė Hill (Juozapinės kalnas), for a long time officially recognised as the highest point in Lithuania at 292.83m. In 2004, the local elevation was remeasured using new GPS technology, bringing bad news for Juozapinė Hill. It was discovered that, 500m away, Aukštojas Hill (Aukštojo kalnas) stood at a whopping 293.84m. Now Juozapinė Hill is the third highest hill, knocked from second position by the remeasuring of unassuming Kruopinė Hill (293.65m) 10km away. Juozapinė Hill has a monument to King Mindaugas on its summit, perhaps a consolatory prize to soothe its bruised ego. Meanwhile, Aukštojas Hill lays claim to the title and was rewarded with new attractions including an observation tower, information board, and sculpture installation called the Balt's Sun Circle symbolising an ancient pagan altar.

Russia and their close ally Belarus. Do not be concerned; visiting the memorial is a legitimate reason to be here. Do not join a queue, rather skip these and continue past the petrol station on your left and look out for the brown tourist sign on the right side of the road. If you are stopped, explain you are going to the memorial (*memorialas*). The memorial is in a layby marked with flags, but the kerb is severe and you should park on the roadside. What has become known as the Medininkai Massacre occurred here in the early hours of 31 July 1991. Members of the OMON unit of the Soviet special police killed seven Lithuanian customs and border guard officers while on duty at the border checkpoint with Belarus. Another customs officer sustained severe wounds but survived. At the time, Lithuania was a newly independent state and bolstering its borders to secure its territory. Acts of intimidation and violence from a disgruntled Moscow were commonplace, but this attack was the most severe and tragic. As with all harassment and aggression from Russia, it strengthened the Lithuanian resolve to defend its independence. The memorial consists of seven crosses dedicated to the victims and the checkpoint building is preserved under a protective glass shelter.

# 5

# Dzūkija

Dzūkija, also known historically as Dainava, is officially one of the five ethnographic regions of Lithuania and encompasses a much larger area than this chapter covers. Our Dzūkija focusses on the lands of southeastern Lithuania where the Dzūkija heritage is strongest. A densely forested region with sandy soils, its unsuitability for large-scale agriculture has preserved old wooden villages, forests and wetlands, diverse habitats and ancient traditions. The draw of Dzūkija is cultural heritage and nature, whether you experience it foraging, hiking, kayaking, birdwatching or cycling. Lithuania's best mushrooms come from Dzūkija region. In fact, mushrooming is a pastime so popular there is even a word for 'inadvertently getting lost in the forest while mushrooming', *nugrybauti*. More forms of recreation are found in the spa resort of Druskininkai, where pampering and medical procedures go hand in hand, and cultural events abound in honour of their favourite son M K Čiurlionis. Small villages and towns offer worthy sights including the lesser-known Museum of Freedom Fights in Lazdijai and really off-the-beaten-track experiences like a visit to eastern Dzūkija and the so-called appendix of Dieveniškės. Over the centuries, southern Lithuania has been the frontline borderland for warfare and hostilities;

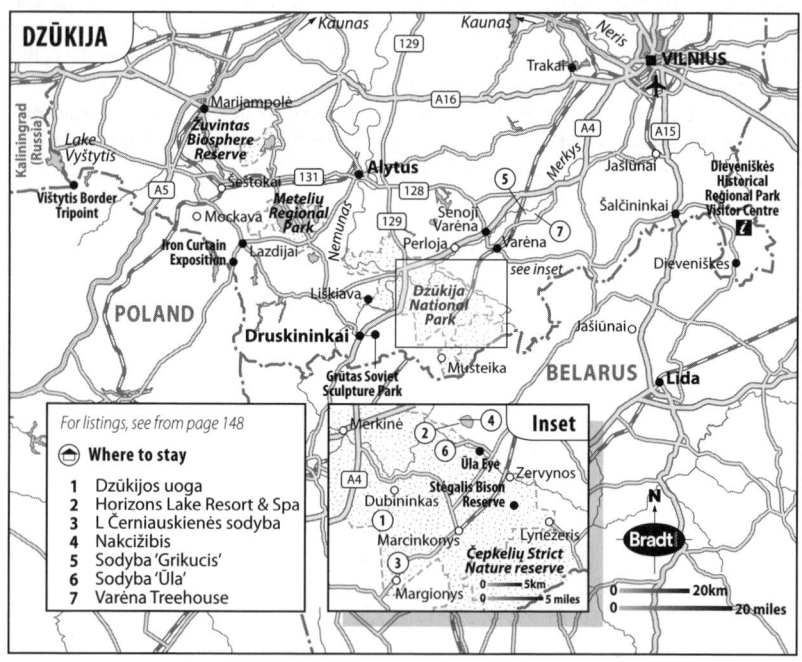

the Grand Duchy of Lithuania and the Teutonic Order, the Russian Empire and Prussia, the USSR and Poland, and today the area of Lithuania and Poland known as the Suwałki Gap is sandwiched between the Russian exclave of Kaliningrad and Belarus. Throughout the border area are remnants of these turbulent times, including old pill boxes and border posts, memorials and graves, and a section of the former Iron Curtain.

## DRUSKININKAI

The oldest health resort in Lithuania is faithful to its roots, still providing curative mud and mineral water treatments whether for relaxation or recuperation. The name Druskininkai is derived from the Lithuanian word *druska* meaning salt, a clear reference to the salty mineral water upon which the town is built. Surrounded by forest and the Nemunas River, laid out generously with wide avenues and landscaped parks, the leafy-green resort is spacious enough to absorb the influx of visitors during the summer season. The main attractions are centred around the pedestrian avenue of Vilniaus alėja, many of which are geared towards families drawn to Druskininkai for the Aquapark, Snow Arena and outdoor recreation. Beyond here you will find high-end wellness spa hotels, peaceful hiking trails, and some curious sights. If you like your comforts, base yourself in Druskininkai and explore the Dzūkija region on day trips.

**HISTORY** Locals were aware of the healing properties of their local salty water long before it became a marketable asset. People noticed sores on their feet healed quicker after wading in certain springs along the Nemunas, springs that were spouting mineral-rich water from 300m deep. News about the healing waters of Druskininkai reached the court of the Grand Dukes and, after examination of the waters by the court doctor, Druskininkai was proclaimed a healing place in 1794. In 1837, Tsar Nicholas I commissioned the first treatment facility known as the Tsar's Hospital, attracting nobles and cultural figures, followed by the masses, and by the late 1800s Druskininkai was the third most popular resort in the Russian Empire (behind the Crimean Peninsula and Caucasus area). During World War I, Druskininkai was on the Eastern Front for three months; it was the scene of intense fighting, during which an estimated 70% of the city was destroyed. By 1920, the Nemunas River was the border between Lithuania and Poland, and Druskininkai a Polish city until its return to Lithuania in 1940 (albeit into the Lithuanian SSR as Lithuania was then annexed into the Soviet Union). Visitors came to Druskininkai from across the Soviet Union, and vast concrete sanatoriums were constructed quickly to accommodate them; the Baltic states were considered 'western' and so attracted inquisitive tourists.

After independence in 1991, arrivals from the USSR abruptly stopped, throwing the local health and tourism industries into disarray. As domestic tourism stabilised, new privatised hotels were renovated and opportunities for budding entrepreneurs flourished. In 2001, the new Grūtas Soviet Sculpture Park opened, attracting international attention and putting Druskininkai on the global tourism map. Meanwhile, a young enthusiastic mayor called Ričardas Malinauskas (son of Grūtas Soviet Sculpture Park mushroom millionaire Viliumas Malinauskas) had been elected and pushed for a bold new plan to diversify from an old-school resort to a contemporary wellness spa and tourism resort, securing investment to create the Aquapark, Snow Arena and the rope park. Tourism was revived and along with Lithuanians and visitors from neighbouring Latvia and Poland came a handful of international guests.

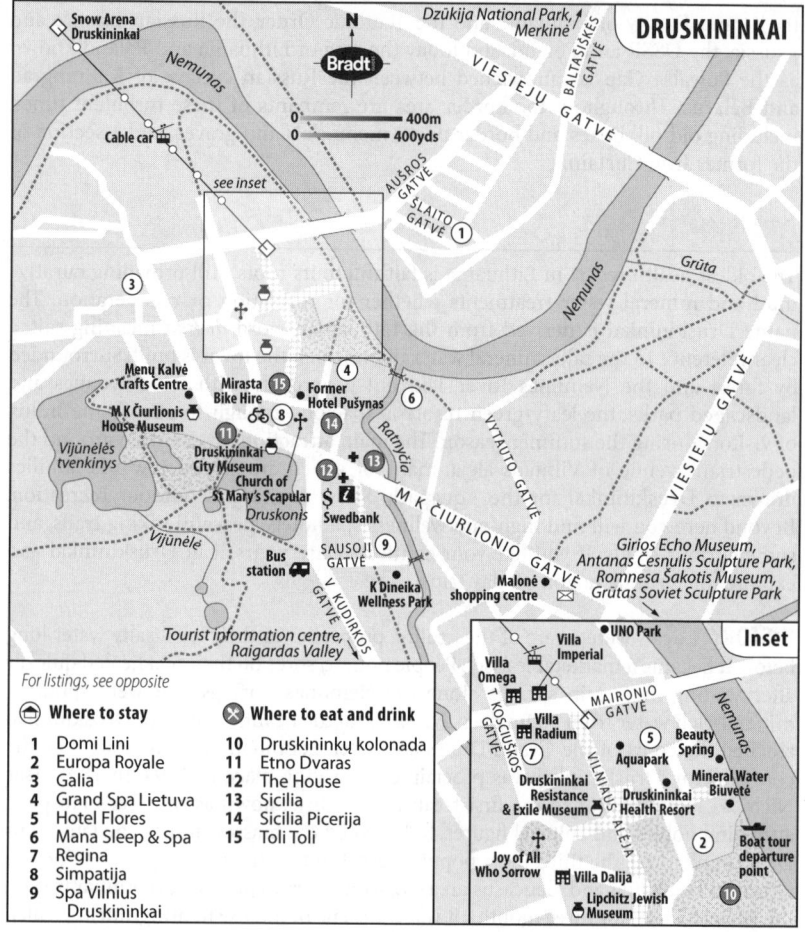

**GETTING THERE AND AROUND** Druskininkai's **bus station** (Druskininkų autobusų parkas; Gardino gatvė 1), in the south of the city centre, is just a 20-minute walk to the Aquapark at the north of the centre. Direct bus services run between Druskininkai and Vilnius (15 times daily; 2hrs 10mins), Kaunas (9 times daily; 2hrs 10mins), Palanga via Klaipėda (twice daily; 6hrs) and Šiauliai (once daily; 5hrs 20mins). Taxis await bus arrivals and the Bolt app is available in town.

There is a good local city bus service connecting the town centre with peripheral parts of town, including to Snow Arena, Grūtas Soviet Sculpture Park and the Raigardas Valley. The latest timetables can be found at w m.stops.lt/druskininkai/#bus/en. Note that the city is leading the way with sustainable public transport and all local buses are electric. Tickets cost €1 one way and can be bought from the driver with cash; from summer 2025, card payments will be accepted too.

**TOURIST INFORMATION** The **central tourist information centre** (Druskininkų turizmo informacijos centras; M K Čiurlionio gatvė 65; w druskininkai.lt; ⊕ 10.00–18.45 Wed–Sun) handles most enquiries for sightseeing, accommodation and booking local guides and activities. There is a second **tourist information centre**

(Druskininkų turizmo ir verslo informacijos centras; Gardino gatvė 3; ⏱ 08.30–17.00 Mon–Fri) on the edge of the city, useful if you are arriving by car or visiting on a Monday or Tuesday, when the central branch is closed.

## WHERE TO STAY  Map, opposite

**Hotel Flores**  (42 rooms) Vilniaus alėja 13-3; w akvapark.lt/en/hotels/flores-hotel. Part of the Aquapark complex, & connected by a glass corridor to that & Druskininkai Health Resort, Hotel Flores is an upmarket, Bali-themed, option for those who want to juggle eastern tranquillity with being in the middle of aquapark fun & a medical centre. You don't have to visit either, but there are special packages with discounted entrance fees & treatments available. €€€€€

❋ **Domi Lini**  (6 apartments) Šlaito gatvė 4; w domilini.lt. These charming self-catering apartments in a quiet residential area are only 10mins' walk from the Aquapark. Sustainability-minded owners Nijolė & Rimas have a background in linen manufacturing, hence the luxurious linen bedding & towels, & 100% green energy & electric car charging at the property. Sauna & BBQ rental available & laundry facilities. Min 2-night stay. €€€€

**Mana Sleep & Spa Hotel**  (79 rooms) Kurorto gatvė 3; w manahotels.lt/druskininkai. The only sleep spa in northern Europe where everything is geared to getting a good night's rest. A minimum 2-night sleep programme could reset your circadian rhythm, sending you home ready for anything. Worst case, it is a pleasant hotel with a spa & smart-beds that track your sleep, or lack of it. €€€€

❋ **Spa Vilnius Druskininkai**  (190 rooms) K Dineikos gatvė 1; w spavilnius.lt. Don't be fooled by the old-school exterior – internally it has been redefined as a luxury wellness spa, planned to perfection for pampering. Guests have access to the spa area & can book extra treatments & procedures for beauty, health & relaxation. Half-board dining is buffet-style, though, which could impede any weight-loss or fitness goals. €€€€

**Europa Royale**  (101 rooms) Vilniaus alėja 7; w europaroyaledruskininkai.lt. This a hotel of 2 parts, one housed in the historic former Tsar's Hospital building from 1894, the other a modern tower-block extension. The carbonic acid baths & therapeutic orthopaedic gymnastics of Tsarist Russia days are long gone, replaced by a contemporary wellness centre. A glass corridor connects the hotel to Druskininkai Health Resort & the Aquapark, making this a good option for families in winter. €€€

**Galia Hotel**  (22 rooms) Dabintos gatvė 3; w galia.lt. A local family-run hotel, Galia's welcoming hosts Agnė & Evgeny are on hand to advise about sightseeing & activities. The 2-bedroom apartments are perfect for families. €€

**Grand Spa Lietuva**  (59 rooms) V Kudirkos gatvė 45; w grandspa.lt. A hybrid of sanatorium & spa hotel, where enemas & urological mud treatments are on offer. Over 100 treatment rooms have a medical & recuperation focus while guests/patients can stay in either of their hotels Lietuva & Druskininkai. Fun can be had in their waterpark. €€€

**Regina Hotel**  (40 rooms) T Kosciuškos gatvė 3; w regina.lt. This cosy, classic hotel in the centre of Druskininkai is ideal for those not in need of the full-blown spa experience, offering a traditional place to rest your head, with a restaurant & summer terrace. Trpl & qrpl rooms for families. €€€

**Simpatija Hotel**  (22 rooms) Vilniaus alėja 2A; w simpatijahotel.lt. Not everyone needs a spa hotel. If you have come to Druskininkai for the nature, history & culture, the Simpatija is a great base. The restaurant Sushi Matters overlooks the Church of Saint Mary's Scapular. Deluxe rooms on the top floor offer sweeping views. €€€

## ✖ WHERE TO EAT AND DRINK  Map, opposite

❋ **The House**  M K Čiurlionio gatvė 61; w thehouse.lt. In the centre of the town, The House is a trendy spot for Lithuanian & international dishes. It's a popular place, too, for lunch or a meal on the pleasant terrace. Remember to ring the bell next to the door when you leave if you enjoyed your meal – very important! €€€€

❋ **Sicilia**  M K Čiurlionio gatvė 56; w sicilia.lt. Lithuanian & Mediterranean restaurant with

an extensive wine menu, & a pleasant terrace for sitting out in summer. Be sure to try their freshly baked bread. €€€€
**Druskininkų kolonada** V Kudirkos gatvė 22; w druskininkukolonada.lt. A cosy restaurant nestled in the old part of Druskininkai in the Nemunas River valley, Kolonada serves a wide range of international cuisine & has live music on Fri & Sat nights. €€€
**Etno Dvaras** M K Čiurlionio gatvė 55; w druskininkudvaras.lt. Lithuanian traditional dishes from all the ethnographic regions of Lithuania are served here. Choose from more than 12 different varieties of Cepelinai, as well as certified culinary heritage dishes. They have their own brewery & serve light, dark & wheat beers. €€€
**Sicilia Picerija** Taikos gatvė 9; w sicilia.lt. The oldest pizza place in Druskininkai opened back in 1998 & is still going strong. Besides pizza you will find a good selection of snacks, salads, soups, pasta & main courses. Take-away pizza service available. €€€
* **Toli Toli** Vilniaus alėja 8; tolitolidruskininkai. This much-loved local restaurant brings a bit of spice to Druskininkai with Middle Eastern flavours & dishes, including vegetarian & vegan options. €€€

**SPORTS AND ACTIVITIES** The array of activities on offer here all year round make Druskininkai a popular family holiday destination. An extensive cycle path network (w druskininkai.lt/en/news/bicycle-paths) surrounds the city with a variety of route lengths incorporating sightseeing and nature. Between May and September, bike hire places pop up across the city. If you prefer an established outlet, visit **Mirasta Bike Hire** (Mirasta dviračiai; Šv. Jokūbo gatvė 3; w dviraciai.mirasta.lt).

A local family business runs **boat tours** along the Nemunas River between Druskininkai and Liškiava village. During the summer months, the *Druskininkai* (V Kudirkos gatvė 22; w gelme-druskininkai.lt; ⊕ May–Oct daily exc Mon; €18/9) departs at 14.30 from Druskininkai dock on the Nemunas River, opposite the Kolonada restaurant. The trip takes 3 hours in total and includes a tour in Liškiava (1h 20mins; entrance to the church basement exhibition incurs an extra charge; page 150).

For sanitoriums and spas, see opposite.

**Aquapark** Druskininkų vandens parkas; Vilniaus alėja; w akvapark.lt/vandens-parkas; ⊕ 10.00–22.00 Sun–Thu, 10.00–23.00 Fri–Sat; €18/9 w/end 2hr session, €13/7 w/day 2hr session, all-day ticket €28/15 (w/end), €19/11 (w/days). The first new attraction to reinvent the resort of Druskininkai, Aquapark has waterslides, waves & a climbing wall, alongside 19 adult-only relaxing bathhouses. Housed in a former Soviet treatment centre, this is the most outlandish concrete building in town, built between 1976 & 1981 in a Brutalist but also rather decorative style (the Former Hotel Pušynas is another unusual example). Tickets are available for 2-, 3- or 4hr slots, or a full day. The bathhouse area of saunas, steam rooms & ice chambers are adult-only & require an additional ticket (€24 w/end 2hr session, €17 w/ day 2hr session). Within the complex is the basic Hotel Aqua (€€), popular with families during w/ ends & holidays when it is most crowded.

**Snow Arena Druskininkai** Nemuno gatvė 2; w snowarena.lt; ⊕ 10.00–19.00 Sun–Thu, 10.00–22.00 Fri–Sat; full-day skiing €31/20) The snow park is half indoors, half outdoors & full of jumps for freestyle skiing, snowboarding & tricks. Open all year round are the main indoor slope (50m wide, 460m long) & the beginners' track (40m wide, 150m long). The outdoor track is open in winter when snowfall & temperature suffice. There is also a snowtubing track, ski instruction, restaurant, café & shop. Professional & national teams train here during summer & autumn. Pay for 2- or 4hr slots, or a full day. W/days are cheaper. Equipment rental is around €18/day for full kit.

**UNO Park** UNO nuotykių parkas; Maironio gatvė 22; w unoparks.lt; ⊕ Apr–Oct; €25/20. UNO is a popular rope park with a selection of difficulty levels suitable for different abilities & age groups. Friendly staff will assist you. Pay extra for the extreme course to whizz over the Nemunas River on a zipwire & complete the 'Elephant Jump'. A fun family activity.

**OTHER PRACTICALITIES** There is a **post office** (M K Čiurlionio gatvė 111) next door to the Malonė shopping centre. Closer to the centre are a **Swedbank** (V Kudirkos gatvė 33) and a group of four **pharmacies** (M K Čiurlionio gatvė 50, 52 & 65) – this is a health resort after all.

### SANATORIUMS AND SPAS

Visitors should be aware of the variety of accommodation and spa experiences available in the resort. Although Druskininkai has successfully reinvented itself as a charming tourism resort with high-end wellness spa hotels perfect for pampering, there are still some throwback experiences to be found and it is important to know this when planning your trip. A **sanatorium** is a resort for recreation with a medical facility for rest and recuperation, often requiring a medical check-up by a doctor at the beginning and end of your stay. In the Soviet Union in the early 1920s a Labour Code was introduced, guaranteeing all workers at least two weeks of annual leave to be taken at a state sanatorium for health benefits. After all, it was in the Communist Party's interest to keep the workforce fit and strong. The collapse of the Soviet Union saw many sanatoriums abandoned, but some survived and continue to thrive to this day. Some are more renovated than others, but all retain a focus on national health patients who have been prescribed treatments or rehabilitation.

It can be quite an experience to visit a sanatorium, but it is best done planned rather than by error, and perhaps just for a day. A sanatorium mud bath can be fun – clinical rather than pampering, but memorable (I'll never forget having mud and moss hosed off by a nurse, firefighter-style, in a sterile cubical). These experiences are gradually being gentrified, driven by revenue and Scandi-chic interior designers being brought in to repackage health treatments in a contemporary wellness image, but they can still be found. For those with genuine ailments who require value-for-money private treatment, Druskininkai is proving a popular medical tourism destination. For those who are visiting for pampering and wellness, choose wisely and you will be in for a real treat.

**Druskininkai Health Resort** (Druskininkų Gydykla; Vilniaus alėja 11; w akvapark.lt/gydykla/druskininku-gydykla; ⏰ 08.00–18.00 Mon–Thu, 08.00–20.00 Fri–Sat, 08.00–17.00 Sun) is the beating heart of the town's spa treatments, its iconic green spa building housing 23 mud-bath and 18 mineral-bath cubicles, treatment pools, salt chambers and corridors of closed doors behind which lie equipment for procedures that may make you feel a bit uncomfortable. If you are staying in self-catering accommodation or a smaller hotel, you are likely to go here for your treatments and should book in advance to guarantee availability. The staff are experienced and professional, and prices competitive.

Several **medical spas** cater more to national health treatments, and international tourists should be aware of these unless they are visiting for specific treatments; at Medical Spa Eglės Sanatorium and Draugystės Sanatorium, expect intestinal showers and electro mud therapy rather than scented candles and ambient music.

At the other end of the spectrum are the high-end **wellness spa hotels** where you can be pampered to your heart's content.

## WHAT TO SEE AND DO
**Druskininkai City Museum** (Druskininkų miesto muziejus; M K Čiurlionio gatvė 59; w druskininkumuziejus.lt; ⊕ 10.00–18.00 daily; €5/3) The history of Druskininkai flows through the rooms of the city museum, housed in the picturesque and prominent Neoclassical Villa Linksma (meaning 'joy'). In the Russian Empire rooms is a rare surviving glass, as old as the city of St Petersburg and used only by kings; it belonged to Augustus the Strong, who proved his strength to Peter the Great at the end of the 16th century. Photographs of radon treatment give you the shudders, along with stories about therapeutic *kumis* (fermented horse milk). The actor Charles Bronson's grandfather was born in a village close by and was a kumis farmer. The interwar years saw the advent of sun parks and nudity areas for the full body tan, the history of which is well covered (or not) in a room dedicated to that era. Exhibits are labelled in English and guided tours are available. On the top floor of the museum is a huge collection of salt cellars, over 2,000 objects from more than 42 countries (take one along to donate if you plan to visit!).

**✷ M K Čiurlionis House Museum** (M K Čiurlionio namai-muziejus; M K Čiurlionio gatvė 35; w ciurlionis.lt; ⊕ 11.00–18.00 Tue–Sat, 11.00–16.00 Sun; €5/2.50) The M K Čiurlionis House Museum is a quaint complex comprising four wooden houses, two of which were owned by the Čiurlionis family. Theirs was a musical household, renowned for their concerts; crowds would sit outside under lilac and apple trees while music drifted through the open windows. It was a simpler time and a highly influential one for Mikalojus Konstantinas, who was just three years old when the family moved here in 1878. The paintings exhibited in the museum are all reproductions; the originals are in the M K Čiurlionis National Museum of Art in Kaunas (page 187). The house includes authentic exhibits thanks to the efforts of Čiurlionis' sisters Valerija and Jadvyga, who preserved Čiurlionis' piano and harmonium among many other family pieces. Bringing Čiurlionis' work into the 21st century is the highly recommended 'Angelų takais' virtual reality experience, which must be booked in advance at an additional €15 per person. An English-speaking guide can be booked for €25 per party.

**Menų Kalvė Crafts Centre** (Druskininkų amatų centras Menų Kalvė; M K Čiurlionio gatvė 27; w acmenukalve.lt; ⊕ 10.00–18.00 Tue–Sat; free) This arts and crafts centre has nine open workshops where you can meet the artists and watch their creations take shape. Crafts include stained glass, designer clothing, silk painting, jewellery making, painting and leather smithing. This active community art incubator runs educational classes, hosts exhibitions and sells handmade artworks in the small shop.

**Joy of All Who Sorrow Church** (Dievo Motinos ikonos 'Visų liūdinčiųjų Džiaugsmas' cerkvė; Laisvės aikštė 1; w cerkov-druskininkai.org; ⊕ service held 09.00 Mon–Sat, 10.00 Sun) Known to visitors and locals alike as the Blue Orthodox Church, this attractive wooden building is all the more striking owing to its isolated location in the centre of the large diamond-shaped Laisvės square. Built in 1865 under the initiative of the deputy governor of Grodno to provide a place of worship for visiting Orthodox holidaymakers, it continues to service the small Orthodox community today. Peek inside to see the wooden carved iconostasis that was brought from Moscow and the icons painted by Moscow masters.

> **WOODEN ARCHITECTURE**
>
> One of the first buildings in Druskininkai to be erected under the auspices of the Russian Empire was the wooden **Joy of All Who Sorrow Church**, otherwise known as the Blue Orthodox Church, on Laisvės alėja (see opposite). It was soon followed by decadent wooden villas built for aristocratic holidaymakers. Frequent fires destroyed many wooden villas, but several fine examples of this period still stand today, though some await investment and improvement. It is a laborious and costly task to renovate a wooden villa, each piece needing to be removed and labelled, restored or replaced, then rebuilt like a huge Lego project. **Villa Dalija** (Laisvės aikštė 21) lies opposite the Orthodox church; it is also known as Villa Maurė (Moorish villa) on account of its design which features latticework arches and ornamental carvings. **Villa Radium** (T Kosciuškos gatvė 7) takes its name from the chemical element, perhaps a nod to its time as the resort's central laboratory during Soviet times. This should not detract from the villa's romantic features reminiscent of wealthy nobles' country estates. Neighbouring villas **Omega** (Maironio gatvė 14) and **Imperial** (Maironio gatvė 16) are overwhelmingly Imperial in style, with grand turrets and detailed fretwork. Until recent years, Villa Imperial housed the popular Širdelė, a famous café that remained unchanged for many decades offering nostalgia, cheap beer and big portions. It was perhaps not in keeping with the health resort ethos, but is missed by many.

**Cable car** (Lynų kelias; Vilniaus alėja 13; w lynukelias.lt; ⊕ 10.00–18.45 Sun–Thu, 10.00–21.45 Fri–Sat; €5.50/4 one way, €2 extra return) The only cable car in Lithuania runs between the Aquapark and Snow Arena. Just over 1km in length and taking 7½ minutes each way, it rises 52m over the Nemunas River and offers scenic views of the resort – a novelty way to travel between attractions, and an eco-friendly transport option. If you don't return on the cable car, there is a cycling and walking path back to the town centre (distance is 3km).

**Druskininkai Resistance and Exile Museum** (Inside the Druskininkai Cultural Centre, Vilniaus alėja 24; w olkm.lt/en/druskininkai-museum; ⊕ 08.00–17.00 Mon–Thu, 08.00–15.45 Fri; free) This small but important museum was set up by former exiles and political prisoners to commemorate and educate about Lithuania's resistance to occupation. Exhibits focus on the brave partisan fighters of the resistance and the deportation of Lithuanians to Siberia. Renovations are planned and the museum will reopen in 2026 with a new look and improved information available in English.

**Beauty Spring** (Grožio šaltinis; on the river path south of the Aquapark) Opened in 1955, this 326m-deep well releases water previously trapped between layers of early Triassic period rock. This water has had some serious steeping down there; one litre of water holds 54g of mineral deposits. This is the saltiest spring in town and you must not drink the water. However, if you wash your hands and face with it, there are purported beneficial properties although it should probably come with a disclaimer that beauty cannot be guaranteed – unless it is in the eye of the beholder. This water is used in therapeutic procedures across the resort.

**Mineral Water Biuvetė** (Mineralinio vandens biuvetė; Vilniaus alėja 9H) Mineral Water Biuvetė's charming yellow building tempts you in, and colourful rays of light stream through the stained-glass windows which represent the famous Lithuanian fairytale *Eglė Žalčių karalienė* (*Eglė, Queen of the Grass Snakes*; page 286). From the depths below, the mushroom-shaped fountain spews curative fresh mineral water which must be sampled – though temper your enthusiasm by recalling why Druskininkai got its name, *druska* (salt). Two different mineral waters can be tried: 'Druskininkai' with 7.06g of mineralisation per litre; and 'Aušra', a lighter version with 2.67g per litre.

**Vijūnėlė Park** (Vijūnėlės parkas; Turistų gatvė 1) Situated between Lake Druskonis and Vijūnėlės tvenkinys (pond) the landscaped park merges with the surrounding forest, full of smooth, winding paths perfect for walking, cycling or trying out the electric scooter rental. Available on the water are rental canoes, pedaloes and paddleboards; meanwhile children are kept busy on the playgrounds. Follow the winding path into the forest to the Old City Cemetery (Druskininkų miesto senosios kapinės), where Lithuanian, Polish and Belarusian graves lie among the wildflowers, or snow depending on the season. The park is host to the annual Daffodil Festival when in late April more than 1 million narcissi bulbs bloom and provide a spectacular sight.

**Former Hotel Pušynas** (Taikos gatvė 13) This is one of the best examples of Socialist-Modernist architecture in Druskininkai (along with the Aquapark building). Built to house the Sūrutis Sanatorium during Soviet times, it was designed in the likeness of a giant pinecone. It is now undergoing reconstruction and, although it will keep its architectural heritage, it will shake off its Socialist past and be transformed into exclusive apartments.

**Lipchitz Jewish Museum** (Žako Lipšico žydų muziejus; Šv. Jokūbo gatvė 17; w museum.lt/lipsicas) Jacques Lipchitz (1891–1973) was a world-famous Lithuanian sculptor of Jewish origin and born in Druskininkai. He lived in exile abroad for most of his life but would always introduce himself as 'I am a sculptor from Lithuania', even when Lithuania was not on the world map having been absorbed into the USSR. A museum has been housed in this charming wooden villa since 1996, but it is currently under renovation and scheduled to reopen in 2026. The renovated museum will present exhibitions about Lipchitz's life and works as a Cubist sculptor, and about Druskininkai's Jewish community and history. At the end of the 19th century about half of Druskininkai's population was Jewish. In August 1942, Druskininkai's 800 remaining Jews were deported to Grodno, Belarus and within weeks were murdered at Treblinka death camp in Poland.

**Church of Saint Mary's Scapular** (Švč. Mergelės Marijos Škaplierinės bažnyčia; Vilniaus alėja 1; w druskininkuparapija.lt; ⏱ services held 18.00 Mon–Fri, 10.00 Sat, 09.00 & noon Sun) This handsome red-brick late Neo-Gothic church (built between 1911 & 1931) sits in Druskininkai's vast main square, surrounded by trees. During the summer of 1915, the church bells were removed and taken deep into Russia by the Tsarist authorities, a strategic move to prevent the Germans melting them down for military purposes. A treasure still resident in the church is a very rare relic of Saint Valentine: a small piece of the saint's bone is kept in a reliquary for all to see or touch. Not only is Saint Valentine revered for love in Lithuania but he also patronises beekeepers, who are held in high regard especially in Dzūkija region.

**K Dineika Wellness Park** (K Dineikos sveikatingumo parkas; Sausoji gatvė 1; f KarolioDineikosParkas; ⏰ park all year round, facilities May–Sep noon–20.00 Thu–Sun; adult €10) This large park was established at the end of the 19th century when fresh air, sun and exercise were deemed vital for good health. It was reorganised in 1952 by Lithuanian psychologist Karolis Dineika to include a water cascade in the Ratnyčėlė River and a bathhouse with sauna, sunbathing areas, walking paths, hammocks, tennis courts and playgrounds – this is a place of relaxation, meditation and active recreation. Everything is planned to maximise wellness.

**Girios Echo Museum** (Girios Aidas Muziejus; M K Čiurlionio gatvė 116; f Girios-Aidas/1439457563004356; ⏰ 10.00–17.00 Wed–Sun; free) In 1972, forester Algirdas Valavičius created this fairytale wooden museum to showcase forestry to the public. Full of tools, carvings and educational displays about the flora and fauna of the Lithuanian forests, the museum's exhibits cover the different varieties of trees, tales about bird (and bat) ringing, and how the conservation team delicately write on dragonfly wings to identify them. Little information is in English, but the interior is still worth a snoop. With advance warning, they could source an English-speaking guide. The surrounding park is well worth a visit and always open, featuring several ethnographic buildings, wooden sculptures, bird boxes (hung on branches so as not to damage the tree) and hiking trails.

### AROUND DRUSKININKAI
**Grūtas Soviet Sculpture Park** (Grūto Parkas; Grūtas village; w grutoparkas. lt; ⏰ Jan–Feb 09.00–18.00 daily, Mar–Apr 09.00–20.00 daily, May 09.00–21.00 daily, Jun–Aug 09.00–22.00 daily, Sep 09.00–20.00 daily, Oct 09.00–19.00 daily, Nov–Dec 09.00–17.00 daily; €15/10) In the immediate aftermath of the collapse of the USSR and restoration of Lithuanian independence, ideological Soviet statues and monuments were eagerly dismantled across the country. Removal was undertaken by the city and town maintenance teams using their trucks and cranes. Some statues remained intact, some were damaged or defaced, others were melted down by enterprising types; but most lay forgotten about in the maintenance yards for years as the nation navigated the turbulent 1990s. During a period of privatisation, the question arose – what to do with these old statues lying in our yards? It was not straightforward: though they may have been pulled from their plinths, they remained on the official state registers as cultural monuments. A political dispute ensued: Are they art or propaganda? Should they be preserved or destroyed? In 1998 the Ministry of Culture announced a tender for initiatives to present these statues in a public arena. Dzūkija-based mushroom millionaire Viliumas Malinauskas won the tender with his proposal to exhibit the statues in their own gulag environment. Grūtas Park was officially opened on 1 April 2001. The intention is to showcase the negative impact of the Soviet system, to educate visitors and younger generations about the cruel imposition of Soviet ideology on the Lithuanian nation. A 2km path takes you through the exposition of statues with guard towers and fragments of deportation camps resembling a Siberian gulag. The main museum collection is housed in the information centre and is full of Soviet memorabilia, propaganda and pseudo-science, which was all engineered to control the occupied nation economically, politically and psychologically. An audio guide, highly recommended, can be hired for €10 and tells the stories behind the statues and exhibits. The café serves traditional dishes and some throwback Soviet cuisine to make you appreciate modern cooking; mushrooms are prevalent of course. Ignore the mini zoo and playground which is not so appealing.

Grūtas Park is 7km north of Druskininkai on the A4 road and well signposted. You can cycle or hike there from Druskininkai on the Žilvinas cycling/hiking trail (8km each way). Public buses 2A, 2B and 2C run daily up to twice an hour; a one-way ticket costs €1 and can be purchased from the driver in cash. The bus stop is in the museum car park.

**Romnesa Šakotis Museum** (Romnesa Šakočių muziejus; Vienkiemių gatvė 3, Jaskonys village; w romnesa.lt/druskininkai; ⊕ Oct–Apr 10.00–17.00 daily, May–Sep 10.00–20.00 daily; €2) *Šakotis* are celebration cakes, perfect for sharing, and for centuries have been baked over open fires on a constantly turning spit which is spoon-fed an eggy batter for many hours until fully cooked. As it cooks, the batter drips and hardens, forming spikes and giving the šakotis its trademark conical shape, earning its other name of 'tree cake'. You can easily spot someone going to a party as they manhandle their šakotis into the car. Baking šakotis is a form of cultural heritage requiring specialist equipment and skill, and the museum – which was opened in May 2015 in conjunction with baking the largest šakotis ever made (3.72m tall and weighing almost 86kg), setting a new Guiness World Record – holds educational workshops making šakotis and other traditional Lithuanian dishes.

The museum is a 4-minute drive from Druskininkai, or a 5km hike or cycle ride along the 'Saulės takas' route to Latežeris. Hourly buses 3B and 3C from Druskininkai stop nearby. The popular Romnesa restaurant is next door for refreshment or a hearty meal.

**✻ Antanas Česnulis Sculpture Park** (Antano Česnulio skulptūrų parkas; Naujasodės gatvė 16, Jaskonys village; w cesnuliusodyba.lt; ⊕ 09.00–21.00 daily; €6/4) A unique sculpture park dedicated to the works of folk artist Antanas Česnulis (b1948), this national treasure is in essence Antanas' garden, where he has let his creative talent loose on a huge scale. A graduate of the National M K Čiurlionis School of Art, he focused on folk art, and during Soviet times his wood carvings were included in many projects including at Witches Hill on the Curonian Spit, the Hill of Crosses, and along the Čiurlionis Road. Antanas' garden is a deep dive into Lithuanian folklore, heritage and crafts. His statues all have a story, best told by Antanas himself. Some installations are weathered or primitive, but others feature movement and music – all are full of symbolism. The charming full-size windmill was constructed by Antanas, and he even handmade the machinery in the mill yard due to a lack of available options. Directions are the same for Romnesa Šakotis Museum as they are only 800m apart.

**Raigardas Valley** (Raigardo slėnis) With Lithuania being a relatively flat country, any ancient geomorphological features be they valleys, lakes or hills have been explained by folklore and, according to legend, many moons ago there was a wealthy city called Raigardas here. The citizens flaunted their wealth and overindulged, which angered Perkunas, the god of thunder, causing him to destroy the city. It collapsed and vanished into the ground taking its citizens with it, creating a deep valley – the salty waters of nearby Druskininkai are the tears of those who were lost. The large Devil's Stone at the valley's edge near Švendubrė is said to block the exit from the underworld.

Nowadays Raigardas, on the Belarus border, is a popular hiking and biking destination. While parking used to be difficult due to trucks queuing to leave Lithuania for Belarus, since the border has been closed it is much quieter. When you are close to the border crossing point, notice the abandoned bicycles and cars.

You can't cross the border on foot, so people left bikes chained to the trees to cycle across the border and then get in their car or hitch a lift on the other side. Since this is border territory – border zones are clearly marked by signs on the trees – it is a legal obligation to have your identity papers (passport or national identity card) on you at all times. You may be asked for these by the border police and asked about your intentions in the area.

The 12km 'Žvaigždžių orbita' cycling and hiking trail from Druskininkai will lead you to Raigardas Valley and nearby Švendubrės village. To visit Raigardas by bus from Druskininkai, take service 5A, 5B, 5C or 5D which depart every hour daily.

## DZŪKIJA NATIONAL PARK

Dzūkija National Park is the largest national park in Lithuania and over 91% of it is forested, mainly with pines. It was established in 1991 to conserve the nature, culture and heritage of the region and to encourage sustainable tourism. Thanks to the region's dense forest and sandy soils, the Soviets could not establish collective farms here, and so its historic wooden farmsteads and traditional villages were preserved. Life in Dzūkija has always been closely connected with the forest: it is one of the country's best mushrooming regions (everyone is free to come and mushroom) and the unique tradition of hollow-tree beekeeping is practised here. The forests played a vital role during Soviet occupation when they became home to thousands of resistance fighters – today, if hiking in the forest, you are likely to come across a former partisan bunker, grave or memorial cross. The star of the show here is nature. People come to unwind, to walk in the woods, kayak on the rivers, to berry pick and birdwatch. Locals aim to keep traditions alive through heritage and crafts projects, ensuring younger generations learn the necessary skills. Subsistence farming continues in villages for both aging locals who have known nothing else, and young families escaping the city and looking for a more wholesome lifestyle in the region – they are the new custodians of traditional Lithuania. While the rural population dwindles, a sense of community is essential; and where they once shared a horse, they now share a car. The historic regional name of Dainava translates as 'land of songs', a worthy name for a region rich in folk-singing traditions. The essence of this was captured beautifully in the independent film *Land of Songs* (2015; w landofsongs.com); it is rarely screened but the online trailer is enough to open your heart to the role of singing in a rural community. Village singing and dance ensembles alongside traditional crafts continue to knit the communities together. The landscape is shared with wholesome named wildlife such as woodlarks, stock doves and European honey buzzards. For visitors, Dzūkija National Park is full of opportunity to experience nature and authentic rural life. The infrastructure is basic (you are advised to bring a picnic) but that is the beauty of this area. Most visitors make no greater demand on the area than to kayak, hike or cycle in nature.

**GETTING THERE AND AROUND** To explore the Dzūkija National Park in depth you need access to a car – it is the only way to cover the distance and reach far-flung sights, especially if time is limited. Visiting by public transport requires a slow-travel approach which is no bad thing.

Intercity **buses** travel from Vilnius and Kaunas to Merkinė (1hr 30mins), also from Druskininkai to Merkinė (30mins) or Varėna (1hr 6mins). Buses will transport bicycles and the national park offers several cycling routes. Merkinė is

25km from Marcinkonys. A direct **train** service from Vilnius to Marcinkonys (1hr 30min) works well for day trips (page 152).

**TOURIST INFORMATION** There are two **visitor centres** for Dzūkija National Park, in Marcinkonys and Merkinė. Each has an exhibition (€2/1). If you are touring the national park area, you can purchase a day ticket (€5/2.50) for entrance to both visitor centres, the Dzūkija Ethnographic Homestead and Drevinės Beekeeping Museum. You are encouraged to make the voluntary donation of €1 and buy a State Park Visitor Ticket (page 6). Both visitor centres sell the necessary permits for kayaking and angling within the national park.

**Marcinkonys** Miškininkų gatvė 61; **w** dnp.lrv.lt; 09.00–17.00 Tue–Fri, 09.00–16.00 Sat. A central hub for exploring the national park. Visit for the flora & fauna exhibition, tourist information, & hiking & cycling route maps. They offer basic accommodation for groups, activity booking & specialist guide services.

**Merkinė** Vilniaus gatvė 3; Dzukijos.Nacionalinis.Parkas; 08.00–17.00 Tue–Fri, 09.00–16.00 Sat. For tourist information covering Merkinė & the Dzūkija region.

**ACTIVITIES** The three main rivers for **kayaking** are the Ūla, Grūda and Merkys. The scenic Ūla River valley is very popular and quotas have been introduced to manage how many people are on the river each day. To kayak on the Ūla with your own craft you need to purchase a permit from one of the Dzūkija National Park visitor centres. The permit is included if you rent a kayak locally. To avoid busy times,

### DZŪKIJA FARMSTEADS    Map, page 136

There's not much Lithuanians like doing more than escaping into the nature, grilling šašlykai, taking a sauna then plunging into the lake, or foraging for berries and mushrooms in the forest. To experience the lifestyle, you need good accommodation. In Dzūkija National Park this is predominantly in the form of rural tourism farmsteads, the majority of which will have self-catering holiday **houses** to rent on their private land. Self-contained holiday house rentals are becoming more available as people buy second homes and rent them out. Rates vary, but in general school holidays and weekends are more expensive. Here are some of the best:

**Horizons Lake Resort & Spa** (4 cabins) Lavysas, southwest of Varėna; **w** horizons.lt. A new generation of rural accommodation bringing contemporary luxury to the wilds of Lithuania – along with a wellness spa on site. €€€€€
**Nakcižibis** (9 cabins) Lavysas, southwest of Varėna; **w** nakcizibis.lt. On the shore of the now-prestigious Lake Lavysas, this modern resort of 2-storey contemporary wooden cabins has access to the sandy lakeshore. Canoe rental available. €€€€
**Varėna Treehouse** (6 treehouses) Šilo gatvė 4, Mielupiai, northwest of Varėna; **w** varenatreehouse.com. These are the first treehouses to be built in Lithuanian woodlands. Services are basic but the accommodation cosy – think Scandi-chic interiors amid the forest, wild but comfortable. The aim is to immerse yourself in nature, relax in the hot tub, or hike/bike. The owners are 3rd-generation caretakers of this land. €€€€
**Margionys** (6 sleeping places) Klojimo gatvė 5, Margionys; **w** margionys.lt. This lovingly restored and very comfortable family homestead in the ethnographic village of Margionys comes complete with

kayaking on a weekday is recommended. The Grūda and Merkys rivers do not have quotas and permits are not required.

**Hiking** is a national pastime in Lithuania, and often the ulterior motive for a spot of mushrooming, berry picking, swimming or grilling. Visitors can pick up hiking trail maps and local advice from the visitor centres, or for advance planning check out the **Baltic Forest Hiking project** (w baltictrails.eu). Consider hiking with a local guide to gain a greater understanding of the nature, culture and local nuances. **Cycling** is growing in popularity in the region, with 12 official marked cycling routes. Search for Dzūkija on w komoot.com. The visitor centres rent bikes and can advise on a suitable route. Bear in mind that sandy forest roads require a little more effort from your muscles.

**Dzūkijos uoga** Viršurodukis 9, between Marcinkonys & Merkinė; w kaimoturizmosodyba.eu. Local experts for foraging & local culinary tours. They also have cabins for overnight stays (see below).

**Grūdos Kayaks** Grūdos baidarės; Naujadvarės gatvė 3, Marcinkonys; w grudosbaidares.lt

**Kayak Rental Dzūkija** Baidarių nuoma Dzūkijoje; Biržų gatvė 5, Žiūrai; w baidariunuoma.lt

**Keliauk Dzūkijoje** w keliaukdzukijoje.lt. Hiking & nature tours in Dzūkija National Park led by fabulous local guide & nature expert Emilis Tamošiūnas.

**LIŠKIAVA** The scenic route between Druskininkai and Merkinė follows road 2519, taking you through Liškiava, a small town dominated by the 17th–18th-century ensemble of the **Liškiava Holy Trinity Church and Dominican Monastery**. Built on

a traditional smoke sauna & large garden. This is a real family holiday home that is rented out, so you are stepping into a local lifestyle in the owners' absence. You are even free to use their tools if you want to teach your city kids how to chop wood. Min stay 3 nights. €€€

**Dzūkijos uoga** (12 sleeping places) Viršurodukis 9, between Marcinkonys & Merkinė; w kaimoturizmosodyba.eu. Located in the tiny village of Viršurodukis where only 5 residents live all year round. Your hosts are experts in foraging experiences (see above) & accommodation is in Nordic-style cabins in the Dzūkija forest. €€€

**L Černiauskienės sodyba** (8 sleeping places) Lina Černiauskienė Homestead; Kapiniškės, near Marcinkonys; w atostogoskaime.lt/apgyvendinimas/linos-cerniauskienes-sodyba. This authentic homestead is located in tiny Kapiniškės village. The crystal-clear Skroblus River runs by the edge of the

garden & host Lina runs masterclasses in buckwheat culinary heritage. €€€

**Sodyba 'Grikucis'** (25 sleeping places) Pamerkiai village, northwest of Varėna; w grikucis.com. Situated on the south bank of the Merkys River, Grikucis is ideally placed for kayaking trips. Hosts Laima & Kostas have a small farm & are well-known for their buckwheat heritage classes (buckwheat pancakes are a must-try). The homestead must be approached from the south bank of the Merkys River if arriving by car; there is only a swing footbridge over the river to the village on the north bank. €€€

**Sodyba 'Ūla'** (20 sleeping places) Trakiškiai village, near Marcinkonys; w atostogoskaime.lt/apgyvendinimas/angeles-raulusaitienes-sodyba-ula. Ideal for kayaking on the Ūla River, which flows past the end of the garden. After a hard day of kayaking, relax in the traditional steam bath followed by a plunge in the river. €€€

the steep slopes of the Nemunas River valley, it was a self-sufficient community with adjoining farm buildings, churchyard and gardens. **Holy Trinity Church** (w liskiavosparapija.lt) is a Baroque beauty in an unusual rural location, but like the city churches it too fell into disrepair during times of occupation and was repurposed as a correctional home for criminal priests and a camp for Polish refugees among other uses. The church organ, made in Warsaw in 1899 by the Polish master Šimanskis, survived. In the church basement you can pay your respects to the Dominican monks encased there in glass coffins and in the basement of the monastery is an exhibition of liturgical heritage (€3/1.50). During the 1990s the complex was restored and the **Liškiava Cultural Centre** (w liskiava.lt) was opened. The team here oversee the site and can arrange guided tours, alongside organising celebrations, retreats and seminars.

Other town sights include **Castle Hill** which was first fortified in the 3rd century BC and **Church Hill**, below which are two pagan stones. Both hills offer fine views of the river valley.

You can also visit Liškiava by taking a boat trip from Druskininkai (page 140).

**MERKINĖ** Strategically located at the confluence of the Nemunas, Merkys and Stongė rivers, Merkinė is one of Lithuania's oldest settlements and has played important commercial and defensive roles in the country's history. During its most prosperous years, Merkinė was the region's main market town for craftsmen, producers and traders, welcoming prominent figures on their way to Trakai or Vilnius. Post-World War II, Merkinė region was a covert hub of partisan activity with freedom fighters hiding out in the surrounding forests and supported by brave locals. Today, it is popular with day trippers and is garnering a reputation for small restaurants specialising in good, honest local food.

Merkinė has a pharmacy, **Gintarinė vaistinė** (Sladkevičiaus gatvė 4), a small IKI **supermarket** (Gardino gatvė 2) and a rather fun bric-a-brac shop, **Merkinės sendaikčių krautuvė** (Vilniaus gatvė 18).

**Getting there and away** Intercity **buses** travel to Merkinė from Vilnius (1hr 30mins, 4 per day), from Kaunas twice a day (2hrs 20mins, 2 per day), and from Druskininkai (36mins, 4 per day). Note that not all services stop in the town centre. Many more services stop at the Merkinės kryžkelė bus stop near the roundabout on the Druskininkai–Vilnius road, 1.5km from the centre. If you are happy with the walk, you have many more bus options including with up to 20 buses daily passing this way from Druskininkai. Buses will transport bicycles.

## ✘ Where to eat and drink

**Dzūkynė** Kauno gatvė 1; dzukyne. This local family-run restaurant serves farm-to-table food, including venison from their own deer farm. Emphasis is on heritage foods & seasonal produce foraged locally or preserved using traditional methods. €€€

**Merkinės fabrikas** Gardino gatvė 28; w merkinesfabrikas.lt. As part of the innovative cultural project Merkinė Factory, you will find Kepsnių Cechas restaurant serving all year round, & in the summer months an outdoor terrace kitchen, Pasaulio puodai (Pots of the World). Diners can enjoy views over the Nemunas River & Merkinės castle mound. €€€

## What to see and do

**Merkinė Regional Museum** (Merkines krašto muziejus; S Dariaus ir S Girėno aikštė 1; w merkinesmuziejus.lt; ⊕ 09.00–18.00 Tue–Sat; €2/1) It is well worth popping in to this small but excellent regional museum, housed in a former Orthodox Church.

The church was built in 1887 during the Tsarist period but was deconsecrated in 1968 and returned to the community as a museum. Note the miniature building to the side of the museum – this is a model of the original 16th-century town hall that stood here previously. The friendly staff can arrange guided walking tours of Merkinė, uncovering local tales of partisans, hillforts and Grand Dukes.

**Merkinė Synagogues** (Merkinės žydų sinagogų vieta, Seinų gatvė 10) Before World War II, there was a complex here of three prayer houses for Merkinė's Jewish community. Today, only one remains and is in the grounds of the local school Vincas Krėvė gimnazija. You cannot go inside but it is visible from the street, where there is an information board. The Jewish history of Merkinė is also covered in the Merkinė Regional Museum. A clearly signposted 15-minute walk from the main town square takes you down Gardino gatvė and into the forest to the Jewish cemetery and Holocaust Memorial.

**Merkinė Cross Hill** (Merkinės kryžių kalnelis; Mokyklos gatvė; ⊕ always open) Merkinė Cross Hill is the nation's largest memorial site to Lithuanian partisans who died fighting for freedom against the Soviet occupiers between 1945 and 1953. Several guerilla fighters are also buried here.

**Black ceramic and craft workshop 'Vienaragių šilas'** (Kauno gatvė 29; w vienaragiusilas.lt; ⊕ check the website; free) Local heritage crafts and traditional black ceramic pottery are kept alive here by ceramic master Džiugas Petraitis. You can pop in and have a look around, buy something from the shop, or sign up to a masterclass workshop and learn the craft yourself. The craft centre is a 5-minute walk from Dzūkynė restaurant.

**Merkinė observation tower** (Merkinės apžvalgos bokštas; ⊕ always open) Take a 2-minute drive or 10-minute walk west from the centre of town along the road to Lazdijai to one of the country's tallest (26m) and most architecturally fun observation towers. It is built around five brown columns resembling pine tree trunks, with 152 steps winding their way up to several bulbous observation decks. From the top deck you are rewarded with panoramic views of Merkinė and the local landscape. The view includes the confluence of the Nemunas and Merkys rivers, Pastraujo Island where cattle and goats were once rafted across for lush summer grazing, and the forest of Merkinė where royals and nobles once hunted.

**Merkinė castle mound** (Merkinės piliakalnis; parking on road 133 at the Merkinė bridge) Merkinė castle mound was of great strategic importance, forming part of the main triangular defence system along with Vilnius and Kaunas. Historical sources dating to 1377 refer to Merkinė castle mound as Merkenpil and Crusaders described it as a major obstacle on their way to Vilnius. Although eroded somewhat, it still provides visitors with a sense of history and a scenic viewpoint over the Nemunas River.

**Merkinė Pyramid** (Merkinės piramidė; Česukai village road off the A4 south of Merkinė; w merkinespiramide.lt; ⊕ 09.00–20.00 daily; free) The result of one man's spiritual journey is now one of the most popular attractions in southern Lithuania. Following several revelations, Povilas Žėkas built this complex of spiritual experience and healing, first constructing a pyramid, which was later covered by a giant glass dome. People come here to meditate, contemplate, pray and to satisfy their curiosity. There is a sense of new-age worship between man and nature. You do not need to be religious – non-believers are welcome too.

**MARCINKONYS** First documented in 1673, Marcinkonys was a settlement predominantly of foresters and their families, living off the land and working locally. In 1862, the Warsaw-to-St Petersburg railway was constructed through the village. It must have been quite a revelation for such a remote community. The original wooden railway station epitomises the Tsarist architecture of the time, although it deserves a bit of an upgrade to service the increasing numbers of day trippers arriving from Vilnius. Marcinkonys is now the end of the line, although the old track continues on, through Belarus, on its way to Warsaw, tracing a journey that is no longer feasible since Lithuanian independence and newly imposed borders.

While Marcinkonys is one of the largest Lithuanian villages in the area, that is not reflected in the size of its population or its amenities. Most people arrive here with a car packed full of provisions for a self-catering holiday or at least with a packed lunch for their hike or bike. The lack of entertainment and attractions ensures Marcinkonys retains a sense of peace, and nature remains top priority.

**Getting there and away** Arriving by **bus** is possible, with the Druskininkai–Varena–Vilnius service running twice a day via Marcinkonys; local buses from Varena–Kabeliai also run twice daily and stop here.

The direct **train** service from Vilnius to Marcinkonys (1hr 30mins each way; adult €7 one way) runs three times a day and is popular for day trips. The route is affectionately called 'the mushroom train' because it stops at all local stops along the way providing easy access to the forest during mushrooming season. Bikes are allowed on the train and there is a snack service. The attractive but basic station is to the south of the town on Kastinio gatvė and a 30-minute walk to the National Park Visitor Centre (page 148). There is no ticket office at Marcinkonys station, but tickets can be bought either on the train or online (w ltglink.lt). The timetable is subject to change, so check in real time.

**✕ Where to eat and drink** The only place in Marcinkonys to buy food is **Pamislyk ir Užeik** (Miškininkų gatvė 55; f; ⊕ noon–17.00 Wed–Sun; €€), open only during the summer season. At all other times there is nothing and you need to be self-sufficient. This cosy café-bakery serves delicious homemade lunches, cakes and good coffee, we encourage you to support them. A small supermarket (Miškininkų gatvė 2; ⊕ 08.00–20.00 daily) sells essentials.

### What to see and do
***Dzūkija Ethnographic Farmstead*** (Dzūkijos nacionalinio parko etnografinė sodyba; Miškininkų gatvė 6, Marcinkonys; w dnp.lrv.lt/lt/informacija-lankytojams/etnografine-sodyba; ⊕ 08.00–17.00 Tue–Fri, 09.00–16.00 Sat; €2/1) Built in 1905, this traditional homestead and barn opened its doors as an ethnographic museum in 1994. The authentic architecture and exhibits tell the story of life in historical Dzūkija from crafting and cooking, to hunting and fishing. Storytelling through folk singing and crafting are the means through which customs and traditions pass down the generations and here you will have chance to hear atmospheric Dzūkijan music and singing (recorded if not a live performance).

***Church of the Apostles St Simon and St Jude Thaddeus*** (Šv. Apaštalų Simono ir Judo Tado bažnyčia; north end of village on road 5003) The yellow

> **ČEPKELIŲ STRICT NATURE RESERVE**
> Welcome to the most safeguarded natural area in Lithuania. This vast area of wetland, bordered to the east by the Katra River and Belarus, covers more than 112km² and is over 10,000 years old. It includes Čepkelių mire, the largest raised bog in the country and home to thousands of species of flora and fauna, including wild rosemary and heathers, black grouse and capercaillies, Lady's Slipper orchids and cut leaf anemones. There is only one path for public access and it is not signposted, resulting in a quest that can feel quite daunting as you drive 5km down a forest road in the hope it is the correct one. It's safe to say that the public are not actively encouraged to come here. Individuals can visit Čepkelių for educational purposes independently from 1 August to 1 March and walk the restricted 1.5km educational trail during daylight hours. From 2 March to 31 July, visitors to Čepkelių must be accompanied by a specialist guide from the Dzūkija National Park and Čepkeliai State Nature Reserve. Excursions incur a fee and can be booked via the Dzūkija National Park Visitor Centre in Marcinkonys via e info@dzukijosparkas.lt. Our advice is to book a professional guide at all times of the year – their expertise will only add to your enjoyment of this very special ecological area.

paintwork of this statuesque wooden church is visible through the trees from the road. Built in 1880, the church's interior is a fine example of sacral folk architecture and the churchyard wall features 14 chapels of the Stations of the Cross. During the Tsarist press ban on Lithuanian literature, the local priest Jonas Šoblickas continued to hold services in Lithuanian language and participated in distributing underground publications. From the large double cross in front of the church, a path leads along the side of the cemetery and past several agricultural buildings to Klonių kalno Gaidžio kopa, an accessible continental dune – it feels rather surreal and out of place here but highlights the sandy composition of the land in this area.

**DZŪKIJAN ETHNOGRAPHIC VILLAGES** There are several attractive ethnographic villages nestled within the forests of Dzūkija National Park. These secluded clusters of authentic Dzūkijan wooden houses (*pirkia*) are approached by sandy tracks; it is courteous, therefore, to park on the edge of the village and explore on foot to avoid congestion and noise for residents. Two smaller villages of **Lyneželis** and **Dubininkas** also have landmark status and are worth visiting if passing nearby.

**Margionys** Margionys is a small but scattered village, with many authentic wooden farmsteads. It is known for its unique All Saints' Day tradition of lighting a fire in the middle of the cemetery from 1 November for ten nights. People gather around to share memories, pray or reflect. Like many rural villages, Margionys has a shrinking population as inherited houses stand waiting to be renovated when funds allow, and others are used only in the holiday season. There are several local attractions for day visitors. The **Barn Theatre** (Margionių klojimo teatras; Klojimo gatvė 6; w klojimoteatras.lt) has been hosting amateur theatre, folk singers and dancers since it was established in 1929. Village legend Juozas Gaidys (1902–86) directed many performances and kept the vision of the barn theatre alive. In 2022 the barn theatre burned down but, incredibly, has since been fully rebuilt and reopened in September 2024. Such a speedy recovery is testament to how well supported and important the venue is to the community. Performances are advertised on the website, though only in Lithuanian. The **Skroblus Trail** is a 12km circular hiking trail starting in Margionys. The route passes through the village of Kapiniškiai, and sights include Bakanauskai swamp, meadows, forests, rivers and Lady's Garden Spring (Bobo daržas šaltinis) – which produces eight litres of water per second, making it the highest-yielding spring in Lithuania. Folklore states that Lady's Garden Spring is where babies are found by parents, a local alternative to the 'delivery-by-stork' theory. Route maps for the trail are available from the Marcinkonys or Merkinė visitor centres (page 148).

**Musteika** Musteika is synonymous with beekeeping. Once famed for its wild apiculture techniques, the village is now home to the **Drevinės Beekeeping Museum** (Drevinės bitininkystės bitynas; Ąžuolo gatvė 1A, Musteika; f Ancient.Varena. beekeeping; ⊕ 08.00–17.00 Mon–Fri, 09.00–16.00 Sat; €1/0.50). The ancient method of hollow-tree beekeeping has been practised in this region of Dzūkija for centuries. Where bees nested in hollow trees, special rope devices would be used to climb the trees to retrieve the honey; the necessary skills were passed down through the generations to keep the practice alive, which was widely used at its peak in the 16th–17th centuries. By the late 1800s, however, when deforestation had changed the landscape, the tradition survived only in densely forested areas. In 2006, the museum was established to protect this endangered cultural tradition by cultivating the craft alongside a healthy apiary. Emphasis is on training and encouraging young beekeepers while raising awareness of the tradition to visitors. A tourist path wends its way through the old hollow trees, considered hallowed for their role as a habitat for bees. This respect for nature is a common theme for Lithuanians and we could all learn a thing or two here. You can buy local fresh honey to show your support and as a souvenir.

**Zervynos** Zervynos is a picturesque linear village and, being one of the oldest (mid 18th century) and best-preserved ethnographic villages, it is akin to an open-air museum – but this is real, prime real estate to be precise. Most buildings have cultural monument status; they are traditional farmsteads made from hefty logs that have survived over the centuries with folk architecture details, yard wells and neatly tended gardens filled with vegetable plots and orchards for subsistence farming. Notice the seven wooden crosses with aprons tied around them, which symbolise the village women's wish not to have illegitimate children. Park on the edge of the village as cars and Zervynos do not go together. It is now common for properties in desirable, historic villages to be bought by wealthy city folk seeking either a second home, investment, or looking to live the idyllic rural life afforded by remote working; but it is still to be seen how this gentrification of the countryside will play out for rural communities. Zervynos has a station on the Vilnius–Marcinkonys railway line, and the village is just a 5-minute walk through the woods on a well-trodden path. Trains are not very regular, so plan how you'll spend your day in advance and pack adequate provisions.

**Stėgalis Bison Reserve** (Stėgalių stumbrynas; head south from Zervynos on Ūlos gatve, bearing right at the fork continue for 2km; ⊕ 08.00–17.00 Tue–Fri, 08.00–16.00 Sat; a viewing platform with information boards is always open; free) European bison were re-established in Lithuania during the 1970s after being hunted close to extinction. A bison reserve was set up near Panevėžys and the herd bred successfully, increasing numbers but not genetic diversity as their isolated habitat amid the dense road network of central Lithuania restricted their movement. This second reserve in Dzūkija was opened in spring 2023 to establish a new herd in southern Lithuania, offering scope for the herd to merge with other bison populations in neighbouring countries as and when small numbers are released into the wild. Visitors can view these magnificent beasts from the observation platform. An official tour must be booked in advance via one of the Dzūkija National Park visitor centres (page 148).

**Ūla Eye** (Ūlos akis; 6km northwest of Zervynos along road 5019, layby parking on the left) Steep wooden steps descend into a picturesque dell, where the Ūla River skirts the base of tall sandy cliffs. From the wooden bridge that crosses the Ūla, common kingfishers that nest in the cliffs can be spotted in the early hours, before hikers and canoeists arrive. A path leads to the Ūla Eye, a hollow of about 4m in diameter and 1m deep filled with clear spring water that bubbles up with great pressure from the central spout, giving the impression it is boiling. The spring is about 4m higher in elevation than the river, so cascades as a small stream down the slope to join the Ūla. The water has a metallic taste and smells of hydrogen sulphide, but according to folklore has magical properties – best experienced by bathing in the waters just before sunset.

## NORTHEAST DZŪKIJA

**DRUSKININKAI TO SENOJI VARĖNA** In 1975, to celebrate the centenary of Čiurlionis's birth, an ensemble of wooden pole sculptures was erected along the roadside of the A4 between Senoji Varėna, his birthplace, and Druskininkai, where his family relocated. The sculptures were individually crafted by master folk artists, inspired by themes and subjects from Čiurlionis's own work. Over time the road became known as **The Čiurlionis Road** (Čiurlionio kelias; w ciurlioniokelias.lt). The route passes the curious village of **Perloja**, which in 1387 was granted a charter by Vytautas the Great, promising that none of the inhabitants could ever become a serf. At the end of World War I, amid the chaos of land disputes between Lithuania, Poland and the Soviet Union, Perlojans declared themselves an independent republic on 23 November 1918. Officials were duly elected and an army raised comprising 300 local men from the surrounding area. Although Polish rule of the area was internationally recognised by 1920, the Republic of Perloja survived until 1923. In 1930, the **Vytautas the Great Monument** (Vytauto Didžiojo paminklas) was erected in the main square to honour their hero. The Soviet authorities attempted several times to destroy the monument, but the cunning Perlojans had reinforced it with steel rods and concrete. It was the only statue of the Grand Duke to survive the Soviet years. It became a symbol of freedom and remains to this day.

If travelling to Dzūkija from Vilnius, the first regional tourist information centre (Varėnos turismo ir verslo informacijos centras; Senoji Varėna; w varenavisit. lt) you'll find is in **Senoji Varėna**, located on the roundabout of the A4/127. The roundabout is memorable for the oversized bright green structure occupying its centre. It is a monument dedicated to artist and composer M K Čiurlionis who was born in Senoji Varėna (Old Varėna) in 1875. The town of Senoji Varėna and the connected new town of Varėna have little to offer tourists, but mycophiles might enjoy the annual mushroom festival on the last Saturday in September.

**DIEVENIŠKĖS** Known as the appendix of Lithuania, this pene-exclave of Lithuania projects into Belarus for approximately 24km, the entrance to the region being only 3km wide. It is said that during a meeting to draw out Europe's new boundaries,

Stalin placed his pipe on the map and no-one was brave enough to move it, hence the unusual shape. In 1939 the region was assigned to Belarus but because the population was predominantly Lithuanian, Belarus voluntarily gave it to Lithuania in 1940. Lithuanian independence had a huge impact on the region, compounded when Lithuania joined the EU and NATO in 2004 and Dieveniškės became the eastern border for both – fences were raised and security cameras installed. It remains ethnically mixed between Lithuanian, Polish and Belarusian and you are likely to hear all these languages on your travels in the region. The population of the main regional town of Šalčininkai is over 70% Polish (census 2021) and is considered the provincial capital of Polish culture in Lithuania.

By far the easiest way to visit and tour the Dieveniškės region is by car. There is a border control (Širvių atraminis punktas) on the road 104 just before the village of Petroškos. You will need to stop and show your passport or personal ID before being allowed into the territory. From there on, you are free to explore the regional tourist sights, and driving routes are surprisingly well signposted in English. Take care not to stray too close to the border; in forests or on rural roads, yellow signs will inform you when you are in border territory. Cameras on the border fence will track you and you may be questioned when leaving the exclave. You should also be prepared to have your vehicle inspected upon leaving the exclave. Dieveniškės appendix makes for an interesting day trip from Vilnius for the curious, who may like something a little edgy, including a border control experience, authentic rural villages and being the only tourist in town.

There is a very scant bus service from Šalčininkai, but at the time of writing this was only once a day and therefore of little use to day visitors.

**Tourist information** The **Dieveniškės Historical Regional Park Visitor Centre** (Centrinė gatvė 2, Poškonys village; ⊕ 09.00–18.00 Mon–Fri, 10.00–15.00 Sat–Sun) is an excellent regional museum full of ethnographic crafts and local history. The staff will be pleased to greet you and share their recommendations for your tour of their home territory.

**What to see and do** The authentic 16th- and 17th-century **linear villages** (Lastaučikai, Poškonys, Grybiškės, Rimašiai) are attractive places to explore, with their cobbled streets and architectural monument wooden houses. Be sure to leave your car at the edge of each village as they were not designed for motor vehicles. There are also several Lithuanian **burial mounds** (Poškonys, Stakai), testimony to the region's tribal inhabitants dating to the 5th century. The region is rich in wildlife and ancient sites, including the villages of Grybiškės and Stakai with their 1,000-year-old oak trees and the century-old six-trunked Grybiškės pine. It is highly recommended to arrange a local guide via the Dieveniškės Historical Regional Park Visitor Centre (see above) for the accompanying local legends and folklore.

For those wanting to stretch their legs, the 1.8km circular **Gauja Educational Nature Trail** is 3km southeast of the town of Dieveniškės on road 3924. It is well signed with information boards as it winds along the Gauja River. In the town of **Dieveniškės** the glossy wood-clad interior of the **Church of the Blessed Virgin Mary of the Rosary** (Švč. Mergelės Marijos Rožančinės bažnyčia; Ašmenos gatvė 3) reflects the light of numerous chandeliers. Visit for an insight into local life. The town has several small convenience shops and a petrol station, too.

Be in no doubt that visiting this region does feel like stepping back in time and there is a fine line between authentic and economically disadvantaged. Single cows by the roadside hint at self-sufficiency; elderly people walking between villages with their shopping means no bus service; few cars on the road suggests lack of wealth. Be sure to buy some snacks in the local shops to support the local economy.

## WESTERN DZŪKIJA

**ALYTUS** Alytus is the historical centre of the Dzūkija region. The modern industrial city straddles the Nemunas River and has little to offer the mainstream tourist, appealing mainly to those with family heritage connections or who are passing through the region. During the early 19th century, Alytus was a divided frontier city. The western bank was part of the Grand Duchy of Warsaw and Kingdom of Poland, the eastern side part of the Vilnius Province of the Russian Empire. Today the contemporary White Rose Bridge spans the river, and at 38.1m it is the highest pedestrian and bicycle bridge in Lithuania and a hit with local extreme sport enthusiasts, who like to bungee jump from it. Little of historical Alytus remains. In 1941 when Germany attacked the Soviet Union, Alytus was ruined and reconstruction was left at the hands of the Soviet authorities, resulting in wide streets and Soviet-Modernist architecture including the Town Hall (Rotušė) and City Theatre (Miesto teatras).

The **tourist information centre** (Alytaus turizmo informacijos centras; S Dariaus ir S Girėno gatvė 1-33; w alytusinfo.lt; ⏰ 09.00–17.00 Mon–Fri) can help with local and regional sights and tours.

**Getting there and away** Buses run approximately every hour between Alytus and Vilnius (2hrs 10mins) and even more frequently between Alytus and Kaunas (1hr). The bus station (Alytaus autobusų stotis; Naujoji gatvė 17K) is on the northern edge of the city, a 50-minute (3.5km) walk to the tourist information centre.

Passenger trains no longer run to Alytus and the railway station is derelict.

**Where to stay and eat**

**Hotel Vaidila** (19 rooms) Rotušės alėja 2; w vaidila.lt. Rooms range from standard to luxury, with 2 larger suites. Guests can dine in the restaurant or beer cellar. €€
**Alytus Camping** (5 cabins) Ulonų gatvė 67A w alytauskempingas.lt. A new & well-maintained campsite with motor home pitches & 5 rental cabins. Facilities include a well-equipped kitchen area, toilets, showers, washing machines/ driers, playground & Wi-Fi. A popular family-run restaurant is next door. €

**Carpe Diem** Rotušės aikštė 16; 🅕 carpediemrestoranas. A classy café by day & restaurant by night, Carpe Diem delivers its own twist on traditional dishes, in a friendly welcoming atmosphere. €€€
**Dzūkų alaus restoranas** Vilniaus gatvė 35; w dzukuainiai.lt. Dzūkų 'brewery restaurant' has an extensive food menu, & a tasting paddle of their beers is recommended. €€€

**Other practicalities** You will find a **pharmacy** (Camelia vaistinė) at Ligoninės gatvė 2 A-1, a **Swedbank** at S Dariaus ir S Girėno gatvė 9, and a **post office** in the northern part of town at Ūdrijos gatvė 1.

**What to see and do**

*Alita Wine Factory* (Miškininkų gatvė 17; w alita.lt; ⏰ prebooked tours only; from €14 pp) Alita was established as a state-owned fruit wine factory in 1963, but it had a major breakthrough in 1980 when it produced the first Lithuanian sparkling wine. 'Alita' became a hugely popular, albeit only, option for an upmarket celebratory drink or to toast a happy occasion. Since then, the company produces the only strong grain drink, Moonshine and the first Lithuanian whiskey, as well as non-alcoholic sparkling wine. The visitor centre hosts factory tours and tastings in English from Tuesday to Saturday, which you can book online (participants must be over 20 years old). A basic factory tour costs €14 per person but can be upgraded to a degustation tour with drinks and snacks for €18 (4 drinks), €22 (5 drinks) or €26 (7 drinks).

**Alytus Regional Museum** (Alytaus kraštotyros muziejus; Savanorių gatvė 6; w alytausmuziejus.lt; ⊕ 09.00–18.00 Mon–Fri, 10.00–16.00 Sat; €1/0.50) Alytus' museum of regional ethnography is refreshingly young and dynamic, innovatively presenting the region's history and heritage. It acts as museum, archive, library and cultural centre, hosting events and educational workshops. Pay an extra €1 for an English audio guide to help you navigate the exhibition. Opposite the museum is the rather charming wooden **Church of the Guardian Angels** – 114 brave volunteers who died for Lithuanian independence are buried in the churchyard.

**Alytus Synagogue and Former Rabbi's House** (Alytaus sinagoga; Kauno gatvė 9; w alytausmuziejus.lt/tema/audiovizualiuju-menu-centras; ⊕ 09.00–18.00 Tue–Fri, 10.00–16.00 Sat) Having survived being ravaged by fire and destructive occupiers over the centuries, this once dilapidated 19th-century synagogue has been reconstructed and is now an audiovisual arts centre. The permanent exhibition 'Shalom, Alytus!' documents the history of Alytus' Jews during the interwar period. Before World War II, Alytus had a considerable Jewish community accounting for approximately 30% of the population. After a four-year, €1 million restoration project, the synagogue is saved and is open to the community and visitors.

**Around Alytus** There are two outstanding areas of natural beauty surrounding Alytus, both havens for waterfowl and other wildlife. As with all national and regional parks, both sites appeal to visitors to consider making a voluntary donation to support their work (w saugoma.lt/en/state-park-visitor-ticket).

✳ **Žuvintas Biosphere Reserve** (Kampelių gatvė 10, Aleknonys village; w zuvintas.lt; ⊕ Tue–Fri 08.00–17.00, Sat 10.00–15.00; €2/1) The importance of the **Lake Žuvintas** area was recognised in January 1928 when the Ministry of the Interior of the Republic of Lithuania imposed restrictions prohibiting the hunting of birds and mammals in the lake's immediate vicinity. Under the initiative of naturalist Tadas Ivanauskas, founder of the Zoological Museum and Zoo in Kaunas, Lake Žuvintas was expropriated from private individuals and ownership transferred to the Faculty of Natural Sciences of Kaunas University in late 1936. In 1937, a guard position was created to protect the lake and its surroundings predominantly from hunters and poachers. The area was granted state protection in 2002 as the Žuvintas Biosphere Reserve, and in 2011 it was included in the World Network of Biosphere Reserves of the UNESCO programme 'Man and the Biosphere' – the first and only Lithuanian site.

**Žuvintas Swamp** along with Lake Žuvintas is the largest wetland in Lithuania and is of great ornithological importance. It is home to one of the country's largest populations of great wagtails, reed buntings and western marsh harriers. Thousands of migrating cranes and geese rest in the reserve, and the reed warbler, one of the rarest songbirds in Europe, breeds in the meadows of Žuvintas. The diversity of flora and fauna, mixed forest and mushroom species is enormous.

The **visitor centre** contains an excellent exhibition with interactive displays about the history and management of the reserve, its habitats and species. You can hire binoculars to use during your visit, and there are telescopes on the viewing platform and several cognitive trails with birdwatching towers.

Žuvintas Biosphere Reserve is located 30km west of Alytus on road 131. It is possible to take a bus from Alytus, but currently there is only one a day, departing Alytus at 06.05. The bus stop is at the end of the access road along which you must walk the final 3km.

**Metelių Regional Park** (Metelių regioninio parko; Seirijų gatvė 2, Meteliai region; w dzukijossuvalkijosstd.lrv.lt/lt/mrp; ⊕ 08.00–17.00 Tue–Fri, 10.00–15.00 Sat; €2/1) Metelių is situated in the basin of the Great Lakes of southern Lithuania – Dusia, the largest of the three, Metelys and Obelija. The lakes are surrounded by estuaries, sandy dunes and marshes, behind which lie sheltering hills and ridges. Lake Dusia's nickname, the 'Sea of Dzūkija', refers aptly to its vast size. The area is home to extremely rare pond turtles which are the symbol of the park and affectionately called 'iron frogs' by Dzūkijans. During the autumn migration season, the park receives an influx of endangered brown ducks and numerous other bird species.

Set in a glass-walled elevated building on the shore of Lake Dusia, the Metelių **visitor centre** is full of facts about the local ecology, and the powerful telescopes mean you can watch birds and wildlife from the comfort of indoors. A 3.5km cognitive hiking trail and two cycling routes begin near the visitor centre. A 3-minute drive or 20-minute walk from the visitor centre is the **Metelių Observation Tower**, where you can enjoy panoramic views of the landscape, best appreciated with binoculars.

## LAZDIJAI

Lazdijai lies 8km from the Poland–Lithuania border, close to the E16/135 which is used by traffic travelling from Augustów in Poland to Lithuania. During Soviet times, Lazdijai was Lithuania's gateway to western Europe, the only way out of the USSR – if you had permission. Although not many international tourists visit the town, it does have several sights worth stopping off for.

There is a daily **bus** between Lazdijai and Vilnius (2hrs 50m) and a more regular bus service between Lazdijai and Kaunas (2 hrs, 4 per day). The new bus station (Lazdijų autobusų stotis, Vilniaus gatvė 48) is less than a 1km walk to the town centre.

**Tourist information** The **main tourist information centre** (Lazdijų turizmo informacinis centras; Kauno gatvė 6A; w lazdijai-turizmas.lt; ⊕ Mon–Thu 08.00–17.00, Fri 08.00–15.45, closed for lunch noon–13.00) is in town. There is also a branch close to the Polish border on road 135 (Lazdiju turizmo informacinis centras Lietuvos-Lenkijos pasienyje; midway between the border & the village of Juozapavas; ⊕ 08.00–18.00 daily).

**Where to stay and eat** If you are one of the few tourists who overnight in Lazdijai, you are likely to stay at **Hotel Gojus** (Kauno gatvė 5; search 'Viešbutis Gojus'; **€€**), a perfectly good basic hotel with clean rooms, friendly staff and a value-for-money restaurant to keep you sated. The restaurant is open to non-residents and is a good option for day visitors too.

**Other practicalities** You will find a **pharmacy** (Camelia vaistinė) at Kauno gatvė 6, a **bank** (Urbo bankas) at Seinų gatvė 41a and a **post office** at Senamiesčio

> **THE SUWAŁKI GAP**
>
> The Suwałki Gap is the area of land between the Russian exclave of Kaliningrad to the west and Belarus to the east, across which the Lithuania–Poland border stretches for 65km. It is the narrowest point between Kaliningrad and Belarus, a major transport and supply route between EU member states and is considered vulnerable amid current geopolitical tensions with Russia and Belarus. Named after the nearby Polish town of Suwałki, the region is sparsely populated with rolling forests, sandy soils, lakes and rivers, popular for rural tourism and hunting. Previously unknown to most people, the Suwałki Gap has featured in news reports as pundits speculate on NATO's position in the region following Russia's invasion of Ukraine.
>
> While military strategies are played out behind the scenes, the area does attract tourists. For some, it is enough to say they've travelled through the 'gap', but if you have the time and inclination to endure rural roads, there are unique historical borderland sights to explore. Where the borders of Lithuania–Poland–Kaliningrad (Russia) meet at the western end of the 'gap' is **Vištytis Border Tripoint** (Wisztyniec – trójstyk granic Polski, Rosji i Litwy). At present, the border point is only accessible from the Poland side on road 651 and the obelisk is cordoned off with razor wire – you can look but not touch. Remember, you are in border territory and under surveillance. Further east, south of Lazdijai on road 135, there is an **Iron Curtain Exposition** (Pasienio rokadinis kelias 'Geležinė uždanga'). Leave the main 135/E16 road at Galadusio gatvė to travel west along the Lithuania–Poland border; a brown tourist sign highlights the junction. After driving for about 2 minutes, you will reach the first information board and fence section; continue for another 10 minutes along the edge of Lake Gaładus to a longer section. Lazdijai was the only border crossing between the USSR and Poland; the fence you see today is reconstructed and represents not the actual border but the fence that secured the border area. This whole area was restricted and inaccessible, the fence was electrified with an alarm system and heavily guarded.

gatvė 1. There is a Circle K **petrol station** to the south of the town at the junction of roads 135/134.

## What to see and do

✳ **Museum of Freedom Fights** (Laisvės kovų muziejus; Vytauto gatvė 18; w lazdijumuziejus.lt; ⊕ 09.00–17.00 Tue–Fri, 09.00–15.45 Sat; €2/1) This is a little-known museum and if you are passing Lazdijai we highly recommend you make time to visit. During the Soviet occupation the NKVD (KGB) established a network of regional detention centres throughout Lithuania, often within their regional headquarters. The aim was to spread fear and mistrust throughout the nation to keep the people in check. In Lazdijai, the NKVD commandeered the home of the Petrauskas family. It provided comfortable lodging for the officers and in the basement they constructed cells for imprisonment and torture. The aim of the detention centre was to extract a confession from the accused, and through interrogation and sadistic treatment they would drive the prisoner to confess even if innocent. The cells are chilling in their authentic state and the museum is thoroughly engaging, covering the partisan movement, guerilla warfare, exile and deportations. The interactive exhibits are on a par with museums in the main cities and is worthy of any detour to get here.

**Lazdijai Regional Museum** (Lazdijų krašto muziejus; Seinų gatvė 29; W lazdijumuziejus.lt; ⏲ 09.00–17.00 Tue–Fri, 09.00–15.45 Sat; €2/1) Housed in the quaint wooden building of the former Žiburis school (1920–36), this is one of the oldest buildings in Lazdijai. Part of the museum is dedicated to the school era, an old classroom filled with desks and artefacts, including a bag of dried peas on which misbehaving pupils were made to kneel. Taking the class is a waxwork dummy of priest Motiejus Gustaitis, who ran the school and was rather a local hero. A separate building in the museum grounds houses the **Motiejus Gustaitis Memorial House** in which you will find hi-tech interactive displays about this influential and progressive priest who allowed girls to attend school, spoke six languages, and authored the first Lithuanian book on language stylistics.

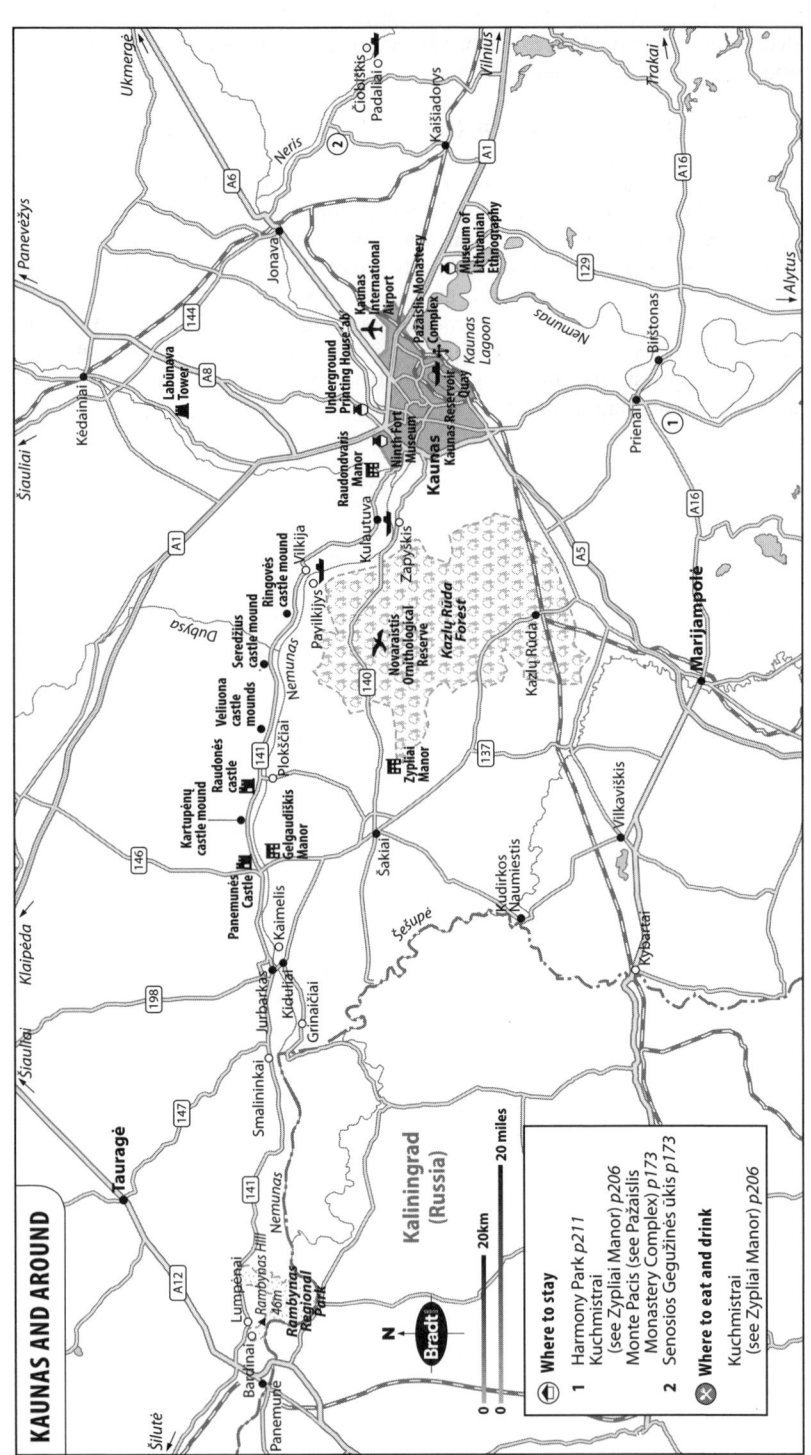

# 6

# Kaunas and Around

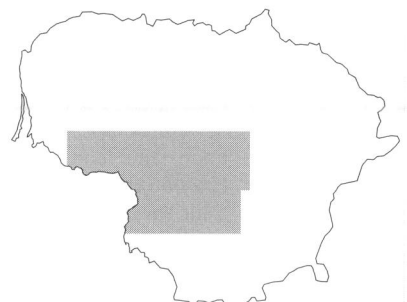

Lithuania's second city, Kaunas is a gateway to the rest of the country. It is located on the main rail and road networks running north–south through the Baltic states, and its airport is a hub for low-cost airlines. Kaunas is a worthy standalone city-break destination, and there are some major sights nearby, including the Ninth Fort and the Museum of Lithuanian Ethnography. Slightly further afield there is the possibility for cultural sightseeing in Kėdainiai, a spa break in Birštonas, hiking in the Kazlų Rūda Forest, exploring the border town of Kudirkos Naumiestis, or enjoying the scenery of the Nemunas River valley route on your way to the coast.

## KAUNAS

Kaunas has long been a cradle of Lithuanian culture and viewed as a rebel town of national resistance by occupiers. During the interwar years, when Lithuania claimed independence in 1918 but then lost its capital Vilnius to Polish annexation, Kaunas became the capital of Lithuania. An influx of native Lithuanians moved to Kaunas, increasing the concentration of Lithuanians in the city all determined to protect their new nation's traditions, culture and identity. Perhaps this is why Kaunas is the home of Lithuanian basketball, buoyed by the spirit of national identity against oppression. The years between the two world wars were a boom time for Kaunas, a period recently recognised when, in 2023 Kaunas's interwar architecture was awarded UNESCO World Heritage list status. Today, Kaunas is a vibrant young city, shaping its own identity as a contemporary city of creativity and design, and balancing a respect for the past while driving innovation though its universities and life science industries. The population of Kaunas is currently 300,000, with an estimated 12% being students. You will find fewer tourists in Kaunas than in Vilnius, but no shortage of first-class museums, sights, dining opportunities and nightlife.

**HISTORY** Evidence suggests that people have lived along the banks of the Nemunas River since the 10th century BC, with organised settlements evident from the 11th to 14th centuries. Kaunas's prime location at the confluence of the Nemunas and Neris rivers provided a strategic location for the transportation of raw materials and trading of goods.

| | |
|---|---|
| 1361 | Kaunas Castle is first mentioned in German historical written sources. |
| 1400 | Around this time, Grand Duke Vytautas the Great builds the Virgin Mary Assumption Church on the Nemunas riverbank – today this is called Vytautas the Great Church (page 181). |

| | |
|---|---|
| **1408** | Grand Duke Vytautas grants Kaunas Magdeburg rights, bringing greater opportunities of commerce and trade. |
| **1441–early 1500s** | During this period, the influential Hanseatic League is based in Kaunas. The Nemunas River has grown in economic importance, connecting inland markets to the Hanseatic cities on the Baltic Sea, and Kaunas becomes a booming trade town. The actual location of the Hanseatic League headquarters in Kaunas is unknown today. Some theories point to Perkūnas House (page 181) and others to the Daugirdas Hotel (page 173), where it is claimed its historical suite overlooking the Nemunas River has carved shelves in the eaves of the window where candles were lit to warn approaching merchants as to whether the customs officers were on duty or not. |
| **1469** | Franciscan monks begin building St George's Church and monastery close to Kaunas Castle, a grand gesture consolidating new religious influences in the city. |
| **1542** | Construction of the town hall building begins as Kaunas continues to grow in both importance and size. |
| **1607–35** | Kaunas city wall is built in response to increasing warfare from neighbouring powers, including the Swedes and Russians. Only a small section remains today in the Musical Theatre Park (page 184). |
| **1664** | Construction of Pažaislis Monastery was granted by the chancellor of the Grand Duchy of Lithuania, Kristupas Pacas (page 194). |
| **1655** | Russia, led by Tsar Alexei Mikhailovich, invades the Grand Duchy of Lithuania from the southeast and occupies Kaunas and Vilnius, the goal being to control the Nemunas and Neris rivers. Equally interested in the strategic importance of the Nemunas and loathe to see Russia take control, the Swedish army invades from the north. The Northern War and Swedish invasion continues into the early 1700s with Russia and Sweden fighting over Lithuanian lands like wolves over a deer. |
| **1795** | Most of Lithuania is occupied by the Russian Empire, the Nemunas River forming the border between the Russian Empire and German Prussia. Imperial Russia begins a huge construction project, fortifying Kaunas with a network of fortresses (page 194). |
| **1812** | 24 June: Napoleon crosses the Nemunas River into Kaunas and watches his 200,000 French troops enter the Russian Empire. Napoleon spends three nights in Kaunas. |
| **1822** | Kaunas Post Office Station is built behind the Town Hall, incorporating Kaunas into the horse-drawn postal route between Warsaw and St Petersburg. |
| **1859** | The construction of Kaunas Railway Tunnel commences (it is still the only train tunnel in Lithuania today) and by 1862, Kaunas is connected to the important transport artery of the Warsaw–St Petersburg railway line. |
| **1895** | The population of Kaunas stands at approximately 70,000, of whom only 7% are Lithuanian. |

| | |
|---|---|
| 1915–18 | During the years of World War I, there is upheaval in Kaunas. In 1915 it takes 11 days for the advancing Germans to force out the Imperial Russian Army. Kaunas is occupied by Germany and street signs are given German names. |
| 1918 | At the end of World War I, Lithuania regains independence. |
| 1919 | Vilnius is annexed by Poland and Lithuania loses its capital city. Kaunas becomes the temporary capital of Lithuania. |
| 1920 | Owing to the loss of Vilnius to Poland, many Lithuanians move to Kaunas and the population rises to over 90,000, of whom 58% are Lithuanian. |
| 1924 | The first Lithuanian Song Festival (page 67) is held in Kaunas, a national celebration that continues to this day. |
| 1939 | Kaunas Basketball Hall (Kauno sporto halė) is opened. It is the first indoor arena for basketball in Europe and testimony to both Kaunas's adoration of the sport and the Lithuanian national team's win at the European Basketball Championship in Riga in 1937. The 1939 championship is hosted here and the title is retained on home ground. Such is the nation's love of basketball that the arena's capacity of 3,500 seated supporters is pushed to the limits with an estimated 11,000 fans in attendance. |
| 1940 | Lithuania is occupied by Soviet Russia. The impact is immediate, with NKVD prisons established to spread fear and mistrust among the population. Deportations of intellectuals and those posing any sign of resistance to Soviet authority begins, with a particularly intense period over 14–19 June 1941. Shops lie empty and food permits called *talonai* are introduced, another exertion of power and control by the occupiers. |
| 1941 | 22 June: Lithuania is occupied by Nazi Germany, after their successful Operation Barbarossa is launched from Poland. The Nazis move fast to exert control and begin their murderous campaign against the Jewish population in July of that year. The Kaunas Ghetto is established, and the Kaunas forts are |

### MODERNIST KAUNAS: ARCHITECTURE OF OPTIMISM, 1919–39

When Vilnius was lost to Poland in 1919, Kaunas was not equipped to accommodate the influx of people and rapid transfer of state institutions that came to the city. A construction boom began, with rapid urbanisation transforming the industrial fortress city into a modern state capital. This was Kaunas's golden age. As a result, the city has a unique concentration of interwar architectural styles for which in September 2023 Kaunas was awarded UNESCO World Heritage list status. While exploring Kaunas you will see many Modernist and Art Deco façades, and it feels completely different to Vilnius even though it is only an hour away. As with many things in Lithuania, you need to understand the story behind the façade to appreciate what you are witnessing. The tourist information office has specialist information and itineraries for those interested in Modernist Kaunas and a tour of the **Art Deco Museum** (page 186) and **Amsterdam School Museum** (page 187) are highly recommended.

| | |
|---|---|
| 1941 | used as extermination camps. Moving into the ghetto for Jews is obligatory, with non-compliance resulting in arrest and probable death.<br>29 October: The largest extermination of Jews in Lithuania in one day occurs at the Ninth Fort (page 192). Large families, including men, women and children, as well as weak, sick and elderly people, are selected and marched to the fort, where they are shot and their bodies dumped in ready-made trenches. That day, between dawn and dusk, 9,200 people are killed (2,007 men, 2,920 women and 4,273 children). Exterminations and transportation to concentration camps continue throughout the war years. Records show that of 30,000 Jews in Kaunas, approximately 2,400 survived the Holocaust. |
| 1944 | Kaunas is again occupied by Soviet Russia, their troops having forced the Nazi German occupiers out. A long period of Soviet occupation begins with Lithuania annexed into the Soviet Union. |
| 1947 | Kaunas Žalgiris basketball club wins gold in the USSR Basketball Championships in Tbilisi, Georgia. Basketball represents an outlet for national pride and solidarity. |
| 1959 | The construction of the Kaunas hydro-electric power plant dams the Nemunas River, creating the Kaunas reservoir (or Kaunas lagoon; *Kauno marios*). At the expense of 35 villages, acres of land, and forced evictions, Kaunas city is now protected from devastating annual floods. |

## KAUNAS AND CHICAGO

The Lithuanian diaspora in Chicago is an example of the significant wave of emigration that occurred in the late 19th century. Occupied by the Russian Empire, Lithuania was economically and culturally oppressed with no respite from this depression in sight; while the USA was a beacon of freedom and opportunity. There were several ways to emigrate. The overland route left via southwestern Lithuania into East Prussia, on to Germany and then to the USA. Alternatively, it was possible to leave by ship from the Baltic sea ports of Riga and Liepāja (called Libau at the time). Most ships arrived in the USA via Ellis Island and many new arrivals continued to Chicago, lured by employment opportunities in industry, mining and farming. Once a community was established overseas, it continued to grow as family and friends joined in search of a new life. Censuses show that by 1890 Chicago was home to 6,000 Lithuanians, more than Kaunas which had 4,000. Chicago remains the largest Lithuanian diaspora in the USA with an active Lithuanian community and approximately 1 million Americans claiming Lithuanian ancestry. No wonder it is fondly known as 'Little Lithuania'.

Back home in Kaunas, the Lithuanian population soared during the post-independence years with 20,000 in 1920 rising to 54,000 in 1923 due to the relocation of many Lithuanians from Vilnius after it was occupied by Poland. Today, family heritage tours of Lithuania for new generations of Lithuanian descendants are a vital way to continue that connection and to keep the history and fighting spirit of Lithuanian democracy and freedom alive.

| | |
|---|---|
| 1972 | 14 May: Nineteen-year-old school student Romas Kalanta sets himself on fire on Kaunas's main street Laisvės alėja in an act of protest against the Soviet occupation of Lithuania. Kalanta becomes a symbol of the Lithuanian resistance throughout the 1970s and 1980s (page 184). |
| 1982 | Laisvės alėja is fully pedestrianised. |
| 1990 | June: Following the Act on the Re-establishment of the Independent State of Lithuania, adopted on 11 March, the first Soviet monuments in Kaunas were pulled down, all of which are now on display at Grūtas Soviet Sculpture Park (page 145). |
| 2015 | Kaunas is designated a UNESCO City of Design and included in the Network of UNESCO Creative Cities, an achievement based on the city's active design industry, design schools and research centres. As Lithuania's second city, it is an important step for Kaunas to create new global connections and to help shape its identity. |
| 2022 | Kaunas is European Capital of Culture. However, as a result of the Covid-19 pandemic, many events are moved online or attended only by local visitors. The anticipated international attention is reduced. |
| 2023 | Kaunas becomes Lithuania's seventh UNESCO World Heritage site, awarded for its Modernist interwar architecture in the city centre. |

## GETTING THERE AND AWAY

**By air** Kaunas International Airport [171 F1] (Kauno oro uostas; Oro uosto gatvė 4; w kaunas-airport.lt) is located 14km north of the city centre. It has become Lithuania's low-cost airline hub thanks mainly to Ryanair, and you can fly direct to Kaunas from more than 20 European cities. The local name of Kaunas airport is Karmėlava and the site was previously a USSR missile launch site (like the Cold War Museum; page 267). The missile bases were all closed under the Intermediate-Range Nuclear Forces Treaty signed between US President Ronald Reagan and Soviet General Secretary Mikhail Gorbachev in 1987. You can still see the old hangars in the forest when on approach to landing. The airport is small, modern and easily navigated with most facilities available.

**Transfers to the city centre** To get to Kaunas city centre, take **bus** number 29 from the bus stop outside arrivals. The timetable works with the flight arrival schedule and the last bus waits for the last plane. The city centre stops serve the main hotels very well. A one-way ticket costs €1 and can be bought from the driver in cash (you must have the exact amount) or you can pay by card on the terminal inside the bus. For travel on to Vilnius, Klaipėda and Riga, a shuttle bus runs from Kaunas airport; up-to-date details are listed on the airport website.

If you prefer to travel by **taxi**, there is a taxi rank outside the arrivals hall; expect to pay €25 to get to the centre. As an alternative, use the Bolt app for your journey. The CityBee and Bolt **carshare** service is also available at the airport; by using either app you can book an available vehicle currently parked at the airport and drive yourself to your destination. There is no guarantee there will be a vehicle available when you arrive, so it is a good idea to prebook your vehicle before your flight departs. You will pay for an additional couple of hours rental while you are in the air, but it will guarantee your vehicle is there upon arrival.

**By train** Kaunas **railway station** [171 H6] (Kauno geležinkelio stotis; M K Čiurlionio gatvė 16; w ltglink.lt) is centrally located with the main pedestrian street of Laisvės alėja a 15-minute walk away. Due to its central location, Kaunas is better served by rail than Vilnius and will continue to be a hub with the construction of the new Rail Baltica service. Currently, the train service between Warsaw, Poland and Lithuania goes via Kaunas (7hrs 30mins, 1 per day; from €20 adult one way). Trains between Kaunas and Vilnius are regular, with more than 20 per day (1hr 20mins; €6.50 adult one way). To travel between Kaunas and Riga by train you must change trains at Kaišiadorys (4hrs, 1 train per day; €20 adult one way). Trains between Kaunas and Klaipėda require a change at Kaišiadorys or Šiauliai (between 4hrs 15mins & 5hrs 15mins, 3 per day; €24 adult one way). A local line also runs between Kaunas and Marijampolė (1hr, 9 per day; €4.90 adult one way). Should you require a taxi from the station, use the Bolt app for cheaper rates and easier communication rather than taking a taxi from the street. Luggage storage is available at the station along with a digital tourist information point, vending machines and public toilets.

**By bus** Kaunas is well served for local, national and international bus travel. Direct express buses run between Kaunas and Riga (4hrs 10mins, 1 per day; €24 adult one way) and there are more daily options with a connection in Vilnius. There is a daily overnight bus service between Kaunas and Warsaw (6hrs 30mins; €22.50 adult one way). Direct buses to Vilnius (1hr 30mins), Klaipėda (2hrs 40mins), Šiauliai (2hrs 50mins) and other Lithuanian cities are daily regular services. Kaunas **bus station** [171 G5] (Kauno autobusų stotis; Vytauto prospektas 24; w kautra.lt/en/bus-stations/kaunas-bus-station) is a modern 24/7 facility with amenities including luggage storage, supermarket, pharmacy, café and a tourism information point. From time to time pop-up concerts and events take place in the bus station too. Intercity and international coach services are provided by companies Kautra (w kautra.lt), Eurolines (w eurolines.lt), Ecolines (w ecolines.lt), Flixbus (w flixbus.lt), Toks (w toks.lt) and Lux Express (w luxexpress.lt). For online schedules and tickets, visit w autobusubilietai.lt.

**By car** Driving from Vilnius to Kaunas along the A1 highway, you will enter Kaunas on Savanorių gatvė which takes you straight into the city centre. Locals joke that this is the longest street in Lithuania, as you will likely have left Vilnius on their Savanorių gatvė too. The same approach into Kaunas applies for travel from Anykščiai, Utena and Ukmergė on the A6 highway. Arriving to Kaunas from Klaipėda, take the ring road direction Warsaw (A5) and take the first exit after crossing the Nemunas River to Aleksotas. This will take you straight down into the Old Town. If you park your car before crossing Vytautas the Great Bridge and cross over to Old Town by foot, you will pay a lower parking rate (and you will be close to Aleksotas Funicular for a view of the Old Town before exploring; page 182). This is also the best way to enter Kaunas from the south. Kaunas traffic is busy and best avoided between the hours of 07.30–09.00 and 16.00–18.00.

**Parking** fees in the city centre apply between 08.00 and 20.00 on weekdays. Parking zones are marked by colour: yellow, red, blue and green, with yellow being the most expensive and green cheapest. Yellow zones are the most central, with green zones being a few streets away from the centre. Pay for your parking either at the parking ticket machine with cash or card, or via the Unipark app. There are also orange and brown zones marking the **low emission zone** of the Old Town where you are charged €2 for entering the zone. This €2 fee is added on to the first hour of parking fees within the zone and payable via the parking meter or parking app. If you do not pay it, be prepared to receive a letter in the post at a later date.

**GETTING AROUND** Kaunas is quite spread out, although everything is still easily walkable if you bring your comfy shoes. When you do need some transport, or fancy a ride on a trolleybus, there are plenty of options.

**By public transport** There is a well-developed network of public transport in Kaunas combining buses and trolleybuses. The website w stops.lt has a very easy-to-use trip-planning tool for bus and trolleybus journeys. Alternatively, you can download the Trafi app for real-time traffic and timetables and the Žiogas app where you can also purchase tickets. The easiest way to buy your bus ticket is by tapping in using your contactless card or phone on the terminal in the bus; tickets can also be purchased from the driver using cash only (exact change of €1 for a one way ticket).

**By taxi and car share** Taxis are distinguished by a 'taksi' sign on the vehicle roof. Make sure the meter is switched on before you start your journey and best to carry cash for payment. It is generally cheaper to call a taxi rather than get in one on the street, even if you call the vehicle parked up in front of you. However, taxi use is declining, with most people preferring to use the Bolt app to book a ride, which is usually much easier and cheaper than a taxi for foreign visitors. Uber is not so prevalent in Kaunas.

Both CityBee and Bolt offer plenty of vehicles for **car sharing** in Kaunas. There are many pick-up and drop-off places in Kaunas; just be sure to park the car in an authorised space as shown in the app.

**By bike and scooter** There are over 106 km of marked **cycling** routes in Kaunas connecting different parts of the town, as well as taking you out of the city for scenic cycling itineraries. It is possible to hire a green Bolt bike using the Bolt app. Be aware, though, that helmets are not available and you have to bring your own. It is also possible to hire **scooters** from locations around the city – use the Bolt app to hire a scooter, pay for it by card, and then leave it at your destination. If you do hire a scooter, be aware that helmets are not available and accidents are very common, sometimes serious.

**TOURIST INFORMATION** The **Kaunas Tourism Information Centre** [171 F3] (Kaunas turizmo informacijos centras; Laisvės alėja 36; w visit.kaunas.lt; ⊕ 09.00–18.00 Mon–Fri, 10.00–16.00 Sat, 10.00–15.00 Sun) is a one-stop shop for maps, guided tours, self-guided routes, recommendations, what's on and souvenirs. They also have handy power packs available to hire.

**WHERE TO STAY** The arrival of large chain hotels in Kaunas has had a big impact on the independent locally owned hotels, which are forced to compete with low prices and strong branding. By choosing a local traditional hotel you will not only benefit from a family-run service and the unique character of Kaunas, but also your money goes directly into the local economy. There is also a new wave of autonomous hotels in Kaunas, with next to no staff, entrance codes and remote help; these might suit some, but not everyone. Wherever you choose, note that you will be asked to pay city tax when checking into your accommodation (€2 pp per night, over 18s only).

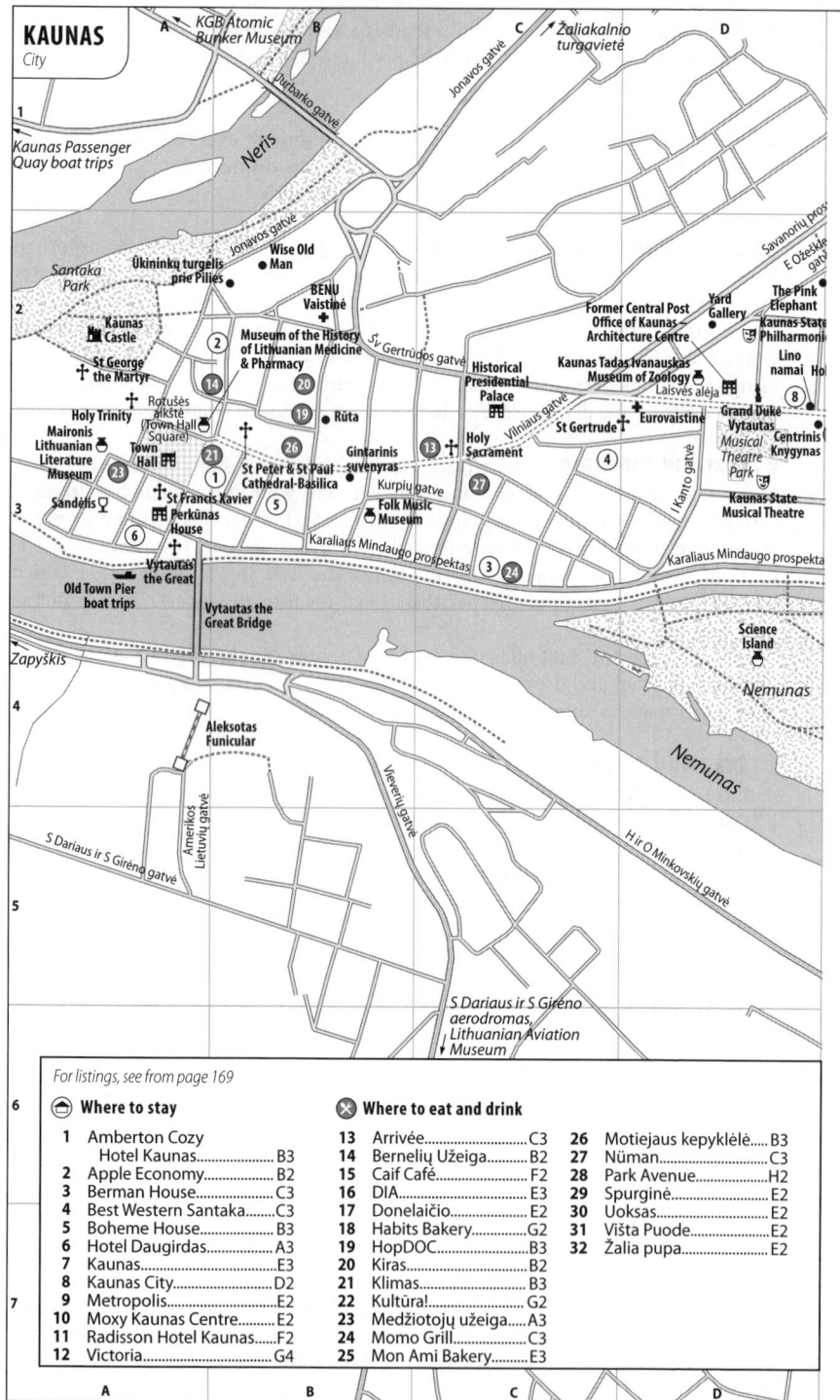

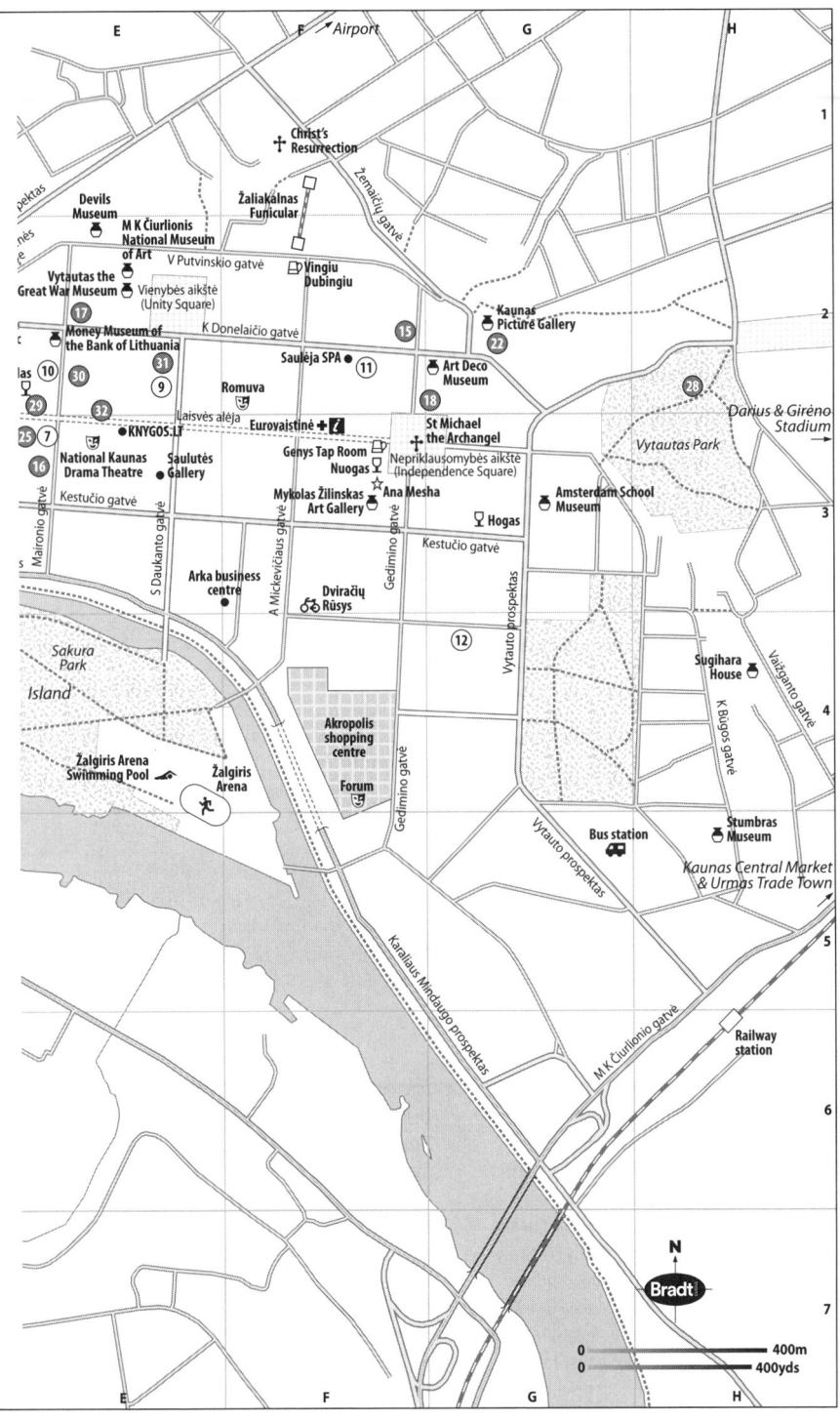

## KAUNAS FESTIVALS

**COURTYARD FESTIVAL** (w kaunaspilnasrenginiu.lt/en) In late May, Kaunas celebrates the local community by holding a huge street party in conjunction with European Neighbours' Day. Communities, organisations and individuals are all invited to bring tables and chairs to Laisvės alėja, set them with a white tablecloth and flowers, then sit down to enjoy a pleasant evening with friends and neighbours surrounded by music and entertainment.

**KAUNAS BIENNIAL** (w bienale.lt) This, the largest international contemporary art event in the Baltic region, consists of exhibitions, an artist residency programme and workshops, as well as public and community arts projects. The 15th Kaunas Biennial will take place between September and November 2025, with the next event planned for 2027, but the time of year might differ.

**KAUNAS BIRTHDAY** (w kaunaspilnasrenginiu.lt/en) The biggest city festival is held every May with celebrations centred around the Kaunas Castle amphitheatre. It incorporates the Courtyard Festival and Putvinskis Street Day, with many more events, performances and celebrations held across the city.

**KAUNAS JAZZ** (w kaunasjazz.lt) Every last weekend in April, Lithuanian and international jazz musicians and fans descend on Kaunas and the city's streets and venues host memorable jazz events.

**PUTVINSKIS STREET DAY** (w kmn.lt/events/putvinskis-street-day-a-living-street) Held on the last Sunday in May, the length of V Putvinskis street fills with a throng of creative activity for the entire family. Activities include workshops, open galleries, music and artistic performances, all of which are free and open to all.

**CHRISTMAS TREE LIGHTING AND CHRISTMAS MARKET** On the last weekend in November, Kaunas Christmas tree is lit in Town Hall Square and the city celebrates with a big concert and the opening of the Christmas market. The Christmas market continues until the first week in January, providing copious amounts of mulled wine and hot chocolate to keep visitors toasty warm while browsing the craft and food stalls.

## Around the Old Town

**Boheme House** [170 B3] (8 apartments) Muitinės 9/J Naugardo 6; w bohemehouse.lt. The only small boutique hotel nestled in the Old Town has jumped on the autonomous band wagon & offers self-check in. Each of the 8 apartments is themed; including the dark, moody & heavily scented 'Parfumerie N°3'; in the monochrome space of 'Architect N°1' you are greeted by a life size **David** by Michaelangelo; and in 'Soloist N°8' is a grand piano which it is perhaps better to have in your own apartment than in your neighbours'. The rooftop terrace is popular & they are renowned for their brunch menu. €€€€

**Amberton Cozy Hotel Kaunas** [170 B3] (27 rooms) V Kuzmos gatvė 8; w ambertonhotels.com/kaunas. With a great location in the heart of the Old Town, this hotel is within walking distance of sights, restaurants & bars. But note that this is a contactless hotel with self-check-in, & if you need assistance, it will be over the phone. Standard dbl rooms are spacious, family rooms sleep max 3 people, & single rooms are characterful. Be aware that top-floor rooms have sloping ceilings. Parking spaces are limited & alternatives in the Old Town are expensive. €€€

**Berman House** [170 C3] (30 rooms) Karaliaus Mindaugo prospektas 17; w bermanhouse.lt. Berman House is a new-generation hotel on the edge of the Old Town area with a self-check-in machine & little contact with human beings. Rooms are compact & practical, designed for a short stay & sleeping as opposed to relaxing in. Be aware that river-facing rooms overlook the busy 6-lane road. €€€

**Best Western Santaka Hotel** [170 C3] (92 rooms) J Gruodžio gatvė 21; w santakahotel.eu. A large but characterful traditional hotel in between the Old Town & Laisvės alėja, the Santaka is perhaps a little old-fashioned but still very popular with locals & groups. Bedrooms are generous in size, & the top-floor corner room with full-height glass windows is worth requesting. A small pool & Finnish sauna are free for guests to use. €€€

**Hotel Daugirdas** [170 A3] (48 rooms) T Daugirdo gatvė 4; w daugirdas.lt. This family-owned hotel in the Old Town is a warren of individual rooms, centred around the light-filled atrium. The hotel has a rooftop bar & a popular restaurant in which they hold 'dinner in the dark' experiences once a week. Rooms are a bit dated, but spacious, & if you are looking for a local independent hotel in Kaunas, this is the best choice. €€€

**Apple Economy Hotel** [170 B2] (14 rooms) M Valančiaus gatvė 19; w applehotel.lt. As stated in the name, this is a basic hotel & perfect for budget travellers. If you are prepared for small, simple rooms, the excellent location will win you over. The family room is a 2-room no-frills apartment that can sleep up to 5 people. If you desire a bigger, better b/fast than provided in the hotel, try one of the nearby cafés in easy walking distance. €€

## Around Laisvės Alėja

**Kaunas Hotel** [171 E3] (85 rooms) Laisvės alėja 79; w kaunashotel.lt. This leading, locally owned hotel on Laisvės alėja provides a warm welcome & a central base for exploring the city. Guests can use the sauna & pool area & dine in the popular Restaurant 55. Larger rooms are in the new extension. €€€

**Moxy Kaunas Centre** [171 E2] (175 rooms) Maironio gatvė 19; w marriott.com/en-us/hotels/kunox-moxy-kaunas-center. A signature Moxy hotel with funky décor. Its central location just off the pedestrianised Laisvės alėja is close to the M K Čiurlionis National Museum of Art & Vytautas the Great War Museum. €€€

**Radisson Hotel Kaunas** [171 F2] (206 rooms) K Donelaičio gatvė 27; w radissonhotels.com/en-us/hotels/radisson-kaunas. For visitors exploring the Old Town, this feels rather on the edge of the city centre, but it has a strong business vibe & offers Radisson quality & services, including a spa, wellness centre & casino. €€€

**Victoria Hotel Kaunas** [171 G4] (91 rooms) Miško gatvė 11; w hotelvictoria.lt/kaunas. Located in a former interwar-period printing house, the Victoria is at the far end of Laisvės alėja from the Old Town. Sauna & jacuzzi can be rented by the hour. €€€

**Kaunas City Hotel** [170 D2] (44 rooms) Laisvės alėja 90; w kaunascityhotel.com. A good economy option in an excellent location on Kaunas's main pedestrian street. €€

**Metropolis Hotel** [171 E2] (41 rooms) S Daukanto gatvė 21; w metropolishotel.lt. Built in the 19th century, the Metropolis was once a landmark hotel with guests including ambassadors & presidents. Those glory days seem a distant memory, although the faded grandeur is all around as you lug your suitcase up the sweeping staircase. It was from here that Japanese ambassador Chiune Sugihara (page 191) continued to issue lifesaving visas in September 1940 after the Japanese consulate was closed; a memorial to him stands outside. €€

### Further afield  *Map, page 162*

As well as these charming options outside the city centre, you can also stay overnight at the simple guesthouse on site at the Museum of Lithuanian Ethnography (page 196).

**Monte Pacis Hotel** (14 rooms) Pažaislis Monastery, T Masiulio gatvė 31; w montepacis.lt. Situated on the Pažaislis Monastery complex (page 194), surrounded by forest & on the shore of the Kaunas Lagoon is this boutique hotel, complete with Michelin-recommended restaurant. Choose from an à la carte or tasting menu in the restaurant, & from standard rooms, apartments or luxury suites in the hotel. €€€

**Senosios Gegužinės ūkis** Beržės gatvė 4, Gegužinė village; w senojigeguzine.lt. Set on a quiet stretch of the Neris River between Jonava & Kernavė, 50km from Kaunas, is this traditional farmstead, where you can experience authentic rural Lithuania. Senosios Gegužinės ūkis is a wooden manor house lovingly built by hosts Rolandas & Neringa, with traditionally decorated guestrooms filled with antiques. Guests stay on a self-catering basis & should bring their own supplies for grilling in the garden or the communal kitchen. A traditional sauna at the bottom of the garden has steps leading down to the Neris River for a dip. The farmstead has received awards for its architectural & cultural heritage, & art exhibitions rotate here every 3 months. €€

**✖ WHERE TO EAT AND DRINK** Kaunas is a city of long-standing establishments popular with locals and a new generation of trendy cafés and exceptional Michelin-recognised restaurants. Much that exists in between either doesn't last long or is best avoided as you can eat very well in Kaunas with a little inside information. Many bars and late-night venues also serve food or snacks into the wee hours (see opposite).

## Around the Old Town

**Medžiotojų užeiga** [170 A3] Rotušės aikštė 10; **w** medziotojai.lt; ⏰ noon–23.00 daily. Being called Hunters' Inn, it's no surprise to find hunting trophies on the walls & a menu heavy on meat, especially local game. It's been here forever & we don't see that changing. €€€€

**Momo Grill** [170 C3] Karaliaus Mindaugo prospektas 18A; **w** momogrill.lt; ⏰ 11.00–22.00 Mon–Fri, noon–22.00 Sat. This contemporary grill restaurant has a farm-to-table ethos & the menu changes regularly in tune with seasonal produce. Located on the edge of the Old Town facing the river – well worth the walk to find it. €€€€

**Bernelių Užeiga** [170 B2] M Valančiaus gatvė 9; **w** berneliuuzeiga.eu; ⏰ 11.00–22.00 Sun–Thu, 11.00–midnight Fri–Sat. A traditional rural tavern-style restaurant serving up heritage dishes that will reliably fill you up without breaking the bank. You must have at least 1 traditional meal like this during your stay in Lithuania – potato pancakes, cepeliniai, or pork cutlet are essential experiences. Finish with their signature black bread ice cream. €€€

**Klimas** [170 B3] Rotušės aikštė 3; **w** restobaras-klimas.tablein.com; ⏰ 18.00–03.00 Wed–Sun, 18.00–02.00 Mon–Tue. Take a seat on the Town Hall Square to enjoy a drink & light snack while watching the world go by. Klimas is a popular bar for cocktails & gets busy later in the evening & at the w/ends. €€€

## Around Laisvės Alėja

**DIA** [171 E3] Maironio gatvė 9; **w** restoranasdia.lt; ⏰ noon–22.00 Mon–Wed, noon–23.00 Thu, noon–midnight Fri–Sat, noon–21.00 Sun. Kaunas should be proud to have such a good selection of Michelin-recommended restaurants, including the family-run DIA. The à la carte menu is full of international influence from carpaccio to Wagyu beef. A tasting menu is available Fri–Sun from €129 pp. €€€€€

**Uoksas** [171 E2] Maironio gatvė 28; **w** uoksas.eu; ⏰ 18.00–22.00 Tue–Thu, 18.00–23.00 Fri, 15.00–23.00 Sat. Modern Baltic cuisine with a Nordic twist – the creative dishes at Uoksas are crafted with care & deserve their Michelin recommendation. Choose from the à la carte menu or book the tasting menu in advance. €€€€€

**Arrivée** [170 C3] Vilniaus gatvė 29; **w** arrivee.lt; ⏰ 17.00–22.00 Wed–Fri, 10.00–14.00 & 16.30–22.00 Sat, 10.00–15.00 Sun. Dining at Michelin-recommended Arrivée is a great opportunity to enjoy fine dining with a French flair, at relatively reasonable prices; & you might just experience the next big thing – up-&-coming chefs practise their craft here. Pleasant summer terrace in the former Dominican monastery courtyard. €€€€

**Donelaičio** [171 E2] K Donelaičio gatvė 66; **w** donelaicio.lt; ⏰ 11.30–22.00 Mon–Tue, 11.30–23.00 Wed–Thu, 11.30–01.00 Fri, 11.00–01.00 Sat, 11.00–22.00 Sun. The menu features a selection of different nationalities' cuisine, so you may be choosing between a curry, fish & chips, mixed grill or tacos. Whatever your preference, it's popular, so make a reservation, especially at w/ends when they have live DJ music either inside or outdoors on the terrace. €€€€

**Numan** [170 C3] Nemuno gatvė 43; **w** numan.lt; ⏰ 17.00–22.00 Tue–Thu, 17.00–23.00 Fri, 15.00–23.00 Sat. Considered a place for a special occasion, they serve up innovative dishes based on good food, creating good emotions. The understated interior is calm, allowing full focus

on your food & company. Awarded a Michelin Bib Gourmand. €€€€
**Park Avenue** [171 H2] Perkūno alėja 4; w park-avenue.lt; ⊕ 11.00–midnight daily. Park Avenue's chef has high standards & creates a flavoursome menu of Asian & European fusion dishes. The restaurant is set in Vytautas Park & surrounded by an ancient grove of oak trees. €€€€
**Višta Puode** [171 E2] S Daukanto gatvė 23; w vistapuode.lt; ⊕ 11.00–midnight daily. Everyone is catered for at the Chicken Pot, whether you're craving milkshakes, snacks, hearty meals or cocktails. Eat either in the cosy restaurant or next door in their pub – the same, homely, food is served in both venues, but the atmosphere is completely different. €€€€
**HopDOC** [170 B3] M Daukšos gatvė 23; w hopdoc.lt; ⊕ 17.00–22.00 Mon, 17.00–midnight Tue–Thu, noon–01.00 Fri–Sat, noon–22.00 Sun. A hipster trendy gastropub liked for its burgers & accompanying cocktails & beers. €€€
**Kultūra!** [171 G2] K Donelaičio gatvė 16; f kauno.kultura; ⊕ noon–22.00 Mon, noon–midnight Tue–Wed, noon–02.00 Thu–Sat, noon–20.00 Sun. There is always a different atmosphere depending on the season or time of day in this combined art gallery & café bar. Popular for lunch & light meals in the evening, it is a reliable, relaxed place for drinks with friends. A hipster alternative young crowd gravitate here & everyone is welcome. €€€
**Žalia pupa** [171 E2] Laisvės alėja 78; f zaliapupa; ⊕ 11.00–16.00 Mon–Fri. The Green Bean is the perfect find for those looking for vegan & vegetarian dishes, or just a delicious healthy meal. €€
**Spurginė** [171 E2] Laisvės alėja 84; f spurginekaunas.lt; ⊕ 08.30–20.00 Mon–Fri, 09.00–20.00 Sat, 10.00–19.00 Sun. If you've heard of the iconic donut joint of Kaunas, that is Spurginė. Come here for a legendary experience – for over four decades they've been serving up donuts with jam, curd or meat fillings here. Accompany that with a signature milky coffee, *kavos su pienu*, for the full experience. €

## Cafés
**Caif Café** [171 F2] K. Donelaičio gatvė 22; f Caifcafe; ⊕ 07.30–20.00 Mon–Fri, 10.00–21.00 Sat, 10.00–19.00 Sun. A small chain of coffee shops offering quick snacks. €€
**Habits Bakery** [171 G2] Laisvės alėja 30; w habits.lt; ⊕ 08.00–17.00 Mon–Fri, 09.00–17.00 Sat–Sun. Contemporary café with smashed avocado & smoothies on the menu, very popular. €€
**Mon Ami Bakery** [171 E3] Laisvės alėja 79; w monami.lt; ⊕ 08.00–20.00 daily. A treat for those with a sweet tooth. Famous for their Napoleon cake – sweet layers of puff pastry & whipped cream. €€
**Kiras** [170 B2] M Daukšos gatvė 27; w kiras.lt; ⊕ 10.00–20.00 daily. Café & vegan bakery with a cheerful retro interior. €€
**Motiejaus kepyklėlė** [170 B3] Vilniaus gatvė 7; f Motiejaus; ⊕ 07.30–18.00 Mon–Sat, 08.30–18.00 Sun. Fresh bread & buns in the heart of the Old Town with a promise that 'in all products, the spice of love is felt'. €€

## ENTERTAINMENT AND NIGHTLIFE
### Bars and clubs
**Ana Mesha** [171 F3] Laisvės alėja 21; f annameshaviesbutis; ⊕ 23.00–05.00 Fri–Sat. Check out the official photos online for a guide to dress code & atmosphere at Kaunas's trendiest club.
**Genys Tap Room** [171 F3] Laisvės alėja 21; w genystaproom.lt; ⊕ 17.00–02.00 Sun–Wed, 17.00–04.00 Thu–Sat. This is the tap room for the local Kaunas craft brewery Genys (it means woodpecker). The beer is great & includes an ever-changing selection of guest beers. Jumbo-sized beer snacks include *kepta duona* (deep fried garlic bread) & *sūrio spurgos* (cheese donuts).
**Hogas** [171 G3] Kęstučio gatvė 6; f HogasKaunas; ⊕ 11.30–23.00 Tue–Wed, 11.30–midnight Thu–Fri, 13.00–midnight Sat, 13.00–22.00 Sun. Hogas is a well-kept secret, but we're letting it out of the bag. Who knew this fantastic courtyard bar was hiding in the shadow of Akropolis shopping mall? Well, now you know. In summer the courtyard area is bustling, & in winter the vaulted bar is cosy. Get there both thirsty & hungry – & prepare to leave later than planned.
**Holas** [171 E2] Laisvės alėja 84b; f hollasbar; ⊕ 17.00–22.00 Mon–Thu, 17.00–01.00 Fri, 11.30–01.00 Sat, 11.30–19.00 Sun. The mantra of Holas is 'food & booze', & its cosy

yet classy interior is perfect for drinks or cocktails with friends. If you find yourself feeling peckish, the kitchen serves Mexican snacks including quesadillas & tacos (€€€). People often don't find this place unless someone has recommended it (& hinted to look in the courtyard), so that is what we are doing.

**Nuogas** [171 F3] Laisvės alėja 21; **f** nuogas. briusly; ⏱ 11.30–22.00 Mon–Tue, 11.30–23.00 Wed–Thu, 11.30–02.00 Fri, noon–02.00 Sat, noon–20.00 Sun. Located in a 19th-century building that was once a grand hotel, this contemporary Art Deco bar is perfect for sipping fashionable cocktails, or eating an Asian fusion meal (€€€€), & if it is the w/end you can burn it all off dancing to the set of a visiting DJ. Ideal for an autumn afternoon as the views from the window are genuinely inspiring.

**Sandėlis** [170 A3] Muziejaus gatvė 8; **f** sandelis.kaunas; ⏱ 18.00–02.00 Fri–Sat. Sandėlis offers the complete package for a good night out: atmosphere, a varied drinks menu, snacks, live music & the night almost always ends with dancing.

✴ **Vingiu Dubingiu** [171 F2] K Donelaičio gatvė 41; **f** VingiuDubingiuAlude; ⏱ 16.00–01.00 daily. Visit Vingiu Dubingiu's relaxed beer garden & take your time sampling their numerous draft & bottled craft beers. A food van (€€) is often parked in the yard providing the necessary to line patrons' stomachs if required. In winter the interior is compact & cosy, with more beer shop vibes than bar, but in all seasons it is the best place for craft beers in Kaunas.

## Cinema

**Forum Cinemas** [171 F4] Karaliaus Mindaugo prospektas; w forumcinemas.lt. Mainstream blockbuster cinema showing current releases in English language.

**Romuva Cinema** [171 F2] Laisvės alėja 54; w kcromuva.lt. The oldest operational cinema in Lithuania, Romuva has been entertaining the city since 1940. The Art Deco building is listed in Kaunas's Modernist architecture ensemble. A mix of mainstream films and arthouse cinema are shown here, with the courtyard hosting outdoor showings in summer.

## Theatre and classical music

**National Kaunas Drama Theatre** [171 E3] Nacionalinis Kauno dramos teatras; Laisvės alėja 71; w dramosteatras.lt. The National Kaunas Drama Theatre is the home of the oldest professional theatre troupe in Lithuania, founded in 1920 & resident in this Modernist building since 1959. Look out for regular English-language performances.

**Kaunas State Musical Theatre** [170 D3] Kauno valstybinis muzikinis teatras; Laisvės alėja 91; w muzikinisteatras.lt. The repertoire at the second largest theatre in Lithuania includes opera, operetta, musicals, classical concerts & dance performances between Oct & May. During the winter, the warm glow from the windows looks so inviting through the trees of the Musical Theatre Park which almost hides the theatre's Neo-Baroque façade. The theatre was originally built in 1892 under the Kaunas governorate of the Russian Empire but has undergone several reconstructions, especially during the interwar years of independence, when it was the venue for touring international artists.

**Kaunas State Philharmonic** [170 D2] (Kauno valstybinė filharmonija; E Ožeškienės gatvė 12 w kaunofilharmonija.lt) An interwar building that was once the Ministry of Justice & the Parliament, has since 2008 been home to the Kaunas State Philharmonic Orchestra. The building's former important roles are both evident in the Neo-Classical exterior that dominates its corner location with grand, towering columns. The Kaunas Symphony Orchestra (w kaunosimfoninis.lt) & Kaunas State Choir (w kvch.lt) are also based here.

## Watching sports

**Darius & Girėno Stadium** [171 H3] (Dariaus ir Girėno stadionas; w stadionas.lt) A renovated multi-use stadium for football & athletics, as well as star-studded concerts. This is where the Lithuanian national football team play & host international teams & their fans.

**Žalgiris Arena** [171 E4] Žalgirio arena; w zalgirioarena.lt. Located on Nemunas Island, this, the largest indoor arena in the Baltics since opening in 2011, hosts basketball games & big-name concerts. Attending a basketball game is a true local experience.

**SHOPPING** The main shopping street in the Old Town is **Vilniaus gatvė**, where a selection of small boutiques and souvenir shops are interspersed by cafés and bars.

A small selection of art and design shops can be found on adjacent M Valančiaus gatvė. Pedestrianised **Laisvės alėja** has a mix of larger stores and boutique shops.

Serious shoppers should visit **Akropolis** [171 F4] (Karaliaus Mindaugo prospektas 49; w akropolis.lt; ⏰ 10.00–21.00 daily), a huge mall, ideal for cool shopping in summer and warm shopping in winter. There are also numerous cafés and restaurants, an ice rink, cinema and other entertainment venues, making this a popular hang-out for young and old alike. The mall was built around several historic houses which are still preserved inside the mall.

### Bookshops
**Centrinis Knygynas** [170 D3] Laisvės alėja 81; w pegasas.lt; ⏰ 10.00–19.00 Mon–Fri, 10.00–17.00 Sat. It's worth popping into this historic bookshop full of character & atmosphere, for a browse of the books, gifts & games.
**KNYGOS.LT** Laisvės alėja 69; w knygos.lt; ⏰ 10.00–20.00 Mon–Fri, 10.00–18.00 Sat, 11.00–17.00 Sun. One of the largest online book shops in Lithuania also has physical stores with a wide range of books, including a small English-language section.

### Markets
**Žaliakalnio turgavietė** [170 C1] Zanavykų gatvė 25H; ⏰ 07.00–15.00 Tue–Sun. One of the oldest markets in Kaunas, it is known locally as Zanavykų turgus, after the name of the street where it is located, a 30-minute walk from Laisvės alėja. At the heart of the market is the meat hall where nothing much has changed since the 1990s.
**Ūkininkų turgelis prie Pilies** [170 B2] Jonavos gatvė 1; 🔲 ukininku_turgelis_prie_pilies; ⏰ 07.00–14.00 Sat. Depending on the season there are about 50 farmers & producers selling fresh meat, cheese, veggies, fruits, smoked fish & salted or fermented products from their stalls here. A true farm-to-table market.
**Kaunas Central Market & Urmas Trade Town** [171 H5] Pramonės prospektas 14; w urmas.net; ⏰ 09.00–18.00 Mon–Fri, 09.00–17.00 Sat, 09.00–15.00 Sun. More than 2,000 stores offer anything & everything that you never knew you needed. Take trolleybus 15 or 16 to Urmas –

though you might need a taxi home to carry all your purchases. You will also see the neighbouring **Verslo centras 1000 litų** (w 1000lt.com) a business centre building designed as a twisted 1,000-litas banknote. Completed in 2008, the façade is constructed of 4,500 pieces of glass & holds the Lithuanian record for the largest stained-glass window.

### Souvenirs
**Saulutės Gallery** [171 E3] (S Daukanto gatvė 17; w saulutesgalerija.lt; ⏰ 09.00–17.00 Mon–Thu, 09.00–16.00 Fri. Find here traditional handmade crafts & gifts from Kaunas folk artists, including painting, blacksmithing, ceramics, weaving, knitting, jewellery & basket ware.
**Gintarinis suvenyras** [170 B3] Vilniaus gatvė 32; w balticbuy.com; ⏰ 10.00–18.30 daily. This shop sells an array of souvenirs, including amber & linen, available to buy online with international shipping if you regret not buying something once you get home.
**Lino namai** [170 D2] Laisvės alėja 88; w linonamai.lt; ⏰ 10.00–19.00 Mon–Fri, 10.00–16.00 Sat. Come here for everything linen, from coasters to curtains, covering both homeware & clothing ranges in contemporary designs.
**Rūta** [170 B3] M Daukšos gatvė 20; w ruta.lt; ⏰ 10.00–18.00 Mon–Fri, 10.00–15.00 Sat. A leading Lithuanian chocolatier, Rūta has been bringing sweetness & smiles throughout Lithuania since 1913. If you can resist eating them yourself, the chocolates make a good gift.

## SPORTS AND ACTIVITIES
### Boat trips
**Laivas Nemunas į Rumšiškes** w laivai.info. Every Sun, May–Sep, there is a regular boat trip to the Museum of Lithuanian Ethnography in Rumšiškės, leaving at 11.00 from Kaunas Reservoir Quay [170 A1] (Kauno marių prieplauka; T Masiulio gatvė 21). The boat ride to the museum takes 1hr 20mins. Take time to explore the museum before the boat departs back to Kaunas at 16.00.

**Laivas Raketa** w laivasraketa.lt. The Kaunas-to-Nida boat service, which was established in 1957, has been restarted by this company. The *Rocket* powers you along the Nemunas River, enters the delta & crosses the Curonian Lagoon to Nida. Kaunas to Nida takes 3hrs 45mins; returning upriver takes an extra 10mins. The service runs Thu–Sun, departing Kaunas Passenger Quay (Kauno keleivinė prieplauka; Raudondvario plenta 107) at 09.00 Thu, Fri & Sat, & departing Nida at 15.30 on Thu, Fri & Sun. The service is very popular & must be booked in advance (from €49 per adult one way, under 12s €39 one way, under 4's free). Note that, if taking a bicycle, you will need to purchase a separate ticket (€21.90) for your bike. There is a car park available at Kaunas Passenger Quay; a ticket is required.

**Nemunas Travel** w nemunastravel.lt. Nemunas Travel operates regular round-trip boat tours (prices from €28/22) from Kaunas to Kačerginė, Raudondvaris & Zapyškis. Tours take 2, 3 or 5hrs & are on the boat *Kaunas*, which takes up to 35 passengers. Audio guides are available on board. Shorter excursions to view the Old Town from the river are available (1hr 20mins, €12/9). All excursions depart from the Old Town Pier [170 A3], near the Vytautas the Great Church (page 181).

**Nemuno Turas** w nemunoturas.lt. Nemuno Turas operates boat tours to Birštonas. A regular boat trip (€31/28 pp) from Kaunas to Birštonas departs Sun between May & Aug. The boat leaves from Kaunas Reservoir Quay [170 A1] (Kauno marių prieplauka; T Masiulio gatvė 21) at 09.00 & the trip takes 4hrs. Upon arrival in Birštonas, you can join a walking tour or have free time to explore the town. At 17.00 a bus takes you back to Kaunas, arriving at Kaunas Reservoir Quay at 17.40.

**Cycling**  To rent bicycles in Kaunas, try the following 2 firms, & pick up maps of local cycling routes from the Kaunas Tourism Information Centre.

**Babilonas**  Žalioji gatvė 38A; w bike.babilonas.lt

### CYCLE RIDE TO ZAPYŠKIS

Zapyškis is an 'up-and-coming village', lucky to have a historic attraction and benefitting from public and private investment into trails, amenities and cafés. In this case, the attraction is the **Old Church of St John the Baptist** (Zapyškio senoji Šv. Jono Krikštytojo bažnyčia; f zapyskiokultura), an iconic 16th-century Gothic church on the flood plain of the Nemunas River. It is one of the oldest brick buildings in Lithuania, no longer used as a church but repurposed as a cultural venue, and it makes for a very pleasant bike ride from Kaunas Old Town.

Cross the Nemunas River via Vytautas the Great Bridge, turn right at the end of the bridge and join the cycle route down on the embankment. Keep the river on your right and cycle until you reach the pine forest and wooden houses of Kačerginė village. If you need a pit-stop here, you are spoilt for choice between the cafés **Velo Baras** (J Biliuno gatvė 2; f velo.kacergine; €€), **Piliakalnio kiemelis** (J Biliuno gatvė 68; €€) and **Kačerga** (J Janonio gatvė 6; f Kacerga; €€). It is another 4km to Zapyškis and lunch at **Scena** (Vytauto gatvė 46; w restoranasscena.lt; €€€) is a tasty reward. Not that the cycling is hard work – most of the 20km from Kaunas Old Town to Zapyškis is flat and easy-going.

Between May and October, pedestrians and cyclists can take the **ferry** *Nevėžis* (w kaunorajonas.lt/keltas-nevezis; adult/bicycle €1/1) from Zapyškis to Kulautuva and cycle back on the opposite bank of the river. Check the ferry timetable to plan your route, but you can always retrace your route back to Kaunas. Look out for **Nemuno7** (w nemuno7.lt), a retired dredger-turned-art-gallery moored near to Zapyškis.

**Dviračių Rūsys** [171 F3] Miško gatvė 30; w dviratispro.lt

## Sightseeing flights

**Audenis Hot Air Ballooning** w skriskimekartu.lt. View Kaunas in blissful silence as you float over the red roofs of the city & the Nemunas & Neris rivers. The flight lasts 1hr & includes an initiation ceremony for becoming an official balloonist. From €133 pp.

**Pilotai.lt** S Dariaus ir S Girėno aerodromas, Karo aviacijos gatvė 36; w pilotai.lt. Brother & sister Ieva Liekytė & Lukas Liekis are local pilots who have grown up around planes, & they offer sightseeing leisure flights over Kaunas in a 2-seater ultralight plane. The view from above is stunning, with many landmarks to look out for from your bird's-eye view. A 30min flight costs from €120 pp.

## Spa

**Saulėja SPA** [171 F2] K Donelaičio gatvė 27; w sauleja.lt. A professional wellness spa offering massages, facials & body treatments; it has a sauna area for private hire.

**OTHER PRACTICALITIES** Following the national pattern, bank branches in the city centre have drastically reduced in recent years. You will need to book an appointment for an English-speaking cashier. Several bank branches including **Swedbank**, **Šiaulių Bankas** and **Luminor** can be found near Arka business centre [171 F3] (Karaliaus Mindaugo prospektas 37). ATMs are widely available. The most central official currency exchange office is **Exchange.lt** [171 F4] (w exchange.lt; Karaliaus Mindaugo prospektas 49) in the Akropolis shopping centre. At the same location is the most central **post office** [171 F4]. The nearest pharmacy to the Old Town is **BENU Vaistinė** [170 B2] (Šv. Gertrūdos gatvė 64); Laisvės alėja has a **Eurovaistinė** pharmacy at both ends, numbers 38 [170 D2] and 99-2 [171 F3].

## WHAT TO SEE AND DO

**Kaunas Castle and around** Built in the 14th century to defend against attacks by crusaders, **Kaunas Castle** [170 A2] (Kauno pilis; Pilies gatvė 17; w kaunomuziejus.lt; ⊕ Sep–May 10.00–18.00 Tue–Fri, 10.00–17.00 Sat, Jun–Aug 10.00–18.00 Tue–Sat, 10.00–16.00 Sun; €4/2) sits strategically at the confluence of the Nemunas and Neris rivers. Not only is it one of the first stone castles in Lithuania, but it is the only one with two rows of defensive walls. Kaunas Old Town developed around the castle, overtaking it in importance when in 1408 the town was granted Magdeburg rights and the heart of the city moved to the current Town Hall Square. During the 16th century, the castle was used as a prison; it is said that the souls of the prisoners have never found peace and haunt the castle by night. Now the castle grounds are patrolled by autonomous lawnmowers and visitors can don a VR headset to visualise the historic setting of the castle, the characters and legends surrounding it.

**Santaka Park** Next to the castle is Santaka Park. *Santaka* means 'confluence', and you can walk down through the park to the point where the rivers meet. Nearby is **Romuvos aukuras**, the altar where ancient pagan rituals once took place and where modern pagans gather to celebrate festivals and important calendrical events. The park also contains a **monument to Pope John Paul II**, commemorating the Mass he held here in 1993, and a **statue of Vytis** on his rearing horse. Vytis is the state emblem of Lithuania, but his origins are from the coat of arms of the Grand Duchy of Lithuania which has led to other former Duchy lands claiming a right to use the symbol. The most recent controversy has stemmed from the Belarusian independent movement designing a special document for their citizens living in exile and using their version of Vytis (named Pahonia).

**Church of St George the Martyr** [170 A2] (Šv. Jurgio Kankinio bažnyčia; Papilio gatvė 7) The large church and adjoining Bernardine monastery to the south of the castle create an imposing ensemble of late Gothic red brickwork. Their construction between 1495 and 1510 initiated the rise of Kaunas town, radiating from the castle area. During Soviet occupation this Roman Catholic church was converted into a medical warehouse. Notice the third floor of the monastery is a neo-Baroque style – it was added atop the original two-floor structure during the interwar period and after some deliberation it has been left in place. Since 2011, the neighbouring friary has contained a simple guesthouse, called Domus Pacis, for pilgrims.

**Town Hall Square and around** Kaunas Old Town is centred on Town Hall Square [170 A3] (Rotušės aikštė), which is surrounded by the historic facades of merchant houses, churches and mansions.

**Kaunas Town Hall** [170 A3] (Kauno rotušė; Rotušės aikštė 15) The elegant Town Hall takes centre stage in Town Hall Square. Since its construction in 1542, the Town Hall has acquired Gothic, Baroque and early Classicist attributes; its graceful 53m-tall tower is the tallest in the Old Town and earned it the nickname 'White Swan', adrift amid the surrounding cobbled streets. You can climb the tower's spiral staircase to peer through small windows across the Old Town. Over the centuries, the Town Hall has hosted markets, fairs, a prison and warehouses; judicial trials have been conducted here, and wax melting furnaces have operated here. Its multifunctional character prevails today and the building now contains the recently renovated **Kaunas City Museum** (Kauno miesto muziejus; w kaunomuziejus.lt; ⊕ 10.00–17.00 Tue–Wed, noon–20.00 Thu, noon–18.00 Fri–Sat, noon–17.00 Sun; €10/5), which tells the story of Kaunas's cultural, industrial and scientific history; in addition to a Tourism Information Centre desk; and the White Hall is an official venue for civil marriages. Download the museum app to hear stories about the exhibits and the history of the building. Opposite the rear doors of the Town Hall is a sculpture dedicated to puppet pioneer Władysław Starewicz. A commemorative plaque is held up by his three main cartoon characters, a stag beetle, an ant and a grasshopper.

**Church of Holy Trinity** [170 A2] (Švč. Trejybės (Seminarijos) bažnyčia; A Jakšto gatvė 1; w kaunoarkivyskupija.lt/kaunas/svc-trejybes-b; ⊕ 14.00–18.00 daily) Tucked away in the northwest corner of Town Hall Square is this Renaissance style church, built between 1624 and 1634. The adjoining priest seminary was added later in 1933. The architectural ensemble provides an attractive backdrop to the Town Hall Square. The inner courtyard garden with carved wooden cross is a contemplative place to sit.

**St Francis Xavier Church** [170 A3] (Šv. Pranciškaus Ksavero (Jėzuitų) bažnyčia; Rotušės aikštė 7; ⊕ 16.00–18.00 Mon–Fri, 07.00–13.00 &16.00–18.00 Sun) The two majestic towers of the Jesuit Church are the centrepiece of the south side of Town Hall Square. When the late 17th-century Baroque church is open, it is possible to access a small observation deck offering views of the square. The interior of the church is modest and most famous for being where historical literary figures Adomas Mickevičius and Jonas Mačiulis-Maironis preached their sermons.

**Museum of the History of Lithuanian Medicine and Pharmacy** [170 A3] (Lietuvos medicinos ir farmacijos istorijos muziejus; Rotušės aikštė 28; w lsmu.

lt/en/about-lsmu/visit-lsmu/museum-of-the-history-of-lithuanian-medicine-and-pharmacy; ⊕ 10.00–17.00 Tue–Sat; €2/1) This fascinating and unexpectedly comprehensive museum takes you back to the days when barbers were surgeons, amputating limbs as well as cropping hair. Medieval medical practitioners were either herbalists closely associated with witchcraft or figures connected to the church, with nuns as nurses and a lot of faith put into healing prayer. In the late 18th century, Kaunas had 'proper' doctors who administered much more scientific treatments, including drilling a hole in the head for a headache – to create an exit for the evil spirits that were causing the pain. The average Kaunas citizen had a relatively short lifespan of approximately 30–40 years; while wealthier nobility and merchants lived longer thanks to imported professional doctors. The museum is housed in an authentic merchant house, with old pharmacy fittings and an impressive yet terrifying collection of historic medical paraphernalia, including some way-past-its-sell-by-date arsenic. As always, a guided tour brings the exhibition to life.

**Maironis Lithuanian Literature Museum** [170 A3] (Maironio lietuvių literatūros muziejus; Rotušės aikštė 13; w maironiomuziejus.lt; ⊕ 09.00–17.00 Tue, Wed & Fri, 09.00–19.00 Thu, 10.00–17.00 Sat–Sun; €8/4) Jonas Mačiulis–Maironis (1862–1932) was one of the most influential figures in Lithuanian literature, widely regarded as the father of Lithuanian poetry and for his role in the National Revival Movement. In 1909, he returned to Kaunas from his theological studies in St Petersburg and took up residence here in the Old Town. Maironis' apartment is an authentic tribute to his life, filled with his furniture and belongings. An introductory film about Maironis is included in the ticket price and an English audio guide is available. Much of the museum is dedicated to Lithuanian literature through interactive media and creative displays of original manuscripts and books of great national importance including copies of the independence movement newspaper *Aušra*. Culture evenings are held in the courtyard during summer.

**Lithuanian House of Basketball** [170 A3; not mapped] (Lietuvos Krepšinio Namai; Santakos gatvė 11; e info@krepsinionamai.lt; w ltu.basketball; ⊕ 10.00–17.00 Mon–Fri, 11.00–16.00 Sat. Housing the national collection of all things basketball, this is an essential destination for basketball enthusiasts, where you can browse the trophies, championship memorabilia, photos, basketballs, shirts, and humungous shoes (size EU52/UK16½/US17). Enquire about prices and to book a tour via email. The adjoining sports bar surely gets raucous when a game is shown, especially a derby game between Kaunas Žalgiris and Vilnius Rytas.

**Perkūnas House** [170 A3] (Perkūno namas; Aleksoto gatvė 6) Perkūnas, or 'Thunder', House is named after the god Perkūnas (the god of thunder), a statue of whom was found in a wall of the building in the 19th century. Perkūnas House is one of the oldest surviving buildings in Kaunas and its impressive red-brick pediment is one of the best examples of Gothic architecture in Lithuania. Built by Hanseatic merchants in the 15th century it has stood the tests of time, fire and war, and today is a Jesuit art school. It is not open to the public, so just admire it from outside.

**Vytautas the Great Church** [170 A3] (Vytauto Didžiojo bažnyčia; Aleksoto gatvė 3; w vytautine.lt) Built in 1400, this is the oldest church in Kaunas and the only Gothic-style church with a cross-shaped plan in Lithuania. It is also known as the Church of the Assumption of the Blessed Virgin Mary. According to historians, Grand Duke Vytautas suffered badly in battle against the Tatars at Vorskla, and almost died by drowning in a river. As an act of gratitude for his survival and return home, he pledged to build a church dedicated to the Virgin Mary. Napoleon's army stored ammunition in the church before their hasty retreat in 1812 and the Russians used it as an Orthodox church in the mid 19th century. Today it is a functioning Roman Catholic church with worship Tuesday to Friday at 17.30, Saturday at 10.00, and Sunday at 10.00, noon and 18.00. Note the water level gauge that was installed in 1877 to monitor the Nemunas River levels especially during the spring flood season. Zero altitude on the gauge is 20.8m above sea level. The waterfront outside the church is where Nemunas River boat tours depart from (page 177).

**Vytautas the Great Bridge** [170 A3/4] (Vytauto Didžiojo tiltas) At one time this was the longest bridge in the world, not because of its distance but because of the time taken to cross it. Between 1795 and 1807 the Nemunas River was the border between the Russian Empire (Kaunas side) and Prussia (Aleksotas side). Russia used the Julian calendar, while Prussia used the Gregorian calendar – there is a 13-day difference between their calendars, so crossing from one side of the bridge to the other side took 13 days!

**Aleksotas Funicular** [170 A4] (Aleksoto funikulieriaus viršutinė stotis; Amerikos Lietuvių gatvė 6; ⊕ 07.00–noon & 13.00–19.00 daily; €1/0.50) This vintage funicular has been transporting citizens of Kaunas from the old city up to the suburbs of Aleksotas since 1935. Its primary intended purpose was to promote development of the Aleksotas district, but for today's visitors the panoramic view over the Old Town and the confluence of the Nemunas and Neris rivers from the observation deck is the main reason to take the trip. The funicular operates every 10 minutes during opening hours and bicycles are transported free of charge.

**Around Vilniaus gatvė** Kaunas's main thoroughfare, **Vilniaus gatvė** links the Old Town to Laisvės alėja and the new town. It was once the medieval road to Vilnius and is lined by a medley of architectural styles – red-brick merchant houses and mansions of wealthy residents, interspersed with interwar and contemporary renovations – replacing the original wooden structures. With plenty of cafés, shops and restaurants, too, it is often lively especially during city events or festivals.

**St Peter and St Paul Cathedral-Basilica** [170 B3] (Šv. apaštalų Petro ir Povilo arkikatedra bazilika; Vilnius gatvė 1; w kaunoarkikatedra.lt) Although it is the biggest Gothic sacral building in Lithuania, stemming from the early 15th century, reconstruction over the years has added Baroque, Classical, Neo-Gothic and Renaissance features. The interior is highly decorative and consists of nine altars, the newest being dedicated to Pope John Paul II after he became the first pope, in 1993, to visit Lithuania. The Pope John Paul II Pilgrimage Route (Jono Pauliaus II pilgrim kelias; w piligrimukelias.lt) was established in his honour and connects the holy sites of Lithuania. Several influential men of the cloth are buried here, including priest and poet Jonas Mačiulis-Maironis, Samogitian (Zemaitija) bishop Motiejus Valančius and Vincentas Sladkevičius, the first cardinal of Lithuania.

**Folk Music Museum** [170 B3] (Tautinės muzikos muziejus; L Zamenhofo 12/Kurpių 12; w kaunomuziejus.lt; ⊕ 10.00–18.00 Tue-Fri, 10.00–17.00 Sat; €4/2) The first (and only) museum in Lithuania dedicated to folk music and its influence on traditional culture contains a collection of over 7,000 exhibits, including traditional musical instruments, audio recordings, photographs, letters and posters. To bring a music museum to life it must be interactive, and here you can learn how *kanklės* (a chordophone instrument related to the zither) are made, sing a *sutartinė* (traditional Lithuanian multipart song), play some instruments, or listen to authentic folk music.

### Church of Holy Sacrament
[170 C3] (Švč. Sakramento bažnyčia; Vilniaus gatvė 31) Both the exterior and interior of this church are testament to the practice of secularisation by occupying forces, an effort to remove faith, community and spirit from the local population. It was originally built around 1678, in Baroque style, on the edge of the Old Town, but the centuries have stripped it of its intended beauty and purpose numerous times – damaged during the Napoleonic Wars in the early 1800s, closed under the Tsarist Russification rules in the mid 1800s, converted into apartments and an Orthodox school, and finally, during the Soviet occupation, used as a cinema, 'Santaka', from 1965 until 1990. Today a small chapel exists in the former cinema bar, while the rest of the church awaits reconstruction.

### Historical Presidential Palace
[170 C3] (Istorinė Prezidentūra; Vilniaus gatvė 33; w istorineprezidentura.lt; ⊕ 10.00–17.00 Tue, Wed, Fri, 10.00–19.00 Thu, 11.00–16.00 Sat–Sun; €5/2.50) If walls could talk, this building could tell many a fascinating story from its 180 years of existence. The ground floor exhibition tells the history of the building with many more important facts than it being the first place with a toilet in Kaunas. The displays are excellent and make Lithuania's political history and path towards modern Lithuanian statehood accessible, even though it is not straightforward. During the Russian Empire occupation, this was the Governor's house from where he managed the difficult province of Kaunas, full of insolent Lithuanians (the National Revival was always close to the surface here). The Nazi invasion saw the palace house the German commander, who hosted exhibitions of anti-Jewish propaganda. During the interwar years of Lithuanian independence, three Lithuanian presidents resided here in the newly titled President's Palace: Smetona, Stulginskis and Grinius – their statues now reside in the garden. And during Soviet times, the palace was a teachers' house and communist ideological centre. Highlights include rare pieces of original Tsarist-period furniture, and gifts presented to the president by international envoys. Book a guide in advance or ask for an audio guide when buying your ticket.

### Around Laisvės Alėja
Laisvės alėja is definitely the longest pedestrian street in Lithuania and one of the longest in Europe. Built in the late 1800s under Russian Empire rule, it runs west to east and is an almost 1.7km-long history lesson in architecture. In English, Laisvės alėja is known as Freedom Avenue or Liberty Boulevard. The wide avenue is lined with shops, cafés, restaurants and bars and is a favourite place to promenade in all seasons.

### Church of St Gertrude
[170 D3] (Šv. Gertrūdos (Marijonų) bažnyčia; Laisvės alėja 101a; w gertrudosbaznycia.lt) Tucked away in the courtyard behind number 101a is the quaint, red-brick Gothic Church of St Getude. It dates back to the 15th century, making it one of the oldest churches in Lithuania, and is a hidden gem that you might stumble across simply by taking a short-cut through a car park. Note the iron cross mounted on the wall opposite the entrance – it is originally from the church tower and is over 450 years old.

**Kaunas Tadas Ivanauskas Museum of Zoology** [170 D2] (Kauno T Ivanausko zoologijos muziejus; Laisvės alėja 106; w zoomuziejus.lt; ⊕ 10.00–18.00 Tue–Sun; €6/3) One of the oldest museums in the country and the only zoological museum in the Baltic states, it was founded in July 1919 by Professor Tadas Ivanauskas (1882–1970), a prominent biologist and zoologist influential in the development of natural science in Lithuania and the establishment of Vytautas Magnus University. The museum consists primarily of taxidermy exhibits, from its collection of approximately 300,000 specimens, and different halls are dedicated to different classes of animal. The oldest exhibits date from 1859 and were made by Ivanauskas's father, Leonardas. The museum is affiliated to the Bird Ringing Centre at Ventės Cape (page 317), also established by Tadas Ivanauskas.

**Former Central Post Office of Kaunas – Architecture Centre** [170 D2] (Kauno centrinis pastas – Architektūros Centras; Laisvės alėja 102) In November 2019, this iconic interwar-period building which housed the Central Post Office was permanently closed. Those who purchased their stamps or paid their heating bills here did so surrounded by valuable examples of national symbolism, including folk accented wood carvings and cornices, motifs of lilies and tulips, and a ceramic floor resembling a folk weaving pattern. The building, constructed between 1930 and 1932, is attributed to the architect Feliksas Vizbaras. His legacy will live on with the reinvention of the building as an architecture centre. At present, the public are welcomed through the doors once again when the building is used to host temporary exhibitions and events. It is expected to be fully renovated in the coming years but look out for pop-up events in the meantime. In front of the building, strolling under the trees is a statue of a dapper gentleman wearing a top hat and carrying a briefcase – this is Jonas Vileišius, a signatory of the 1918 Act of Independence of Lithuania and former mayor of Kaunas.

**Musical Theatre Park** [170 D3] (Muzikinio teatro parkas; Laisvės alėja) At first glance, this is a normal park with benches and a play area for children, but look closer and you will find it is packed with historical references. At the front of the park, alongside the pavement of Laisvės alėja is a monument in honour of Romas Kalanta (1953–72), a Kaunas student whose public act of self-immolation protesting the Soviet regime made him a symbol of the Lithuanian resistance. The grand building to the rear of the park is Kaunas State Musical Theatre (page 176). To the right of the theatre is the last remaining fragment of the old city's defensive wall. The most recent installation is an illuminated fountain in the centre of the park, making this a popular place to while away the hours on a summer's evening.

**Statue of Grand Duke Vytautas** [170 D2] (Paminklas Vytautui Didžiajam; Laisvės alėja) Vytautas the Great (Vytautas Didysis) is Lithuania's long-time national hero. During his reign as Grand Duke of the Grand Duchy of Lithuania (1392–1430), Vytautas always strived for a free and independent Lithuania. He fought many wars against Lithuania's adversaries: the Tatars, Russians, the Golden Horde, and the Teutonic Knights against whom his military might was confirmed with victory at the Battle of Žalgiris (Grunwald) in 1410. The original statue was erected in 1930 to commemorate 500 years since Vytautas the Great's death and was created by sculptor Vincas Grybas. It was removed during Soviet times and never found; this replacement was erected in 1990.

## STREET ART IN KAUNAS

The **Wise Old Man** (Jonavos gatvė 3) by Gyva Grafika was the first large form of street art in Kaunas. Installed in 2013, it is dedicated to the Kaunas-born father of the Fluxus movement, Jurgis Mačiūnas (incidentally, there is a farmer's market held in front of the mural every weekend morning). Since then, street art has become prolific under an organised movement. In 2014, the **Nykoka Street Art Festival** took place to bring colour to the city and liven up grey public spaces, and in 2015 the Kaunas City Municipality launched a campaign (w nykoka.lt) – known locally as 'street art tinder' – to connect artists with property owners willing to host art on their walls. They mutually agree on the design and, once approved, it is funded by the municipality. Every year the number of art installations increases, a combination of professional artworks and dedicated spaces for legal self-expression. After all, in 2015 Kaunas was designated a UNESCO City of Design (w designcities.net/city/kaunas), where creativity flourishes and expression is encouraged. The tourist information office has self-guided tour maps of Kaunas street art, but you will be hard-pressed not to see any during your visit. Some of the most iconic pieces include **The Pink Elephant** (E Ožeškienės gatvė 18A, 2014) by Vytenis Jakas, whose huge pink elephant image was worked around the existing graffiti scrawl of young lovers 'Deima + Arūnas' (who are now immortalised together even if they've since split up). **Contemporary Ladies** (A Mickevičiaus gatvė 37; 2015) by Linas Kaziulionis brightens up a wall of Kaunas University of Technology with renditions of two of Leonardo da Vinci's leading ladies (Lady with an Ermine and La Belle Ferronnière) meeting up to play chess and listen to music.

For a full immersion into Kaunas's urban art scene, visit **Yard Gallery** [170 D2] (Kiemo galerija; E Ožeškienės gatvė 21A (backyard); w yard.gallery), an accidental project that was started ten years ago by local artist and resident Vytenis Jakas. Motivated by modern life becoming unfriendly and isolated, a lack of care for communal spaces and detachment from the local history, Jakas held an event to spring clean the yard. People shared stories and memories, they brought out photos of old residents, and the community felt revived. With the support of other residents, Jakas began to transfer photos of the Jewish families who previously lived here on to the courtyard walls. Gradually, more and more pieces of art have appeared in the courtyard, bringing a fascinating feeling of optimism, colour and community. If you visit, please respect the residents' peace and quiet.

***Money Museum of the Bank of Lithuania*** [171 E2] (Lietuvos banko muziejus; Kauno filialas; Maironio gatvė 25 w pinigumuziejus.lt; ⊕ 09.00–15.15 Tue–Wed, 11.00–17.00 Thu, 09.00–14.00 Fri; free) It was the 1920s, Lithuania had lost its capital Vilnius to Polish annexation, and Kaunas was ill-prepared to host the government departments and national infrastructure required to run a newly independent nation. A building boom followed and in 1928 the interwar Neo-Classical Kaunas branch of the Bank of Lithuania was built. It is the only building erected during that period to retain its original purpose. After admiring the exterior, you can pop inside for a quick look around as it still has operational counters in the main hall. Look up at the murals, reminiscent of Wedgwood pottery, on the ceiling. To access the museum, you need to book a guide in advance. The free guided tour includes displays of currency previously used in Lithuania, including Russian Empire roubles, German marks and Lithuanian litas. Visit the vault from Milners London–Liverpool, and the beautifully restored governor's apartment on the top floor.

**Memorial to Jan Zwartendijk, Honorary Consul of the Netherlands** (Laisvės alėja 29) Jan Zwartendijk (1896–1976) was a Dutch businessman and honorary consul of the Netherlands in Lithuania in 1940. During his tenure as honorary consul, Zwartendijk issued up to 2,345 'visas for life' to Jewish refugees for entry to the Dutch Caribbean island of Curaçao. He operated without the consent of the Dutch government and, although there were no diplomatic relations between the Netherlands and Japan at the time, he cooperated with the Japanese vice-consul Chiune Sugihara (page 191), who issued transit visas for onward travel to Curaçao via Japan. It is estimated they saved between 6,000 and 10,000 lives, issuing visas for whole families at incredible speed, knowing their consulates would be closed by the authorities imminently. Upon his return to the Netherlands, Zwartendijk never spoke of his courageous role, but in 1997 he was posthumously awarded the title of Righteous Among the Nations by Yad Vashem, the World Holocaust Remembrance Center. Often in the shadow of the more recognised Sugihara, his memorial and highlighted recognition is a welcome addition to Kaunas's historical sights. A spiral of light installed among the trees, designed by Dutch artist Giny Vos in 2018, the memorial to Zwartendijk stands outside his former office at Laisvės alėja 29.

## Around Nepriklausomybės aikštė

If Nepriklausomybės aikštė doesn't roll off your tongue, you can call it **Independence Square** [171 F3]. This is fast becoming a trendy area for hanging out with friends in cafes and bars, and music events are often held here in the summer months.

### St Michael the Archangel Church
[171 F3] (Šv. arkangelo Mykolo (Įgulos) bažnyčia; Nepriklausomybės aikštė 14) Known locally as *soboras*, which translates quite plainly to cathedral, this Neo-Byzantine-style church has split local opinion for more than 100 years. It is also known as 'the garrison church', having been built in 1895 as an Orthodox Church for the Kaunas Fortress soldiers under orders of Russian Tsar Alexander III. In 1919, independence from the Russian Empire saw it reconfigured into a Catholic church; under Soviet occupation all crosses were removed and it became a stained-glass and sculpture gallery; today it has been reconsecrated as a Catholic church.

### Mykolas Žilinskas Art Gallery
[171 F3] (Mykolo Žilinsko dailės galerija; Nepriklausomybės aikštė 12; w ciurlionis.lt; ⊕ closed for reconstruction at time of writing) Built in 1989, the gallery houses the extensive private collection of the late art collector Mykolas Žilinskas (1904–92). Works date from the 17th to 20th centuries and vary from fine art to applied art, predominantly from Europe and Asia. It is now a branch of the M K Čiurlionis National Museum of Art. As you approach the gallery from Nepriklausomybės aikštė, you can't help but notice the sculpture *Man* (*Žmogus*), an iconic statue by sculptor Petras Mazūras of a naked man. He was unveiled in 1991 and stands with his arms open wide with no inhibitions – although on occasion he does get dressed up or accessorised for fun or as a political statement.

### Art Deco Museum
[171 G2] (Art Deco muziejus; Gedimino gatvė 48; w artdecomuziejus.lt; ⊕ daily, for tours; €25 pp) The rich collection of interwar

architecture that characterises Kaunas's streets is complemented by this lovingly and painstakingly restored 1929 apartment. Chosen for its original layout, the apartment is decorated true to its era and filled with authentic furniture, accessories and household objects that ooze character and style from this period of optimism. The owners of this privately funded architectural endeavour, Karolis Banys and Petras Gaidamavičius, have achieved something quite extraordinary. Tours are experiential: it's like being invited to a soiree at a stranger's house, sampling their lifestyle and being enamoured by their stories. Either join a 2-hour public group tour (fixed-time English tours are bookable online), though book early as dates are limited and sell out; alternatively, book a private tour for maximum 17 guests for €425.

**Amsterdam School Museum** [171 G3] (Amsterdamo Mokyklos muziejus; Vytauto prospektas 58-6; w amsterdamomokyklosmuziejus.lt; ⊕ daily, for tours; €25 pp) The second project of Art Deco afficionados Banys and Gaidamavičius (see opposite) is housed in the only Amsterdam School architectural-style building in Kaunas. Built in 1928 by wealthy industrialists, the once luxurious property had become communal social housing under the Soviets but retained the original layout. Upon purchasing your ticket online, you will receive pre-renovation photos to set the scene. Furnished with Art Deco, Modernist and Amsterdam School pieces, the apartment here is more sumptuous than its sister Art Deco Museum. Tours take the same experiential format; either join a 2-hour public group tour in English (bookable online; advance purchase is a must) or book a private tour for maximum 20 people (€450).

**Kaunas Picture Gallery** [171 G2] (Kauno paveikslų galerija; K Donelaičio gatvė 16; w ciurlionis.lt; ⊕ 10.00–18.00 Tue & Fri–Sun, 11.00–19.00 Wed–Thu; €8/4) A subdivision of the M K Čiurlionis National Museum of Art (see below), the gallery houses Lithuanian and international art alongside a community exhibition space titled 'Backup Stories'. Key attractions include the Fluxus room featuring works by renowned artists including Jurgis Mačiūnas (father of the Fluxus movement), Jonas Mekas and George Brecht; and the Japanese artist Ay-O's installation *Black Hole*, which makes your whole body feel like a 'protruding finger' as you tentatively navigate a route in the pitch black.

## Around V Putvinskio gatvė
**Devils Museum** [171 E2] (Velnių muziejus; V Putvinskio gatvė 64; w ciurlionis. lt; ⊕ 11.00–17.00 Tue–Wed & Fri, 11.00–19.00 Thu, 10.00–17.00 Sat–Sun; €8/4) Officially titled A Žmuidzinavičius Creations and Collections Museum, this is a unique Kaunas wonder and the only devil museum in the world. Professor Antanas Žmuidzinavičius (1876–1966) collected devil-related paraphernalia and artefacts resulting in an exhibition of more than 3,000 devils from over 70 countries of the world. When you are prepping and packing for your trip to Lithuania, feel free to include a local devil from your hometown as visitors are welcome to contribute pieces to the collection.

**M K Čiurlionis National Museum of Art** [171 E2] (Nacionalinis M K Čiurlionio dailės muziejus; V Putvinskio gatvė 55; w ciurlionis.lt; ⊕ 10.00–18.00 Tue & Fri–Sun, 11.00–19.00 Wed–Thu; €10/5, free last Sun of the month) Established in 1921, this is one of the oldest and largest art museums in Lithuania, dedicated to the life and works of Lithuania's most prominent artist and composer Mikalojus Konstantinas Čiurlionis and housing a vast collection of his paintings, drawings and manuscripts. You are encouraged to book a museum guide to interpret the folklore and symbolism embedded within the artworks. The Angelų takais (Trail of Angels; w angelutakais.lt; €20/13) immersive virtual-reality headset experience is a beautiful introduction to Čiurlionis and highly recommended. Tickets are best booked in advance online as it is very popular. Other permanent exhibitions include: 'Lithuania – the Land of the Crosses', dedicated to the Lithuanian heritage skill of cross-crafting and sun crosses; 'Lithuanian Art of the 14th to 19th centuries'; and 'Archaics: Lithuanian Folk Art of the 18th to 20th centuries'. Externally, the building, which houses two of Kaunas's great museums, is an example of Modernist interwar architecture built with patriotic purpose: the art museum façade resembles a giant crown, and that of the Vytautas the Great War Museum is guarded by two cast-iron lions commissioned by Count Jonas Tiškevičius. During periods of oppression, the building was an ideological bastion and symbol of independent Lithuania.

**Vytautas the Great War Museum** [171 E2] (Vytauto Didžiojo Karo Muziejus; K Donelaičio gatvė; w vdkaromuziejus.lt; ⊕ 10.00–17.00 Tue–Sun, 10.00–19.00 Wed; €5/2.50) Proudly named after one of the greatest warrior lords of medieval Lithuania, the Vytautas the Great War Museum contains exhibitions dedicated to military art in prehistoric Lithuania, uprisings of the 18th and 19th centuries, anti-Nazi and anti-Soviet resistance, and a collection of weaponry from various ages. The Lituanica Memorial Hall displays the wreckage of the doomed transatlantic flight plane *Lituanica* and personal effects of pilots Steponas Darius and Stasys Girėnas (page 193). To the front of the war museum is the **Garden of War**, centred around an eternal flame (Amžinoji ugnis) with a monument to the *Fallen for Lithuania's*

### MIKALOJUS KONSTANTINAS ČIURLIONIS   Vika Ross

During his tragically brief life cut short at the age of 36 (1875–1911), Mikalojus Konstantinas Čiurlionis honed and shared his exceptional musical and artistic gifts and thereby made an indelible contribution to Lithuania's cultural landscape. Often referred to as the Godfather of Lithuanian music and art, Čiurlionis was not only a prolific composer and artist, he was also a staunch advocate for the renewal, preservation and proliferation of Lithuanian culture in all its forms. Born in the small town of Varėna on the outskirts of Druskininkai, Čiurlionis grew up surrounded by the fairy-tale landscape of the region of Dzūkija. Druskininkai remained his beloved home-base despite extensive travels and lengthy stays in other parts of Europe.

The first-born son of a church organist, Čiurlionis followed in his father's footsteps by learning to play the piano and organ when he was not yet of school age. The prodigy was 'discovered' by a noble patron, Prince Michał Ogiński, who made it possible for Čiurlionis to attend the Mykolas Oginskis Orchestra School in Plungė during his early teens where he learned to play a variety of instruments. He furthered his musical studies at the Leipzig Conservatoire. Following the death of his patron, Prince Oginiski, Čiurlionis was forced to leave his music studies behind and he instead opted to devote himself to the study of art which he pursued at the Warsaw School of Drawing under the guidance of various teachers.

Fame and fortune largely eluded him during his lifetime but – in the spirit of a true artist – he was driven to produce authentic works of art until he was physically and emotionally spent and exhausted.

*Freedom* (Žuvusiems už Lietuvos laisvę) and the *Grave of the Unknown Soldier* (Nežinomo Kareivio Kapas), all surrounded by statues of prominent Lithuanians and traditional wooden crosses and pole shrines honouring those who have lost their lives in war. The garden was destroyed by the Soviets and restored using public donations between 1988 and 1990. Nearby is the *Freedom Monument* (Laisvės paminklas) where remembrance ceremonies gather. On the garden wall is the *Star Seeder* (Sėjėjas), created illegally in 2008 by street artist Morfai by strategically stencilling stars on a wall behind the existing statue of a seed spreader by sculptor Bernardas Bučas. After dark, when the light is right, it all makes beautiful sense. The stars were illegal graffiti and painted over, but the love of locals and visitors resulted in them being permanently restored.

The war museum has a **Branch of Military Equipment** at the Sixth Fort (page 195) and they also manage the **Underground Printing House 'ab'** (page 196).

**Unity Square** [171 E2] (Vienybės aikštė) This contemporary communal space next to the Vytautas the Great War Museum has recently been renovated. It is a well-loved space for youngsters to hang out on skateboards, for children to play in cooling fountains during the summer months, with plenty of seating and landscaping. Surrounded by Vytautas the Great University and Kaunas Technical University buildings, this makes a popular place for students to socialise. Look out for the large, shiny stainless-steel sculpture in the south of the square – it is a tribute to the Lithuanian letter ė and called *Taškas*. The declining use of correct punctuation in computing and tech is a major problem, and the sculpture highlights the importance of using the Lithuanian alphabet correctly.

The love of his life, his wife Sofija – a cultural force in her own right – was Čiurlionis' passionate partner who worked ardently with her husband to preserve and promote Lithuanian culture. The dynamic duo sought to lasso creative Lithuanians in the neighbouring countries back into the fold of the country's cultural scene. At the time, Polish and Russian influences had a major impact on the flourishing of Lithuanian language and culture, and Čiurlionis advocated for a renewal of cultural pride and appreciation.

Rooted in the traditional Lithuanian landscape, mythology and folk traditions of his homeland, Čiurlionis' artistic and musical creations are often described as ethereal, mystical and sometimes haunting. Čiurlionis was thought to have synaesthesia which can be loosely defined as having the ability to 'see' music and to 'hear' in colours and in images. He was considered a trailblazer with his avant-garde style in both his artistic and musical creations. His creative legacy – in Lithuania and abroad – has continued to expand since his passing well over a century ago. Some have likened Čiurlionis to Van Gogh. Both artists died young under tragic circumstances, suffered mentally and financially near the end of their lives and were especially prolific in their final chapters.

Through his singular style in both his artistic and musical compositions, Čiurlionis carved out an unparalleled niche which is now deeply integrated in Lithuania's artistic tapestry and a great source of national pride. For a deeper dive into Čiurlionis' life and creative output, you are recommended to visit the **M K Čiurlionis National Museum of Art** in Kaunas (page 187) or the **M K Čiurlionis House Museum** in Druskininkai (page 142).

***Žaliakalnas Funicular*** [171 F1/2] (Žaliakalnio funikulieris; Lower Station, V Putvinskio gatvė 22; ⏰ 07.30–17.30 Mon–Fri; one-way ticket €1 in cash) This funicular has been transporting locals and visitors up and down, down and up since 1931 – they made them to last in those days. The original wagons feature sturdy wooden benches and accommodate 25 passengers. A one-way trip takes 1 minute 40 seconds and is the ideal way to ascend the hill to visit Christ's Resurrection Church. The upper station is at Aušros gatvė 6.

***Christ's Resurrection Church*** [171 F1] (Kristaus prisikėlimo bazilika; Žemaičių gatvė 31A; w prisikelimas.lt; ⏰ Mar–Sep 11.30–18.30 Mon–Fri, 11.00– 18.30 Sat–Sun, Oct–Feb noon–18.00 Mon–Fri, 11.00–18.00 Sat–Sun; entrance to the observation deck €5/3) In 1922, during Lithuania's interwar independence and with Kaunas as the temporary capital, locals wanted to construct a new church as a symbol of their thanks to god. The vast size of the church reflects the scale of their gratitude – it is the biggest basilica in the Baltics. Construction began in 1932 but was halted by the Soviet occupation and the building confiscated and utilised as the Kaunas Radio Factory. In 1990 the building was returned to the church and it was finally completed and consecrated in 2004. Standing tall over the city (the tower is 70m tall), it is an iconic symbol of independence and interwar sacral architecture. From the observation deck there is a panoramic view of the city; note that entry is €2 cheaper if you take the stairs rather than the lift. Return to the city centre via the funicular, or walk down the pleasant 256 steps of Šilelio laiptai stairs to V Putvinskio gatvė.

***Nemunas Island*** [170 D4] A short walk across the bridge from Karaliaus Mindaugo prospektas brings you to Nemunas Island, an area of trees and parkland with circular hiking and cycling tracks. In late spring the blossoms of **Sakura Park** bring a burst of early colour. Facilities on the island include **Žalgiris Arena**, the home of basketball club Žalgiris – the presence of hordes of fans will indicate when there is a game on. Next door to the arena is Olympic size **Žalgiris Arena Swimming Pool** [171 E4] (Žalgirio arenos baseinas; w zalgirioarenosbaseinas.lt). Outdoor tennis courts are also available to hire.

***Science Island*** [170 D4] (Mokslo Sala; Karaliaus Mindaugo prospektas 50; w mokslosala.lt; ⏰ 10.00–19.00 Tue–Sun; €17/12) Nemunas Island's newest attraction is this state-of-the-art science and innovation centre, created to inspire, educate and entertain all ages to engage with STEM, especially the younger generations of innovators and entrepreneurs. Displays are in Lithuanian and English, exhibits are interactive, and against the shiny clinical laboratory-style backdrop there are people of all ages enjoying science. Since this is a new and popular attraction, it is advisable to book in advance online for an allocated entrance time slot. Note that if you want to experience the centre's star attraction **Planetarium** (currently in Lithuanian only), you should also book a slot online; it is an additional €8/6.

## City centre outskirts
***Stumbras Museum*** [171 H5] (Stumbro muziejui; K Būgos gatvė 7; w stumbras. lt; ⏰ must be booked in advance) Established in 1906 under Russian Empire rule as 'Kaunas State Wine Warehouse No. 1' and later merged with the Stumbras liquer factory under Soviet nationalisation, the factory has been producing Lithuanian spirits non-stop. Since privatisation and modernisation in the post-independence

years, the company have taken many more Lithuanian brands on board and become more experimental with flavours such as 'young potato vodka' and vodka made from quince ('Lithuanian lemons'). The museum tells the story of Lithuanian drinking culture and includes tastings of several of their branded beverages (you must be over 20 years old to participate in tastings). Tours cost from €23 per person and should be booked in advance via the website.

**Sugihara House** [171 H4] (Vaižganto gatvė 30; w sugiharahouse.com; ⊕ Apr–Oct 10.00–17.00 Mon–Fri, 11.00–16.00 Sat–Sun, Nov–Mar 11.00–15.00 daily; €6/3) Chiune Sugihara (1900–86) was the Japanese vice-consul to Lithuania between 1939 and 1940. His main role was to spy on German and Russian troop movements and report back to Tokyo. The situation was grave; Russia had invaded Lithuania, Polish and Lithuanian Jews who had sought safety in Kaunas were in danger and living in hiding, the city was full of soldiers and tanks, and options to escape were limited, with emigration quotas to Palestine and the USA full. Foreign consulates were to be closed imminently, so time was precious. Plans were construed between Jewish refugees and the Dutch honorary consul to Lithuania, Jan Zwartendijk (page 186) to issue visas for the Dutch Caribbean island of Curaçao. To travel to Curaçao, a transit visa was needed via Japan; vice-consul Sugihara agreed with Zwartendijk to supply these, going against the orders of the Japanese government. And so began the 'visas for life' scheme. It cost a nominal fee of 2 Lithuanian litas per visa, and they issued approximately 2,139 visas for families, saving an estimated 6,000–10,000 mainly Jewish lives. People fled across the width of the USSR to get to Japan. Not one person went on to Curaçao, as most applied for visas to free countries from Japan. The museum is housed in the interwar villa that was the former Japanese Consulate and home of the Sugihara family. It is run by the Diplomats for Life Foundation (Sugiharos fondas 'Diplomatai už gyvybę') to keep the story of Sugihara alive and acts as an important link between Lithuania, Japan and Israel. In 1984, Sugihara was awarded the title Righteous Among the Nations by Yad Vashem, the World Holocaust Remembrance Center.

At the museum, you are welcomed with a 20-minute documentary film. The displays are mainly in English, but prebooking an English-speaking guide is highly recommended.

**Lithuanian Aviation Museum** [170 C6] (Lietuvos aviacijos muziejus; Veiverių gatvė 132; w lam.lt; ⊕ 10.00–17.00 Mon–Fri, 10.00–16.00 Sat; €2/1) In the former passenger terminal of Darius and Girėno Airport (prior to that, Aleksotas Airport) is this modest aviation museum. The airport is no longer used for commercial flights, but at its peak this was Kaunas's international airport used for internal USSR flights. Nothing flew west and all international connections had to be made via Moscow. Now it is a pilot school and home to private planes, search and rescue, and the aerobatic club.

The museum is undergoing renovations, the first newfangled attraction being a flight simulator (€6 for 10mins). The outdoor exhibits will remain and, although it may look like a graveyard of old planes, each has a story to tell. One of the stars of the show is a Blue Antonov – a model that was in production for 50 years with no changes made. This plane was hired privately and used to secretly coordinate the Baltic Way (page 116) by radio, and to film it – the aircraft appears on the documentary dropping flowers on to the Baltic Way participants below, a cover for taking to the sky for communications and filming. The film was handed to ground crew and covertly distributed to inform the world of this peaceful protest.

The museum collection also contains a replica of Darius and Girėnas' *Lituanica* plane (see opposite), which was made for the 50th anniversary of their doomed flight and is flown at air shows and on anniversaries. The new museum will also have a dedicated section to gliding. The town of Prienai near Birštonas (page 210) produces world-class gliders at the LAK Lithuanian Aviation Plant. From 1927 the factory produced gliders for the whole of the USSR, post-independence it extended its reach to export gliders around the world, and in 2022 every winner of a gliding championship used Lithuanian gliders.

**Getting there** To get to the museum, take **bus** 6, 6A or 6B from 'Karaliaus Mindaugo' bus stop, alighting at 'S Dariaus ir S Girėno aerodromas' bus stop. There are several buses an hour. By **car** it is a 10-minute drive from Kaunas centre, south on road 130 (Veiverių gatvė).

**KGB Atomic Bunker Museum** [170 A1] (KGB atominio bunkerio muziejus; Raudondvario plentą 164 A (in the yard); w atominisbunkeris.lt; ⊕ private bookings only) An outstanding private collection of historical memorabilia is presented in the former nuclear bunker of a factory. The inextricably tangled world of the KGB used the latest technology to spy on the public and on each other; mistrust, accusation and persecution were rife. The descent 6m underground echoes the secrecy and uncertainty of living during such times, the musty smell and cool air adding to the atmosphere. The bunker rooms are crammed full of paraphernalia, each exhibit able to elicit a unique or outrageous story from your guide. The huge collection includes an impressive array of gas masks, mobile chemical laboratories, medical instruments, radio communications, listening devices, hidden cameras, surveillance equipment, assassin's weapons including a lipstick gun, and so much more. The museum may feel like you're in a props room of a theatre or behind the scenes of a James Bond movie, but this is real and shows a true aspect of life in the Soviet Union. Since the bunker does not keep regular opening hours, you must prebook a scheduled tour via the website.

To get to the museum, take **bus** 7 or 11 from 'Laisvės alėja' bus stop, alighting at 'Atominio bunkerio muziejus B' bus stop. There are several buses an hour. By **car** it is a 10-minute drive from Kaunas centre, heading west on road 141 (Raudondvario plentas). Turn right into the IKI supermarket car park and head towards the back right corner of the car park, where there is a passageway through which you can drive and then parking for the bunker is on the right near the entrance.

**Ninth Fort Museum** (Kauno IX forto muziejus; Žemaičių plentas 73; w 9fortomuziejus.lt; ⊕ 09.00–17.00 Tue–Sun; €8/4) The ninth fort of the Kaunas Fortress is by far the best-preserved section of the city fortifications and has served a sombre array of uses since its construction between 1902 and 1913 by the army of the Russian Empire. The earth ramparts and buildings were built to a high specification to defend the empire's western frontier, so it was an embarrassing shambles when the whole fortress fell to the German army in 11 days (although such an easy takeover is the reason it is so well preserved). Limited combat and a hasty retreat resulted in little damage, making it ideal to be repurposed as Kaunas's hard labour prison in 1924. From 1940 to 1941 it was an NKVD prison, and during the Nazi occupation it was turned into a death camp where an estimated 50,000 people were murdered. After World War II, the fort became a Soviet prison, before being chosen in 1958 to become a museum 'to commemorate the victims of the terror of the Lithuanian bourgeois-nationalists and the German fascist invaders'

## LITUANICA

The *Lituanica* was a modified Bellanca CH-300 aircraft used in the 1933 non-stop transatlantic flight from New York, USA, to Kaunas, Lithuania, by Lithuanian American pilots Steponas Darius and Stasys Girėnas. Having emigrated from Lithuania to the USA during Imperial Russian rule, the men, both proficient aviators, aspired to showcase Lithuania's capabilities and national identity to the world. They dedicated their flight to the newly independent Lithuania:

> Young Lithuania! Inspired by Your spirit, we embark on a mission we have chosen. May our success strengthen Your spirit and confidence in Your own powers and talents!

On 15 July 1933, they departed Floyd Bennett Field, New York, and successfully crossed the Atlantic ocean, covering a distance of 6,411km, only to crash near Pszczelnik in Poland on 17 July, 650km from their destination of Kaunas. The reason for their tragic crash is not certain but possibly was due to engine defects, a navigation error or adverse weather conditions. When their bodies were returned to Lithuania, Darius and Girėnas were mourned as national heroes.

Not long after the tragedy, it was mooted by the Lithuanian community in Chicago to finance another attempt at the flight, and they soon had a Lockheed Vega aircraft named *Lituanica II* and pilot Felix Waitkus (Feliksas Vaitkus in Lithuanian) on board. On 21 September 1935, Waitkus took off from Floyd Bennett Field to cross the Atlantic, and although he failed to get to Kaunas due to exhaustion and low fuel, he landed successfully and safely near Ballinrobe, Ireland, and became the sixth person to complete a solo flight across the Atlantic.

The salvaged wreckage of the original *Lituanica* is on display at the Vytautas the Great War Museum (page 188) and a replica can be seen at the Lithuanian Aviation Museum (page 191), both in Kaunas. The Energy and Technology Museum (page 116) in Vilnius has a model of the plane with an information display on its roof; and there is a monument to Darius and Girėnas in Marquette Park in Chicago, USA.

– in other words to push a version of history that supported Soviet ideology. In June 1984 the museum was extended and the domineering 32m-tall monument in memory of Nazi victims (by sculptor Alfonsas Vincentas Ambraziūnas) was installed. Unofficially, this became an illegal rock-climbing hotspot for youngsters. It was only once the wind of change arrived in 1988 and the mood of independence started to take hold that the exhibitions in the museum started to change and the narrative began to show the atrocities of both Nazi and Soviet occupations, feeding the independence movement. To this day, the museum presents the traumatic history of Lithuania with a view to educate and encourage awareness and resistance to external threats so that history will not be repeated. For visitors, this is a cold harsh history lesson and a reminder of what is at stake when fascist leaning or imperialistic leaders are in power.

**Getting there** To get to the Ninth Fort, take **bus** 23 from 'Kauno pilis' bus stop direction Voškoniai, alighting after 20 minutes at '9-ojo forto muziejus' bus stop.

There are several buses an hour. **By car** the Ninth Fort is easily accessible from the A1 north of Kaunas, follow signs for 'IX Fortas'.

**Further afield** Many of these sites around Kaunas come under **Kaunas Region Tourist Office** (Pilies takas 1, Raudondvaris; w kaunorajonas.lt) and detailed information about the wider area is available from the website.

***Pažaislis Monastery Complex*** (Pažaislio vienuolynas; T Masiulio gatvė 31; w pazaislis.org; ⊕ 10.00–16.30 Tue–Fri, 10.00–15.30 Sat, Nov–Mar closed Sun–Wed; €6/3) Under the patronage of Grand Duchy of Lithuania chancellor Kristupas Žygimantas Pacas (1621–84), this Baroque church and monastery ensemble was built for the Camaldoese monks of Kaunas. Italian architects were commissioned to design the complex, with craftsmen and artists brought from Lombardy to

### KAUNAS FORTRESS

In 1879, Russian Tsar Alexander II approved the military proposal to construct a fortress in Kaunas to defend the western border of the Russian Empire. It was to consist of forts, batteries, warehouses, barracks, hospitals and churches, and in 1891 alone more than 400 buildings were constructed (there is a good chance that any historic red brick building you see on the outskirts of Kaunas, whether in ruin or renovated, originated from the fortress construction). It sounds impressive, but in 1915 the whole fortress succumbed in just 11 days to a more technically advanced German army. Some sections of the fortress continued to be used for military and penal purposes, but most forts had suffered damage and fell into disrepair, remaining in that state today. If you visit the abandoned forts, be very careful for your own safety and also the protected bat species that now occupy them. Also, avoid visiting between October and April when the bats are hibernating (in particular, forts I, II, III, IV and VIII).

**FORT I** (Šiltnamių gatvė, Kazliškiai) Damaged by German artillery during World War I, Fort I was the location during the interwar years of a gas chamber used to execute criminals. It is the westernmost and least urban of the forts and was left to rack and ruin. After recent improvements of the fort building and surrounding territory there are ad hoc tours and art events held here.

**FORT II** (Pilviškių gatvė 24) In an urban location, the surrounding suburban streets follow the original pentagonal fort plan and the Fort II ruins and territory are now encircled by houses and gardens. The fort suffered major damage during both world wars.

**FORT III** (Titnago gatvė 43A, Seniava) One of the better-preserved examples, Fort III is in a residential area and looked after by the local community. Before the bats' annual return, it is used to host events and there is a permanent exhibition of Lithuanian military equipment.

**FORT IV** (Plytinės gatvė 15, Rokai) Constructed to withstand the frontline of enemy fire, Fort IV played a relatively small role in defence. About 4,000 Jews were killed here under Nazi occupation. Some of the buildings are flooded so explorers should take great care.

Kaunas to create the superb examples of decorative marble, sculptures and frescoes that have survived to this day; though periods of occupation did take their toll. Napoleon's army stole statues and artefacts in 1812. Tsarist authorities closed the monastery in 1831, accusing the monks of supporting insurgents, and the complex was given to the Orthodox community. In 1915 German soldiers based at the monastery removed the copper roof to be smelted for military use. A period of respite during the interwar independence years saw the Sisters of the Congregation of St Casimir from Chicago oversee repairs; however, in 1948 they were evicted by Soviet authorities who converted it into an archive and neurological hospital. Between 1967 and 1992, Pažaislis was a branch of the M K Čiurlionis Art Museum and underwent restoration, before being returned to the safe hands of the Sisters again. Sadly, patron Kristupas Pacas did not live to see the finished ensemble and requested to be buried as a sinner at the entrance so that everyone would walk over him.

**FORT V** (Rūko gatvė 11) Complex and expensive due to the hilly terrain, Fort V was mostly unscathed by combat until an unexplained explosion occurred during World War II. The grounds are used today by a local sports club.

**FORT VI** (K Baršausko gatvė 101; w vdkaromuziejus.lt/en/military-engineering-division/history; ⏰ 10.00–17.00 Tue–Sun; €5/2.50) Having survived World War I intact, Fort VI served as a military prison during the interwar years, and during World War II about 35,000 prisoners of war were killed here. It is now managed by the Vytautas the Great War Museum (page 188) and houses their Branch of Military Equipment including infantry vehicles, radars and a Su-7 fighter plane.

**FORT VII** (Archyvo gatvė 61; w septintasfortas.lt) There was no military action at this fort. During the Nazi occupation it was converted into a concentration camp, where more than 5,000 Jews were killed. During Soviet occupation the fort was plundered. Now it is a private venture focused on children's summer camps and educational activities. Individuals can visit for free, but a guided tour must be booked in advance.

**FORT VIII** (Pryšmančių gatvė 2C) Built in 1889 to protect against attacks from the northwest, Fort VIII was constructed in concrete, covered in earth, and was the first to have electricity. However, its position was weak and so it was used only as a barracks and warehouse. Ammunition stores were detonated during World War I causing extensive damage. Efforts to reinvent the fort as a cultural venue have included light installations and pyrotechnic acrobatic shows held here, while the grounds are used as a community garden. It is also known as Linkuva.

**NINTH FORT** See page 192.

**FORT X** (Romainių g. 18) Although unfinished before World War I, Fort X saw much action and was strategically important. The retreating Russian army blew it up during World War I so only remnants exist today.

*For more information about Kaunas Fortress, visit* kaunotvirtovesparkas.

A guided tour must be booked in advance, or for an informal self-guided visit you can pay on arrival.

For accommodation at the monastery complex, see page 173.

**Getting there** Pažaislis is 9km from Kaunas city centre and served by **trolleybus** line 12. Disembark at the last stop, 'Perašiūnai', from where it is a 20min walk to the monastery. If you arrive by **car**, you can use the large free on-site car park. An 8.5km **cycle** route connects Kaunas railway station and Pažaislis Monastery, passing the Sixth Fort and going via Petrašiūnai.

***Museum of Lithuanian Ethnography (Rumšiškės)*** (Lietuvos etnografijos muziejus; L Lekavičiaus gatvė 2, Rumšiškės; w lemu.lt; ⊕ Apr 10.00–17.00 daily; May–Sep 10.00–18.00 daily, Oct–Mar 10.00–16.00 daily; €10/5, free last Sun of the month) Step back in time in the bucolic Lithuanian countryside, where genuine wooden farmsteads, barns, mills and yards have been relocated and represent the five ethnographic regions of Lithuania: Dzūkija, Aukštaitija, Suvalkija, Žemaitija and Lithuania Minor. Whether spring flowers are blooming, autumn leaves are falling or snow covers the ground, the pastoral scenes are charming and the hardships of days of yore are thoroughly romanticised. Established in 1966 and commonly known as 'Rumšiškės', this is one of the largest open-air ethnographic museums in Europe. There are more than 90,000 exhibits, and within the exhibits are master crafts workshops, a Siberian yurt educating about deportations and resistance, and a wonderful traditional sauna (w dvaropirtis.lt). A 7km circular walking or cycling route covers the main sights. Crafts workshops and sauna experiences must be booked in advance, and there is also the option to stay overnight at the museum in a town square building set up as a basic guesthouse (€€). Also in the town square, a restaurant (€€€) serves snacks and light meals. Note that you will need cash to make any crafts purchases. The interior exhibitions are open May to September; at all other times it is outside only.

**Getting there** The museum is located on the A1/E85 highway, 25km east of Kaunas and 79km west of Vilnius. Parking is available at the museum.

**Buses** travelling between Kaunas and Vilnius do stop at the 'Rumšiškės' bus stop on the A1/E85, 1.8km (25min walk) from the museum. Minibuses to Rumšiškės run from Kaunas bus station to the museum bus stop 'Muziejus' between May and September at weekends and during school holidays. At other times, the closest bus stop is 'Rumšiškės paviljonas' – minibuses heading to Rumšiškės from Kaunas bus station stop here, 500m from the museum entrance.

Between May and September, a private **boat service** 'Nemunas' (w laivai.info) departs every Sunday at 11.00 from Pažaislis pier on the Kaunas Lagoon to the open-air museum. It arrives at the museum at 12.10 and leaves at 16.00 for the return journey.

***Underground Printing House 'ab'*** (Pogrindinė spaustuvė 'ab'; Spaustuvės gatvė 2; w vdkaromuziejus.lt/paslaugos-2; ⊕ tours must be prebooked; free) This fascinating, raw piece of modern history is not your run-of-the-mill tourist attraction, and for those interested in Cold War history, it is a must-see offering a unique insight into how people used their skills to fight oppression, in this case through words.

The Underground Printing House is named 'ab' after Vytautas Andziulis and Juozas Bacevičius. Between 1980 and 1990, the two men were inspired to

> **ČIOBIŠKIS–PADALIAI MANUAL FERRY**
>
> At the western end of Čiobiškis village on road 4305 is the **Čiobiškis–Padaliai manual ferry** (Čiobiškio–Padalių keltas). The only one of its kind in Lithuania, the ferry (more of a platform really) is attached to a steel cable suspended across the river. When the ferry is released, the river current powers it across to the other side, while the ferry master controls it with a rudder. The current 'vessel' is called *Nerimi* and has been in service since 1978. It takes two cars plus pedestrians, and the crossing takes 5 minutes. You must pay in cash to the ferry master (he is the latest generation of the family of ferry masters). The service runs between spring and early November as it cannot operate when ice forms on the river. If the ferry master is not there, you must go the long way around.

fight against the propaganda of Soviet occupation by producing underground publications, which were disseminated in their thousands across the country by a network of brave volunteers. Andziulis built the summer house you see today and, along with Bacevičius, undertook the most remarkable covert construction of an underground printing house in his garden. Andziulis' wife, Birutė, was lookout and went to great lengths to keep it hidden from their children. The stories are best kept for your own experience.

The printing house is now a branch of the Vytautas the Great War Museum, but the site itself is in the garden of a private home, so please do not visit without a pre-arranged appointment (booked via the museum; see page 188 for contact details), and certainly do not enter the grounds without permission. You are advised to visit with a guide or translator as the host does not speak English, and note that the visit involves climbing in and out of a tricky entrance to access the underground section. If you are able to, it is well worth it.

## KĖDAINIAI

Albeit small, Kėdainiai is one of the most attractive old towns in Lithuania and in recent years it has benefited from investment; sprucing up the streets, renovating facades, and an increase in small businesses and attractions have put Kėdainiai on the tourist map. The uniqueness of Kėdainiai is a result of its multi-cultural history, each resident community having left their mark on the town. Located on the Nevėžis River, Kėdainiai grew into a respectable town on the boundary of the ethnographic regions of Žemaitija and Aukštaitija, in large part due to the town's connection with the powerful noble Radvila (Radziwiłł) family from 1445 to 1655. Particularly intriguing is the town's surprise connection to Scotland. In 1630, emigrating Scots arrived in Kėdainiai and settled down, with a population of about 130 Scottish residents living in Kėdainiai until 1750. They brought with them their Calvinist protestant faith and new scholarly ideas, and today you will find buildings named after former Scottish residents: George Anderson house, the house of George Bennet, and the cellar of Alexander Gordon. From the mid 18th century, Kėdainiai's influx of Catholic believers and Jewish scholars added to the cultural melting pot. The Jewish community, called *qahal*, was the biggest and most influential in northwestern Lithuania, and Kėdainiai developed a reputation for Talmud studies. During the 19th century, Kėdainiai was incorporated into the Russian Empire and benefitted from being situated on the new Warsaw-to-

St Petersburg railway line, opening opportunities for industrial development and agricultural production. Kėdainiai has historically been involved in the production of vegetables and its nickname is the 'Cucumber Capital of Lithuania'.

**GETTING THERE AND AWAY** From Kaunas it is a 50km **drive** north to Kėdainiai along roads A1 and 1906. You can make a short stop en route along road 1906 to see the Labūnava Tower (page 200).

Kėdainiai is served by regular **buses** from Kaunas (1hr, several buses per hour). The bus station (Kėdainių autobusų stotis; J Basanavičiaus gatvė 93) is a 30-minute walk south from the Old Town.

Kėdainiai is on the Vilnius–Klaipėda and Kaunas–Šiauliai **train** lines with direct services between Kėdainiai and Vilnius (1hr 30mins; 6 trains per day), Klaipėda (3hrs; 3 per day) and Kaunas (57mins; 2 per day). The train station (Kėdainių geležinkelio stotis; S Dariaus ir S Girėno gatvė 3) is a 40-minute walk north from the Old Town.

**TOURIST INFORMATION** Kėdainiai Tourism Information Centre (Kėdainių turizmo ir verslo informacijos centras; Didžiosios Rinkos aikštė; w kedainiutvic.lt; ⊕ 08.00–18.00 Mon–Fri, 09.00–17.00 Sat, 10.00–15.00 Sun) should be your first port of call for a map, advice on the sights, what's on and how best to spend your time in Kėdainiai.

## WHERE TO STAY AND EAT

**Grėjaus namas** Didžioji gatvė 36; w grejausnamas.lt. 'Gray's House' is named after Scot Jokūbas Grėjus (Jacob Gray), who lived here in Kėdainiai in the early 18th century. It is a modest but well-maintained hotel with restaurant & sauna area. Tartan & bagpipes feature in the décor, complementing the authentic 18th-century cellars & painted vaults. €€

**Kavos namai 'Kavamanija'** Didžioji gatvė 26; ⓕ kavamanija. A trendy little café set up by an enterprising young team, 'Coffeemania' offers freshly ground coffee & pastries to break up your sightseeing. €€

**Uršulė** Didžioji gatvė 22; ⓕ Restoranas.Ursule. This independent restaurant serves hearty traditional meals in a contemporary setting. The waiting staff are friendly & so is the wheeled robot server that delivers to your table! We hope it is still in employment when you visit as it is quite entertaining. €€

## WHAT TO SEE AND DO

**Kėdainiai Regional Museum** (Kėdainių krašto muziejus; Didžioji gatvė 19; w kedainiumuziejus.lt; ⊕ 11.00–18.00 Wed–Fri, 10.00–17.00 Sat, 10.00–15.00 Sun; €3/1.50) Established in 1922 during the interwar period of independence and on a wave of national, regional and local pride, the museum once had a huge collection but it was greatly depleted during the years of occupation that followed. It still houses 50,000 local objects of interest and is the best place to start your tour of Kėdainiai for a historical overview. The regional museum is responsible for most of the main sights in the town, including some not listed here; but you can find further details about the **Wooden Sculptures of Vytautas Ulevičius Museum** and **Janina Monkutė-Marks Museum** on their website.

**Great Market Square** (Didžiosios Rinkos aikštė) The Great Market Square is large in area and surrounded by quaint buildings, compensating for their size with their vibrant colours. The most distinctive buildings are the Glazier's Houses, with their 17th-century Dutch-style façades immediately catching your eye. They currently house a souvenir, art and craft shop called Stiklių namas (Glass House).

The attractive Town Hall (Kėdainių rotušė) stands out and highlights the damage suffered by the town where once stood equally grand buildings. The monument in the square is called *Skrynia* (Chest) and is dedicated to the noble Radvila family. It symbolises the treasury of the Grand Duchy of Lithuania which was brought to Kėdainiai in 1655 by Jonušas Radvila (immortalised in the monument) to protect it from invading Swedes and Russians.

**Evangelical Reformed Church** (Kėdainių evangelikų reformatų bažnyčia; Senoji gatvė 3; w ref.lt) Construction of a new Renaissance-style Evangelical Reformed Church was initiated by Kristupas II Radvila in 1631 and completed by his son Jonušas XI Radvila in 1652. The church has suffered little damage over the centuries, and its intricately carved oak pulpit and oak panels in Dutch Mannerism style are original. The crypt contains the restored Mausoleum of Dukes Radvilas, the only surviving example from the 17th-century belonging to nobility from the Grand Duchy of Lithuania. The ornate tin sarcophagi contain the remains of Kristupas Radvila Perkūnas (1547–1603) – known as 'the Thunderer', and one of the greatest military heroes of Lithuania – and his grandson Jonušas Radvila (1612–55). Services are held once a month in the church, but it is also open to visitors.

**Traditional Crafts Centre Arnet's House** (Tradicinių amatų centras Arnetų name; Radvilų gatvė 21; w kedainiumuziejus.lt; ⊕ 08.00–17.00 Mon–Fri; free) Arnet's House was built by Scottish merchant John Arnet in the mid 17th century. The exterior and interior layout are authentic, including Lithuania's sole-surviving example of a small vaulted room which was a residential toilet. The building is state-owned and managed by the Kėdainiai Regional Museum; they offer traditional craft workshops, including ceramics, egg painting, paper cutting, weaving and wood carving. Regular folk art exhibitions are hosted in the centre and entry is free to the exhibitions. There is little information in English, so you may prefer to visit with a pre-booked guide, especially if wanting to participate in a craft class.

**Synagogues** (Senosios Rinkos aikštė) Located on the Old Market Square are two synagogues. The **Great Summer Synagogue** was built in the late 18th century, replacing the previous wooden synagogue which was destroyed by fire. It currently houses an art school. The **Small Winter Synagogue** was built next door in the early 19th century and named so because it was heated and used in the colder months. It is sympathetically restored and retains some original features dating from its construction in 1837: the men's room complete with four columns and place for the bimah; a rectangular Aron Hakodesh niche; and a women's gallery with rectangular tapering niches. A permanent exhibition tells the Jewish history of Kėdainiai including the Holocaust. The synagogue is also a **Multicultural Centre** (Paeismilgio gatvė 12B; w kedainiumuziejus.lt; ⊕ 11.00–18.00 Wed–Fri, 10.00–17.00 Sat, 10.00–15.00 Sun), which hosts a variety of events and concerts throughout the year. A memorial plaque states that for a short period during World War II Kėdainiai became a refuge for Mir Yeshiva, a leading Jewish spiritual academy. Close to the synagogues, on the square, are two memorials in honour of the Kėdainiai Jews who were killed during the Holocaust and one in honour of the locals who risked their lives to save Jews. There is also a third surviving synagogue building, **Smilgos Street Synagogue** (Kėdainių Smilgos gatvė sinagoga), and a walk along Zydų gatvė (Jewish Street) offers a glimpse of the former Jewish houses and shops in their characteristic red brick.

**Kėdainiai Minaret** (S Dariaus ir S Girėno gatvė 5D) Possibly the most asked question at the town's tourism information office is 'Why is there a minaret in Kėdainiai?' Erected in 1880 by Russian general Eduard Totleben, who owned an estate in the town, the minaret was built to commemorate his service in the Russo–Turkish war (although locals believe such a folly must be in honour of a Turkish lover).

**Labūnava Tower** (13km south of Kėdainiai on road 1906, south of the village of Labūnava) Early records about the tower exist in chronicles of the crusaders in 1364 and later references to Labūnava Manor from the 16th century, but it is modern history for which it is remembered. After World War II several families connected with the partisan resistance movement lived in the tower, and when celebrating Christmas in 1946 they were attacked by Russian soldiers resulting in 11 of them being killed and others arrested. The plaque in front of the tower is a first-hand account of the event as told by a survivor.

## NEMUNAS RIVER VALLEY

The Nemunas River flows west from Kaunas, finally discharging into the Curonian Lagoon at its nature-rich delta. The river valley provides a scenic route for those travelling leisurely to the coast, or for a day trip from Kaunas. Česlovo Ražanausko Bridge in Kaunas (highway A5) is the last bridge crossing until you reach Jurbarkas 83km away, although there are several small ferry crossings at Zapyškis and Vilkija. The main scenic route is along road 141, which takes in castles, villages and viewpoints. This route is often called 'the Panemunė road' and holds great historical importance not only for its strategic role in defending Lithuania but also as the main route taken by the book smugglers who risked their lives transporting banned Lithuanian literature from Prussia (page 38).

**RAUDONDVARIS** The architectural ensemble of **Raudondvaris Manor** (Raudondvario dvaras; Pilies takas 1; w raudondvariodvaras.lt; ⊕ 08.00–17.00 Tue–Fri, 10.00–16.25 Sat; €2/1) is a 17th-century Renaissance treasure resided in over the centuries by several noble families. It consists of a castle with tower, an orangerie, estate buildings, stables and an icehouse, all of which have been carefully restored. The estate is now a centre for culture and arts, containing a museum, events venue and an art incubator to support young artists and small-to-medium enterprises. Tours of the estate are available in English (€5 for 1hr) or you can use their 'Dramatour' audio guide (€3). A restaurant operates in the orangerie.

**VILKIJA** Vilkija is an attractive small town and the only one fully built on a slope in this very flat country. A visit to **Juškos Museum of Ethnic Culture** (Antano ir Jono Juškų etninės kultūros muziejus; Kauno Mažoji gatvė 2; ◼ AntanoirJonoJuskumuziejus; ⊕ 08.00–17.00 Mon–Sat; €2/1) is a cheerful experience and will offer a boost to a small rural museum that honours the priest, ethnographer and folklorist Antanas Juška (1819–80). From Vilkija it is possible to take the small ferry *Vilkynė* across the Nemunas River to Pavilkys (€1 per pedestrian, €6 per car one way; cash only).

**RAUDONĖ CASTLE** (Raudonės Pilis; Pilies gatvė 1, Raudonė; w raudone.lt/ turistams; ⊕ 09.00–17.00 Fri–Sun; €1.50/1) Raudonė Castle is more manor house than castle, appearing more residential than defensive, but this is largely because

> **CASTLE MOUNDS**
>
> The Nemunas River has historically been a border, a frontier and natural defence. You will notice numerous castle mounds (*piliakalnis*) along its route, once topped with wooden hillforts that played a critical role in defending against invading enemies. **Ringovės** mound had a wooden castle atop until 1364, where today you will find a pagan fire pit where sacred fires are lit on pagan festival dates. **Seredžius** mound (also known locally as Palemonas Hill) dates from the 13th century. The original wooden castle suffered numerous attacks by the Brotherhood of the Cross, its final restoration being in 1412 immediately after the Battle of Žalgiris. You can park at the foot of the mound and climb 300 wooden steps to the top for a spectacular panorama of the Nemunas River and Dubysa River valley. **Veliuona** consists of two mounds next to each over. It is believed that this is where Grand Duke Gediminas died during battle, and one of the mounds is named 'Gediminas' Grave'. Finally, **Kartupėnų** is where Bisenės Castle once stood, the first line of defence against attacks from the Teutonic Knights of Prussia.
>
> For more information, read the comprehensive study of Lithuanian hillforts at w *piliakalniai.lt*.

it was badly damaged in World War II, and after reconstruction it was used as a school for many years. Today it is used mainly for events and workshops, but it is possible for visitors to climb the tower and be rewarded with panoramic views.

**PANEMUNĖS CASTLE** (Panemunės pilis; Vytenų 53, Skirsnemunės village; w panemunespilis.com; ⏲ May–Oct 10.00–18.00 Tue–Sun, Nov–Apr 10.00–17.00 Wed–Sun; €4/2) By far the most visited attraction along the Nemunas River valley route, this Renaissance castle was built in 1610 by a Hungarian merchant called Eperias. Contrary to the previous wooden castles that stood on this site and saw much military action between the Grand Duchy and Teutonic Knights, the newly built 17th-century castle was built as a residence. Due to the misfortunes of various owners, conflicts and occupations, the castle fell into disrepair and underwent a slow and costly process to restore it. As a branch of the Vilnius Academy of Arts it now operates as a museum, art gallery and artists' residence. Visitors can explore the apartment of the Governor of Žemaitija, the castle kitchen and apothecary. The surrounding parkland is perfect for a picnic or you can buy lunch locally. During the summer season a café opens in the orangerie. During the summer a private sightseeing boat service (Laivas Bisena; Vytėnų prieplaukos aikštelė, Jurbarkas region; f laivasBisena; €100 for 1hr) is available to hire from Panemunės Castle. Note that, although they share similar names, Panemunės Castle is 78km away from the settlement of Panemunė on the Kaliningrad (Russia) border – there are numerous Panemunės in Lithuania as Panemunė means 'by the Nemunas River' and it's a long river!

**JURBARKAS** The castle at Jurbarkas (formerly known as Georgenburg by the Teutonic Order) was destroyed by Grand Duke Vytautas in 1403 and never rebuilt. For centuries Jurbarkas was a small settlement reliant on the trade of passing merchant vessels on the Nemunas River. With the construction of the railways and less reliance on the Nemunas, Jurbarkas suffered a decline, its significance as a transport hub and industrial town revived only with the construction of a new bridge across the Nemunas River in 1978. Between the 18th and early 20th century, Jurbarkas had a significant Jewish population and was famed for its wooden synagogue – but this, like most of the community, did not survive the horrors of World War II. There is not much for international tourists in Jurbarkas and most visitors have a family heritage connection to the area. The **Tourism and Business Information Centre** (Vydūno gatve 19; w jurbarkas.info) should be your first port of call for local information and advice. If you do need a place to overnight, **Hotel Jurbarkas** (w hoteljurbarkas.lt; €€) is a retro experience, which done properly could become an attraction itself.

### NEMUNAS RIVER BORDER ZONE

Approaching from Jurbarkas, **Smalininkai** is the first village on the Lithuanian side of the Nemunas where the river becomes the Lithuania–Russia (Kaliningrad) border. It is the first (or last) village of the ethnographic region of Lithuania Minor and has distinct Prussian heritage with Germanic architecture; large-scale old Prussian photos have been installed on some of the buildings. Walk down Kranto gatvė to see the water measurement station which has been monitoring the level of the Nemunas since 1811, and an official Lithuania territory border post.

After the village of Lumpėnai, turn off the 141 towards Bardinai. You are entering Rambynas Regional Park within which is **Rambynas Hill** (Rambyno kalnas), a sacred hill of significant importance to Lithuanian pagans where the ancient Baltic gods were worshipped. Traditionally, St John's Day (Joninės) midsummer celebrations are held here and the fire pit lit. From the viewpoint at the top of the hill you can see across the Nemunas to Kaliningrad. Wooden steps allow for exploration down to the riverbank.

**Panemunė** holds nothing for tourists except curiosity and fascination with border territory. Prior to Russia's invasion of Ukraine in 2022, this border crossing was open to those with a Russian visa to enter and exit Kaliningrad. Now the border is closed to vehicles and sanctions have stopped all goods traffic, but it is still possible to cross the bridge on foot. On the opposite riverbank is the Russian town of Sovetsk, formerly known as Tilsit in Prussia. It is so close, you can hear children laughing and car engines, but it feels a world away. On both sides of the Nemunas, fishermen sit patiently, hoping for a catch. Astride the Nemunas is the historical Queen Louise Bridge, witnessing yet another period of turbulent history since its construction in 1907. Queen Louise of Prussia was the wife of King Frederick Wilhelm III and was revered for her extraordinary meeting with Napoleon in Tilsit, 1807, where under the orders of her husband she begged the French emperor to be lenient with Prussia after suffering heavy military and territorial losses. Berlin was occupied by France, and Queen Louise and the king had fled to Memel (Klaipėda). Napoleon made no concessions, and a peace treaty was signed here. Two days prior, a second peace treaty had been signed between Napoleon and Russian Emperor Alexander I, on a neutral raft in the middle of the Nemunas. The bridge was heavily damaged during World War II but retains one of its original arches on the Russian side.

If you visit this area, remember you are in border territory and can be asked for your personal identification by border guards.

> **THE MOLOTOV LINE**
>
> Between 1940 and 1941, the Soviet Army began an unprecedented military construction project called the Molotov Line. It was an epic scramble to fortify the western border of the Soviet Union and consisted of individual reinforced concrete defensive structures, now commonly known as pillboxes. The line ran from the Baltic Sea to the Carpathian Mountains, but many structures were not completed in time for 22 June 1941, when Nazi Germany attacked the Soviet Union in Operation Barbarossa and the defensive system failed. In Lithuania, the Molotov defensive line stretched from Palanga to Druskininkai, via the north of Klaipėda, Tauragė, Jurbarkas and Kalvarija, continuing into Belarus after Druskininkai. These indestructible monoliths still exist although they are often hidden in undergrowth, happily forgotten. In the city centre of Tauragė is an example of a Molotov Line pillbox, easily accessible at Prezidento gatvė.

At Jurbakas you have the option to speed up your travel to the Lithuanian coast by leaving the river valley and heading north on road 198 to join the main A1 highway. Alternatively, continue on road 141 along the Nemunas River which becomes the Lithuania–Kaliningrad (Russia) border until the river delta.

**TAURAGĖ** Primarily an industrial city and hub of services for the region, Tauragė doesn't make it on to the itinerary of many tourists, but if you are passing by there are several reasons to stop. Few buildings survived the extensive damage of World War I, but one of those that did was Tauragė Castle (*Tauragės pilis*), which now houses the **Tauragė Regional Museum 'Santaka'** (Tauragės krašto muziejus; Dariaus ir Girėno gatvė 5; w tauragesmuziejus.lt; ⊕ 09.00–17.00 Tue–Thu, 09.00–15.45 Fri, 10.00–16.00 Sat; €6/2). A rather splendid museum with fresh contemporary exhibitions, its open depository of ethnographic artefacts and restoration workshop are of particular interest. A second branch of the museum, the **Exile and Resistance Museum** (Tremties ir rezistencijos muziejus; Prezidento gatvė 38; ⊕ 09.00–17.00 Tue–Thu, 09.00–15.45 Fri, 10.00–16.00 Sat; €2/1) is housed in the former NKVD (KGB) building and provides a valuable education on the horrors of exile in labour camps and the danger faced by partisans; and there is an interactive interrogation room to reinforce what the country went through – for those who do not carry the memories first-hand. If you require a bed for the night, the **Tauragė Hotel** (Vytauto gatvė 83; w tauragehotel.lt; €€€) has had a major makeover and is the best option in town.

## SOUTH OF THE NEMUNAS RIVER

The region west of Kaunas and south of the Nemunas River covers much of the Suvalkija (or Sudovia) ethnographic region of Lithuania. It is the least developed region for tourism, but changes are afoot and the existing eclectic mix of sights are being complemented with a new focus on culinary heritage and manor houses.

**KAZLŲ RŪDA FOREST** When travelling west from Kaunas south of the Nemunas River, you will pass through Kazlų Rūda Forest, one of Lithuania's largest forests covering an area of 555km². Popular for hiking, mountain biking and foraging, it is a mixture of natural woodland and managed forest, although even Lithuanian managed forest can feel very natural. You will notice the different stages of growth;

young saplings are planted in rows, but the weaker ones are weeded out, resulting in an uneven distribution of trees and space for the forest floor to grow thick with moss, plants and small shrubs. The terrain is sandy, making the forest roads soft and root-riddled; these are maintained by villagers who need access to their remote farmsteads dotted within the forest.

The forest holds some secrets deep within it, not your usual tourist sights but interesting certainly for those interested in military history. Remnants still exist of Kazlų Rūda Soviet military airbase (Gulioniškės region). Once an important airfield and headquarters of a paratrooper division, now it attracts weekend quad bikers and drone operators, who make use of the large expanse of derelict concrete surrounded by trees. It was at this military polygon that the Soviet Army would transport tanks by helicopter and deposit them by parachute as the soft sandy ground provided a gentle landing. Nearby in the thick forest and not easy to access or find is the abandoned Brezhnev villa and bunker, an emergency shelter for Soviet officials. It is privately owned and plans for the site are unknown.

The forest is rich with flora and fauna, and to the north is **Novaraistis Ornithological Reserve** (w visitlekeciai.lt/en/novaraistis-ornithological-reserve), a vast former peat bog, famous for migrating common crane and breeding spotted crake, along with black-tailed eagles and sedge warblers. There is an observation tower and car park. The forest also contains numerous memorial sites to the brave Lithuanian resistance, many of whom were based in Kazlų Rūda Forest – the thick forest being the perfect hideaway for animals, birds and partisans.

**ŠAKIAI** A relative newcomer to the tourism industry for domestic, let alone international tourists, and that is part of this region's appeal. Šakiai was once a busy crossroads, the Šakiai smuklė inn welcoming weary travellers journeying between Poland, Koenigsberg (Kaliningrad) and Žemaitija. Notably, of the 20 signatories of Lithuania's Act of Independence in 1918, three of them were from Šakiai (five in total were from the Suvalkija region). More recently, between 1992 and 1995 Lithuanian linen flax was exported through Šakiai to the USA, where it was used in the production of US dollar banknotes. And who would guess that Šakiai is home to Lithuania's one and only Circus School (f sakiaicircus).

The **Šakiai Tourism and Business Information Centre** (Šakių turizmo ir verslo informacijos centras; V Kudirkos gatvė 61; w visitsakiai.lt; ⏰ 08.00–17.00 Mon– Thu, 08.00–15.45 Fri) will be pleased to welcome you on weekdays.

The old market square of Šakiai contains a 24-bell **carillon**, made by Dutch bell casting specialists Royal Eijsbouts and installed in 2015. It will play on request if you feed it €1. A walk around the town circles the scenic Lake Šakiai, an artificial lake resulting from the drainage of the surrounding swamp areas. A unique statue honours the Lithuanian alphabet on Nepriklausomybės gatvė. If you are in search of a snack, head to **Laimė bakery and patisserie** (V Kudirkos gatvė 61; w cukrainelaime.lt; ⏰ 07.45–18.00 Mon–Fri, 08.00–20.00 Sat, 09.00–20.00 Sun), where they sell the biggest croissants we've ever seen.

**ZYPLIAI MANOR** This historic manor house in Lukšiai village, 8km east of Šakiai, is a restoration project with a difference. The early 19th-century Classicist manor was altered extensively as it passed between numerous noble family owners, becoming a substantial estate. After World War I, such noble entitlement was lost and the manor was used for practical purposes, including an agricultural school and hospital of which maintenance was poor and the estate soon deteriorated. Thanks to the foresight of sculptor Vidas Cikana who moved to Lukšiai in 1981 and

## THE FOREST BROTHERS

The Forest Brothers (Miško broliai) were the most prominent resistance group in Lithuania during the period of Soviet occupation after World War II. They were an organised group of armed freedom fighters who fought a guerrilla war against the Soviet occupiers between 1944 and the early 1950s. Their aim was to restore Lithuanian independence, a vast challenge for a small resistance, but these were patriotic individuals who felt compelled to act against the occupation of their homeland. Ultimately, they believed that help would come from the west to support their fight for freedom, but it never did. The network of partisans was sophisticated, operating in regional divisions, platoons and units. They were well armed, having stolen or bought weapons from Soviet soldiers, and they conducted sabotage on Soviet infrastructure and attacks on Soviet forces and their collaborators. The safest place for the partisans was in the extensive, thick forests where they constructed secret bunkers and hideouts. Brave members of the local population supported the partisans by delivering food, medical aid and information, and risked their own lives as the Soviets waged a campaign of terror on those who assisted the resistance with public displays of torture, execution or deportation. The same fate befell captured partisans and their family members. An estimated 30,000 partisans died in Lithuania; all of them are deigned national heroes. Notable partisans included Adolfas Ramanauskas, codename Vanagas (hawk). Ramanasukas was a teacher who refused to submit to orders of the Soviet police to spy on his students. He joined the resistance and became an influential leader. In 1956 he was betrayed by a colleague and suffered brutal torture then execution. Another partisan leader, Juozas Lukša, escaped to the west to encourage more support for Lithuania's resistance movement and was parachuted back into Lithuania and eventually killed in 1951. He wrote a chilling first-hand account of his experience as a partisan, *Fighters for Freedom*, under the pseudonym Juozas Daumantas. Lukša was killed to the east of Kazlų Rūda Forest; the site is marked with a memorial (Partizano Juozo Lukšos Daumanto žūties vieta, Pažėrai village, road 1933).

Their legacy is remembered in the excellent regional resistance museums, but nothing brings home their struggle more than visiting a partisan bunker in the depths of the forest. You will find these all over Lithuania, marked with brown signs 'Partizanų bunkeris'; but be prepared to navigate unruly sandy or rutted roads to get there. Some of the main memorials include Lydžio rinktinės partizanų bunkeris (Pagramančio forest, Šilalė region), Punios šilo partizanų bunkeris (Strazdynė, Alytaus region), and Prisikelimo apygardos štabo bunkeris (Daugėliškių forest, Raseiniai region). You will usually find a Lithuanian flag, a wooden or metal cross, and memorial plaque. Notice the double *cross of* Vytis, which is a symbol of Lithuanian statehood, banned by the Soviets and used by the partisans. Many bunkers have been reconstructed, and you may be able to open the trap door and climb down a wooden ladder for a glimpse into their tough existence – imagine the freezing cold winters spend here. Also look out for a chimney or air vent nearby; theses were often disguised as tree stumps. Forests are sacred in Lithuanian mythology. They provide game animals, mushrooms and berries for sustenance, and for the partisans they provided sanctuary and a strategic advantage. One more reason for the Lithuanian love and respect of the forest.

became its mayor, the estate was transferred to the local authority and it became a well-maintained cultural centre and museum. Several things set Zypliai Manor apart. First of all, is the top-floor exhibition of crafts, the result of an innovative idea to host an annual master crafts workshop. All artworks created are donated to the exhibition, resulting in over 22 years' worth of superior craftwork on display and increasing every year. Second is the manor house kitchen and hotel, **Kuchmistrai** (12 rooms; Zypliai Manor, Beržų gatvė 3, Lukšiai village; w kuchmistrai.lt; €€€€; €€€€). Life has been ushered back into the manor house kitchen, creating a unique dining experience based on regional and national culinary heritage and incorporating the traditional cuisine of nobles and peasantry. A tasting menu of multiple courses accompanied by local berry wines and acorn coffee is authentic and delicious. If you choose to imbibe the local beers or liquors and need a place to stay, they also have a small hotel, Zyplių dvaro oficina, in a separate estate building. The rooms are beautifully decorated and complement the dining experience.

**NORTH OF ŠAKIAI** Running along the south bank of the Nemunas River are several small places of interest, which, when combined, make a pleasant day trip from Šakiai.

**Plokščiai** is a small village that hit the headlines in 2005 when a Russian jet crashed here. It was one of six military aircraft flying from St Petersburg to Kaliningrad, but this one allegedly got lost and ran out of fuel. The pilot ejected on the northern bank of the Nemunas River, while the plane crashed on the south side. Plokščiai is also known for its 'river road' called *Vaiguvos upė-gatvė*. Several farmsteads up this small valley can only be accessed by vehicle by driving along the narrow river bed. Before you travel all this way to navigate it yourself, be aware that you are not permitted to do so and unless you have a feisty, compact off-road vehicle you could find yourself in trouble. Alternatively, there is a path beside the river which is a pleasant walk.

**Gelgaudiškis Manor** (Gelgaudiškio dvaras; Parko gatvė 5; f GelgaudiskioDvaras; €4 pp with advance booking) has been renovated into a multi-purpose venue. You can visit the manor house, take a tour of the interior and admire the lovingly restored ceilings and woodwork, or enjoy the estate hiking trail.

**Kiduliai** is a small town where you can cross the Nemunas River to Jurbarkas via the only bridge west of Kaunas (road 137). If you are looking for lunch, **Winery Vilkenta** (Sodų g. 26, Kiduliai; w kiduliuvynas.lt; €€€) is your best option. They specialise in making craft wines from local berries, and dandelion wine is their speciality. Their cosy restaurant and summer terrace serve a traditional menu of hearty grub. English might be off the menu but persevere. Heading east from the Kiduliai crossroads along road 3807 you will come to Kaimelis. **Kaimelis Manor** (w kaimeliodvaras.lt) is currently being restored by period property entrepreneurs Petras and Karolis, who did outstanding jobs with the Art Deco Museum and Amsterdam School Museum in Kaunas (page 187). It is currently closed for renovation but is certainly one to watch for the near future. In the meantime you can follow their progress at 📷 kaimeliodvaras and admire the hard work and dedication needed for this level of restoration.

**Grinaičiai** is the most western village on the south bank of the Nemunas River, before the border with Kaliningrad (Russia). Here you can explore the Sudargas castle mounds and discover a surprising tribute to American author J D Salinger. Salinger's great-grandfather Hyman Joseph Salinger was born in Sudargas in 1828, and this connection is acknowledged with an outline sculpture extending out towards the Nemunas. Salinger was of Jewish descent and there was a big Jewish community here during the early 1800s. Immediately next to the car park are some weathered Jewish gravestones, remnants of a Jewish cemetery. Be aware that you are now in border territory and could be stopped and asked to show your identity document. This route was once famed as the main smuggling route for fuel between Kaliningrad and Lithuania, but the border is now closed.

**KUDIRKOS NAUMIESTIS** It's been in Prussia, Poland, the Russan Empire and independent Lithuania, occupied by Nazi Germany, occupied by the Soviet Union and since 1990 part of independent Lithuania again. This is borderland at its finest and the unconventional tourist will enjoy getting up close and hopefully not personal with the Lithuania–Russia (Kaliningrad) border. Like a moth to the flame (but a wise moth, who keeps its distance from said flame) some visitors will enjoy peering through the old rickety iron gates and barbed wire that block the former border crossing over the Šešupė River. The open ground on both sides of the river may appear naïvely vulnerable until you spot the numerous security cameras on the Lithuanian side. Nearby, the **Potato Museum** (Bulvės muziejus; Bažnyčios gatvė 34; ⊕ May–Sep; for prices & to book a tour email e valjona@gmail.com or call ✆+370 687 47791) pays homage to the Lithuanian potato with an educational tour and tastings. The tour is in Lithuanian only, so it's best done with a guide. To the north of the town are the **Pranas Sederevičius Sculptures** (Prano Sederevičiaus skulptūrų ansamblis; P Mašioto gatvė 37–39). Pranas Sederevičius (1905–79) was a folk sculptor, who, between 1951 and 1979, created probably the best display of primitive folk art in Lithuania. Luckily, the sculptures survived Soviet occupation, including a statue of J F Kennedy. Nothing quite prepares you for the scale of the 21 sculptures that are crammed into Sederevičius' former private garden. It is still a private house, so stay on the pavement unless invited in and don't disturb the residents.

The town was renamed from Naumiestis to Kudirkos Naumiestis in 1934 in honour of Vincas Kudirka, a Lithuanian patriot and composer of the Lithuanian national anthem. He lived here from 1895 to his death in 1899 and is buried in the town cemetery. The **Vincas Kudirka Museum** (Vinco Kudirkos muziejus; V Kudirkos gatvė 29; w lnm.lt/en/museums/vincas-kudirka-museum; ⊕ 10.00–17.00 Tue-Sat, 10.00–15.00 Sun; €4/2) is a branch of the Lithuanian National Museum and presents the history of the town, tells of Vincas Kudirka and hosts temporar exhibitions.

**KYBARTAI** Kybartai is one of the main border crossing points between Lithuania and Kaliningrad (Russia). Sanctions on Russian goods has had an impact, but it is currently still operational for restricted road traffic, and transit trains between Kaliningrad and mainland Russia cross the border here. The town is centred around the border crossing. Its main industry is customs and freight processing, and has been since it began to develop around 1865 alongside the St Petersburg to Warsaw railway line when Kybartai was on the border between the Russian Empire and Prussia. Kybartai developed into a busy town of trade and commerce with a large Jewish population, most of whom were victims of a mass Nazi execution in 1941. Many of the remaining buildings from this period are distinctly German or Jewish in their style.

The road south from Kybartai (186) follows along the Russian border and heads to Lake Vyštytis, which is carved in two by the international border. The **Vyštytis Regional Park** is an isolated recreational area surrounded by rolling landscapes and borders the three countries of Lithuania, Russia and Poland. The **Vyštytis Regional Park Visitor Centre** (Vytauto gatvė 8, Vyštytis; w vistytis.lt; ⊕ 08.00–7.00 Tue–Fri,

10.00–15.00 Sat) has trail maps and local information. The staff there can also advise on how to reach the restored **Vyštytis Windmill** (Vištyčio vėjo malūnas), which is 2km east from the town centre. If you are in need of snacks, there is a general store in Vyštytis; otherwise follow the lakeshore road to Camping Viktorija (Poilsiavietė/ Kempingas 'Viktorija'), where they have a snack bar during the summer season. Do not be tempted to travel this way to visit the border Tripoint (Lithuania–Russia– Poland) as it is only accessible from the Polish side; you can cross into Poland via road 5144.

**VILKAVIŠKIS** This southwest borderland region of Lithuania suffered much turmoil and devastation being regularly on the front line of battle. Consequently, it experienced huge emigration as people were displaced from disputed territories and fled to safety. As a result, many Lithuanians who live abroad have connections to this region and returning for family heritage trips continues to be popular. Accommodation options are quite limited, so it is common to visit for a day trip, and it is advised to take a guide or at least a Lithuanian speaker who can help translate as the best family research results always come from local conversations.

In his book, *Thirty Days in Lithuania in 1919*, Reverend Peter P Saurusaitis describes the damage he witnesses, suffered by Lithuania during World War I, when he returns to his home town of Vilkaviškis:

> I saw that Lithuania is more devastated than Belgium. The Germans crossed through Belgium once only, while Lithuania had been the regular battlefield for the German and Russian armies. It was alternately captured and recaptured by the contending armies. When the Russian army was fleeing it destroyed whatever opportunity afforded, likewise the German army in its retreat carried everything in its wake, pillaged, burned and destroyed whatever it could not take. I noticed in particular one village which had been, only a few trees were visible. Numerous farm houses had been destroyed and burned to the ground. People now live in huts made partly of straw, old boards and clay. Not only the war, but nature has made changes in Lithuania. Rivers, such as the Seimena and Sirvinta, are only brooks. As we approached Vilkaviskis, my native town, the passengers called my attention to the station. My imagination failed to picture the rudely constructed hut as the same station of former years, which had been entirely destroyed by the invading army.

Vilkaviškis had a population of around 3,500 Jewish people at the beginning of 1941; by the end of the year, more than 3,400 of them had been murdered. A visit to the **Jewish cemetery** (Vilkaviškio senosios žydų kapinės; Kapų gatvė 83) provides a sombre reminder of their prominence in the town before the Holocaust. The cemetery, which was in use between 1875 and 1942, is the only record of the Jewish community's presence here.

Vilkaviškis has an unusual story concerning two churches. The original **Cathedral of the Blessed Virgin Mary** (Švč. Mergelės Marijos Apsilankymo katedra; Vytauto gatvė 14; w vilkaviskioparapija.lt) was damaged beyond repair during World War I. The Soviets did not allow the cathedral to be rebuilt, so only in 1991 were plans to reconstruct the cathedral started. It was consecrated in 1998 and features contemporary stained-glass windows. During the independent interwar years, the Catholic parishioners were without their cathedral and the local Russian population was in decline, hence how an Orthodox church came to be given to the Catholic community in 1922 and why the **St Cross Catholic Church** (Šv. Kryžiaus bažnyčia; Vysk. A Karoso gatvė 2) looks like a typical Orthodox church; but the tower and dome are topped with Catholic crosses.

Only 4km from the city centre is **Paežeriai Manor** (Paežerių dvaras; Dvaro gatvė 6, Paežerių; w paezeriai.info; ⊕ Apr–Sep 09.00–17.00 Tue–Fri, 10.00–18.00 Sat, 11.00–16.00 Sun, Oct–Mar 09.00–17.00 Mon–Fri; €3/2), located on the south shore of Lake Paežerių and home to the Vilkaviškis Regional Suvalkija Cultural Centre that includes the regional history museum. In addition, the **Vilkaviškis Tourism and Business Information Centre** (Vilkaviskio turizmo ir verslo informacijos centras; J Basanavičiaus aikštė 7; w vilkaviskisinfo.lt; ⊕ 08.00–17.00 Mon–Fri) runs a 'Made in Vilkaviškis' project, which highlights local producers and craftspeople who can be visited.

**MARIJAMPOLĖ** Marijampolė is known locally as Miami, a nickname stemming from the city's booming second-hand car market – while perhaps not as large as that of its American namesake, it's one of the biggest in Europe. Marijampolė's relationship with the auto trade started rather dubiously during the 1990s. It was here that second-hand cars from western Europe ended up, either for onward sale or broken down and sold for spare parts. For Lithuanians, the luxury of owning a new Western car was still a dream. The supply chain relied on damaged vehicles or old bangers purchased for a song and patched up enough to run local errands; yet they offered a sense of freedom to those ditching their Russian Moskvich for an albeit old German BMW. A thriving sector of insurance brokers supported the car dealing industry. Today, alongside its legitimate second-hand car trade, Marijampolė is predominantly an industrial town with a large ice-cream plant and sugar-processing factory, supported by local sugar beet farming – all of which are key local employers. It is a service centre for the region and the city centre is pleasant with good amenities for residents, providing a good overnight stop if travelling in the region or between Lithuania and Poland.

The **Marijampolė Tourism Information Centre** (Vytauto gatvė 17; w marijampoletic.lt; ⊕ 08.00–17.00 Mon–Fri) is ready to help visitors, unless you visit at the weekend. The city's highlights include the Neo-Gothic **railway station** (Stoties gatvė 2), built in 1923–24 and retaining many original features while still a functioning train station. The renovated **Choral Synagogue** (P Butlerienės gatvė 5; w mmlsc.lt; ⊕ 11.00–18.00 Tue–Fri, 10.00–15.00 Sat) houses an art gallery dedicated to artist Beatričė Kleizaitė-Vasaris and an education centre. The newly

### MALONNY

The annual street art symposium MaLonNy (think Marijampolė, London and New York; w malonny.lt) brings artists from the UK and USA to Marijampolė usually in July, where they join a team of local artists and volunteers to create street art throughout the city. Founded in 2014 by Lithuanian American artist Ray Bartkus, the annual festival has been cause for celebration. The impact has generated a new interest in Marijampolė as an art destination and is attracting mainly domestic tourists. It has made art accessible to the local community and brought an injection of colour and creativity to the city. Keep your eyes peeled for artworks as you walk around the city, including *Floating World* by Bartkus himself which is painted upside down above water, the true image being seen in the reflection.

renovated **Mercure Marijampolė Hotel** (J Basanaviciaus aikštė 8; w accor.com; [€€€] is a good place to overnight if needed.

## BIRŠTONAS

The pretty spa town of Birštonas is tucked away in one of the river loops of the Nemunas Loops Regional Park; the river acts like a moat, almost surrounding the town, adding to the feeling of escape and indulgence. The resort is on a smaller scale compared with its counterpart Druskininkai, and with fewer attractions it is less geared towards entertainment, and more towards recreation. Birštonas is a simpler escape, a place to unwind with excellent wellness treatments, a focus on healthy living, and many opportunities to enjoy nature. Bring your book, bike or both to make the most of Birštonas.

**HISTORY** During the Grand Duchy of Lithuania era covering the 13th to 18th centuries, Birštonas was a royal estate used primarily for hunting by the Grand Duke and his noble entourage. After partition by the Russian Empire in 1795 and the discovery of saline springs, it was granted resort status and flourished as a

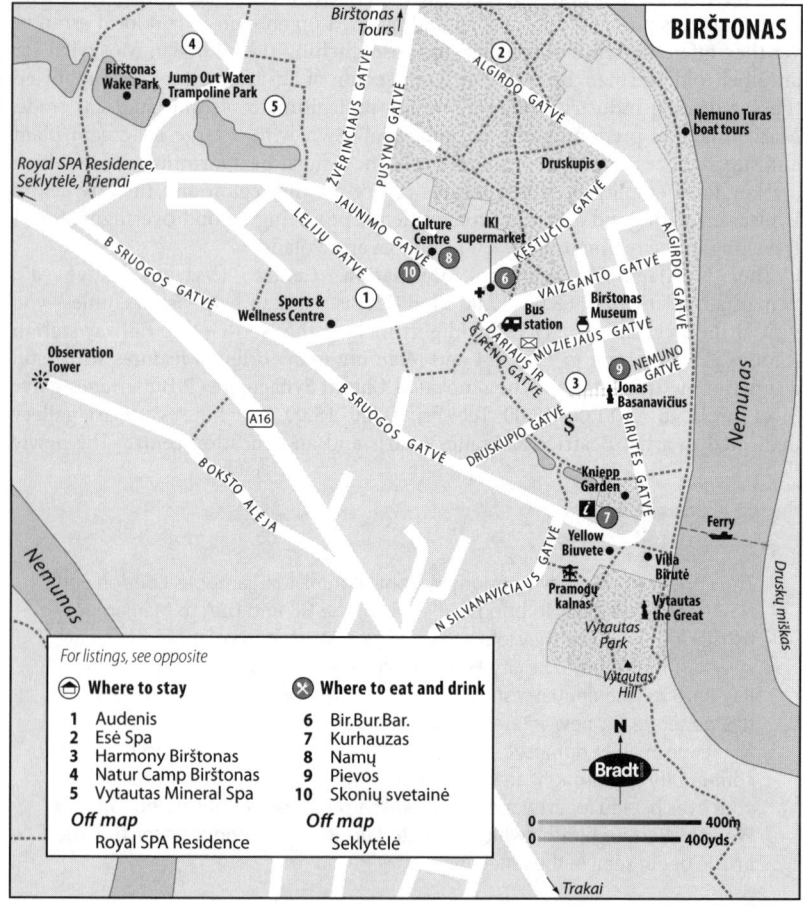

popular health resort. The border between the Russian Empire and German Prussia ran along the Nemunas River and during World War I Birštonas was both damaged and neglected. The newly independent state of Lithuania had no budget for repairs, but in stepped the Red Cross, which signed an agreement to manage and invest in Birštonas as a health resort. Simultaneously, other societal shifts were underway as the new government encouraged the division of large estates and redistribution of land and property to individuals. The annexation of Druskininkai to Poland in 1919 meant that Birštonas was now Lithuania's premier health resort and there followed a golden era for Birštonas. New hotels, spas, mud baths and treatment facilities were all established, and tourists flocked here.

In 1959, Birštonas was affected by the damming of the Nemunas River for construction of the Kaunas hydro-electric power plant. The original Vytautas spring outlet was flooded, and the surrounding concrete structure (built to protect the outlet from ice damage and freezing during the winter) was subsequently submerged too. This concrete structure was nicknamed *banginukas* (whale) on account of its whale-like shape – and hence the town's coat of arms today features a whale. During the Soviet period Birštonas suffered decline, but since independence it has been forging its own identity as a resort that is calm, cosy and close to nature.

**GETTING THERE AND AWAY** Buses run regularly between Birštonas and Kaunas (57mins), Vilnius (2hrs) and for Klaipėda you must change bus at Kaunas or Prienai. Birštonas bus station (Birštono autobusų stotis; Vaižganto gatvė 2) is centrally located and has good facilities, including a café and supermarket close by. You can travel to Birštonas by **boat** on Sundays from Kaunas Reservoir Quay (Kauno marių prieplauka; T Masiulio gatvė 21; w nemunoturas.lt; €31/28). The boat departs at 09.00 and arrives Birštonas at 13.00. The return journey to Kaunas is by bus, departing Birštonas at 17.00, arriving back to the quay at 17.40. If travelling by **car**, from Kaunas the direct route is via road 130 and takes 40 minutes.

**TOURIST INFORMATION** The Birštonas Tourist Information Centre (Birštonas turizmo informacijos centras; B Sruogos gatvė 4; w visitbirstonas.lt; ⏰ 09.00–18.00 Mon–Fri, 10.00–18.00 Sat, 10.00–17.00 Sun) has a friendly team to welcome you and advise on guided tours, self-guided routes, what's on and souvenirs.

 **WHERE TO STAY** *Map, opposite, unless otherwise stated*

**Esė Spa** (40 rooms) Algirdo gatvė 34; w esehotel.lt. A small-scale spa hotel, surrounded by pine trees & fresh crisp air, this hotel has everything you need to be pampered, relax & eat well: a small spa, swimming pool, restaurant, summer terrace & kids' indoor play area. You can even check their website to see how busy the pool is. €€€

**Harmony Birštonas** (14 rooms) S Dariaus ir S Girėno gatvė 2; w harmonypark.lt/harmony-park-birstonas. A branch of the Harmony Park Resort, this small luxury hotel in the centre of Birštonas has large, spacious rooms & an on-site restaurant. Free transfers are available between the hotel & resort to use their impressive spa facilities. €€€

**Harmony Park** [map, page 162] Vazgaikiemis, Preinai region; w harmonypark.lt. Located 16km west of Birštonas & occupying a huge private estate is this luxurious holiday resort. Accommodation includes a luxury hotel complete with opulent spa, a selection of villas & a campsite. On-site facilities include restaurants, a farm, tennis & padel courts, mini-golf & horseriding (including their own hippodrome). Very popular with families & equestrian fans. €€€€

**Royal SPA Residence** (150 rooms) Pakalnės gatvė 3; w royal-spa.lt. Situated outside of town, Royal SPA Residence is popular for its large spa centre with a wide range of treatments. It is located on the edge of the resort, a 40min walk to the centre, but has the advantage of being close to the Nemunas River & amid the pine forests close to the observation tower & hiking trails. €€€

**Vytautas Mineral Spa** (164 rooms) Karalienės Barboros alėja 2; w vytautasmineralspa.lt. This is a big wellness spa hotel, meaning they can offer a multitude of spa packages & treatments, then you can eat well in the gastrobar or restaurant. The selection of rooms & suites all come with complimentary robe & slippers. The library is a must-see with its lunar landscape décor. €€€

**Audenis Hotel** (13 rooms) Lelijų gatvė 3; w audenis.lt. Convenient for exploring the resort & for those not requiring on-site spa facilities, this centrally located, small family-run hotel has its own restaurant. Spa treatments can be taken at the large spa centres in town (Versmės sanatorija is the closest & Eglės sanatorija is 15mins' walk away). €€

**Natur Camp Birštonas** Karalienės Barboros alėja 1; w naturcamp.lt. A pleasant, welcoming campsite with tent places, campervan hook-ups, 3 cabins with shared facilities, 7 pods with en-suite shower & WC & 6 glamping bell tents with dbl beds. On-site bar with kitchen, renowned for their homemade stew on Sat evening & pancakes on Sun morning. Mobile climbing wall & nearby wake park too. €€

## ✴ WHERE TO EAT AND DRINK  *Map, page 210*

**Kurhauzas** B Sruogos gatvė 2; ◨ restoranaskurhauzas; ⏰ noon–22.00 Fri, noon–23.00 Sat, noon–22.00 Sun. Kurhauzas is not just a restaurant but an art gallery too, housed in a historical wooden building that serves as an arts space for exhibitions. There's a small seating area inside & a large terrace overlooking the church. €€€

**Namų** Jaunimo gatvė 4; ◨ namurestoranasbirstonas; ⏰ noon–21.00 Thu, noon–23.00 Fri–Sat, noon–22.00 Sun. Located in the Cultural Centre, serving up European food with the option to dine in the courtyard or on the roof terrace. €€€

**Pievos** J Basanavičiaus aikštė 16; w pievosbirstone.lt; ⏰ 09.00–21.00 Mon–Thu, 09.00–22.00 Fri–Sat, 09.00–20.00 Sun. A charming medley of plant shop & café, Pievos is perfect for coffee, snacks or a meal any time of day. €€€

**Seklytėlė** Prienų gatvė 10; w sonata.lt/seklytele; ⏰ 10.00–22.00 daily. A wholesome, Lithuanian menu with all the favourites, including kepta duona for starters, daily soup with fresh bread, meat cutlets, chicken Kyiv, all served with fried potatoes or rice & fresh vegetables. Eat in the cosy indoors in winter, or on the spectacular terrace overlooking the Nemunas River in summer. €€€

**Bir.Bur.Bar.** S Dariaus ir S Girėno gatvė 24; ◨ birburbar. This is the place for burgers & ribs in Birštonas. Located on the upper floor of IKI supermarket. €€

**Skonių svetainė** Jaunimo gatvė 3; ◨ SkoniuSvetaine. A small family-run restaurant & a great spot for lunch during the day, it has a small seating area inside & a shaded terrace outside. €€

**SPORTS AND ACTIVITIES** The tourist information centre offers advice and maps for hiking, cycling, kayaking and cross-country skiing routes around Birštonas. Alongside relaxing in the resort, these activities will add to your nature therapy. Some hotels also have bicycles for hire.

**Audenis Hot Air Ballooning** Birštonas; w skriskimekartu.lt. Though based in Birštonas, pilot Žydrūnas Kazlauskas & his team arrange hot-air balloon trips across Lithuania. Join a small group or book an exclusive flight. From €133 pp to join a small group flight.

**Birstonas Tours** Pusyno gatvė 75; w birstonastours.lt. A local provider of bicycle (€5/hr or €15/day) & kayak rental (€15/day Mon–Fri, €20/day Sat–Sun), they also run a regular City Tour of Birštonas by electric vehicle (40mins; €7/3) with audio guides in English.

**Birštonas Wake Park** Next to Natur Camp Birštonas, Karalienės Barboros alėja; birstonaswake.lt; ⏰ Jun–Sep 10.00–22.00; €12 for a 20min ride. Try wakeboarding at this very popular small wake park. Advance booking is required. At the far end of the course is a small pontoon area set aside for swimming.

### HOT-AIR BALLOONING IN LITHUANIA

Hot-air ballooning is a popular pastime in Lithuania; in fact, Lithuania ranks within the top five countries in the world for the number of balloons per capita. This fascination and love for ballooning stems from the country's strong aviation traditions, and perhaps living in a relatively flat country provides the motivation to take to the skies for gloriously uninterrupted views.

Birštonas is the ballooning capital of Lithuania with 360° clear airspace. The town of Prienai, close to Birštonas, is home to Prienai airfield and the Lithuanian Aviation Plant (w lak.lt), where they have produced world-class gliders since 1969. The story goes that, decades ago, a glider was sold to Hungary and the recipient paid for it with two hot-air balloons. After making connections with the ballooning community in Poland, staff at the glider plant soon learned the ballooning basics. In 1988, the first Lithuanian ballooning championships were held and Lithuanian balloonists began to compete in international competitions, inspired by the opportunity to travel and developing their passion for the sport. In 1999, Lithuanian balloonist Gintaras Šurkus won bronze in the World Hot Air Ballooning Championships, putting Lithuania on the map. Lithuania continues to produce champions, some of whom come from multi-generational families of pilots; and Lithuanian pilots work worldwide.

The season for hot-air ballooning is May to October. If you book a flight, you must be prepared to be flexible as safety is paramount and depends on the weather conditions among other factors. Flights normally take off around 06.00 or 18.00, with pick-up 1 hour before. A flight lasts approximately 1 hour. Baskets usually take up to 6 passengers and a flight costs between €100 and €150 per person. You can pay extra for an exclusive flight. You can also take off from Trakai, Kaunas and Vilnius. These flights involve more aerial sightseeing of the cities or castle but must satisfy additional conditions before take-off owing to their proximity to more urban areas, airports and the Belarus border. Flights over Vilnius Old Town are widely publicised but they are also the least likely to be realised as the airport and Belarus are very close. If your flight is redirected to Trakai, Kaunas or Birštonas, it is for good reason and will still be an extraordinary experience.

**Boat tours** From Apr to early Oct, 07.00–sunset, a small ferry operates from Birštonas close to Tulpės Sanatorija across to Druskų miškas (salt forest) on the opposite bank of the river, where there are hiking trails & a circular cycling route. Take a picnic. Local company **Nemuno Turas** (w nemunoturas.lt) runs regular 1hr sightseeing cruises (from the riverbank next to Eglės sanatorija) on their boat *Algirdas*, exploring the Nemunas loops.

**Jump Out Water Trampoline Park** Next to Natur Camp, Karalienės Barboros alėja; jumpoutbirštonas; ⊕ Jun–Sep 11.00–19.00 daily; €10 pp/hr. A very popular trampoline park & inflatable obstacle course on a small lake. Operates only in good weather.

**Pramogų kalnas** N Silvanavičiaus gatvė 4; w pramogukalnas.lt; ⊕ May–Sep 11.00–19.00 Mon–Fri, 10.00–19.00 Sat–Sun. A small-scale amusement park with rides & attractions for all ages, including a summer sledging toboggan. Pay separately for each ride; the toboggan run is €5/3.

**Sports & Wellness Centre** Sporto ir sveikatingumo centras; Kęstučio gatvė 14; w birstonosportas.lt; ⊕ 08.00–21.00 Mon–Fri, 09.00–17.00 Sat–Sun. Visitors can rent the tennis courts or use the gym; pop into the reception to make a booking. The main sports facilities here focus on basketball, rowing & athletics, so you might see some national athletes training.

**OTHER PRACTICALITIES** You will find a Gintarinė **pharmacy** at S Dariaus ir S Girėno gatvė 24, inside the IKI supermarket. The **post office** is on the same street at number 14. The only **bank** branch is Šiaulių Bankas (Druskupio gatvė 1), but don't expect much (if anything) in English. There is a Swedbank cashpoint at the IKI supermarket.

## WHAT TO SEE AND DO
**Observation Tower** (Birštono apžvalgos bokštas; Bokšto alėja 25; **f** birstono. bokstas; ⊕ 06.00–19.00 daily; free) Standing proud at 55m tall, this is the tallest observation tower in Lithuania. From the top, a panoramic view extends for miles beyond the Nemunas River as it loops to distant towns and thick forests. First, you must conquer the 300 steps to the top (there is no lift). At the entrance to the stairwell is a counter to manage the number of people on the tower at any given time. You can even check online (**w** visitbirstonas.lt/en/sightseeing-places/birstonas-observation-tower) to see how busy it is. If you need refreshments before or after you tackle the tower, there is a pop-up café next to the tower in the summer months. To get to the tower from Birštonas, follow the signposted route from near Versmės sanatorija which takes you over the pedestrian bridge to avoid the road.

**Culture Centre** (Birštono kultūros centras; Jaunimo gatvė 4; **w** birstonokultura.lt; ⊕ 08.00–17.00 Mon–Fri) As its name suggests, the Culture Centre is the hub of cultural events in Birštonas. It is also home to an outstanding, and very large (22m x 7m), example of stained-glass art, by Vytautas Švarlis. Created in 1980, when under Soviet occupation 7% of the Culture Centre budget had to be spent on an art installation, *Lietuva* (Lithuania) depicts patriotic themes: the Grand Duchy defending against crusaders, and traditional life skills such as weaving, fishing, medicine and music. Look for the hand that is subtly turned to the left – was it a silent protest? You can see the window from outside as it is floodlit, but it is better from inside with the light behind it. The window is on the national heritage register.

**Druskupis** (Algirdo gatvė 21; ⊕ 24/7) Set amid the tall pine trees is this mineral water graduation tower, where people can sit inside the curved structure and experience open-air inhalation of healthy 'sea air'. Mineral water trickles down the walls of the tower and evaporates naturally due to the temperature or wind, in effect creating a salty 'sea air' that is beneficial to those within 50–80 m of the tower.

> **BIRŠTONAS JAZZ FESTIVAL**
>
> The very first Birstonas Jazz Festival (**w** birstonasjazz.lt) was organised in 1980 by Culture Centre director Zigmas Vileikis. At that time, Lithuania was occupied by Soviet Russia under Brezhnev's rule. Jazz music was viewed as the music of freedom, of rebellion and of underground movements, so it was neither encouraged nor flaunted. The larger cities were reluctant to host a jazz festival, so brave Birštonas did just that. And the festival continues to this day, still under the supervision of director Zigmas Vileikis, and is held biannually on the last weekend of March, unless Easter bumps it into April. Attracting more than 3,000 visitors, the festival's intense 72 hours of jazz features Lithuanian and international artists, adding music therapy to the list of Birštonas' feel-good treatments.

Admire the wooden architecture of Druskininkai spa resort, including the colourful Joy of All Who Sorrow Church PAGE 143

above (SCP/S)

Modernist Kaunas's 'Architecture of Optimism' was inscribed on the UNESCO World Heritage List in 2023. Pictured: Kaunas Central Post Office PAGE 165

below (BV/S)

| | |
|---|---|
| above (LC/LT) | Now UNESCO listed and of great archaeological importance, Kernavė was the medieval capital of the Grand Duchy of Lithuania PAGE 129 |
| left (RT/S) | Tour the decommissioned Ignalina Nuclear Power Plant, film location for the hit television series *Chernobyl* PAGE 239 |
| below (VG/S) | The Ninth Fort lies on the outskirts of Kaunas, a solemn reminder of occupation and resistance PAGE 192 |

The Hill of Crosses is a powerful symbol of Lithuanian faith, identity and independence PAGE 258 above (LZ)

An outstanding collection of Soviet-era antiquities are housed in the KGB Atomic Bunker Museum PAGE 192 below left (SC)

Visit the hideouts, bunkers and memorials that honour the Forest Brothers resistance fighters PAGE 205 below right (SC)

above right (MU/S)  Wood carving is an ancient craft protected under law; visit artisans at the Museum of Lithuanian Ethnography PAGES 37 & 196

above left (MU/S)  The Baltic Sea produces the finest amber; hunt for your own on the beach, see amber on display at a museum, or create your own amber piece in a workshop PAGE 36

left (RA/S)  In Trakai, be sure to try the local speciality, *kibinai* PAGE 125

below (BV/S)  Held every July, the Archaeological Days festival in Kernavė sees craftspeople, traders, musicians and re-enactors set up a medieval camp around the open-air museum PAGE 130

White storks are not only the national bird of Lithuania, they are also a much-loved symbol of summer PAGE 8 — above (SA/S)

Ethnographic crafts are a feast of colour and artisan skill, the best collections often found in regional museums like the Šiauliai History Museum PAGE 256 — below (SC)

Labanoras is one of many attractive villages in Lithuania's Aukštaitija region PAGE 228 — bottom left (SC)

The festival of Užgavėnės is held in February to celebrate the end of winter; there is an excellent exhibition of traditional masks at Plateliai Manor in Žemaitija National Park PAGES 62 & 268 — bottom right (MU/S)

above (SB/LT) Cycling is the perfect way to explore the Curonian Spit PAGE 304

left (SC) Lake Plateliai in Žemaitija National Park, where you can swim, sail or dive PAGE 267

below (SB/LT) Aukštaitija National Park's diverse network of waterways are best explored by kayak PAGE 231

Zarasai Observation Wheel provides the ideal viewpoint over Lake Zarasas PAGE 241 above (SC)

Observation towers are scattered across Lithuania, but Kirkiliai Observation Tower near Biržai is one of the most attractive PAGE 247 below (MNS/S)

top (LJ/S) — Sunset over the dunes at Nida PAGE 313

above left (S/S) — Palanga Pier originally had train tracks running its length to service ships; today it is a focal point of the resort and a popular place year-round to sit or stroll PAGE 285

above right (YB/S) — Melnragė, a Blue Flag beach area north of Klaipėda, is home to the *Walking with Fish* statue PAGE 300

below (SC) — Remnants of Fachwerk architecture in the port city of Klaipėda hint at the region's Prussian history PAGE 299

**Birštonas Museum** (Birštono muziejus; Vytauto gatvė 9; w birstonomuziejus.lt; ⊕ 10.00–18.00 Tue–Sat, 10.00–16.00 Sun; €3/1.50) The displays at the Birštonas Museum are mostly in Lithuanian, so for non-Lithuanian speakers a visit here is largely an opportunity to appreciate the historic wooden villa Ramunė in which it is housed, and speculate about old photographs and artefacts. A second branch of the museum, **Birštonas Museum of Sacral Art** (Birštono sakralinis muziejus; Birutės gatvė 10; ⊕ 10.00–18.00 Tue–Sat, 10.00–16.00 Sun; €2/1) is dedicated to the history of the church and its clergy in Birštonas.

**Statue of Jonas Basanavičius** (J Basanavičiaus aikštė 1) It is a rare thing for an original statue of a patriotic figure like Basanavičius to have survived occupation. It became normal for such monuments to be destroyed or removed in an attempt to erase national identity. But every time Soviet officials visited Birštonas, a box was placed over Basanavičius's head and they were told the statue had been removed for renovation. So, survive it did, and the statue, created in 1939 by sculptor Antanas Aleksandravičius, remains in place today, untouched and unscathed.

**Statue of Vytautas the Great** (Vytauto Didžiojo paminklas; B Sruogos gatvė 1) Sometime during the Soviet era, a large stone was transported to Lithuania from Ukraine destined to become a statue of Lenin. That plan was never realised and the stone was put away in storage and forgotten about. After independence, the stone resurfaced and in a show of patriotism Grand Duke Vytautas was the chosen subject for a new statue, with one shortfall – there was not enough stone to carve the full height of his horse, hence the unusual block-style plinth. Vytautas stands facing west ready to face his Crusader enemies. It is considered good luck to touch the horse's right nostril.

**Villa Birutė** (Birutės vila; B Sruogos gatvė 1A; ⊕ 09.00–18.00 Tue–Fri, 10.00–18.00 Sat, 10.00–17.00 Sun; free) Villa Birutė is a mineral water pavilion. During opening hours, you can come here free of charge and simply sit, listen to the fountain, and inhale the air, slightly scented with minerals from the mineral vaporisation wall. It is a quiet place for relaxation so do respect other visitors. Toilets are also available.

**Kniepp Garden** (Kneipo sodas; B Sruogos gatvė 2B; ⊕ 24/7) German priest Sebastien Kniepp (1821–97) believed that 'Water cures everything; water works wonders; prevention is better than cure', a philosophy that is promoted in Birštonas. Wellness is central to strengthening your constitution and boosting your immune system, and a holistic approach of hydrotherapy, exercise, phytotherapy, harmony and nutrition will give the best results. The Kniepp Garden is designed with self-treatment areas – information boards will guide you on how to take a hand treatment (alternating your hands in a cold water bath), a reflexology treatment (barefoot walking path), and a leg procedure to help circulation (by wading in a cold-water pool). The park will be a pleasant find for cold-water swimmers, as it is focused on cold water treatment and its role in building resistance and strengthening the immune system.

**Yellow 'Biuvete'** (Geltonoji biuvetė; B Sruogos gatve 3; ⊕ during the warmer months 07.30–19.00 daily; free) This curious folly from the 19th century is built above the spring 'Vytautas'. Go inside and sample fresh Vytautas mineral water, but beware it has the nickname of 'salty tears'. There is only a tap, so bring a cup or bottle if you want to indulge in more than a taste (the water must be consumed within 2 hours of being drawn from the depths). Vytautas water is bottled and sold throughout the country along with Birutė water, named after Grand Duke Vytautas's wife.

**Vytautas Hill** (Southern point of Vytautas Park) In the late 14th century, Birštonas Castle stood atop this steep-sided castle mound with sweeping views across the Nemunas River and surrounding forest. The castle was one of Grand Duke Vytautas's hunting estates, regularly hosting princes and nobles for both entertainment and diplomacy. Access to the summit is by sturdy wooden steps with handrails.

# 7

# Aukštaitija

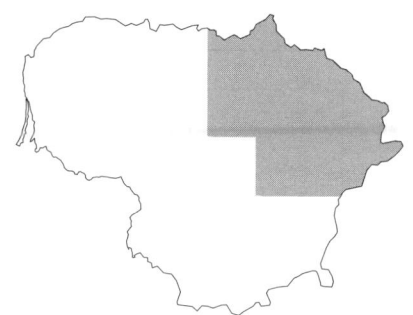

Aukštaitija (*owk-shtay-tia*) is the largest ethnographic region in Lithuania and officially is a more extensive area than is covered in this chapter, which has been designed with tourism in mind. But it felt a travesty to call this chapter northeast Lithuania, rather than Aukštaitija!

Bordering Latvia to the north and Belarus to the east, this is a land of lakes and rolling landscapes, referred to as the Aukštaitija highlands – not for height but for its location in the upper basin of the Nemunas River. Western Aukštaitija is known as the breadbasket of Lithuania, its rich fertile soils supporting expansive arable farming and wealthy farmers. Those travelling through this flat landscape will be rewarded with dramatic wide, open skies. Rounded boulders are reminders of the glacial forces that sculpted this area. Deposited by the retreating ice millennia ago, they continue to torment those working the land, and piles of boulders lie on field boundaries having been removed to enable cultivation. Glacial boulders were also put to good use in the construction of manor houses and farmstead foundations.

To the east, the terrain is a combination of gentle hills, lakes, swamps and forests, dotted here and there with summer houses and holiday homes. With the largest concentration of lakes in the country, this Lithuanian lake district is adored by nature lovers and outdoor enthusiasts alike. Tourism has become an important industry here and the facilities are constantly improving, although development is restricted and attitudes remain true to the local approach that nothing counteracts modern life better than enjoying a simple, rural way of life in nature.

Aukštaitija is home to some unique Lithuanian experiences: astronomical stargazing, ethnocosmology, riding a narrow-gauge railway, long-distance kayaking on interconnected waterways, visiting a decommissioned nuclear power plant, listening to Sutartinės archaic polyphonic singing, and more. Exploring the region can be tricky by public transport, but for those blessed with time it is perfect for slow travel, although you will need to be open to hitchhiking to cover routes not served by local buses. Car is king in this region if you want to get off the beaten track (we're talking forest tracks and gravel roads), and the hummocky terrain makes it the most interesting and picturesque region for touring.

## ANYKŠČIAI

Anykščiai has experienced its fair share of turbulence over the centuries (unfair seems more appropriate). A strategic trading location on the Šventoji River and on the land route between Vilnius and Riga no doubt helped with the growth and development of the town, but it also attracted unwelcome attention from Teutonic marauders in the days of knights on horseback. Evidence of this early history can be seen in the many castle mounds that are scattered throughout the region – if you think you've spotted one, you probably have. During the early 20th century there was a sizeable

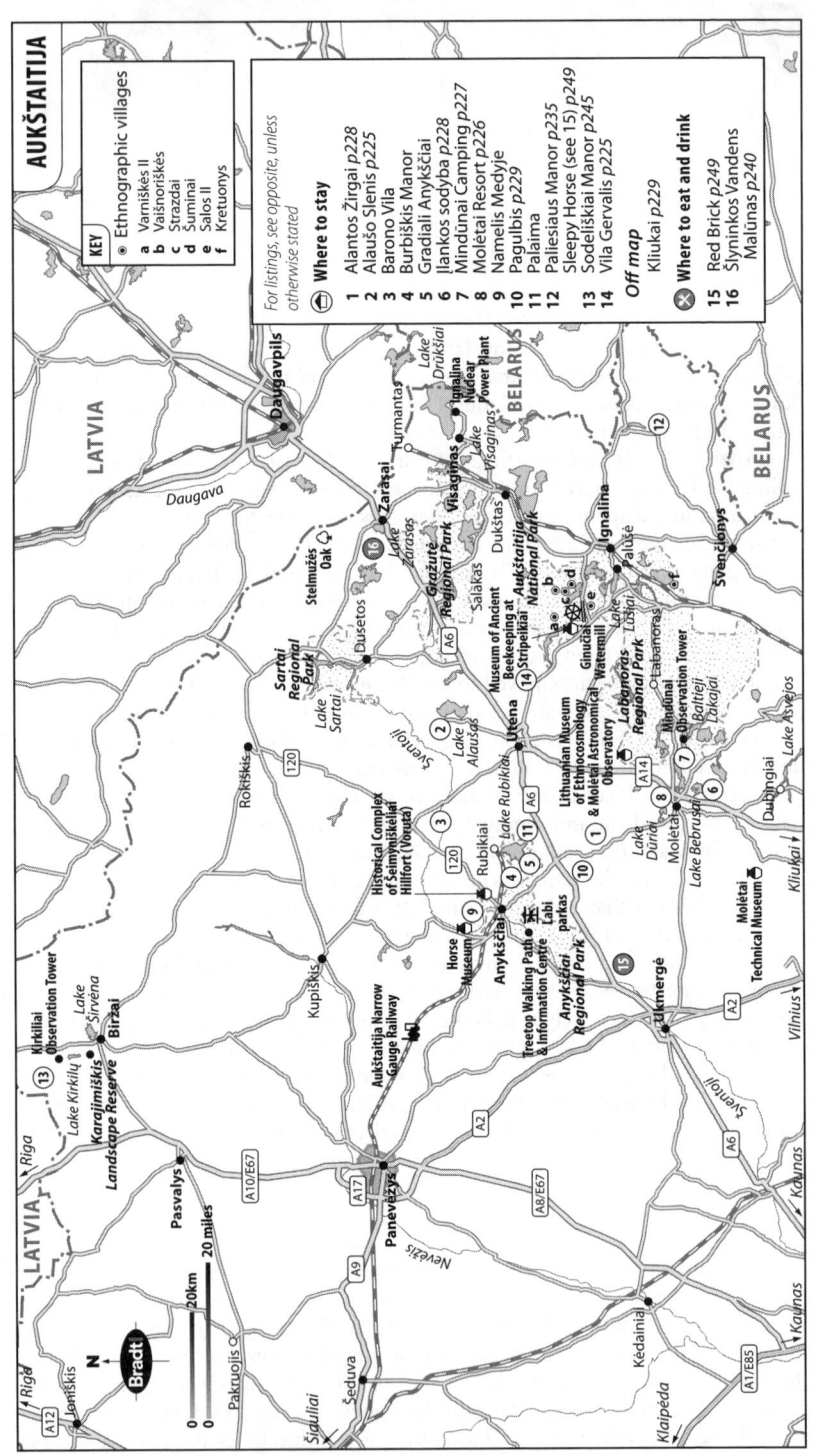

Jewish population in Anykščiai, and a familiar fate befell them as in many cities, towns and villages across Lithuania. In the summer of 1941, German Nazis assisted by local collaborators killed around 1,500 Jews in Anykščiai. During this period, the city centre and bridges were destroyed, with any development during the period of Soviet occupation that followed characterised by brutal, unsympathetic architecture.

Perhaps in response to these dark periods of history, Anykščiai has been home to many Lithuanian poets and writers – a place of tortured souls often bears the fruit of creativity. No doubt, their inspiration came from the same pride held by the local community today – that they live in one of the most attractive regions of Lithuania. It was the local poet Antanas Baranauskas who in 1859 wrote his masterpiece *Anykščių Šilelis* (The Anykščiai Forest), in which he waxed lyrical about the overwhelming connection that Lithuanian people have with their forests and woodland. He was greatly concerned about the forest's demise due to deforestation and is credited with saving it by raising awareness and changing attitudes – he was ahead of his time. In 1938, Anykščiai was awarded resort status and has been a popular holiday destination for domestic tourism ever since. Recent infrastructure improvements, new attractions and excellent accommodation options in and around the city now make Anykščiai one of the most appealing rural resorts for international visitors wanting to experience lesser-known Lithuania.

Anykščiai is a social city with a small-town feel in part due to the shops and services centred around the main square, behind which are cobbled streets lined with historic wooden houses in various states of renovation and dilapidation. The atmosphere is quite charming, especially if you allow time to fix your hunger or thirst at the tiny restaurant 5 Taskai (page 221). Chat with the owners who gave up their high-flying lifestyle in Vilnius to move to Anykščiai and open this little gem. You know times have changed when Lithuanian rural towns are attracting young entrepreneurs from the capital to invest in a lifestyle business. This is wonderfully exciting and the success of these endeavours will have a huge impact on the future of rural areas.

**GETTING THERE AND AWAY** The bus station (Anykscių autobusu stotis; A Vienuolio gatvė 1) has direct **bus routes** to the main cities of Vilnius (2hrs; twice daily) and Kaunas (2hrs; four times daily). It is located opposite the tourist information centre and is only a short walk across the bridge to the city centre. Getting to Anykščiai **by car** is straightforward, with driving times to/from Vilnius of 1hr 30mins (head north on road A2/E272, taking the A6/E262 east at Ukmergė) and Kaunas 1hr 40mins (leave Kaunas on road A6/E262).

**TOURIST INFORMATION** The **Anykščiai Tourism Information Centre** (Muziejaus gatvė 1; w visitanyksciai.lt; ⊕ 08.00–17.00 Mon–Thu, 08.00–16.00 Sat) lists events and activities on its website and has a useful downloadable app – search for Anykščiai in your app store. To get acquainted with the surrounding regional park, the displays in the **Anykščiai Regional Park Visitor Centre** (J Biliūno gatvė 55; w anyksciuparkas.lt; ⊕ 09.00–18.00 Tue–Fri, 08.45–16.30 Sat) are worth seeing and the staff can advise on the best hiking trails, cycling routes and camping places – the majority of which are around Lake Rubikiai and along the Šventoji River.

**WHERE TO STAY** Anykščiai accommodation options make the most of the quiet, natural areas on the edge of the city but are no further than a short walk or cycle ride from the main sights and amenities of the city centre. Further afield you will find some very comfortable resorts within the Anykščiai Regional Park for a more rural retreat.

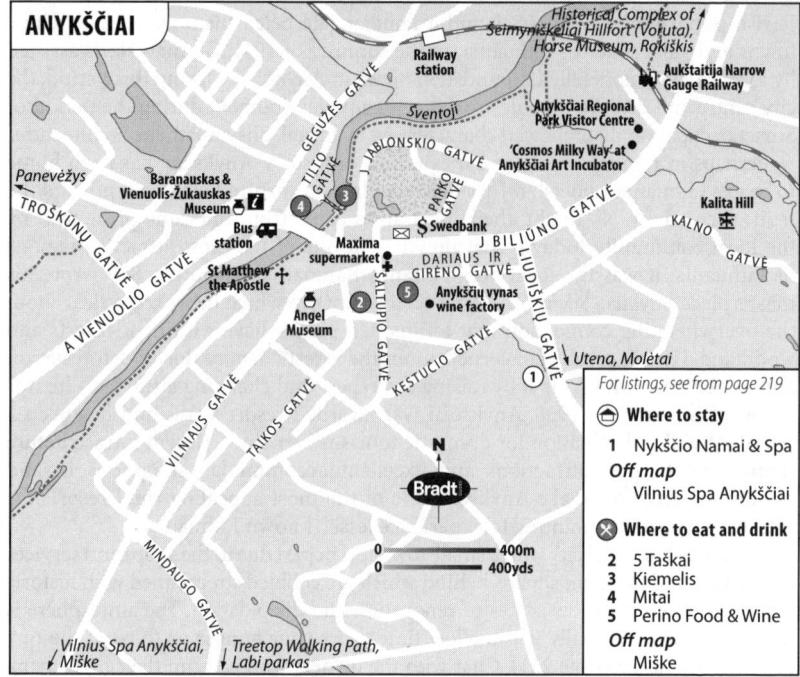

## In and around the centre
Map, above, unless otherwise stated

**⁕ Vilnius Spa Anykščiai** (47 rooms) Vilniaus gatvė 80; w spavilnius.lt. What was once a Soviet recreation camp for employees of the Lithuanian gas board has been utterly transformed into an award-winning spa & wellness hotel. The weight of the world lifts here, with the only considerations being which spa treatments to indulge in, what seasonal dish to choose in restaurant Miške, & whether to walk or cycle the 2.5km along the river into the city after lunch. The friendly staff & small scale of this hotel make it one of the best. Very family-friendly too. €€€€

**Namelis Medyje** [map, page 218] (2 treehouses, 3 cabins, 1 large house) Elmos 8-oji gatvė 2, Šeimyniškeliai; w namelis-medyje.lt. 'Anykščiai Treehouse' is located next to the cycle path between the centre & the Horse Museum. The treehouses are straight out of a kid's dream, where their room is built around a tree & connected to the adults' room via a bridge. Treehouses & cabins sleep 2 or 4 people & the main house, which is an old grain barn, sleeps 10 with access to a communal dining kitchen. Sauna available for rental. Self-catering is centred around an outdoor grill. It is a 4km cycle ride or walk to the city centre. €€€

**Nykščio Namai & Spa** (28 rooms) Liudiškių gatvė 18; w nykscionamai.lt. This renovated tourist-class hotel in the centre has a spa & sports facilities, including a basketball hall, tennis courts & bowling alley. €€€

## Further afield
Map, page 218

**Barono Vila** (11 rooms, apartments & villas) Elnio gatvė 12, Butėnų region; w baronovila.lt. On route 120 between Anykščiai and Rokiškis is this holiday complex of self-catering small villas with 2 or 3 bedrooms, or the Grand Villa with boutique-hotel-style rooms & apartments. It's popular with groups & weddings, so w/ends are often busy & best avoided. Private lake for boating & swimming, no loud music after midnight. €€€€

**Burbiškis Manor** (11 rooms) Parko gatvė 1B; w burbiskis.lt. 8km east of Anykščiai is this 19th-century manor house renovated into a museum & small hotel with unique guest rooms, one of which is a quadruple. There is also a restaurant, small spa area (€60/hr), & tours of the manor are available to guests & non-residents (€5 pp). €€€

**Gradiali Anykščiai** (22 rooms) Klykūnai region; w anyksciai.gradiali.com. On the southwestern shore of Lake Rubikiai, 13km east of Anykščiai, is this recreation complex with restaurant, sauna, playgrounds & games room to keep families happy. Accommodation is in villas, comprised of en-suite rooms or apartments with all mod cons. Professional chefs & staff can be hired. €€€

**Palaima Hotel** (5 rooms, 1 cottage) Ežero gatvė 8d, Mačionių village; w palaima.ch. A lakeside retreat, on the eastern shore of Lake Rubikiai, this hotel has a Swiss-chalet theme & rooms styled in calm pastel colours. The separate cottage sleeps 6. The restaurant is open to non-residents & Sun brunch is popular (€35 pp). Activities include walking with alpacas, paddleboarding, sauna, handicraft workshops & berry picking. Children are only allowed if the whole site is booked exclusively. €€€

## ✖ WHERE TO EAT AND DRINK  Map, opposite

**Miške**  Vilnius Spa Anykščiai; Vilniaus gatvė 80; f restoranasMiske; ⏱ 12.30–22.00 daily. The menu is creative, healthy & sustainable, with many ingredients coming from the hotel kitchen garden. Charming summer terrace with outdoor grill in summer. €€€€

**5 Taškai**  S Daukanto gatvė 5; f 5taskai; ⏱ noon–21.00 Fri–Sat, noon–18.00 Sun. People travel from far & wide for the tiramisu here, their pasta is homemade & the mushroom sauce made with freshly foraged mushrooms from the local forest. The interior is a tad bijou but which adds to the homely atmosphere & personal service. Larger families or groups of friends might struggle here. Book in advance or have a back-up plan. €€€

**Kiemelis**  Paupio gatvė 10; f restoraneliskiemelis; ⏱ 11.00–20.00 Sun– Thu, 11.00–22.00 Fri–Sat. Known as a little restaurant, or *restoranėlis*, this is a cosy place for lunch & has a reputation for its show-stopping desserts. €€€

**Mitai**  Tilto gatvė 2; ⊙ mitai.restoranas; ⏱ 11.30–17.00 Mon, Tue & Thu, 11.30–23.00 Fri, noon–midnight Sat, 11.00–20.00 Sun. The location is lovely, with a pleasant terrace from which to enjoy a drink & snack overlooking the river. €€

**Perino Food & Wine**  Dariaus ir Girėno gatvė 8; f perino.skanu; ⏱ 11.00–15.00 Mon, 11.00–20.00 Tue–Thu, 11.00–22.00 Fri, noon–22.00 Sat, noon–18.00 Sun. Located in the complex of Anykščių vynas wine factory (w anyvynas.lt), this makes an excellent lunch stop before or after a wine tour & tasting. €€

**ACTIVITIES**  There are two main centres of family fun in Anykščiai, both of which offer a variety of activities and amusements for all ages.

Close to the centre, **Kalita Hill** (Kalita kalnas; Kalno gatvė 25; w visitanyksciai.lt/kalita-hill; ⏱ 10.00–19.00 daily; €3 pp Mon–Fri, €4 pp Sat–Sun) offers year-round fun, at speed. In summer you can ride the alpine rollercoaster toboggan run and kids will love the playground; while in winter you can ski, sled or tube down the hill. Equipment is available to hire and instructors can be booked for tuition.

On the way to the Treetop Walking Path from the city centre, you pass **Labi parkas** (Skapiškių gatvė 5; w labiparkas.lt; ⏱ May–Sep 10.00–20.00 daily; €16/8 Mon–Fri, €20/10 Sat–Sun), an amusement park full of family activities. If you have kids, good luck not stopping. Offering unlimited fun on an all-day ticket, there are rides, a maze, climbing, junior driving, mini golf and upside-down houses. Sustenance to keep the energy levels up is available at the snack bar and pizzeria.

**OTHER PRACTICALITIES**  There is a branch of **Swedbank** (J Biliūno gatvė 11) in the centre of town, along the street from the **post office** (J Biliūno gatvė 5). Next to the **supermarket** Maxima is a Camelia Vaistinė **pharmacy** (Dariaus ir Girėno gatvė 1-44).

**WHAT TO SEE AND DO** When exploring the city centre be sure to visit the cobbled side streets of S Daukanto and Sinagogos gatvės, the remaining area of Anykščiai's Old Town. Along with the original red-brick houses on the main square, these streets offer a glimpse of what the city looked like prior to 1941, when life was centred around a bustling marketplace surrounded by small Jewish shops.

## In and around the city centre

**Church of St Matthew the Apostle** (Šv. apaštalo evangelisto Mato bažnyčia; Vilniaus gatvė 8; w anyksciuparapija.lt) The red-brick Neo-Gothic twin towers of this early 20th-century church dominate the city skyline and at 79m tall, they make this officially the nation's tallest church. For a view of the city, you can climb the 186 steps up to the observation deck at 33m. In 1999, a new organ was installed, featuring 2,600 pipes and 45 voices. Built in 1925 and shipped to Anykščiai from Southampton, it is considered one of the best organs in Lithuania.

**Angel Museum** (Angelų muziejus; Vilniaus gatvė 11; w amenucentras.lt; ⊕ May–Jun 10.00–17.00 daily, Jul–Aug 10.00–17.00 Sat–Sun, Sep–Oct 10.00–16.00 Sat–Sun, Nov–Apr 10.00–16.00 Mon–Fri; free) Lithuania's first angel museum opened in July 2010, centred on the private collection of cultural figure Beatričė Kleizaitė-Vasaris. More than 109 angel ornaments and sculptures made from glass, wood, ceramics and other materials are exhibited, with the collection constantly being added to by prominent Lithuanian artists and folk artists (you are welcome to bring an angel to donate). The museum also houses the **Anykščiai Sacred Art Centre**, which displays the valuable collection of Anykščiai pastor Monsignor Albert Talačka (1921–99), including paintings and more than 4,000 books and manuscripts from the 17th to 20th centuries.

**Baranauskas and Vienuolis-Žukauskas Museum** (A Baranausko ir A Vienuolio-Žukausko memorialinis muziejus; A Vienuolio gatvė 2; w baranauskas. lt; ⊕ Jul–Aug 10.00–18.00 daily, Sep–Jun 08.00–17.00 daily; €3/2) This memorial museum for prominent Lithuanian literary figures may well attract more Lithuanian visitors than international ones. It was here in the granary, during the summers of 1858 and 1859, that the bishop and poet **Antanas Baranauskas** (1835–1902; page 219) wrote his best-known work, the poem *Anykščių šilelis* (The Forest of Anykščiai). The museum houses Baranauskas' furniture and books, keeping his memory preserved for future generations. The museum is also dedicated to **Antanas Vienuolis-Žukauskas** (1882–1957), who was born in Anykščiai and became one of Lithuania's foremost writers of the 20th century. His grave is in the garden. One of the main joys for a tourist when visiting a memorial museum like this, is the privilege of seeing inside a traditional wooden house which you pass so often on your travels in Lithuania.

**'Cosmos Milky Way' at Anykščiai Art Incubator** ('Cosmos Paukščių takas'; J Biliūno gatvė 53; w pauksciutakas.eu; ⊕ 09.00–18.00 daily; €3/1.50) Enjoy this mirror-and-lights optical illusion designed to make you feel immersed in the solar system. Costing €3 for approximately 5 minutes, it is popular for taking selfies in the colour-changing light show. The surrounding art incubator buildings host numerous artists and handicraft specialists, whose wares are displayed and for sale.

**Aukštaitija Narrow-Gauge Railway 'Siaurukas' and Museum** (Stoties gatvė 4A; w siaurukomuziejus.lt; ⊕ May–Sep 10.00–18.00 Mon–Fri, 10.00–19.00

Sat–Sun, Nov–Apr by prior appointment only; €5/4, rides extra) In 1862 the Warsaw-to-St Petersburg railway was completed – a Russian gauge railway line servicing goods and passenger trains with grand stations ready to greet the wealthy and noble who could afford to buy tickets. To service the main railway line from provincial areas, industrial centres or agricultural sites, a network of narrow-gauge branch lines was established. The stretch of track between Panevėžys and Rubikiai (68.4km) was opened in 1899 and in its heyday transported tens of thousands of passengers and tonnes of freight each year. Today, this is the last remaining section of functioning narrow-gauge track in Lithuania and is fondly called 'Siaurukas'. The name comes from the Lithuanian word *siauras* meaning narrow; *siaurukas* is a diminutive form of siauras. Having been removed from the national network, it was saved by local supporters for its tourism potential, and its success as a popular attraction continues to grow. The main museum for the railway is at the original wooden station complex at Anykščiai (Siauruko muziejus) with a good selection of exhibits, and for €1 you can ride a handcar or rail-bicycle. During the summer months a pop-up café bar, Reisas XIX (f reisas.baras), operates at the station. Regular train rides on the narrow-gauge railway currently operate between Anykščiai and Rubikiai between May and October only, on Saturdays and Sundays (departing Anykščiai at 11.00, arriving Rubikiai 11.50, returning at 13.50 and arriving Anykščiai at 14.40; €12/8). To book train tickets online, go to w siaurukas.eu. At Rubikiai you have free time to swim in the lake, hire a pedalo, hike, picnic or enjoy lunch at **Žuvienės pašiūrė** (w zuvienespasiure.lt; ⊕ 11.00–21.00 Sat–Sun; €€). Look out for special train journeys, starting from either Panevėžys or Anykščiai stations, often with a novelty theme and incorporating a stop at one of the smaller wooden stations for an event, including Santa Trains throughout December, or the 'Beaužole Train' wine festival held in November. They even have a sauna and hot-tub carriage for private hire.

## Further afield
*Historical Complex of Šeimyniškėliai Hillfort (Voruta)* (Šeimyniškėlių piliakalnio kompleksas; J Biliūno gatvė 97A; w baranauskas.lt; ⊕ May–Oct 10.00–17.00 daily; €4/3) Honouring Grand Duke Mindaugas, the only king of Lithuania, Šeimyniškėliai mound is the most researched castle mound in the country with archaeological finds dating from the 13th and 14th centuries. Evidence suggests that here stood a large wooden fortress, with some historians attributing it to the historical mention of King Mindaugas' castle Voruta. The reconstructed fort offers fun for all ages with archery and medieval costumes to try, while the exhibition details the history of the hillfort. It is a 3.5km walk from the city centre to the fort, straight along J Biliūno gatvė.

✳ *Horse Museum* (Arklio muziejus; Muziejaus gatvė 4, Niūronys village; w arkliomuziejus.lt; ⊕ May–Sep 09.00–18.00, Oct–Apr 09.00–17.00; €5/3) You don't need to be a horse fanatic to enjoy this idyllic rural scene – it is as much an open-air ethnographic museum as a horse museum. It was founded in 1978 by agronomist Petras Vasinauskas (1906–95), and the traditional barns and farmsteads on the site house collections of agricultural tools, vintage vehicles and wood carvings. Inside some barns craftspeople demonstrate weaving, breadmaking, wood carving and blacksmithing. It is possible to arrange a horse ride, or a turn in a horse-drawn carriage (or sleigh in the winter months); and there is a restaurant for refreshments. To get to the Horse Museum, take the cycle path from the Church of St Matthew the Apostle upstream for 8km. If driving, leave the centre on J Biliūno gatvė, following the brown signs for Arklio muziejus.

> **MINIATURE TRAIN**
>
> A novelty tourist train runs between the city centre and Treetop Walking Path, picking up at A Baranausko aikštė 16b in the city centre. One-way takes 20 minutes and costs €1.50. There are scheduled stops along the route, clearly marked by a blue train sign. Tickets can be purchased from the driver.

**Treetop Walking Path and Information Centre** (Medžių lajų tako kompleksas; Dvaronys village; w anyksciurp.lrv.lt; ⊕ Apr–Sep 09.30–20.00 daily, Oct 09.30–18.00 daily, Nov–Mar 09.30–17.00 daily; €5/2.50) Opened in the summer of 2015, this unique project was driven by Anykščiai's then-mayor, Sigutis Obelevičius, a committed environmentalist and keen gardener. Not only is it a magnificent structure, sympathetically built within the forest, but it also provides spiritual and sensual immersion into the hidden heights of the canopy 20m above the forest floor. The 300m walkway leads visitors through pine, spruce, birch and oak, the trees often within touching distance. Breathe in the pure fresh air. Information boards inform about the forest flora and fauna alongside quotes from A Baranauskas' ode *The Anykščiai Forest*. The walkway's finale is a 34m-high observation tower with panoramic views of the Šventoji River and surrounding forest landscape. Today the Treetop Walk is one of the most visited attractions in Lithuania. Since its humble beginnings when chaos reigned due to no parking, food or toilets, there is now a car park and an information centre with everything you need. You can even book an educational walk with a guide. Access to the walkway is by stairs or lift, but the lift does not work between November and March or if the temperature falls below 0°C. It is the only observation tower accessible by lift in Lithuania. The tree-top walk is easily accessible on foot or by bike, starting at the Church of St Matthew the Apostle in Anykščiai and cycling or walking 5km downstream along the foot- and cycle path.

They say from small acorns large oak trees grow – and that is exactly what happened with Anykščiai's tourism potential after the success of the Treetop Walk. New life has been breathed into old attractions, including the impressive **Puntukas Stone** located close to the car park. It is the second largest boulder in Lithuania – a glacial erratic transported by glacial ice and deposited here when the ice melted. Its composition is Rapakivi granite originating most probably from Finland. It measures 6.9m long by 6.7m wide and is 5.7m tall, weighing approximately 446 tonnes. On the face of the boulder are carved the resemblances of the ill-fated trans-Atlantic pilots Steponas Darius and Stasys Girėnas (page 193) by sculptor Bronius Pundzius.

# UTENA

Utena developed as an industrial city alongside the Warsaw-to-St Petersburg railway and continues to be a successful industrial centre with the added bonus of being a gateway to Lithuania's lake district. Evidence of its earlier history as a strategic town in the Grand Duchy of Lithuania and as a thriving Jewish town is virtually non-existent, having been destroyed repeatedly over the centuries. Today, Utena is known both domestically and internationally for being home to Utenos Brewery. Facilities in Utena host more business travellers than tourists, but the basics are catered for. **Utena Tourism Information Centre** (Bažnyčios gatvė 1; w utenainfo. lt; ⊕ 09.00–13.00 & 14.00–18.00 Mon–Sun) can advise on accommodation and recommend tourist routes.

**GETTING THERE AND AWAY** Utena is well connected with **bus** services to Vilnius (1hr 45mins, 11 daily), Kaunas (2hrs 45mins; 3 daily), Molėtai (30mins; 8 daily) and Zarasai (50mins, 5 daily). The bus station (Utenos autobusų stotis; A Baranausko gatvė 7; w utenosap.lt) is a 1km walk to the tourism information centre. Utena is a straightforward drive **by car** from Vilnius (1hr 30mins; north on road A14), making it a popular weekend escape from the city. From Kaunas, it is a 2-hour drive along road A6/E262.

## WHERE TO STAY AND EAT

**Alaušo Slenis** [map, page 218] (8 cabins) Pakrantės gatvė 53, Bikuškios village; w alausoslenis.lt. 15km northeast of Utena is this very well-kept country resort surrounded by a deer park & on the shore of Lake Alaušas. Guests stay in individual cabins & have access to the facilities, including tennis courts, play area, swimming, pedaloes & the on-site restaurant. €€€

**Vila Gervalis** [map, page 218] (9 rooms) Ežero gatvė 29, Klykiai region. 12km east of Utena is this small country hotel on Lake Klykių, complete with spa area, beach, tennis courts, boat hire & lake swimming. It is a popular weekend & holiday destination for active leisure. €€

**Burgundija** J Basanavičiaus gatvė 55; burgundijarestoranas.utena. Named after the wine, 'Burgundy' is a French-style restaurant though their homecooked French-fusion meals can be accompanied by wines from around the world. It's quite formal, but daily lunch menus are good value for money. €€€

**Food Lab** J Basanavičiaus gatvė 54; foodlab. utena. Bringing a bit of a hipster vibe to Utena, this gastrobar is very popular for its delicious burgers, healthy salads & soups. €€€

**Liūtas ir Avelė** Maironio gatvė 4; liutasiravele. Café-bistro serving creative dishes, daily lunch specials & the best b/fast-brunch in town. Vegetarian & vegan options are available. €€€

## WHAT TO SEE AND DO

**The Centre of Brewing Excellence** (Utenos Brewery; Pramonės gatvė 12; e utenosalus@svyturys.lt; w svyturys.eu; ⊕ for prebooked tours in English; €15 pp, min age 20 years) Beer aficionados can experience a tour and tasting at the Utenos Brewery which has been brewing some of the household names in Lithuanian beer for decades. The local water is soft and pure, perfect for brewing lager pilsner-style beers. In 2001, two of the major Lithuanian breweries – Utenos Alus and Švyturio Alus – merged, and in 2008 they were bought out by brewing conglomerate Carlsberg, causing more than a little distress to local beer drinkers as to the long-term plans for their favourite tipples. Thankfully, both brands still exist today, although a true faithful will tell you they've never tasted the same since the takeover. The brewery has a museum with some English information, but for a tasting experience, lasting approximately 2 hours, you must book in advance via the website.

**Utena Regional Museum** (Utenos krastotyros muziejus; Utenio aikštė 3; w utenosmuziejus.lt; ⊕ 10.00–18.00 Tue–Fri, 10.00–17.00 Sat; €2/1) Having recently celebrated its 95th anniversary, this museum has got showcasing their local history, culture and folklore down to a fine art. Clear chronological displays guide you along, with snapshots of days gone by and examples of local textiles and straw gardens. Several smaller departments of the museum are based in surrounding villages, including a ceramics museum, crafts centre and ethnographic farmstead – although these cater more to local Lithuanian visitors, details can be found on the website.

**Freedom Struggle Museum** (Laisvės kovų muziejus; Stoties gatvė 39; w utenosmuziejus.lt/laisves-kovu-muziejus/; ⊕ 10.00–16.00 Tue–Sat; €2/1) Housed in the former narrow-gauge railway station, a 20-minute (1.5km) walk from the tourism information centre, this small but informative museum covers resistance in Lithuania when the country was occupied and hidden behind the Iron Curtain. The staff are super storytellers, so do not shy away from their offer to guide you round. There is a small exhibition about the former Panevėžys-to-Švenčionėliai narrow-gauge railway line.

**Old Posting Station Complex** (J Basanavičiaus gatvė 36) Dating from the 1830s, this is the oldest brick building in Utena and one of the best surviving examples of a posting station built along the Warsaw-to-St Petersburg postal route. Tsar Nicholas I himself stayed here, in the days when horses would be changed, travellers rested, post sorted and carriages loaded. Today it houses the Utena Art School (Utenos meno mokykla; w menas.utena.lm.lt).

## MOLĖTAI

The town of Molėtai has long been the gateway to this region of recreation famed for its more than 300 lakes dotted amid the pine forests. Recent investment, including a new technology centre, has seen positive repercussions for the town with a new hotel and improved infrastructure. Young workers are relocating here for a more family-oriented lifestyle, and summer houses are being bought by city folk. Situated in a slightly hilly locale and centred around two small lakes, the town is scenic, walkable and a good option for those wanting to stay in a town rather than rural accommodation while exploring the nearby Labanoras Regional Park and Aukštaitija National Park.

The **Molėtai Tourism Information Centre** (Inturkės gatvė 4; w infomoletai.lt; ⊕ 08.00–18.00 Mon–Fri, 09.00–18.00 Sat, 10.00–14.00 Sun) has excellent route maps, VR experiences and local souvenirs. The team can help you plan your visit or advise when in town.

**GETTING THERE AND AWAY** Regular direct **buses** are to Vilnius (1hr 15mins; 10 per day), Utena (30mins; 8 per day), Rokiškis (2hrs 15mins; 4 per day) and Zarasai (1hr 45min; 1 per day). Molėtai **bus station** (Vilniaus gatvė 2) is a 10-minute walk from the tourist information centre. Molėtai is just over 1 hour's drive **by car** from Vilnius. Its convenient location means the roads can be very busy on a warm summer's Friday evening as people head to the lake district for the weekend. Similarly, the return route on Sunday evening can be slow and congested.

 **WHERE TO STAY AND EAT** Accommodation choices in and around Molėtai continue to improve with several contemporary options attracting new clientele, but for many visitors to this region a farmstead is the ultimate idyllic escape (page 228). There are some small cafés, kebab shops and a sushi bar in the centre of Molėtai, but the main restaurants are in the hotels.

**Molėtai Resort** [map, page 218] (4 cabins, 4 rooms) Kampų gatvė 22; w moletairesort. lt. 2km from the centre of Molėtai & set amid the pine trees on the shore of Lake Dūriai is this contemporary resort. The 4 cabins sleep 2, 6 or 8 people with kitchenettes for self-catering. Above the restaurant are 4 dbl rooms. B/fast is served in the Amora restaurant, which is also open to non-residents for lunch & dinner – its Thai–European cuisine is extremely popular, so table reservations are advised (closed Mon). On-site facilities for guests include tennis courts, bicycle, paddleboard & boat rental, sauna & hot tub rental. **€€€€**

### ROADS AROUND MOLĖTAI

The Vilnius–Molėtai road was constructed from reinforced concrete slabs strong enough to land a plane on, basically a Soviet runway. The rubber sealant used between the slabs has not fared well due to extreme temperature fluctuations causing expansion; hence for many years there have been 'deformed surface' warnings, plus it's noisy to drive on. Work to upgrade the road is underway and due for completion by the end of 2025, after when the ride will be much smoother and the story filed away in the history annals and travel guides. The smaller roads around Molėtai are renowned for their winding, undulating characteristics which are unusual for Lithuania, and therefore drivers often get carried away with speed. Drive with special care as visibility is not great. Cycling on these roads is not recommended. The scenery is delightful, though. Of particular note is road 119 from Molėtai to Anykščiai which has minimal asphalt, blind bends, and drivers must go half off the road on to gravel to avoid oncoming traffic – purposefully slowing people down on what could be a fast, dangerous road. Some people love the way it weaves through the undulating landscape; for many locals it is their only experience of carsickness.

**Molėtai Hotel** (24 rooms) Ąžuolų gatvė 8; w moletaihotel.lt. A modern & fresh business-style hotel a short walk from the town centre – perfect for visitors needing a central location or who want to explore the region from contemporary accommodation. The town swimming pool, sauna & tennis courts are next door. The hotel has its own restaurant, Pušyne, while another option is next door at the swimming pool pizzeria, Restoranas Ežerai. €€€

**Senoji Užeiga** (6 rooms) Vilniaus gatvė 29; w senojiuzeiga.lt. A small guesthouse in the centre of town with 2 suites, 3 dbl rooms & 1 sgl, a popular restaurant & the town laundry, so handy if you need to wash your smalls. Rooms are Scandi-style décor & b/fast in the garden in summer is charming. €€€

**Mindūnai Camping** [map, page 218] Mindūnų kempingas; w ignaturas.lt/en. The oldest camping site in Molėtai region is in a prime location on the shore of Baltieji Lakajai, a clean lake perfect for fishing & swimming. The site has lodges for 6–8 people, room rental, campervan hook-ups & tent pitches. There's plenty to keep visitors busy – you can rent a sauna, hot tub, pedalo, paddleboard, kayaks or bikes, & the site is next door to Mindūnai Observation Tower (page 230) & in the territory of Labanoras Regional Park. €

**OTHER PRACTICALITIES** In Molėtai you will find an **ATM** and **pharmacy** at the IKI **supermarket** (Vilniaus gatvė 95); an alternative **pharmacy** is closer to the centre (Vilniaus gatvė 67) near the **post office** (Vilniaus gatvė 43).

**WHAT TO SEE AND DO** The town of Molėtai encompasses two lakes: Pastovis and Pastovėlis. Walking or cycling along the **trail** that circumnavigates the lakes is a pleasant way to spend some time here. The paths are good, and illuminated in the evening. Choose from a short route of 4km or a longer one of 5.5km. Along the way you encounter various sculptures, bridges, Spring Hill, the Sculpture Park, a playground, beaches and bathing areas, and benches on which to rest and watch the birds.

Next door to the tourist information centre, the **Molėtai Regional Museum** (Moletu krasto muziejus; Inturkės gatvė 4; w moletumuziejus.lt; ⊕ 09.00–17.00 Tue–Sun; €4/2) is housed in a striking contemporary building having been renovated in 2021. At the time of writing, the museum is a work in progress, and currently the main exhibits are those of the **Molėtai Art Gallery** (w moletumuziejus.

## AUKŠTAITIJA FARMSTEADS  *Map, page 218*

Lithuanians love spending time in nature, whether it's fishing, mushrooming, hiking, or gathering with friends and family with the necessary components of grill, sauna and lake. The number of farmsteads where foreign tourists can experience this is increasing – these are some of the best for English-speaking guests in Aukštaitija. For more information about rural tourism, see page 59.

**Alantos Žirgai** (4 cabins) Utenos gatvė 9, Alanta region (20km north of Molėtai); w alantoszirgai.lt. On the edge of the pretty town of Alanta is this well-kept ecological farmstead & Žemaitija horse-breeding stud. There are 4 cottages to rent, 3 of which surround the small lake & 1 is more private by the river. It is 3.8km to Alanta Manor art gallery & museum (w zukasalanta.lt) which can be walked or cycled, with a stop in Alanta town to visit the church & wooden synagogue. The Neoclassical Alanta Manor has an impressive collection of vintage cups & saucers, used for hosting tea ceremonies. Their goal is to restore an original wood panelled reception room where tea ceremonies were originally conducted. €€€€

**Įlankos sodyba** (5 cabins) Žvejų gatvė 50, Šaukšteliškiai region (9km south of Molėtai); w ilankossodyba.lt. A family-friendly homestead on the southern shore of Lake Bebrusai with individual well-equipped cabins (some are more recently renovated), all with a sauna. The family owners live on site & speak English. You can rent a boat, paddleboard, or take a boat tour on the homemade vessel *Švyturys*, which has a sauna & grill

lt/moletu-dailes-galerija). Opposite the museum, in their distinctive red brick, are Molėtai's historic Jewish houses still functioning to this day with shops on the ground floor and accommodation above.

## AROUND MOLĖTAI

To explore the region around Molėtai, you need a car or to be a competent cyclist. Public transport only runs between the main towns, leaving the remote tourist sites tricky to access. Several sites of interest are within the Labanoras Regional Park, a delightful region of wooden farmsteads with productive gardens filled with fruit trees, vegetable plots and colourful flowerbeds.

**MOLĖTAI TECHNICAL MUSEUM** (Molėtų Technikos Muziejus; 16km southwest of Molėtai on road 172 opposite Molėtai Aeroclub; Tumenčizna region; w mtm.lt; ⊕ 10.00–18.00 Sat, 11.00–17.00 Sun, closed w/days; €9/5) Molėtai Technical Museum is home to an impressive private collection of vehicles spanning decades of motoring in Lithuania. More than 250 exhibits of cars, trucks, emergency vehicles, motorbikes and more are laid out in the museum's halls and yards, including popular Soviet-made Moskvich and VAZ cars and Western cars of the 1980s. The museum can arrange an English-speaking guide (€25/hr); this must be organised in advance but will be worth it to hear the stories behind these cars. You can ride in a VAZ 2106 or Moskvich 2140 around the site for €30 per person (and it is possible to try driving too). A snack bar opens on site in the summer months.

**LABANORAS REGIONAL PARK** In the heart of the Labanoras Regional Park is the quaint village of **Labanoras**. Its long-standing **Hotel Labanoras and restaurant**

on board. The clear water & sandy shore are perfect for swimming, the playground & hammocks adding to the holiday atmosphere. The owner runs the nearby Meniškas kaimas (w meniskaskaimas.lt) traditional crafts centre, where you can learn about black ceramics, felting, candle making & basket weaving. €€€
**Kliukai** (4 cabins) Gervių gatvė 37, Kliukai region (16km south of Molėtai); w kliukai.lt. A childhood summer holiday spot has been developed by the entrepreneurial family owners, who now share it with guests. 4 cottages (sleep 4–6) surround the pond, & the library building has a cosy communal lounge & kitchen/dining area. €€€
*\** **Pagulbis** (31 sleeping places) Pagulbis, Alanta region (halfway between Anykščiai & Molėtai on road 119); pagulbis.lt. This beautifully renovated ethnographic homestead provides an authentic trip down memory lane for many Lithuanians. Although modern comforts are to hand, the whole place is grounded in history, nature & antiquities. It's a very popular venue for weddings & parties, thanks to the large barns perfect for music & cultural events, so weekends can be tricky or are best avoided. During the week, the traditional log-built guesthouse rooms can be booked individually; note that b/fast & dinner must be prebooked. A bunkhouse is available for basic group accommodation. Nestled at the bottom of the orchard is a rustic smoke sauna, built around a living tree. Guests can use the sauna for an additional charge and must book it in advance as it takes time to be prepared. A local self-guided walk includes a visit to the quaint Janonys Chapel. €€€

(Seniūnijos gatvė 29; w hotellabanoras.lt; €€; ⊕ restaurant closed Mon & Thu; €€€€) can be a lunchtime hotspot in an area with few eateries – the prices reflect this, but the atmosphere is bucolic and filled with pastoral antiquities. Stop here for lunch and a walk around the village, or overnight and make use of their kayak rental and traditional sauna. The wooden Catholic Labanoras church (Svc. Mergeles Marijos gimimo baznycia) is set against the backdrop of wooden farmsteads. Pick up local maps and advice from the **Labanoras Regional Park Visitor Centre** (Labanoro regioninio parko lankytojų centras; w aparkai.lt; ⊕ 08.00–17.00 Mon–Thu, 08.00–15.45 Fri) and learn about the Labanoras Forest via their interactive exhibition (€2/1).

The visitor centre staff can recommend hiking and biking trails throughout the regional park (an off-road bike is essential) for discovering the lesser-visited lakes and forests. The main cultural sights of the regional park lie in the northwestern area; two are linked to the regions' optimal dark skies and the other offers panoramic views of the region best appreciated during daylight hours.

*\** **Lithuanian Museum of Ethnocosmology** (Žvaigždžių gatvė 10, Kulionys village; w etnokosmomuziejus.lt; ⊕ 08.00–16.30 Mon–Fri; €8/4) Welcome to the only museum in the world dedicated to ethnocosmology. This otherworldly place on Kapeliai Hill is uniquely concerned with the relationship between mankind and the cosmos, with particular focus on the cosmic world worshipped by ancient Lithuanians – they overtly worshipped the moon, sky, stars and sun. There is strong evidence of a connection between ethnography and cosmology in Lithuanian ancient culture. An offshoot of the neighbouring Molėtai Astronomical Observatory (page 230), the museum was built in 1990, when cultural specialists and astronomical scientists recognised the intertwined behaviours of ethnographic

and cosmological beliefs, symbolism and spiritual practices in ancient cultures and their lasting legacies. Tours of the museum run regularly during opening hours; it is advisable to book online in advance for an English-speaking tour. The museum is very well presented and will keep young and old entertained. There are two telescopes for stargazing, a spaceship-style café, and the view from the 32m-high observation deck is memorable.

**Molėtai Astronomical Observatory** (Žvaigždžių gatvė 12, Kulionys village; w mao.tfai.vu.lt/sci/en/info-for-visitors) Lithuania was recently ranked third in Europe for its dark skies, making it perfect for stargazing, and here on Kaldiniai Hill visitors can do just that. The observatory is managed by Vilnius University and used mainly by the astrophysics department and for hosting research courses and symposiums; however, keen visitors can also book an excursion and stargazing session. This must be done by emailing (e moletu.observatorija@gmail.com) in advance to arrange a visit, which will depend on the weather conditions on the day. The observatory itself is a bit old school, but if you book an English-speaking excursion you will get a valuable insight into astronomy, and hopefully a clear night will reveal some celestial wonders.

**Mindūnai Observation Tower** (Mindūnų apžvalgos bokštas; ⊕ always open; free) At the time of writing, this was the second tallest observation tower in Lithuania, but new towers are always on the agenda and Mindūnai is expected to slide down the rankings in the near future. Note that the tower is also known as Labanoras Regional Park Tower as it is located in Labanoras Regional Park territory, next to Mindūnai Camping (page 227) on the shore of Baltieji Lakajai. Climb the steps for a panoramic view of the surrounding lakes and forests; but be warned, this tower can feel wobbly when the wind is up. The view is particularly pleasant at sunset when the sky's colours reflect off the lake's surface. To reach the tower from Molėtai, travel 11km east on road 114 and make a right turn at the village of Mindūnai. Note that on the main road in Mindūnai village is the restaurant **Vilkasalė** (f sodybaVilkasale; €€€), which is a good option for lunch when exploring the area.

**ASVEJOS REGIONAL PARK** This regional park is set around **Lake Asvejos**, the longest lake in Lithuania at 21.9km long. The lake is long, deep and narrow and, before the construction of a beautifully engineered wooden bridge in 1934 (Asveja tiltas), was quite an inconvenience for those without a boat, but with a need to get to the other side. Large sections of the lakeshore are designated nature reserve, making this a popular birdwatching area. The family-owned boat ***Laumaris*** (e laumarisdubingiai@ gmail.com; f search 'Laumaris Dubingiai') runs regular tours of the lake from May to September, departing from the beach next to the bridge. The tour lasts 1½ hours, with beanbag seating on the open top deck, binoculars provided, and a coffee machine if you would like to purchase refreshments. It's a very popular trip, including a stop for a paddle in warm weather, so it is best to book in advance (max 12 people).

On the opposite side of the bridge are steps leading up **Dubingiai Mound** (Dubingių piliavietė), a significant and historically important defensive castle mound of the 14th century, benefitting from being on a promontory that is almost an isolated island. In 1415, a stone castle was built atop the mound under the orders of Grand Duke Vytautas to strengthen Vilnius fortifications. During the 16th century, the castle was upgraded to a luxurious palace and became the seat of the Radvila family, some of whom are buried in the churchyard belonging to the former castle; the outline of the church foundations having been reconstructed. The palace no longer exists, destroyed by attackers during the 17th and 18th centuries. Instead, on the site of the castle foundations stands an unexpected concrete structure: the **Dubingiai Castle Exposition** (Dubingių piliavietė; ⊕ May–Sep 08.00–17.00 Mon–Fri, 10.00–15.00 Sat; €2/1) underneath which are the original foundations with excavation finds on display. Plans to reconstruct the castle are underway, but no time schedule has been announced as yet. A path leads around the summit of the castle mound and information boards explain the history and fragments of ruins. When you come across the information board close to some wide steps being reclaimed by the earth, you are at the entrance to the former summerhouse of President Antanas Smetona. Constructed in 1938 during the inter-war period when this was the Lithuania–Poland border, the summerhouse was used for diplomatic meetings and officials' accommodation, but Smetona himself never stayed. The wooden villa burned down in 1944 and was never rebuilt.

For more information on the regional park, plus maps and local advice, pop in to the **Asvejos Regional Park Visitor Centre** (Asvejos regioninio parko lankytojų centras; Radvilų gatvė 1; w asvejosparkas.lt; ⊕ 09.00–18.00 Tue–Fri, 10.00–15.00 Sat), housed in a historic wooden house in the village of Dubingiai. Over the road is the restaurant **Radvilų Rezidencija** (Radvilų gatvė 4; ⊕ 10.00–16.00 Tue–Fri, 10.00–21.00 Sat, 10.00–20.00 Sun; €€€), a popular choice for drinks, snacks and main meals either in the dining room or on the terrace.

## AUKŠTAITIJA NATIONAL PARK

This, the oldest national park in Lithuania was established in 1974 when Lithuania was under Russian occupation and a satellite state of the Soviet Union (Lithuanian Soviet Socialist Republic), hence its original name, the Lithuanian Soviet Socialist Republic National Park. Those shackles were shed with independence in 1990, and in 1991 the park was renamed in honour of the Aukštaitija ethnographic region. Whatever the name or governing authority, the aim of the national park has always been to protect the landscape of lakes and forests, along with numerous rare species of flora and fauna of which 195 are found in the Red Data Book of Lithuania endangered species. You might come across roe deer, elk, hares, wild boar, foxes and pine martens, wild orchids including Lady's Slipper, and more than 110 types of edible mushroom. The territory of the national park contains the largest number of pre-historic settlements in Lithuania; fortifications, castle mounds and barrows, and original layouts of historic villages, though often these subtle sights of days gone by are overshadowed by the natural landscape. The interconnected network of 127 lakes and rivers, formed millennia ago by glaciers, attracts many visitors during the spring, summer and autumn for watersports, while the rolling landscape and wild nature attract hikers, cyclists, foragers and campers. The resort of Palūšė is where most routes on land and water begin.

Note that if visiting out of season between October and April, you will find many places closed. If staying in the national park, your closest regional centre for facilities such as a bank, pharmacy or supermarket is Ignalina (page 234).

**GETTING THERE AND AWAY** For visitors to Aukštaitija National Park the main hub of information and amenities is Palūšė. You can gather excellent tourist information from the visitor centre and many trail, road and water routes start from here. **Buses** stop in the centre of the village close to the visitor centre. Services run daily between Ignalina bus station and Palūšė village (10mins; 4 per day) and connect with the train service from Vilnius. There is one bus each day to/from Kaunas (3hrs). **Driving** to the national park undoubtedly gives you more independence to explore. Expect the journey between Vilnius and Palūšė to take just under 2 hours, from Kaunas just under 2 hours 30 minutes. The main **parking** for private cars is at the Aukštaitija National Park Visitor Centre.

**TOURIST INFORMATION** The **Aukštaitija National Park Visitor Centre** (Lūšių gatvė 16; w aparkai.lt; ⏰ 09.00–18.00 Mon–Fri, 10.00–16.00 Sat) is in Palūšė. They are a valuable resource for up-to-date maps of hiking and cycling trails, kayaking and sailing itineraries, and scenic driving routes, as well as providing help in finding suitable farmstead or campsite accommodation and local activity providers. You are encouraged to buy a voluntary visitor ticket for €1, €5 or €25 (available via the website or in person at the centre) – contributions go towards the protection and conservation of the park.

**WHERE TO STAY AND EAT** Palūšė is the main centre within the national park for accommodation, but the watermill in the village of Ginučiai (see opposite) offers an alternative, unique, experience. For accommodation just outside the park, in Ignalina, see page 235.

**Palūšės Kempingas** Miko Petrausko gatvė 1A, Palūšė; w paluseskempingas.lt; ⏰ May–Oct. Tucked away behind the church, the site has 10 pitches for motorhomes & caravans, 10 pitches for tents & 5 cabins with a total capacity of 30 beds. A motorhome/caravan pitch is €27/night for 2 people; a tent is €21/night for 2 people; electric hook-up €5. €

**Palūšės žuvų rukykla** Lūšių gatvė 22, Palūšė; 📷 paluses_piratai; ⏰ May–Sep 10.00–20.00 daily, Oct–Apr Sat only. Here you can get fresh smoked fish every day during the summer season. They smoke fish twice a day, & also serve other grill dishes, including 6 types of homemade burger. Try their own *gira* brewed on site. €€

**Palūšės valtinė baras** Lūšių gatvė 1, Palūšė; 📘 palusesvaltinebaras; ⏰ May–Sep 10.00–20.00 Wed–Sun. A seasonal summer bar at the marina, it's a good choice for a drink & snack. It gets lively here in summer season with concerts held Jun–Aug. Opening hours can be affected if the weather is bad. €

**SPORTS AND ACTIVITIES** The Aukštaitija National Park Visitor Centre has excellent route maps and descriptions for **self-guided hikes** of various distances within the national park. The most popular leisurely hike from Palūšė is a 40-minute walk along the lakeshore to Meironys village, incorporating a **wooden sculpture trail** carved by local folk artists in 1977 – a leaflet from the visitor centre explains each of the works. For a guided hike, try local provider **Tiki Inn** (📘 tikiinn) or regional experts **LitWild** (w litwildtravel.com), who are based in Visaginas but arrange outdoor activity and nature tours throughout the national park.

**Cycling**
**Aukštaitijos dviratis** Miko Petrausko gatvė 1A, Palūšė; w paluseskempingas.lt/paslaugos-ir-kainos; ⏰ May–Sep 08.00–21.00 daily) Bike rental for €20/day Mon–Fri & €25/day Sat–Sun. Electric bikes also available. Rentals are arranged from the Palūšės Kempingas site.

**Fishing** There is no commercial fishing, so you must bring your own equipment & purchase a fishing licence online (w alisas.

lt) or from any Perlas lottery ticket terminal in any supermarket.

**Watersports and boat tours**
**Aukštaitijos laivai** Lūšių gatvė 1, Palūšė; w aukstaitijoslaivai.lt; ⏰ May–Sep 10.00–21.00 Wed–Sun. Offers regular boat tours May–Sep; advance booking is advised. Also boat, kayak, canoe & SUP rental.

**Baidarių uostas** Lūšių gatvė 29, Palūšė; w baidariuuostas.lt; ⏰ May–Sep

08.00–20.00 daily. Arranges kayak, canoe and paddleboard (SUP) rental; €30/day per kayak/canoe Mon–Fri, €35/day Sat–Sun; SUP €8/hr).

**Palūšės laivai** Lūšių gatvė 29, Palūšė; w paluseslaivai.lt; ⏱ May–Sep 08.00–20.00 daily. Has small leisure boats for hire & offers boat tours in the national park.

## WHAT TO SEE AND DO

**Palūšė** The pretty town of Palūšė is the main resort of Aukštaitija National Park and the starting point for many visitors – first stop, the visitor centre. A brief visit should also involve a visit to the church, a stroll along the shore of Lake Lūšiai, and perhaps a snack or lunch in a café. A longer visit will allow time to explore the cycling or hiking trails (of varying lengths) or take to the water by rowing boat, canoe, kayak, yacht, paddleboard, or on a scenic cruise. Multi-day tours – biking, hiking or on the water – are popular and can be arranged by local companies. At the end of the day, Palūšė can be blessed with some stunning sunsets. During winter the resort is quiet, with few facilities open, except for during the **Winter Smelt Festival**. Held at the end of February, this is the only time when fishing for freshwater smelt is legal. It is a cultural heritage event using traditional fishing methods of lowering a net into the water via a hole in the ice, and there is of course opportunity to sample the fresh catch.

Sitting atop a hillock overlooking Lake Lūšiai and the village, the **Church of St Joseph** (Palūšės Šv. Juozapo bažnyčia; Miko Petrausko gatvė 1; w musuparapija.lt/ paluse) is Lithuania's most iconic church and one of the oldest surviving wooden folk ensemble churches in the country. It has even appeared on the back of the 1 litas banknote. It is a protected architectural monument, an astonishing legacy to Reverand Juozas Baziliauskas, who built it in 1750 using only an axe to cut and shape the timber. The wooden bell tower, added in 1800, has an octagonal base reminiscent of medieval Lithuanian castle towers. If the door is open, be sure to take a look inside; you will be welcomed by the priest or a parishioner. It is a place of peace and calm in what can be a busy tourist hotspot in the summer season. Mass is held on Saturdays at noon.

**Ginučiai Watermill** (Ginučių vandens malūnas; Ginučių gatvė 24, Ginučiai; w aparkai.lt; ⏱ May–Sep 10.00–18.00 Wed–Sun; €1.20/0.60) This fine 19th-century watermill is the main attraction of Ginučiai village. Situated next to the Srovė River, this was a fully functioning watermill producing flour and electricity for the village until 1968. Restored in 1978, it is a rare example of authentic milling equipment, and during the summer the museum is open to the public. The mill also contains several guest rooms (**€€**) for rental during the summer season for approximately €50 per night; but guests must be of a hardy nature to spend a night here – the devil lives in watermills according to legend. Rooms can be booked via the Aukštaitija National Park Visitor Centre in Palūšė. Refreshments can be found at nearby **Gervinė café** (Malūno gatvė 28; f gervine.lt; ⏱ May–Oct; €€).

**Šiliniškis Observation Tower** (Šiliniškių (Ginučių) apžvalgos bokštas); ⏱ always open; free) Only 2km from Ginučiai on road 1423 heading east is the 60m-tall Šiliniškis Observation Tower, which is actually a telecommunications tower built in 2004. If you are willing and able to climb the steel stairs to the viewing platform (30.5m), you will be rewarded with a panoramic view that highlights the hummocky landscape of the Šiliniškes ridge, known to locals as the 'dragon's spine' and unusual compared with the usual flat horizon seen from most Lithuanian observation towers.

\* **Museum of Ancient Beekeeping at Stripeikiai** (Stripeikių bitininkystės muziejus; Stripeikių region; w biciumuziejus.lt; ⊕ May–mid Sep 10.00–18.00 Tue–Sun; €6/3, audio guide in English €3) Stripeikiai is one of the oldest villages in the national park, certainly pre-dating its first written mention in the Livonian Chronicles of 1357. The hilly and remote region was one of hunting, fishing, foraging and beekeeping – all livelihoods providing the necessary resources to survive; any excesses, in this case honey and wax, could be traded. Opened in 1978, the beekeeping museum has long been the most-visited attraction in the national park. Set in the charming grounds and outbuildings of an idyllic rural homestead, the museum provides a wealth of knowledge about ancient and contemporary beekeeping. Locally made products are available to buy as souvenirs. To find the museum, you need to follow the brown tourist signs and have the confidence of a local to drive along the sandy forest tracks. One route is from Ginučiai: head up north out of the village and follow the Bytininkystės muziejus signs (5km from Ginučiai).

**Ethnographic villages** Acknowledged as architectural monuments for their historic layouts and authentic buildings, ethnographic villages are like living open-air museums. There are several dotted around the national park which can be visited along the main circular hiking, cycling or driving routes available from the visitor centre. The village of **Salos II** is designated a cultural reserve, a scattered village on a peninsula which can be explored on an off-road bike ride or on a hike. Four other villages – **Šuminai**, **Strazdai**, **Vaišnoriškės** and **Varniškės II** – are similarly scattered villages, lacking a centre, with traditional farmsteads and well-tended gardens irregularly spread out. The village of **Kretuonys** lies 18km south of Palūšė and is a single-street village lined with 20 homesteads, barns and outbuildings. These are all examples of old rural lifestyles, of days gone by, slowly being inherited by a younger generation who must choose whether to sell their very desirable property, keep it as a holiday home, or embrace rural life and settle in the countryside. When visiting these settlements, it is preferable to leave your car on the edge of the village and take a leisurely and less intrusive walk to appreciate the architecture and atmosphere.

## IGNALINA

Ignalina lies just outside the eastern boundary of Aukštaitija National Park but plays an important role as a service and transport hub for the park. Located on the all-important Warsaw-to-St Petersburg railway, the city was built around the timber industry from the 19th century onwards, but industry and employment declined in the post-Soviet years and steps are being taken to replace this with tourism. The city was hard hit when the region's Ignalina Nuclear Power Plant closed down and the cheap energy that had benefitted local residents for decades was gone. Note that the city of Ignalina is not the place for visiting the decommissioned nuclear power plant – that is another 38km northeast from the city. Visaginas is the closest destination to the power plant.

The **Ignalina Tourism Information Centre** (Ignalinos rajono turizmo informacijos centras; Ateities gatvė 18 A; w ignalina.info; ⊕ 09.00–18.00 Mon–Sat) offers local English-speaking guides, maps and help with transport connections.

**GETTING THERE AND AWAY** Buses run several times daily between Ignalina and Vilnius (2hrs 3mins; 9 per day), Visaginas (35mins; 11 per day) and Palūšė (10mins;

4 per day). The train station (Ignalinos geležinkelio stotis; Geležinkelio gatvė 19) is located directly opposite the bus station (Ignalinos autobusų stotis) from where it is a 650m walk to the tourist information centre. Direct trains run regularly between Vilnius and Ignalina (1hr 38mins; 7 per day). In contrast to the train, driving **by car** to Ignalina from Vilnius will take you just under 2 hours, but you will have the benefit of independent exploring with your own transport.

 **WHERE TO STAY AND EAT**

**Lake & Library Hotel** (10 rooms) Turistų gatvė 30B; w lahotel.lt. Located on the edge of town by the lakeside & public beach area, a 20min walk from the town centre, the Lake & Library Hotel is a contemporary building with stylish décor with accommodation in dbl rooms, suites & 2-bed family rooms. B/fast is served in their cosy café & can be ordered in advance (check whether it is included in the rate when you book). Parking is a short walk away. €€€

**Žuvėdra Hotel** (8 rooms) Mokyklos gatvė 11; w zuvedra.com. In the centre of town, with grounds sloping down to the lake with access for swimming, this is an older, traditional hotel popular with both business & leisure travellers. €€

**Romnesa Ignalina** Centro gatvė 5, Strigailiškis village; w romnesa.lt; ⏰ 10.00–19.00 daily. A very popular, traditional restaurant & Aukštaitija's home to the šakotis tree cake. The rustic décor even includes a ceiling shaped like giant šakotis branches hanging down. You can book a šakotis-making experience over the restaurant fire (popular with groups; €175 for 0–25 people) lasting 45mins. Or you can simply savour their hearty snacks & dishes. €€€

**Laisvės 65** Laisvės gatvė 65; aguonadecor; ⏰ 11.00–17.00 Wed–Thu, noon–02.00 Fri–Sat. A trendy café & bar, for coffee & cake during the day or drinks & live music in the evening at w/ends. €€

## PALIESIAUS MANOR

A 30km drive southeast from the town of Ignalina (or 114km northeast from Vilnius) is the beautifully restored **Paliesiaus Manor** ✱ (Paliesiaus dvaras; Dvaro gatvė 7, Paliesiaus region; w paliesiausdvaras.lt; ⏰ open all year round). Tucked away in a hidden corner of Lithuania close to the Belarus border and with little other than nature surrounding it, this is a rural retreat with emphasis on treat. A former manor and estate of the 17th-century noble family Tiškevičius, before World War II it was officially in Belarus and during the Soviet occupation was nationalised and neglected for decades. In 2014 the manor, outbuildings and estate gardens were restored by private owners and it has been reinvented with several surprise features. Not only are there several charming **guest rooms** (nine in the manor house and four larger ones in the wooden barn building; €€€€), the restaurant serves a local seasonal menu supplied with fresh produce from local farmers, there is a boutique shop selling chic Nordic and Baltic clothing and gifts, and it has an impressive wine cellar. But the crowning glory that sets this manor house apart is the Concert Hall in the ruins of the former stable building; the original red-brick walls are covered in a contemporary glass enclosure where two Steinway pianos await the next guest performers. Classical music concerts are held at weekends, with guests able to reserve dinner and an overnight stay to complete this unique experience. The manor also runs well-being weeks when guests come to relax or recuperate in beautiful surroundings, perhaps for weight-loss, lifestyle changes, or physio – the treatments being delivered one-to-one by professionals.

**WHAT TO SEE AND DO** Ignalina is primarily a gateway to the Aukštaitija National Park and a hub of services for the surrounding rural communities. To understand the historical and current role of the city, visit **Ignalina Regional Museum** (Ignalinos krašto muziejus; Ateities gatvė 43; w ignalinosmuziejus.lt; ⊕ 09.00–17.00 Tue–Fri, 10.00–16.00 Sat; €4/2), which preserves and promotes the ethnic culture of the region. The interactive model village of Palūšė teaches about the ancient art of winter smelt fishing. The museum is one of many places of interest and beauty around Ignalina on the easy **'8 Lakes of Ignalina' hiking route** (12km). The route map is on the tourism information centre website. For decades, Ignalina has been known as the heart of winter sports in Lithuania, not least because it is one of the snowiest regions of the country. The **Lithuanian Winter Sports Centre** (Lietuvos Žiemos Sporto Centras, Sporto gatvė 6;  LietuvosZiemosSportoCentras; ⊕ 08.00–21.00 Mon–Fri, 10.00–18.00 Sat) has long been popular with groups for training or educational stays, but individual guests are also welcome. Winter facilities include several slopes with lifts for downhill skiing, long distance cross-country ski tracks, a biathlon circuit, skiing and snowboarding lessons, and a large snow park. They also open in summer for tennis, basketball and Nordic walking.

# VISAGINAS

Construction of Lithuania's youngest city started in 1975, purpose-built to house the new Ignalina Nuclear Power Plant workers, their families and the supporting community. Originally called Sniečkus after the leader of the Lithuanian Communist Party, the city was renamed Visaginas post-independence in 1992 after a local village. Visaginas was a Soviet architect's dream, an ideological city designed for pedestrians, prepared for nuclear incidents, of identikit apartment blocks surrounded by a forest of tall fir trees. It is rumoured that the city was designed in the shape of a butterfly but only half was completed; however, there is no proof of this and the shape is also reminiscent of an old imperial fortress. Whatever its name, the city has always been the most Russian city in Lithuania. Specialist workers were moved here from across the Soviet Union, a melting pot of nuclear scientists, engineers, administrators and cleaners alongside workers to support the local infrastructure. Russian was the dominant language and still is; more than half the population were not born in Lithuania. Closure of the nuclear power plant between 2004 and 2009, once employing 5,500 people, had a huge impact on the city. The plant now has 1,600 employees, whose number will continue to diminish as decommissioning progresses. Many specialists left to work at other nuclear plants in Russia, others moved away for work or education, reducing the population from its peak of 33,000 to just 18,000. To many Lithuanians this area was a mysterious place and there was no reason to visit, their curiosity piqued only alongside an international audience after Visaginas and the power plant were used as film locations for the HBO drama series *Chernobyl*. Tourism has certainly increased as a result and we highly recommend you book a local guide alongside an official tour of the power plant. A quirky non-nuclear highlight of the Visaginas calendar is the annual **Visaginas International Country Music Festival** (w visaginocountry.lt) held in August and attracting acts from across the world, a sure sign that Visaginas is open to new initiatives.

**GETTING THERE AND AWAY** Visaginas **train station** (Visagino geležinkelio stotis; Pasmalvės 2) is located 3km west of the city, a 30-minute walk from the centre. A direct train runs between Vilnius and Visaginas (destination Turmantas, 2hrs

10mins; 6 per day), with an adult return ticket from Vilnius in standard class costing €17.20 (concessions €8.60). Direct **buses** operate between Visaginas and Vilnius (2hrs 40min; 9 per day) and Kaunas (4hrs 15min, twice per day). Visaginas bus station (Visagino autobusų stotis; Parko gatvė 12A) is a short walk from the tourist information centre.

**TOURIST INFORMATION** Visaginas Tourism Information Centre (Parko gatvė 7; w visitvisaginas.lt; ⏰ 08.00–16.30 Mon–Fri, 09.00–13.00 Sat) can arrange excursions with local guides all year round – they are highly recommended to bring the city to life through stories. Local family business **Litwild** (w litwildtravel. com) offers guided tours of Visaginas, visits to the Ignalina Atomic Energy Control Room Simulator (page 239) and arranges official tours of Ignalina Nuclear Power Plant (page 239).

 **WHERE TO STAY AND EAT**

**Hotel Kornealita** (30 rooms) Jaunystės gatvė 1; w kornealita.lt. The main hotel used by foreigners has everything you need; a selection of sgl, dbl & deluxe rooms with use of the spa, gym & bike rental for an extra charge. The on-site restaurant is popular with locals too. €€

**Bear & Boar** Taikos gatvė 72a;  BearBoarPizza; ⏰ 15.00–23.00 Thu–Fri, 11.00–midnight Sat, 11.00–21.00 Sun. Owned by former Olympic sprint canoeist Evgeny Shuklin, this place is loved for its pizza & craft beers from their **Bear & Boar Brewery** ( bearboarbrewery). €€€

**Bunker** Veteranų gatvė 5;  bunkerfood.lt; ⏰ 16.00–23.00 Mon–Thu, 14.00–midnight Fri, noon–midnight Sat, noon–23.00 Sun. Burgers & tacos served up with beer & cocktails in a cosy interior in winter or on the summer terrace in warmer months. €€

**OTHER PRACTICALITIES** An **ATM** can be found at Swedbank (Veteranų gatvė 5). An IKI **supermarket** is close by in the Domina Shopping Mall (Veteranų gatvė 2), inside which is also a Gintarinė Vaistinė **pharmacy**.

**WHAT TO SEE AND DO** By far the best way to explore this quirky, purpose-built city is on foot – walk around it, get up close to the architectural styles and feel the current energy of the city. Our best advice is to book a local guide. Not only will they help you navigate the labyrinth of similar-looking apartment blocks and numerous roads with the same names, but they will also bring the city to life with their anecdotes and stories. But we include a self-guided walk below for those wanting to explore independently.

**A walk around Visaginas** Start your walk at the **crane statue and clock** (Sedulinos alėja/Parko gatvė traffic island), which is close to the bus station and has parking nearby. Perched up high, with wings spread, the metal bird peers down on Visaginas' main pedestrian area, Sedulinos alėja. Today this crane – symbolising prudence and vigilance – is the symbol of Visaginas city, but in a former life the very same sculpture was a stork and the emblem of the city of Sniečkus. The electronic display beneath the statue informs passers-by of the time, date and temperature, but during its 'stork' era this was the city Geiger counter, displaying local radiation levels. The city also had a siren system to alert residents of dangerous levels of radiation; it is still tested twice a year. Cross over the road to enter the pedestrianised town centre area of Sedulinos alėja, and continue along until you reach the **city's memorial stone** (Parko gatvė 7, outside the tourist information centre). On 10 August 1975, this large stone, whose shape has a likeness to the outline of Lithuania, was placed by builders as a cornerstone of the new city. That date has been Visaginas' birthday ever since. The **singing fountain** (Sedulinos alėja 5) is a focal point of the city in summer. It is a popular hang-out spot, especially when the fountain entertains with music and a colourful light show. Notice the impressive **mosaic wall art** nearby at number 6. It depicts the four elements of earth, air, water and fire alongside the evolution of humans from cave paintings to the discovery of the atom. Created in 1990 and designed by Viktoras Tatarenko, the mosaic was inspired by the red brick of the surrounding utilitarian housing. Take the path left of the mosaic building and continue along past the central flower beds, slowly down the gently descending steps, until you reach the pedestrian crossroads; to your right, tucked away in the bottom corner of the apartment block is a sign saying 'Biblioteka'. This is Visaginas' library where you can see the **Visaginas First City Plan** (Visaginas biblioteka, Sedulinos alėja 14/3; ⏲ 11.00–19.00 Tue–Fri, 10.00–17.00 Sat). Go inside, walk along the corridor and round to the left to find the original city plan mounted on the wall on your left. This was the architects' vision for a carefully planned city serving the workers of the new nuclear power plant and their families. The library also has a selection of publications about Visaginas, some of which are in English. Upon exiting the library, turn right and follow Visagino gatvė pedestrian zone, pass through the underpass and the trees to the shore of Lake Visaginas. This is Visaginas' **public beach** (Visagino ežero paplūdimys) complete with play areas, swimming pontoon, a water slide and changing areas. From the beach, a network of paths weave through the forest back to the city centre and residential areas. To continue this walking tour you can be adventurous and navigate the scenic forest paths keeping the lakeshore on your right for about 10–15 minutes until you leave the forest and join Jaunystės gatvė (or you can exit the forest before then and walk along Jaunystės gatvė). When you reach Jaunystės bus stop on the opposite side of the road, cross over, then follow the path to the left of the apartment blocks straight ahead of you. When the path joins the road continue along the road to the right and turn right at the small supermarket. Straight ahead you can now spot **Jono Krikštytojo Gimimo cerkvė orthodox church** (Sedulinos alėja 73A). Religion was not accommodated in the city design as it was banned under Communist rule, so Visaginas was secular in design, with no religious centre like most Lithuanian towns and cities. Some Visaginas citizens risked their jobs and reputations by travelling to other towns to practise their faith in established places of worship. Soon after independence, community churches were built in Visaginas, including this curious place of worship squeezed in between the two tallest apartment blocks. Continue along the road until it bends to the right; here you should turn left on to the path running to the left of the play area. Continue along, keeping the basketball courts on your right. Over to the left is the area called **Open Gallery** (Draugystės gatvė 10). where huge examples of open-air art adorn the apartment block walls. Of particular interest is the abandoned school building to the far right which has artworks in the window spaces ranging from artistic photography to cultural statements. The larger installations are thought-provoking graffiti-style works of art. Leave this area by heading towards the Norfa supermarket on Draugystės gatvė, keep the supermarket on your right and follow the curve of the road until the junction. Head over the pedestrian crossing and continue straight along Tarybų gatvė for about 1 minute, when on your right immediately after passing some trees the area opens up and you will see a yellow-and-red building (it is a school) with a ramp leading up to a door – this is **Visaginas City Museum** (Visagino miesto muziejus, Tarybų gatvė 23; w visaginomuziejus.lt; ⏲ 09.00–17.00 Wed–Sun; €4/2). This newly opened museum focuses on the recreation of a local apartment including household objects during Soviet times, providing a trip down memory lane for many Lithuanians and a fascinating insight into domestic life in the Soviet era for international visitors. The photography exhibitions have intriguing names like 'My Reaction to the World's Largest Nuclear Reactor', and interactive stories told via old telephones are planned to accompany the images.

### Ignalina Atomic Energy Control Room Simulator (LOK - Ignalinos AE valdymo bloko simuliatorius, Ramybės gatvė; w vrpc.lt/iae-valdymo-skydas)
Located within the rather old-school recreation centre Visagino Parkas is the Ignalina nuclear power plant control room simulator, where staff were trained before graduating to the live site. At the time of writing, it is not functional and its future is uncertain but you can still visit. Visagino Parkas is a 7-minute drive from the centre of Visaginas along road 1417, but you are strongly recommended to arrange your visit via the tourist information centre as an English-speaking guide will be required. A full tour of the actual power plant will be a better experience for those with a genuine interest in the power plant operations.

### * Ignalina Nuclear Power Plant (10km from Visaginas; tours can be arranged via Visaginas Tourism Information Centre (page 237), recommended if you need transport to be included; or book directly with the Ignalina Atomic Energy Communications Centre: e info@iae.lt; w iae.lt)
Construction of the Ignalina Nuclear Power Plant started in 1978 on the southern shore of Lake Drūkšiai. The region needed a new source of energy and the location was stable, undeveloped and next to the biggest lake in Lithuania (through which runs the Lithuania–Belarus border). Four RBMK-type reactors were planned and in 1983 the first reactor, Unit 1, was switched on. In 1986 as Unit 2 reached completion, disaster struck at the Chernobyl nuclear power plant in Ukraine, with the devastating explosion of a similar RBMK-type reactor. Work on Unit 2 at Ignalina was halted while authorities assessed the risks; operations finally began in 1987. At this time, Unit 3 was 60% complete but work was paused and finally suspended in 1989, the future of the plant being called into question as the Lithuanian independence movement and ecological awareness were on the rise.

One of the environmental impacts of Ignalina's location was the cyclical use of Lake Drūkšiai's water. It took 28 days for the whole of the lake's water to pass through the nuclear plant's clean water system when it was discharged back into the lake the water was 3°C warmer. This had a detrimental effect on the lake's ecosystem, though it did result in the region producing an inordinate number of champion rowers who could practise all year round due to the lack of ice on the lake. A condition of Lithuania's accession to the European Union in 2004 was to close Ignalina Nuclear Power Plant down, and in December 2004 Unit 1 was shut down, followed by Unit 2 in 2009. Ignalina is the first nuclear power plant to be decommissioned and completely dismantled, including the reactor core. Estimated to cost €3.5 billion, the process involves complex radiological waste disposal to achieve the planned transformation into a brownfield site by 2038.

Since the plant was used as a film location for the successful TV series *Chernobyl*, visitor numbers have increased although getting on a tour can be tricky due to limited opportunities. At the time of writing, there were two options for visiting the site on weekdays only: a guided tour of the visitor centre and visit to the canteen; or a full guided tour of the plant including restricted areas which involves donning protective clothing and a personal dosemeter (you must be aged over 18, will need personal ID, and the route of the tour depends on which areas are safe to visit as they are planned around decommissioning work). All tours must be prebooked (page 237). For those who aren't able to visit in person, there is a virtual tour online (w virtual.iae.lt). Our personal highlights of an Ignalina Nuclear Power Plant restricted zone tour include being advised not to lick any surfaces, the radiation test plates to check hands outside the toilet doors, standing in a narrow corridor 600m long, the overwhelming scale of the reactor hall and turbine hall, and seeing a moose on our approach to the plant. It is a unique and memorable excursion which one day will no longer be available.

## ZARASAI

Zarasai is a picturesque city in the northeast of Lithuania, surrounded by a hilly landscape and seven lakes – the nickname of Lithuania's Switzerland is perhaps a bit stretched but it is certainly a pretty region. Zarasai is only 4km from the Lithuania–Latvia border and on the main A6 road which continues up to Daugavpils in Latvia. The few international visitors who make it to this far northeastern corner of the country will be pleasantly surprised by the amenities on offer. Much is made of the largest lake, Lake Zarasas, with abundant watersports, new boardwalks and trails, and observation points; and the Great Island is a bustling venue for cultural events in summer. The city centre is assembled around the leafy green horseshoe-shaped park area of Sėlių aikštė (Sėlių square), overlooked by the Blessed Virgin Mary of the Assumption Church. This region was dominated during the 15th and 16th centuries by the Selonian Baltic tribe, the name Zarasai coming from the Selonian word for lakes, *ezerasai*. In 1836, Russian Tsar Nicholas I visited the town and was so impressed he took the liberty of renaming it after his son Alexander – Novo Aleksandrovsk. It only returned to Zarasai in 1918 after Lithuanian independence.

The **Zarasai Tourism Information Centre** (Sėlių aikštė 22; w visitzarasai.lt) can help with excursions, workshops, lakeshore walks and tourist routes through the Zarasai region.

**GETTING THERE AND AWAY** Direct **buses** that run between Zarasai's bus station (Zarasų autobusų stotis; Savanorių gatvė 7) and the cities of Vilnius (2hrs 35mins; 3 per day) and Kaunas (3hrs 50mins; 2 per day). Expect the journey by **car** between Vilnius and Zarasai to take just over 2 hours; having your own vehicle will make exploring the surrounding region easier.

 **WHERE TO STAY AND EAT**

**Brut Wine Hotel** (6 rooms) Vytauto gatvė 10; f brutwine.zarasai. The main hotel in Zarasai is small but spick & span. The rooms are above the hotel **Bistro Zarasai** (f bistrozarasai), which is handy unless there is a private party that you are not invited to; in this instance you need to eat elsewhere & might need the complimentary earplugs conveniently placed by your bed. €€

**RestoBaZar** Sėlių aikštė 4; f restobazar; ⏰ 11.00–22.00 Mon–Thu, 11.00–01.00 Fri, noon–01.00 Sat, noon–22.00 Sun. Bar & grill serving burgers, ribs & salads with a summer terrace overlooking Sėlių aikštė. A kids' corner keeps the little ones entertained. €€€

**Šlyninkos Vandens Malūnas** [map, page 218] Štadviliai village; f slyninka; ⏰ 10.00–17.00 Wed–Fri, 10.00–18.00 Sat–Sun. For something a little different, 4.5km out of the city is Šlyninkos historic water mill, where you can explore the old mill workings full of antiquities & eat a hearty lunch at the traditional tavern. To get here leave Zarasai on Šiaulių gatvė at the back of Sėlių aikštė, then turn left at the 5305, direction Štadviliai; the water mill is signposted to the left as you approach the village. €€€

**Monopolis** Sėlių aikštė 8; ⏰ 11.00–21.00 Mon–Thu, 11.00–23.50 Fri–Sat. With a menu of traditional Lithuanian staples, the main pull here is the view from the terrace at the rear of the restaurant. Enjoy a cool drink or hearty meal overlooking Lake Zarasas. €€

## WHAT TO SEE AND DO

**Zarasai Regional Museum** (Zarasų krašto muziejus; D Bukonto gatvė 20; w zarasumuziejus.lt; ⏰ 10.00–18.00 Wed–Fri, 10.00–16.00 Sat; €6/3) This is the place to learn about Zarasai and the local region's history and culture through permanent and temporary exhibitions. The museum collection was established in 1934 thanks to the foresight of local teacher S Jauniškis, and although the collection was destroyed and diminished during periods of occupation and upheaval, there are many exhibits showcasing the people and place of Zarasai. As with all regional museums, great pride is shown in local stories and influential residents from the area; this understandably flourishes after years of oppression.

**Zarasai Observation Wheel** (Zarasų apžvalgos ratas; directly opposite the Zarasai Regional Museum on D Bukonto gatvė; ⏰ always open; free) Built in 2011, this unique observation platform juts out from the top of the sloping lakeshore and curves right round in a helicoidal (circular) path, 100m long and 17m above the ground. Your attention flicks between its architectural complexity and the scenic view of the lake. If you descend the steps to the lakeshore, there is a path for leisurely walking and cycling around Lake Zarasas. During the evening, the wheel path is illuminated, adding another artistic quality to the design and function of what is now a very popular attraction and a symbol of the city. Hats off to the architect Šarūnas Kiaunė who designed it.

**Great Island in Lake Zarasas** (Zaraso ežero Didžioji sala) Great Island is one of the largest islands in Lithuania, covering 44ha and is a central focus of cultural events and recreation for the city. There is a large car park where Didžiosios salos gatvė begins, along which you can cycle or walk on to the island. Immediately on your left is **Wake Inn Zarasai** (w wakeinn.lt/wake-inn-zarasai) home to the largest wakeboarding track in the Baltics with camping pods, a café bar and various sports on offer. Around the island are hiking paths, beaches and pontoons for swimming. On the southern peninsula is **Zarasai Kupolė** (cupola), a subterranean dome-shaped event space reminiscent of a huge hobbit house. The curved, minimalist interior has excellent acoustics, with many artistic and cultural events taking place here. In warmer months, the nearby open-air amphitheatre hosts performances and festivals too, all coordinated by Zarasai Culture Centre (w zkc.lt).

**Šarūnas Sauka and Nomeda Saukienė Art Gallery** (Š Saukos ir N Saukienės galerija; D Bukonto gatvė 1; w zarasumuziejus.lt/saruno-saukos-ir-nomedos-saukienes-galerija; ⏰ 10.00–18.00 Wed–Sat, 10.00–16.00 Sun; €6/3) Multi award-winning artist couple Šarūnas and Nomeda are originally from Vilnius but have become honorary Zarasai citizens since relocating here. Their art gallery opened in 2023 and includes 42 pieces of work showcasing the surreal fragility of life and death via imagery of various body parts and random objects. Whether this is your artistic dream or nightmare, it's thought-provoking and there's much to explore and ponder in each exhibit. Come with an open mind and perhaps not with the kids.

**Zarasai Public Beach** (Zarasaičio ežero paplūdimys; Dariaus ir Girėno gatvė 2B; ⏰ always; free) Zarasai is home to one of Lithuania's oldest outdoor swimming pools with a diving board. Built in 1933, it became a well-known facility for swimmers and divers to train, with both local coaches and athletes working with the national teams. Originally, the tower was a wooden structure but in 1965 it was replaced with a concrete one and it gained a unique 10m-high diving board. The area becomes the heart of Zarasai during the warm summer months. It is not on the larger lake of Lake Zarasas but on the neighbouring smaller lake of Lake Zarasaitis on the opposite side of road A6 from the Zarasai Observation Wheel.

## AROUND ZARASAI

**STELMUŽĖS OAK** (Stelmužės ąžuolas; Ąžuolo gatvė 14, Stelmužė village) This mighty oak tree is one of the oldest oaks in Europe, estimated to be between 1,500 and 2,000 years old. It is one of the most famous in Lithuania, with an impressive girth measurement of approximately 9.5m, taking nine adults to fully hug the tree. It has witnessed a lot of history over the centuries and has been the subject of local legends. One claims the tree trunk to be the entrance to the underworld, and some say there is treasure buried underneath. Perhaps there is a message there – does greed lead you to the underworld? Oak trees are sacred in Lithuania, and this one is very special. It is certainly looking its age, with supports in place to prevent heavy branches breaking away from the trunk. The good news is that seedlings from the oak have been successfully propagated and will hopefully live long and healthy lives of their own in the Lithuanian forests. The tree stands in the grounds of the **Stelmužė Lord Jesus Cross Church** (Stelmužės Viešpaties Jėzaus Kryžiaus bažnyčia; ⊕ May–Sep), a historic wooden church built in 1650. Inside, there are some particularly ornate Baroque-style ornaments and reliefs worthy of a visit. A car park area is nearby.

To visit Stelmužės, leave Zarasai on road 117 heading north, after 4.5km turn right on road 5304, direction Stelmužė. After 9km, passing through the village, look out for the brown tourist signs to the oak tree and church.

**SARTAI REGIONAL PARK** Sartai Regional Park is a protected region of managed forests, wetlands and lakes, including its namesake Lake Sartai, which has the longest shoreline of any lake in Lithuania (almost 79km). It is an area popular for hunting, fishing and foraging but is most well known, even internationally, for its annual horse race (see opposite). For more information about the region, visit **Sartai Regional Park Visitor Centre** (Vytauto gatvė 5; w sartai.info; ⊕ May–Sep 09.00–18.00 Tue–Fri, 09.00–16.45 Sat, 10.00–15.00 Sun) in Dusetos.

One of the highlights of the regional park is **Sartai Lake Tower** (Sartų ežero apžvalgos bokštas; Ščiūrių gatvė 16b, Baršėnų region; ⊕ 09.00–22.00 daily). It is one of the older observation towers in Lithuania and also one of the tallest at 33m. Its slim build and steep, narrow steps accentuate its height, and the views from the top are worth the climb. Lake Sartai is an intricate lake with many inlets and promontories that result in an interesting view. It is especially beautiful at sunrise or sunset, and in autumn when the forests are a spectacle of russets and yellows. Be careful in wet weather as the steps can be slippery, and note the opening times as the tower is on private property. It is approached from the north of Lake Sartai; if travelling along road 3608, the turn off for the tower is between the village of Baršėnai and the junction with road 117. Turn off at the brown sign for 'Apžvalgos bokštas'.

The town of Dusetos lies on the southern end of Lake Sartai and is home to an impressive contemporary art gallery. The **Dusetos Art Gallery and Cultural Centre** (Kultūros centras Dusetų dailės galerija; Vytauto gatvė 54; w dusetukultura. lt; ⊕ 09.00–17.00 Wed–Fri, 10.00–17.00 Sat–Sun) showcases high-quality artwork

> **SARTAI HORSE RACE**
>
> The annual Sartai Horse Race (w sartaidusetose.lt) has been held in Dusetos for over 120 years. In its long history, since 1905, there have been some exceptions – obstacles of war, Covid-19 and climate change have all prevented the event going ahead at one time or another.
>
> The unique characteristic of this traditional trotting event, held in early February, is that the racing takes place on ice, customarily on the frozen Lake Sartai; but in recent years milder temperatures have resulted in the lake not freezing over. This has not deterred event organisers, however, who have moved the race to dry land at the Dusetos hippodrome (Dusetų hipodromas), though still on a natural ice track. But the ideal conditions needed to form the ice track – ten days of temperatures lower than -5° – are becoming rare and unreliable, putting the future of the race at risk. Reconstruction of the hippodrome is being considered, so perhaps a technical solution will be found to help the tradition survive. We must wait and see…
>
> When the Sartai horse race is held, large crowds arrive to watch, all wrapped up warm in their winter layers. The event is attended by visiting dignitaries too. Traditional food and drink are on sale, and folk art stalls and music groups add to the special atmosphere.
>
> Since there is always a risk that the horse race could be cancelled due to mild conditions, consider this in your trip planning.

from local artists through permanent and temporary exhibitions. Local artists, many of whom have toured internationally, have benefitted from this outlet and support network for over 25 years, and Dusetos has established a solid reputation in the Lithuanian art world.

**GRAŽUTĖS REGIONAL PARK** South of Zarasai and west of Visaginas, Gražutės Regional Park is one of Lithuania's quietest – a peaceful oasis of wetlands and wilderness with few people. It is popular for fishing owing to its abundance of pike, perch and roach, and is particularly beautiful in autumn when the deciduous trees put on a spectacle of colour. Although quiet, the park is still accessible with hiking trails and boardwalks, maps of which can be picked up at the **Gražutės Regional Park Visitor Centre** (Laisvoji aikštė 14; w grazutesparkas.lt; ⊕ 08.00–noon & 12.45–16.45 Tue–Fri, 09.00–noon & 12.45–16.45 Sat) in Salakas village. This should be your first stop if visiting the park. Not only do they help with regional park information, but the centre also houses an unexpected museum of the sea! The private collection of more than 5,000 seashells and marine artefacts, belonging to local resident Vida Žilinskienė, make up the **V Žilinskienės Maritime Museum** (V Žilinskienės Jūrų muziejus; ⊕ same hours as the visitor centre; free), a rather delightful tribute to an eccentric local collector.

## ROKIŠKIS

When you mention Rokiškis, what springs to mind is cheese. Rokiškio sūris (w rokiskio.com) is the largest cheese producer in the Baltic states; it is an important local employer and a flagship Lithuanian brand which exports to a worldwide market. What started out as a small dairy was developed into a specialised factory by the Soviets in 1964, and independence took it to the next level on a global stage.

There is no opportunity to visit the factory, though there is a rather lacklustre milk truck exhibition outside. Aside from cheese, Rokiškis is a pleasant town with a noble legacy handed down from the influential Krošinskis, Tyzenhaus and Pšezdzecki families, who ruled the area between the 16th and 19th centuries. This was a region of large estates and wealthy landowners, with Jewish merchant towns thriving on trade between the Lithuanian farming estates and the Latvian city of Riga – the third largest city in the Russian Empire. The size of Rokiškis' central Independence Square is evidence of the huge markets that took place here, and their importance is marked by the architectural grandeur of Rokiškis Manor and the Church of St Matthew the Apostle at either end.

**GETTING THERE AND AWAY** The bus station (Rokiškio autobusų stotis; Panevėžio gatvė 1; w rokiskioap.lt) is a 2km walk to the tourism information centre. Daily direct **buses** serve Rokiškis from both Vilnius (3hrs 10mins; 6 per day) and Kaunas (3hrs 25mins; 3 per day).

**TOURIST INFORMATION** The **Rokiškis Tourism Information Centre** (Rokiškio turizmo informacijos centras; Nepriklausomybės aikštė 8-3; w rokiskiotic.lt; ⊕ 09.00–18.00 Thu, 10.00–17.00 Sat, 10.00–15.00 Sun) website is currently only in Lithuanian so you should email them directly to request information in English.

## WHERE TO STAY AND EAT

**Pagunda** (18 rooms) Respublikos gatvė 45; ⓕ kavinepagunda. Pagunda's main feature is that it is currently the only hotel in Rokiškis. Therefore, if you need a bed in town, you will probably end up here. It can be booked via the tourism office or via hotel booking websites; direct contact is not so easy. More of a practical option than a leisure one. €€

**Pesto** Taikos gatvė 10; w restoranaspesto.lt; ⊕ 11.00–22.00 Tue–Fri, 11.00–23.00 Sat, 11.00–21.00 Sun. Homemade pizzas & good coffee keep locals & visitors happy in this popular Italian restaurant. Pasta dishes are available too & we love that *kepta duona* (fried black bread with garlic) is on the menu to remind you this is Lithuania! €€€

**Pupelė** Nepriklausomybės aikštė 12; ⓕ pupelerokiskis; ⊕ 10.00–22.00 Mon–Thu, 10.00–23.00 Fri–Sat, 11.00–21.00 Sun. Housed in a standalone wooden house with three sets of painted window shutters adorning the façade, a warm welcome awaits you at 'The Bean', along with snacks, hot mains & pizzas. Terrace & children's play area. €€€

**Senas Grafas** Nepriklausomybės aikštė 6-8; w senasgrafas.lt; ⊕ 10.00–22.00 Mon–Thu, 10.00–23.00 Fri–Sun. The 'Old Count' is something of a social hub, morphing between sports bar, music club & restaurant & they have a guesthouse located in a nearby wooden residential house with 5 bedrooms. The restaurant can arrange tastings of local cheeses & other delicacies if booked in advance. €€€

**WHAT TO SEE AND DO** Unique to Rokiškis, the old tradition of **painting shutters** was revived in the early 2000s by artist Arūnas Augučis. Ever since, more than 300 sets of shutters have been painted by local, national and international artists, encouraging community spirit and bringing colour and interest, and visitors, to the city. Often the designs are connected with the owners' interests, or the building's use. Enjoy admiring the shutters on a stroll that may take you to streets you would otherwise overlook.

**Rokiškis Regional Museum** (Rokiškio krašto muziejus; Rokiškis Manor; Tyzenhauzų gatvė 5; w muziejusrokiskyje.lt; ⊕ 10.00–18.00 Tue–Sun; €7/3) Housed in Rokiškis Manor, the regional museum covers the history of Rokiškis with diverse exhibits, but it also presents a very strong overview of Lithuanian history and culture with many national customs and events explained clearly – from medieval history and sun crosses, to the press ban, authentic outfits, Old Believers and occupations. You may need more time here than expected, especially if you pay the extra €1 for the audio guide – highly recommended. The manor is approached from the town centre via Tyzenhauzų gatvė, a pedestrian causeway cutting across the lake. The main manor house building – it's the one with the grand Classical façade directly ahead when you enter the manor park – contains the museum. The stone buildings either side of the manor are home to additional exhibitions and the estate administration.

**Church of St Matthew the Apostle** (Šv. apaštalo evangelisto Mato bažnyčia; Nepriklausomybės aikštė 1; w rokiskioparapija.lt; ⊕ 10.00–17.00 daily) Built between 1866 and 1885, the Neo-Gothic church was commissioned by Count Tyzenhauz, but he did not live to see it completed – a common problem back in those days. Construction costs were understood to be spiralling out of control, but the family's modest answer when asked about the cost of the church was that 'God knows, so we don't need to'. The stepped parapet of the façade is striking and particularly beautiful at sunset when the retiring sun streams through the openings and the tower windows. The church interior contains exceptional hand-carved woodwork.

## BIRŽAI

Tucked away in the northeast of Lithuania, close to the Latvian border, Biržai city and the surrounding lands once defended the northern territories of Lithuania from invaders. Today, it is a pleasant town beside Lake Širvėna, Lithuania's first dammed reservoir created in 1589 and traversed by the country's longest pedestrian bridge. The region is synonymous with craft beer, the Big Z (Žydrūnas Savickas, Lithuania's most successful strongman) and sinkholes. International visitors are not so common, but for those who stop en route to other destinations or stay in the locality, Biržai is worth exploring for a day. The **tourist information centre** (J Janonio gatvė 2; w visitbirzai.lt; ⊕ May–Sep 08.00–17.00 Mon–Fri, 10.00–14.00 Sat–Sun, Oct–Apr 08.00–17.00 Mon–Thu, 08.00–15.45 Fri) should be your first port of call for booking a local guide to the town or region.

**GETTING THERE AND AROUND** Direct **buses** run between Biržai and Vilnius (3hrs 5mins; 9 per day), Kaunas (3hrs 40mins; 6 per day) and Panevėžys (1hr 15mins; 15 per day). The centrally located bus station (Biržų autobusų stotis; J Basanavičiaus gatvė 1; w birzuap.lt) is behind the post office building, accessible from Vytauto gatvė and convenient for the sights. **Driving** to Biržai from the capital takes approximately 2 hours 40 minutes, and slightly less from Kaunas (2hrs 25mins).

 **WHERE TO STAY AND EAT**

**Butenas Hotel** (16 rooms) Tylos gatvė 2; w butenas-hotel.lt. This is a simple, yet cosy family-run hotel, with 14 standard rooms & 2 suites. Ask for a lake-view room to make your stay a bit more special. An on-site restaurant & bar make evenings easy. **€€**

**Sodeliškiai Manor** [map, page 218] (32 rooms) Sodeliškių dvaro sodyba; Sodeliškių gatvė 1A, only 14km north of Biržai on road 1305; w sodeliskiudvaras.lt. To find such a treasure trove of amenities in what feels like the middle of nowhere is quite extraordinary. Hotel accommodation is in a separate building to the main manor house which houses the restaurant & spa. This largely keeps hotel guests away from any functions – it is very popular for weddings & parties at w/ends. Book half-board accommodation if you want to dine here in the

evening. The spa & ethnographic museum (an authentic Aukštaitija homestead complete with windmill) are free for guests. Entry to the antique technical museum, with exhibits ranging from prams to planes, is an extra €4/2. The traditional sauna by the pond can be booked for an additional cost & with advance notice. The grounds, sports & playground areas are free to use. €€
**Biržų kempingas** J Basanavičiaus gatvė 69A; birzaicamping. This campsite is on the edge of Biržai on the shore of Lake Širvena & close to the longest pedestrian bridge in Lithuania. The beach is suitable for swimming, & local walking & cycling paths ideal for exploring. There are 20 pitches for motorhomes/caravans, 100 places for tents, & 5 cabins. Open season is 1 Mar–1 Oct. Quieter on w/days. €
**Beer Route 'Alaus kelias'** Alyvų gatvė 8; w rinkuskiai.lt. The restaurant at the Rinkuškiai brewery offers a traditional full menu for dining, or you can experience the 'Beer Route' beer tasting experience of 9 different locally brewed beers & accompanying beer snacks. To recreate the tasting experience for your dedicated driver at home, you can purchase the beers to take away.€€€
**Portfolio** Rotušės gatvė 12; portfoliobirzai. Sit among the artworks at this café-gallery in the centre of town. Their vegetarian daily menu (*dienos meniu*) is a good option for lunch. €€

**WHAT TO SEE AND DO** A walk or cycle around **Lake Širvėna** is the best way to experience and appreciate the highlights of Biržai. From Biržai castle is a pleasant hiking trail along the shore of the lake which leads to the recently built **Apaščios vinguotasis tiltas** – a curved bridge installation over the Apaščia River. From here it is a short walk to the start of **Širvėnos ežero tiltas**, the longest pedestrian footbridge in Lithuania at 525m long. It was built for workers from Biržai to commute to the linen factory Siūlas, built in the grounds of Astravas Manor in 1928. Today, the bridge is a popular attraction and adds novelty to a local walk for tourists visiting Biržai Castle and Astravas Manor.

**Biržai Regional Museum** (Biržų krašto muziejus; w birzumuziejus.lt; May–Sep 10.00–18.30 Wed–Sat, 10.00–17.30 Sun & Tue, Oct–Apr 09.00–17.30 Wed–Sat, 09.00–16.30 Sun & Tue; €5/2.50) On a promontory of Lake Širvėna, bordered on both sides by the Agluona and Apaščia rivers, **Biržai Castle** occupies the site of a former fortress, the shape of which is best viewed from above or on a map. The fortress structure is accessed via a red-brick bridge and gateway across the dry moat, a detail that emphasises the defensive importance of this location and construction. Biržai was the seat of the Radviliškis family (Radzwili or Radvila) and it was Duke Kristupas Radvila (1547–1603) who built this impressive bastion fortress to protect his lands, complete with a church, arsenal, warehouses and barracks, all planned for strategic defence during the period when Swedes were attacking from the north. The Swedes successfully destroyed the fortress a number of times during the 17th and 18th centuries; each time it was rebuilt with stronger ramparts by successive Radvila generations. The current castle was rebuilt from ruin in the 1980s, with late-Renaissance-style architecture. It became the local library and then home of the Biržai Regional Museum. The halls of the castle are filled with exhibits of local history, culture, art and folklore. The arsenal houses a permanent warfare exhibition, including mortar from the 17th-century Northern War. Ask for the free English audio guide.

**Astravas Manor** (Astravo dvaras; Astravo gatvė; look out for the small red-brick gatehouse). Astravas Manor or Palace was built in the mid 1800s by the Tiškevičius family, having purchased the Duchy of Biržai lands from the Radvila family. As Biržai Castle was in disrepair, they built this Italianate villa as their main residence, and it remained in the family until 1930 when it was incorporated into the linen factory, which still exists in the grounds today. It is not possible to see the interior of the manor; simply enjoy the grounds which are open and free all year round.

**Biržai Narrow-Gauge Railway Station** (Cnr Stoties & Kęstučio gatvės) There is nothing official here at the time of writing, but the station and depot buildings, water tower, 750mm-gauge track and a new train are in place and catch the eye of passers-by. The track was constructed in 1921 and ran between Biržai and Gubernija near Šiauliai until its closure in 1996. One to watch for the future…

### Further afield

***Cow Cave*** (Karvės ola; near Mantagailiškis village) Leaving Biržai centre on road 1303, before you reach Mantagailiškis turn left following signs for Karvės ola. You are now in **Karajimiškis Landscape Reserve** about 4.5km from the centre of Biržai, and where there is the highest density of sinkholes in Lithuania. Residents of Biržai region never utter the phrase '*Kad tu prasmegtum*' (to be swallowed up by the earth) because that could actually happen here. Not that people have been swallowed up by the earth, but here as the name Cow Cave suggests, there has been one bovine victim. There are an estimated 9,000 sinkholes in the Biržai region and every year more appear in the fields, meadows, farmsteads and forests. They are noticeable as small hollows, or areas of shrubs in the middle of open land. At Cow Cave, a steel staircase descends into the sinkhole, giving a basic overview of the geology of this area which is eroded over time by subterranean water channels, creating underground tunnels and caves that eventually collapse.

***Kirkiliai Observation Tower*** (Kirkilų apžvalgos bokštas; 7km north on the 1305, turn right at Kirkilų cemetery) Kirkiliai is widely regarded as one of the most attractive observation towers in Lithuania. The tower is shaped like an ancient canoe standing on end, its gentle curve reflected in Lake Kirkilų, around which are many circular lakes formed in sinkholes. The landscape is really quite unique and tranquil, although the surrounding trails are popular with hikers. The tower is 32m tall, with an observation platform at 30m, and provides a great opportunity to count sinkhole features from above.

## PANEVĖŽYS

Officially the capital of Aukštaitija, Panevėžys lies midway between Vilnius and Riga and was transformed from a modest town to a manufacturing centre during the 1960s and 70s. With the population boom that followed, the historic centre of wooden houses became surrounded by apartment blocks; the incorporation of a substantial network of cycle paths made Panevėžys Lithuania's most bike-friendly city. Today, Panevėžys is an administrative capital where the surrounding population visit for shops and services. Tourists tend to have a family heritage connection or come to visit a specific attraction, although hotels and restaurants are used to welcoming international business guests.

The **Panevėžys Tourism Information** website is currently run by the Panevėžys Development Agency (**w** panevezysnow.lt) and offers excellent information on events and services available in the city.

**GETTING THERE AND AWAY** The bus station (Panevėžio Autobusų Stotis; Savanorių aikštė 5) is in the city centre and served by direct **buses** to/from Vilnius (2hrs; 19

per day), Kaunas (2hrs 10mins; 18 per day) and Šiauliai (1hr 25mins; 10 per day). Panevėžys **train station** (Panevezio gelezinkelio stotis; Kerbedžio gatvė 9) is the beginning of the railway line to Mažeikiai, via Radviliškis and Šiauliai where you can connect to the main line routes for Vilnius, Kaunas, Klaipėda and Riga. It is a 2.2km walk from the train station to the tourism information centre. Panevėžys will have a passenger station and freight terminal on the new Rail Baltica high-speed trainline, and although the station will be a small distance out of the city to the west, it is expected to have a positive impact on the city.

##  WHERE TO STAY AND EAT

**Conviva Hotel** (10 rooms) Laisvės aikštė 16; w conviva.lt. A small, cosy hotel in the city centre with classic sgl or twin/dbl rooms plus a larger suite. B/fast is taken in the hotel café N°7. €€€

**Hotel Romantic** (70 rooms) Kranto gatvė 24; f romantichotel.spa.konferencijos.restoranas. dejavu. In a converted historic flour mill dating from 1841, the hotel is divided into 3 sections with business class, mid-range & economy room categories. Small spa area & Déjà vu restaurant (closed Mon). €€€

**Riverside Restaurant** Kranto gatvė 36-101; f riverside.panevezys; ⊕ 11.30–22.00 Tue–Thu, 11.30–02.00 Fri–Sat. For finer dining, cocktails & a trendy atmosphere, this is the place. There is seating on the terrace overlooking the river in summer. €€€€

**Akordai** Laisvės aikštė 26; ⊙ akordai_ panevezys; ⊕ 11.00–22.00 Mon–Thu, 11.00–midnight Fri, noon–midnight Sat, noon–21.00 Sun. This city-centre venue has a solid reputation for good food that fuses Italian & Lithuanian cuisine, live music & drinks with friends. €€€

**Špunka Old Barrel Pub** Savanorių aikštė 5b; f spunkaoldbarrelpub; ⊕ 16.20–midnight Thu, 16.20–02.00 Sat–Sun, 16.00–22.00 Sun. Local draft beers, pub food, good music & friendly staff, what more do you need to fill you up & lift the spirits? €€€

**Kavos dėžutė** Laisvės aikštė 15-18; f kavosdezute; ⊕ 07.30–18.00 Mon–Fri, 10.00–17.00 Sat, 10.00–14.00 Sun. A creative coffee shop, where they don't just make coffee, cake & snacks, but you can reach for a book or listen to a fellow patron tinkling the ivories of the in-house piano. €€

## WHAT TO SEE AND DO

**Panevėžys Local History Museum** (Panevėžio kraštotyros muziejus; Vasario 16-Osios gatvė 23; w paneveziomuziejus.lt; ⊕ 10.00–18.00 Tue–Fri, 11.00–16.00 Sat; closed last Fri of the month; €4/2) The local history museum offers an updated and well-presented exposition of the city over the years, from archaeology, ethnography, occupation and deportation, to independence and famous locals. One stand-out exhibit is the aerial photograph taken by a German reconnaissance aircraft in July 1944, showing targets and destruction inflicted – a stark reminder of the damage done in these contested lands. Another department of the museum is the **Exhibition of the Resistance to the Soviet Occupation and the Sąjūdis Movement** (Respublikos gatvė 17; ⊕ 10.00–18.00 Tue–Fri, 11.00–16.00 Sat; free), which details life under Soviet occupation through authentic artefacts and accounts, including the activities of the local resistance movement. It is housed in the former premises of the Panevėžys branch of the Sąjūdis independence movement.

**Panevėžys Narrow-Gauge Railway 'Siaurukas' Station** (Geležinkelio gatvė; w siaurukas.eu) The narrow-gauge railway station can be accessed from the main station by crossing over the tracks on the footbridge. Although the Aukštaitija Narrow-Gauge Railway does run between Panevėžys and Anykščiai, there are currently no regular services; only special-event trains run between Panevėžys and Anykščiai and they require prebooking via the website. For full details about the Aukštaitija Narrow-Gauge Railway, see page 222.

**Stasys Modern Art Museum** (Respublikos gatvė 40; **f** stasysmuseumlt; ⊕ 11.00–19.00 Tue–Sat, noon–17.00 Sun; €8/4) It's safe to say this is not going to be everyone's cup of tea, but for modern art lovers it is a must-see: a contemporary gallery of modern art, centred around the works of globally acclaimed Lithuanian artist Stasys Eidrigevičius and featuring those of other renowned artists. For those just accompanying said modern art lovers, the architecture, rooftop panoramic view and café should hold your interest long enough.

## UKMERGĖ

Ukmergė is one of the oldest towns in Lithuania, first mentioned as a settlement in 1333 in the Livonian Chronicle of H Vartberges. It was originally called Vilkmergė, because of its position at the confluence of the Vilkmergėlė stream and Šventoji River, but has been known as Ukmergė for many centuries. Although the city lacks major attractions, its streets are full of evidence of a varied history, including the 13th-century castle mound, cobbled streets, wooden buildings, Jewish merchant houses, and townhouses that once belonged to wealthy landowners. Like most settlements across Lithuania, Ukmergė was a thriving market town with a significant Jewish population, approximately 10,000 of whom were murdered during the Nazi occupation. Ukmergė's prime location amid fertile agricultural lands and on a major crossroad of the Warsaw-to-St Petersburg road saw it develop into an important staging post and merchant centre in the 19th century. Today, it is a successful manufacturing centre and known for **Vilkmergės Brewery** (**w** vilkmergesalus.lt), whose craft beers and ciders you will find across the country.

**GETTING THERE AND AWAY** Ukmergė's bus station (Ukmergės autobusų stotis; Vytauto gatvė 111) is located 2.5km northeast of the city centre, better placed for visiting the hospital rather than the tourist attractions. Direct **buses** connect with

> **✴ RED BRICK AND FARMERS CIRCLE**
>
> **Red Brick** [map, page 218] (Žirgyno gatvė 1, Radiškis; **w** red-brick.lt; €€€€€) is an unexpected Michelin Green Star restaurant in the fields of Lithuania, representing the new generation of farm-to-table sustainable farming and new Baltic cuisine of Lithuania. Guests enjoy an 'immersive culinary experience' focused on the innovative use of local, seasonal produce in a charming setting. The **Sleepy Horse** (€€€), a 15-room guesthouse in the former stables, provides accommodation on site, with the added bonus of their homecooked breakfast too. Also on site are a farm shop and event spaces in the former barn and mill. The complex is part of **Farmers Circle** (**w** farmerscircle.lt), an organic, sustainable farm of over 600ha committed to producing fresh and delicious seasonal produce all year round. They are true pioneers in the drive towards an organic, sustainable and nature-based environment and society.
>
> To visit the farm or to dine/stay at Red Brick you are advised to book in advance via the website. It is an hour's drive north of Vilnius, and 20mins northeast of Ukmergė on road E262. When in Vilnius, you can sample the farm's bounty at their venues in Senatorių Pasažas, including a delicatessen, wine bar and restaurants 14Horses and Nineteen18 (pages 84 and 85).

Vilnius (1hr 5mins; 15 per day), Kaunas (1hr 22mins; 7 per day) and Šiauliai (2hrs 20mins; 7 per day).

**TOURIST INFORMATION** The **Ukmergė Tourism Information Centre** (Ukmergės turizmo informacijos centras; Kauno gatvė 1; w ukmergeinfo.lt; ⊕ 09.00–18.00 Tue–Fri, 09.00–16.45 Sat) is on the corner of Kauno gatvė and Vienuolyno gatvė in front of the Church of the Holy Trinity (Švč. Trejybės bažnyčia). The staff can arrange activities with local suppliers that are difficult to arrange directly, including a visit to the private military heritage site Kopūstėliai former missile base (unauthorised entry to the site is not allowed).

 **WHERE TO STAY AND EAT**

**Big Stone Hotel** (22 rooms) Kauno gatvė 5; w bigstonehotel.lt. Ideally located in the city centre, with contemporary standard & deluxe rooms. The hotel restaurant gives a big nod to Ukmergė's Jewish heritage with a Jewish kitchen serving specialities including *forshmak* & *imberlach*. €€

**Laurentroom Apartments** Deltuvos gatvė 10b; w laurentroom.lt. Across Ukmergė Laurentroom has a wide range of self-catering apartments, an autonomous 'hotel' & a hostel. The 'old town' apartments are well located & well equipped with comforts including Wi-Fi, heated floors & coffee machines. €€

**Aš būsiu čia** Kauno gatvė 29; f asbusiucia; ⊕ 11.00–21.00 Tue–Thu, 11.00–01.00 Fri–Sat, 11.00–20.00 Sun. Translated as 'I will be here', this is the place to be for finger-licking pub food & live music under the title of Rockmergė, although artists cover all genres. €€€

**Greita** Kęstučio alėja 2; f KavineGreita; ⊕ 08.00–20.00 Mon–Thu, 08.00–22.00 Fri, 09.00–22.00 Sat, 10.00–20.00 Sun. A friendly, cosy café serving fresh traditional snacks & lunches. €€

**Coffee Spot** Žuvų gatvė 3; w coffeespot.lt. For freshly made teas, coffees, frappuccinos, milkshakes, delicious cakes & desserts in trendy surroundings. €

**WHAT TO SEE AND DO**

**Ukmergė Castle Mound** (Ukmergės piliakalnis; Piliakalnio gatvė 5) Ukmergė castle mound is one of only two castle mounds in a city centre in Lithuania, something Ukmergė locals are quite proud of (the other is Gediminas Castle in Vilnius; page 95). This was the heart of Ukmergė (Vilkmergė) in the 13th century, when a wooden fortress topped the mound and served to defend the region from attacks by Teutonic Knights and the Livonian Order. Today it is a focal point of the city, where people gravitate for a stroll around the illuminated walkway that circles the summit, or to sit and admire the view at sunset.

**Ukmergė Regional Museum** (Ukmergės kraštotyros muziejus; Kęstučio alėja 9; w ukmergesmuziejus.lt; ⊕ Jun–Aug 10.00–18.00 Wed–Sat, 10.00–17.00 Sun, Sep–May 09.00–17.00 Tue–Fri, 09.00–16.00 Sat; €2/1) Ukmergė's regional museum provides a comprehensive overview of the region's history from the Stone Age to contemporary living, tracking wars, uprisings and historical events that have shaped the area. A strong emphasis is placed on ethnographics, largely because many everyday objects were ubiquitous and touch the memory of many people. These include wooden utensils, crafts and textiles that showcase the traditional skills and designs of the region. Immediately in front of the museum is a fountain with music choreography. Standing at the museum entrance with the fountain in front of you, turn left and walk along the street, past the memorial, until you get to Pakalnės gatvė, where you will find the little statue of Keksas the dog (Šuo Keksas) – rub his nose and he will remember your smell and give you protection for life!

# 8

# Žemaitija

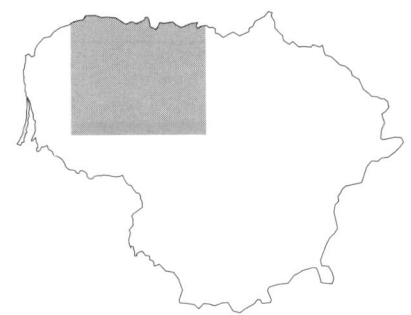

Žemaitija is the Lithuanian name for the ancient land of Samogitia in northwest Lithuania, though ancient Samogitia covered a much larger area than today's Žemaitija ethnographic region. It was bordered to the north by the Livonian Order and to the south by the Teutonic Order, both of which had expansionist plans and wanted to convert Samogitia to Christianity, leading to numerous battles and invasions. Between 1345 and 1382, Samogitia was attacked by Teutonic crusaders about 70 times, and by Livonians 30 times, with tensions reaching a finale in 1410 at the Battle of Žalgiris (Grunwald), where the Polish–Lithuanian Commonwealth armies defeated the Teutonic Order. Samogitia had proven itself to be a land of warriors and resistance, and this defiance towards foreign influence has been key to Samogitia remaining a distinct region with its own surviving dialect, culture and customs, and why it was the last area of Lithuania to be converted from paganism to Christianity. Later, between 1422 and 1795, the Duchy of Samogitia was the only independent territory in the Grand Duchy of Lithuania to be granted duchy status.

Just as the lands of Samogitia differed to those of today's Žemaitija, the territory covered by this chapter is slightly different to the current official ethnographic region of Žemaitija. For the purposes of modern-day tourism, rather than launching crusades, this chapter covers the majority of Žemaitija, with the exception of the northern Lithuanian coast, and some blurred border areas which may appear in other chapters. We refer to the region as both Samogitia and Žemaitija, with Samogitia used when referencing the region's ancient history and traditions.

These days, Žemaitija is the most ethnically homogenous region of Lithuania with a strong cultural identity evident in its architecture, customs and food. Even through centuries of occupation, local traditions have endured and formed the backbone of a wider, national identity. Notice that many signs here are in both Lithuanian and Samogitian (eg: Telšiai/Telšė) as the ancient dialect undergoes a revival. The capital of Žemaitija is Telšiai, although Šiauliai is the largest city, and both are surrounded by Lithuania's large eastern plateau, dotted with wooden farmsteads, villages and folk architecture churches, alongside modern wind farms and large-scale agriculture. Visitors are drawn to Žemaitija by the headline attractions of the Cold War Museum and Hill of Crosses, often doing both in one day. But you will get much more from your visit if you slow down and stay a while. Embrace those quirky museums, sit by a lakeshore at sunset or sunrise surrounded by birdsong and wildlife sounds, savour authentic dishes, and feel grateful to experience this little corner of the world.

## ŠIAULIAI

Šiauliai usually only appears on an international visitor itinerary for its proximity to the headline tourist attraction of the Hill of Crosses, which lies 12km out of the city.

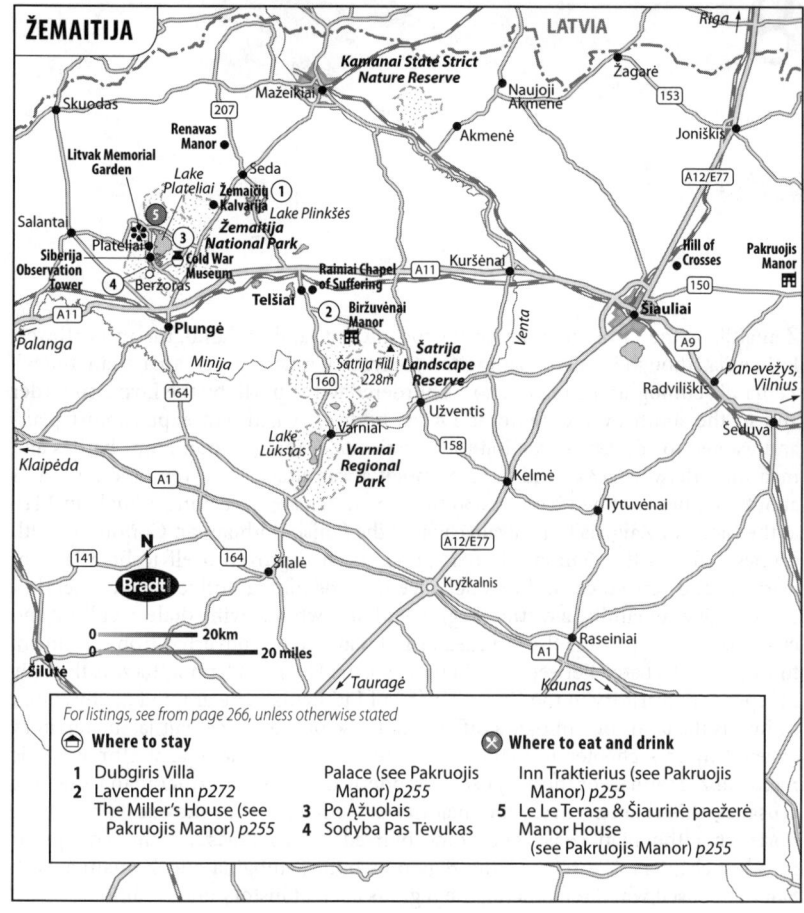

For listings, see from page 266, unless otherwise stated

**Where to stay**
1. Dubgiris Villa
2. Lavender Inn p272
   The Miller's House (see Pakruojis Manor) p255

3. Po Ąžuolais
4. Sodyba Pas Tėvukas

Palace (see Pakruojis Manor) p255

**Where to eat and drink**
Inn Traktierius (see Pakruojis Manor) p255
5. Le Le Terasa & Šiaurinė paežerė Manor House (see Pakruojis Manor) p255

Šiauliai is the hub for local public transport to the Hill of Crosses, and perhaps a place for a quick wander and bite to eat if time allows. It offers the opportunity to experience a real Lithuanian city – it's the country's fourth largest – and has an abundance of unusual museums and local spirit. A full day or overnight stay is recommended.

**HISTORY** Known as the city of the sun, Šiauliai was first mentioned in the Livonian Chronicles as the 'city of Saulė' when describing the 1236 Battle of the Sun which was fought nearby between pagan Samogitians and the Catholic Livonian Brothers of the Sword – the Samogitians were victorious.

During the second half of the 19th century, Šiauliai underwent a transformation with the construction of road and rail networks, making the city an important crossroads within the Russian Empire and resulting in large-scale industrial development. In the same period, locals played an important role in the Lithuanian National Revival movement, the local newspaper *Aušra* being one of the main mediums through which the independence movement communicated. During the press ban *Aušra* was printed in Koenigsberg (Kaliningrad) and smuggled to Šiauliai, hence its main street Tilžės gatvė runs all the way to former Tilsit (now Panemunė) on the Lithuania–Kaliningrad (Russia) border.

During the independent interwar years, Šiauliai lost much of its trade with Russia and a rail connection to Klaipėda was constructed to open up access to new Western markets. With logistical importance comes vulnerability, and during World War I more than half of the city's buildings were destroyed – Šiauliai has no Old Town. The city recovered to become northern Lithuania's main economic and cultural centre, but during World War II, as the Red Army advanced from the east, this was the front line between Nazi Germany and Russia. Over 80% of its buildings were damaged, making Šiauliai the most war-torn city in the country.

As was the case in all Lithuanian cities, towns and villages, Šiauliai lost the majority of its Jewish population during the Nazi occupation. In July 1941, a Jewish ghetto was established and by July 1944 the inhabitants had been either killed locally or sent to their deaths at Nazi concentration camps. In 1939, Siauliai had approximately 8,000 Jewish residents, but by the end of World War II only about 500 had survived.

Šiaulia was rebuilt during the interwar period and later during Soviet occupation, and the architecture reflects this, with wide streets and large Modernist buildings. The city became one of the USSR's manufacturing hubs, a centre of Soviet technology exporting TVs, bicycles and electronics (notice the link between former factories and current museums). Locals formed a highly skilled workforce, many of whom relocated abroad when Lithuania joined the EU, but are now moving home as they realise the balanced lifestyle their revived hometown now offers.

**GETTING THERE AND AWAY** Šiauliai is served by direct **buses** to/from Vilnius (3hrs 20mins; 10 per day), Kaunas (2hrs 45mins; 12 per day), Panevėžys (1hr 25mins; 10 per day) and Palanga (2hrs 15mins; 3 per day). The bus station (Šiaulių autobusų stotis; Tilžės gatvė 109) is a short walk from the tourism information centre.

The **train station** (Šiaulių geležinkelio stotis; Dubijos gatvė 44B) is a little further away, 1.5km from the tourism information centre. Šiauliai has long been a key station for passenger and freight trains on the main routes of Vilnius–Riga, Vilnius–Klaipėda and Kaunas–Šiauliai. It will remain an important part of the east–west rail route, but it is uncertain how the existing slower line via Šiauliai will be affected once the new high-speed north–south Rail Baltica service opens via Panevėžys. Currently there are rail services between Šiauliai and Vilnius (2hrs 16mins; 8 per day), Kaunas (2hrs; 2 per day), Klaipėda (2hrs 6mins; 7 per day) and Riga (1hr 49mins; 1 per day).

**TOURIST INFORMATION** The **Šiauliai Tourism Information Centre** (Siauliu turizmo informacijos centras; Vilniaus gatvė 213-90; w visitsiauliai.lt; ⊕ 09.00–18.00 Mon–Fri, 10.00–16.00 Sat, 10.00–14.00 Sun) is run by an enthusiastic team keen to share their city. It contains excellent interactive exhibits in the **Balts Road** educational section, covering the history and culture of the region in a fun, accessible way. Bike rental is also available.

**WHERE TO STAY** *Map, page 254*

Hotels in Šiauliai accommodate more business travellers and NATO soldiers than tourists, so cosy boutique hotels are yet to materialise. For location and service, the following are our recommendations for where to lay your head and refuel.

**Park Hotel** (14 rooms) S Lukauskio gatvė 5A; w parkhotelsiauliai.lt. Renovated in 2021, the Park Hotel is a cosy contemporary property in a leafy green area of the city centre. Dbl & quad rooms; small spa & gym. **€€€**

**Saulys Hotel** (42 rooms) Vasario 16-osios gatvė 40; w saulys.lt. A business-class hotel in the centre with a small spa zone & a smart restaurant serving European cuisine. **€€€**

**Hotel Šiauliai** (30 rooms) Draugystės prospektas 25; w hotelsiauliai.lt. A throwback to the old days, this hotel still has a travel agency, hairdressers & nightclub on site. Stay here for a bit of nostalgia & a cheap rate. €€

## ✖ WHERE TO EAT AND DRINK  *Map, below*

The dining scene in Šiauliai is constantly improving and you can eat well for less here. Interestingly, the local brewery is Gubernija (w gubernija.lt), but we have not found its beers for sale locally. If you solve this mystery of why or where, please let us know.

**Bleu de Frenkel**  Chaim Frenkel Villa, Vilniaus gatvė 74; bleudefrenkel_restoranas; ⊕ noon–21.00 Mon, 11.00–22.00 Tue–Thu, 11.00–23.00 Fri–Sat, 11.00–21.00 Sun. Come

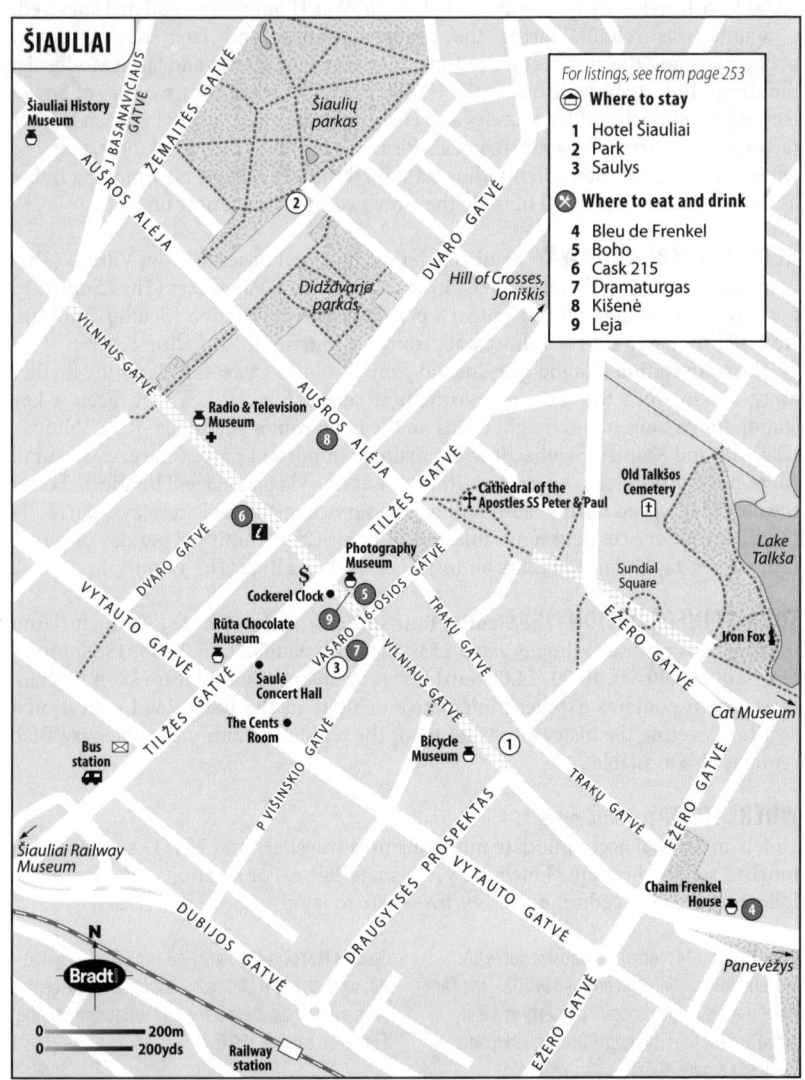

## ✶ PAKRUOJIS MANOR

A 40km drive east of Šiauliai amid the northern plains of central Lithuania lies **Pakruojis Manor** (Pakruojo dvaras; Parko gatvė 1, Pakruojis; w pakruojo-dvaras.lt). The 19th-century manor complex and parkland is dedicated to reviving manor life for all to enjoy. Within the estate are two hotels, a restaurant, museums, crafts and artisans. The main manor house is home to the boutique-style **Palace Hotel** [map, page 252] (11 rooms; €€€€€) boasting lavishly decorated Classical en-suite rooms full of antiques and certainly fit for a baron or baroness. A short walk from the manor house is **The Miller's House Hotel** [map, page 252] (22 rooms; €€€) offering charming cosy accommodation with triples and quads for families. Next door is the **Inn Traktierius** (€€€), a typical rustic tavern serving wholesome dishes, regional beers, and breakfast of course. For more upmarket and opulent dining, the **Manor House Restaurant** (€€€€) opens in the main manor house at weekends or for special occasions; book in advance to guarantee a table. Spa services are available, including massage, treatments and sauna. Note that the price of overnight accommodation at Pakruojis Manor includes tickets for any event being held during your stay. And events are commonplace here, because entertainment is the name of the game – not in a wild party fashion, but more akin to a cultural extravaganza. First of all is the celebration of Pakruojis Manor's history through the **Manor Farm**, including horseriding, a technical museum and falconry. Then back in the manor house are **crafts workshops**, including a perfumer, dressmaker, potter and beekeeper. **Pakruojis Manor Distillery** creates infused spirits using estate-grown botanicals. A portrait photographer is also on hand with vintage props to capture your stay. Alongside these permanent activities, Pakruojis hosts an array of **festivals** throughout the year which fill the grounds with spectacular entertainment, including a colourful Spring Flower Festival (April–May), winter festivals and a Brewing Festival.

here to experience fine dining (& fine wines) in the beautiful Art Nouveau atmosphere of Chaim Frenkel Villa. Summer seating on the terrace overlooks the gardens. Booking is advised for evenings & w/ends. €€€€
**Dramaturgas** Vasario 16-osios gatvė 42; f dramaturgas.siauliai; 11.30–23.00 Sun–Thu, 11.30–04.00 Fri–Sat. A classy industrial design brings the drama, world cuisine dishes bring the colour & DJs at the w/end bring the dancing. One of the trendiest places in the city. €€€€
**Boho** Vilniaus gatvė 134; f boho.siauliai; 11.00–23.00 Sun–Thu, 11.00–midnight Fri–Sat. This warm & welcoming place has a sugary-sweet ambience, also serving European dishes alongside its desserts. €€€

**Cask 215** Vilniaus gatvė 215; f cask215; 11.00–23.00 Mon–Thu, 11.00–midnight Fri, noon–01.00 Sat, noon–20.00 Sun. Burgers & ribs are on the menu at this gastropub, with cocktails or beer to wash down hefty servings of meat. €€€
**Leja** Vilniaus gatvė 138; f LejaCafe; 11.00–23.00 daily. Creative dining, smart but relaxed, attracts families on special occasions for a treat. Perfect for a lighter, less meaty lunch or dinner. €€€
✶ **Kišenė** Aušros alėja 13; f BarasKisene; 11.00–midnight Mon–Fri, 15.00–midnight Sat–Sun. Kišenė is one of the oldest pubs in Šiauliai – a friendly bohemian bar with a true pub spirit & local character, serving pub food & good beers. €€

**ENTERTAINMENT** **Saulė Concert Hall** (Saulė koncertų salė; Tilžės gatvė 140; w saule.lt) is the main venue for indoor events throughout the year, including song and dance performances, drama and music concerts. The building houses Lithuania's largest stained-glass window, by legendary artist Kazys Morkunas (1929–2008), an explosion of colour covering 200m$^2$ and depicting scenes from the historic 1236 Battle of the Sun (Saulės Mūšis). The window is best appreciated from inside the building with daylight behind it.

**OTHER PRACTICALITIES** There is a **post office** (Tilžės gatvė 109) on the ground floor of the Saulės Miestas centre, and nearby a **bank** (Vilniaus gatvė 193) and **pharmacy** (Vilniaus gatvė 174).

**WHAT TO SEE AND DO** Šiauliai has a disproportionate number of quirky museums, too many to list here, so if you are curious (telephony, cinema, angel or water management enthusiasts listen up), enquire at the tourist information centre for details.

**Šiauliai 'Aušros' Museum** (w ausrosmuziejus.lt) The museum was started in 1923 and named after the first Lithuanian language newspaper, *Aušros*. It is now an umbrella organisation for multiple local museums in Šiauliai, finding strength through partnership and shared resources.

* **Šiauliai History Museum** (Šiaulių istorijos muziejus; Aušros alėja 47; w ausrosmuziejus.lt/sam-education-center; ⊕ 10.00–18.00 Tue–Fri, 11.00–17.00 Sat–Sun; €5/2.50) Although housed in this same place since the 1930s, the museum was revamped in 2019 with great success. The history of the region is told through clear displays, with many local stories and personal contributions. The highlight must be the open repositories on the top floor; it is an ethnographic treasure trove. Artefacts in beautiful condition, including intricately hand-woven sashes, traditional clothing, dolls, baskets, ceramics and woodwork, are carefully stored behind glass. Larger objects, including lovingly painted dowry chests, sun crosses and Užgavėnės masks (page 62), are openly displayed. Many of these handcrafted items would have been used traditionally when negotiating a dowry, so it was important for boys and girls to learn the skills necessary to showcase or attract attention in this way. A boy might ornately carve a towel hanger, while a girl would embroider a towel, to the best of their abilities, hoping for a good match. Substituting someone else's superior craftmanship for one's own in order to appear a better catch was not unheard of – only to be found out once they were committed to married life. The top floor is accessible by lift.

**Chaim Frenkel House** (Chaimo Frenkelio vila; Vilniaus gatvė 74; w ausrosmuziejus.lt/chaimas-frenkelis-villa; ◨ ChaimoFrenkeliovila; ⊕ 10.00–18.00 Tue–Fri, 11.00–17.00 Sat–Sun; €5/2.50) Chaim Frenkel (1851–1920) was one of the most successful industrialists in Šiauliai. Born into a Jewish family, he was expected to become a rabbi, but his instincts led him to drop out of his studies and learn the skill of leatherwork; at the age of 25 he established his leather factory on this site. His innovative approach saw the factory thrive, and with approximately 1,000 employees it was one of the largest leather-processing and shoe factories in the world. Frenkel's wealth enabled him to pursue various philanthropic projects, including setting up the city's first hospital and several Jewish schools. He and his wife, Dora, commissioned the building of their fine Art Nouveau villa in 1908, along with the surrounding gardens. The exterior of the villa is eye catching, and the interior does not disappoint having been painstakingly restored true to its authentic

Art Nouveau and Jugendstil style, including curved woodwork, geometric patterns and intricately decorated ceilings. During World War II, when Nazi Germany occupied Lithuania, a Jewish ghetto was established close to the Frenkel factory. Chaim had passed away, but Dora remained at the villa until she was forced to move to the ghetto, where she died. All Jewish workers at the factory were laid off, but it was soon apparent that their skills were needed to continue the production of leather for the Nazi regime, providing salvation for some. An exhibition focuses on the interwar period in Šiauliai, when production at the factory was at its peak; and the city's Jewish heritage – upon which more focus is planned as Šiauliai has an active Jewish community and many visitors to the villa have Jewish connections. The villa houses art exhibitions, concerts, cultural events and film festivals. A free audio guide in English is available and an official 1-hour tour in English can be booked in advance. The villa also has a fine dining restaurant, Bleu de Frenkel (page 254).

The former factory buildings run alongside the villa grounds and along the footpath are highly informative information boards telling the story of the Frenkel enterprise. Look out for the collection of shoes that has been created along the iron railings. The grounds include a rose garden and are open to the public. Every summer a music festival is held in the grounds, with concerts throughout July and August (check their Facebook page for details). The villa is on the edge of the city centre, a 20 minute walk from the tourism information centre.

**Bicycle Museum** (Dviračių muziejus; Vilniaus gatvė 139; w ausrosmuziejus.lt/bicycle-museum; ⊕ 10.00–18.00 Tue–Fri, 11.00–17.00 Sat–Sun; €5/2.50) This is a niche little museum, another legacy of Šiauliai's former industrial glory – the city was the centre of bicycle manufacturing in the USSR under the local bicycle factory Vairas. It is nothing flashy, but a genuine tribute to the bicycle, full of nostalgia and interesting facts, and of course you can try a selection of different bikes. See if you can spot the homemade bicycles. Ask for the free audio guide in English.

**Radio and Television Museum** (Radijo ir televizijos muziejus; Vilniaus gatvė 174; w ausrosmuziejus.lt/radio-and-television-museum; ⊕ 10.00–17.00 Wed–Fri, 11.00–17.00 Sat–Sun; €2/1) This quirky small museum is well worth a visit, and, if you have time, pay extra for a guided tour (€10 per group) to bring these inanimate objects to life. Kids of today will be bemused at the size of the apparatus and clunky buttons of old. The museum pays homage to Šiauliai's history as a television-manufacturing centre from the 1970s until the factory closure in 1993. At its peak the Šiauliai television factory had 8,000 employees, producing the first Lithuanian monochrome and later colour 'Tauras' television sets. Supporting the factory were recreation facilities, a health centre, a local newspaper and housing complex.

**Šiauliai Railway Museum** (Šiaulių geležinkelio muziejus; Dubijos gatvė 26; w ltgmuziejus.lt; ⊕ 09.00–noon & 13.00–18.00 Tue–Sat; €4/2) Since its launch in 1971 the museum collection has grown to over 6,000 pieces. Indoors, old photographs show life on the historic railways, railway paraphernalia is on display, and a model railway prompts many visitors to revisit the dream of building their own in the attic/garage/shed. The outdoor exhibits steal the show, with two steam locomotives, a collection of coaches and machinery. The downside for international visitors is that the museum guides might not speak English, so you will need to improvise with a translation app, or book a local guide to act as translator through the tourist information centre.

**Rūta Chocolate Museum** (Rūtos šokolado muziejus; Tilžės gatvė 133; w ruta.lt; ⏰ 10.00–19.00 Tue–Fri, 10.00–17.00 Sat; €5/3) Rūta is the last remaining chocolate manufacturer of Šiauliai (there were ten during the interwar period). Standard entry gains you access to the museum to learn about chocolate and how it came to Lithuania. But you can upgrade your ticket to include a guide and a chocolate workshop (€25/18), for chocolate tastings and to create your own chocolate, or bypass the museum and go straight to the sweet stuff with a chocolate-workshop-only ticket (€20/15). Professional chocolatier classes are also available.

**Photography Museum** (Fotografijos muziejus; Vilniaus gatvė 140; w fotomuziejus.lt; ⏰ 10.00–18.00 Tue–Fri, 11.00–17.00 Sat–Sun; €5/2.50) This private museum focusses not only on photography exhibitions but also on preserving Lithuanian visual heritage, and has amassed a collection of more than 150,000 objects – photographs, prints and equipment are all stored here – with rotating exhibitions covering local, national and international photography of contemporary and historical subject matter. The museum also runs creative workshops for small groups. The building is of distinctive interwar-period design with a flat roof, upon which you can visit the camera obscura for an additional €1 per person. The roof terrace affords wide-ranging views of the city centre.

**Cathedral of the Apostles St Peter and St Paul** (Šv. apaštalų Petro ir Pauliaus katedra; Aušros takas 3; w siauliukatedra.lt) Restored and reconstructed many times since it was first built from wood in 1445, the cathedral now dominates the Šiauliai skyline with its statuesque 70m-tall tower. It is possible to access a viewpoint up the tower, but this needs to be prebooked with a guide and the best chance is at the weekend – contact the tourist information centre for guidance on this. During

> **THE HILL OF CROSSES**
>
> Always open to visitors, the Hill of Crosses (Kryžių kalnas) is Lithuania's iconic pilgrimage site. You do not need to be religious to appreciate the significance of this symbol of faith and resilience of the Lithuanian people, or to be awestruck by the sheer number of crosses, crucifixes, rosaries and religious statues that have been placed here. The practice of bringing crosses here – originally a castle hill called Jurgaičiai Mound – is believed to have started in the 19th century after the failed uprising against the Russian Empire in 1863–64. The Tsar's government banned the public display of crosses, ripping them down and causing great insult to Lithuanians. The effect was counter-productive, stirring up feelings of defiance and strengthening individuals' faith. People began to place crosses on the hill; it became a symbol of faith, of resilience and of national identity.
>
> During the period of Soviet occupation atheism was actively promoted and religion, especially Roman Catholicism, was suppressed. The Soviets destroyed the site several times in an attempt to quash religious faith and national identity. But they underestimated the resilience of the Lithuanian people and it was always rebuilt – placing a cross here was a powerful act of resistance.
>
> Today the Hill of Crosses is a national monument and one of the most-visited attractions in Lithuania, attracting thousands of pilgrims and tourists every year. Climb the steps up and into the hill, exploring smaller paths, strewn with crucifixes and rosaries, that wind through the crosses. Take time to read the messages and note the global audience that has visited this spiritual site. On a windy day the

the Soviet occupation, access to the tower was forbidden to prevent espionage as Šiauliai airport is only 6.5km away and can be seen from the viewpoint. The airport was one of the largest military airports in the Soviet Union, but today it is home to the Lithuanian Air Force and a NATO airbase. It was only in 1997 that the church became a cathedral after Pope John Paul II instructed the founding of Šiauliai Diocese. Inside, the cathedral is pure and simple in white. On the exterior, be sure to look for the sun-dial clock on the right side of the church.

**Cat Museum** (Katinų muziejus; Žuvininkų gatvė 18; w gamtininkucentras.lt/katinu-muziejus; ⏲ 09.00–17.00 Tue–Fri, 09.00–16.00 Sat; €5/3) If you are a cat lover and in Šiauliai, how can you not visit the cat museum? It was founded in 1990 by Vanda Kavaliauskienė (1923–2011), and her legacy lives on here. There are real cats to pet and an array of cat-themed collectibles, including a stained-glass window of cats. As with most collectible themed museums, feel free to bring a cat trinket to donate to the collection, though be prepared to take it home again if they already have it. Either way, it'll be a half-hour well spent if you like cats.

**The Cents Room** (Centų kambarys; Šiauliai Academy Information Centre, Vytauto gatvė 84; w biblioteka.vu.lt; ⏲ 25 Jun–31 Aug 08.00–17.00 Mon–Thu, 08.00–15.45 Fri, rest of year 08.00–19.00 Mon–Fri, 10.00–15.00 Sat; free) The Cents Room is another unique oddity for Šiauliai. Thanks to the collaborative creativity of the Union of Non-Governmental Organizations of Šiauliai (SANOS), the university rector, library director, a student and a sculptor (Vilius Puronas), this tribute to the Lithuanian litas centai coin was unveiled on 16 February 2015 (Independence Day). A total of 157,130 cents are stuck to the walls (worth around €1,000 today). Since 2012, here also resides the largest book in Lithuania, *Aukuras Salduvei* (Altar for Salduvė), which can be

crosses gently tinkle in the wind. Since independence, visitor numbers have increased dramatically, resulting in the mass of crosses spreading beyond the mound. In 1993, Pope John Paul II visited, a highly significant event for Lithuania. He performed mass in front of a huge crowd from the nearby small chapel that was constructed specially. He also later encouraged the construction of the Franciscan Monastery close by.

At the **Hill of Crosses Information Centre** (Šiaulių rajono turizmo informacijos centras; w siauliurajonas.lt; ⏲ Apr–May 09.00–18.00 daily, Jun–Aug 09.00–19.00 daily, Sep 09.00–18.00 daily, Oct–Mar 09.00–17.00 daily) facilities include a souvenir shop, refreshments and toilets. It is a short walk along a well-paved and illuminated footpath, with benches available should a rest be needed.

The **Hill of Crosses** is 11.5km north of Šiauliai, on the eastern side of the main A12/E77 highway. The drive is straightforward: turn off the highway after 10km and follow the brown sign 'Kryžių kalnas'. Parking costs €1 per car. If visiting by **bus**, note that public buses between Šiauliai and Joniškis run almost hourly, but not on Sundays. The bus stop is on the highway at the third stop from Šiauliai, called 'Domantai' (€1.50 one way). It is a 2km walk to the hill from the bus stop. Be sure to check the bus times carefully to ensure your onward or return journey is possible. A bicycle track is adjacent to the A12/E77 highway between Šiauliai and Joniškis – follow the brown signs when you get 10km north of Šiauliai or 30km south of Joniškis.

found in the reception area on the first floor. The book is dedicated to the history of Lithuania and is written in a special ink that will not fade for 300 years.

**Šiauliai Boulevard** (Vilniaus gatvė) Locals will tell you that in 1975 Šiauliai was brave: it was the first city in Lithuania to pedestrianise its central street, and only the third city to do so in Europe, after Rotterdam in 1972 and Erfurt in 1973. Originally built in the 18th century, Vilniaus gatvė was a historical road running from east to west, and crossing Tilžės gatvė, which runs north to south. At this crossroads, you will find the **Cockerel Clock** (Laikrodis gaidys), a popular meeting place where, in its prime, the lofty cockerel would flap its wings and announce the time every hour. Having lost the will to live during Soviet times, the cockerel was revived in 2003 and now proudly welcomes visitors to Šiauliai at noon and 18.00. Reclaiming the street from vehicles to create the 1.28km-long boulevard has transformed the area and created a central hub of commerce and leisure. You will find most services available here, including restaurants and cafés, many of which spill out on to the boulevard in summer.

**Around Sundial Square** (Saulės laikrodžio aikštė, Ežero gatvė 64) Here stands the tallest **sundial** in Lithuania, built in 1986 to commemorate Šiauliai's 750th anniversary. It towers an impressive 18m and is topped with the golden statue of *The Archer* (Šaulys), whose long shadow tells the time on sunny days (how liberating to switch off from time on cloudy days). The area also includes an amphitheatre and temple-style entrance. Walk through neighbouring Old Talkšos Catholic cemetery with its ethereal crypts and mausoleums, before arriving at the shore of Lake Talkša where you will find another iconic sculpture of the city – the **Iron Fox** (Geležinė lapė), designed by sculptor Vilius Puronas and standing here, proudly posing for selfies, since 2009. From the southern end of pedestrianised Vilniaus gatvė, at Hotel Šiauliai, it is a 500m walk along S Šalkauskio gatvė to the square.

## JONIŠKIS

Joniškis is a typical northern Lithuanian market town dating back to the 16th century. The town experienced its heyday during the 19th century when it thrived on trade between the Lithuanian agricultural producers of flax and tobacco and the commercial hub and port of Riga. The town had a significant Jewish population, all of whom were murdered or fled during the Nazi occupation of World War II, and today the Joniškis synagogue complex is one of the main attractions for visitors and those with Jewish heritage.

Located on the main road A12/E77 between Šiauliai and Riga, Joniškis is on the route taken to visit the Hill of Crosses (30km south of Joniškis), though traffic through the town centre has recently been relieved by the construction of a bypass. While the bypass has improved the town centre for the local population, it has caused a reduction in passing trade. But do stop off here if you can for a slice of real life, to grab a local lunch and see some lesser-visited sights. These include the quirky, independent **Basketball Museum** (Joniškio krepšinio muziejus; Livonijos gatvė 3; \+370 612 89 986; pre-booking essential; €5 pp) and the **Joniškis Synagogue Complex** (Miesto aikstė 4A-B; w joniskiomuziejus.lt) consisting of the White and Red synagogues, both restored and housing exhibitions about Jewish culture in Joniškis, as well as the town's history. You will also find a small **Table Tennis Museum** in the Šiaurės Vartai hotel (see opposite). For an in-depth dive into Joniškis' history visit **Joniškis History and Culture Museum** (Joniškio istorijos ir kultūros muziejus;

Vilniaus gatvė 6; w joniskiomuziejus.lt; ⏰ 08.00–noon & 12.45–18.00 Mon–Thu, 08.00–noon & 12.45–16.45 Fri, 10.00–noon & 12.45–16.00 Sat; €4/2).

**GETTING THERE AND AWAY** Direct **buses** run between Joniškis and Vilnius (3hrs 55mins; 2 per day), Kaunas (3hrs 45mins; 1 per day) and Šiauliai (55mins; 16 per day). The bus station (Joniškio autobusų parkas; Vilniaus gatvė 54) is located south of the city, a walkable 1.3km from the tourist information centre.

The **train station** (Joniškio geležinkelio stotis; Stoties gatvė 26) is similarly located south of the city – it is a short walk between the bus and train stations for connecting services. It is on the main line between Vilnius and Riga. One train per day runs from Joniškis to Riga (1hr 12mins), and one train per day runs from Joniškis to Vilnius (1hr 45min). Once the new route of the high-speed Rail Baltica service opens, Joniškis will no longer be on the main international line and at the time of writing it is uncertain how services will be affected.

**TOURIST INFORMATION** The **Joniškis Tourism Information** (Joniškio turizmo ir verslo informacijos centras; Žemaičių gatvė 9; w visitjoniskis.lt; ⏰ 08.00–18.00 Mon–Fri, 08.00–16.45 Fri, 10.00–14.00 Sat) can help plan your visit whether short and sweet or more involved.

 **WHERE TO STAY AND EAT**

**Šiaurės Vartai** (18 rooms) Upytės gatvė 5a; w siauresvartai.lt. The main central hotel, this is a family-run business with sgl, dbl & larger deluxe rooms. Sauna available for hire (€50 for 3hrs). Also, the unexpected home to Joniškis' small Table Tennis Museum, which is free to visit – enquire at the hotel reception. **€€**

✱ **Virtienių restoranėlis**  Miesto aikštė 1; virtieniurestoranelis; ⏰ 08.30–18.00 Mon–Wed, 08.30–18.00 Fri, 10.00–17.00 Sat. This restaurant is famous for its traditional *virtieniai* dumpling dishes. Every grandma in the region had their own dumpling filling recipe & creations varied from house to house. Local kids would be raised on virtieniai at least once a week, with curd & tarragon the basic filling. At the restaurant you will find at least 21 different fillings on the menu. Order a selection & you will get 7 dumplings, each the size of a match box, & the fillings will only be revealed when you cut the dumplings apart. Perfect for a lunch stop during your journey. **€€**

## ŽAGARĖ  *with Sarah Mitrikė*

Žagarė is a historic border town, first documented in 1254, making it almost as old as Riga. With a pre-World War I population of more than 14,000 compared with today's figure of just over 1,000, it is no surprise that Žagarė has a large diaspora around the world, many of whom are Jewish and return to visit the birthplace of their ancestors and to make their own connections with the land. Local history is treasured; and the thriving, close-knit community full of artistic souls continues to buck the trend of declining rural towns with its own slow revolution and as a vibrant cultural hub hosting annual festivals and attracting new creative residents. Surrounded by the nature of Žagarė Regional Park, the town itself is divided by the Švėtė River between old and new Žagarė, as symbolised by the two keys which make up its coat of arms. The cobbled streets and red-brick buildings of the Old Town centre are reminders that Žagarė was an important Jewish shtetl, the large central square playing an important role for market trading.

**GETTING THERE AND AWAY** The bus station (Žagarės autobusų stotis; Kęstučio gatvė 31) is served by direct **buses** to/from Joniškis (40mins; 6 per day) and Kaunas

(4hrs 25mins; 2 per day), with an additional stop made at the Church of St Peter and St Paul on Kęstučio gatvė. If travelling **by car** from Joniškis, you will arrive through the avenue of old oaks. Park at the regional park visitor centre as the town is best explored on foot.

**TOURIST INFORMATION** The excellent **Žagarė Regional Park Visitor Centre** (Žagarės regioninis parkas; Malūno gatvė 1; ZagaresRegioninisParkas; 08.00–17.00 Tue–Fri, 10.00–15.00 Sat) at Žagarė Manor can arrange general sightseeing, Jewish history and nature tours; these must be booked in advance. Activities including bike rental, fishing, hiking and birdwatching are also available. Contact Maarten, Žagarė's local resident Belgian (w balticguides.com), for local guided tours and also airport transfers to Žagarė.

 **WHERE TO STAY**

**Anas Namas** (2 rooms) Naujoji gatvė 12; w booking.com/hotel/lt/anas-namas. This centrally located self-catering guest house has 2 bedrooms, 1 bathroom, a dining area & fully equipped kitchen, together with a terrace & garden. €€

**Sodyba Prie Malūno Dolce Vita** Raktuvės gatvė 28; SodybaPrieMalunoDOLCEVITA; camping May–Sep. Lithuanian-Italian artisan couple Jurga & Seba run this welcoming homestead, where on site they also create authentic Italian pizzas at their pizzeria, Dolce Vita ( Mar–Nov w/ends only; €€), & Venetian glass beads & jewellery in their craft studio, Laboratorio d'arte. You can camp (tent or caravan/camper) or rent a static caravan in the garden next to their old windmill, not far from Žvelgaitis hill & the lake. Shower, toilet & laundry room. €

**Žagarė Campsite** Malūno gatvė 1; zagarecampsite. Located adjacent to the manor house in the grounds of a former dairy, this quirky campsite has tent pitches & motorhome/camper areas. Facilities include shower, toilet, small kitchenette & hammocks. €

**Žagarė Manor** (28 beds) Malūno gatvė 1. Have you ever spent a night in a museum? Well, you can in Žagarė. Within Žagarė Manor (Žagarės dvaras), above the regional park visitor centre, you can overnight in one of their sgl/twin guest rooms or dorms sleeping up to 8. Bathrooms, & a kitchenette for preparing your own meals, are separate in the corridor. A unique experience for €20 pp per night. €

 **WHERE TO EAT AND DRINK**

**Švedlaukis Café** Miesto aikštė 27; 11.00–14.00 Mon–Fri. Located on the main square, with extra seating in the courtyard behind, this is an ideal place to stop for lunch. Simple daily lunch menu. €€

**Žagarė Bagels** (Žagarės Beigeliai) Mikse Studio, Šiaulių gatvė 12; zagares_beigeliai. Once a month, Mikse Studio transforms into a pop-up artisan bagel café so you can taste the Jewish heritage of Žagarė for yourself. At other times you can place an order in advance. Contact them in advance of your visit to check their opening times or arrange an order. €

**WHAT TO SEE AND DO**

**Žagarė Manor and Park** (Žagarės dvaras; Malūno gatvė 1; 08.00–17.00 Tue–Fri, 10.00–15.00 Sat opening hours; €2/1) There has been a manor house in Žagarė since the first half of the 16th century. The present building, though, including the ensemble gatehouses and impressive neighbouring horse stud, were rebuilt in the 19th century under the ownership of nobleman Count Naryshkin – hence its former name of Naryshkin Palace and Park. The architectural style is noticeably different to other Lithuanian manors, as Naryshkin was influenced by the motherland of his English wife, with some materials even imported for certain elements. The paths of the surrounding park are said to display the coat of arms of the Naryshkin family, when viewed from above. The ground floor houses the Žagarė Regional Park Visitor Centre (see opposite).

**Pan House** (Edmundo Vaičiulio puodų namas; P Cvirkos gatvė 31; w visitjoniskis.lt/house-of-pots-with-museum-in-zagare-2; donations welcome) The creator of this unique museum, Edmundas Vaičiulis, is as characterful and unique as the place itself. This is Žagarė's version of Narnia. Vaičiulis' collection of local historic memorabilia ranges from the obvious pots and pans adorning his house roof to an original copy of the Torah. Combined with his own sculptures, wood carvings including masks, and other artistic creations, it is a truly eccentric experience. For entry, knock on the gate.

**Žagarė Synagogue Complex** (Žagarės sinagogų kompleksas; P Avižonio gatvė 7A) Žagarė undeniably has a tragic past, the mass grave site on the edge of town bearing the bodies of more victims of the Holocaust than there are living residents of the town today. But it keeps Jewish culture alive here through heritage days and other events. One of the remaining synagogue buildings (there were nine) and the bath house are undergoing renovation, and a memorial walk from the town to the mass grave site takes place annually at the end of September together with the Šiauliai Jewish Community.

**Scarecrow Factory** (Kaliausių Fabrikėlis) Švėtės gatvė 22; f zagares.kaliauses. The guardian angels of the annual Cherry Festival (see below) are the scarecrows that pop up all over town during the summer months to protect the annual crop of delicious fruits. You can get involved anytime of the year by taking part in a workshop at folk artist Aušra's Scarecrow Factory, located on the bank of the Švėtė River, followed by a sampling of tasty local cherry jam. Aušra is a member of the Lithuanian Folk Art Union and also offers doll-making workshops in her doll museum (Lėlių namai; Vilniaus gatvė 6). Visits and workshops must be organised in advance by contacting Aušra via Facebook.

## ŽAGARĖ FESTIVALS

**CHERRY FESTIVAL** (Žagarės vyšnių festivalis; f ZagaresVysniuFestivalis) Having both a variety of cherry tree (Žagarvyšnė) and a cherry liqueur (Žagarės vyšnių) named after the town, Žagarė has long been known throughout Lithuania, though not many knew where the town was, or had reason to visit – until the arrival of the Žagarė Cherry Festival in 2005. The festival takes place every year on the third weekend of July, with a full 3-day programme of events across the town, including a large market and entertainment in the main square during the day, and moving to the main stage by Lake Žvelgaitis for pop concerts on both Friday and Saturday nights. Concert tickets are €5.

**FRINGE FESTIVAL** w zagarefringe.com. Žagarė was Lithuania's Capital of Culture in 2015, and to mark the occasion a new festival was born. Tapping into friends' networks and the World Fringe Network, this festival brings contemporary culture into the heart of this unique rural environment, turning old buildings and street corners into venues for a weekend, with performers, artists and musicians from all over the world. It is a biennial festival which takes place on 'odd years' in May.

> **WOODEN CHURCHES OF LITHUANIA**
>
> Lithuania has hundreds of wooden churches and chapels dotted across the country, most dating from the 18th and 19th centuries. It is astounding that so many have survived, having been at the mercy of fire, lightning, conflict, vandalism, anti-religious authorities and neglect. Whatever your religious position, these often-colourful monuments to folk architecture are a joy to stumble across in villages, towns or remote locations. Some are plain and simple, others more elaborate; all are well maintained by dedicated local parishioners and priests. The size of a church reflected the size of the local population when it was built, with many now feeling oversized for today's depleted rural settlements. However, they remain the hub of communities and testify to Lithuania's strong Catholic faith. The interiors vary tremendously, as unique in style as their exteriors, and incorporate folk art often determined by the available skills of local craftspeople.
>
> During your travels, you will see many smaller road shrines, carved saints and pole shrines along most routes. Less common are wooden Orthodox churches, synagogues and mosques, some of which have suffered badly over the years and either await renovation or are beyond saving. The wooden churches of Lithuania have been well catalogued online by Sakrali Lietuva (w sakralilietuva.lt), an excellent project that documents the sacred wooden architecture of Lithuania. The region of Žemaitija has a large concentration of well-preserved wooden churches, so do stop and take a walk in the grounds, or peek inside if the church is open. Lithuania's faith is strongly connected to its national identity, both of which have had to fight oppression to exist today.

**Second Church of St Peter and St Paul** (Žagarės II-oji Šv. apaštalų Petro ir Povilo bažnyčia; Švėtės gatvė 1) This church is known locally as Barbora's Church after a devout young woman called Barbora of Žagarė (1578–1604), who died tragically young. She had many miracles attributed to her. It is said that long ago the church burned down, her body was inside and unlike the others who turned to ash, her body remained intact (this was confirmed by a physical examination in 1963). It was also believed that those who prayed through her intercession experienced recovery from illness, so much so that in 2005 the process for her beatification and canonisation was begun. Her body was removed from the crypt during the Soviet occupation, but now there is a replacement coffin in place and you can see the heavily worn ground where, for hundreds of years, people have come to kneel and ask for her healing and help.

**Mūšos Tyrelis Nature Trail** (Mūšos Tyrelio pažintinis takas; w visitjoniskis.lt/swamp-musos-tyrelis-trail) Located 15km south of Žagarė, but within the Žagarė Regional Park territory, this is the longest boardwalk (7km) through a swamp in Lithuania and it was established to protect the unique local flora and fauna from extinction. There are information stands along the route, which navigates past the only natural lake in the district. Trust us, a hike through swampland is far better than it might sound!

## NORTHERN ŽEMAITIJA

Few international tourists visit northern Žemaitija along the border of Lithuania and Latvia. There are no major attractions, although each town or city has its own regional museum proudly showcasing its history, ethnography and archaeological finds. Most foreigners found exploring this area are on a family heritage tour, or in the region for business and on their day off. It is a popular region with locals who seek a rural lifestyle in a quieter corner of the country. The town of **Akmenė** is divided into three zones named I, II and III simply because it developed in size, Akmenė I being the oldest part, and II and III coming later. Akmenės II is home to the **Kamanai State Nature Reserve Visitor Centre** (Pušų gatvė 2; ⊕ 08.00–17.00 Tue–Fri, 10.00–15.00 Sat) where you can learn about, and arrange access to, the **Kamanai State Strict Nature Reserve** (Kamanų valstybinis gamtinis rezervatas), a land of wetland, swamps and rich biodiversity 10km northwest of the visitor centre. It is forbidden to enter the reserve without permission, but those who do visit are rewarded with an oasis of peace and unspoilt nature that can be viewed from the 30m-tall observation tower.

The main town of **Mažeikiai** is an industrial town dominated by its huge oil refinery plant, the only one in the Baltic countries. Although the refinery itself is about 20km west of the town, Mažeikiai is heavily dependent on it for employment. To visit or find out more, contact the **Mažeikiai Tourism and Business Information Centre** (Mažeikių turizmo ir verslo informacijos centras; Vasario 16-osios gatvė; w visit.mazeikiai.lt). A 30km drive southwest of Mažeikiai is **Renavas Manor** (Renavo dvaras; w renavodvaras.lt), the only renovated manor house in the region that is open to the public and a popular venue for weddings and private parties. It was once famed for its library collection and, although the manor was nationalised and converted into offices for a Soviet collective farm, the interior is beautifully restored and the library gallery and spiral staircase are a unique highlight.

## ŽEMAITIJA NATIONAL PARK

Established soon after independence in 1991, Žemaitija National Park (Žemaitijos nacionalinis parkas) is famed for its natural beauty and rich cultural heritage. Most tourist sites and places of interest are centred around Lake Plateliai (Platelių ežeras), the largest lake in Žemaitija region and the clearest lake in Lithuania – characteristics that attract abundant wildlife, swimmers and scuba divers. In 2008 the lakeside town of **Plateliai** won a European Commission EDEN (European Destinations of Excellence) award for its unique traditional customs, and it is a highlight to learn about their annual celebration of Užgavėnės. The small, quaint town offers activities, cultural museums and refreshments and is often the starting point for touring the national park. Within the park are numerous hiking routes, opportunities to swim in the lakes, observe nature, birdwatch, and relax in rural farmstead accommodations. The ethnographic heritage of this region is proudly on display and sightseeing comes naturally as you tour – rustic wooden farmsteads, forest glades and dappled light, wildflower meadows, glistening lakes, castle mounds, folk architecture and road shrines. Not only is cultural heritage a visual delight, it should also be sampled in a local restaurant serving traditional seasonal dishes – then you will be a true friend of Samogitia. Look out for *šiupinys* (a pot of mashed potatoes, boiled peas, pieces of pork and boiled cereals) or *cibulynė* (a cold soup made with fried herring, lots of onion, vinegar and cold water).

**GETTING THERE AND AWAY** Plateliai bus station (Platelių autobusų stotis; cnr Žemaičių Kalvarija gatvė & Stoties gatvė) is more of a bus stop, in the centre of the town with everything in walking distance. Local **buses** 24A, 24B, 24C, 25A, 25B operate between Plungė bus station and Plateliai, approximately two buses per day on each route mostly in the morning and late afternoon/evening to service commuters.

**TOURIST INFORMATION** The Žemaitija National Park Visitor Centre (Žemaitijos nacionalinis parkas; Didžioji gatvė 8, Plateliai; w zemaitijosnp.lt; ⊕ 08.00–17.00 Mon–Thu, 08.00–15.45 Fri; entrance €1) has an exhibition about Samogitia and plenty of useful tourism information.

## WHERE TO STAY AND EAT

**Dubgiris Villa** [map, page 252] (14 rooms) Pušynės gatvė 28, Uikių region; w dubgiris.lt. This hunting-lodge-style country hotel is situated on the western shore of Lake Plinkšės, just outside the national park. Lake Plinkšės is a tranquil nature reserve, where sunset accompanied by birdsong is a memorable experience. From the site, you can cycle, hike to Panų kalno wooden chapel, swim, hire a rowing boat, or read your book. In addition to its 12 dbl rooms & 2 luxury suites, it has a good on-site restaurant, spa area with sauna & hot tub, pleasant grounds leading to the lake & a jetty for swimming. The separate 'Mother-in-Law's' cabin sleeps up to 20 guests & has its own sauna. The restaurant is open to non-guests too (⊕ noon–21.00 Fri, noon–22.00 Sat, noon–20.00 Sun; €€€€). Birdlife & wildlife are in abundance locally, but hunting is popular & the hotel is filled with hunting trophies. Note that you need to call or use the intercom to open the entrance barrier. €€€

**Po Ąžuolais** [map, page 252] (14 guesthouse rooms, 5 apartments, 1 cabin) Plokštinės gatvė 20, Paplatelė region; w sodybapoazuolais.lt. Family friendly & family run, a rural complex of self-catering holiday accommodation & restaurant, with a big spa area including swimming pool & sauna. Very close to the Cold War Museum. Choose from guesthouse rooms, 1- & 2-bedroom apartments, or the larger cabin 'Smilga' sleeping up to 6. The on-site restaurant (€€€) is open to non-residents. €€€

**Sodyba Pas Tėvukas** [map, page 252] (4 cabins, 11 rooms) Plungės gatvė 42, Beržoras region; w pastevukus.lt. Located on Lake Beržoras in historic Beržoras village, 'Homestead at Granny's'

is one of the founders of rural hospitality in Lithuania, now run by the 2nd generation of this hospitality-driven family. Mother-&-daughter chefs Marija & Jurgita are known locally for their certified culinary heritage tasting experience. This is available from Sep to mid-Jun & must be prebooked with a minimum of 10 people (€35 pp). It is highly recommended if you want to understand & experience Samogitian cuisine. At all other times, there is no catering here; their accommodation is self-catering & comprises traditional thatched-roof homestead buildings converted into comfortable en-suite cabins, overlooking the lake. €€€

**Plateliai Žalgiris Yacht Club** (30 rooms) Ežero gatvė 40, Plateliai; w plateliuose.lt. During the summer season, the yacht-club offers accommodation in en-suite dbl, trpl & qdpl rooms, in its building with views of the marina, pier & public beach. Next door is the club's restaurant, Kavinė Burė (€€€). €€

**Le Le Terasa** [map, page 252] Miškų gatvė 2, Paežerės Rūdaičių region; ✦ leleterasa;; ⊕ noon-19.00 Sun–Thu, noon–20.00 Fri–Sat. Le Le Terasa is a quaint restaurant on the north shore of Lake Plateliai. It's a popular spot to stop for a snack or lunch when cycling around the lake, or on a warm evening to dine on the terrace overlooking the lake & marvel at the sunset's reflection. International menu, including a good selection of pizzas. Their surrounding farmstead **Šiaurinė paežerė** (w plateliuezeras. lt; €€€) also has several self-catering cabins (sleep 2–5), en-suite rooms with a lake or garden view & lake- or forest-side apartments (sleep 6–8). €€€

## SPORTS AND ACTIVITIES

**Cycling** Cycling has long been a popular mode of transport in these parts, even before the completion of the 22km cycle path that circumnavigates Lake Plateliai. Fully paved and signposted, with information boards on the nature, heritage and other sites of interest not to be missed, the path has become a very popular attraction. Across the road from the Žemaitija National Park Visitor Centre in Plateliai, you will find **Dviračių Nuoma** (Didžioji gatvė 3, Plateliai), a pop-up shop which has been hiring out bicycles during the summer season for over 15 years. They have a good selection of adult and children's bicycles for rent; child seats or trailers are also available.

**Diving** Lake Plateliai is clear, deep and harbours some interesting underwater features making it ideal for diving. It is believed that the lake was once much smaller and islands that are now submerged have structures and ruins to explore, including a sunken yacht and the remains of a 15th-century bridge among other interesting objects. **Oktopusas Diving Club** (Oktopusas Nardymo Centras; next to the Plateliai Žalgiris Yacht Club; w oktopusas.lt) offers lessons on roped routes, guided dives at all levels of difficulty, and equipment rental. Lifeguards are on duty during the diving season.

**Watersports** Plateliai Žalgiris Yacht Club (Platelių Žalgirio jachtklubas; Ežero gatvė 40, Plateliai; w plateliuose.lt; ⊕ 11.00–23.00 Mon–Thu, 11.00–midnight Fri, noon–01.00 Sat, noon–20.00 Sun) is the main place for water sport activities on Lake Plateliai, offering sailing boats, paddle boards, pedaloes and kayaks for hire by the hour, half day or full day. This is also the main public **swimming** area during the summer months.

**OTHER PRACTICALITIES** The nearest facilities, including bank, pharmacy, supermarket and post office, are in Plungė (page 269).

## WHAT TO SEE AND DO
✴ **Cold War Museum** (Šaltojo karo muziejus; Šilinės gatvė 4, Plokščių region; w zemaitijosnp.lt/en/expositions; ⊕ May–Sep 10.00–19.00 daily, Oct & Apr 10.00–17.00 daily, Nov–Mar 10.00–17.00 Tue–Sun; €12/6 inc guided tour; audio guide service €4 extra) Plokštinė Missile Base was constructed in 1960 under top-secret conditions. Not even local residents of Plokščiai village knew about it, and if they had their suspicions, they knew to keep quiet. Most work was undertaken at night-time and no machinery was used – that would have attracted too much attention. Instead, the base was dug out manually by more than 10,000 conscripted Soviet soldiers, many of whom were Estonian. The extracted earth was dumped along the roadside and is still visible as mounds at the side of the road today. The surrounding area was a strict nature reserve, which was crucial in controlling access and retaining secrecy for such a clandestine operation. Between 1963 and 1978, at the height of the Cold War between the USSR and USA and their respective allies, four medium-range R-12 (SS-4) ballistic missiles were installed here, each equipped with two megatons of thermonuclear warheads and aimed at cities in western Europe. As diplomatic tensions mounted, the USSR threatened to move their nuclear weapons within range of the USA. It is understood that several of the R-12 missiles from Plokštinė were secretly moved by train to the Black Sea, from where they were shipped to Cuba – an event that became known as the Cuban Missile Crisis. After the collapse of the Soviet Union the base was abandoned, visited only by woodland animals, urban explorers and metal thieves – you can see where failed attempts were made to remove the diesel engine in the generator room by cutting it up (they certainly underestimated the risk to their health in such a toxic environment at the time). The displays at the Cold War Museum are excellent and informative, and you can easily spend half a day reading everything. It is chilling to stare into the

23m-deep empty missile silo, to watch the videos of nuclear weapon testing, read the anti-West propaganda, and to think about history's habit of repeating itself. All visitors must either join a guided tour or take an audio guide. The guided tours in English are fixed at noon and 16.00 daily and run between May and September, but you should check beforehand on the website. If you miss the guided tour time, the audio guide is excellent and allows you to linger longer at the exhibits. Sturdy shoes are needed as the ground can be uneven, and as most of the tour is underground you'll need to watch out for low ceilings. If you are curious but unable to visit, check out the virtual tour on the museum's website.

The museum is accessible via the circular cycle path around Lake Plateliai, but bear in mind that it is on the opposite side of the lake to Plateliai village, 11km there and 11km back. If arriving by car, the road is asphalt and there is parking available.

## Around Lake Plateliai

**Beržoras** Historic single-street village Beržoras boasts one of the oldest wooden churches in Lithuania. Built in 1746, **St Stanislaus Church** (Šv. Vyskupo Stanislovo bažnyčia) is an exceptional example of folk architecture and is complemented by 14 Ways of the Cross around the village. On the feast days of Blessed Virgin Mary (Scapular) of Mount Carmel on 16 July (nearest Sunday), Assumption of the Blessed Virgin Mary on 15 August, and Feast of the Exaltation of the Holy Cross on 14 September (nearest Sunday), a procession begins at 10.30 and follows the route of Beržoras Calvary. At all other times you can explore the village independently.

**Siberija Observation Tower** (Siberijos apžvalgos bokštas) Between Beržoras and Plateliai, this observation tower is worth a stop. Climb to the top of its 15m-high staircase for a view of Lake Plateliai and the surrounding Siberian Wetland (which you have to cross on boardwalks to reach the tower), another simple, natural place of beauty and biodiversity.

**Plateliai** Several hours can easily be spent in Plateliai; otherwise its attractions and activities can be enjoyed during a longer, more leisurely stay in the region. **Plateliai Manor** (Platelių dvaro svirnas; Didžioji gatvė 22; ⊕ 10.00–1700 Tue–Sat; €4/2 inc exhibition & crafts centre) is a cultural complex set among the manor estate buildings. Here you will get acquainted with the history of Plateliai, the nature and ethnography of Samogitia, local traditions and the personalities who have influenced the region. Housed in the manor stable is the star attraction. Užgavėnės, the Lithuanian equivalent to Shrove Tuesday or Mardi Gras, is an ancient festival rooted in the spring equinox and celebrates the end of winter and beginning of spring (page 62). After Christianisation, the dates of the festival were altered slightly to fit with the Christian calendar, but the ancient customs and traditions were preserved and Užgavėnės continues to be the most important festival in Žemaitija. The **Užgavėnės Mask Exhibition** (Užgavėnių kaukių ekspozicija; Didžioji gatvė 24) is the first and only museum dedicated to Užgavėnės masks (*lyčyna*). It is a colourful, whacky, and sometimes creepy display of craftsmanship. Every year a mask-carving competition is held for master carvers – there are over a dozen mask-makers in the Samogitia region. Up to 35 different artists compete and some 140 masks are submitted. Alongside its growing collection of masks, the museum is filled with tales of mask making, pancake eating, bonfire burning and the defeat of 'evil' winter. You can visit the museum and browse the masks any time of year (and make your own souvenir mask too), but of course nothing compares to being in Lithuania for Užgavėnės and attending a procession or festival when these garish masks are brought to life!

In the former vegetable cellar of the manor house is **Plateliai Manor Traditional Crafts Centre** (Platelių dvaro sodybos tradicinių amatų centras; Didžioji gatvė 19), a small exhibition showcasing a variety of traditional crafts, but for now most of the information is in Lithuanian only.

**St Peter and St Paul's Church** (Šv. Apastalu Petro ir Pauliaus baznycia; Didžioji gatvė 15) is a well-preserved example of a wooden church in regional folk architecture style. Although it has been reconstructed since being built in the 15th century, it is rich with sacral heritage and a visit inside to see the Baroque altars should not be missed. As is the case with many churches, archaeological finds suggest that prior to Lithuania's conversion to Christianity, this was a place of pagan worship and sacrifice.

**Litvak Memorial Garden** (Litvakų Žemė Memorialas; on road 2302 on the right side 1.1km south of the roundabout with road 3217) Litvak Memorial Garden is a poignant memorial created by the Jakovas Bunka Charity and Sponsorship Fund (f JBfund.lt; see page 271 for more details on the folk artist Jakovas Bunka). The garden is laid out in the shape of Lithuania, with metalwork apple trees marking the location of Lithuanian Jewish (Litvak) communities that were destroyed between 1941 and 1944 during the Holocaust. Folk artist Artūras Platakis crafted these trees, adorned with metal apples which are inscribed with the names of families lost from that region, city, town or village. Litvak families from around the world can request their family to be included in the garden. There is a plan to create an authentic Jewish farmstead next to the garden, but the memorial apple trees with Litvak names and stories of their fate will remain the focus here.

**Žemaičių Kalvarija** (Samogitian Calvary) Tucked away in the northeastern territory of Žemaitija National Park is one of the most sacred places in Lithuania. First mentioned in historic chronicles of 1253 and known as Gardai, this is one of Lithuania's oldest settlements. It was in the early 17th century during the Grand Duchy of Lithuania that Bishop Jurgis Tiškevičius, along with the Dominicans, built a **Calvary** (Way of the Cross) comprising 19 chapels, after which the Dominicans established a monastery here. The current **Basilica of the Visitation of the Virgin Mary** (Švč. Mergelės Marijos Apsilankymo bazilika) dates from the early 1800s and forms part of the Pope John Paul II Pilgrimage Route of Lithuania (w piligrimukelias.lt). Every July the **Great Samogitian Calvary Celebration** is held, attracting over 70,000 pilgrims who walk the Way of the Cross.

# PLUNGĖ

Plungė was historically an important seat of Samogitian nobility, centred since the late 19th century around the Oginski Manor and Park. With the construction of a new railway line connecting it to Klaipėda to the west and Vilnius to the east, Plungė developed rapidly and became a thriving industrial city. Today the railway continues to serve modern industries including wheel manufacturing, a bread factory and a large frozen fish plant. Little of Plungė's Old Town remains, but you can get a sense of the historic town on J Tumo-Vaižganto gatvė, which is still lined with wooden houses and old Jewish merchant houses. Most international tourists visit Plungė for the Samogitian Art Museum before moving on to Žemaitija National Park, but with a new hotel option in town, Plungė makes a great base for those who want the creature comforts of a contemporary hotel while exploring the region.

**GETTING THERE AND AWAY** Plungė is on the Vilnius–Klaipėda **train** line with services between Plungė and Vilnius (3hrs 45mins; 2 per day), Klaipėda (1hr; 5 per day), Šiauliai (1hr 9mins; 5 per day) and Kretinga (28mins; 5 per day). It feels like you are on the outskirts of the city when you arrive at Plungė train station (Plungės geležinkelio stotis; Stoties gatvė 29), but it is only a short walk to the tourist information centre.

Daily **buses** run between Plungė and Vilnius (5hrs 15mins; 3 per day), Kaunas (4hrs 15mins; 4 per day), Klaipėda (1hr 40mins; 6 per day) and Telšiai (35mins; 4 per day). The **bus station** (Plungės autobusų parkas) is adjacent to the train station. Local buses 24A, 24B, 24C, 25A, and 25B run between Plungė bus station and Plateliai; there are roughly two buses a day for each service, running mainly in the morning and late afternoon to serve commuters.

By 2026 there will be a new **cycle path** between Plungė and Plateliai in Žemaitija National Park via the Kaušenai Holocaust Memorial.

**TOURIST INFORMATION** The friendly staff at **Plungė Tourism Information Centre** (Plungės turizmo informacijos centras; Dariaus & Girėno gatvė 27; w visitplunge. com; ⊕ 08.00–17.00 Mon–Fri, 10.00–15.00 Sat–Sun) will welcome you to Plungė and advise on city and regional sightseeing, experiences and activities.

 **WHERE TO STAY AND EAT**

✵ **Oginski Hotel** (23 rooms) Dariaus ir Girėno gatvė 10; w oginskihotel.lt. By far the best accommodation option in Plungė, the Oginski occupies a prime location opposite Plungės Manor Park & next to Plungė Waterfall on the Babrungus River. Superior rooms all have a river view. The family room has 2 separate bedrooms. The Flow restaurant & terrace is highly recommended. €€€
**Flow** Oginski Hotel, see above;
RestoranasFlow; ⊕ 11.00–15.00 Mon, 11.00–21.00 Tue–Thu, 11.00–22.00 Fri–Sat, 11.00–20.00 Sun. Creative World cuisine is served up in this contemporary restaurant that spills out on to the riverside terrace in summer. The w/day lunch menu (available 11.00–15.00) should be among your Plungė highlights. €€€
**Skalvija Plungė** Vytauto gatvė 3; interinas; ⊕ 10.00–17.00 Sun–Tue, 10.00–22.00 Wed–Sat. On the menu at this cellar restaurant are traditional Samogitian dishes, guaranteed to both fill & warm you up. €

**OTHER PRACTICALITIES** There is a centrally located **post office** (Dariaus ir Girėno gatvė 2) along the street from a major **bank** (Dariaus ir Girėno gatvė 5), while nearby is a **pharmacy** (Gintarinė vaistinė, Telšių gatvė 1-1A).

**WHAT TO SEE AND DO**
**Oginski Manor** (Oginskio dvaras) itself, also referred to as Oginski Palace (Oginskio rūmai) or Plungės Manor (Plungės dvaras), was commissioned by Mykolas Mikalojus Oginskis (1849–1902) and built between 1873 and 1886. The Neo-Renaissance architectural ensemble consists of ten buildings and is surrounded by leafy green Plungė Park (Plungės parkas). The Oginskis were a noble family of the Grand Duchy of Lithuania, and Mykolas had a strong interest in social and cultural life, having a positive impact on the town of Plungė. He accumulated a large art collection along the way. It was here that he established a music school, attended by a certain Mikalojus Konstantinas Čiurlionis, whose further studies in Warsaw were supported by Oginski – a valuable contribution to Čiurlionis becoming Lithuania's

most eminent composer. Notice the antique furniture throughout the manor – the Oginksi family were avid collectors so their furniture was not of their period but much older. The estate's **Orangerie and Clocktower** is a romantic red-brick building inspired by the Palazzo Vecchio in Florence, hence the Florentine style. It was built in 1846 by the noble Zubov family. After decades of neglect, since 2012 it has been renovated and now contains Plungė public library. The 12m-tall clocktower houses an unusual manual clock that needs winding up every three days. Both locals and tourists are welcome to visit.

✷ **Samogitian Art Museum** (Žemaičių dailės muziejus; Mykolo Oginskio rūmai, Parko gatvė 3A; w zdm.lt; ⊕ May–Sep 10.00–18.00 Tue–Sun, Oct–Apr 10.00–17.00 Tue–Sat; €5/3) Taking centre stage among Plungė's attractions, the Samogitian Art Museum has been resident in Oginski Manor since 1994. The museum showcases the work of Samogitian artists from the 20th and 21st centuries. Many of these works focus on ethnographic art, some almost resembling stained glass, with heavy definition and storytelling. The odd watercolour or work in a lighter medium are exceptions. Notable artists displayed here include Ignas Budrys (1933–99) and Antanas Lipskis (1917–2013). Exhibitions change regularly, so check the website if you are looking for something specific. Every four years the museum hosts the **World Samogitian Art Exhibition** to unite Samogitian artists from around the world – 2024 was the most recent one.

**Plungė centre** The city centre is a short walk from Oginski Manor and park along the pedestrian street of Laisvės alėja which is lined with quaint wooden houses. Where Laisvės alėja meets Vytauto gatvė stands a monument to **St Florian** (Šv. Florijonas), the Catholic saint who guards against fires. Plungė was ravaged by fires throughout its history, so residents put their faith in the saint to protect them. During the Soviet occupation the original sculpture was removed, but a new sculpture by folk artist Valdas Stumbras was installed soon after independence in 1990.

At the western end of Vytauto gatvė is the **Church of St John the Baptist** (Šv. Jono Krikštytojo bažnyčia), a Neo-Romanesque, twin-towered church. The number of confession booths in this church exceeds expectation and suggests it once had a lot of priests or a naughty congregation. An information board describes how M K Čiurlionis lived with his wife in the living room of the neighbouring rectory for several months during 1909.

**Kaušenai Holocaust Memorial** (Holokausto aukų atminimo vieta; 3km west of Plungė on road 3201) There are scores of memorials across Lithuania that remember and honour Jewish Holocaust victims, but this one is rather unique. Jakovas Bunka (1923–2014) was the last Jew living in Plungė, having survived ordeals most of us cannot imagine. Deported to Siberia, drafted into the Soviet army, and losing his close family – he experienced the worst of this period of history. During the interwar period, Plungė's population was half Jewish, but shortly after the Nazi invasion of Lithuania in June 1941, on 15 and 16 July 1941 about 1,800 Jews were murdered and buried here. The victims' names are engraved on the memorial walls. Along with fellow wood carvers, Bunka created oak wood carvings of harrowing faces, emaciated figures in chains, depicting the pain and despair of the individual and the community. During the Soviet occupation it was common practice for the Russians to repurpose such Jewish memorials for propaganda purposes. As happened here, they constructed a concrete obelisk as the central memorial, stating that USSR citizens were murdered here, therefore victimising the USSR and encouraging a brotherhood with Israel. Often these obelisks have new plaques placed on them, likely covering up a red star icon of the former USSR. For Jewish tours of Plungė, a descendent of Bunka runs local tours that can be arranged via the Plungė Tourism Information Centre.

## TELŠIAI

A treasure within the rolling farmland of Samogitia, the historic city of Telšiai is spread across seven small hills at the northern end of Lake Mastis. Its picturesque, atmospheric Old Town market square is edged with old Jewish merchant houses and wooden-house-lined streets lead off the market square. Telšiai has a long history as a centre of education and religion, and today it is home to the Telšiai Faculty of Vilnius Academy of Arts. Students' works are showcased at the **VAA Telsiai gallery** (VDA Telšių galerija; Kęstučio gatve 3-2; w vda.lt/telsiu-galerija; ⊕ noon–18.00 Tue–Sat). As the capital of Samogitia/Žemaitija there is a strong focus here on preserving and promoting Samogitian cultural heritage and history; note that the local signs are in both Lithuanian and Samogitian. Here you can eat authentic regional dishes, visit traditional wooden churches, learn about pagan Lithuania, and experience a city and region with a strong local flavour.

**GETTING THERE AND AWAY** Telšiai is served by direct **buses** to/from Vilnius (5hrs 30mins; 2 per day), Kaunas (3hrs 40mins; 5 per day), Klaipėda (2hrs 45mins; 4 per day) and Palanga (1hr 40mins; 1 per day). The bus station (Gedimino gatvė 1) is west of the city centre, a 16-minute walk from the tourist information centre.

The **train station** (Stoties gatvė 35) is north of the town centre, also 1.2km from the tourist information centre. It is on the direct Vilnius–Klaipėda line and has scheduled services to/from Vilnius (3hrs 39mins; 2 per day), Klaipėda (1hr 18mins; 5 per day), Šiauliai (47mins; 5 per day) and Kretinga (1hr 4mins; 5 per day).

**TOURIST INFORMATION** The **Žemaitija Tourism Information Centre** (Žemaitijos turizmo informacijos centras; Turgaus aikštė 21; w visit.telsiai.lt; ⊕ May–Oct 09.00–18.00 Mon–Fri, 11.00–19.00 Sat–Sun, Nov–Apr 08.00–16.00 Mon–Fri) is housed in an attractive former weigh house building at the top of the market square (Turgaus aikštė). Alongside maps, leaflets and souvenirs there is a small museum collection of over 5,000 teddy bears! That makes sense when you learn that the symbol of Telšiai and the region of Samogitia is a bear; according to legend bears played a role in raising Samogitian children. Enquire about the town trail that takes you around the main sights while hunting for 58 bears along the way. You will find the biggest bear in town at the bottom of Turgaus aikštė at the **Clock Tower** (Laikrodžio bokštas) from which the warrior bear guards the town.

## WHERE TO STAY

**Lavender Inn** [map, page 252] (11 rooms) Viešvės gatvė 19A, Viešvėnai I village; w lavenderinn.lt. Not in Telšiai, but a 7km drive southeast from the centre, this guesthouse & restaurant is full of scents & hues of lavender of course. The restaurant is open all year round, although only for residents in the winter months. The lavender ice cream is delicious. Each room has a theme including Lavender, Sky & the artist Mondrian, the piece de resistance being the Fling Apartment that certainly makes this place less *Ladies in Lavender* & more *Fifty Shades of Grey*. **€€€**

**Dharma Stay** (12 apartments) Birutės gatvė 1; w dharmastay.lt. Located on the 2nd & 3rd floors above Harmony Lounge Restobar are well-equipped apartments from dbl room size to quads with a sofa bed, all in contemporary décor with kitchenette & washing machine. Rooms have keycode access & the only staff are those working in the restaurant. Small spa area must be booked in advance. B/fast from 09.00 when the Restobar opens. €€

**Sinchronas** (7 rooms) Turgaus aikštė 24; w sinchronas.lt. The best hotel in Telšiai with comfortable rooms, homely décor & popular top-floor restaurant with panoramic views across Lake Mastis. Turkish bath & jacuzzi area for private rental. Rooms have either a city or lake view. €€

## ✴ WHERE TO EAT AND DRINK

**Abatija** Katedros aikštė 3; [f]; ⊕ 14.00–21.00 Tue–Thu, 13.00–midnight Fri–Sat, 13.00–21.00 Sun. A romantic cellar restaurant; white tablecloths, candles & low-arched ceilings set the scene for high-end European dishes. €€€€
**Džiugo Namai** Respublikos gatvė 49; w dziugashouse.lt; ⊕ 10.00–21.00 Sun–Fri, 10.00–22.00 Fri–Sat. This is the restaurant outlet for local delicacy Džiugas sūrio. Since 1924, the award-winning cheese has been made by the local dairy (& Telšiai's biggest employer) Žemaitijos Pienas. A pleasant restaurant & café in which to order a sample cheeseboard & wine or try cheese ice cream. Suitable for vegetarians too. Downstairs is a small museum dedicated to the company's cheese-making history, full of interesting facts, including how they play Čiurlionis classical music to the cheese while it is maturing. €€€

**Kavinė Senamiestis Telšiuose** Turgaus aikštė 11; [f] kavinesenamiestistelsiuose; ⊕ 11.00–20.00 Mon–Thu, 11.00–23.00 Fri–Sat, 11.00–16.00 Sun. This is the place to come for traditional Samogitian dishes. Regional specialities include Kraujiniai vėdarai (blood sausage), kastinis (soured-milk-based sauce), cibulynė (onion & herring soup) & kanapinė (cannabis seeds). You can order individual dishes from the main menu, or prebook a full Samogitian tasting experience (particularly popular with foodies & those with Lithuanian heritage who are transported back to grandma's cooking). €€€
**Prezo kepyklele** Turgaus aikštė 17A; w prezo.lt; ⊕ 08.00–19.00 Mon–Fri, 08.00–14.00 Sat. Tasty pastries, hot drinks & people watching from the big glass windows overlooking the market square. €

**OTHER PRACTICALITIES** There is a **post office** (Plungės gatvė 4) inside the Rimi supermarket, a **bank** (Turgaus aikštė 24A) opposite the tourism information centre and a **pharmacy** (S Daukanto gatvė 1A) inside the Maxima supermarket.

## WHAT TO SEE AND DO
**Samogitian Museum 'Alka'** (Žemaičių muziejus Alka; Muziejaus gatvė 31; w muziejusalka.lt; ⊕ 09.00–18.00 Tue–Fri, 11.00–18.00 Sat–Sun; €8/6) The word 'alka' means a place of sacred worship. The most important museum for the ethnographic region of Samogitia, it received its name back in 1932 when the History Fellowship 'Alka' established it. The museum collection includes well over 100,000 exhibits including fine art, photographs, archaeological finds, textiles, folk art, agricultural and household objects, sun crosses, wood carvings, and more. All are documented, preserved and exhibited here, unlocking the stories and cultural background to many of the sights you will see during your travels in the region. It is a pleasant walk (just over 1km) along the lakeshore from the city centre to the museum.

✱ **Samogitian Village Museum** (Žemaičių kaimo muziejus; Malūno gatvė 5; w muziejusalka.lt; ⊕ Nov–Apr 08.00–16.00 Mon–Fri, May–Oct 09.00–18.00 Mon–Fri, 11.00–19.00 Sat–Sun; €4/2) This small ethnographic open-air museum showcases 19th-century rural Samogitian wooden homesteads, gardens and barns, complete with authentic artefacts and special breed Samogitian horses. Since it was opened in 1960, the museum has been passing on stories and traditions to new generations. It is brimming with history – and more than 25 different types of peony. If you are staying in Telšiai, walk or cycle the 2.8km from the city centre along the lakeshore path to the museum on the western side of Lake Mastis. Enquire at the tourist information centre or your hotel for local bicycle hire options.

**Telšiai Yeshiva** (Telšių ješiva; Iždinės gatvė 11; w muziejusalka.lt/telsiu-jesiva; ⏰ by appointment only; €4/2) Yeshivas were the highest of Jewish educational institutions and Telšiai Yeshiva, established in 1875 and attributed to Rabbi Eliezer Gordon (1841–1910), became one the most important in the Jewish diaspora. Over 5,000 rabbis from around the world came to Telšiai to study the Torah and Talmud. Along with Kaunas (Vilijampolė) and Panevėžys yeshivas, during World War II they were re-established in Israel and the USA – the Telšiai Yeshiva still exists in Cleveland, Ohio. Telšiai's Jewish population of 2,800 suffered brutally under the Nazi occupation in 1941, a ghetto was quickly established and by the

### A DAY TOUR FROM TELŠIAI

If you have a car, or are a suitably proficient cyclist for a full day of touring, the region south of Telšiai including **Varniai Regional Park** and **Šatrija Landscape Reserve** provides a pleasant overview of Samogitian countryside and culture. With a little preplanning you could also include some unusual activities.

The main cultural sights when visiting Varniai from Telšiai on road 160, begin 4.5km out of the city at the roadside **Rainiai Chapel of Suffering** (Rainių Kančios koplyčia; w muziejusalka.lt), a beautiful memorial to tragic events. In June 1941, 76 political prisoners were murdered by Soviet soldiers and collaborators in the nearby forest. The frescoes by artist Antanas Kmieliauskas are impressive. In Varniai town is the **Samogitian Diocese Museum** (Žemaičių vyskupystės muziejus; S Daukanto gatvė 6; w muziejusalka.lt/museum-of-the-diocese-of-samogitia; ⏰ 09.00–18.00 Tue–Fri, 11.00–18.00 Sat–Sun; €6/3). Located in the 18th-century former Varniai priest seminary, the museum has been a branch of the Samogitian Museum 'Alka' since 1999 and has recently undergone renovation. It now houses the Sacral Heritage Exposition previously in Telšiai and covers the turbulent history of the Diocese of Samogitia through personal accounts and stories. Ascending the bell tower offers panoramic views of Varniai (additional €2). Nearby, the **Church of St Alexander** (Šv. Aleksandro bažnyčia; Vytauto gatvė 10; w varniuparapija.lt) offers an opportunity to visit a Samogitian wooden church built in 1770 in traditional Lithuanian folk architecture.

Be sure to stop at the **Varniai Regional Park Visitor Centre** (Varnių regioninio parko lankytojų centras; Dumbrių gatvė 3, Ožtakiai village; w saugoma.lt/en/objects/objects-varniai-regional-park-visitor-center; ⏰ 08.00–17.00 Tue–Fri, 10.00–15.00 Sat) to pick up some route maps and local advice. Of note is the small, winding Virvyčia River which passes through the park – it is scenic and popular for kayaking. Kayak rental can be arranged with **Angelų malūnas** (w angelumalunas.lt). Head west to **Lake Lūkstas** (Lūkstas Ezeras) for a leisurely walk. Or you can get dirty in **Sietuvos kūlgrinda** – an ancient stone road that is submerged by swamp and it is possible to walk along the 250m-long route feeling the flat stones beneath your feet as you wade through a very natural mud bath. Centuries ago, these secret roads were of great strategic importance, providing escape routes for locals to flee quickly from foreign invaders; today you are advised to wear old clothes and book a local guide through the visitor centre.

end of the year all had been murdered except for 64 Jewish women who escaped. The newly renovated yeshiva now hosts a Jewish museum, exhibitions and events. A guided tour with an English-speaking guide is available but must be booked in advance (€20).

**Telšiai Cathedral** (Šv. Antano Paduviečio katedra; Katedros aikštė 2; w telsiukatedra.lt) The cathedral location is high above the city on Insula Hill (Insulos kalva) and since 1624 it has been the most impressive sacral complex in Samogitia. What began as a modest wooden Church of St Anthony of Padua, developed into a considerable complex after rebuilding was required following episodes of fire and war. In 1924, Pope Pius XI established the ecclesiastical province of Lithuania and the Diocese of Telšiai, and the church was transformed into a cathedral. Originally surrounded by a Bernardine Monastery, this was closed

Return to Telšiai via asphalted roads 223 and 194, or if you have a good road map or gps maps, take the unsigned gravel roads cross country towards Pašatrija. Here you will find **Šatrija Hill** (Šatrijos kalnas; 228m), part of the surrounding Šatrija Landscape Reserve. At first glance, this is yet another of Lithuania's ubiquitous glacially formed mounds, upon which Baltic tribes built a hillfort to defend their territories. But Šatrija Hill is special. It is one of the most famous archaeological sites in Lithuania, with a wealth of finds, including tombs, funeral urns, amber ornaments and stone axes. Evidence of early settlements here is believed to date back to 2BC. Šatrija was one of the most important pagan sites of worship in Samogitia, before paganism was erased by the introduction of Christianity. A path and steps lead to the summit, and wide-open views of the surrounding plateau accentuate the hill's modest height. On the summit is a firepit altar (*alka*) and flag of the eternal flame guards. On a smaller, adjacent hill is a circular wooden building which houses Šatrija's eternal flame (Amžinoji Šatrijos Ugnis). An army of dedicated volunteers keep the flame permanently alight, each signing up to 24-hour shifts or longer to guard the flame. Inside is a central firepit, the smoke from which floats upwards through the blackened chimney; wooden bench seating edges the walls on both sides and a basic bed fills the back wall. Every morning before sunrise, the volunteer carries embers from the eternal flame up to the firepit on Šatrija Hill and a fire is lit for the gods and left to burn out. This is the only eternal pagan fire in the Baltic countries, so volunteers travel from beyond Lithuania to watch the fire, motivated not only by a spiritual link between the earth and the gods, but by the solitude, silence and sanctuary the role provides.

Heading back to Telšiai on road 4605, make a final stop at **Biržuvėnai Manor** (Biržuvėnų dvaro sodyba; Dvaro gatvė 4, Biržuvėnai village; w birzuvenudvaras.lt; ⊕ 09.00–18.00 Tue–Sat). A rebuilt 18th-century manor which at the time of writing had been taken over by the Telšiai tourism team and it is planned to be a combination of art gallery, museum, guesthouse and function rooms. At the time of writing, visitors can explore the manor grounds and admire the wooden exterior, but tours of the interior at not available. Take a walk in the surrounding parkland or along the Virvyčia River. As you approach Biržuvėnai Manor on road 4630 from the 4605, you will pass the manor's road shrine (Biržuvėnų dvaro sodybos koplytstulpis). Shortly after, as you turn right towards the manor, look over the old manor wall on the left to see the World War I German graves.

in 1853 by the anti-Catholic Russian authorities and only in 1927 was it reopened as a priests' seminary and Bishops Palace. Today there are only three priests residing here. The Cathedral of St Anthony of Padua interior is unusually decorative and contains a rare example of a double altar and full circle balcony. The crypt is always open, and you can pay your respect to the three bishop martyrs who were killed by Soviet soldiers. The huge copper plated doors are carved with intricate scenes of Christianity in Samogitia. Opposite the ornate white church gates, check out the wall-mounted carillon and carved stonework on the Telšiai Culture Centre (Telšių kultūros centras).

# 9

# The Coast

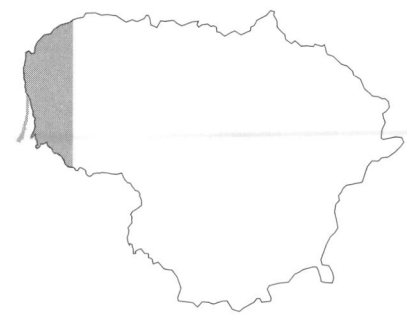

The coastal region is a surprise highlight for many first-time visitors to Lithuania. The Baltic Sea coastline stretches for 90.6km from the Lithuania–Latvia border in the north to the Lithuania–Russia border in the south. Including the inland Curonian Lagoon coastline, this extends to a total of 262km of beaches, dunes, marshes and fens. In ancient times, this was the land of the Curonian Baltic tribe and legacy of their influence on the Baltic coast is evident in archaeological finds, local mythology and regional names: Curonian Spit (Kuršių nerija), Curonian Lagoon (Kuršių marių) and Kurzeme (Courland) in Latvia. The Curonian Spit is a 98km-long natural wonder, granted UNESCO World Heritage Site status in 2000 for its commitment to protecting its vulnerable natural environment and cultural heritage. Visitors flock to the Curonian Spit National Park to walk in the sand dunes, pick berries in the forest and bathe in the Baltic Sea, while locals navigate the fine balance between conservation and dependency on a tourism economy. Shared equally between Lithuania and the Russian territory of Kaliningrad, the spit and lagoon are divided in half by an international border which has been closed and under close surveillance since Russia's full-scale invasion of Ukraine in 2022. Tourism continues to thrive on the Lithuanian side.

The mainland coastline is dominated by the historic port city of Klaipėda and the summer capital resort town of Palanga. At an inconspicuous location named Nemirseta between Klaipėda and Palanga lies an easily overlooked trench in the forest which was once a border of great historical influence. To the north, including the resort of Palanga, was the Russian Empire-occupied lands of Lithuania's Žemaitija ethnographic region. To the south, including Klaipėda, was the German Empire of East Prussia, encompassing the ethnographic region of Lithuania Minor. Free from occupation and division, what were contested lands for centuries are now united and lead the way in recreational tourism, hospitality and bucolic landscapes perfect for birdwatching, hiking and cycling adventures. The Baltic Coastal Hiking Route (page 45) and EuroVelo Cycling Trails (page 281) are new assets to the region, providing the necessary infrastructure for self-guided and self-propelled touring.

The Baltic Sea has its own notable characteristics. The water is brackish, meaning low salinity, containing one fifth of the salt content of other oceans. The water temperature in summer hovers around 20–22°C and the Lithuanian coastline has a shallow sandy shelf along its fine sandy beaches.

There is a marked difference between the seasons. On a warm summer weekend much of the country migrates to the coast, making midweek and the shoulder seasons of spring and autumn appealing times to visit. Although many outdoor attractions close outside of the summer season many permanent ones remain open and prices are often lower. Winter can be bitter and wild, but the contrast of snow-covered dunes, frozen seascapes and crystalised beaches with the warmth of

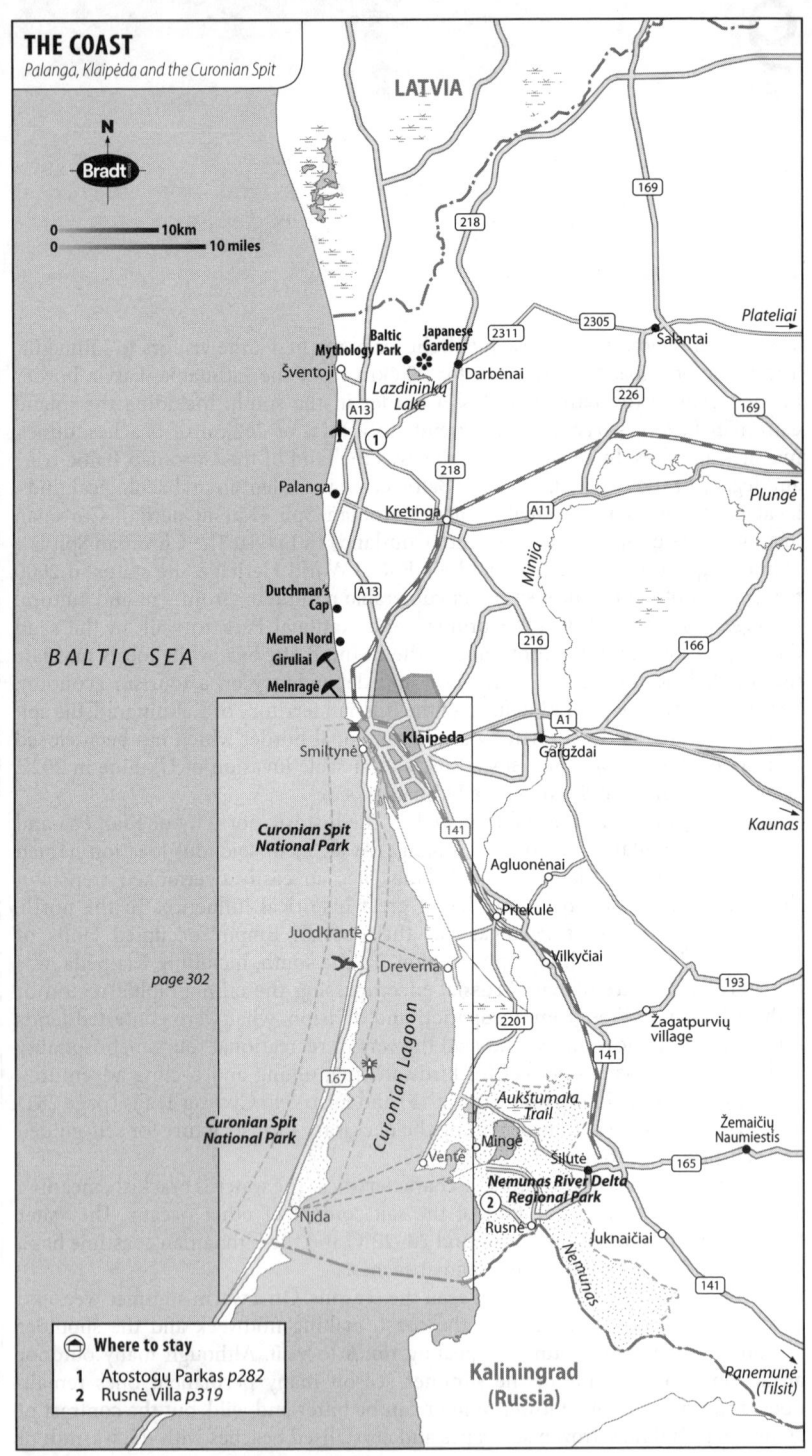

a reduced-rate luxurious spa hotel can be a marvellous combination. Whatever the season, a walk along the shore of the Baltic Sea is a must – keep your eyes peeled for precious fragments of amber as you stroll.

## PALANGA

The name Palanga brings a smile to Lithuanian faces. The promise of summer sun, swimming and *šaltibarščiai* (cold beetroot soup) has helped everyone get through the winter months for generations.

In 1824, Mykolas Tiškevičius (of the Polish noble family Tyskiewicz) acquired the Palanga region and the family continued to preside over it until their properties were appropriated by the authorities in 1940. Their wish to establish a recreational resort gradually took shape with the construction of their grand residence and gardens, the pier, J Basanavičiaus gatvė, a new church, health sanatoriums, wooden villas for guests to stay and venues for entertainment. During Lithuania's second Russian occupation, Palanga was a premier resort in the Soviet Union attracting curious souls from St Petersburg and Moscow to experience the western periphery of the USSR. Accommodation was predominantly in the form of state-owned sanatoriums and holiday centres, built for workers to holiday with their families, with the best accommodation saved for Communist Party members. Locals went to significant efforts to keep influential guests happy, even planting mushrooms along a path if they requested to go mushrooming. Consequences could be severe if they were not shown the best time.

Summer season is short, with a lot of fun to be had and energy expended between June and September. Off season, Palanga's local population is a modest 18,000 and a more sedate atmosphere prevails, making it an appealing weekend escape and when good deals can be found. To escape the crowds, head south from J Basanavičiaus gatvė along Meilės alėja (Love Alley) and you will be rewarded with pine forests, parkland and sleepier residential areas.

These days Palanga has something for everybody: some come to Palanga to party and need round-the-clock sustenance; some come to rejuvenate and rebalance in a zen-filled spa hotel; others are families looking for activities and entertainment, or those who have been prescribed downtime at the seaside to recuperate. Somehow, Palanga welcomes them all and sends them home fulfilled, dreaming of their next visit.

To quote the Tiškevičius family motto '*Deligas quem diligas*' ('Choose what you love') – many choose Palanga.

### GETTING THERE AND AWAY

**By air** Located just 6km north of the town centre, **Palanga Airport** (Palangos Oro Uostas; Liepojos plenta 1; w palanga-airport.lt) offers a small selection of international direct flights, enabling visitors to access western Lithuania and Latvia. The airport is small and easy to navigate; car rental companies are located in the arrivals hall, where you will also find ATMs and vending machines.

The **bus** stop for connections to Palanga or Klaipėda is in front of the airport, slightly to the left. Minibus number 31 (Palanga Airport–Palanga–Klaipėda) is scheduled to service flight times. Ticket prices reflect a preference for electronic payment: if paying the driver in cash, it's €4; via Klaipėda City app, €3; and by bank card, €2.50. To take a bus north to Šventoji, you need to cross to the other side of Liepojos plenta, slightly to the left. Bus number 3 (Palanga Airport–Šventoji) will take you north and runs regularly between the hours of 06.57 and 22.47.

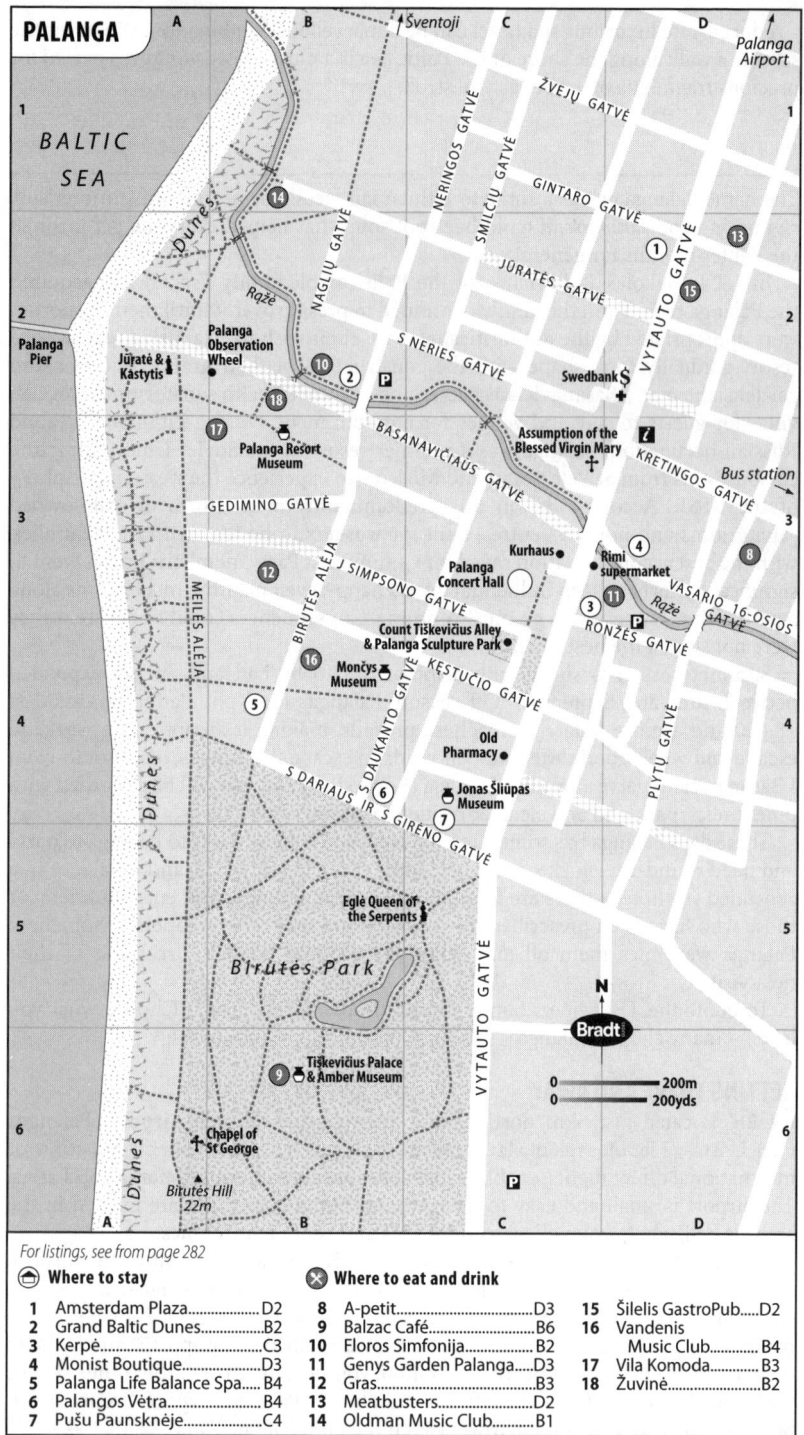

For listings, see from page 282

### 🛏 Where to stay

1. Amsterdam Plaza.................D2
2. Grand Baltic Dunes.............B2
3. Kerpė...................................C3
4. Monist Boutique.................D3
5. Palanga Life Balance Spa..B4
6. Palangos Vėtra....................B4
7. Pušu Paunsknėje................C4

### ❌ Where to eat and drink

8. A-petit.................................D3
9. Balzac Café..........................B6
10. Floros Simfonija................B2
11. Genys Garden Palanga.....D3
12. Gras......................................B3
13. Meatbusters........................D2
14. Oldman Music Club...........B1
15. Šilelis GastroPub................D2
16. Vandenis Music Club........B4
17. Vila Komoda.......................B3
18. Žuvinė..................................B2

**Local taxis** operate at the airport when a flight arrival is due; it takes 12 minutes to drive to Palanga centre, and expect to pay €8. If you are without cash, the **Bolt** taxi service app is available in the area. **CityBee** cars can be picked up at the airport, but availability is not guaranteed (page 57).

**By bus** Direct **buses** serve Palanga from Klaipėda (25mins; 36 per day), Kaunas (3hrs; 12 per day) and Vilnius (4hrs; 10 per day). A bus to Liepāja in Latvia departs from the Lidl car park (Klaipėdos plenta 59; w liepajasture.lv/satiksme; Jun–Sep departs at 16.40 on Mon, Wed, Fri, Sat & Sun, Oct–May Wed, Sat & Sun only). For bus travel to Riga, connect via Klaipėda.

Palanga's bus station [280 D3] (Palangos autobusų stotis; Klaipėdos 42; w palkom.lt/autobusu-stotis) is on the eastern edge of the town centre, a 15-minute walk to the tourist information office and a 30-minute walk to the pier.

**By car** Getting to Palanga by car is straightforward. It is a short distance off the main road A13 which runs from the Lithuania–Latvia border to the north, to Klaipėda in the south. The main A1 highway joins the A13 just before Klaipėda, making it a smooth drive from Kaunas (2hrs 30mins) and Vilnius (3hrs 30mins). These times can be greatly affected if travelling to the coast at peak times, especially Friday evenings when the weather forecast is good.

**GETTING AROUND** The easiest ways to explore Palanga are **on foot** or **by bike**. The city is very walkable with clearly marked pedestrian zones. Bicycle hire is widely available and will enable you to explore further or more quickly, including the leafy residential areas, and to make use of the excellent cycle tracks along the coast. Note that cycling is not permitted along J Basanavičiaus gatvė in the summer season. When hiring a bicycle, insist on getting a bike helmet as part of your hire.

If car transport is needed, you have the option of finding and communicating with a **local taxi** on the street (don't expect English to be spoken); or use the **Bolt** app to book a taxi service, pay online, and even choose your vehicle type or whether it has an extra, eg: baby car seat. If you want to explore further afield and with more independence, **CityBee** short-term car hire operates in the city and are bookable via the app (page 57).

> **EUROVELO CYCLE ROUTES**
>
> Lithuania's coastline incorporates more than 100km of the European cycle route network EuroVelo (w en.eurovelo.com/lithuania). The EuroVelo 10 Baltic Sea Cycle Route enters Lithuania from Russian exclave Kaliningrad at the border crossing south of Nida on the Curonian Spit and follows the coast north into Latvia. The EuroVelo 13 Iron Curtain Trail follows a similar route. At the time of writing the border with Russia is closed and a long diversion around Kaliningrad oblast is needed. It is now common to start or end the journey in Nida.
>
> A third route, EuroVelo 11 East Europe Route, traverses eastern Lithuania, entering the country from Poland via the Suwałki Gap (page 160), passing through Vilnius and exiting into Latvia close to Zarasai.
>
> The local specialists for cycling holidays in Lithuania are **Baltic Bike Travel** (w bbtravel.lt) who offer self-guided and guided tours, along with bike rental and transportation services.

**TOURIST INFORMATION** The **Palanga Tourism Information Centre** [280 D3] (Palangos turizmo informacijos centras; Vytauto gatvė 94; w visit-palanga.lt; ⏱ 08.00–18.00 Mon–Fri, 10.00–16.00 Sat, 10.00–15.00 Sun) has a variety of themed routes for sightseeing in Palanga, including by bike or with a focus on amber. Be sure to try their virtual reality headsets.

**WHERE TO STAY** Gone are the days of older ladies standing on the roadside and waving you down as you enter Palanga, hoping to tempt you to stay in their spare room for your summer break and their summer cash boost. When choosing your accommodation, be aware that central Palanga can be noisy in summer, weekends can be crazy busy, and hotels are not keen on one- or two-night stays in summer. Not mentioned here are the large sanatorium hotels on the edge of town as these are not so appealing to the leisure tourist.

**Amsterdam Plaza** [280 D2] (29 rooms) Vytauto gatvė 79; w amsterdamplaza.lt. In the heart of Palanga, this boutique hotel has standard rooms & luxurious suites, all including access to the small spa (09.00–21.00). Its highly rated restaurant has an à la carte menu & summer terrace. €€€€€

**Palanga Life Balance Spa** [280 B4] (84 rooms) Birutės alėja 60; w palangahotel.lt. A luxury oasis located in a quiet area, designed for relaxation of the highest standard & the only hotel in the world to have a 5° inclined floor. We are still struggling to understand why. Their luxury apartments in cottages are perfect for families & those wanting privacy. Non-residents can book the spa centre. €€€€€

**✵ Pušų Paunksnėje** [280 C4] (19 rooms) S Dariaus ir S Girėno gatvė 23; w pusupaunksneje.lt. A long-standing characterful, upmarket favourite located in a quiet area of Palanga close to Birutės Park, this hotel has 8 luxury dbls, 4 luxury family suites & 7 junior suites. Plus pool, sauna & spa area. €€€€€

**Monist Boutique Hotel** [280 D3] (30 rooms) Vytauto gatvė 88A; w monist.lt. Here, emphasis is placed on tranquillity, slow travel & a boutique experience. Spa packages are available. If you missed b/fast (inc), they serve a classy brunch, like everything else here, best enjoyed slowly. €€€€

**Atostogų Parkas** [map, page 278] (103 rooms) Venecijos 2, Žibininkai village; w atostoguparkas.lt. The biggest holiday resort in western Lithuania boasts 16 swimming pools & the largest amber sauna in Europe. Accommodation is in the hotel, or in wooden cottages with basic facilities & optional extras like take-away food delivery, grill rental or a hot tub. All-inclusive rates with buffet dining are available. Additional activities include bike rental, padel tennis, spa centre & sauna sessions with an expert sauna master (page 92). Great fun for families who like to be kept busy. Located 6km from Palanga centre. €€€

**Grand Baltic Dunes** [280 B2] (100 rooms) Birutės alėja 26; w grandbalticdunes.com. Apartment-style rooms make this a good option for longer stays or basic self-caterers. They also have connecting rooms for families. Professional holiday photo shoots can be arranged for an unusual holiday souvenir. €€€

**Kerpė** [280 C3] (23 rooms) Vytauto gatvė 76; w kerpehotel.lt. A comfortable & cosy smaller hotel with a small spa, plunge pool & terrace restaurant, Kerpė is a good value-for-money option. €€€

**Palangos Vėtra** [280 B4] (36 rooms, 1 apartment) S Daukanto gatvė 35; w palangosvetra.lt. An array of rooms are available here, from bijou economy dbls to a VIP apartment, all including morning access to the sauna area. Popular outdoor summer terrace. €€€

**✕ WHERE TO EAT AND DRINK** Many hotels have reliable restaurants open all year round. Pop-up restaurants and summer terraces appear each year in new guises. The opening times listed are for summer; check their websites for winter hours.

**Vila Komoda** [280 B3] Meilės alėja 5; w vilakomoda.lt; ⏱ 09.00–14.00 Mon–Tue, 09.00–14.00 & 17.00–23.00 Wed–Sat, 09.00–23.00 Sun. The Italian neo-Renaissance-style Vila

Komoda was commissioned for the Tiškevičius family in 1895 & is now listed as a cultural heritage property of the Republic of Lithuania. Today the modern cuisine served here gives a respectable nod to Lithuanian culinary heritage, and was awarded a recommendation by the Michelin Guide in 2024. Head to the rooftop terrace to watch the sunset. €€€€

**Floros Simfonija** [280 B2] Birutės alėja 22; w florossimfonija.lt; ⊕ 11.00–23.00 Mon–Thu, 11.00–midnight Fri, 10.30–midnight Sat–Sun. Known for its large summer terrace, Floros Simfonija is very family friendly place with a varied menu of European dishes. €€€

✱ **Gras** [280 B3] Žilvinas Hotel, Kęstučio gatvė 32; w restoranasgras.lt; ⊕ 10.00–22.00 Mon–Thu, 10.00–23.00 Fri–Sat, 10.00–21.00 Sun. Smart but relaxed, the friendly atmosphere here contrasts with the rather brutal architecture of the hotel. Suitable for brunch, lunch or dinner; families welcome. Modern European cuisine. €€€

**Meatbusters** [280 D2] Gintaro gatvė 43; w meatbusters.lt; ⊕ 10.00–22.00 Sun–Thu, 10.00–23.00 Fri–Sat. On a mission to make burgers healthier with sprinklings of sprouts & pickled extras, Meatbusters offer reliably good gastropub portions & prices that locals love. Vegan & vegetarian burgers too. €€€

**Šilelis GastroPub** [280 D2] Vytauto gatvė 112; ☏+370 609 33601; ⊕ 10.00–midnight daily. A retro vibe emanates from the vintage 'šilelis' portable TVs dotted around the place, in which both cool & old-school punters enjoy snacks, meals, draft beers & cocktails. Take-away available. €€€

**Žuvinė** [280 B2] J Basanavičiaus gatvė 37A; w zuvine.lt; ⊕ 11.00–midnight daily. If we tell you the Lithuanian for fish is *žuvis*, you can guess what features mainly on the menu. Here you'll enjoy relaxed but upscale dining, with a good wine list to complement the fish dishes. €€€

**A-petit** [280 D3] Plytų gatvė 7; ▮ apetitpalanga; ⊕ 09.00–22.00 daily. A very family-friendly, reasonably priced restaurant for lunch or dinner. The daily lunch is recommended & make sure you leave room for something sweet. €€

✱ **Balzac Café** [280 B6] Amber Museum (Tiškevičius Palace), Vytauto gatvė 17; ▮ BalzacLietuva; ⊕ 11.00–17.00 daily. A rare phenomenon in Lithuania – a café inside a museum. French-style coffee, cakes & snacks can be enjoyed inside the palace or on the terrace overlooking the formal gardens. €€

✱ **Genys Garden Palanga** [280 D3] Ronžės gatvė 5; ▮ genysgardenpalanga; ⊕ 16.00–02.00 daily. For a laid-back atmosphere & live music, this is the place to be – a hipster beer garden serving craft drinks & a food court for those with munchies who don't want to lose their in-demand seat. €€

**Oldman Music Club** [280 B1] Jūratės gatvė 2A; ▮ oldmanpalanga; ⊕ closed Mon. This place can be a restaurant, a bar, a café, a cinema, or a concert venue depending on when you visit. The food is of a higher quality than you might ordinarily expect from a music venue. Check their Facebook page for event listings & times. €€

**Vandenis Music Club** [280 B4] Birutės aleja 47; w vandenis.lt; ⊕ 10.00–22.00 Mon–Thu, 10.00–midnight Fri, 09.30–midnight Sat, 09.30–22.00 Sun. A music club with a retro feel & a varied music programme, Vandenis offers b/fast, lunch & dinner menus with their homemade pizza a favourite with regulars. Home delivery is available if you prefer a quiet night in. €€

**ENTERTAINMENT** The main venue for indoor events and concerts throughout the year is **Palanga Concert Hall** [280 C3] (Palangos koncertų sale; Vytauto gatvė 43; w palangosks.lt), whose repertoire covers everything from live music acts, theatre, comedy and children's entertainment. In summer, the whole city buzzes with outdoor events and pop-up venues, providing no end of entertainment. You may want to consider this when choosing accommodation.

**OTHER PRACTICALITIES** There is a **post office** [280 C3] (Malūno gatvė 10) inside the Rimi supermarket. A **bank ATM** can be found outside the tourist information centre [280 D3] (Vytauto gatvė 94), and a **Swedbank** branch [280 D2] (Vytauto gatvė 61) and **pharmacy** [280 D2] (Vytauto gatvė 59; w eurovaistine.lt) are convenient for the city centre.

> **PALANGA FESTIVALS**
>
> Palanga likes to party and every national holiday, be that Easter, Christmas, Midsummer or national holidays, can be cause for celebration here. You choose whether this appeals or to avoid. Summer season feels like one long festival, but attending a low-season event can be a memorable experience and can offer good value for money.
>
> The **Palanga Smelt Festival** (Palangos stinta mugė; w palangosstinta. lt) celebrates the heritage of the seaside every February with fishing and barbecuing competitions, crafts, performances and plenty of opportunities to sample smelt or *stinta*, the small, delicate fish plentiful at this time of year.
>
> The **St George's Day Festival** (Jurginės) held the weekend after 23 April (St George's Day) sees regional troupes in traditional dress celebrate with a 'sing-off' around Birutės Park, culminating in a sunset bonfire celebration on the beach next to the pier.

**WHAT TO SEE AND DO** Palanga is best explored on foot. Following this order of attractions will get you acquainted with the resort, but you will need several days in town if you are to make the most of the museums on offer.

**J Basanavičiaus gatvė** [280 C3] The heart and soul of Palanga, J Basanavičiaus gatvė lies perpendicular to the Baltic shore and leads from the city centre straight to the pier. This 950m pedestrianised strip is devoted to entertainment, restaurants and bars – no wonder the street is nicknamed the biggest restaurant in Lithuania – and is a place for promenading throughout the seasons. Originally named Tiškevičius gatvė, after the patron of Palanga, Count Tiškevičius, this boulevard was the route along which aristocrats and wealthy nobles built their summer villas in spacious plots; exceptional examples located at numbers 26, 28, 30, 32 and 34 showcase the wooden architecture and **Fachwerk** influence of the late 19th and early 20th centuries. In 1942, the boulevard was renamed after Jonas Basanavičius (1851–1927), a highly regarded cultural and political figure and proponent of Lithuanian national identity and independence.

Further along, at number 43, the **Palanga Observation Wheel** [280 B2] (Palangos apžvalgos ratas; w palangosapzvalgosratas.lt; ⊕ summer 10.00–23.00 daily, winter noon–dark; €15/10) stands proud as the largest and newest big-wheel ride in the Baltics, a novel way to get a birds-eye view of the resort and appreciate the endless stretch of sandy beach heading off into the distance. One ride involves three rotations; there is a supplement for sunset rides and upgrades to VIP gondolas with prosecco are also available.

✳ **Palanga Resort Museum** [280 B3] (Palangos kurorto muziejus; Birutės alėja 34A; w kurortomuziejus.lt; ⊕ Oct–Apr 10.00–19.00 Tue–Sat, May–Sep 10.00–19.00 Wed–Sun; €3/1.50) The local name for the splendid villa in which this museum is housed is 'Alnapilis' (The Otherworld) on account of the former owner Countess Sophia Tiškevičienė's (1837–1919) dabbling in the spiritual world. Her seances were given ethereal gravitas by the sound of the unique wind organ installed in the tower. Visit on a winter evening for added mystique. Exhibits unveil the history of Palanga as it developed into a seaside resort, from prudish costumes and bathing machines to the modern resort of today – the interactive photo booths provide fun souvenir opportunities.

✳ **Palanga Pier** [280 A2] (Palangos tiltas) Palanga Pier was originally built in 1892 for Count Tiškevičius's boat *Feniksas* to dock. Practically, the pier was needed for shipping bricks and featured a horse-drawn railway out to the far end, but its development as a port was limited due to shallow waters – a blessing for the resort's recreational potential. The present 470m L-shaped pier dates from 1997, its predecessor having been destroyed by severe storms four years earlier. The wooden boards are well trodden as it is a popular place to stroll in all seasons and at all times of day. The street lamps lining the pier reflect in the water and fishermen's rods are always propped along the railings hoping for a catch. Watching a sunset from the pier is an absolute must-do in Palanga.

**Statue of Jūratė and Kastytis** [280 A2] (Pier end of J Basanavičiaus gatvė) Since 1961, this much-loved statue of the legendary sea goddess Jūratė and fisherman Kastytis has reminded passers-by of their tale of love and woe. In 1842, author Adomas Liudvikas Jucevičius (1813–46) published this local legend in his book *Memories of Samogitian Land*, and in 1920 the story was poeticised by Jonas Mačiulis-Maironis (1862–1932) in the ballad 'Jūratė and Kastytis'. A firm favourite of Lithuanian literature, the legend tells of an amber palace on the bed of the Baltic Sea from where Jūratė ruled over the waters and all creatures. Learning her fish were dying at the hands of the fisherman Kastytis, she rose from the depths to warn him away but got caught in his fishing net. As their eyes met, it was a case of love at first sight and she invited him to return with her to the amber palace. When Perkūnas, god of all gods, saw Jūratė meddling with a mortal, he was incensed and cast his fire arrow directly at the amber palace, smashing it to smithereens. Kastytis met his end in the watery depths and Jūratė was imprisoned in an underwater cave. Her tears of grief for Kastytis have been washing up on the shore as grains of amber ever since. The sculpture was created by Nijolė Gaigalaitė (1928–2009) and is a symbol of the resort.

**Meilės alėja** [280 A3] Meilės alėja, or Love Avenue, leads south from the statue of *Jūratė and Kastytis* into Birutės Park. Behind the pine trees and dunes and running south of Palanga Pier for 500m is the Blue Flag **Palanga Beach** (Palangos paplūdimys), a haven of clean sand and swimming water. Beyond the Blue Flag beach, both north and south, the sand stretches far and wide along the whole coastline. At the southern end of Love Avenue, among the pine trees and undergrowth towards the beach, are the remains of a **defence pill box**, a reminder of darker times in this peaceful park.

### Tiškevičius Palace and Birutės Park
**Tiškevičius Palace** [280 B6] (Tiškevičų rūmai; Vytauto gatvė 17; ⊕ gardens & park always open & free; entry to palace interior is via admission to the Palanga Amber Museum – page 286) Tiškevičius Palace was commissioned by Count Feliksas Tiškevičius (1869–1933) in 1897 as a primary residence for the family. The Neo-Renaissance façade and terrace are approached by an elegant double staircase, its centrepiece a lion statue alongside which Palanga children traditionally have their photo taken. During the summer months, the terrace is a venue for evening serenade music concerts and during the day provides outdoor seating for Balzac Café (page 283). The formal gardens, central fountain and statue of *Christ Blessing* by Danish sculptor Berthel Thorwaldsen are best appreciated from the elevated terrace, although the beauty of the park extends well beyond the manicured flower beds and lawns.

Countess Tiškevičienė, Antanina Korzbok-Łącka (1870–1951) was a devout Catholic and the palace's octagonal side chapel was added in 1907 to enable the family to start and end the day with prayers. The subtle palace interior was filled with precious pieces of art, paintings, books and the exclusive amber collection of Count Tiškevičius. In 1939, when Nazi Germany gave Lithuania an ultimatum to leave the Klaipėda region, the Tiškevičius family fled Palanga, ultimately settling in Canada. The palace suffered damage during the war years; then, during post-war Soviet occupation, it was nationalised; and since 1963 it has housed the Palanga Amber Museum.

**Palanga Amber Museum** (Palangos gintaro muziejus; w lndm.lt/en/pgm; ⊕ Sep–May 10.00–18.00 Tue–Sat, 10.00–17.00 Sun, May–Sep 10.00–20.00 Tue–Sat, 10.00–19.00 Sun; €8/4) Palanga Amber Museum celebrates the story of amber from formation to processing via a wealth of amber artefacts, including rare 'inclusions' – amber with preserved insects trapped inside. Highlights include the 'Sun Stone' (saulės akmuo), Europe's third largest piece of amber weighing in at 3.524kg, which has been stolen twice; a still bagged-up delivery of amber jewellery which never made it to the Ireland–USSR Friendship Festival in 1986, but turned up in Dublin Airport's unclaimed baggage in 2015; and an amber toilet. There's also a museum shop and café (page 283) which you do not need a ticket to visit.

✴ **Birutės Park** [280 B5] (Birutės parkas; ⊕ 24hrs; free) A lush 100ha parkland, sandwiched between the beach and Vytauto gatvė, Birutės Park wraps around Tiškevičius Palace. Created in 1897 by famous French landscape architect Edouard Francois Andre (1840–1911) and continued by his son Rene Edouard Andre (1867–1942), the park was previously called Palanga Botanical Park, reflecting the 500 different varieties of exotic trees and shrubs planted here. Small ponds, picture-perfect white bridges and well-kept forest make the park popular for strolling and picnics. The bronze statue of *Eglė Queen of the Grass Snakes* [280 C5] (Eglė žalčių karalienė), created in 1960 by sculptor Robertas Antinis, is a focal point and honours the ancient folk tale of the young girl Eglė, who after enjoying a swim with her sisters finds a grass snake in her clothing. The grass snake gives Eglė an ultimatum: that he will leave her clothing only if she agrees to marry him. Keen to get rid of the pesky snake, she agrees – without considering the consequences. Reluctantly, Eglė marries the snake who transpires to be a rather handsome man called Žilvinas, and they live with their offspring in an underworld. Their story goes horribly wrong when Eglė returns to visit her parents, her protective brothers kill Žilvinas and, through despair and some enchanting, Eglė turns herself and her children into a variety of trees. Such a summary does not do the story justice, but the overarching theme is one of connection to nature which is still prevalent in the Lithuanian character today. Eglė remains a popular girl's name.

At the south end of the park, **Birutės Hill** [280 A6] (Birutė kalnas) is the highest dune in Palanga and once a pagan place of worship and ritual. Birutė (c1330–82), after whom the park and the hill are named, was a priestess who became Grand Duchess of Lithuania. Legend has it, that Birutė had promised herself to the gods and was protecting the sanctuary when Lithuania's Grand Duke Kestutis fell for her. They wed and she bore Grand Duke Vytautas the Great. Birutė was honoured long after her death, and her name lives on. With the introduction of Christianity and to suppress paganism, a statement **Chapel of St George** [280 A6] was built on Birutės Hill in 1506. The current chapel was built here in 1869–70 and houses a statue of the Virgin Mary brought from Lourdes. Below the chapel hill is a replica of the Lourdes grotto, included at the personal request of Countess Antanina Tiškevičienė during the estate landscaping in 1898.

**Jonas Šliūpas Museum** [280 C4] (Jono Šliūpo muziejus; Vytauto gatvė 23A; w lnm.lt/en/museums/jonas-sliupas-museum; ⊕ 10.00–17.00 Wed–Fri, 11.00–17.00 Sat, 11.00–16.00 Sun; €4/2) This small branch of the Lithuanian National Museum commemorates the life of Lithuanian activist Jonas Šliūpas (1861–1944). Born in the Kretinga region, Šliūpas fled Lithuania in 1884 ultimately to the USA, where he stayed for 35 years working tirelessly to raise the profile and support of the Lithuanian diaspora for their homeland. During the inter-war period he returned to Palanga and was city mayor on and off between 1933 and 1941, until fleeing in 1944 to Germany. The 19th-century villa housing the museum was his mayoral home during that time.

**Old Pharmacy** [280 C4] (Senoji vaistinė; Vytauto gatvė 33; w senojivaistine.lt; ⊕ 09.00–21.00 Mon–Sat, 09.00–18.00 Sun) The Old Pharmacy is one of Palanga's finest wooden buildings and the oldest operating chemists shop in Lithuania. It was founded in 1827 by Wilhelm Johann Grüning, who is credited with inventing the recipe for the herbal tincture '999' (Trejos devynerios), which is still taken by many Lithuanians as a remedy for various minor ailments. Interior highlights are the original wooden cabinets and murals.

**Mončys Museum** [280 B4] (Mončio namai muziejus; S Daukanto gatvė 16; w antanasmoncys.com; ⊕ 11.00–17.00 Wed–Sun; €3/1.50) Modern art lovers will appreciate this museum, a tribute to the eminent Lithuanian émigré artist Antanas Mončys (1921–93), who, in 1991, donated his personal collection of artworks to Palanga city. Over the years more pieces and personal effects were added and the museum opened in 1999. Having left Kretinga region in 1944 and settled in Paris, his exposure to the Avant Garde art movement influenced his modernist sculptures.

**Count Tiškevičius Alley** [280 C4] (Grafų Tiškevičių alėja; Kęstučio gatvė 2 to J Simpsono gatvė 1A) The paved and well-lit Count Tiškevičius Alley passes through the contemporary exhibits of **Palanga Sculpture Park**. Rotarians from around the globe may be surprised to encounter a statue of Paul Harris, the founder of Rotary International, donated to the sculpture park by Lithuanian rotary clubs. The elegant couple immortalised in bronze at the northern end are Count Feliksas Tiškevičius and Countess Antanina Tiškevičienė with their dog. Of note, is the untypical street name J Simpson gatvė, named after James Simpson, a Scottish professor at Edinburgh University who acted as an independent mediator overseeing the international redrawing of the Lithuania–Latvia border post World War I. Simpson cast the deciding vote to give Palanga to Lithuania, and a street was named in his honour.

Also on Count Tiškevičius Alley, is the **Kurhaus** [280 C3] (Palangos kultūros centras; Grafų Tiškevičių alėja 1; w palangoskultura.lt; ⊕ check their website for events & times). Built by the Tiškevičius family in 1877 to accommodate and entertain their guests, the Kurhaus was Palanga's first hotel and entertainment hub, complete with a billiard room and reading room. In 2002 it was severely damaged by fire and has been sympathetically restored using authentic designs and techniques – particularly the ornate woodwork on the rear section. Today it is a cultural and youth centre for local concerts and events.

**Church of the Assumption of the Blessed Virgin Mary** [280 C3] (Mergelės Marijos Ėmimo į dangų bažnyčia; Vytauto gatvė 51; ⊕ 08.00–19.00 daily) One of few monuments to grace the Palanga skyline, the church's four-angled tower is 24m tall and climbing its approximately 100 steps will reward you with a panoramic view of the city from the **observation deck** (⊕ 09.00–17.30 Mon–Sat, 13.30–17.30 Sun; free). The red-brick vaulted ceiling of the church interior is striking and, along with the colourful stained-glass windows behind the altar, brings an unusually warm feel to the church.

## AROUND PALANGA

**ŠVENTOJI** Some 12km north of Palanga, Šventoji is an old fishing village that has attempted to reinvent itself over the centuries. Archaeological evidence suggests it was a more strategically important port than Palanga in the 17th century and prospered from the British and Danish shipbuilding and timber trades. However, development of the port of Šventoji located at the mouth of the eponymous river has always been hindered by excessive deposits of sand. Today, the small harbour is being improved to moor private leisure boats to support the tourism infrastructure and recreational demand spilling over from Palanga. A cheaper alternative to Palanga, the resort is more frequented by locals and it is popular for cycling day trips from Klaipėda (35km) or Palanga (12km). The centre has a small selection of shops, supermarket, restaurants and bars. Set in the dunes, the **Fisherman's Daughters** statue (Žvejo dukros; access path starts behind the new port authority building at Šventoji harbour at time of writing), created in 1982 by sculptor Zuzana Pranaitytė, depicts three long-haired girls looking out to sea, waiting for their father to return. A recent revelation by the artist's niece claims the three girls represent Lithuania, Latvia and Estonia looking to the west for help during the Soviet occupation, thus attributing the statue with an even stronger national identity. Spanning the Šventoji River at the north of the resort, the **Monkey Bridge** (Beždžionių tiltas; Kopų gatvė) has been reconstructed since it was first built in 1973 but remains a symbol of the village. As well as providing an essential crossing for pedestrians and cyclists, it attracts budding photographers especially at sunset. After the bridge, the track continues north to the **Samogitian Sanctuary** (Žemaičių alka; on the coastal path, 500m north of Monkey Bridge; parking on Kuršių takas, Šventoji), a reconstructed medieval pagan sanctuary based on archaeological records. The 12 oak pillars are approximately 2m tall and were individually carved by Lithuanian folk artists in 1998. Each pole corresponds to an ancient Balt god or goddess, including Thunder, the Devil and the Moon. When the sun goes down at the end of the day, the shadows cast by the poles indicate the festivals of the Baltic calendar as the site is arranged as a paleo-astronomic observatory. Today, neo-pagans use the site for celebrating festivals, including Midsummer.

**BALTIC MYTHOLOGY PARK** (Baltų mitologijos parkas; Sausdravų village, Kretinga region; BaltuParkas; ⊕ 10.00–22.00 daily; €5/2) Close to Lake Lazdininkų and Darbėnai town, 20km northeast of Palanga, is this educational park dedicated to the understanding of the ancestral Balts' close relationship with nature. Mythological deities and symbols are laid out in a pyramid-shape woodland walk and sculpture trail which offers an insight into ancient beliefs and customs. Anywhere with a 'pit of happiness' exudes good energy. Sculpture fans and ethnographic souls will not be disappointed.

**JAPANESE GARDENS** (Japoniškas sodas; Sodų gatvė 10, Mažučiai village; w japangarden.lt; ⊕ 10.00–20.30 daily; €12/7) To the west of Darbėnai, you'll find a beautifully designed and well-tended Japanese garden of soft landscaping, easily enjoyed from the self-guided plan. Seasonal highlights include vibrant acers and blossom trees, and the recommended tea ceremony can be enjoyed all year round for an additional €3 per person. Professional photoshoots in the garden are available. Pause to consider customs rules before buying a bonsai tree in the gift shop.

**SALANTAI** The town of Salantai is not a tourist destination in itself, but, if you find yourself passing through on the way from Palanga to Plateliai and in need of refreshment, there is a local experience waiting for you at **Pakalnutė** (M Valančiaus gatvė 3; \+370 445 58703; ⊕ 10.00–20.00 daily; €€). This old-school restaurant, which rates highly with food critics, serves up homely fare – but there's no menu and no English. The owners will tell you what you should eat, and other customers will help translate or you can guess with some key words. There is seating outside in summer, surrounded by trees and the church tower nearby.

**KRETINGA** Most of the major regional dynasties have had a hand in Kretinga's history, including Chodkevičius (Chodkiewicz), Sapiega, Masalskiai, Potockiai, Zubov and Tiškevičius. One of the oldest towns in Lithuania, the Kretinga we see today is that of the Tiškevičius family, who, in 1875, transformed the original manor house into their namesake palace complete with a splendid winter garden. Since independence, Kretinga has forged its way as a cultural centre of art, folk and music festivals. For visitors staying in Palanga or Klaipėda, it makes for a pleasant day out; and for those with Lithuanian heritage, the water mill exhibition of the Kretinga Museum is a beautiful insight into ancestral traditions and crafts which revive the memories and stories of long-lost relatives.

It is a 3-minute walk to the Kretinga Museum from both bus and train stations. Walk via J Basanavičiaus gatvė to avoid the main road (cross the Akmena River via the footbridge at house number 47) and visit the **tourist information centre** (Kretingos turizmo informacijos centras; Vilniaus gatvė 2B; w visitkretinga.lt; ⊕ 08.00–18.00 Mon–Fri, 09.00–15.00 Sat–Sun) and the **Church of the Annunciation of the Blessed Virgin Mary** (Vilniaus gatvė 2) on the way.

**Getting there and away** To reach Kretinga, take the number 51 bus from Klaipėda bus station, or the number 60 from Palanga bus station; both have regular departures daily. Several trains depart Klaipėda train station to Kretinga (25mins) every day.

## What to see and do

✴ ***Kretinga Museum and Winter Garden*** (Kretingos muziejus; Vilniaus gatvė 20; w kretingosmuziejus.lt; ⊕ museum: 10.00–18.00 Wed–Sun; Winter Garden: Jun–Aug 10.00–18.00 Mon, 10.00–20.00 Tue–Sun, Sep–May 10.00–18.00 Tue–Sun; €8/4) For centuries, Kretinga residents were encouraged by public figures to keep historical artefacts, and in 1935 teacher Juozas Žilvitis donated his collection and founded the city museum. The main collection is now housed in the prominent Kretinga Manor (also known as Tiškevičius Palace), former home of numerous Lithuanian noble families about which there are genealogical displays. There is limited exhibition information in English, though the new basement archaeology displays are an exception.

The **Winter Garden** is the only one of its kind in Lithuania – a haven of exotic plants, intertwined with spiral staircases and water feature grottos. It was destroyed in World War II but painstakingly restored by the staff of the Kretinga Agricultural College. The details can be admired when having a leisurely coffee or lunch in the Winter Garden's restaurant, **Pas Grafą** (w pasgrafa.lt; ⊕ Jun–Aug noon–18.00 Mon, noon–23.00 Tue–Sun, Sep–May noon–23.00 Tue–Sun; €€€). A walk around the park estate takes in an astronomical calendar and sun clock, and stone sculptures.

The museum's ticket office is in the car park on the opposite side of Vilniaus gatvė to the palace. Your ticket includes entry to the whole museum complex, including the **Traditional Craft Centre** (Vilniaus gatvė 37), which surrounds the car park and hosts craft workshops and demonstrations. Exit the car park and turn left to visit the **Water Mill** (Vandens malūnas), which hosts a small but exquisite collection of ethnographic crafts and heritage objects with detailed explanations about their use and traditions. On the lower level is a small café and sweet shop.

## KLAIPĖDA

Klaipėda is a medley of maritime heritage with so many layers of history and influence that few sights have a straightforward story. For much of its history, Klaipėda was the German city of Memel, the most northeastern frontier city of the German Empire, Prussia. In 1918, at the end of World War I, Prussia collapsed and the Memel region was placed under the protectorate of the Entente States. As Memel's future was being debated, in 1923 Lithuania made a bold move, seizing the territory and annexing it into Lithuania. They met little resistance. Lithuania had gained strategic access to the Baltic Sea, and Memel became the Lithuanian city of Klaipėda. The name Klaipėda is believed to have ancient roots, originating from the language of a Curonian tribe: *klaip* (bread) and *ėda* (eat). Despite being forced to navigate further 20th-century occupations by Nazi Germany and Soviet Russia, Klaipėda has been forging its Lithuanian identity ever since – not an easy task for the country's third largest city, with its diminishing population (202,000 in 1989 to fewer than 160,000 in 2024). After independence in 1990, most tourists were of German heritage visiting their ancestral homeland in Memel region and hospitality services were focused towards German-speaking guests. Today, Klaipėda's tourism appeal has broadened to a worldwide audience curious to discover the Lithuanian seaside for its beaches, culture, history and attractions – the latter three being useful on a day of inclement weather, making Klaipėda a good base for exploring the coast.

As Lithuania's only seaport, Klaipėda is a gateway for both cargo and passengers. For those arriving or departing Lithuania by international ferry with their own car, or as part of a no-fly itinerary, you are following in the sails of 18th-century British timber merchants. A much-anticipated modern cruise terminal enabled the city's inclusion in Baltic Sea cruise itineraries, raising the profile of the city but unfortunately providing few benefits to the local community. Most cruise-ship passengers take an organised day trip to the Curonian Spit and see nothing (nor spend anything) in Klaipėda. Similarly, those touring Lithuania by land often use Klaipėda as a launch point to the Curonian Spit and miss out on this delightful smaller city and the heritage of this oft-contested territory. During summer season, it can be easier (and cheaper) to find a short hotel stay in Klaipėda than in Palanga or Nida.

### GETTING THERE AND AWAY
**By air** Klaipėda is served by **Palanga Airport** (page 279), located approximately 25km north of the city on the main A13 (E272) highway which runs to the Latvia border. Minibus number 31 (1hr 10mins; €2.50) runs from Palanga Airport to

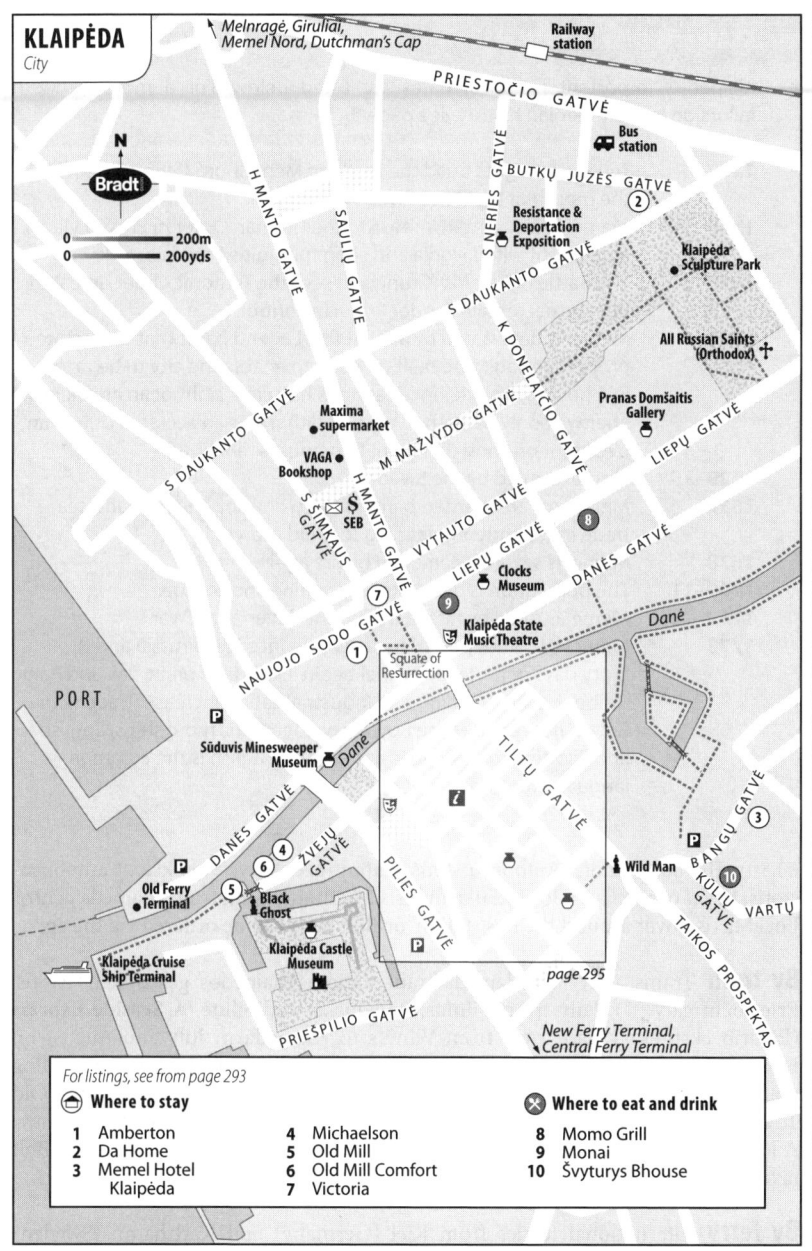

Klaipėda train and bus stations, the timetable scheduled to suit the flight times. A taxi ride will take about 35 minutes; expect to pay in the region of €28.

**By bus** There are daily direct bus services to Klaipėda from Vilnius, Kaunas, Telšiai, Šiauliai, Liepāja and Riga; and daily local buses to/from Palanga, Kretinga and Nida. Bus numbers 3, 8 and 17 are regular services to the city centre (adult

## KLAIPĖDA HISTORY TIMELINE

Klaipėda's important historical dates are listed below. For a more in-depth incursion into Lithuanian history, see page 9.

| | |
|---|---|
| **1252** | Teutonic Knights build the castle of Memelburg (Memel castle) at the mouth of the Danė River. |
| **1328** | Memel region is transmitted to the German Order in Prussia via an agreement with Livonia and soon fully joins Prussia. |
| **1410** | The Battle of Žalgiris (Grunwald) sees the Teutonic Order defeated but Memel remains under Prussian control. |
| **1540** | Memel is devastated by a great fire. Legend has it that a law stated properties had to be built of wood to enable the city to be razed in 6 hours so the defence cannons had clear sight of an attacking enemy. It only happened once and that was an accident due to an oversight on wind direction. Two houses remained. |
| **1629–35** | Memel is ruled by the Swedes. |
| **1657** | Merchants are granted permission to develop the port and sea trade independently, leading to rapid growth. |
| **1678** | Memel is severely damaged by fire again. |
| **1709–11** | The population is decimated by famine and plague. |
| **1757–62** | Memel is ruled by Russia during the Seven Years War. |
| **1773** | Memel becomes part of the new province East Prussia and the glory days of trade for Memel begin. Exports of grain, flax and Baltic timber for shipbuilding and industrialisation increase. Trade with Britain flourishes as the Royal Navy demands more ships, English and Scottish communities appear and English is the common language for trade. |

€0.80). The bus station (Autobusų stotis; Butkų Juzės gatvė 9; w klap.lt/autobusu-stotis; ticket office: ⊕ 05.30–19.50 daily) is a 20-minute walk from Klaipėda centre. Local taxis hover around the bus station, or Bolt taxis can be ordered via the app.

**By train** Trains arrive to Klaipėda train station (Klaipėdos geležinkelio stotis; Priestočių gatvė 1) daily from Vilnius, Radviliškis and Šilutė. A **Seaside Express** (Pajūrio ekspresas) train runs from Vilnius to Klaipėda in July and August on Fridays, Saturdays and Sundays. Station amenities include a luggage store, vending machines and a ticket information centre. Take bus number 8 to get to the Old Town and city centre (adult €0.80); otherwise it's a 20-minute walk to the centre. A local taxi can usually be found at the front of the station, or you can order a Bolt taxi via the app.

**By ferry** International ferries from Kiel (Germany) and Karlshamn (Sweden) arrive at Klaipėda Central Ferry Terminal (Centrinis Klaipėdos terminalas; Baltijos pr. 40; w ckt.lt) located 4km south of the city centre. There are basic facilities for passengers. Bus numbers 3 and 9 will take you to the city centre.

**By car** If travelling by car, you will arrive in Klaipėda on road A1 from the east, 168 from the north and 141 from the south. Follow the signs for 'centras' and be aware of the speed limits reducing as you get closer to the centre. **Parking** in Klaipėda is

| | |
|---|---|
| 1808 | For one year, Memel is the capital of Prussia due to the occupation of Berlin by Napoleon. King Friedrich Wilhelm III of Prussia decamps to Memel. |
| 1854 | Another fire destroys a large part of the city. |
| 1864–1904 | The Russian Empire bans Lithuanian-language books, but they continue to be printed in neighbouring Prussia and Memel is a smuggling route into Lithuania. |
| 1873 | The King Wilhelm Channel is constructed to join the mouth of the Nemunas River with Memel port. |
| 1918 | Post-World War I the territory of Lithuania Minor is integrated into Lithuania proper via the Act of Tilsit. |
| 1919 | The Treaty of Versailles confiscates the Memel region from Prussia and places it under the jurisdiction of the Entente States with French administration. |
| 1923 | The Klaipėda Revolt – an uprising of the local pro-Lithuanian population in Memel petitioning to join Lithuania – is successful. Memel joins Lithuania and is renamed Klaipėda. |
| 1939 | Nazi Germany annexes Klaipėda region, and Hitler arrives on his ship *Deutschland* to give a hardline speech from the drama theatre balcony. Germany invades Lithuania in June 1941. |
| 1944 | The Battle of Memel. Soviet Russia forces Nazi Germany back to the west. |
| 1945 | At the end of World War II, Lithuania is annexed into the USSR as the Soviet Socialist Republic of Lithuania. Industrialisation moves fast as Klaipėda is now Soviet Russia's only ice-free Baltic port. |
| 1990 | Lithuania gains independence from Russia. |

arranged in green, yellow, red and blue zones, priced from low to high respectively. You can pay per hour via the roadside machines or download the Unipark app for a speedy way to pay.

**GETTING AROUND** Klaipėda is a small city and easily explored on foot. Local buses operate within the city with most sights no more than a couple of stops away. If car transport is needed, using the **Bolt** app to book a taxi service is most convenient.

**TOURIST INFORMATION** Visit **Klaipėda Tourism Information Centre** (Klaipėdos turizmo informacijos centras; Turgaus gatvė 7; w klaipedatravel.lt; ⊕ Sep–May 09.00–18.00 Mon–Fri, 10.00–16.00 Sat, Jun–Aug 10.00–16.00 Sat–Sun) for help with accommodation, sightseeing tours, transport options and local events.

 **WHERE TO STAY** *Map, page 291, unless otherwise stated*

✳ **Michaelson Hotel** (16 rooms) Žvejų gatvė 18A; w hotelmichaelson.com. The Michaelson family were early 19th-century merchants whose warehouses now house a luxury boutique hotel & spa, as opposed to grain & flax. The hotel is located on the dockside between Klaipėda Castle & the Old Ferry Port only a short walk from the city centre. The restaurant is recommended to non-residents. **€€€€**

✳ **Victoria Hotel** (105 rooms) S Šimkaus gatvė 2; w hotelvictoria.lt/klaipeda. This grand hotel, contemporary in style, was once an 18th-century tavern where traders changed their horses, then a meeting place for the Prussian cultural elite – the composer Wagner stayed here, Hitler drank coffee here, then the Soviets split it into units & it was abandoned for over 20 years. These days there are classical music concerts in the atrium & an Instagram-loved Zebra in the rooftop bar. The daily business lunch is recommended. €€€€

**Amberton** (254 rooms) Naujojo Sodo gatvė 1A; w ambertonhotels.com/klaipeda. A big chain hotel, Amberton somehow retains a whiff of its former Intourist days, not least due to its harsh exterior & casino–nightclub combo. The 20th-floor restaurant & 21st-floor rooftop bar are cocktail-central at sunset, offering panoramic views of the region & the satisfaction of being at the very top of the skyline in Klaipėda. €€€

**Hotel Rėja** [map, opposite] (50 rooms) Teatro gatvė 1; w hotelreja.com. Housed in a historic building dating from 1855, the recently refurbished interior is elegant & worthy of their Design Hotel status. 2 suites have private terraces. Hotel gastropub The Fat Cat is well loved by locals & guests alike. €€€

**Old Mill Comfort Hotel** (21 rooms) Žvejų gatvė 20; w oldmillcomfort.lt. Sister hotel to the neighbouring Fachwerk-style **Old Mill Hotel** (w oldmillhotel.lt) with spacious, contemporary rooms. Check-in & b/fast services are shared between the two during low season. The walk between hotels is via the chain bridge, which is regularly opened to allow boats into the dock. The opening schedule is displayed next to the bridge & takes 15mins. €€€

**Da Home Hotel** (6 rooms) Butkų Juzės gatvė 14-8; w dahome.lt. Located near the Klaipėda Sculpture Park & train station, Da Home is a new-generation 'urban hotel' with self-check-in dbl & family quad rooms. There's a communal lounge & mini kitchen for guests. €€

**Euterpė Hotel** [map, opposite] (35 rooms) Daržų gatvė 9; w euterpe.lt. The name stems from a Renaissance tile depicting mythical muse Euterpė, found during archaeological excavations close to the hotel. This story is a nice detail, but the hotel's strengths are the simple pleasures of a well-run independent hotel including an attractive summer courtyard. €€

**Memel Hotel Klaipėda** (50 rooms) Bangų gatvė 4; w memelhotel.lt. On the inland side of the Old Town at the beginning of a residential area, & close to the Bhouse brewery, this small, simple hotel has very reasonable prices for a central stay. €€

## WHERE TO EAT AND DRINK
*Map, opposite, unless otherwise stated*

**Momo Grill** [map, page 291] w momogrill.lt/en/klaipeda; ⏰ 11.00–21.00 Mon, 11.00–22.00 Tue–Thu, noon–22.00 Fri–Sat. High-end seasonal kitchen serving burgers, grills & creative dishes. Save room for the crème brulé – highly recommended. €€€€€

**Meridianas** [map, page 291] Moored on the left bank of the Danė River; w restoranasmeridianas.lt; ⏰ 11.00–22.00 Mon–Thu, 11.00–midnight Fri, noon–midnight Sat, noon–21.00 Sun. Meridianas is popular both for its novelty factor, located on board a historic ship, & for its high-quality Mediterranean menu. A business lunch menu is available 11.00–15.00 Mon–Fri. Children's menu also available. Highly recommended, so book in ahead if you'd like to dine on board one of Klaipėda's iconic landmarks (page 298). €€€€

**Monai** [map, page 291] Liepų gatvė 4; w restoranasmonai.lt; ⏰ 11.30–22.00 Tue–Fri, 11.00–22.00 Sat, 11.00–16.00 Sun. Klaipėda's first Michelin-recommended restaurant, Monai has a relaxed atmosphere with delicate & stylish dining. The daily lunch menu could easily be the highlight of your day. €€€€

**Stora Antis** Tiltų gatvė 6; w storaantis.lt; ⏰ 18.00–22.30 Fri–Sat. This small family-run restaurant has a legendary reputation for serving creative Lithuanian food in their architectural monument cellars. Open w/nds only. €€€

**Švyturys Bhouse** [map, page 291] Kūlių Vartų gatvė 7; w svyturysbrewery.lt/gastro-baras; ⏰ 16.00–midnight Mon–Thu, 16.00–midnight Fri, 13.00–02.00 Sat, 13.00–23.00 Sun. Since 1784, Svyturys beer has been quenching the thirst of Klaipėda residents. During World War II when Klaipėda (Memel) was under German control, the Russians bombed the city heavily causing widespread damage. Knowing the importance of beer to local morale, the Švyturys brewery was a priority reconstruction project. In 1999 the iconic beer brand was controversially bought by Carlsberg, with production moved to Utena & the brewery building converted to apartments. Thankfully, the scent of hops prevails & the small-scale Red Bricks Brewery is now housed here along with the excellent Bhouse gastro-bar. Brewery tours are available in English between 10.00 & 20.00 Tue–Sat if prebooked. €€€

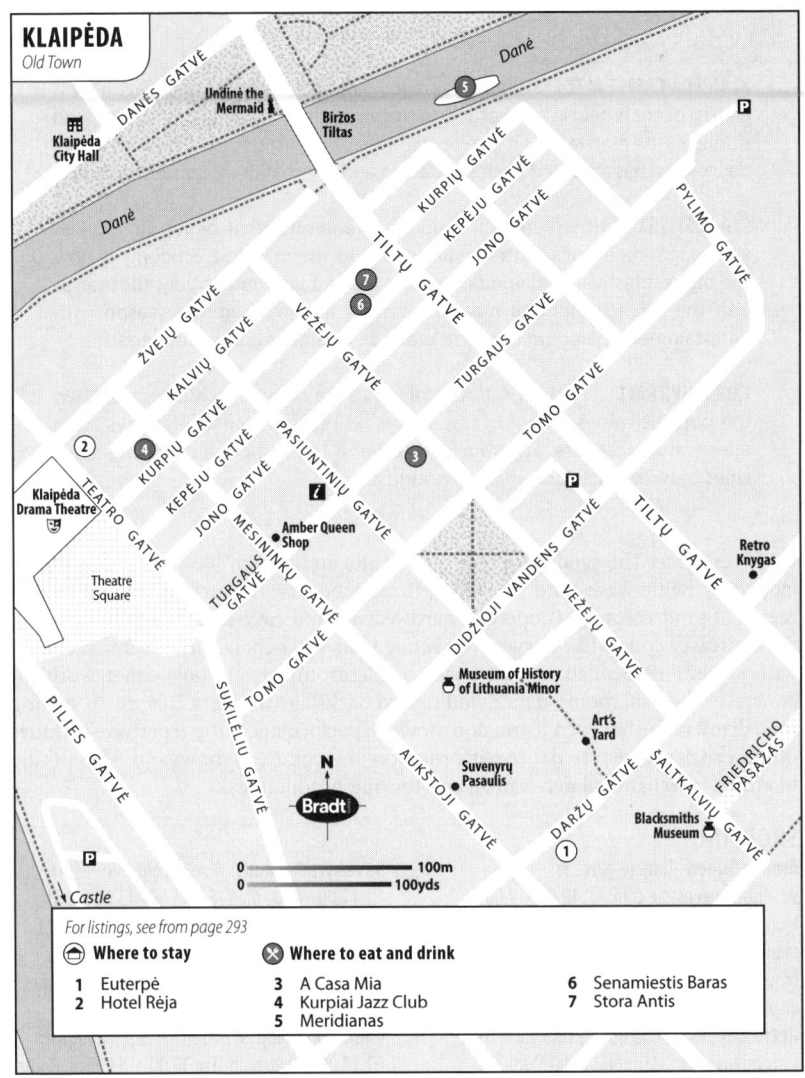

**A Casa Mia** Turgaus gatvė 10; w acasamia. lt; ⏰ 14.00–22.00 Mon–Sat. Chef Francesco & partner Gabriele have created a home-from-home feeling at their authentic Italian restaurant & deli shop. Simple works – quality without compromise. €€

**Kurpiai Jazz Club** Kurpių gatvė 1A; kurpiai; ⏰ noon–midnight daily. Where good food meets good music, especially jazz. Their daily lunch menu (€7) is served noon–15.00 & helps break up a day of sightseeing. €€

**Senamiestis Baras** Kepėjų gatvė 13; senamiestis.baras; ⏰ 10.00–23.00 daily. When in Klaipėda this is the place for must-taste 'Old Town Fingers' (cheese), herring 'in a medieval way' and rum with tea 'grog'. A local lunchtime favourite. €€

**ENTERTAINMENT** A multi-million-euro renovation has created a truly unique concert hall in the shape of **Klaipėda State Music Theatre** (Klaipėdos valstybinis muzikinis teatras; Danės gatvė 19; w klaipedosmuzikinis.lt), taking creative design

> ### KLAIPĖDA FESTIVALS
>
> **KLAIPĖDA CASTLE JAZZ FESTIVAL** (Klaipėdos pilies džiazo festivalis; w jazz.lt) This annual event is held in June or July in the grounds of Klaipėda Castle, although during castle renovations it is relocated to Teatro aikštė. Since 1994, this three-day festival has attracted both Lithuanian and international jazz performers.
>
> **SEA FESTIVAL** (Jūros šventė; w klaipedossventes.lt) What began in 1934 as a propaganda event to attract youngsters to the maritime academy is now the biggest festival in Klaipėda. Held on the last weekend in July, thousands visit the city to celebrate maritime history and the summer season with entertainment including concerts, craft fairs, parades and sailing regattas.
>
> **TALL SHIPS RACE** (w tallships.lt) A highlight of the calendar in Klaipėda is when the port welcomes a fleet of traditional sailing ships for several days amid a festival atmosphere. The ships race around the Baltic Sea, stopping at six cities between late June and early August.

to the extreme. The sand-sculpted walls of the auditorium look like they've been lapped by Baltic waves and provide optimal acoustics. All surfaces are covered in reems of sand-coloured (hopefully hardwearing and easy-clean) carpet, including the staircase's conch-like curves. The venue seats 700 people and is fully accessible, with screens embedded in seat backs. Underground is a whole other world of concrete rehearsal rooms, dance studios and backstage wonders. It is worth visiting for a drink in the bar even if you don't watch a performance. The repertoire includes opera, classical concerts, dance performances and children's shows and is beginning to attract international performers and touring productions.

## SHOPPING

**Amber Queen** Turgaus gatvė 3; w amberqueenstore.com; ⊕ 10.00–19.00 Mon–Sat, 10.00–16.00 Sun. Buy amber jewellery manufactured locally in their Klaipėda factory while browsing the many interesting amber exhibits on display. Factory tours are available if prearranged.

**Retro Knygos** (Retro Books) Tiltų gatvė 19; w retroknygos.lt; ⊕ noon–18.00 Mon–Fri, noon–16.00 Sat. It's worth a browse in this quirky independent bookshop which stocks a random selection of retro publications & collectibles too – you may be lucky & find a gem. Opening hours are a guide, not totally reliable.

**Suvenyrų Pasaulis** Aukštoji gatvė 5; ⊕ 11.00–18.00 Mon–Fri, 11.00–15.00 Sat. The painted shutters lure you in with the promise of traditional Lithuanian souvenirs & handicrafts – that's exactly what they stock, among some other questionable items.

**VAGA Bookshop** H Manto gatvė 9; w vaga.lt; ⊕ 10.00–19.00 Mon–Fri, 10.00–16.00 Sat. Books, gifts, souvenirs, postcards & coffee all in one place. They also sell a small selection of English-language books covering travel & history mainly.

**OTHER PRACTICALITIES** The central **post office** (H Manto gatvė 7) is in the new town and there is a branch of **SEB Bank** at the same address. A little further along the street there is a **pharmacy** (H Manto gatvė 11) inside the Maxima **supermarket**.

## WHAT TO SEE AND DO
**North of the Danė River** The right bank of the Danė River is known as Naujamiestis (New Town). The area lost many historic buildings during periods

of conflict and remains a tad battle-scarred with open spaces and Soviet construction. Liepų gatvė offers a glimpse of the area's former beauty, with examples of Jugendstil architecture (German Art Nouveau); the building at number 7 is particularly fine.

**\* Sūduvis Minesweeper Museum** (Laivas-muziejus 'Sūduvis'; Danės gatvė; w muziejus.lt/en/ship-museum-suduvis; ⏰ Jun–Aug 11.00–19.00 Tue–Sat, 11.00–17.00 Sun, May & Sep 11.00–17.00 Wed–Sun, Oct–Apr 11.00–17.00 Fri–Sun; €5/3) Sūduvis is a Lindau-class minehunter of the Lithuanian Naval Force. The ship was gifted in 1999 by Germany to Lithuania to assist the newly established Lithuanian Marine Corp to clear local waters safely. There are an estimated 8 million mines still in the Baltic Sea, although it is unlikely any will still be active. The vessel is now docked permanently in Klaipėda and is a visitor attraction belonging to the Lithuanian Sea Museum. Visitors can explore the ship and learn about the dangerous missions of minesweeping and minehunting. On the last Sunday of every month free tickets are available online. A mine-hunting escape room experience is available for small groups (3–7 people; €60 per group; must be booked in advance – e edukacija@muziejus.lt).

***Klaipėda City Hall*** (Rotušė; Danės gatvė 17) This historical building was built in the late 18th century in a Classical style and originally occupied by the Danish consul. Its place in history was secured when King Friedrich Wilhelm III of Prussia and Queen Louise resided here during the Napoleonic Wars (1807–08) when Napoleon's army had invaded Prussia and forced the royal family to flee northeast to Klaipėda. A commemorative bas-relief plaque of Queen Louise was unveiled on the building in 1999. In 1846 the city magistrate bought the building and it became Klaipėda City Hall. Since 2011, it is home to working offices for the Mayor of Klaipėda and municipality staff.

***Square of Resurrection*** (Atgimimo aikštė; Naujojo Sodo gatvė) This large, angular space feels frozen in time. The harsh architecture that surrounds the square includes the former Intourist hotel building, which still operates as a hotel, albeit with a new 'K'-shaped building on the city skyline. Since Lenin's statue was removed in 1991 and deposed to Grūtas Soviet Sculpture Park (page 145), nothing much has changed. The clockface of the Klaipėda State Music Theatre (page 295) dominates the eastern side of the square, below which is the *Arka* (arch) sculpture commemorating Lithuania Minor joining Greater Lithuania in 1918, the broken end symbolising the territory lost to Kaliningrad (Russia).

**\* Clocks Museum** (Laikrodžių muziejus; Liepų gatvė 12; w lndm.lt/en/lm; ⏰ closed Mon; adult €5) Housed in a grand residence once belonging to an English trader, this impressive collection of timepieces is a branch of the Lithuanian National Museum of Art. The museum traces the evolution of timekeeping and the fashions and technologies of clocks and watches. It also presents a different angle on the history of the Klaipėda region; in 1944, knowing the Russians were advancing towards the region, East Prussians abandoned their houses and fled west. Clocks, being large, cumbersome objects, were often left behind; many of them were ornate and valuable, having belonged to wealthy merchants. These were collected, commandeered or casually left to one side by locals, but there was definitely a disproportionate number of attractive and valuable clocks in the region. During the Soviet occupation, the secretary of the Communist Party organised an exhibition of clocks, encouraging locals to bring in their treasured timepieces to be showcased. They never got them back, and today those clocks account for a large proportion of the museum exhibits on display today. The walled garden has more horology examples, including sundials, and it was here in the garden that the first Klaipėda Jazz Festival (page 296) was held and small music events are often hosted here.

**Pranas Domšaitis Gallery** (Prano Domšaičio galerija; Liepų gatvė 33; w lndm.lt/en/pdg; ⊕ 10.00–18.00 Tue–Wed, noon–20.00 Thu, 10.00–18.00 Fri–Sat, 10.00–16.00 Sun; €5/2.50) Born Franz Domscheit in the Memel region under Prussian rule, Pranas Domšaitis (1880–1965) assumed his Lithuanian name in 1937, having been labelled a 'degenerate artist' by the Nazi regime. He fled to South Africa in 1949 and became one of the most acclaimed Lithuanian artists living in exile. His work was influenced by European modern art and contemporary Expressionism. Over 200 of his artworks are displayed alongside temporary exhibitions.

**Klaipėda Sculpture Park** (Klaipėda skulptūrų parkas; surrounded by the streets K Donelaičio, Liepų, Trilapio and S Daukanto; w mlimuziejus.lt/en/museum/sculpture-park; ⊕ at all times; free) From 1820 to 1975 this site was one of the city's main cemeteries, until the Soviet occupiers destroyed it. The Sculpture Park, also known as Martynas Mažvydas Sculpture Park, was created in 1975 and contains more than 110 unique granite sculptures. Since independence, several authentic gravestones have been restored, but it is worth noting that over 40,000 people are buried here. Exit the park at the **Orthodox Church of All Russian Saints** (Klaipėdos Visų Rusų Šventųjų parapija; Liepų gatvė 45).

**Resistance and Deportation Exposition** (Tremties ir rezistencijos ekspozicija; S Nėries gatvė 4; w mlimuziejus.lt/en/museum/resistance-and-deportation; ⊕ by appt only, call ✆+370 464 10527; free) At the time of writing this small but fascinating exhibition, housed in the former residence of the Soviet Committee for State Security (KGB), must be prebooked. In the basement cells, 8,268 people were detained, tortured or killed between 1945 and 1954. Today, they house an exhibition dedicated to the resistance movement, political prisoners and partisans of western Lithuania during 1945–54. Authentic objects are displayed, and the recordings of conversations with first-hand account witnesses are chilling.

## South of the Danė River
**Biržos Tiltas** (Exchange Bridge) Biržos Tiltas was named after the adjacent stock exchange and was a lucrative asset for the city – every ship wanting passage up the Danė River was charged a fee for the bridge to be opened. The bridge has been rebuilt many times in response to battle damage or the need for upgrading. Below its northwest support lives the sculpture of *Undinė the Mermaid*, a gift to the city from the Lithuanian Maritime Academy in 2014. Rub the snake bracelet on her right wrist and supposedly your dreams will come true. Do let us know.

**Meridianas** (Moored on the left bank of the Danė River; w restoranasmeridianas.lt) Visible from Biržos Tiltas, the *Meridianas* is essentially a restaurant (page 294) aboard a historic ship. Built in Turku, Finland, in 1947, it was one of 26 vessels built to service Finland's war reparation agreement with the Soviet Union. Moored in Klaipėda, for 20 years she was a training vessel for the maritime school before being bought by a private owner and opened as a restaurant. Her fate has been in the balance a number of times, but as an icon of the city, she has been saved time and time again. To board the ship you must be a customer of the restaurant, but the information boards along the quayside illustrate the history of the ship and the painstaking restoration process endured to keep her afloat and in use.

**Friedricho Pasažas** (◉ friedrichopasazas) This quaint pedestrian arcade of restaurants and cafés retains the atmosphere of the historic Friedrichstadt area of the city, where once coachmen and craftsmen rested and refuelled; now tourists do. Entrance is either from Tiltų gatvė 26, marked by the **statue of the Wild Man**, or from the opposite end at the Blacksmith's Museum on Šaltkalvių gatvė

✳ **Blacksmiths Museum** (Kalvystės muziejus; Šaltkalvių gatvė 2; w mlimuziejus.lt/en/museum/blacksmiths-museum; ⏱ 10.00–18.00 Wed–Sun; €2.20/1.20) During the 1970s, one of Klaipėda's main cemeteries was demolished by the Soviets, determined to repurpose the land and ultimately remove the cultural heritage of the region. Very few residents with ancestral connections remained in Klaipėda post-World War II, affording cultural monuments little or no protection. But local blacksmith Dionyzas Varkalis (1934–2022) did manage to salvage a huge amount of cemetery metalworks, including burial crosses, fencing and gates, often of highly decorative quality, and he established a museum in the abandoned blacksmith's workshop of Gustav Katzke (1868–1944), where the collection honours both craftsmen and the deceased. Varkalis' rebellious streak is evident in the design of the museum which subtly resembles a church, banned under the anti-religious Soviet regime. Perhaps this was sweet revenge, having lent his clocks to the Communist Party and never getting them back (page 297). At the entrance to the museum is the **Klaipėda History Wall**, a display of local student artworks to commemorate the 770th anniversary of the city.

**Museum of History of Lithuania Minor** (Mažosios Lietuvos istorijos muziejus; Didžioji Vandens gatvė 2; w mlimuziejus.lt/en/museum/the-history-museum-of-lithuania-minor; ⏱ 10.00–18.00 Wed–Sun; €3.40/1.70) Here, the focus is on the ethnographic region of Lithuania Minor and the amalgamated culture of the German and Lithuanian populations living together under Prussian rule. Part of the exhibition highlights the important role played by East Prussia as a source of Lithuanian literature and printed materials during the ban imposed by Imperial Russia across occupied Lithuanian territory.

## FACHWERK ARCHITECTURE

Within Lithuania, this distinctive timber-framed architecture of German influence is unique to Klaipėda. Fachwerk buildings are constructed with an exposed timber frame, which is filled in with brick or wattle-and-daub. These historic and unusual buildings are a legacy of the German Prussian history of Klaipėda during its Memel years, and their scarcity highlights the damage that was done to the city during wartime. The best remaining examples are in the area known as **Art's Yard** (located within Daržų, Aukštoji, Didžioji Vandens, Bažničių and Vežėjų streets) which is home to small galleries, studios, the **Culture Communication Centre** (Bažnyčių gatvė 4; w kkkc.lt) and the **Klaipėda Ethno-Culture Centre** (Etnokultūros centras; Daržų gatvė 10; w etnocentras.lt), which arranges events, exhibitions and craft workshops.

***Teatros aikštė*** (Theatre Square) Formerly a market square for traders, butchers' huts and fish stalls, Theatre Square is the cultural heart of Klaipėda, hosting concerts, fairs and festivals throughout the year. At the head of the square is **Klaipėda Drama Theatre** (Klaipėdos dramos teatras; w kdt.lt/en), an active venue for contemporary and classic productions. The theatre's most infamous performance was Adolf Hitler's victory speech delivered from the balcony when Nazis seized the city in March 1939. In front of the drama theatre is a fountain and **statue of Ann from Tharau** (Taravos Anikė) dedicated to the German poet Simon Dach (1605–59), who was born in Klaipėda and whose love for Ann inspired his poetry. The statue is a replacement since the original went missing in World War II, possibly removed to prevent her having her back to the Führer on the balcony.

✳ **Klaipėda Castle Museum** (Klaipėdos pilis; Priešpilio gatvė 2; w mlimuziejus.lt/en/museum/castle-museum; ⊕ 10.00–18.00 Wed–Sun; €4.40/2.20) Built in 1252 by the Teutonic Order and named Memelburg, over the centuries Klaipėda's castle experienced routine attacks, fires and rebuilding. Since losing its strategic importance in the 1800s, the castle was demolished. Evidence of the former castle can be spotted throughout the Old Town; locals eagerly incorporated this new source of fire-resistant construction material into their buildings and castle rocks can be spotted where plaster has worn away. Today the castle is in a state of rebuild. Everything above ground was lost and one corner turret is currently being reconstructed, skirting controversy as to whether this is money well spent. The engaging underground exhibitions in the bastion passages track the history of the castle and Klaipėda from the 13th century, while **Museum 39/45** is an outstanding exhibition focusing on Klaipėda during World War II.

**Black Ghost sculpture** (Juodasis vaiduoklis; Chain bridge, Žvejų gatvė 22) The *Black Ghost* has been terrifying late arrivals to the nearby hotels since 2010. A 16th-century legend tells of a dark, windy night when a soldier on duty at the castle was approached by a spectral figure in a dark cloak. The apparition spoke, warning the soldier that the city was not prepared for a long siege. Reporting back to his seniors, leverage was given to the spectre's words and the city's stores of grain were increased, ensuring the city survived the following harsh years. Nowadays the *Black Ghost* still lends a hand, providing distraction and photo opportunities for tourists and cruise-ship day-trippers stuck in the bottleneck when the adjacent chain bridge is opened.

## AROUND KLAIPĖDA

The stretch of coastline north of Klaipėda has several worthwhile attractions and beaches to explore. Road number 2217 follows the coastline and bus numbers 4 and 6 from Klaipėda Old Town stop regularly along the way (sixth stop for Melnragė, 12th for Giruliai); most stops have an obvious path leading to the beach.

**MELNRAGĖ BEACH** Melnragė has two beach areas with the same name, distinguished as Melnragė I and Melnragė II. **Melnragė II** offers the best beach experience. Being Klaipėda's mainland Blue Flag beach, it attracts big crowds on scorching summer weekends as the plentiful facilities include sports activities, changing facilities and duty lifeguard. **Melnragė I** is closer to Klaipėda and a good option for a cultural rather than sun-worshipping experience. A short walk along the North Pier is the unusual **Walking with Fish** (*Pasivaikščiojimas su žuvimi*) statue. It was created by local blacksmiths from steel sheets and depicts a man walking into the wind, holding his hat on tight, his coattails flapping, as he follows a jaunty looking fish parading ahead of him. You may well find yourself emulating him, as the wind can be powerful. Walking north along the beach, the remnants of the World War II German observation post **Battery Nordmole** interrupt the natural beach, although it is now largely consumed by sand.

## ✕ Where to eat and drink

**Baltas Ruonis** Vėtros gatvė 8, Melnragė I; baltas.ruonis.restoranas; ⏱ noon–23.00 Mon–Fri, 11.00–23.00 Sat–Sun. This buzzing beach restaurant attracts beach & non-beach lovers alike for their creative menu, cocktails & music. Expect sunset to be extra busy. €€€

**GIRULIAI BEACH** A further 4km north from Melnragė is the quieter beach of Giruliai backed by forests and wooden villas. There are numerous parking areas along the main road, the northern-most having toilets and a café; otherwise facilities are scarce. Bus stops along the length of the beach are regularly served by bus number 4 from Klaipėda. At the far north of Giruliai beach is a nudist beach.

**MEMEL NORD** (Šiaurės Baterijos gatvė; Kukuliškių kaimas; memelnord; ⏱ noon–20.00 Mon-Sun; €2 pp) After annexing Klaipėda region in 1939, Nazi Germany planned the construction of two coastal defence batteries – Memel Süd (never built) and Memel Nord. Consisting of a central command building flanked by two artillery blocks, Memel Nord was in use until 1955 by Nazis and Soviets, providing defence and deterrence to enemy ships and aircraft. Since 2002, it has operated as a raw military museum with no modern glossy displays – a visit here simply involves clambering around the concrete monstrosity, viewing rusty relics of war and embracing the true spirit of the place thanks mainly to the theatrics of the military-style guide. It's advisable to message in advance to ensure it will be open for your visit.

Memel Nord is 10km north of Klaipėda, on the beach side of road 2217 in between the villages of Giruliai and Kukuliškiai. Driving from Klaipėda, turn left on to Šiaurės baterijos gatvė just after the Giruliai bus stop laybys on both sides of the road; parking is further along this road. It is a short walk through the pine trees to the dunes, where you will find the museum.

**DUTCHMAN'S CAP** (Olandų kepurės) The highest seashore cliff in Lithuania acquired its name from its distinctive shape when seen from the sea. At a height of 25m, it was for centuries used as a landmark for fishermen and sailors; today it is a launch spot for paragliders. The beach below is rocky and traversed by streams, more frequented by hikers than sunbathers. Rather than scouring the beach for amber here, keep your eyes peeled for mammoth tusks. A single intact tusk was found protruding out of the shoreline here in 2024 and one assumes another is still to be found.

Dutchman's Cap is a further 2km drive north from the Memal Nord junction on road 2217; there's a car park on the roadside. Olandų kepurės bus stop is here also, with the coastal route served by regular bus service 24 between Klaipėda and Karklė/Kunkiai.

## THE CURONIAN SPIT

The Curonian Spit (Kuršių nerija) is a 98km-long sand spit separating the Baltic Sea from the Curonian Lagoon. Connected to the mainland at its southern end, it was formed about 7,000 years ago by sand deposits being washed north from the Samland peninsula (now the Kaliningrad oblast). The steady supply of sand established a sandbank that emerged first as small islands; then, as vegetation became established and increased the rate of sand deposition, the long strip of dunes developed. Reckless deforestation by the timber trade in the 18th century and a lack of understanding of the consequences resulted in a critical situation for the spit. The dunes were unstable with sand movement and depletion at critical rates, causing whole villages to be relocated to avoid being buried by sand. Throughout the 19th century an intensive programme of planting was implemented, stabilising the dunes with grasses, shrubs and trees. As a result, the fragile landscape seen today is wholly influenced and managed by human efforts, recognised by UNESCO as a World Heritage Site in 2000.

In 1944, the Russian Red Army marched on Klaipėda region, pushing Nazi Germany back towards the west. Evacuation orders had been underway since 1943 and many locals, particularly those with German-Prussian nationality, took an incredibly dangerous gamble and fled across the frozen lagoon to travel onwards down the spit to the German territory of Koenigsberg (now Kaliningrad). For those Lithuanians who remained, hopeful that the Red Army would liberate them from the horrors of Nazi Germany, it was the beginning of a new chapter of Soviet occupation and terror. Soviet plans for the spit involved fishing and forestry industries but thankfully they left few scars on the landscape.

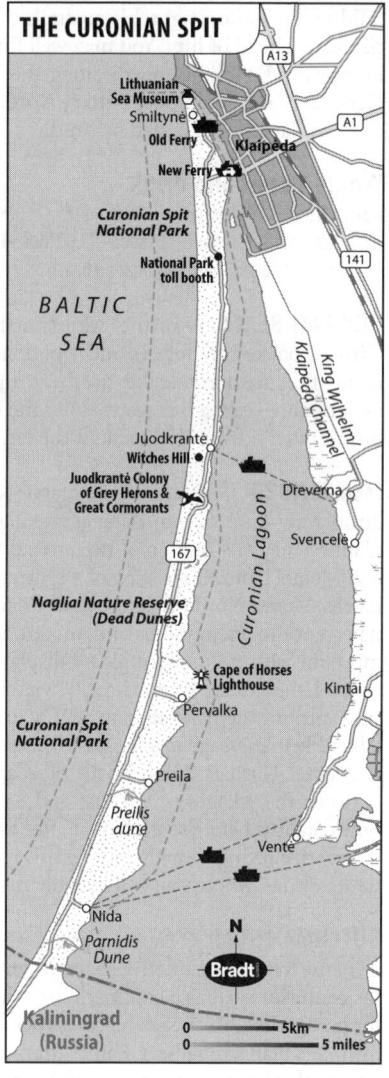

All but the northernmost 7km of the Lithuanian side of the spit is within the Curonian Spit National Park, established in 1991. The region is also known as Neringa – the name of the municipality, named after the mythological giantess who created the spit by gathering sand in her apron and building the protective sandbar to shelter fishermen from the fierce storms of the Baltic Sea.

The four main settlements of Juodkrantė, Pervalka, Preila and Nida are located on the sheltered lagoon side, with a permanent population of approximately 2,500. Tourism and fishing are the main industries and source of income for locals, who face the universal challenge of being priced out of the property market in their home region as second homes and holiday rentals take over. The traditional fishermen's houses are now prime real estate, a world apart from the tough life and basic conditions of their former occupants, whose initials remain on many houses along with the year of construction. Traditional ethnographic houses tend to face the lagoon and have intersecting wooden gable features often carved with birds or horses to protect against evil spirits. The houses are typically painted in bright colours, or a traditional brown with vibrant blue-and-white details, and are surrounded by well-tended gardens which often include a smokehouse for fish.

The Curonian Spit is officially the sunniest place in Lithuania, and the tourism industry provides a lucrative short season for local businesses. The lure of the sea, smoked fish, sand dunes, forest walks and hunting for amber on the beach all continue to attract visitors. New accommodations being established alongside attractions and restaurants opening all-year round are gradually extending the tourist season into the winter months when ice fishing on the frozen lagoon and cross-country skiing on the beach replace sunbathing. The main tourist season on the spit runs from late May to September. This is when hospitality comes alive, but outside of these times can be a wonderful time to visit too, though you may find your options are limited. The larger hotels remain open throughout the year but very few other restaurants stay open unless there is a special event like the Stintapūkis Festival (w visitneringa.com) held annually in mid-February to celebrate traditional Curonian ice fishing and enjoy the locally caught smelt fish – a winter festival to certainly lift the spirits.

## GETTING THERE AND AWAY

**By ferry** The most popular way to visit the spit for **pedestrians and cyclists** (bikes go free) is by ferry to Smiltynė via the **Old Ferry Terminal** (Senoji perkėla; Danės gatvė 1, Klaipėda; w keltas.lt; ⊕ 07.00–22.00; €1.70 pp), located a short walk from the centre of Klaipėda. Tickets are sold from machines or the ticket office, with departures every 30 minutes in summer and hourly in winter. There's a café with a roof terrace to occupy any waiting time. The crossing takes just 5 minutes, and upon arriving at the spit it is easy to explore Smiltynė on foot, join the cycle path that goes south all the way to Nida, or take one of the regular bus services immediately in front of the ferry port to the spit villages.

The **car and bus ferry** departs from the **New Ferry Terminal** (Naujoji perkėla; Nemuno gatvė 8, Klaipėda; w keltas.lt; ⊕ 24hrs; €23.20 per car) located 2.5km south of Klaipėda centre. The ferry operates 24/7 with an hourly service between 22.00 and 05.00 and every 20 minutes between 05.00 and 22.00. The journey takes 5 minutes, arriving at the New Ferry Terminal in Smiltynė.

In the summer months, the Curonian Spit villages are served by small **private passenger ferry services** criss-crossing the lagoon. These are usually timed to allow for a day trip from the mainland to the spit, departing first thing in the morning and returning in the evening. However, you can use these services to create an independent tour of the lagoon region, which is particularly good for cyclists as almost all ferries accept bikes on board (€3/bike). Details of each ferry service are listed under the villages they serve.

**By bus** Intercity buses to Nida are available daily from Vilnius (TOKS buses; w toks.lt; adult one way €29; 6hrs) and Kaunas (Kautra buses; w kautra.lt; adult one way €26; 4hrs). Find timetables and buy online tickets at w autobusubilietai.lt. The service is direct and the ferry crossing included in the fare.

## GETTING AROUND
If you need a **private taxi** service on the spit, it is best booked in advance (see w neringatours.lt).

**By bus** Between May and September, buses run along the spit from Smiltynė Old Ferry Terminal to Nida. They take 1 hour and run hourly from 07.10 on weekdays and 09.10 at weekends. They are less regular in low season. Tickets can be purchased on the bus by cash or card, or online at w autobusubilietai.lt – an adult fare to Nida costs €6, and to Juodkrantė €3. All buses service the villages along the spit, but not all of them divert into Pervalka.

**☀ By bike** Cycling is by far the most enjoyable way to explore the Curonian Spit, with upgrades to cycle paths and signage ongoing. Alongside the EuroVelo routes (page 281) that run the length of the spit and beyond, there are local routes that can be done separately or combined (see w bicycle.lt/seasideroute). Cycling day tours between the villages, with a local lunch while watching the waves lap may appeal to a wider audience than an epic endurance challenge. There are many places to hire bikes in Nida and Juodkrantė.

**By car** After arriving by ferry in Smiltynė, a 7km drive south along the spit brings you to the Curonian Spit National Park **toll booth**. The ecological tax payable depends on the season, but electric cars are free all year round. You can pay in cash or by card at the booth, or in advance online via w neringa.unipark.shop (passenger car inc all occupants: Jun–Sep €30, Oct €10, Nov–Apr €5, Mar–May €10). There is no limit on the number of cars entering the national park but traffic congestion and limited parking is a problem. Visitors are strongly encouraged to leave the car behind and make use of the regular public transport and newly upgraded cycle paths instead.

**TOURIST INFORMATION** Online tourist information is available at w visitneringa.com and there are physical tourist offices in Juodkrantė and Nida. The **Nida Culture and Tourism Information Centre 'Agila'** (Nidos kultūros ir turizmo informacijos centras 'Agila'; Taikos gatvė 4; ☏ +370 469 52345; ⏰ 09–18.00 daily) can help with booking tours, finding accommodation as well as birding, wildlife and activity suppliers. The **Juodkrantė branch** (L Rėzos gatvė 8B; ☏ +370 469 53490; e juodkrante@visitneringa.lt; ⏰ 09.00–18.00 Tue–Sat) is within the Ludwig Reza Culture Centre (page 307).

**PRACTICALITIES** Most facilities serving the spit are in Nida. The **post office** (cnr Taikos gatvė 13 & Kopų gatvė 22; w post.lt) stands out with its bas relief of a historic postal wagon and horses, a tribute to the European postal road that ran along the spit from the mid 17th century to 1833. Nida's Maxima **supermarket** (Naglių gatvė 29A) has an **ATM** (SEB Bank) and a **pharmacy**. The only **petrol station** on the spit is in Nida (leave Nida heading south on Taikos gatvė, at the main road Nidos-Smiltynės turn left, and the petrol station is immediately on the left). Card payments are widely accepted but it is recommended to carry enough cash for a meal just in case. Insect repellent is essential in the warmer months as mosquitoes and midges thrive here. Avoid weekends if possible as they are busier, more expensive and likely to have a minimum number of nights stay.

**SMILTYNĖ** Officially part of Klaipėda city, Smiltynė is the most northern section of the Curonian Spit and is a favourite day trip for Klaipėda residents thanks to the reliable Old Ferry service for pedestrians and cyclists.

The main attraction is the **Lithuanian Sea Museum** (Smiltynės 3; w muziejus.lt; ⏰ Oct–Apr 10.30–17.00 Fri–Sun, May 10.30–18.00 Wed–Sun, Jun–Aug 10.30–18.00

> ### CURONIAN SPIT NATIONAL PARK
>
> Since 1991 it has been the responsibility of the Curonian Spit National Park to preserve the spit's cultural and natural heritage, to balance conservation with access and to enable the community to thrive without detrimental effects on the environment. Covid-19 lockdowns were a surprising success for the national park. Maintenance work on hiking trails and cycle paths progressed with no interruption from tourist traffic, a renewed interest and support for nature and the outdoors secured funding, and locals will confess it was idyllic to be quietly cut off for a little while.
>
> The spit focuses on slow tourism; the great outdoors, birdwatching, nature tours, hiking, cycling, the beach and heritage culture, including local gastronomy. The infrastructure to enjoy these activities is gradually improving with observation decks, trails, birdwatching towers, upgraded cycle paths, cultural events, architectural preservation orders on traditional buildings and strict control on dwindling fish stocks. Just as the vegetation holds the dunes together, this infrastructure holds the community together.
>
> A variety of mammals inhabit the spit, including moose (the symbol of the Curonian Spit), foxes, roe deer and wild boar. If driving at dusk and dawn, take particular care looking out for wildlife on the roads. Migrating birds get funnelled along the narrow peninsula, a highway along which around 15 million birds pass each year. Birdwatchers from all around the world visit during the migration season of September and October hoping to see sandpipers, terns, sanderlings or calidris. There are ten pairs of wild white-tailed eagle and 11 pairs of sea eagle currently on the spit.

Tue–Sun, Sep 10.30–18.00 Wed–Sun; Jun–Aug €13/6.50, Sep–May €9/4.50, free on the last Sun of the month) Repurposing the 19th-century Nerija Fort (w muziejus.lt/en/nerija-fort) as a museum of the sea has been extremely successful. The fort was constructed to defend the sea gate, but it never saw any military action. For those interested in military history over marine life, it is worth a visit to walk around the hexagonal ramparts and explore the casemates. Soldiers and equipment (including much unexploded ordnance) are long gone and since 1979 the Lithuanian Sea Museum has been housed here. Consistently ranked as one of the top museums in Lithuania, it has seen much modernisation and improvement over recent years. Attractions include a well-presented modern **Aquarium**, the highlight of which is an underwater tunnel through the sturgeon tank. The **Dolphinarium** (w muziejus.lt/en/dolphinarium; Jun–Aug €17/12, Sep–May €9/6) has performances by their Black Sea dolphins three or four times daily in summer, and at other times they specialise in dolphin-assisted therapy sessions. In the grounds of the museum are a **fishing boat exhibition** and **ethnographic fisherman's homestead**. The museum is also home to the **Baltic Sea Animal Rehabilitation Centre** (w muziejus.lt/en/bjgrc; €6/3) specialising in the rescue and rehabilitation of seals and monitoring local seal populations. The additional fee includes a compulsory guided tour; you should book in advance as numbers are limited. Museum facilities include a fast-food café and gift shop. Tickets can be booked online or at the museum ticket office. The sea museum is a 20-minute walk (1.6km) from the Old Port Smiltynė (Senoji perkėla Smiltynė) and half of that allows for viewing the outdoor exhibitions. Alternatively, a selection of novelty transport runs between the port and museum, including a miniature train, tuk-tuk and horse-drawn carts (pay the driver directly).

> **THE LOST VILLAGES**
>
> Fourteen villages were lost to the shifting sands of the Curonian Spit between the 17th and 19th centuries. There is nothing sinister to the story, and those expecting to spot a roof poking through the sand will be disappointed as there was plenty of time to pack up and move; in fact most houses were dismantled and moved to new locations. All other traces of the former settlements are well and truly gone, submerged by the sand. Even the main settlements of Nida and Juodkrantė are not in their original locations. The spit's vulnerability was aggravated during this time by the harvesting of the natural forest for the timber trade, being cheaper than the mainland and in great demand by Europe for shipbuilding. After a mass afforestation effort at the end of the 19th century, the dunes have since stabilised and modern environmental management practice should ensure that villages will not be lost again. The wooden grave markers along the Nagliai Nature Reserve trail are an artwork installation from 2020 to commemorate the buried villages, alongside information boards.

**Smiltynė beach** (Smiltynės paplūdimys) is easily the most scenic beach close to Klaipėda and the summer crowds are evidence of this. When alighting the Old Ferry, follow the pavement along the left side of the bus parking, cross the pedestrian crossing and follow the forest footpath for 1.5km to the beach. At the beach turn left to head towards the general beach, beach bar, nudist beach or men-only beach areas. Turn right for the pet-friendly beach.

**JUODKRANTĖ** Juodkrantė is the first resort after entering the Curonian Spit National Park, a long colourful town of characteristic fishermen's houses and villas. From the 1840s Juodkrantė started to develop as a resort, but it was between 1860 and 1890 when boom-time hit. Driven by a demand for amber, German company Stantien & Becker began dredging the lagoon for amber on a huge industrial scale, something the spit had never experienced before. At its peak in the 1880s there were 230 vessels and 22 dredgers scouring the floor of the Curonian Lagoon. They collected 2.5 million tonnes of raw amber, including a treasure trove of Mesolithic and Neolithic amber artefacts. Alongside their lucrative excavations, wealthy businessmen built grand villas and a spa in contrast to the modest local fishing village homesteads, which remain a unique architectural feature specific to Juodkrantė.

**Getting there** Most people travel to Juodkrantė via road or cycle path, but **seasonal passenger ferries** operate from Dreverna (w dreverna.lt/keltas; Jun–Sep; €9/5) and Klaipėda (ferry *Benas*; w klaipedanida.lt; Jun–Sep; €16/10).

**Where to stay and eat**

**Kuršių Kiemas** (20 rooms) (also known as Vila Bachmann) Miško gatvė 11; w neringatravel.lt. A grand villa in its day, this hotel is now a practical option popular with families, & has rental bikes & a BBQ area where you can grill your own fish. €€€
**Vila Flora** (15 rooms) Kalno 7a; w vilaflora.lt. Housed in a historic wooden villa from the 19th century, Vila Flora's qdpl rooms are good for families. The terrace restaurant is open daily (⏱ 09.00–23.00; only at w/ends in low season). €€€
**Juodasis Kalnas** Ievos kalno gatvė 22; ฀ RestoranasJuodasisKalnas; ⏱ 09.00–2200 daily. For seafood lovers to sample local delicacies on a calm summer terrace. €€€

**Malka Pizza & Grill**  L Rėzos g 1, Long Pier; 
[f] MalkaPizzeria; ⏱ 12.30–23.00 daily, summer only. This seasonal terrace restaurant is a family favourite, with people flocking here for the traditional pizzas baked in an outdoor oven. €€

## What to see and do

**Witches Hill** (Raganų Kalnas; L Rėzos gatvė; w raganukalnas.lt; ⏱ always open; free) Juodkrantė is home to one of the spit's most popular attractions – an open-air sculpture trail of witches, devils, gods and goddesses from Lithuanian folklore. This area of dunes was once known as 'Blond Eva' on account of its golden sands and for centuries was a place to celebrate pagan festivals, in particular Midsummer. Since forestation was necessary to stabilise the dunes, the steep parabolic dunes are now covered in a forest of fir trees casting shadows and shafts of sunlight over their sandy roots. The mystical significance and woodland habitat inspired woodcarvers and blacksmiths from all over the country to create more than 80 sculptures embodying the characters of Lithuanian legends and fairytales. The collection has grown since inception in 1979 and is regularly being renewed and restored via annual woodworking symposia. You can choose from a short or long route and in summer you will need insect repellent for both. Half of the sculptures represent good, the other half evil, but to be frank a lot of Lithuanian folklore has a sinister twist. Visiting with a local guide will bring these characters and their stories to life. The entrance is at the southern end of the long, stretched-out village of Juodkrantė, with parking nearby and also the Raganų kalnas bus stop.

**Pamario Gallery** (Pamario galerija; L Rėzos gatvė 3; w lndm.lt/en/mm/; ⏱ Jun–Sep 11.00–18.00 Tue–Sat, 11.00–16.00 Sun; €5/2.50) A seasonal branch of the Lithuanian National Museum of Art, the Pamario Gallery brings annual exhibitions, events and workshops to Juodkrantė in summer. A permanent outdoor exhibition of modern Lithuanian sculptures is located between the gallery and lagoon shore.

**Ludwig Reza Culture Centre** (Liudviko Rėzos Kultūros centras; L Rėzos gatvė 8B; w lrezoskc.lt; ⏱ 10.00–18.00 Tue–Sun, closed Sun in low season; €1/0.50) Martin Ludwig Reza (1776–1840) was a notable Lutheran pastor and professor of East Prussia who was a prominent advocate of the Lithuanian language in Lithuania Minor and a publisher of Lithuanian texts. This small museum is dedicated to his life. The historical photographs of daily life on the spit are enlightening, but for most people the main reason to visit here is the tourist information centre which shares the same building.

**Juodkrantė Colony of Grey Herons and Great Cormorants** (Juodkrantės pilkųjų garnių ir didžiųjų kormoranų kolonija) Some 3km south of Juodkrantė along the main road 167 is one of the largest colonies of great cormorants in Europe. More than 2,000 cormorants nest and breed here between February and October, the impact of their residency eerily evident in the denuded trees and barren landscape due to their acidic droppings stripping the leaves from trees and vegetation. A viewing platform with information boards is accessible via steep wooden steps. The noise can be deafening, and if you come by car be sure to check the paintwork is clean after your visit as the birds' excrement acts like paint-stripper. Originally, a grey heron colony inhabited this area, but they were forced out by the aggressive cormorants. A reduced colony of grey herons still inhabit the peripheral forest areas, returning to breed just after the cormorants around the month of March.

❋ **NAGLIAI STRICT NATURE RESERVE** (Naglių gamtinis rezervatas) Nagliai Strict Nature Reserve was established in 1994 to preserve the fragile landscape of the **Dead Dunes** (Negyvosios kopos) and the rare flora and fauna that inhabit them. The reserve is an area 9km long by 2km wide, with the tallest dune 50m tall. The dunes have stopped moving due to the mass afforestation of the 19th century and creation of a dune ridge that protects the area. Vegetation including mosses, lichens and coastal grasses has become established and given the dunes a grey tone, hence they are also referred to as the grey dunes. As a result of the strong prevailing wind from the west and an influx of tourists, the fragile ecosystem is under constant threat of erosion and measures have been taken during peak summer season to manage access. A 1.1km **educational trail** (Apr–Sep 09.00–17.00 daily; €5 pp) contains the impact of tourism and is overseen by four official dune guards.

**PERVALKA AND PREILA** Pervalka and Preila are quiet village resorts on the lagoon shore made up mainly of second homes and holiday rentals. In Pervalka, the main sight is the **Cape of Horses Lighthouse** (Žirgų rago švyturys), built in 1900 on an artificial island in the lagoon and still operating to this day. A 5km circular trail starts from the northern end of the main street, Pervalkos gatvė, follows the lagoon shore around the Cape of Horses (Žirgų ragas) offering the best views of the lighthouse, and returns through the deciduous **Birštvynas forest** of pines, alders and birches. Seasonal summer restaurants pop up in the village alongside the permanent and very popular **Vėjopačio Užeiga** (Pervalkos 19A; ☏+370 611 15627;

### BEACHES ON THE CURONIAN SPIT

Each settlement in the Curonian Spit National Park has a well-maintained beach on the Baltic Sea side of the spit, several regularly being awarded Blue Flag status. Numerous well-marked paths guide pedestrians from the villages across to the beaches on the western shore (approx 15mins' walk). The beaches are free spaces with good facilities but officially they are divided into clearly marked sections. The beaches of Juodkrantė, Pervalka, Preila and Nida each has a designated nudist beach (*nudistų paplūdimys*), women-only beach (*moterų paplūdimys*) and pet-friendly beach (*šunų paplūdimys*) alongside their general beaches. There is a men-only beach at Smiltynė (*vyrų paplūdimys*). Nida beach is the most accessible, with a specialist sea-bathing wheelchair available. Parking for the beaches is often free or payable at €0.60 per hour. Expect to pay €5 for beach bed rental.

Strict **beach rules** apply:

- Red flag means swimming is forbidden. Yellow flag warns it is dangerous to swim. Red/yellow flag signals a lifeguard is on duty.
- Do not litter.
- Do not damage plants or the dune reinforcement structures.
- Alcohol is not permitted at the beach.
- Use of inflatables in the sea is prohibited.
- Use of power kites is forbidden in beach territory.
- Use of professional kites is prohibited.
- Sports and games to be played only in designated areas.
- Use a life vest when using a paddleboard (SUP).
- Pets are allowed only on designated beaches.

**e** jolanta.mitkute@gmail.com; **f** uzgaida; €€), a cosy home restaurant open all year round but which requires a reservation in advance (min 1hr's notice needed). Seasonal fish is their speciality, much to the pleasure of their cat Mandarinas who is a local celebrity.

The village of Preila sits on the lagoon shore beneath **Preilis dune** (artist's dune). To help alleviate visitor numbers to the other dunes, a recently installed stairway gives access to the dune summit where a circular boardwalk and benches offer far-reaching views.

**NIDA** Nida is without doubt the most charming resort in Lithuania and well worth the extra effort needed to visit. In the late 19th century, this remote fishing community attracted a group of artists from Koenigsberg art school to study the dune landscapes. Since the students were not wealthy clientele, local guesthouse owner Friedrich Blode agreed to take payment for lodgings in the form of paintings and he became a regular host of visiting artists. When his son, Hermann Blode, took over the guesthouse at Skruzdynės gatvė 2, it was welcoming artists, composers, writers and musicians (including Sigmund Freud and Thomas Mann) and became known as the hub of Nida artists' colony. The halcyon days of these free-thinkers and expressionists ended in 1944 as the front line approached and the house was abandoned, but the connection with German culture remained strong and until recently German tourists dominated visitor numbers to the Curonian Spit. Life in Nida revolves around the port, and after hiking, biking or museum tours a relaxing sail on the lagoon to witness the dunes from the water is recommended. Even with the trappings of modern life, Nida holds on to the nostalgia of times gone by.

**Getting there** For those who choose to travel to Nida by private car via the New Ferry, you should consider the parking options with your accommodation in advance. Nida bus station is in the town centre and is the terminus for all services along the spit. Most hotels are within walking distance and local taxis park nearby.

**Seasonal passenger ferries** connect Nida directly with Klaipėda (ferry *Benas*; **w** klaipedanida.lt; Jun–Sep €21/15), Ventė (**w** pamariopramogos.com; May–Sep; €15/7 one way), Mingė (**w** mingeskaimas.lt; Jun–Aug; €20/15 one way) and Šilutė (**w** kde.lt; Jun–Sep; €15/12 one-way). These are perfect for day trips across the Nemunas Delta, touring by bike around the Curonian Lagoon, or completing the section of the Baltic Coastal Hiking Route (page 45), which circumnavigates the lagoon.

In summer, a **hydrofoil** passenger service runs from Kaunas to Nida (**w** laivasraketa.lt; €69 plus extra for luggage/bikes), sailing Thursday to Sunday, departing Kaunas at 09.00 and departing Nida at 15.30. The journey takes 3 hours 45 minutes each way, and there is a bar on board.

**Where to stay** *Map, page 310*

In summer season there are a whole host of places to stay in Nida; spare rooms are rented out, tents are pitched in gardens and locals decamp to host tourists. The season is short and lucrative.

* **Nidos Namai** Taikos gatvė 41; **w** nidosnamai.lt. A small exclusive development of Scandi-style self-catering holiday cottages with all mod cons, washing machines, wood burner & terrace. 1- to 3-bedroom cottages sleep 1–7 persons & are available for short & long stays. Strict 22.00–08.00 quiet time. **€€€€**

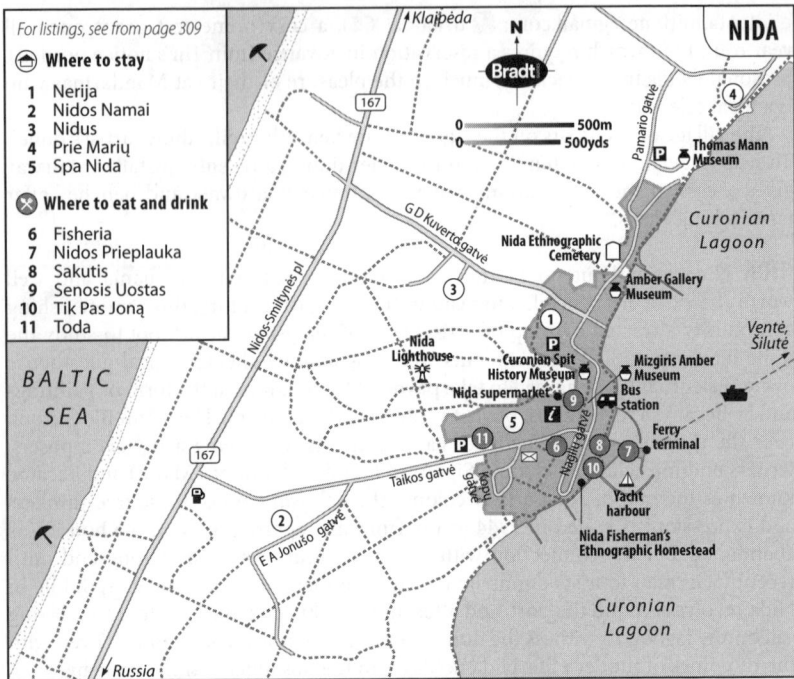

**Prie Marių** (5 rooms) Purvynės gatvė 9; w priemariunida.lt. Prie marių means 'by the lagoon' & this traditional guesthouse offers quaint dbl-room accommodation with modern trimmings & a buffet b/fast. Ask for a lagoon-view room. €€€€

✹ **Spa Nida** (39 rooms) Taikos gatvė 18; w spanida.lt. The newest hotel in Nida, tucked away in a quiet residential area boasts smart facilities, including a spa with pool, sauna & treatments. Spacious 1- & 2-bedroom apartments. **Restaurant '22 mylios'** is scrumptious & healthy. This newcomer will hopefully prompt other hotels to renovate. €€€€

**Nerija** (57 rooms) Pamario gatvė 13; w neringahotels.lt. This comfortable family-feel hotel in the centre of Nida is nothing fancy, but the location & summer terrace earn its popularity. €€€

**Nidus** (26 rooms) G D Kuverto 15; w nidus.lt. Hidden in the forest, Nidus is loved by both local & international guests but is perhaps resting on its laurels. It is a 15min walk east to the centre of Nida or west to Nida beach. €€€

## ✕ Where to eat and drink *Map, above*

A lot of places feel like pop-up bars or restaurants because of the seasonality and use of terraces, small buildings for take-aways and outdoor grill places.

✹ **Toda** Taikos gatvė 32B; todarestoranas; ⏱ 16.00–23.00 daily. A culinary delight hidden among the pine trees, bringing creative & exotic dishes to Nida with a relaxed ambience. Reservation in advance essential. Best not to be in a rush. €€€€€

✹ **Nidos Prieplauka** Naglių gatvė 16; w nidosprieplauka.lt; ⏱ 10.00–midnight daily. Boasting an iconic location on the harbour with commanding views of the lagoon, this is a bustling place for all, with a contemporary menu & cocktails alongside a friendly welcome. €€€€

**Fisheria** Taikos gatvė 5; fisherianida; ⏱ 10.00–22.00 Sun–Thu, 10.00–23.00 Fri-Sat. Seafood steals the show here of course, & if you were to judge a place on its mackerel paté, this would be a winner. Creative & playful fish dishes served up in a homely environment. €€€

**Sakutis** Naglių gatvė 14A; [f] sakutis; ⊕ noon–21.00 Mon–Fri, 10.00–23.00 Sat–Sun. Traditional Lithuanian dishes including grilled meat, fish & salads with views overlooking the port. €€€

**Senosis Uostas** Naglių gatvė 29D; w senasis-uostas.lt; ⊕ Apr–Oct 10.00–22.00 Sun–Thu, 10.00–23.00 Fri–Sat. Reliably feeding a seemingly endless flow of guests during the summer season is no trouble for the team at 'The Old Port'. Their varied menu of satisfying Lithuanian specialities will warrant a walk up the dunes to burn off the calories. The weekday business lunch (noon–15.00 Mon–Fri) is a bargain at €4.50. €€

**Tik Pas Joną** Naglių 6-1; [f] tikpasjona; ⊕ 10.00–21.00 daily. Simple but delicious is the theme at this well-established family-owned business, specialists in smoked fish. A local experience. €€

**What to see and do** The collection of wave-battered fishing boats moored and bobbing in the **harbour** are a reminder that Nida is primarily a fishing community. Were it not for the gifts of the sea, the historic homesteads, now museums or guesthouses, would not have existed. The northern wharf shelters fishing vessels, sightseeing ships offering boat tours of the Curonian Lagoon and ferry services across to the Nemunas Delta, Klaipėda and Kaunas (page 309). The southern wharf is home to private yachts, appearing more luxurious and exclusive every year, reflecting the country's entrepreneurial successes. Extending north and south from the harbour following the water's edge for 2.3km is the **promenade**, a must-visit location for a stroll, jog or cycle.

**Thomas Mann Museum** (Thomo Manno kultūros centras; Skruzdynės gatvė 17; w neringosmuziejai.lt/en/thomas-mann-museum; ⊕ Jun–Sep 10.00–18.00 daily, Oct–May 10.00–17.00 Tue–Sat; €3/1.50) German author Thomas Mann and his wife Katia were 'seized by the indescribable peculiarity and beauty of nature, and the fantastic world of shifting dunes' when visiting Nida in 1929. Mann spent

> **WEATHERVANES**
>
> The unique symbol of Neringa region and the Curonian Lagoon is a curious object steeped in history and tradition, admired by visitors but not often understood. An outdoor exhibition of weathervanes lines the promenade either side of Nida port from May to September. Over 80 distinct designs are displayed, each telling a different story about its owner.
>
> Weathervanes were devised in the 19th century by the inspector of fishing licences in the lagoon territory, Ernstas Berbomas. There were 133 villages on the surrounding shores of the lagoon and he devised a system to identify boats and their respective villages using a colour-coded system: black-and-white signs for the Curonian Spit, red-and-white for the eastern shore of the lagoon, and yellow-and-blue for the southern villages. Geometric shapes were used to distinguish between settlements. Each boat had to display its sign on the mast and could only fish in its designated waters. Fishermen got creative, and by replacing the original tin and cloth signs with wood, they carved symbols, objects from nature, elements of faith and love, and personalised their signs with artistic expression.
>
> As fishing methods modernised, the traditional flat-bottomed *kurėnas* sail boats were replaced, making the weathervanes redundant. The legacy of these local icons was revived in the 1990s when national heritage and identity was permitted to thrive, and in 2004 the open-air exhibition was erected along the Nida waterfront.

the prize money from his Nobel Prize in Literature building a summer house for the family in Nida, and they were warmly welcomed by the locals. Unfortunately, after spending only three summers there, they fled to Switzerland due to the rising anti-Semitic movement in Nazi Germany; Katia was Jewish. Over the following years, their idyllic summer house was used by army officers and was nationalised, becoming a hunting lodge. Saved and repaired by the Lithuanian Writer's Union in the 1950s, it is now a museum and cultural centre dedicated to the life and works of Thomas Mann and a venue for literary and music events, including the Thomas Mann Festival held every July (w mann.lt). There is a bus stop at the museum, but not all buses stop there.

**Nida Ethnographic Cemetery** (Nidos etnografinės kapinės ir krikštai; Pamario gatvė 43) Alongside Prussian metal crosses inscribed with German gothic font, Nida's historic cemetery from the 19th and 20th centuries contain the unique wooden grave markers called *krikštai* – the oldest form of grave marker in Lithuania. More than just a memorial, the krikštas is believed to provide a connection between the living world and the afterlife and is always placed at the feet of the deceased to help their soul ascend. Traditionally, male krikštai were made from 'male' trees such as oak, birch and ash, with female krikštai being crafted from 'female' trees like aspen, fir and linden. Decorative symbols also differed: birds and horses for men, hearts and plants for women. The names of the departed in the cemetery are a mix of Germanic and Lithuanian and the dates suggest short, harsh lives.

**Amber museums** For those curious to learn about Baltic amber, there are two dedicated museums in Nida. **Mizgiris Amber Museum** (Mizgirių gintaro muziejus; Naglių gatvė 27; w ambergallery.lt; ⊕ 10.00–19.00 daily; €12/6) is a new exhibition featuring an educational multimedia presentation included in the ticket price. The dark atmosphere and display case lighting really set off the exhibits and the story of amber is narrated via a headset for English speakers. The **Amber Gallery Museum** (Gintaro galerija muziejus; Pamario gatvė 20; w ambergallery.lt; ⊕ 10.00–19.00 daily; €2.50/1.20) is a more traditional exhibition, where you can arrange an amber workshop if booked in advance. The gallery also offers souvenirs and jewellery for purchase if your masterpiece is not up to scratch. For more on Baltic amber, see page 36.

**Curonian Spit History Museum** (Kuršių nerijos istorijos muziejus; Pamario gatvė 53; w neringosmuziejai.lt/en/curonian-spit-history-museum; ⊕ Jul–Aug 10.00–17.00 Tue–Sun, Sep–Jun 10.00–17.00 Tue–Sat; €2/1) When it first opened in 1969, the Curonian Spit History Museum was greatly limited by Soviet ideology and told only of practical history such as geography or economy, ignoring the local culture and heritage. Since 2002, the museum has displayed the human and cultural life of the spit, with a most memorable insight into the now-discontinued gory art of crow-catching.

\* **Nida Fisherman's Ethnographic Homestead** (Nidos žvejo etnografinė Sodyba; Naglių gatvė 4; w neringosmuziejai.lt/en/nida-fishermans-ethnographic-homestead; ⊕ Jul–Aug 10.00–17.00 Tue–Sun, Sep–Jun 10.00–17.00 Tue–Sat; €2/1) This is a simple but evocative museum of days-gone-by, when life in Nida revolved around fishing, family and productive gardens. Houses were typically single-storey, often separated into two living quarters when the eldest child married, and everything was managed by the woman in case her husband didn't return from a fishing trip. Locals spoke Curonian when fishing, German at church and Lithuanian at home. Bucolic in summer, dangerous in winter – the house could be damaged or moved by drift ice blown in from the lagoon. The house feels very authentic, filled with traditional homelife artefacts and fishing equipment, including some very big boots. But it is the solid timbers and worn floors of the building, heavy with history, that capture your imagination of the dedicated life of a fisherman.

**Nida Lighthouse** (Nidos švyturys; Švyturio gatvė 8; w neringosmuziejai.lt/en/nidos-svyturys; ⊕ Jun–Aug noon–18.00 daily, Sep–May noon–18.00 Wed–Sun; €5/3) Situated atop Urbis Hill since 1853, the lighthouse offers far-reaching views of Nida if you are willing to climb 132 steps to the small balcony. The lighthouse is lit only on special occasions.

**Nida Beach** (Nidos paplūdimys) The Blue Flag beach at Nida on the Baltic Sea side of the spit is a highlight for many visitors. For naturists, Nida nudist beach at the southern end of the main beach was recently ranked by US news outlet CNN as one of the best nude beaches in the world. The area is clearly marked both at the beginning of the footpath leading from the road, and when walking along the beach. Watch out for the border territory signs and respect that the area of beach beyond here is strictly prohibited.

✳ **Parnidis Dune** (Parnidžio kopos) Parnidis Dune forms the southern boundary of the settlement of Nida, an impressive hulk of a dune beyond which is uninterrupted nature until the Kaliningrad (Russia) border. Parnidis is a white dune, alive in the sense that it is still drifting due to the lack of vegetation securing the pure sand. The prevailing wind from the sea constantly shifts sand from the dune eastwards, depositing it in the lagoon. A well-trodden path continues for 1.5km from the southern end of the promenade and summits the dune via steep wooden steps. At the top since 1995 sits a **sundial-calendar**, a prominent 13.8m granite obelisk at its centre. Wooden boardwalks have been constructed to guide and restrict public access to the dune, with several observation platforms affording stunning views. Parnidis Dune is the only place in Lithuania where you can observe the sun rising and setting over water. The French philosopher and writer Jean-Paul Sartre and the writer Simone de Beauvoir came to Nida in June 1965, visiting Lithuanian artists and intellectuals. A photograph of Sartre taken during the trip was recreated as a sculpture titled *Windward*, explaining why you will find him permanently poised on the dune since 2018. Walking in the dunes is permitted,

> **THE LITHUANIA–RUSSIA BORDER**
>
> Since early 2022 after Russia's invasion of Ukraine, the border between Lithuania and Russian exclave Kaliningrad has been closed. Monitoring and surveillance on the Lithuanian side have been increased and it is advised not to go snooping. If you are in the border area, be prepared to be approached by Lithuanian border guards and asked to show your personal identification.
>
> During Soviet Russia's occupation of Lithuania, every evening the coastal beaches were raked smooth at 23.00 and at 06.00 the next morning a patrol inspected for signs of activity, attempts to escape or smuggling. The same routine of fenced and raked beaches continued up the coast of Latvia and Estonia, as this was the external border of the USSR.

following the guidance shown on the information boards. A longer route takes you around the periphery of Parnidis Dune, via the **Valley of Silence** – the location of a former prisoner-of-war camp between 1870 and 1872, although no physical evidence has ever been discovered. The area is marked by primitive wooden crosses and often referred to as the 'valley of death'; these morbid references are based more on myth than fact. Beyond this area the Lithuanian dunes continue, rolling into the grey dunes of Grobštas Nature Reserve and more importantly the border zone with Russia – it is strictly prohibited to go beyond the clearly marked border territory signs.

The dune can also be accessed from the west by car or bicycle along E A Jonušo gatvė; there is a small parking area and a path up to the sundial, lined with souvenir stalls.

## SOUTH OF KLAIPĖDA

Until recently, the eastern shore of the Curonian Lagoon was primarily the reserve of birdwatchers and visitors with family heritage connections. This is former Prussian territory and the German influence on the region is evident in the faded German shop signs, Lutheran churches and gravestones with Germanic names etched in Gothic font. Prussian Lithuanians were called 'Lietuvininkai' and the ethnographic region became known as Lithuania Minor (Mažoji Lietuva) from the mid 16th century onwards. This quiet corner of Lithuania, known for recreational tourism and bird migration routes, holds many secrets from a tumultuous past as a contested borderland. In the 13th century the region was invaded by north-advancing Teutonic Knights, and the incessant war between the Grand Duchy of Lithuania and the Teutonic Order ensued until the signing of the Treaty of Melno in 1422. The new Prussia–Lithuania border region was relatively stable, even when lands of the Grand Duchy of Lithuania were annexed into the Russian Empire in 1795. As the border fluctuated, so did the local population; Germans retreated when they knew Russians were coming and Lithuanians repopulated when the Germans left. Communities continued to shift over the centuries. In 1918, at the end of World War II, Lithuania declared its independence and Lithuania Minor demanded unification with Lithuania proper via the Act of Tilsit. The Nemunas River was a natural border and everything north of the river was claimed as Lithuania (except for the city of Memel and its surrounding region). As a result, much Lithuania Minor territory was lost to Germany (in present-day Kaliningrad, Russia) and Poland. You will find German more widely spoken in the region than English due to historically larger numbers of German tourists, but this is changing. Tourism amenities are improving, but there is still a rustic charm of this lesser-known backwater. When the weather is not beach-worthy, the region provides a cultural and culinary day out with Lithuania Minor famed for its farmstead restaurants and hospitality.

A snapshot of days gone by in Lithuania Minor can be glimpsed at the **Agluonėnai Ethnographic Homestead Museum** (Agluonėnų etnografinė Sodyba; Klojimo gatvė 9, Agluonėnai; w gargzdumuziejus.lt/agluonenu-etnografine-sodyba; ⊕ Apr–Oct 11.00–18.00 Tue–Sat, Nov–Mar 11.00–18.00 Tue–Fri, 11.00–15.00 Sat; €5/2.50), a beautifully restored and well-curated historic farmstead depicting authentic rural life and harking back to the days when it was built in 1898. Since 1983 it has also been home to a barn theatre, where local song and dance troupes perform usually during local festivals. The museum is located close to Račkauska Sodyba restaurant in the village of Agluonėnai, a 30-minute drive south of Klaipėda on road 141.

## KING WILHELM CANAL

The King Wilhelm Channel (also known as Klaipėda Channel) starts at Lankupiai, where it branches off from the Minija River. Lankupiai lock controls the water levels in the channel as it flows northeast in a straight line, passing Dreverna and reaching Klaipėda at Malkų Bay. The objective of the channel was to offer an alternative route for ships which were vulnerable to damage from the dangerous storms of the Curonian Lagoon. It greatly shortened the time for timber and cargo transportation. The channel is approximately 27km long, 28m wide and 1.7m deep and was manually dug by French prisoners of war between 1863 and 1873. There is a memorial to the French prisoners at the Klaipėda end. The canal takes its name from the Prussian King (Kaiser) Wilhelm I who reigned at the time.

It is possible to book a **canoe tour** of the Wilhelm Canal with local activity operator **Wet Weim** (for further information, see w wetweim.com/all-canoe-tours/wilhelm-canal).

## WHERE TO STAY AND EAT

**Račkauska Sodyba & 'Agluona' restaurant** Kantvainų gatvė, Agluonėnai; w rackauskusodyba.lt; ⏱ 11.00–22.00 daily. A family-run farmstead with 3 cottages to rent (each sleep 2–4 people), one of which is fully modernised & upgraded. There's a spa area for hire & the on-site restaurant Agluona has been famous for its grill for over 15 years. €€€

**Česlovo vynas** Virkytų 1, Žagatpurvių region; w ceslovovynai.lt; ⏱ 10.00–22.00 Tue–Fri, 10.00–15.00 Sat. Česlovo vynas is proud to be the first family wine-maker in Lithuania, producing high-quality organic fruit wines using berries & fruits grown on their organic certified farm. The shop is available to visit during opening hours, but tastings (90mins) must be booked in advance via the website. €€

**Mėmelio vynas** (Memel Wine) Pjaulių g 16, Priekulė; w memeliovynas.lt. This small craft winery focuses on manual production & local raw materials to create limited-edition wines. Tours & tastings lasting 1–3hrs (in English) are available if booked in advance. Stockists of their wine are listed on the website. €€

**Sotus Vilkas Vilkyčiai** Vilkyčių gatvė 4, Vilkyčiai; w sotusvilkas.lt/vilkyciai; ⏱ 11.00–21.00 Mon–Thu, 11.00–23.00 Fri, 10.30–23.00 Sat, 10.30–21.00 Sun. A local favourite serving up Lithuanian cuisine in generous portions with an outdoor terrace in warm weather. How anyone manages 3 courses here is a mystery. €€

**OTHER PRACTICALITIES** Be aware this region is sparsely populated and services limited. Although most places will accept card payments, in the event of needing cash the only **ATMs** are in Šilutė. **Petrol stations** are in Priekulė and Šilutė, along with **pharmacies** and **supermarkets**.

**DREVERNA** A once-quiet fishing port of homesteads and gardens is now a purpose-built holiday resort, **Dreverna Recreation and Entertainment Port** (Drevernas Uostas, w dreverna.lt). Contrary to the usual isolated holiday farmstead in the Lithuanian countryside, this is mass tourism Lithuania-style. Year-round accommodation is in basic holiday cottages situated along the water's edge, and in summer there are also 'living modules' in repurposed shipping containers and a campsite. Along with the swimming pool, saunas and slides, you can hire a boat, canoe or paddleboard, and a daily passenger ferry service runs to Juodkrantė on the Curonian Spit (page 306). Views of the Curonian Spit and lagoon can be enjoyed from the 15m-tall Dreverna observation tower.

**SVENCELĖ** (w svencele.com) What was once a small, local fishing area has been transformed into a prestigious artificially created resort for water sports. Affluent young professionals and hipsters from the cities come here to party and power kite. A brave new world of futuristic box-shaped houses and apartments line newly dug access channels to/from the lagoon and moored boats replace parked cars. Properties are private second homes, but private holiday rentals are expected to appear on the market. The 'town centre' is built of repurposed shipping containers which house a basic seasonal hotel, pop-up restaurants and water sports providers. The season runs from May to October. The conditions here make Svencelė the best place in Europe, and one of the best in the world, for kitesurfing – shallow, fresh water and wind being the key components for success. You can bring your own equipment or hire it from one of the water sports schools who offer kitesurfing, windsurfing and wakeboarding.

**NEMUNAS RIVER DELTA REGIONAL PARK** (w saugoma.lt/en/territories/nemunas-delta-regional-park) The ecological importance of the Nemunas River delta was promptly recognised post-independence and was granted regional park status in 1992. The park is a waterscape which encompasses the delta, the shallow bays of the Curonian Lagoon, smaller rivers, lakes, wetlands and raised bogs, all connected by a network of reclaimed land, polders, dykes and drainage channels, some of which experience seasonal flooding in spring. It is recommended to take to the water on an organised boat tour of the Nemunas delta or a kayaking adventure to embrace slow travel and give attention to the dragonflies, wildflowers and the families labouring in their hay meadows. Bicycle touring works well here, in thanks to quiet gravel roads and most boat services accepting bikes for a modest fee of about €3 per bike. The regional park is a haven for ornithologists and a guided tour with an expert is essential. The highlights of the delta can be done comfortably in a day trip from Klaipėda. Most amenities in the region are seasonal, operating between late May and September, so if visiting in low season be sure to prebook with local suppliers in advance to ensure they can accommodate you.

**CAPE OF VENTĖ** Ventė Cape (Ventės Ragas) is an absolute must for those interested in ornithology and for non-birders too. This hook of land is the most southern end of the Curonian Lagoon eastern shore and projects out into the lagoon pointing towards Russian waters. On a clear day, the dunes of the Curonian Spit are visible, while water sports enthusiasts mingle with fishing vessels and border patrol boats on the lagoon.

**Getting there and away** Bus 46 from Klaipėda (Klaipėda–Priekulė–Kintai–Ventė) runs three times daily on weekdays and twice at weekends, taking approximately 2 hours with regular stops at local villages. After exiting the bus, follow the road keeping the lagoon on your right; you will walk past **Jono žuvis parduotuvė** shop and cafe (Marių gatvė 18, Ventė) on your left, which is where you should park if arriving by car. You can also arrive by ferry from Nida (w pamariopramogos.com; May–Sep; adult €15, bike €3).

### Where to stay and eat

**Šturmų Švyturys** (9 rooms) Švyturio gatvė 7, Šturmai w sturmusvyturys.lt; ⏰ 13.00–21.00 daily. This long-established hotel & restaurant is popular with day-trippers looking for lunch & those wanting to overnight in comfort. The restaurant is famous for its daily catch being presented on ice & resulting in a last-minute menu of fresh fish. You select the fish you would like

baked in the fireplace just for you. Guest rooms – dbls, tpls & quads – are blue, maritime themed. Some rooms have single beds shaped like boats, for children. There's also a separate fishermen's cabin with 2 sgl beds. B/fast inc. €€€
**Ventainė** Marių gatvė 7, Ventė; **w** ventaine.lt; ⏲ 09.00–21.00 daily. A busy complex of basic hotel, campsite & villas, with a well-established restaurant serving European cuisine. Water sports including paddleboards, kayaks & jet skis can be booked in advance & they run a small daily ferry service to Nida in summer season for pedestrians & bikes, allowing guests to opt for a day trip to Nida direct from the site. €€€
**Ventragis** Marių gatvė 24, Ventė; **f** ventragis; ⏲ 11.00–20.00 Sun–Thu, 11.00–23.00 Fri–Sat. Ventragis is another iconic local restaurant, this one in a prime location overlooking Ventė lighthouse & the Ventė Cape Ornithological Station bird-ringing nets. The outdoor terrace is perfect for when the weather is kind. Reliably high standard in food & service. €€€

**What to see and do** Opened in 1929 by Lithuanian naturalist Tadas Ivanauskas, **Ventė Cape Ornithological Station** (Ventės Rago ornitologinė stotis, Marių gatvė 24; **w** vros.lt/en; ⏲ 10.00–20.00 daily) was one of the first bird-ringing stations in the world and still operates today to monitor and understand better the behaviour of migratory birds. The cape is an important resting place for migrating birds, especially in autumn, and home to the largest bird trap in the world. The 'Big Trap' is a single-chamber trap used to capture birds flying in a southwest direction; here they are carefully and quickly extracted, ringed and released. Their movements are then able to be tracked and monitored by specialist ornithological research programmes. Regulars include starlings, Eurasian siskins and common chaffinches. Visitors can explore the interactive ornithological exhibition and climb the lighthouse (built in 1863). Keen birdwatchers are advised to arrange a guide and comprehensive tour in advance via the website.

**Boat tours of the Nemunas Delta** (**w** pamariopramogos.com) depart from the pier daily from May to September at noon and take 2 hours. They also offer a **ferry service to Nida** for pedestrians and bicycles.

**MINGĖ** As quaint as it is, the nickname 'Venice of Lithuania' is a little generous. Wooden fishermen's houses flank each side of the Minija River, each with steps or a jetty to the water's edge where a boat is moored instead of the family car. Opposite neighbours visit each other by boat, or by crossing the ice on foot in winter, as there is no bridge. Well, there is a bridge but it crosses a tributary rather than the main river (a mishap between Moscow central planning and local implementation). Perhaps this was a stroke of luck, retaining a remote and peaceful Mingė village. Most houses are second homes or holiday rentals, but there are a few permanent residents left. There are no amenities, so you should bring everything you need for your stay. Note also the approach roads on both sides of the river are gravel roads.

Mingė was once the only place in the world where you could get a ferry to Nida, Klaipėda, Liverpool and New York, and the best way to see Mingė and the Nemunas delta region is still from the water. **Sightseeing boat trips to Nida** (**w** mingeskaimas.lt; adult €30 return, bike €3) run from June to August daily and at weekends in September, departing Mingė at 09.00 and returning from Nida at 17.30. The sailing takes 2 hours.

🏠 **Where to stay** Housed in a former school building, **Ėvė Mingė** (3 apartments; Mingės village, road 4228; **w** mingeseve.lt; €€) is brimming with artefacts of historical interest which are brought to life by the hosts' stories. The bygone era of East Prussia feels close when you stay here.

> ### AUKŠTUMALA TRAIL
>
> A worthy place to stretch your legs, the Aukštumala Trail (Aukštumalos pažintinis takas, road 4217 between the Mingė junction and Šilutė) is an accessible trail leading through 'One of the most famous raised bogs in the World!' A boardwalk takes you out into the vast expanse of the Aukštumala bog. Rare bird species including golden plovers, great grey shrikes and wood sandpipers breed here and flocks of cranes and geese visit during the annual migration seasons. Continue to the second tower for panoramic views and information boards.

**ŠILUTĖ** Once a staging post and trading centre between the port of Klaipėda (Memel) and border town of Panemunė (Tilsit), Šilutė is today a regional hub providing the delta region with practical amenities including banks, ATMs, supermarkets, pharmacy and a petrol station (be advised to fill up here before you go exploring). Šilutė is a tree-lined town dotted with examples of Prussian architecture in varying states of repair and disrepair. The **tourist information office** (w siluteinfo.lt) is based in the **Šilutė Hugo Scheu Museum** (Šilutė Hugo Šojus Museum; Lietuvininkų gatvė 4; w silutesmuziejus.lt; ⊕ Jun–Sep 10.00–18.00 Tue–Fri, 10.00–16.00 Sat–Sun, Oct–May 10.00–18.00 Tue–Fri, 10.00–16.00 Sat–Sun), which is the flagship museum for local history and restoration of local cultural objects. The **Evangelical Lutheran Church** (Lietuvininkų gatvė 21; w silutesparapija.lt) has a visually striking blue altar and frescoes painted by Professor Richard Pfeiffer (1878–1962) of the Koenigsberg Academy of Arts. The village of Macikai is a short drive from Šilutė centre, where you will find the location of former World War II concentration camp **Stalag Luft VI** (Macikų koncentracijos stovykla; Vilties gatvė; w silutesmuziejus.lt/en/maciku-lageriai/the-macikai-complex). Little evidence remains of the camp itself, but there is a small museum housed in the former solitary confinement unit. You must pre-book your visit via the Šilutė Hugo Scheu Museum (✆+370 441 62207; e info@silutesmuziejus.lt). When exiting the museum, head along the road diagonally to the left for approximately 450m to the cemetery, where you will find an information board detailing the history of the camp and its former location. The cemetery is the resting place for a number of allied nationalities who died as prisoners of war.

**Getting there and away** Šilutė is on the former Memel (Klaipėda)–Koenigsberg (Kaliningrad) railway line, which now terminates at Šilutė station (Šilutės geležinkelio stotis; Geležinkelio gatvė 4). Direct **trains** from Klaipėda run four times daily, taking 51 minutes; a one-way adult ticket costs €5.

**Buses** run regularly between Šilutė and Klaipėda; the journey takes 1 hour and costs €6 for an adult one way. Change in Klaipėda for local buses to Palanga, Nida, Tauragė and long-distance buses to Kaunas, Vilnius and Riga. Šilutė bus station (Šilutės autobusų stotis) is at Tilžės gatvė 22.

From late June, a **ferry** service between Šilutė and Nida operates daily, departing Šilutė small ship port (Uosta gatvė 9) at 08.30 and returning from Nida at 18.00. The crossing takes 2 hours, parking is free for the day, and tickets can be booked online (w kde.lt; €15/12 one-way).

**Where to stay and eat** Accommodation in Šilutė is limited and basic, with most tourists to the region choosing to stay in more rural locations. Šilutė does, however, serve a purpose, with most guests being German tourists interested in the former

Prussia connection, or individuals on family heritage tours who want a base from which to explore local history.

**Hotel Deims** (43 rooms) Lietuvininkų gatvė 70; w deims.lt. A no-frills basic hotel in the centre of Šilutė with a restaurant. €€

**Hotel Gilija** (16 rooms) Vytauto gatvė 17; w silutesgilija.lt. Slightly more upmarket than the Deims, Gilija boasts a swimming pool & sauna but neither are guaranteed to be in working order. €€

**Kitchen Inn** Saulės akligatvis 10; KitchenInn; 11.00–22.00 daily. Regularly the top choice for food in Šilutė, serving a reliable menu of burgers, pasta & fries. €€

**RUSNĖ ISLAND** Whether Rusnė Island (Rusnės sala) is an actual island is up for debate. This is reclaimed land, formed from sediment deposited by the Nemunas River as it enters the Curonian Lagoon and drained via an extensive network of canals, polders and pumps. The area is prone to flooding and in 2019 a new elevated section of the only access road to Rusnė was opened (road 206 from Šilutė to Rusnė). Considering how much the landscape here is managed and influenced by humans, it required a determined effort by naturalists and ornithologists to restore native meadowlands needed to support various species of birds. The town of Rusnė has 1,500 inhabitants with the bare minimum of amenities as locals depend on nearby Šilutė for most services.

For **tourist information**, there is no physical office on Rusnė Island, only an online resource: w salarusne.lt.

**Getting there and away** Two **buses** a day depart Klaipėda, at 06.00 and 11.00 Mon–Sat; the journey time to Rusnė Island is 1 hour 40 minutes. The same service picks up en route in Šilutė at 07.20 and 12.20. Buses run regularly between Šilutė-Rusnė-Šilutė to suit working hours and school commuting times. Vinardo Taksi is Rusnė's local **taxi** service (K Donelaičio gatvė 9; +370 441 76005). Bolt taxi service is available locally but with fewer drivers so you may need to wait for availability. Expect a Bolt taxi from Šilutė to Rusnė to cost €5.50.

**Where to stay and eat**

**Rusnė Villa** [map, page 278] (9 rooms) Pakalnės gatvė 82, Pakalnė village; w villarusne.lt. The best hotel accommodation on the island is not in Rusnė town. Instead it has a rural location near Pakalnė village &, in keeping with its 'romantic & dreamy' image, is often booked up with weddings at w/ends. Private guides for birdwatching, nature tours & night-hiking can be booked in advance. The restaurant is open all year round. €€

**Prie Peterso Tilto** Šilutės gatvė 13; w rusnepetersas.lt; 11.00–22.00 daily. Pub grub in Rusnė in a Prussian-style building with menus in English. Popular with groups. Fish soup is regularly recommended. €€

**What to see and do**

*A short walk around Rusnė* Joining the river path from Šilutės gatvė, there is an unexpected monument to **Mahatma Ghandi** and his close friend Hermann Kallenbach. Kallenbach grew up on Rusnė and Ghandi referred to him as his 'soulmate'. They are immortalised at the place where the original bridge to Rusnė once spanned the Nemunas River before it was destroyed in World War II. An outdoor exhibition of **old flood vehicles** displays how innovative locals coped with seasonal floodwaters before a land viaduct was constructed in the 1960s. You are now in border territory both on land and in the water. As you reach the furthest point of the landmass (Rusnės salos pradžia) and the Lithuanian border post marker, directly opposite you is Kaliningrad, Russia. It can feel a bit strange as there is no physical barrier and there will often be Lithuanians fishing opposite Russians fishing on the far bank. Look around closely and you will see there are hi-tech surveillance cameras on the Lithuanian side. The landlocked **ancient Lithuanian boat *Vytinė*** looks a bit lacklustre but the new audio guide installation will lift your spirits with its very loud legends of Rusnė. Upon reaching the road, cross over the bridge and follow the footpath on your right along the riverbank. This is the **Skirvytėlė ethnographic area** (Skirvytėlės etnografinis kaimas), an open-air museum of traditional wooden houses. At Žvejo gatvė turn off the path through the homestead to visit the **Ethnographic Fisherman's Homestead** (Žvejo sodybos muziejus; ✆ +370 441 58169) – book in advance and visit with a guide who can translate the tales and traditions. Back on the river path, continue to the suspension bridge (Kabantis tiltas per Pakalnę), cross the Pakalnė River and return to the town on the opposite side.

***Uostadvaris Lighthouse*** (Uostadvario švyturys) Leaving Rusnė on Nemuno gatvė, with the Atmata River on your right, follow road 4204 for 10km to reach the Uostadvaris Lighthouse. Parking is on the roadside. Uostadvaris (w uostadvaris.lt) is a small marina with several boat-trip companies offering trips around the delta. It is also a base for the border patrol boats and local fishing boats. You can climb to the top of the historic lighthouse to admire the view. Owing to land reclamation, the lighthouse is no longer on the coast and became redundant, being replaced by Ventė Lighthouse. Unfortunately, this place is still awaiting an entrepreneur to open a café.

**ŽEMAIČIŲ NAUMIESTIS** A small town east of Šilutė on the 165 road, Žemaičių Naumiestis was a border town, bustling with multicultural traders, Lithuanian, German and Jewish. Their legacy is fully evident in the remaining architecture – a wooden Catholic church (1782), a stone synagogue (1816) and a Protestant church (1842). The town is often used as a filming location due to its authentic architecture and atmosphere, and it is not without its own script-worthy story. Following the failed uprising against the Russian Empire in 1863, Lithuanian-language publications in the Latin alphabet were banned and Žemaičių Naumiestis became an important distribution point for banned literature.

**JUKNAIČIAI** Welcome to the remnants of a communist utopia. Juknaičiai was purpose built in the 1960s as a model Soviet rural community based around a collective farm and it became a showcase collective farm in the Soviet Union. Visiting Soviet officials were taken to Juknaičiai and shown the cinema, hotel, swimming pool, landscaping, unusual water tower and quality housing – it masked how most people really lived. Unfortunately, a fire destroyed the wellness centre in 2006. Restoration work is underway, but although it is making slow progress, Juknaičiai is worthy of a quick stop if you are travelling on the 141 road between Šilutė and Panemunė.

# Appendix 1

## LANGUAGE

You should always give some basic words of Lithuanian a go. Your efforts will be warmly welcomed even if they conjure up a smile from the locals.

**PRONUNCIATION** In general, Lithuanian is a phonemic orthography, meaning that it is pronounced as it is written. Do this and you will have a good chance to be understood. Beyond this, pronunciation becomes complex with numerous rules and nuances including being a pitch-accent language, so how you pronounce a word can completely change its meaning. Consonants can be palatised or non-palatised depending on whether they are followed by a vowel. For those looking to learn Lithuanian thoroughly see the reading and course recommendations below. We joke that Lithuanian can be stressful to learn, literally – left stress, right stress or wavy stress!

**The alphabet** The Lithuanian alphabet, or *abėcėlė*, is based on the Latin script and has 32 letters. There are 12 vowels, 20 consonants, no Q, W or X, and 9 letters have diacritics, eg: Š.

| | | | |
|---|---|---|---|
| A, a | is in **a**pple | K, k | as in **k**ick |
| Ą, ą | as in f**a**ther | L, l | as in **l**ick |
| B, b | as in **b**ig | M, m | as in **m**oth |
| C, c | like 'ts' in an**ts** | N, n | as in **n**ip |
| Č, č | like 'ch' as in **ch**ip | O, o | as in g**o**at |
| D, d | as in **d**ark | P, p | as in **p**ick |
| E, e | as in g**e**t | R, r | is always trilled or rolled |
| Ę, ę | like the 'ai' in **air** | S, s | as in **s**ky |
| Ė, ė | like the 'a' in l**a**te | Š, š | like **sh** in **sh**oe |
| F, f | as in **f**irst | T, t | as in **t**ape |
| G, g | as in **g**old | U, u | as in p**u**t |
| H, h | as in **h**ello | Ų, ų | as in tr**u**e |
| I, i | as in p**i**t | Ū, ū | also as in tr**u**e |
| Į, į | as in f**ee**t | V, v | as in **v**ote |
| Y, y | as in m**ea**d | Z, z | as in **z**ip |
| J, j | like the 'y' in **y**es | Ž, ž | like the 's' in mea**s**ure |

Note the two common digraphs:

| | |
|---|---|
| Dz | like 'dz' in frien**dz**one |
| Dž | like 'j' in **J**ohn or 'g' in **G**eorge |

> **LANGUAGE TRIVIA**
>
> For many years the longest Lithuanian word was 37 letters long: *nebeprisikiš kiakopūsteliaujantiesiems*, meaning 'for the ones who no longer cannot have enough of picking wild sorrel'.
> In 2018, a new generation came up with their longest word of 43 letters: *nebeprisivaizdotinklaraštininkaujantiesiems*, meaning 'for the ones who no longer cannot have enough of video blogging'.

Common dipthongs are:

| | | | |
|---|---|---|---|
| ai | like 'ai' in **ai**sle | ui | like 'ooey' in ph**ooey** |
| au | like 'ow' in h**ow** | uo | like the 'uo' in the Italian |
| ei | like 'ay' in d**ay** | | word b**uo**no |
| ie | like 'ea' in p**ie**r | | |

Tripthongs can appear as endings:

| | |
|---|---|
| iai | like '**ay**' in d**ay** |
| iau | like 'eow' in m**eow** |

**BASIC GRAMMAR** Lithuanian distinguishes between proper and common nouns, with only proper nouns capitalised. Some nouns can be both. Lithuanian has no articles. It has three genders: masculine, feminine and neutral. There are no strict rules for the gender of words, but some general guidelines are that masculine nouns in the nominative case usually end in -*s* and feminine nouns usually end in -*a* or -*ė*. Lithuanian is a highly inflected language, meaning that word endings change to indicate the word's function in the sentence. There are seven cases; nominative, genitive, dative, accusative, instrumental, locative and vocative. There are four main tenses: present, past, past iterative and future. The language also has aspect markers: perfective and imperfective. The most common sentence structure in Lithuanian is subject-verb-object. There are many grammar exceptions that must be learned by heart at school, and not even native speakers master them all perfectly.

## USEFUL WORDS AND PHRASES
### Essentials

| | |
|---|---|
| Yes | *Taip* |
| No | *Ne* |
| Please | *Prašau* |
| Thank you | *Ačiū* |
| Don't mention it | *Neminėkite šio* |
| Cheers! | *Į sveikatą!* |
| I don't understand | *Nesuprantu* |
| Please would you speak more slowly | *Prašau kalbėti lėčiau* |
| Do you understand? | *Ar suprantate?* |

### Greetings

| | |
|---|---|
| Good morning | *Labas rytas* |
| Good afternoon | *Laba diena* |
| Good evening | *Labas vakaras* |

Hello — *Labas*
Hi — *Sveiki*
Goodbye — *Viso* gero (formal), *Iki/Atia* (informal)
How are you? — *Kaip sekasi?*
Pleased to meet you — *Malonu susipažinti*
My name is… — *Mano vardas…*
What is your name? — *Koks tavo vardas?*
I am from…UK/USA — *Aš esu iš Jungtinės Karalystės/Jungtinių Amerikos valstijų*

## Questions

| | | | |
|---|---|---|---|
| How? | *Kaip?* | Where? | *Kur?* |
| How much? | *Kiek* | Which? | *Kuris?* |
| What is it? | *Kas tai yra?* | Who? | *Kas?* |
| What? | *Ką?* | Why? | *Kodėl?* |
| When? | *Kada?* | | |

## Numbers

| | | | |
|---|---|---|---|
| 1 | *vienas* | 16 | *šešiolika* |
| 2 | *du* | 17 | *septyniolika* |
| 3 | *trys* | 18 | *aštuoniolika* |
| 4 | *keturi* | 19 | *devyniolika* |
| 5 | *penki* | 20 | *dvidešimt* |
| 6 | *šeši* | 21 | *dvidešimt vienas* |
| 7 | *septyni* | 30 | *trisdešimt* |
| 8 | *aštuoni* | 40 | *keturiasdešimt* |
| 9 | *devyni* | 50 | *penkiasdešimt* |
| 10 | dešimt | 60 | *šešiasdešimt* |
| 11 | *vienuolika* | 70 | *septyniasdešimt* |
| 12 | *dvylika* | 80 | *aštuoniasdešimt* |
| 13 | *trylika* | 90 | *devyniasdešimt* |
| 14 | *keturiolika* | 100 | *šimtas* |
| 15 | *penkiolika* | 1,000 | *tūkstantis* |

## Time

| | | | |
|---|---|---|---|
| What time is it? | *Kas tai yra?* | today | *šiandien* |
| It's…o'clock | …*valanda* | tonight | *šiandien vakare* |
| morning | *rytas* | tomorrow | *rytoj* |
| evening | *vakaras* | yesterday | *vakar* |

## Days of the week

| | | | |
|---|---|---|---|
| Monday | *Pirmadienis* | Friday | *Penktadienis* |
| Tuesday | *Antradienis* | Saturday | *Šeštadienis* |
| Wednesday | *Trečiadienis* | Sunday | *Sekmadienis* |
| Thursday | *Ketvirtadienis* | | |

## Months

| | | | |
|---|---|---|---|
| January | *Sausis* | May | *Gegužė* |
| February | *Vasaris* | June | *Birželis* |
| March | *Kovas* | July | *Liepa* |
| April | *Balandis* | August | *Rugpjūtis* |

| September | *Rugsėjis* | November | *Lapkritis* |
| October | *Spalis* | December | *Gruodis* |

## Getting around
### Public transport

| | |
|---|---|
| I'd like… | Aš norėčiau |
| …a one-way ticket | …bilieto į vieną pusę |
| …a return ticket | …bilieto pirmyn ir atgal |
| I want to go to… | Norėčiau keliauti į… |
| How much is it? | Kiek tai kainuoja? |
| What time does it leave? | Kada išvyksta? |
| What time is it now? | Kiek dabar valandų? |
| The train has been… | Traukinys… |
| …delayed | …vėluoja |
| …cancelled | …atšauktas |
| | |
| 4x4 | varoma keturiais ratais |
| airport | oro uostas |
| arrival/departure | atvykimas/išvykimas |
| bicycle | dviratis |
| boat | laivas |
| Bon voyage! | Gero kelio! |
| bus | autobusas |
| bus station | autobusų stotis |
| car | mašina |
| ferry | keltas |
| first class | pirma klasė |
| from/to | iš/į |
| here/there | čia/ten |
| minibus | mikroautobusas |
| motorbike/moped | motociklas/mopedas |
| plane | lėktuvas |
| platform | platforma |
| port | uostas |
| railway station | geležinkelio stotis |
| second class | antra klasė |
| sleeper | miegamoji kajutė |
| taxi | taksi |
| ticket office | bilietų kasa |
| timetable | maršrutų grafikas |
| train | traukinys |

### Private transport

| | |
|---|---|
| I have broken down | Sugedau |
| I'd like…litres | Man reikėtų…litrų |
| Is this the road to…? | Ar šis kelias veda į…? |
| Please fill it up | Prašau, užpildykite |
| Where is the service station? | Kur yra autoservisas? |
| | |
| diesel | dyzelinis kuras |
| unleaded petrol | bešvinis benzinas |

## Road signs
| | |
|---|---|
| danger | pavojinga |
| detour | Apylanka |
| entry | įvažiavimas |
| exit | išvažiavimas |
| give way | duokite kelią |
| keep clear | neužstatyti eismas |
| no entry | draudžiamas |
| one way | vienpusis eismas |
| toll | Kelių mokestis |

## Directions
| | |
|---|---|
| Where is it? | Kur tai yra? |
| Go straight ahead | Eikite tiesiai |
| Turn left | sukite į dešinę |
| Turn right | sukite į kairę |
| …at the traffic lights… | prie šviesoforo |
| …at the roundabout | žiede |
| north | Šiaurė |
| south | Pietūs |
| east | Rytai |
| west | Vakarai |
| behind | už |
| in front of | priekyje |
| near | netoli |
| opposite | kitoje pusėje |

## Street signs
| | |
|---|---|
| closed | uždaryta |
| entrance | įėjimas |
| exit | išėjimas |
| information | informacija |
| open | atidaryta |
| toilets | Tualetas |
| …men's/women's (WC) | …vyrų/moterų |

## Accommodation
| | |
|---|---|
| Could you please write the address? | Gal galėtumėte užrašyti adresą? |
| Do you have any rooms available? | Ar turite laisvų kambarių? |
| How much it is per night/person? | Kokia kaina žmogui per naktį? |
| I am leaving today | Išvykstu šiandien |
| I'd like… | Norėčiau |
| …a single room | vienviečio kambario |
| …a double room | dviviečio kambario |
| …a room with two beds | kambario su atskiromis lovomis |
| …a room with a bathroom | kambario su vonios kambariu |
| …to share a dorm | noriu bendrabučio kambario |
| Is there… | Ar yra… |
| …hot water? | …karštas vanduo? |
| …electricity? | …elektra? |
| Is breakfast included? | Ar pusryčiai įskaičiuoti? |
| Where is the bathroom? | Kur galėčiau rasti vonios kambarį? |
| Where is a cheap/good hotel? | Kur rasti pigų/gerą viešbutį? |
| Where is the toilet? | Kur galėčiau rasti tualetą? |

## Eating out
| | |
|---|---|
| Do you have a table for…people? | Ar turėtumėte stalą…žmonių? |
| I am a vegetarian | Aš vegetaras |
| Do you have any vegetarian dishes? | Art urite vegetariškų patiekalų? |
| Please bring me… | Gal galėčiau gauti… |
| …a fork/knife/spoon | Gal galėčiau gauti šakutę/peilį/šaukštą |
| Please may I have the bill? | Sąskaitą prašau |

## IN AN EMERGENCY

| | |
|---|---|
| Help! | Padėkite! |
| Call a doctor! | Iškvieskite daktarą! |
| There's been an accident | Įvyko nelaimė |
| I'm lost | Pasilydau |
| Go away! | Pasitraukite! Eikite šalin! |
| police | policija |
| fire | gaisras |
| ambulance | greitoji pagalba |
| thief | vagis |
| hospital | Ligoninė |

## Food and drink

### Basics
| | | | |
|---|---|---|---|
| bread | duona | pepper | pipirai |
| butter | sviestas | salt | druska |
| cheese | sūris | sugar | cukrus |
| oil | aliejus | | |

### Fruit
| | | | |
|---|---|---|---|
| apple | obuolys | mango | mangas |
| banana | bananas | orange | apelsinas |
| grape | vynuogė | pear | kriaušė |

### Vegetables
| | | | |
|---|---|---|---|
| broccoli | brokolis | onion | svogūnas |
| carrot | morka | pepper | pipiras |
| garlic | česnakas | potato | bulvė |

### Meat and fish
| | | | |
|---|---|---|---|
| beef | jautiena | mussels | midijos |
| chicken | vištiena | pork | kiauliena |
| goat | ožkiena/ožkos mėsą | salmon | lašiša |
| | | sausage | dešrelės |
| lamb | aviena | tuna | tunas |
| mackerel | skumbrė | | |

### Drinks
| | | | |
|---|---|---|---|
| beer | alus | tea | arbata |
| coffee | kava | water | vanduo |
| fruit juice | vaisių sultys | wine | vynas |
| milk | pienas | | |

## Shopping

| | |
|---|---|
| How much is it? | Kiek tai kainuoja? |
| I don't like it | Man nepatinka |
| I'd like to buy… | Norėčiau nusipirkti |
| I'll take it | Norėčiau |
| I'm just looking | Aš tik žiūriu |

| | | | |
|---|---|---|---|
| It's too expensive | *Per brangu* | | |
| Please may I have… | *Gal galėčiau gauti…* | | |
| Do you accept… | *Ar priimate…* | | |
| …credit cards? | *…kredito korteles?* | | |
| I need a bag | *Gal galėčiau maišelį* | | |

bigger — *didesnis*
less — *mažiau*
more — *daugiau*
smaller — *mažesnis*

## Communications

| | | | |
|---|---|---|---|
| I am looking for… | *Ieškau…* | tourist office | *turizmo informacijos centras* |
| bank | *banko* | | |
| church | *bažnyčios* | | |
| embassy | *ambasados* | | |
| bureau de change | *valiutos keitykla* | | |
| post office | *pašto* | | |

## Health

| | | | |
|---|---|---|---|
| I am ill | *Aš sergu* | antiseptic | *antiseptikas* |
| I am… | *Aš esu…* | condoms | *prezervatyvai* |
| …asthmatic | *…asmatikas* | contraceptive | *kontraceptikai* |
| …diabetic | *…diabetikas (sergu diabetu)* | diarrhoea | *viduriavimas* |
| | | doctor | *daktaras* |
| …epileptic | *…epileptikas* | nausea | *pykinimas* |
| I'm allergic to… | *Aš alergiškas…* | paracetamol | *paracetamolis* |
| …bees | *…bičių įgėlimui* | pharmacy | *vaistinė* |
| …nuts | *…riešutams* | prescription | *receptas* |
| …penicillin | *…penicilinui* | sunscreen | *saulės kremas* |
| | | tampons | *tamponai* |
| antibiotics | *antibiotikai* | | |

## Travel with children

| | |
|---|---|
| Are children allowed? | *Ar galima su vaikais?* |
| Do you have… | *Ar turite* |
| …a children's menu? | *…vaikų meniu?* |
| …infant milk formula | *pieno kūdikiams* |
| Is there a baby changing room? | *Ar yra kūdikio vystymo kambarys?* |
| babysitter | *vaikų auklė* |

### LANGUAGE COURSES

Vilnius University runs two- and four-week Lithuanian language courses every summer. For further information, see w flf.vu.lt/en/lsk/courses/summer-course.

*Learn and Speak Lithuanian* by Teresė Ringailienė (Šviesa, 2020) is a recommended book for studying Lithuanian and includes audio exercises online.

highchair　　　　　　　　　　aukšta kėdutė (vaiko kėdutė)
nappies　　　　　　　　　　　sauskelnės
potty　　　　　　　　　　　　puodelis

**Other useful vocabulary**

and/some/but　　　ir/keli/bet　　　　good/bad　　　　　geras/blogas
beautiful/ugly　　　gražu/bjauru　　　hot/cold　　　　　karštas/šaltas
boring/interesting　nuobodus/įdomus　my/mine/ours/yours　mano/mūsų/jūsų
difficult/easy　　　sunkus/lengvas　　old/new　　　　　senas/naujas
early/late　　　　　anksti/vėlai　　　this/that　　　　　šitas/tas
expensive/cheap　　brangu/pigu

# Appendix 2

## FURTHER INFORMATION
### BOOKS
### History and politics

Butterwick, Richard *Lithuania: A Short History* Hurst, 2025. An enjoyable and accessible introduction to the complex history of Lithuania by Richard Butterwick, Professor of Polish-Lithuanian History at the School of Slavonic and East European Studies, University College London.

Clarke, Charles (ed.) *Understanding the Baltic States: Estonia, Latvia and Lithuania since 1991* Hurst, 2023. Analysing the role of the Baltic states since their independence in 1990–91, their significance in European security, and their commitment to freedom and democracy along the borderlands of the EU and Russia.

Frost, Robert *The Oxford History of Poland-Lithuania: Volume I: The Making of the Polish-Lithuanian Union, 1385–1569* Oxford, 2018. Recommended reading for those requiring a comprehensive overview of the Polish-Lithuanian Commonwealth.

Galeotti, Mark *Teutonic Knight vs Lithuanian Warrior: The Lithuanian Crusade 1283–1435* Osprey, 2023. Bringing to life the three main battles of the Lithuanian crusades: Voplaukis in 1311, Kaunas in 1362, and Grunwald (Žalgiris) in 1410.

Lieven, Anatol *The Baltic Revolution: Estonia, Latvia, Lithuania and the Path to Independence* Yale University Press, 1994. An excellent overview of the history of the Baltic states. No longer the only comprehensive book covering Baltic history, but it is still one of the best.

Lukša, Juozas *Forest Brothers: The Account of an Anti-Soviet Lithuanian Freedom Fighter, 1944–1948* Central European University Press, 2009. A physical copy is difficult to get hold of, but Lukša's account has also been translated and published under his code name Daumantas, Juozas (*Fighters for Freedom: Lithuanian Partisans versus the USSR*) and can be read online at w partizanai.org/failai/pdf/fighters-for-freedom.pdf

Sayers, Nick *The Jews of Lithuania: A Journey through the Long Twentieth Century* Vallentine Mitchell, 2024. A welcome history of the Jews in Lithuania covering why the Jewish population was so numerous in the late 19th century, to the Holocaust, and emigration.

Snyder, Timothy *The Reconstruction of Nations: Poland, Ukraine, Lithuania, Belarus 1569–1999* Yale University Press, 2003. This historical overview of the wider region provides a solid basis for understanding current geopolitics.

Thomson, Clare *The Singing Revolution* Michael Joseph, 1991. An informative, accessible and personal account covering the lead-up to the Baltic states' independence from the Soviet Union.

### Language and culture

Briedis, Laimonas *Vilnius: City of Strangers* Central European University Press, 2009. A literary walk through the streets of Vilnius including quotes from the artistic, cultural and political icons who visited over the centuries.

Druchunas, Donna and Hall, June *The Art of Lithuanian Knitting* Trafalgar, 2017. Showcasing Lithuanian knitting through wholesome stories and inspiring with patterns and techniques for 25 designs.

Ringailienė, Teresė *Learn and Speak Lithuanian* Šviesa, 2020. One of the best companions to learning Lithuanian with clear exercises and online link for pronunciation and listening skills. Tricky to find online, but available in Lithuanian bookstores.

Zak, Zuza *Amber and Rye: A Baltic Food Journey, Estonia Latvia Lithuania* Murdoch, 2021. Authentic Baltic recipes that have been passed down the generations, complete with stories, cultural traditions and a new contemporary twist.

## Fiction

Carey, Edward *Alva and Irva* Picador, 2012. Although not directly about Lithuania, the fantasy city of Entralla is clearly based on Vilnius and the charming story about two twin sisters contains many a quirk that would feel at home in Lithuanian literature.

Gavelis, Ričardas *Vilnius Poker* Open Letter, 2009. A dystopian novel about life under Soviet rule, the protagonist descending into paranoia and mental decline under absurd scenarios. Dark and troubling but born out of real historical events.

Kunčinas, Jurgis *Tula* Pica Pica, 2016. Set in Užupis, the bohemian quarter of Vilnius, this is a modern-day classic of Lithuanian literature that has been translated and distributed internationally. It won the Lithuanian Writers' Union prize in 1993. A book filled with curious characters, tragic love and surreal storytelling.

Putrius, Birutė *Lost Birds* Birchwood Press, 2015. Enjoyable short stories weave a tale of emigration from Lithuania to Chicago in the wake of World War II, establishing community and a new life in the USA, and finally a return to free Lithuania.

Sepetys, Ruta *Between Shades of Gray* Penguin, 2010. This debut novel by American-Lithuanian author Sepetys tells the story of Lina, who is deported from her home in Kaunas to Siberia during the first wave of Soviet Russian deportations in 1941. The book was a New York Times bestseller, a Carnegie Medal nominee, and was adapted into a film titled *Ashes in the Snow*.

Škėma, Antanas *White Shroud* Vagabond Voices, 2018. Published in Lithuania in 1988 where Škėma has achieved cult status, this is modernist fiction telling the story of a Lithuanian émigré poet working as a bellboy in a New York hotel during the 1950s.

Zwi, Rose *Last Walk in Naryshkin Park* Spinifex, 1998. Although it might be difficult to source, this tragic account of the Jewish town of Žagarė sheds light on the local experience of many Lithuanian cities, towns and villages across Lithuania during the Holocaust.

**MAPS** Lithuanian map publisher **Briedis** (w briedis.lt) has wide range of national, regional and city maps. Latvian map publisher **Jana Seta** (w kartes.lv) also covers Lithuanian regions and cities.

## WEBSITES

w **bilietai.lt** What's-on listings, concert and event tickets in Lithuania.

w **investlithuania.com** For those looking to do business in Lithuania.

w **lietuvosgamta.lt** Dedicated to natural heritage sites that do not make it on to main sightseeing itineraries; trees, stones, mounds and springs – all have cultural and spiritual importance stemming from the old Lithuanian paganism. More than 160 sites are listed here along with their mystical folklore and legends.

w **lithuania.travel** The main portal for Lithuanian tourism including itineraries, sightseeing, hotels and events.

w **lithuanianculture.lt** Promoting Lithuanian culture worldwide through events and study programmes.

w **lrt.lt/en/news-in-english** English-language news portal of Lithuanian Radio and Television covering current affairs and cultural articles. You can sign up for email bulletins.

w **ltfai.org** A Canadian organisation keeping Lithuanian folk art traditions alive, the website has good overviews of the different types of applied art.

w **tablein.lt** Recommended for making restaurant reservations online.

# JOURNEY BOOKS
## CONTRACT PUBLISHING FROM BRADT GUIDES

## DO YOU HAVE A STORY TO TELL?

- Publish your book with a leading trade publisher
- Expert management of your book by our experienced editors
- Professional layout, cover design and printing
- **Unique** access to trade distribution for print books and ebooks
- Competitive pricing and a range of tailor-made packages
- Aimed at both first-timers and previously published authors

"Unfailingly pleasant"... "Undoubtedly one of the best publishers I have worked with"... "Excellent and incredibly prompt communication"... "Unfailingly courteous"... "Superb"...

For more information – and many more endorsements from our delighted authors – please visit: **bradtguides.com/journeybooks**

Journey Books is the contract publishing imprint of award-winning travel publisher, Bradt Guides. All subjects are considered for Journey Books, not just travel. Our contract publishing is a complement to our traditional publishing, not a replacement, and we welcome traditional submissions from new and established travel writers. Please visit **bradtguides.com/write-for-us** to find out more.

# Index

Page numbers in **bold** indicate major entries; those in *italic* indicate maps.

accommodation 58–60
activities
  Aquapark 139, **140**, 143, 144
  Aukštaitija Narrow-Gauge Railway
  'Siaurukas' and Museum 57, 118,
  **222–3**, 248
  Belmontas Adventure Park 119
  boat tours 140, 178, 182, 213, 232–3, 317
  cycling 46, 48, 78
  family amusement parks 213, 221
  golf courses 131
  hiking trails **7**, 45, 124, 130, 132, 146,
    147, 149, 153, 154, 156, 159, 227, 232,
    246, 264, 308, 318
  hot-air ballooning 92, 179, 212, **213**
  Liepkalnis 119
  rope parks 119, 140
  Snow Arena Druskininkai 140
  Treetop Walking Path and Information
    Centre 224
  watersports 124, 231, 232–3, 240, 267,
    316–17
Adamkus, Valdas 16
air travel 47–8
airlines 48
airports 47
Alytus 157–9
amber **36**, 66, 99, 279, 285–6, 306, 312
Anykščiai 217–24, *220*
  accommodation 219–21
  activities 221
  getting there and away 219
  restaurants 221
  sights 222–4
  tourist information 219
art 32–4
arts and entertainment 66–7
Asanavičiūtė, Loreta 19
Aukštaitija 217–50

Aukštaitija National Park 231–4
Aukštaitija Narrow-Gauge Railway 57, 118,
  **222–3**, 248
Aukštojas Hill 3, 135

Baltic Chain *see* Baltic Way, The
Baltic Trails 45
Baltic Way, The 15, 19, 21, 31, 76, 93,
  116, 191
Baltušis, Juozas 39
Basanavičius, Jonas 215, 284
basketball 2, 41–2, 90, 163, 165–6, 176, 181,
  190, 260
beaches 134, 238, 241, 277, 285, 300–1,
  303, 306, **308**, 313
beekeeping **9**, 144, 154, 234
Benedictsen, Dane Meyer 10
Bičiūnienė, Monika 33
Bielinis, Jurgis 38
birds, birdwatching **7–8**, 44, 46, 158–9,
  230, 262, 305, 307, 317, 319
Birštonas *210*, 210–16
  accommodation 211–12
  activities 212–13
  getting there and away 211
  history 210–11
  jazz festival 214
  restaurants 212
  sights 214–16
  tourist information 211
Biržai 3, **245–7**
bison 8, 154–5
bogs and swamps 3, 124, 153, 154, 158, 204,
  264, 265, 274, 318
book smuggling 10, **38**, 40, 109, 200
bookshops 91, 177, 296
border zones 3, 22, 47, 134–5, 146–7, 156,
  202, 206–8, 313–14, 319–20
budgeting 56

Budrys, Algis 39
Bunka, Jakovas 269, 271–2
bus travel 49–50

Camino-Lituano 45
camping 59, 84, 123, 157, 212, 227, 241, 246, 262, 317
Cape of Ventė 316–17
car travel 50–1, 57–8
castle mounds 130, **201**, 206, 250
cemeteries 64, **111**, 299
charities 70
Christianity **30**, 63, 74, 94, 96, 100, 106, 251, 269, 275–6, 286
Christmas 30, **64**, 81, 172
churches and cathedrals
    Assumption of the Blessed Virgin Mary, Church of the (Vilnius) 288
    Cathedral of the Apostles St Peter and St Paul (Šiauliai) 258–9
    Christ's Resurrection Church (Kaunas) 190
    Dominican Church of Apostles St Philip and St Jacob (Vilnius) 112
    Dominican Church of the Holy Spirit (Vilnius) 109
    Gates of Dawn (Vilnius) 106
    Holy Sacrament, Church of (Kaunas) 183
    Holy Trinity, Church of (Kaunas) 180
    Holy Trinity Uniate Church (Vilnius) 105
    Orthodox Cathedral of the Theotokos (Vilnius) 101
    Russian Orthodox Church of the Holy Spirit (Vilnius) 105–6
    St Anne, Church of, and Bernardine Monastery Complex (Vilnius) 98
    St Casimir, Church of (Vilnius) 104–5
    St Catherine's Church (Vilnius) 108
    St Francis Xavier Church (Kaunas) 180
    St George the Martyr, Church of (Kaunas) 180
    St George's Church (Vilnius) 110
    St Gertrude, Church of (Kaunas) 183
    St Matthew the Apostle, Church of (Anykščiai) 222
    St Michael the Archangel Church (Kaunas) 186
    St Nicholas, Church of (Vilnius) 107
    St Nicholas' Orthodox Church (Vilnius) 102–3
    St Parasceve Orthodox Church (Vilnius) 102
    St Peter and St Paul Cathedral-Basilica (Kaunas) 182
    St Peter and St Paul, Church of (Vilnius) 97
    St Theresa, Church of (Vilnius) 106
    St Virgin Maria's Church (Vilnius) 104
    Telšiai Cathedral 275–6
    Vilnius Cathedral 94
    Vytautas the Great Church (Kaunas) 181–2
Cinzas, Eduardas 39
city tax 59
Čiurlionis, M K 103, 142, 155, **187–9**
climate 2, **4**, 8
conservation 4–9
cultural etiquette 69
culture 32–42
    cinema 40
    literature 37–9
    music 40–1
    painting 32–4
    sport 41–2
    traditional arts and crafts 34–7
Curonian Lagoon 200, 277, 309, 311
Curonian Spit, The *278*, 301–14, *302*
    getting around 303–4
    getting there and away 303
    tourist information 304
currency 2, 55–6

Dainava *see* Dzūkija
Darius, Steponas and Girėnas, Stasys 193
democracy 22–3, 166
deportations, Soviet 14, **15**, 17, 18, 20, 30, 40, 65, 75, 112, 143, 161, 165, 196, 298
diaspora, Lithuanian 26, 34, 166
dietary requirements 61
Dieveniškės 155–7
disability, travelling with a 53–4
dog, travelling with your 55
Donelaitis, Kristijonas 37
Dreverna 306, **315**
driving *see* car travel
Druskininkai 26, 44, 131, **137–47**, *138*, 149, 150, 152, 155, 188, 203, 211
    accommodation 139
    activities 140
    getting there and around 138
    history 137

restaurants 139–40
sanatoriums and spas 141
sights 142–7
tourist information 138
Dubingiai 230–1
Dzūkija 5, 6, 8, 9, 45, 57, 61, *136*, **136–61**, 144

Easter 30, 34, 43, 59, 62, **63**, 102, 284
eating out 62
economy 23–5
education 26, 31, **32**
embassies and honorary
    consuls 47
ethnographic regions 5
etiquette *see* cultural etiquette
European Union 3, 24, 47, 65, 76, 132, 134,
    239
Europos Parkas 132–3
exchange rate 2

Fachwerk architecture 284, 294, **299**
famous Lithuanians 26
farmsteads *see* rural tourism
fauna *see* wildlife
ferry travel 50, 292
festivals **62–5**, 67, 80–1, 112, 123, 127, 130,
    144, 155, 172, 209, 214, 223, 233, 236,
    255, 257, 263, 268, 284, 296, 303, 312
flag, Lithuanian 65
flora 7
food and drink 60–2
foraging 7
Forest Brothers 16–17, 40, 65, 75, 111–12,
    143, 147, 160, 196, 200, 203, **205**, 248, 298
freedom fighters *see* Forest Brothers
freedom fighting 16–18
funiculars 95, 182, 190

galleries *see* museums and galleries
Gavelis, Ričardas 39
genealogy and family research 46
Geographical Centre of Europe, The 132
geography 3–4
Gerlikienė, Petronėlė 33
Ginučiai 232–4
gods and goddesses 9, 27, 30, 36, 102, 146,
    181, 285, 288, 307
Gorbachev, Mikhail 18–19, 21, 31, 167
government and politics 23
Grand Duchy of Lithuania 9, 37, 95, 121,
    128, 129, 137

Grand Dukes
    Alexander 74
    Algirdas 101, 106
    Casimir 104
    Gediminas 73–4, **93**
    Jogaila 30, 74, 100
    Kazimierz 98
    Kernius 129
    Kestutis 126, 286
    Mindaugas 9, 64, 94, **96**, 223
    Sobieski, John 103
    Vytautas 125, 126, 128, 155, 163–4,
        181–2, **184**
    Žygimantas Augustas 107
Gražinytė-Tyla, Mirga 41
Grinaičiai 206–7
Grinius, Kazys 183
Griškevičius, Petras 18
Grušaitė, Gabija 39
Grūtas Soviet Sculpture Park 112, 137,
    **145–6**, 167
Gudaitis, Antanas 33

health 51–2
highlights 44
Hill of Crosses 258–9
historical timelines 20–1, 163–7,
    292–3
history 9–22
Holocaust 14, 25, 28–9, 108, 151, 166, 186,
    191, 199, 208, 263, 269, 270–1

Ignalina 234–6
Ignalina Nuclear Power Plant 4, 25, 40, 234,
    236, 237, 239–40
independence 1918 9–20, 20, 23, **62**, 101
independence 1990 19–21, 167
internet 68
Iron Curtain 17, 160, 281
itineraries, suggested 44–6

Jakas, Vytenis 185
Jewish Lithuania 46, **28–9**, 144, 151, 158,
    185, 186, 191, 197–200, 208, 244, 253,
    256–7, 260–3, 269, 271, 274–5
Jewish Vilnius 74–5, 87, 99, 104, **108–9**,
    110, 117, 129
Joniškis 48, 259, 260–1
Juknaičiai 320
Juodkrantė 306–7
Jurbarkas 5, 200, 201–3

Kalanta, Romas 18, 167, 184
Kalpokas, Petras 33
Karaites, The 125
Karvės Ola 247
Kaunas 11–12, *162*, 163–97, *170–1*
   accommodation 169–74
   activities 177–9
   bars and clubs 175–6
   festivals 172
   getting around 169
   getting there and away 167–9
   history 163–7
   restaurants 174–5
   shopping 176–7
   sights 179–97
   tourist information 169
Kaunas Fortress 194–5
Kaunas Hydroelectric Power Plant 4
Kaunas lagoon 166, 196
Každailis, Arvydas 33–4
Kaziukas Fair 34, 43, 66, **80**, 105
Kazlų Rūda Forest 203–4
Kėdainiai 197–200
Kernavė 129–30
kids, travelling with 54–5
King Wilhelm Canal 315
Klaipėda 11, *278*, 290–301, *291*, *295*
   accommodation 293–4
   entertainment 295–6
   festivals 296
   getting there and away 50, 290–3
   history 292–3
   restaurants 294–5
   sights 296–301
   tourist information 293
Kmita, Rimantas 39
Kondrotas, Saulius Tomas 39
Kretinga 289–90
Kudirka, Vincas 2, 111, 207
Kudirkos Naumiestis 207
Kunčinas, Jurgis 39
Kybartai 49, 207–8

Labūnava 200
lakes
   Asvejos 230
   Drūkšiai 239
   Dusia 159
   Galvė 121, 124
   Green Lakes (Vilnius) 133–4
   Kirkilų 247

Plateliai 265–8
Sartai 242, 243
Širvėna 246
Zarasas 241
Žuvintas 158
Landsbergis, Vytautas 18–19
language 26–7, 321–7
language ban *see* book smuggling
Lazdijai 50, 136, **159–61**
Levickis, Martynas 41
LGBTQIA+ travellers 54
Liškiava 149–50
Lithuania Minor 5, 202, 277, 299, **314**
Lithuanian Song and Dance Festival 41, **67**, 96, 117
Lituanica 193
Lukiškės Prison 112–13
Lukša, Juozas 40, 205

Mačiūnas, Jurgis 32, 185
Maironis, Jonas Mačiulis **181**, 182
Mamontovas, Andrius 41
manual ferry 197
Marcinkevičius, Justinas 39
Marcinkonys 152–3
Margionys 153–4
Marijampolė *162*, 209–10
Markevičius, Marius 40–1
Mažeikiai 265
Mažvydas, Martynas 37, 298
media 68–9
medical 51–2
Medininkai 134–5
Memel 290, 292, 299
Mekas, Jonas 39
Meras, Icchokas 39
Merkinė 150–2
Michelin restaurants 60
Mickevičius, Adomas 98
Midsummer **63**, 130, 133, 202, 284, 288, 307
Mieželaitis, Eduardas 39
Milosz, Oscar 39
Mingė 317
Mockava 48–9
Modernist Kaunas 165
Molėtai 226–31
Molotov Line, The 203
Molotov–Ribbentrop Non-Aggression Pact 12–13, 19, 21, 65, 75–6, 98
money 55–6

Morkunas, Kazys 256
museums and galleries
   Adomas Mickevičius Museum (Vilnius) 98
   Amber Museum and Gallery (Vilnius) 99
   Amsterdam School Museum (Kaunas) 187
   Antanas Česnulis Sculpture Park 146
   Art Deco Museum (Kaunas) 186–7
   Auto Museum (Vilnius) 118
   Automatika Cold War Bunker (Vilnius) 118
   Bastion of Vilnius Defensive Wall 105
   Bicycle Museum (Šiauliai) 257
   Biržai Regional Museum 246
   Blacksmiths Museum (Klaipėda) 299
   Cat Museum (Šiauliai) 259
   Chaim Frenkel House (Šiauliai) 256–7
   Chodkevičius Palace (Vilnius) 102
   Church Heritage Museum (Vilnius) 98–9
   Clocks Museum (Klaipėda) 297–8
   Cold War Museum 267–8
   Curonian Spit History Museum (Nida) 312
   Devils Museum (Kaunas) 187
   Energy and Technology Museum (Vilnius) 116
   Folk Music Museum (Kaunas) 182–3
   Gediminas Castle Tower and Ducal Palace (Vilnius) 95
   Grūtas Soviet Sculpture Park 145–6
   Historical Presidential Palace (Kaunas) 183
   Horse Museum (Anykščiai) 223
   House of Signatories (Vilnius) 101
   Jonas Šliūpas Museum (Palanga) 287
   Kaunas Picture Gallery 187
   Kaunas Tadas Ivanauskas Museum of Zoology 184
   Kazys Varnelis House Museum (Vilnius) 114
   Kėdainiai Regional Museum 198
   KGB Atomic Bunker Museum (Kaunas) 192
   KGB Museum *see* Museum of Occupations and Freedom Fights
   Klaipėda Castle Museum 300
   Lithuanian Aviation Museum (Kaunas) 191–2
   Lithuanian House of Basketball (Kaunas) 181
   Lithuanian Money Museum of the Bank of Lithuania (Vilnius) 111
   Lithuanian Museum of Ethnocosmology 229–30
   Lithuanian National Museum Complex (Vilnius) 95–7
      Castellan's House 96–7
      House of Histories 97
      New Arsenal 96
      Old Arsenal 97
   Lithuanian Railway Museum (Vilnius) 118
   Lithuanian Sea Museum (Smiltynė) 304–5
   Lithuanian Theatre, Music and Cinema Museum (Vilnius) 107–8
   Lukiškės Prison (Vilnius) 112–13
   M K Čiurlionis House Museum (Druskininkai) 103
   M K Čiurlionis National Museum of Art (Kaunas) 187–8
   Maironis Lithuanian Literature Museum (Kaunas) 181
   Marija and Jurgis Šlapelis Museum (Vilnius) 101
   Markučiai Manor (Vilnius) 119
   Memel Nord 301
   MO Museum (Vilnius) 114
   Molėtai Technical Museum 228
   Mončys Museum (Palanga) 287
   Money Museum of the Bank of Lithuania (Kaunas) 185–6
   Museum of Ancient Beekeeping at Stripeikiai 234
   Museum of History of Lithuania Minor (Klaipėda) 299
   Museum of the History of Lithuanian Medicine and Pharmacy (Kaunas) 180
   Museum of Illusions (Vilnius) 107
   Museum of Lithuanian Ethnography (Rumšiškės) 196
   Museum of Occupations and Freedom Fights (Vilnius) 111–12
   Mykolas Žilinskas Art Gallery (Kaunas) 186
   National Museum of Art (Vilnius) 114–15
   Nida Fisherman's Ethnographic

Homestead 312–13
Ninth Fort Museum (Kaunas) 192–4
Office of the President of the Republic of Lithuania (Vilnius) 110
Palace of the Grand Dukes (Vilnius) 94–5
Palanga Amber Museum 286
Palanga Resort Museum 284
Panevėžys Local History Museum 248
Parliament of the Republic of Lithuania (Vilnius) 113
Pažaislis Monastery Complex 194–6
Photography Museum (Šiauliai) 258
Radio and Television Museum (Šiauliai) 257
Rokiškis Regional Museum 244–5
Romnesa Šakotis Museum 146
Rūta Chocolate Museum (Šiauliai) 258
Samogitian Art Museum (Plungė) 271
Samogitian Museum 'Alka' (Telšiai) 273
Samogitian Village Museum (Telšiai) 273–4
Šiauliai 'Aušros' Museum 256–7
Šiauliai Railway Museum 257
Stasys Modern Art Museum (Panevėžys) 249
Stumbras Museum (Kaunas) 190–1
Sūduvis Minesweeper Museum (Klaipėda) 297
Sugihara House (Kaunas) 191
Thomas Mann Museum (Nida) 311–12
Tuskulėnai Memorial Complex and Peace Park (Vilnius) 117
Ukmergė Regional Museum 250
Underground Printing House 'ab' 196–7
Utena Regional Museum 225
Vytautas the Great War Museum (Kaunas) 188–9
Yard Gallery (Kaunas) 185
Zarasai Regional Museum 241
music 40–1
Musteika 154

names 27
Napoleon 74, 79, 98, 103, 104, 110, 117, 164, 195, 202, 293, 297
NATO 134, 156, 160
national parks 6
  Aukštaitija National Park *218*, 231–4
  Curonian Spit National Park *278, 302*, 305
  Dzūkija National Park *136*, 147–55
  Trakai Historical National Park 6, **120–8**
  Žemaitija National Park 6, 45, *252*, 265–9, 270
natural history 4–9
nature reserves
  Čepkelių Strict Nature Reserve 153
  Grobštas Nature Reserve 314
  Kamanai State Nature Reserve 265
  Karajimiškis Landscape Reserve 247
  Nagliai Strict Nature Reserve 308
  Novaraistis Ornithological Reserve 204
  Šatrija Landscape Reserve 275
  Stėgalis Bison Reserve 154–5
  Žuvintas Biosphere Reserve 158–9
Nazi occupation 14–15
Nemunas Island 190
Nemunas River 4, 5, 7, 137, 140, 143, 151, 163–4, 166, 178, 182, 200–3
Nemunas River valley 200–3
Neris River 4, 78, 92–3, 130–2, 163–4
Nėris, Salomėja 39
New Year's Eve 64–5
Nida 309–14, *310*
  accommodation 309–10
  getting there 309
  restaurants 310–11
  sights 311–14
  tourist information 304

oak trees **7**, 242
observation towers 7, 151, 159, 204, 214, 224, 230, 233, 242, 247, 265, 268, 315
Oginskis, Mykolas Mikalojus 270
opening times 68
Operation Barbarossa 14, 21, 75, 165, 203

Pacas family 103, 164, 194–5
Paganism **30**, 62–4, 73–4, 96, 101, 126, 129, 135, 179, 201, 251–2, 272, 275
Pakruojis Manor 255
Palanga *278*, 279–90, *280*
  accommodation 282
  festivals 284
  getting around 281
  getting there and away 279–81
  restaurants 282–3
  sights 284–8
  tourist information 282
Paliesiaus Manor 235
Palūšė 231–4

Panemunė 252, 318
Panemunės Castle 201
Paneriai 128
Panevėžys 247–9
Partisan resistance *see* Forest Brothers
people 25–6
Perloja 155
Pervalka 308–9
Pitrėnas, Modestas 41
Plateliai 265–9
Plungė 269–72
politics 23
Pope John Paul II 18, 117, 179, 182, 259, 269
postal services 68
Preila 302, **308–9**
Prussia 5, 9–11, 38–9, 164, 182, 202, 211, 290, 292–3, 297, 299, 302, 314–15, 318
public holidays 57, 62–5

Radauskas, Henrikas 39
Radvila (Radziwiłł) family 108, 110, 115, 197, 199, 230, 246
Radvilavičiūtė, Giedra 39
Rail Baltica 48, 49, 168, 248, 253, 261
Rambynas Hill 202
Raudondvaris 178, 194, **200**
Reagan, Ronald 18, 167
red tape 47
regional parks
   Anykščiai 219, *220*
   Asvejos 230–1
   Dieveniškės Historical 156
   Gražutės 243
   Labanoras 226–30
   Metelių 159
   Nemunas Loops 210
   Nemunas River Delta 316
   Neris 130–2
   Pavilniai 119
   Rambynas 202
   Sartai 242–3
   Varniai *252*, 274
   Verkių 133–4
   Vyštytis 207–8
   Žagarė 261–4
religion and beliefs 27–30
resorts around Vilnius 127
responsible travel 70
restaurants 53, 54, 56, 61, 63, 64, 68
Rokiškis 24, 29, 220, **243–5**

rural tourism 59, 148–9, 228–9
Rusnė Island 319–20
Russian Empire 74, 95, 97, 112, 137, 143, 157, 164, 182, 183, 192, 194, 197, 207, 211, 244, 252, 258, 277, 293, 314, 320

Sabaliauskaitė, Kristina 39
safety 52–3
St George's Day 43, 284
Sąjūdis **19**, 21, 31, 75, 117, 248
Šakiai 204–7
šakotis 61, 66, 146, 235,
Salantai 289
Salinger, J D 206
Samogitia *see* Žemaitija
Sarbievijus, Motiejus Kazimieras 37
Sartai horse race 243
Saulė, Battle of 20, 256
sauna 92
Seimas *see* Parliament of the Republic of Lithuania
Senieji Trakai 120, 127–8
Senoji Varėna 155
Šepetys, Rūta 15, 39
Šerelytė, Renata 39
shopping 65–6
Šiauliai 251–60, *254*
   accommodation 253–4
   getting there and away 253
   history 252–3
   restaurants 254–5
   sights 256–60
   tourist information 253
Šilutė 318–19
Simpson, James Young 11, 287
sinkholes 3, 245, 247
Škėma, Antanas 39
Šlepikas, Arvydas 39
Smetona, Antanas 12, 13, 18, 20, 28, 183, 231
Smiltynė 304–6
Smuglevičius, Pranciškus 33, 97, 100
Sniečkus, Antanas 18, 236–7
Soviet occupation 12–14, 15, 16–19
spa resorts 3, 137, 210
sport 41–2
Sruoga, Balys 39
statues and monuments
   Barbora Radvilaitė (Vilnius) 107
   Frank Zappa (Vilnius) 108–9

Grand Duke Vytautas (Kaunas) 184
Jūratė and Kastytis (Palanga) 285
Memorial to Jan Zwartendijk, Honorary Consul of the Netherlands (Kaunas) 186
talking statues 100
Žibintininkas Lamplighter (Vilnius) 100
Stelmužės Oak 242
storks 2, **8**
street art 89, 185, 209
Stripeikiai 234
Struve Geodetic Arc 4
Sugihara, Chiune 13, 115, 173, 186, **191**
Suvalkija 5, 61, 111, 196, 203–10
Suwałki Gap, The 50, 137, **160**
Svencelė 316
Šventoji 288–9
synagogues 28–9, 74, 104, 106, 108–9, 151, 158, 199, 202, 209, 228, 260, 263, 264, 320

talking statues 100
Tauragė 203
taxis 58
telephone 68–9
television 69
Telšiai 50, 251, **272–6**
textiles 35–6
ticks 51–2
tipping 55, **56**, 62
Tiškevičius family 126, 128, 188, 235 246, 269, 279, 283, 284, **285–7**, 289
tour operators **46–7**, 79
tourist information 46
*see also individual locations*
town twinning 24
train travel 48–9, 56–7
Trakai 17, 28, 40, 44, 57, 74, 79, 92, **120–8**, *122*, 131, 213
   accommodation 123
   activities 124
   festivals and fairs 123
   getting there and around 121–2
   restaurants 123–4
   sights 124–8
   tourist information 123
Trakų Vokė 128
travelling positively 70

Ukmergė 24, 50, 86, 168, 219, **249–50**

UNESCO 40, 67, 73, 104, 129, 158, 165, 167, 277
Urbšys, Juozas
Utena 27, **224–6**, 294
Užgavėnės 37, **62**, 256, 265, 268
Užupis 44, **102–3**, 84, 87, 111, 330

vaccinations 51
Vaitkusm, Jonas 40
Valančius, Bishop Motiejus 38, 182
Varnelis, Kazys 33, **114**
Vesconte, Pietra 30
Vilkaviškis 208–9
Vilkija 200
Vilnius 72, **73–119**, *82–3, 85, 120*
   accommodation 79–84
   activities 91–3
   art galleries 114–15
   banks 93
   bars and clubs 87–90
   cafés 87
   cinemas 89
   concert venues 89–90
   festivals 80–1
   getting around 77–8
   getting there and away 76–7
   history 73–6
   Jewish Vilnius 108–9
   markets 90–1
   museums 95
   nightlife 87–90
   parks 96
   pharmacies 93
   post office 93
   restaurants 84–7
   shopping 90–1
   sights 93–119
   theatres 90
   tour operators 79
   tourist information 78
Vilnius Pass 78, 95
Vilnius TV Tower 19, 22, 76, 78, 113, **117–18**
Vilnius University 10, 20, 37, 40, 74, **99–100**, 230, 327
Vingis Park 66, 67, 75, 113, **117**
Visaginas 25, 27, 57, **236–40**, 243
visas 47

weathervanes 311
what to take 55

when to visit 43–4
wildlife **4–9**, 147, 158, 159, 304, 305
Witches Hill 37, 146, **307**
wooden architecture 113, **143**, 264, 284
wooden churches 44, 134, 153, 158, 242, **264**, 268, 269, 274
World War I **10–11**, 28, 75, 110, 137, 155, 165, 194–5, 208, 211, 253, 275, 287, 290, 293
World War II **12**, 22, 25, 28–9, 34, 39, 65, 75, 104, 106, 110, 150–1, 195, 200, 202, 253, 257, 293, 294, 300, 314, 318
Yeltsin, Boris 19–20

Zapyškis **178**, 200
Žagarė 46, 51, **261–4**
Žagarė Cherry Festival 41, **263**
Žalgirio Arena 41, **176**
Zarasai 33, **240–3**, 281
Zdebskis, Juozas 17
Žemaičių Kalvarija 269
Žemaičių Naumiestis 320
Žemaitė 37–8
Žemaitija 3, 5, 61, 196, 197, **251–76**, *252*
Zervynos **154**, 155
Žmuidzinavičius, Antanas 33, 187
Zwartendijk, Jan 13, **186**, 191
Zypliai Manor 204–6

## INDEX OF ADVERTISERS

Baltic Holidays 1st colour section
Regent Holidays inside front cover
Wanderlust 328

# THE BRADT STORY

## In the beginning

It all began in 1974 on an Amazon river barge. During an 18-month trip through South America, two adventurous young backpackers – Hilary Bradt and her then husband, George – decided to write about the hiking trails they had discovered through the Andes. *Backpacking Along Ancient Ways in Peru and Bolivia* included the very first descriptions of the Inca Trail. It was the start of a colourful journey to becoming one of the best-loved travel publishers in the world; you can read the full story on our website (**bradtguides.com/ourstory**).

## Getting there first

Hilary quickly gained a reputation for being a true travel pioneer, and in the 1980s she started to focus on guides to places overlooked by other publishers. The Bradt Guides list became a roll call of guidebook 'firsts'. We published the first guide to Madagascar, followed by Mauritius, Czechoslovakia and Vietnam. The 1990s saw the beginning of our extensive coverage of Africa: Tanzania, Uganda, South Africa, and Eritrea. Later, post-conflict guides became a feature: Rwanda, Mozambique, Angola, and Sierra Leone, as well as the first standalone guides to the Baltic States following the fall of the Iron Curtain, and the first post-war guides to Bosnia, Kosovo and Albania.

## Comprehensive – and with a conscience

Today, we are the world's largest independently owned travel publisher, with more than 200 titles. However, our ethos remains unchanged. Hilary is still keenly involved, and **we still get there first**: two-thirds of Bradt guides have no direct competition.

But we don't just get there first. Our guides are also known for being **more comprehensive** than any other series. We avoid templates and tick-lists. Each guide is a one-of-a-kind expression of an expert author's interests, knowledge and enthusiasm for telling it how it really is.

And a commitment to wildlife, conservation and respect for local communities has always been at the heart of our books. Bradt Guides was **championing sustainable travel** before any other guidebook publisher. We even have a series dedicated to Slow Travel in the UK, award-winning books that explore the country with a passion and depth you'll find nowhere else.

## Thank you!

We can only do what we do because of the support of readers like you – people who value less-obvious experiences, less-visited places and a more thoughtful approach to travel. Those who, like us, take travel seriously.

**Bradt** GUIDES
**TRAVEL TAKEN SERIOUSLY**